Expanding the Frontiers of Visual Analytics and Visualization

John Dill • Rae Earnshaw • David Kasik •
John Vince • Pak Chung Wong
Editors

Expanding the Frontiers of Visual Analytics and Visualization

Springer

Editors
Professor John Dill, BASc, MS, PhD
School of Interactive Arts & Technology
Simon Fraser University
Surrey, British Columbia
Canada
dill@cs.sfu.ca

Professor Rae Earnshaw, PhD, FBCS, FInstP, FRSA, CEng, CITP
Informatics Research Institute
Centre for Visual Computing, School of Computing, Informatics and Media
University of Bradford
Richmond Road
Bradford, BD7 1DP
UK
R.A.Earnshaw@bradford.ac.uk

David Kasik, BA, MS
Visualization and Interactive Techniques
The Boeing Company
South Trenton Street
Seattle, WA 98124
USA
david.j.kasik@boeing.com

Professor John Vince, MTech, PhD, DSc, FBCS, CEng
Bournemouth University
Poole, BH12 5BB
UK
john.a.vince@btinternet.com

Dr Pak Chung Wong, BS, MS, PhD
Pacific Northwest National Laboratory
Richland, WA 99352
USA
pak.wong@pnnl.gov

ISBN 978-1-4471-2803-8 e-ISBN 978-1-4471-2804-5
DOI 10.1007/978-1-4471-2804-5
Springer London Dordrecht Heidelberg New York

British Library Cataloguing in Publication Data
A catalogue record for this book is available from the British Library

Library of Congress Control Number: 2012936987

Printed on acid-free paper

Springer is part of Springer Science+Business Media (www.springer.com)

Jim Thomas, 1946–2010

Foreword

Jim Thomas—An Appreciation

It is fitting that so many of Jim Thomas's friends and colleagues have written papers and gathered them together in this book as a lasting tribute. Jim was exceptional—he was one of the most friendly, cheerful and determined people I have ever known. He was a maker of things to happen. He saw challenges and needs—and acted on them. He was a doer. He was one of the computer graphics community's most dedicated volunteers. An early workshop he organized led to the UIST conferences. He founded a new field of research. He understood the power of positive thinking, using it as he relentlessly pursued his goals with a contagious enthusiasm and vision that drew folks—including me—to join with him in that pursuit.

Jim spent a year with me in the early 1980s when I was at The George Washington University. Jim and I collaborated on software development and networking, and I came to know and respect him. We interacted frequently thereafter, and my respect for Jim continued to grow. He was awesome.

But first, a few facts. Jim was born in 1946, earned the BS in Mathematics (Eastern Washington University, 1968) and the MS in Computer Science (Washington State University, 1970), worked at General Motors Research Lab until 1976, and then at the Department of Energy's Pacific Northwest National Laboratory (PNNL). He officially retired in mid-2009, continuing to be professionally active until his sudden death on August 6, 2010.

As an activist volunteer, Jim's most notable contributions were as ACM-SIGGRAPH 1980 conference program chair, ACM-SIGGRAPH 1987 conference co-chair, ACM-SIGGRAPH Chair from 1987 to 1992, *IEEE Computer Graphics and Applications* Editor-in-Chief from 1999 to 2002 and IEEE Visualization conference co-chair in 2003 and 2004. Jim served the United States as a Science Adviser to the Department of Homeland Security and to the Army's Simulation, Training and Instrumentation Command.

Many of Jim's technical interests converged to what I believe time will judge to be his most lasting contribution—articulating and tirelessly developing the discipline of Visual Analytics—using data analysis and information visualization to turn data into actionable knowledge. While computer graphics was at the center of most of Jim's work, he realized that Information Visualization is only one part of a more complex process that starts with analyzing, organizing, and abstracting massive amounts of data and presenting the data via information visualization in ways that support our human cognitive processes of analysis and reasoning that lead to insights.

With support from the Department of Homeland Security, Jim recruited and convened a series of workshops involving about 30 thought leaders in the constituent disciplines that contribute to Visual Analytics. They went on to write the defining book *Illuminating the Path: The Research and Development Agenda for Visual Analytics*, which Jim co-edited.

The legacies of Jim's determined development of Visual Analytics are amazingly impressive. Working with and through others, we now have:

- National Visualization and Analytics Center at PNNL,
- Annual Visual Analytics Conference as part of IEEE VisWeek,
- FODAVA (Foundations of Data Analysis and Visual Analytics) research initiative of the US National Science Foundation and Department of Homeland Security, led by Georgia Tech and involving over 60 university researchers in the United States,
- The CCIDADA (Command, Control and Interoperability Center for Advanced Data Analysis) DHS Center of Excellence, led by Rutgers with many university partners,
- The VACCINE (Visual Analytics for Command, Control, and Interoperability Environments) DHS Center of Excellence, led by Purdue, also with many university partners, and
- Similar research programs in Canada, the EU, Australia and New Zealand.

Jim's career trajectory prepared him well for this seminal contribution. His longest-standing interest was of course computer graphics itself, going back to his early days at General Motors Research Labs and carrying throughout all his professional work and to his many service contributions to SIGGRAPH and IEEE.

Jim was fascinated with BIG DATA. Back in the late 1970s and early 1980s he co-led the ALDS (Analysis of Large Data Sets) project. I saw ALDS at PNNL, running on a Digital VAX/780 computer and Ramtek 9400 color raster display. ALDS was the precursor of systems that integrate statistical analyses and information visualization—complete with what were then called "self-describing data sets" and what we now call XML-tagged data. And of course it was done jointly with statisticians. I consider ALDS to be the precursor of PNNL's decade-later ThemeScape system, which used statistical analysis of large collections of text documents to create a visual overview of the document's themes.

Another of Jim's interests was Interaction. He appreciated its centrality to computer graphics. Concerned that SIGGRAPH's Conference on Computer Graphics and Interactive Techniques was too much about modeling and rendering and not enough about interaction, Jim organized the 1980 workshop on Graphical Interaction Techniques at the Battelle conference center in Seattle. This brought together about 30 thought leaders in graphics interaction; the proceedings were highly influential in defining the field. Jim had the vision and drive to make the conference happen, and figured prominently in formulating the intellectual content of the workshop report. The intellectual seeds nourished at that conference led to the creation of the UIST (User Interface and Software Technology) conference series that continues to this day, under the joint aegis of ACM-SIGCHI and ACM-SIGGRAPH.

Jim left us too early, at the age of 64. But he left us with lasting intellectual and organizational contributions. Beyond that, for me and for many others, he left us with a wonderful example of leadership—always positive, always supportive, always goal-focused. I wrote a toast for the party celebrating Jim's life: "To one of the most friendly, cheerful and determined guys I have ever known—that was his key to success professionally and in life—may we all learn from Jim."

Thank you Jim, for all you did for us and for all you taught us.

Georgia Tech
Atlanta, Georgia, USA
November 2011

Jim Foley

Preface

The concept of this book arose out of discussions among the editors on how best to honor the contributions of Jim Thomas to the fields of visual analytics and visualization. It was agreed that a book would be appropriate as a number of summaries of his work had appeared in journals. It was also agreed it should be forward looking rather than simply reflect on his many seminal contributions to the field. One of his favorite sayings was "*The best is yet to come*" and this volume was put together in this spirit. It therefore seeks to explore the frontiers of visual analytics and visualization, concentrating on the new research that is paving the way for future developments and applications.

We are very grateful to all the people who responded to our invitation to contribute and who completed their chapters very efficiently. In a number of cases they involved collaborators, or members of their research group, as co-authors of their papers and we therefore also thank the co-authors for their various contributions.

The following were the invited contributors to this volume—

Prof Mike Bailey, Oregon State University, USA
Prof Mark Billinghurst, University of Christchurch, New Zealand
Prof Ken Brodlie, University of Leeds, UK
Prof Chaomei Chen, Drexel University, USA
Kris Cook, Pacific Northwest National Laboratory, USA
Prof Peter Eades, University of Sydney, Australia
Prof Jose L. Encarnacao, Technical University of Darmstadt, Germany
Prof Peter S. Excell, Glyndwr University, UK
Prof Dieter W. Fellner, Fraunhofer IGD and Technical University of Darmstadt, Germany
Prof James D. Foley, Georgia Institute of Technology, USA
Prof Mikael Jern, Linkoping University, Sweden
Prof Daniel A. Keim, University of Konstanz, Germany
Michael Kluse, Pacific Northwest National Laboratory, USA
Prof Tosiyasu L. Kunii, Morpho Inc and University of Tokyo, Japan
Prof Haesun Park, Georgia Institute of Technology, USA

Dr Jon Peddie, Jon Peddie Research, USA
Theresa-Marie Rhyne, Computer Graphics Consultant, USA
Prof Bill Ribarsky, University of North Carolina, USA
Dr Lawrence J. Rosenblum, National Science Foundation, USA
Prof Ben Shneiderman, University of Maryland, USA
Prof Gabriel Taubin, Brown University, USA
Prof Daniel Thalmann, Nanyang Technological University, Singapore
Prof Bodo Urban, Fraunhofer IGD, Rostock, Germany
Prof Dr Frank Van Reeth, University of Hasselt, Belgium
Dr Turner Whitted, Microsoft Research, USA
Prof Jian Jun Zhang, Bournemouth University, UK

Further chapters were contributed by the co-editors.

The book begins with the dynamics of evolving a vision based on some of the principles that Jim Thomas and colleagues established and in which his leadership was evident. It is then followed by chapters in the areas of visual analytics, visualization, interaction, modeling, architecture, and virtual reality. The book concludes with the key area of technology transfer to industry. Each chapter contains a summary of the paper in an Abstract. These Abstracts are also visible on the web in the electronic book corresponding to this volume.

We thank Springer for publishing this book and for their support and assistance in the editorial and production processes. We particularly thank Beverley Ford, Helen Desmond and Ben Bishop who dealt with a number of complex issues speedily and efficiently.

Simon Fraser University, Surrey, BC, Canada — John Dill
University of Bradford, Bradford, UK — Rae Earnshaw
The Boeing Company, Seattle, WA, USA — David Kasik
Bournemouth University, Poole, UK — John Vince
Pacific Northwest National Laboratory, Richland, WA, USA — Pak Chung Wong

Contents

List of Contributors

Editors

John Dill Simon Fraser University, Surrey, Canada

John Dill is an emeritus professor in the School of Interactive Arts and Technology at Simon Fraser University, Burnaby, Canada. He is also a founder and chief scientist of ThoughtShare Communications. His research interests include information visualization, visual analytics, design visualization, haptic rendering, and intelligent graphics interfaces. He received a BASc in engineering physics from the University of British Columbia, an MS from North Carolina State University, and a PhD in engineering science from the California Institute of Technology. He is active in ACM's SIGGRAPH.

http://www.siat.sfu.ca/faculty/John-Dill/

Email: dill@cs.sfu.ca

Rae Earnshaw University of Bradford, Bradford, UK

Rae Earnshaw is professor of electronic imaging at the University of Bradford since 1995. He was Dean of the School of Informatics (1999–2007) and Pro Vice-Chancellor (Strategic Systems Development) (2004–2009). He has been a Visiting Professor at Illinois Institute of Technology, George Washington University, USA, and Northwestern Polytechnical University, China. He is a member of ACM, IEEE, CGS, Eurographics, and a Fellow of the British Computer Society. He has authored and edited 35 books on computer graphics, visualization, multimedia, design, and virtual reality, and published over 150 papers in these areas. He is on a number of Editorial Boards of international journals and a Top Management Program Fellow of the Leadership Foundation. He has a PhD in computer science—computer graphics—from the University of Leeds, UK.

http://www.inf.brad.ac.uk/home/rae.php

http://sites.google.com/site/raearnshaw/

Email: R.A.Earnshaw@bradford.ac.uk

David Kasik The Boeing Company, Seattle, WA, USA

David J. Kasik is a Boeing Senior Technical Fellow specializing in visualization and interactive techniques. His interests include visualization of geometric and non-geometric data, all types of interactive and display devices, combining basic research with practical implementation and increasing awareness of the impact of computing and technology innovation outside the computing community, especially for K-12 students. Kasik has an MS in computer science from the University of Colorado and a BA in quantitative studies from the Johns Hopkins University. He is a member of the IEEE Computer Graphics and Applications editorial board. He is a member of the IEEE, ACM, ACM SIGGRAPH, and ACM SIGCHI.

Email: david.j.kasik@boeing.com

John Vince Bournemouth University, Poole, UK

Prof John Vince began working in computer graphics at Middlesex Polytechnic in 1968. His research activities centered on computer animation software and resulted in the PICASO and PRISM animation systems. Whilst at Middlesex, he designed the UK's first MSc course in Computer Graphics, and developed a popular program of short courses in computer animation for television designers. In 1986 he joined Rediffusion Simulation as a Research Consultant and worked on the development of real-time computer systems for commercial flight simulators. In 1992 he was appointed Chief Scientist of Thomson Training Simulation Ltd. In 1995 he was appointed Professor of Digital Media at the National Centre for Computer Animation at Bournemouth University, and in 1999 he was made Head of Academic Group for Computer Animation. He has written and edited over 28 books on computer graphics, computer animation and virtual reality. He was awarded a DSc by Brunel University in recognition of his work in computer graphics.

http://www.johnvince.co.uk/

Email: john.a.vince@btinternet.com

Pak Chung Wong Pacific Northwest National Laboratory, Richland, WA, USA

Pak Chung Wong is a project manager and chief scientist in information analytics at the Pacific Northwest National Laboratory in Richland, Washington. His research background is in visualization and visual analytics with focuses on extreme scale data analytics, graph analytics, multimedia analytics, and national security analytics. Currently, he serves on the editorial boards of IEEE Computer Graphics and Applications (CG&A) and Information Visualization (IVS). In 2012, he will co-chair the IEEE VisWeek Conference in Seattle, Washington and the SPIE Visual Data Analysis (VDA) Conference in San Francisco, California. In the past, he has served as a conference chair, program chair, and/or papers chair at visualization conferences from IEEE Visualization (Vis), IEEE Information Visualization Conference (InfoVis), and IEEE Symposium on Visual Analytics Science and Technology (VAST). He received a PhD in computer science from the University of New Hampshire.

http://www.pnnl.gov/wong

Email: pak.wong@pnnl.gov

Invited Authors (in alphabetical order)

Mike Bailey Oregon State University, Corvallis, USA

Mike Bailey is a Professor of Computer Science at Oregon State University. His areas of interest include scientific visualization, high performance computer graphics, GPU programming, and solid freeform. Mike received his PhD from Purdue University in Computer Graphics and Computer Aided Design in 1979. From 1979–1981 he was a member of Sandia National Laboratories' Technical Staff, specializing in developing CAD/graphics tools for mechanical designers. From 1981–1985, Mike was a faculty member at Purdue University, where he taught and conducted research in the areas of computer graphics and computer aided mechanical engineering. He was promoted to Associate Professor in 1985. Later in 1985, Mike became the Director of Advanced Development at Megatek Corporation, where he managed a group of engineers who were charged with developing Megatek's next generation of computer graphics technology. From 1989–2004 Mike was the Director of Visualization at the San Diego Supercomputer Center and an adjunct professor at the University of California San Diego. Mike enjoys teaching and has taught a variety of college classes to over 4,100 students. He has been awarded 9 university teaching awards, including 5 Teacher of the Year awards from UCSD's Computer Science seniors. He has also presented numerous technical papers and short courses at a variety of conferences and workshops. Mike is a member of the Association of Computing Machinery (ACM), the Special Interest Group on Computer Graphics (ACM-SIGGRAPH), the Institute of Electrical and Electronics Engineers (IEEE), and the American Society of Mechanical Engineers (ASME). He has served on a number of conference committees, including co-chairing the 1991 SIGGRAPH international conference and the 2001 IEEE Visualization conference.

http://web.engr.oregonstate.edu/~mjb/WebMjb/mjb.html

Email: mjb@eecs.oregonstate.edu

Mark Billinghurst HIT Lab NZ, University of Canterbury, Christchurch, New Zealand

Prof. Billinghurst is Director of the Human Interface Technology (HIT) Laboratory in New Zealand. His research focuses primarily on advanced 3D user interfaces such as wearable computers, shared space interfaces, and multimodal input. He has a BCMS (Bachelor of Computing and Mathematical Science) (first class honors) in 1990 and a Master of Philosophy (Applied Mathematics & Physics) in 1992 from Waikato University. He completed his PhD in 2002 in Electrical Engineering, at the University of Washington, under the supervision of Professor Thomas Furness III. As part of the research for his thesis entitled "*Shared Space: Exploration in Collaborative Augmented Reality*", Prof. Billinghurst invented the Magic Book—an animated children's book that comes to life when viewed through a lightweight head-mounted display.

http://www.hitlabnz.org/index.php/people

http://www.hitl.washington.edu/people/person.php?name=grof

http://www.canterbury.ac.nz/ucresearchprofile/Researcher.aspx?researcherid=87070

Email: mark.billinghurst@canterbury.ac.nz

Ken Brodlie University of Leeds, Leeds LS2 9JT, UK

Ken Brodlie's research interests cover the spectrum of visualization as a discipline—from foundations to applications; from systems to algorithms; from scientific visualization to information visualization; from data visualization to computational steering; from abstract visualizations to modeling reality. A recent unifying theme has been the use of visualization in e-science—with a number of research projects funded under the UK e-Science initiative. This work aims to extend current visualization systems in three directions: collaborative visualization, computational steering, and the incorporation of visualization in Web- and Grid-based environments. It has been carried out within the wider *Visualization and Virtual Reality Research Group* at Leeds, and is done in close collaboration with a number of staff and students at Leeds; with colleagues at other universities through joint research projects; and with industry—in particular, *NAG Ltd.* He gained a BSc in Mathematics from the University of Edinburgh and an MSc and PhD in numerical analysis from the University of Dundee. He is now formally retired but as Emeritus Professor at the University of Leeds, he retains his visualization research interests.

http://www.comp.leeds.ac.uk/kwb/

http://www.comp.leeds.ac.uk/kwb/research.html

Email: K.W.Brodlie@leeds.ac.uk

Chaomei Chen College of the Information Science and Technology, Drexel University, Philadelphia, PA, USA

Dr. Chaomei Chen is an Associate Professor in the College of Information Science and Technology at Drexel University. He is a Chang Jiang Scholar (visiting professor) at Dalian University of Technology, China since 2008 and has been a visiting professor at Brunel University in the United Kingdom (2002–2008). He received his bachelor degree in mathematics from Nankai University, China, his MSc in computation from the University of Oxford and his PhD in computer science from the University of Liverpool. His research interests include information visualization, visual analytics, knowledge domain visualization, mapping scientific frontiers, and theories of scientific discoveries and creativity. Dr. Chen is the author of *Turning Points: The Nature of Creativity* (Springer, 2011), *Information Visualization: Beyond the Horizon* (Springer, 2004, 2006) and *Mapping Scientific Frontiers: The Quest for Knowledge Visualization* (Springer, 2003). He is the founder and the Editor-in-Chief of the journal *Information Visualization* and an editorial board member of *Journal of Informetrics*. Dr. Chen has published over 170 peer-reviewed publications in journals and conference proceedings in multiple disciplines of computer science and information science, including *Proceedings of the National Academy of Sciences* (PNAS), *IEEE Computer*, *IEEE Transactions on Visualization and Computer Graphics* (TVCG), *IEEE Computer Graphics and Applications* (CG&A), *Journal of the American Society for Information Science and Technology* (JASIST), *Journal of Informetrics* (JOI), *Information Processing & Management* (IP&M), and *Scientometrics*. His work has been cited over 4,700 times on Google Scholar. He is the principal investigator of research grants and contracts from the National Science Foundation (NSF) and other government agencies and industrial sponsors such as Pfizer. His earlier research was funded by the European Commission, the Engineering and Physical Sciences Research Council (UK), and the Library and Information Commission (UK). Dr. Chen created the widely used software http://cluster.cis.drexel.edu/~cchen/citespace for visualizing and analyzing emerging trends in scientific literature. CiteSpace has been used by users in over 3,800 cities of 105 countries.

http://www.pages.drexel.edu/~cc345

Email: cc345@drexel.edu

Kristin Cook Pacific Northwest National Laboratory, Richland, USA

Kristin Cook has managed research and development projects in information visualization and visual analytics at Pacific Northwest National Laboratory for fifteen years. She led the development of the initial version of the IN-SPIRE visual information analysis software, which is now in use in both government and commercial industry. She is co-editor of "*Illuminating the Path: The Research and Development Agenda for Visual Analytics*", published in 2005 by IEEE Press.

http://nvac.pnl.gov/

Email: Kris.Cook@pnl.gov

Peter Eades University of Sydney, Sydney, Australia

Peter Eades is a professor in the School of Information Technologies at the University of Sydney, Australia. He has been Professor of Computer Science, the University of Newcastle, 1992–1999, Program Leader, NICTA, 2003–2005, Research Director, HxI Initiative, 2006, and Distinguished Researcher, National ICT Australia, 2006. His research interests are in the areas of graph drawing, network visualization; graphs and related combinatorial structures, information visualization, and algorithms. He is working on scalable visual analytics for uncertain dynamic networks. He has a PhD in Mathematics from the Australian National University.

http://sydney.edu.au/engineering/it/~peter/

Email: peter.d.eades@gmail.com

J. Encarnação TU Darmstadt, Darmstadt, Germany

José Luis Encarnação was born in Portugal, passed there the school "Escola Salesiana do Estoril", and is living in the Federal Republic of Germany since 1959. He was since 1975 a full professor of Computer Science at the Technische Universität Darmstadt and the head of the Interactive Graphics Research Group (TUD-GRIS). Since October 2009 he is Professor Emeritus of the Technische Universität Darmstadt. From 1987 to 2006 he was the founding director of the Fraunhofer Institute for Computer Graphics (IGD) in Darmstadt. He founded in 1999 the INI-GraphicsNet (International Network of Institutions for Computer Graphics), today a network of legally independent but closely cooperating research entities in Germany, Italy, Panama, Portugal and Spain, that signs since 2010 under the new name GraphicsMedia.net. Professor Encarnação was one of the founders of EUROGRAPHICS, the European Association for Computer Graphics; from 1980 to 1984 he was its chairman. From 1985 to 1991 he was chairman of its Professional Board. Professor Encarnação holds a diploma (Dipl.-Ing.) and a doctorate (Dr.-Ing.) in electrical engineering from the Technical University of Berlin where he completed his studies as a holder of a scholarship of the Gulbenkian Foundation. In 1967, he started his career in computer graphics at the Technical University of Berlin. Before coming to Darmstadt, he held research and academic positions at the Heinrich-Hertz-Institute in Berlin (1968–1972) and at the University of Saarbrücken (1972–1975). From 1995 to 2001 he was an elected member of the Senate of the Fraunhofer-Gesellschaft, Munich and from 2002 to 2006 he was a member of the Advisory Board (Präsidium) of this German Association for Applied Research. From July 2001 to October 2006 he was the chairman of the Fraunhofer ICT Group (Information and Communication Technology Group consisting of 17 institutes with about 3,000 employees and a total budget of about 190 million EURO in 2005). From 2001 to 2007 Professor Encarnação was member of the EU-advisory board of the EU 6th and 7th framework program for the information technology area (ISTAG). He was chairman of this board from 2002 to 2004 and vice-chairman from 2005 to 2007. Besides several honors, he was awarded with the German Federal Service Cross in 1983, with the German Federal Service Cross First Class in 1995 and with the Big Cross of the Order of Merit of the Federal Republic of Germany in 2006. The country of Portugal honored him with the "Ordem Militar de Santiago de Espada" in 2001. The German Federal State of Hesse awarded to him the "Hessischer Kulturpreis" in 2000 in recognition of his scientific achievements. In 2001 he was elected full academy member of the "Berlin-Brandenburgische Akademie der Wissenschaften" (BBAW, the former Leibniz Academy) and in 2002 he became a full academy member in the German academy of science and technology (acatech). For outstanding technical and scientific achievements he received among other awards the Karl-Heinz-Beckurts Award in 1989. He was the recipient of the Steven A. Coons Award from ACM-SIGGRAPH (USA) in 1995 and the recipient of the Konrad-Zuse-Medal by the German Computer Society (GI) in 1997. Professor Encarnação is today active as a Senior Technology and Innovation Adviser to

Governments, multinational companies, research institutions and foundations. He is also strongly involved in the development of Research Agendas and Innovation Strategies for Socio-Economic Development in Emerging Economies.

http://www.gris.informatik.tu-darmstadt.de/home/members/encarnacao/index.de.htm

http://www.igd.fraunhofer.de/

http://www.graphicsmedia.net/

Email: jl_encarnacao@t-online.de

Peter S. Excell Dean, Institute for Arts, Science and Technology, Glyndwr University, Wrexham, Wales, UK

Peter Excell joined Glyndwr University in 2007: he was previously Associate Dean for Research in the School of Informatics at the University of Bradford, UK, where he had worked since 1971. He obtained a BSc in Engineering Science from Reading University in 1970 and was awarded his PhD from Bradford University in 1980 for research in electromagnetic hazards. His long-standing major research interests have been in the applications and computation of high-frequency electromagnetic fields, but he has broadened his interests in recent years to include mobile communications content and usage scenarios: these interests have led to numerous research grants, contracts and patents. His principal recent work in the classical area has been in the computation and measurement of electromagnetic fields due to mobile communications terminals: this commenced in 1991, with a large-scale study of procedures for testing of mobile telephones. He was a leading partner in a pan-European project developing standardized test and simulation procedures for evaluation of the coupling between a mobile phone and the human body. This led to major successes in the development of the hybrid field computation method and novel designs for mobile communications antennas. His current work includes studies of advanced methods for electromagnetic field computation (including the use of high performance computing), the effect of electromagnetic fields on biological cells, advanced antenna designs for mobile communications, and consideration of usage scenarios for future mobile communications devices. The latter topic is being developed in conjunction with colleagues from wider discipline areas, analyzing human communications in a 'holistic' way and developing new ways of using mobile multimedia devices. There has been fruitful new collaborative work on design of content for mobile screens and on integration of mobile devices with garments. He is a Fellow of the British Computer Society, the Institution of Engineering and Technology and of the Higher Education Academy, a Chartered IT Professional and Chartered Engineer, a Senior Member of the Institute of Electronics and Electrical Engineers, an Associate Fellow of the Remote Sensing and Photogrammetry Society, and a member of the Association for Computing Machinery, the Applied Computational Electromagnetics Society, and the Bioelectromagnetics Society.

http://www.newi.ac.uk/computing/research/PE.htm

http://kn.theiet.org/communities/electromagnetics/exec-team/peter-excell.cfm

Email: p.excell@glyndwr.ac.uk

D.W. Fellner Fraunhofer IGD and Technische Universität Darmstadt, Darmstadt, Germany

Dieter Fellner is a professor of computer science at the Technical University of Darmstadt, Germany, and the Director of the Fraunhofer Institute of Computer Graphics (IGD) at the same location. Previously he has held academic positions at the Graz University of Technology, Austria, the University of Technology in Braunschweig, Germany, the University of Bonn, Germany, the Memorial University of Newfoundland, Canada, and the University of Denver, Colorado. He is still affiliated with the Graz University of Technology where he chairs the Institute of Computer Graphics and Knowledge Visualization he founded in 2005. Dieter Fellner's research activities over the last years covered algorithms and software architectures to integrate modeling and rendering, efficient rendering and visualization algorithms, generative and reconstructive modeling, virtual and augmented reality, graphical aspects of internet-based multimedia information systems and digital libraries. In the latter field he has initiated/coordinated the first strategic initiative on 'General Documents' (funded by the German Research Foundation DFG, 1997–2005) followed by a DFG-Research Center on 'Non-Textual Documents' (2006–2011). In 2006 he initiated a new funding initiative on 'Visual Computing' funded by the Austrian Ministry BMVIT. In the areas of Computer Graphics and Digital Libraries Dieter Fellner is a member of the editorial boards of leading journals in the respective fields and a member of the program committees of many international conferences and workshops. He is a member of the EUROGRAPHICS Association where he serves in the Executive Committee and as Chairman of the Publications Board, ACM, IEEE Computer Society, and the Gesellschaft für Informatik (GI) where he serves as a member of the extended Board of Directors and as Chairman of the Graphics Chapter (Fachbereich Graphische Datenverarbeitung). In 2009 he became a member of the Academia Europaea. Furthermore, Dieter Fellner is an adviser for the German Scientific Council, the German Research Foundation, and the European Commission (as a member of ISTAG, the IST Advisory Group to the European Commission).

http://www.gris.tu-darmstadt.de/home/members/fellner/index.en.htm

Email: d.fellner@igd.fraunhofer.de

J.D. Foley Georgia Institute of Technology, Atlanta, USA

Dr. Foley is Professor in the College of Computing, and Professor in the School of Electrical and Computer Engineering. He earned the PhD in Computer Information and Control Engineering at the University of Michigan and the BSEE at Lehigh University, where he was initiated into Phi Beta Kappa, Tau Beta Pi and Eta Kappa Nu. Dr. Foley first came to Georgia Tech in 1991 to establish the Graphics, Visualization & Usability Center, which in 1996 was ranked #1 by US News and World Report for graduate computer science work in graphics and user interaction.

In 1996, he became director of Mitsubishi Electric Research Lab in Cambridge and then in 1998 chairman and CEO of Mitsubishi Electric ITA, directing corporate R&D at four labs in North America. He returned to Georgia as Executive Director and then CEO of Yamacraw, Georgia's economic development initiative in the design of broadband systems, devices and chips. Dr. Foley is a Fellow of ACM and IEEE, an inaugural member of the ACM/CHI Academy, and recipient of the biannual ACM/SIGGRAPH Stephen Coons Award for Outstanding Creative Contributions to Computer Graphics. The graphics textbooks he has co-authored are widely used and have been translated into six foreign languages. In 1992, the Georgia Tech College of Computing graduate students named him, "most likely to make students want to grow up to be professors." In July 2001, Dr. Foley became chairman of the Computing Research Association—an organization of over 200 computer science and computer engineering university departments, professional societies and industrial research labs.

http://www.cc.gatech.edu/fac/Jim.Foley/foley.html

http://en.wikipedia.org/wiki/James_D._Foley

Email: foley@cc.gatech.edu

Mikael Jern Media and Information Technology, National Centre for Visual Analytics, Linköping University, Linköping, Sweden

From 1970–1976 Prof Jern worked with Professor Hertz at the University of Lund. Together they invented the Color Graphics System based on the first ink jet plotter for raster based visualization software in the world. In 1980 he founded UNIRAS addressing industry needs with a more general-purpose raster graphics approach. UNIRAS became a world leading supplier of Visual Data Analysis. Jern coordinated several EC projects in the domain of knowledge-based information visualization and also consulted with the EC Commission as a technical expert. He has published more than 200 technical papers and books in visual computing and visualization application areas. At SIGGRAPH 1993 he was elected a "pioneer of computer graphics" based on his breaking new ground research together with Hertz in raster graphics. In 1999 he was appointed professor in information visualization at Linköping University. His latest research interest includes cutting-edge geovisual analytics methods with storytelling. In 2008 he founded the Swedish National Centre for Visual Analytics http://ncva.itn.liu.se with partners Unilever, SMHI, OECD, Ericsson, Statistics Sweden and Eurostat. His research in geovisual analytics and embraced by OECD is acknowledged through many scientific papers and invited presentations. In 2010 his entrepreneurship led to the second spin-off company NComVA.

http://ncomva.com

Email: mikael.jern@liu.se

Daniel A. Keim University of Konstanz, Konstanz, Germany

Daniel A. Keim is full professor and head of the Information Visualization and Data Analysis Research Group in the Computer Science Department of the University of Konstanz, Germany. He has been actively involved in data analysis and information visualization research for about 20 years and developed a number of novel visual analysis techniques for very large data sets. He has been program co-chair of the IEEE InfoVis and IEEE VAST symposia as well as the SIGKDD conference, and he is member of the IEEE InfoVis and VAST steering committees. He is an associate editor of Palgrave's Information Visualization Journal (since 2001) and the Knowledge and Information System Journal (since 2006), and has been an associate editor of the IEEE Transactions on Visualization and Computer Graphics (1999–2004) and the IEEE Transactions on Knowledge and Data Engineering (2002–2007). He is coordinator of the German Strategic Research Initiative (SPP) on Scalable Visual Analytics and the scientific coordinator of the EU Coordination Action on Visual Analytics. Dr. Keim got his PhD and habilitation degrees in computer science from the University of Munich. Before joining the University of Konstanz, Dr. Keim was associate professor at the University of Halle, Germany and Technology Consultant at AT&T Shannon Research Labs, NJ, USA.

http://www.informatik.uni-konstanz.de/~keim/

Email: Daniel.Keim@uni-konstanz.de

Michael Kluse Senior VP, Battelle and Laboratory Director, Pacific Northwest National Laboratory, Richland, USA

Michael Kluse is Director of Pacific Northwest National Laboratory, operated by Battelle for the U.S. Department of Energy (www.pnnl.gov). He also is Senior Vice President of Battelle. Mr. Kluse is responsible for setting the vision and strategic direction of PNNL, an organization of more than 4,900 staff members with an annual business volume of more than $1.1 billion. He has focused the Laboratory on advancing the frontiers of science and solving some of our nation's most complex challenges in energy, the environment, and national security. Mr. Kluse previously served as Vice President of Battelle's Defense Engineering business, Vice President and General Manager of Battelle's Navy Sector, and Associate Laboratory Director of PNNL's National Security Directorate. Mr. Kluse serves on the boards of the Council on Competitiveness Energy Security as well as several business, technology and educational boards in Washington state. Mr. Kluse holds a BS degree in Systems Analysis from Miami University, and an MS degree in Industrial and Systems Engineering from The Ohio State University.

http://www.pnl.gov/about/kluse_bio.asp

Email: mkluse@pnl.gov

Tosiyasu L. Kunii Iidabashi First Tower 31F, Morpho, Inc., 2-6-1 Koraku, Bunkyo-ku, Tokyo 112-0004, Japan

Tosiyasu L. Kunii is currently Chief Technical Adviser of Morpho Inc., Distinguished Professor and Adviser of Beihang University in Beijing, Honorary Visiting

Professor of University of Bradford in UK, and Professor Emeritus of the University of Tokyo and of the University of Aizu. He was Professor and Director of IT Institute at Kanazawa Institute of Technology from 2003 to 2008, Professor of Hosei University from 1998 to 2003. Before that he served as the Founding President and Professor of the University of Aizu dedicated to computer science and engineering as a discipline, from 1993 to 1997. He had been Professor of Department of Computer and Information Science at the University of Tokyo from June 1978 until March 1993, after serving as Associate Professor at Computer Centre of the University of Tokyo in October 1969. He was visiting professors at University of California at Berkeley in 1994 and University of Geneva in 1992. He received the 1998 Taylor L. Booth Education Award the highest education award of IEEE Computer Society given to one individual a year. He is a Life Fellow of IEEE and Fellow of IPSJ. He has published over 50 books and around 500 refereed papers in computer science. Dr. Kunii was Founder and Editor-in-Chief of The Visual Computer: An International Journal of Computer Graphics (Springer-Verlag) (1984–1999), and International Journal of Shape Modeling (World Scientific) (1994–1995), and was Associate Editor of IEEE Computer Graphics and Applications (1982–2002). He is Associate Editor-in-Chief of The Journal of Visualization and Computer Animation (John Wiley & Sons) (1990–) and on the Editorial Board of Information Systems Journal (1976–2008). He received his BSc in 1962, MSc in 1964 and DSc in 1967 all from the University of Tokyo.

http://www.morphoinc.com/

http://www.kunii.net/

Email: kunii@ieee.org

Haesun Park Computational Science and Engineering, Georgia Institute of Technology, Atlanta, USA

Haesun Park is professor at Georgia Institute of Technology and Director of the NSF/DHS FODAVA-Lead (Foundations of Data and Visual Analytics). Her current research interests are in numerical algorithms, data and visual analytics, scientific computing, bioinformatics (gene selection), missing value estimation, protein structure prediction, text analysis, parallel computing. Previously she was Program Director of the Division of Computing and Communication Foundations at the National Science Foundation and before this was professor in the Dept of Computer Science and Engineering at the University of Minnesota. She has a BS in mathematics from Seoul National University and MS and PhD degrees in computer science from Cornell University.

http://www.cc.gatech.edu/~hpark/

Email: hpark@cc.gatech.edu

Jon Peddie Jon Peddie Research, Tiburon, CA 94920, USA

Jon Peddie is president of Jon Peddie Research. Dr. Jon Peddie is one of the pioneers of the graphics industry, starting his career in computer graphics in 1962. After the successful launch of several graphics manufacturing companies, Peddie began JPA in 1984 to provide comprehensive data, information and management expertise to the computer graphics industry. In 2001 Peddie left JPA and formed Jon Peddie Research (JPR) to provide customer intimate consulting and market forecasting services. Peddie lectures at numerous conferences on topics pertaining to graphics technology and the emerging trends in digital media technology and has been named one of the most influential analysts. He is frequently quoted in trade and business publications, and contributes articles to numerous publications and has appeared CNN and TechTV. He is the author of several books including "Graphics User Interfaces and Graphics Standards" (1992), "High Resolution Graphics Display Systems" (1994), "Multimedia and Graphics Controllers" (1994), and a contributor to "Advances in Modeling, Animation, and Rendering" (2002) and a Contributing editor to "Handbook of Visual Display Technology" (2009).

http://www.jonpeddie.com/

http://www.jonpeddie.com/about/who-we-are

http://www.glgroup.com/Council-Member/Jon-Peddie-2643.html

Email: jon@jonpeddie.com

Theresa-Marie Rhyne SCII, University of Utah, Salt Lake Sity, USA

Theresa-Marie Rhyne is a recognized expert in the field of computer-generated visualization and a consultant who specializes in applying artistic color theories to visualization and digital media. She is currently consulting for the Scientific Computing and Imaging Institute (SCII) at the University of Utah. In the 1990s, as a government contractor with Lockheed Martin Technical Services, she was the founding visualization leader of the US Environmental Protection Agency's Scientific Visualization Center. In the 2000s, she founded the Center for Visualization and Analytics and the Renaissance Computing Institute's Engagement Facility (renci@ncsu) at North Carolina State University. Rhyne is the editor of the Visualization Viewpoints Department for IEEE Computer Graphics & Applications Magazine and serves on the Advisory Board of IEEE Computer magazine. She received a BS degree, two MS degrees, and the Degree of Engineer in Civil Engineering from Stanford University. She entered the computer graphics field as a result of her computational and geographic modeling research in geotechnical and earthquake engineering. She is also an internationally recognized digital media artist who began creating digital media with early Apple computers, including the colorization of early Macintosh educational software. She is a senior member of the IEEE Computer Society and of the Association for Computing Machinery (ACM).

http://en.wikipedia.org/wiki/Theresa-Marie_Rhyne

Email: theresamarierhyne@gmail.com

William Ribarsky The University of North Carolina at Charlotte, Charlotte, USA

William Ribarsky is the Bank of America Endowed Chair in Information Technology at UNC Charlotte and the founding director of the Charlotte Visualization Center. Since 2009, he has been Chair of the Computer Science Department. He is also Principal Investigator for the DHS SouthEast Regional Visualization and Analytics Center. His research interests include visual analytics; 3D multimodal interaction; bioinformatics visualization; virtual environments; visual reasoning; and interactive visualization of large-scale information spaces. Formerly, he was the Associate Director for External Relations of the Georgia Tech GVU Center. Dr. Ribarsky is the former Chair and a current Director of the IEEE Visualization and Graphics Technical Committee. He is also a member of the Steering Committees for the IEEE Visualization Conference and the IEEE Virtual Reality Conference, the leading international conferences in their fields. He was an Associate Editor of IEEE Transactions on Visualization and Computer Graphics and is currently an Editorial Board member of IEEE Computer Graphics & Applications. Dr. Ribarsky co-founded the Eurographics/IEEE visualization conference series (now called EG/IEEE EuroVis) and led the effort to establish the Virtual Reality Conference series. For the above efforts on behalf of IEEE, Dr. Ribarsky won the IEEE Meritorious Service Award in 2004. In 2007, he will be general co-chair of the IEEE Visual Analytics Science and Technology (VAST) Symposium. Dr. Ribarsky has published over 130 scholarly papers, book chapters, and books. He has received competitive research grants and contracts from NSF, ARL, ARO, DHS, EPA, ONR, AFOSR, DARPA, NASA, NIMA, NIJ, U.S. DOT, and several companies. He received a PhD in physics from the University of Cincinnati.

http://coitweb.uncc.edu/~ribarsky/

Email: ribarsky@uncc.edu

Lawrence J. Rosenblum National Science Foundation, Washington DC, USA

Lawrence J. Rosenblum has been Program Director for Graphics and Visualization at the National Science Foundation since 2004. From 1994 to 2004, he was Director of Virtual Reality (VR) Systems and Research at the Naval Research Laboratory (NRL) and Program Officer for Visualization and Computer Graphics at the Office of Naval Research (ONR). From 1992 to 1994, he was Liaison Scientist for Computer Science at the ONR European Office, based in London, UK. Rosenblum is currently on the editorial boards of IEEE CG&A and IJVR and has served on both the editorial boards of IEEE TVCG and several other journals. He was the Chairman of the IEEE Visualization and Graphics Technical Committee (VGTC) from 1994–1996 and is currently a VGTC Director. Rosenblum received an IEEE Outstanding Contribution Certificate for initiating and co-founding the IEEE Visualization Conference (now VisWeek). In 2008, he received the IEEE VGTC Visualization Career Award. He has served on the conference, program, and steering committees of numerous international conferences. Rosenblum is a Senior Member of the IEEE and a member of the IEEE Computer Society, ACM, and SIGGRAPH. He received his PhD in Mathematics from the Ohio State University http://en.wikipedia.org/wiki/Ohio_State_University in 1971.

http://en.wikipedia.org/wiki/Lawrence_J._Rosenblum

Email: lrosenbl@NSF.GOV

Ben Shneiderman Dept of Computer Science & Human and Computer Interaction Lab, University of Maryland, College Park, MD 20742, USA

Ben Shneiderman is a Professor in the Department of Computer Science, Founding Director (1983–2000) of the Human-Computer Interaction Laboratory, and Member of the Institute for Advanced Computer Studies at the University of Maryland at College Park (full resume). He has taught previously at the State University of New York and at Indiana University. He was made a Fellow of the ACM in 1997, elected a Fellow of the American Association for the Advancement of Science in 2001, and received the ACM CHI (Computer Human Interaction) Lifetime Achievement Award in 2001. He was elected to the National Academy of Engineering in 2010: "For research, software development, and scholarly texts concerning human-computer interaction and information visualization." Dr. Shneiderman is the author of Software Psychology: Human Factors in Computer and Information Systems (1980). His comprehensive text Designing the User Interface: Strategies for Effective Human-Computer Interaction (1st edition 1987, 2nd edition 1992, 3rd edition 1998, booksite Addison-Wesley Publishers, Reading, MA), came out in its 4th edition in April 2004 with Catherine Plaisant as co-author. The fifth edition appeared in March 2009. His 1989 book, co-authored with Greg Kearsley, Hypertext Hands-On!, contains a hypertext version on two disks. He is the originator of the Hyperties hypermedia system, which was produced by Cognetics Corp., Princeton Junction, NJ. Since 1991 his major focus has been information visualization, beginning with his dynamic queries and starfield display research that led to the development of Spotfire (Christopher Ahlberg, CEO). He was a Member of the Board of Directors (1996–2001). Spotfire grew to 200 employees and during Summer 2007 was bought by TIBCO. Dr. Shneiderman developed the treemap concept in 1991 which continues to inspire research and commercial implementations. The University of Maryland's Treemap 4.0, developed in cooperation with Catherine Plaisant, has been licensed by the HiveGroup, and remains available for educational and research purposes. Dr. Shneiderman remains as a Technical Adviser for the Hivegroup and he was a Computer Science Adviser (1999–2002) to Smartmoney which implemented the widely used MarketMap for stock market analyses. He has a BS from the City College of New York and an MS and PhD from the State University of New York at Stony Brook.

http://www.cs.umd.edu/~ben/

Email: ben@cs.umd.edu

Gabriel Taubin Brown University, Providence, RI 02912, USA

Gabriel Taubin earned a Licenciado en Ciencias Matemáticas degree from the University of Buenos Aires, Argentina, and a PhD degree in Electrical Engineering from Brown University. In 1990 he joined IBM, where during a thirteen years career in the Research Division he held various positions, including Research Staff Member and Research Manager. In 2003 he joined the Brown University School of Engineering as an Associate Professor of Engineering and Computer Science. While on sabbatical from IBM during the 2000–2001 academic year, he was appointed Visiting Professor of Electrical Engineering at the California Institute of Technology. While on sabbatical from Brown during the Spring semester of 2010, he was appointed Visiting Associate Professor of Media Arts and Sciences at MIT. Prof. Taubin is the current Editor-in-Chief of the IEEE Computer Graphics and Applications Magazine, he serves as a member of the Editorial Board of the Geometric Models journal, and has served as associate editor of the IEEE Transactions of Visualization and Computer Graphics. Prof. Taubin was named IEEE Fellow for his contributions to the development of three-dimensional geometry compression technology and multimedia standards, won the Eurographics 2002 Günter Enderle Best Paper Award, and was named IBM Master Inventor. He has made significant theoretical and practical contributions to the field now called Digital Geometry Processing: to 3D shape capturing and surface reconstruction, to geometric modeling, geometry compression, progressive transmission, signal processing, and display of discrete surfaces. The 3D geometry compression technology that he developed with his group was incorporated into the MPEG-4 standard, and became integral part of IBM products.

http://mesh.brown.edu/taubin/

Email: taubin@brown.edu

Daniel Thalmann Institute for Media Innovation, Nanyang Technological University, Singapore, Singapore

Prof. Daniel Thalmann is with the Institute for Media Innovation at the Nanyang Technological University in Singapore. He is a pioneer in research on Virtual Humans. His current research interests include Real-time Virtual Humans in Virtual Reality, crowd simulation, and 3D Interaction. Daniel Thalmann has been the Founder of The Virtual Reality Lab (VRlab) at EPFL. He is coeditor-in-chief of the Journal of Computer Animation and Virtual Worlds, and member of the editorial board of 6 other journals. Daniel Thalmann was member of numerous Program Committees, Program Chair and CoChair of several conferences including IEEE VR, ACM VRST, and ACM VRCAI. Daniel Thalmann has published more than 500 papers in Graphics, Animation, and Virtual Reality. He is co-editor of 30 books, and co-author of several books including "*Crowd Simulation*" and "*Stepping Into Virtual Reality*", published in 2007 by Springer. He received his PhD in Computer Science in 1977 from the University of Geneva and an Honorary Doctorate (Honoris Causa) from University Paul-Sabatier in Toulouse, France, in 2003. He also received the Eurographics Distinguished Career Award in 2010.

http://research.ntu.edu.sg/expertise/academicprofile/pages/StaffProfile.aspx?ST_EMAILID=DANIELTHALMANN

http://people.epfl.ch/daniel.thalmann

Email: daniel.thalmann@epfl.ch

danielthalmann@ntu.edu.sg

Bodo Urban Fraunhofer IGD, Joachim-Jungius-Str. 11, 18059 Rostock, Germany

Bodo Urban is Head of the Competence Center "Interactive Document Engineering" at Fraunhofer IGD in Rostock since 2008. Until 1990 he was research associate at the Computer Science Department of the University of Rostock, 1991 he moved to the new founded Rostock Division of the Computer Graphics Center, and 1992 he became responsible for the new founded Rostock Division of the Fraunhofer IGD. In 1998 he was appointed to Professor of Multimedia Communication at the Computer Science Department of the University of Rostock. Bodo Urban is a member of GI, ACM, IEEE and Eurographics. He is a reviewer and member of many program committees of international conferences and workshops as well as member of several executive committees and advisory boards. He received a MSc (Dipl.-Math.) in Mathematics and a PhD (Dr.-Ing.) in Computer Science from the University of Rostock, Germany in 1978 and 1983, respectively.

http://www.igd.fraunhofer.de/en/Institut/Abteilungen/Interactive-Document-Engineering/Mitarbeiter/Prof-Dr-Ing-Bodo-Urban

Email: bodo.urban@igd-r.fraunhofer.de

Frank Van Reeth Expertise Centre for Digital Media, Hasselt University – tUL – IBBT, Wetenschapspark, 2, BE-3590 Diepenbeek, Belgium

Frank Van Reeth is Professor of computer science at Hasselt University in Diepenbeek, Belgium since 1993. He is Deputy Managing Director of the Expertise Centre for Digital Media (EDM), a research institute of about 80 people at Hasselt University. He obtained a MSc in computer science in 1987 at the Free University of Brussels and a PhD in computer science at Limburgs University Centre (now Hasselt University) in 1993. His research interests include computer graphics, computer animation, networked virtual environments, human computer interaction and multimedia technology. He published over 120 scientific papers in the above domains. He is a frequent member of the Program Committee of international conferences such as "IEEE Virtual Reality", "Computer Graphics International" and "Computer Animation and Social Agents". Frank Van Reeth has been active in the R&D as well as project management in more than 10 European research projects and has been involved in numerous bilateral industrial research projects. He has served on many review committees (European Commission, IWT (Flanders), EPSRC) evaluating research proposals in the above domains. Currently he is the chairman of the computer science department at Hasselt University and serves as deputy director of the Future Internet research department of the IBBT. Frank Van Reeth is also cofounder of 8 spin-off companies.

http://www.edm.uhasselt.be/people/show/frank.van_reeth

Email: frank.vanreeth@uhasselt.be

Turner Whitted Microsoft Research, Redmond, USA

Turner Whitted is a Principal Researcher at Microsoft studying the architecture of graphics systems. He was a member of the computer science faculty at the University of North Carolina at Chapel Hill from 1983 until 2001 as well as a cofounder and director of Numerical Design Limited. Prior to that he was a member of the technical staff in Bell Labs' computer systems research laboratory where he introduced the notion of using recursive ray tracing to implement global illumination. In the past he has served on the editorial boards of IEEE Computer Graphics and Applications and ACM Transactions on Graphics, and was papers chair for SIGGRAPH 97. He is an ACM Fellow and a member of the National Academy of Engineering. He earned BSE and MS degrees from Duke University and a PhD from North Carolina State University, all in electrical engineering.
Email: jtw@microsoft.com

Jian J. Zhang National Centre for Computer Animation, Bournemouth University, Bournemouth, UK

Jian J. Zhang is Professor of Computer Graphics at the National Centre for Computer Animation, Bournemouth University and leads the Computer Animation Research Centre. He has worked at various universities including Bristol University, University of Newcastle upon Tyne, Chongqing University, Queens University of Belfast and Brunel University. Prof. Zhang has secured over 4 million pounds (GBP) in research grants from the EPSRC, AHRC, the GWR, the Wellcome Trust and other funding organizations. His research focuses on a number of topics relating to 3D virtual human modeling, animation and simulation, including geometric modeling, rigging and skinning, motion synthesis, deformation and physics-based simulation. He is also interested in graphics applications in medical visualization and sports simulation. Prof. Zhang has chaired numerous international conferences and symposia, and serves a number of editorial boards. Prof. Zhang has given over 30 invited talks and keynote presentations internationally. He is a member of both AHRC and EPSRC peer review colleges. Prof. Zhang is a co-founder of the EPSRC funded Centre for Digital Entertainment (CDE) jointly with the University of Bath. The CDE is a multimillion pound organization with the goal of producing the next generation of technical leaders in the area of computer games, computer animation and digital effects.

http://nccastaff.bournemouth.ac.uk/jzhang/

Email: jzhang@bournemouth.ac.uk

Co-authors (in alphabetical order)

Rodolfo Allendes Osorio Depto. de Ciencias de la Computación, Fac. de Ingeneria, Universidad de Talca, Talca, Chile

Rodolfo Allendes' main interests are the use and development of visualization methods applied in multidisciplinary scientific research, especially in terms of incorporating uncertainty to visualization and evaluating the effectiveness of such methods. Rodolfo gained a BSc in Engineering from the Universidad de Talca, Chile, and an Integrated degree of MSc and PhD in multidisciplinary informatics from the University of Leeds, UK.

G. Baduza SAP Research Internet Applications & Services, Pretoria, South Africa

Gugulethu Baduza is a Masters Research Associate at SAP Research Internet Applications and Services Africa, based in Pretoria, South Africa. She has studied at Rhodes University for her Bachelor of Commerce, Bachelor of Commerce (Hons) and is currently doing her Master of Commerce (Information Systems) still at Rhodes University. She has been involved the following living labs which have contributed to her knowledge of living labs, Smart Energy LL (SAP), Rustica LL (SAP), Siyakhula LL (Rhodes). Her main research areas include, rural development, ICT4D, community needs, ICT4D strategy, impact assessments. Recent activities have included conducting ethnographic research, observations studies, developing user manuals for GUI's developed for projects, implementation of software, training users to use the software, conducting needs assessments and conducting impacts assessments.

Email: gugulethu.baduza@sap.com

Fatih Calakli Brown University, Providence, RI 02912, USA

Fatih Calakli received his bachelor's degree in Electrical Engineering from Bogazici University, Turkey, in 2007. He is currently a PhD student working under the supervision of Professor Gabriel Taubin in Electrical Sciences and Computer Engineering at Brown University. His main research interests are computer vision, computational photography and digital geometry processing with particular interest in 3D shape capturing, surface reconstruction, and geometric modeling. His doctoral work involves developing inexpensive tools and efficient algorithms to create digital models of real-world objects.

http://www.lems.brown.edu/~fc/

Nancy Chinchor ChinchorElectric, Orange City, USA

Dr. Nancy Chinchor has degrees in Mathematics and Linguistics with continuous work experience in Computer Science. Currently she assists the US government in carrying out research in advanced analytics aided principally by visualization and the underpinning disciplines. She did a stint in computational linguistics founding the field of text extraction with the community. Prior to that she did CAD/CAM and graphics jobs. Some of her early work was embedded software in the brakes on Washington DC subway cars.

Email: chinchoreclectic@gmail.com

Jaegul Choo Computational Science and Engineering, Georgia Institute of Technology, Atlanta, USA

Jaegul Choo received the Bachelor's degree in electrical engineering from Seoul National University, Korea, and the Master's degree in electrical and computer engineering from Georgia Institute of Technology, USA. Currently, he is a PhD candidate in the school of computational science and engineering at Georgia Institute of Technology. His current research interests include data mining, machine learning, and visual analytics.

Stuart Cunningham Glyndwr University, Wrexham, Wales, UK

Stuart Cunningham joined Glyndwr University in 2003. He was awarded the BSc degree in Computer Networks in 2001, and in 2003 was awarded the MSc Multimedia Communications degree with Distinction, both from the University of Paisley (UK). In 2009 he was awarded the degree of PhD in Data Reduced Audio Coding by the University of Wales (UK). His research interests cover a broad range of computing and creative hybrids and include: audio compression techniques; human-computer interaction and audio for health and wellbeing; sound design; wireless network security; and the socio-economic impact of leading-edge technologies. Stuart is a Fellow of the British Computer Society (BCS) and Chartered IT Professional (CITP), Member of the Institution of Engineering & Technology (IET) and Member of the Institute of Electrical and Electronics Engineers (IEEE). Stuart was also a member of the MPEG Music Notation Standards (MPEG-SMR) working group. In his spare time, Stuart is an avid mountain biker and performs in a Pink Floyd tribute band named *Pink Lloyd*.

Email: s.cunningham@glyndwr.ac.uk

Steven Drucker Microsoft Research, Redmond, USA

Dr. Steven M. Drucker has been at Microsoft Research for over 16 years. He is currently a Principal Researcher and manager of the Visual User Experience group at Microsoft Research (MSR) focusing on human computer interaction for dealing with large amounts of information. He is also an affiliate professor at the University of Washington Computer Science and Engineering Department. Before coming to Microsoft, he received his PhD from the Computer Graphics and Animation Group at the MIT Media Lab in May 1994, an MS from the MIT AI Lab, and a ScB in Neurosciences from Brown University. He has demonstrated his work on stage with Bill Gates at the Consumer Electronics Show (CES); shipped software on the web for gathering and acting on information collected on the web; filed over 108 patents; and published papers on technologies as diverse as exploratory search, information visualization, multi-user environments, online social interaction, hypermedia research, human and robot perceptual capabilities, robot learning, parallel computer graphics, spectator oriented gaming, and human interfaces for camera control.

J.H.P. Eloff SAP Research Internet Applications & Services, Pretoria, South Africa

Prof. Dr Jan Eloff is currently appointed as the Research Director of SAP Meraka UTD. In this role, his main focus is on conducting research for the creation of new software platforms for emerging economies. He is appointed as a Chief Researcher at the CSIR (Meraka) and as an Extraordinary Professor in Computer Science at the University of Pretoria. He is also a board member of SoftstartBTI, an ICT entrepreneurial development company in South Africa. A PhD (Computer Science) was awarded to him in 1985. Since then he worked on and managed many industry related projects and served as an expert adviser on information security.

http://www.cs.up.ac.za/~eloff

http://za.linkedin.com/in/janeloff

Steven K. Feiner Columbia University, New York, USA

Steven K. Feiner is Professor of Computer Science at Columbia University, where he directs the Computer Graphics and User Interfaces Lab and co-directs the Columbia Vision and Graphics Center. His research interests include human–computer interaction, augmented reality and virtual environments, 3D user interfaces, knowledge-based design of graphics and multimedia, mobile and wearable computing, computer games, and information visualization. His lab created the first outdoor mobile augmented reality system using a see-through display in 1996, and has pioneered experimental applications of augmented reality to fields such as tourism, journalism, maintenance, and construction. Prof. Feiner is coauthor of *Computer Graphics: Principles and Practice* and of *Introduction to Computer Graphics*, received an ONR Young Investigator Award, and was elected to the CHI Academy. Together with his students, he has won the *ACM UIST Lasting Impact Award* and best paper awards at *ACM UIST*, *ACM CHI*, *ACM VRST*, and *IEEE ISMAR*. He is currently program co-chair for *IEEE Virtual Reality 2012* and for *Foundations of Digital Games 2012*. Feiner received a PhD in Computer Science from Brown University in 1987.

http://www.cs.columbia.edu/~feiner/

Email: feiner@cs.columbia.edu

Fabian Di Fiore Expertise Centre for Digital Media, Hasselt University – tUL – IBBT, Wetenschapspark, 2, BE-3590 Diepenbeek, Belgium

Fabian Di Fiore is a visiting professor in computer science at Hasselt University (UHasselt) in Belgium. He obtained a MS in computer science in 1997 at the University of Leuven and a PhD in computer science at Limburgs University Centre (now Hasselt University) in 2004. His research activities are concerned with computer animation, non-photorealistic rendering and animation, highly stylized drawn animation and visual computing. He published over 30 scientific papers in the above domains. He is a frequent member of the Program Committee of international conferences such as "Motion in Games" and "Computer Animation and Social Agents". Fabian Di Fiore has been active in the R&D as well as project management in several research projects.

Email: fabian.difiore@uhasselt.be

Fabian Fischer University of Konstanz, Konstanz, Germany

Fabian Fischer is Research Associate and PhD student at the Computer Science department of the University of Konstanz (Germany) and is employed by the Data Analysis and Visualization Group lead by Prof. Dr. Daniel A. Keim. He has received his MSc degree in Information Engineering by the same university in 2011, where he also received his BSc in 2008. His research interests are in the field of visual analytics, network security, real-time applications, and system administration.

http://infovis.uni-konstanz.de/~fischer/
Email: Fabian.Fischer@uni-konstanz.de

Eddy Flerackers Expertise Centre for Digital Media, Hasselt University – tUL – IBBT, Wetenschapspark, 2, BE-3590 Diepenbeek, Belgium

Prof. Dr. Eddy Flerackers is a full professor in Computer Science at Hasselt University. He obtained a Master degree in Physics (1973) from the Catholic University of Leuven and a PhD in Physics (1980) at the Free University of Brussels. His current research interests include Computer Graphics, Multimedia & Communication Technology and Human-Computer Interaction. He co-authored more than 90 international publications. He is promoter of several PhD projects in computer science at Hasselt University and was member of the PhD jury of over 30 PhD projects. He is the managing director of the Expertise Centre for Digital Media, a research institute at Hasselt University with 60 researchers. He is also a member of the Research Council of the university. Eddy Flerackers has been project leader of 5 ERDF-projects (European Regional Development Fund, with a total contract volume of more than 12 M€) and project leader/participant in more than 25 European Framework Research Projects. He has been project leader of numerous research projects with the industry. He is initiator of multiple spin-off companies and is president (or member) of the Board of several of these spin-off companies. He is a Fellow of the Virtual Reality Society and a member of ACM, IEEE, CGS and Eurographics. Currently, he is also an associate editor of Virtual Reality journal and a member of the editorial board of The Visual Computer.

Email: Eddy.flerackers@uhasselt.be

Deborah Gracio Director, Computational and Statistical Analytics Division, Pacific Northwest National Laboratory, Richland, USA

Deborah K. Gracio is Director for the Computational and Statistical Analytics Division in Pacific Northwest National Laboratory's National Security Directorate. She has led the research, development, and management of multiple cross-disciplinary, multi-laboratory projects focused in the basic sciences and national security sectors. As the director of the Data-Intensive Computing research initiative, she built a program that identified PNNL as the leader in addressing the challenges of high-throughput streaming data and multi-source analytics focused on problems in the fundamental science and national security domains. Ms. Gracio received an R&D 100 Award in 1999 and a Federal Laboratory Consortium Award in 2000 for the Molecular Sciences Software Suite, a software product now used by institutions worldwide. She is currently a Senior Member of the Institute for Electrical and Electronics Engineers and served on the IEEE Information Systems Strategy Council. She earned BS and MS degrees in Electrical Engineering from Washington State University.

http://www.pnnl.gov/nationalsecurity/technical/computing/

Seok-Hee Hong University of Sydney, Sydney, Australia

Seok-Hee Hong is an associate professor and principal research fellow in the School of Information Technologies at the University of Sydney, Australia. She has been a Project Leader at NICTA, 2004–2007. Her research interests include graph drawing, network visualization, visual analytics, and algorithms. She is working on scalable visual analytics for uncertain dynamic networks. She has a PhD in Computer Science from Ewha University in Korea.

http://sydney.edu.au/engineering/it/~shhong

Email: shhong@it.usyd.edu.au

Haiyan Hou WISELab, Dalian University of Technology, Dalian, China

Dr. Haiyan Hou is an associate professor of the School of Science Studies and Management of Science & Technology of Dalian University of Technology, China. She is currently a visiting professor at the iSchool of Drexel University. She earned her PhD degree in Science Studies and Management of Science in Dalian University of Technology in 2006. Her research interests include mapping knowledge domains of scientific disciplines and discoveries. She has published more than 50 papers in *Journal of Informetrics*, *Scientometrics*, and Chinese journals such as *Science Studies* and *R & D Management*. She led and participated in projects funded by the Chinese National Natural Science Foundation. She is an Editorial Board Member of COLLNET Journal of Scientometrics and Information Management, a member of the Chinese National Society of Science and Technology Management, a member of COLLNET member (a global interdisciplinary research network), and a member of the council of Institute of Quantitative Economics of Liaoning Province, China.

Zhigang Hu WISELab, Dalian University of Technology, Dalian, China

Zhigang Hu is a PhD student at Dalian University of Technology, China. He is currently a visiting doctoral student at the iSchool of Drexel University. He earned his BA degree in Management Science at Beijing Normal University in 2006 and his Master degree in Philosophy of Science at the Graduate School of the Chinese Academy of Sciences in 2009. His research areas include citation analysis, scientific collaboration, and information visualization. He has published several papers in *The Science of Science and the Science and Technology Management*, *Journal of the China Society for Scientific and Technical Information*, and *Journal of Management Sciences in China.*

Keehyoung Joo Korea Institute for Advanced Study, Seoul, Korea

Keehyoung Joo is research professor at Center for Advanced Computation, Korea Institute for Advanced Study, Korea. His research interests are protein structure prediction/determination, bioinformatics, global optimization. Previously he was assistant professor of School of Computational Sciences, Korea Institute for Advanced Study. He has a BS, MS and PhD degrees in physics from Sungkyunkwan University, Korea.

Email: newton@kias.re.kr

Simon J. Julier University College London, London, UK

Simon J. Julier is a Senior Lecturer in the Virtual Environments and Computer Graphics Group, Department of Computer Science, University College London. He has a MEng and a DPhil from the University of Oxford, UK. Before joining UCL in 2006, he worked for nine years in the VRLab at the Naval Research Laboratory, Washington DC where he served as the co-investigator on the Battlefield Augmented Reality System project. His research interests lie at the cross roads between information fusion and information presentation. He has published in mixed reality, augmented reality, nonlinear estimation, multi-target tracking, distributed estimation, and mapping and localization. He co-chaired IEEE VR 2006 and IEEE ISMAR 2008. He serves on the Steering Committee for ISMAR.

http://www.cs.ucl.ac.uk/staff/s.julier/

Email: S.Julier@cs.ucl.ac.uk

J. Kohlhammer Fraunhofer IGD, Darmstadt, Germany

Jörn Kohlhammer heads the department of Information Visualization and Visual Analytics, a team of 15 researchers, at the Fraunhofer Institute for Computer Graphics (IGD) in Darmstadt, Germany. For five years he worked as a scientist at a Fraunhofer-Center in Providence, RI, USA in the area of context-based information visualization. His work on decision-centered visualization brought him back to Germany and to Fraunhofer IGD. He received his doctoral degree from the Technical University of Darmstadt in 2005 and a Master of Science degree in Computer Science from the Ludwig-Maximilian-University Munich in 1999. His interests include semantics-based and decision-centered information visualization, visual business intelligence, and visual analytics, especially their various industry applications. He served as co-chair of the IEEE VAST in 2009.

http://www.igd.fraunhofer.de/IVA

D. Kok SAP Research Internet Applications & Services, Pretoria, South Africa

Danie Kok is the Head of the SAP Research Internet Applications and Services Africa, based in Pretoria, South Africa. He is also Joint Chief Executive Officer of the SAP Meraka Unit for Technology Development. He was responsible for both the establishment of SAP Research Pretoria and the SAP Meraka Unit for Technology Development (UTD). SAP Research Pretoria and UTD focus their research on new business opportunities for SAP linked to appropriate technologies for emerging economies. It similarly, in terms of its collaboration agreement with the SA Government, contributes to advanced human capital development, whilst also studying the impact technology (ICT) can have on socio-economic development. He initiated various research projects since the establishment of the Research Centre—in the health, education and training, VSE (SMME) and civil society sectors. All research projects are addressing issues related to the technology (ICT) needs of these sectors in emerging economies; solutions to obstacles preventing/hindering the utilization of technology; appropriate hardware, application software and communication infrastructures, ease of use of technology solutions and the impact ICT can have on development. His experience in higher education, further and distance education and training, organizational and partnership development spans a period of 25 years. In various roles, ranging from Vice-Principal at Technikon SA to Development, Marketing and Communication Director at various Universities and Colleges, he developed an expert understanding of the higher and further education sectors and the developmental needs of emerging regions. He was responsible for the establishment of SAP Research Pretoria in SA and was appointed Director in 2005. Danie graduated from the University of Pretoria with a BA Political Science Degree in 1977 and has subsequently completed a Business Development Program (University of Pretoria) and an Advanced Executive Program (University of South Africa). His research interest relates to the introduction and utilization of technology to increase access, particularly for individuals previously deprived of such opportunities, to quality learning (education), as well as the development and utilization of appropriate technology solutions, characterized by simplicity and ease of use that could open new markets for SAP and facilitate socio-economic development in emerging regions.

http://www.sap.com/about/company/research/index.epx

Email: danie.kok@sap.com

Minkyung Lee HIT Lab NZ, University of Canterbury, Christchurch, New Zealand

Minkyung Lee is Manager in Technology Strategy Office at KT. Her research interests include 3D multimodal interfaces and user behavior modeling. She has a BcEng (Bachelor of Engineering) in 2002 from Kyunghee University and a Master of Science in 2004 from GIST. She completed her PhD in Computer Science in 2010 at the University of Canterbury, New Zealand, under the supervision of Professor Mark Billinghurst.

Fuxin Li Computational Science and Engineering, Georgia Institute of Technology, Atlanta, USA

Fuxin Li received the Bachelor's degree from Zhejiang University in 2001 and the PhD degree in the Institute of Automation, Chinese Academy of Sciences in 2008. He is a postdoctoral researcher in the department of Computational Science and Engineering, Georgia Institute of Technology. He had spent two years as a research scientist in the University of Bonn, and won the PASCAL Visual Object Challenge in image segmentation for 2009 and 2010. He has published about 20 research papers in machine learning, computer vision, pattern recognition and proteomics. He is a member of the IEEE.

Shengbo Liu WISELab, Dalian University of Technology, Dalian, China

Shengbo Liu is a PhD student at Dalian University of Technology. He earned his bachelor degree in computer science at Southwest University in China. He is a member of the WISElab in Dalian University of Technology. He is currently a visiting doctoral student at the iSchool of Drexel University. His research areas include co-citation analysis, complex network analysis, knowledge measurement, and information visualization. He has published more than 10 papers on related topics in China.

Mark A. Livingston Naval Research Laboratory, Washington DC, USA

Mark A. Livingston has been a researcher at the Naval Research Laboratory since 2001; since 2007, he has led the Virtual Environments and Visualization group. He directs and conducts research on interactive graphics, including augmented reality and visual analytics, focusing on human factors and applications. He received his doctorate in 1998 from the University of North Carolina at Chapel Hill, where he helped develop augmented reality systems for intra-operative ultrasound and laparoscopic imagery visualization. He is a member-at-large of the Executive Committee of the IEEE Technical Committee on Visualization and Graphics, on program, conference, or steering committees for the IEEE International Symposium on Mixed and Augmented Reality, IEEE Virtual Reality, and SPIE Visualization and Data Analysis, among others. The work described in this chapter on depth perception and X-ray vision led to an Alan Berman Research Publication Award at NRL in 2003 and an Honorable Mention at IEEE Virtual Reality in 2006.

Email: mark.livingston@nrl.navy.mil

Adriano Lopes CITI / Depto. Informática, FCT, Universidade Nova de Lisboa, Lisbon, Portugal

Adriano Lopes graduated with the BSc degree in electrical engineering and informatics in 1986 and the MSc degree in computer science in 1993, both from the University of Coimbra, Portugal. In 1999, he received the PhD degree in scientific visualization from the University of Leeds, United Kingdom. He was a lecturer on the Faculty of Science and Technology at the University of Coimbra. In 2002 he joined the Department of Informatics of the Faculty of Science and Technology,

New University of Lisbon, Portugal, where he is also a member of the Research Center for Informatics and Information Technologies (CITI). His teaching and main research interests are in visualization and computer graphics. He is a member of the Eurographics Association.

Patrik Lundblad Media and Information Technology, National Centre for Visual Analytics, Linköping University, Linköping, Sweden

Patrik Lundblad is a PhD student in Information Visualization at NCVA (Swedish National Center for Visual Analytics) working in close collaboration with SMHI (Swedish Meteorological and Hydrological Institute). His area of research involves Information- and Geo-visualization applied to the area of meteorology and statistics. Together with SMHI he has worked on visualizing weather in combination with safety and optimization of ship voyages, giving the shipping operators better insight into their ships performance and how the weather influences a voyage. He has also created a web-enabled application for road weather visualization, a tool for analyzing and communicating information about road weather conditions particularly during the Swedish winter months that is used by the Swedish Road Administration. With OECD he developed the PISA 2009 country profiles application which contains visualizations of key indicators for the 65 countries that took part of the 2009 PISA assessment. Together with the team at the spin-off company NComVA he is now developing statistical software used by the statistics community to make statistics data more easily available for the public users.

Email: Patrik.lundblad@liu.se

Florian Mansmann University of Konstanz, Konstanz, Germany

Dr. Florian Mansmann is a post-doctoral fellow at the University of Konstanz. He received a Bachelor degree in “Information Engineering” from the University of Konstanz in 2003 and a Master’s degree in “Business Information Management” from the Vrije Universiteit Brussels in 2004 and a PhD in computer science from the University of Konstanz in 2008. His research interests include network security, geographic analysis and real-time analysis with a focus on knowledge discovery, information visualization and visual analytics methods. Besides actively teaching visualization and knowledge discovery courses, he is a team leader for several visual analytics projects in network security and geographic analysis. He serves as a program committee member of VizSec, EuroVA and IEEE InfoVis and chairs the Discovery Exhibition 2011.

http://infovis.uni-konstanz.de/~mansmann/

Email: Florian.Mansmann@uni-konstanz.de

C. Merz SAP Research Internet Applications & Services, Pretoria, South Africa

Christian Merz acts as a manager in SAP’s Research Center in Karlsruhe, Germany. Currently he is directing the *Internet of Services (IoS)* research group that is looking into future service e-trading and delivery mechanisms. The portfolio includes the

THESEUS/TEXO project one of the largest publicly funded interventions to implement the *IoS* vision. In addition he is working in the research field "applications for emerging economies" trying to establish sustainable business and technology models for socio economic development in emerging countries. He leads SAP's involvement in the *African Cashew Initiative* focusing on IT supported smallholder farmer groups. In 2006 he acquired and led the EU funded project *Collaboration at Rural* (C@R) that stimulated economic development of small and micro enterprises in rural Africa through the innovative concept of *Virtual Cooperatives*. Other project experiences comprise interoperability in business networks (EU project ATHENA), e-learning platforms to educate in-service teachers and healthcare solutions in rural South Africa. He joined SAP Research 11 years ago and contributed innovative solutions in the area of Ubiquitous Computing before he concentrated on Knowledge Management, Human Computer Interaction and Collaborative Working Environments. Christian started in 1997 as an SAP employee and consulted SAP customers internationally on SAP implementations for about 3 years. He received his Diploma in Physics from the Albert-Ludwigs-University in Freiburg, Germany.

Email: christian.merz@sap.com

Christian Peter Fraunhofer IGD, Joachim-Jungius-Str. 11, 18059 Rostock, Germany

Christian Peter is senior scientist at the Competence Center "Interactive Document Engineering" of the Fraunhofer IGD in Rostock. He obtained his Master's Degree (Diploma) in Electrical Engineering in 1996 from the University of Rostock, Germany. From 1997 to 2000 he was researcher at the Computing Laboratory of Oxford University, UK in the field of hardware development and systems design for novel sensor technologies. Since 2000 he is with Fraunhofer IGD in Rostock, focusing his research on the development of intelligent, self-contained, non-obtrusive sensors for affect-related physiological parameters and the analysis and application of the obtained data. Mr. Peter is initiator and co-organizer of a workshop series on Emotion in Human-Computer Interaction and serves on the scientific committee of several conferences, workshops and symposia related to affect and emotion in human-computer interaction. He is a member of the BCS, Eurographics, and the Humaine Association, and contributes to the emotion sub-group at the World Wide Web consortium's (W3C) MMI activity.

http://www.igd.fraunhofer.de/en/Institut/Abteilungen/Interactive-Document-Engineering/Mitarbeiter/Dipl-Ing-Christian-Peter

http://emotion-research.net/Members/ChristianPeter/

Email: christian.peter@igd-r.fraunhofer.de

Anthony Peurrung Associate Laboratory Director, National Security, Pacific Northwest National Laboratory, Richland, USA

Anthony Peurrung is the Associate Laboratory Director for the National Security Directorate at Pacific Northwest National Laboratory (www.pnnl.gov/nationalsecurity/). His Directorate of 1,190 staff members is responsible for delivering high-impact, science-based, practical solutions to clients to prevent and counter acts of terrorism and the proliferation of weapons of mass destruction. Dr. Peurrung has been a member of the US Department of Energy's Radiation Detection Panel and held the senior non-federal leadership role representing the DOE laboratory complex during the standup of the US Department of Homeland Security's radiological/nuclear countermeasures science and technology program. His research has entailed such topics as special nuclear material detection and characterization and fundamental advances in the areas of neutron detection and gamma-ray spectrometry. Dr. Peurrung has a BS degree in Electrical Engineering from Rice University and a PhD degree in Physics from the University of California, Berkeley.

Email: aj.peurrung@pnl.gov

M. Przewloka SAP Research Internet Applications & Services, Pretoria, South Africa

Martin Przewloka serves as Senior Vice President at SAP and is responsible for the Global SAP Research Program of Future Internet Applications and Services that includes SAP's research program of ICT solutions for Emerging Markets and Economies. During his tenure with SAP, Prof. Przewloka held various management roles. Previously, he was the Senior Vice President of Showcase & Trial Solutions as part of SAP Marketing; responsible world-wide for all SAP demo and presentation solutions, infrastructures, and services. Formerly, Prof. Przewloka was responsible for several SAP industry solutions as well as for SAP ERP, one of the SAP flagship products. Prof. Przewloka is based at the SAP headquarters in Walldorf Germany, and he holds university degrees in physics, economics, and medical physics from the universities of Giessen/Germany, Geneva/Switzerland and Kaiserslautern/Germany. Furthermore, he holds a professorship in computer sciences from the University of Applied Sciences of Giessen/Germany and has another professorship at Provadis School of International Management and Technology, Frankfurt/Germany.

Email: martin.przewloka@sap.com

Jean Scholtz Pacific Northwest National Laboratory, Richland, USA

Dr Jean Scholtz is a researcher at the Pacific Northwest National Laboratory. She was recruited to come and work on the Visual Analytics Science and Technology (VAST) contest by Jim Thomas when she retired from the National Institute of Standards and Technology. Her research interests are in developing metrics and methodologies for evaluating interactive systems. She has applied this to varied domains including information systems for intelligence analysts, visual analytics systems and human-robot interaction systems. She holds a PhD in Computer Science from the University of Nebraska.

Email: Jean.Scholtz@pnnl.gov

T. Schreck Universität Konstanz, Konstanz, Germany

Tobias Schreck currently is an Assistant Professor for Visual Analytics with the Department for Computer and Information Science at University of Konstanz, Germany. Between 2007 and 2011, he was a Postdoc researcher at Technische Universität Darmstadt, Germany, where he headed a research group on Visual Search and Analysis. He obtained a PhD in Computer Science in 2006, and a Master of Science degree in Information Engineering in 2002, both from the University of Konstanz. Tobias Schreck works in the areas of Visual Analytics, Information Visualization, and Digital Libraries. His research interests include visual search and analysis in time-oriented, high-dimensional, and 3D object data, with applications in data analysis and multimedia retrieval. He co-authored more than 70 scientific publications. He served as a co-organizer for the Eurographics Workshop on 3D Object Retrieval in 2010 and 2011, and as a poster and publicity co-chair for IEEE Visweek in 2009 and 2011, respectively.

http://cms.uni-konstanz.de/informatik/schreck/

Nick Schultz Oregon State University, Corvallis, USA

Nick Schultz was born and raised in Portland, Oregon and went to Oregon State University. At Oregon State, he graduated Cum Laude with a Bachelors of Science degree in Computer Science. He then went on to graduate school at Oregon State and obtained his Masters of Science in Computer Science with the majority of his work pertaining to computer graphics. While working on his Master's degree, he worked for the Bioengineering Department developing scientific visualizations. After graduation in June of 2011, Nick accepted a position with Intel Corporation where he develops graphics hardware simulation software.

Han-Wei Shen The Ohio State University, Columbus, OH, USA

Han-Wei Shen is an Associate Professor of Computer Science and Engineering at The Ohio State University, where he heads the Graphics and Visualization Study (GRAVITY) research group. His research interests include data analysis and visualization, computer graphics, and high performance computing. Having worked in the areas for nearly two decades, he has authored over one hundred technical papers on a variety of topics in scientific visualization, information visualization, and visual analytics. He has served on the editorial board for numerous journals including IEEE Transactions on Visualization and Computer Graphics. He has also been a guest editor for several special issues of IEEE Computer Graphics and Applications. He was a program co-chair for IEEE Pacific Visualization 2009–2010, and IEEE Visualization 2008–2009. He joined Ohio State in 1999. Previously he worked at NASA Ames Research Center from 1996 to 1999. He received his PhD from the Scientific Computing and Imaging Group at University of Utah in 1998. He is the recipient of NSF Career Award and DOE's Early Career Principle Investigator Award.

J. Edward Swan II Mississippi State University, Starkville, USA

J. Edward Swan II is a Professor of Computer Science and Engineering, and an Adjunct Professor of Psychology, at Mississippi State University. He holds a BS (1988) degree in computer science from Auburn University and MS (1992) and PhD (1997) degrees in computer science from the Ohio State University, where he studied computer graphics and human-computer interaction. Before joining Mississippi State University in 2004, Swan spent seven years as a scientist at the Naval Research Laboratory in Washington, DC Swan's research has been broad-based, centering on the topics of augmented and virtual reality, perception, human-computer interaction, human factors, empirical methods, computer graphics, and visualization. Currently, Swan is studying perception in augmented and virtual reality, including depth and layout perception and depth presentation methods, as well as empirical techniques for evaluating and validating visualizations. His research has been funded by the National Science Foundation, the National Aeronautics and Space Administration, the Naval Research Laboratory, and the Office of Naval Research. Swan is a member of ACM, IEEE, the IEEE Computer Society, and ASEE.

http://www.cse.msstate.edu/~swan/

Email: swan@cse.msstate.edu

H. Ugail Centre for Visual Computing, University of Bradford, Bradford, UK

Prof. Hassan Ugail, is the director for the Centre for Visual Computing at Bradford. He has a first class BSc Honors degree in Mathematics from King's College London and a PhD in the field of geometric design from the School of Mathematics at University of Leeds. Prof. Ugail's research interests include geometric modeling, computer animation, functional design, numerical methods and design optimization, applications of geometric modeling to real time interactive and parametric design and applications of geometric modeling to general engineering problems. Prof. Ugail has 3 patents on novel techniques relating to geometry modeling, animation and 3D data exchange. He is a reviewer for various international journals, conferences and grant awarding bodies. His recent innovations have led the formation a university spin-out company Tangentix Ltd with investments from venture capitalists. He has recently won the vice-chancellor's award for knowledge transfer for his outstanding contribution to research and knowledge transfer activities.

http://scim.brad.ac.uk/staff/?u=hugail

Email: h.ugail@bradford.ac.uk

T. von Landesberger Technische Universität Darmstadt, Darmstadt, Germany

Tatiana von Landesberger is currently a Postdoc researcher at Technische Universität Darmstadt, Germany, where she leads a research group on Visual Search and Analysis. She obtained a PhD in Computer Science in 2010 from Technische Universität Darmstadt, Germany. After finishing master studies of economic and financial mathematics at Univerzita Komenskeho, Bratislava, Slovakia in 2003, she worked for two years at the European Central Bank, Frankfurt, Germany. Tatiana von Landesberger's main research topics are Visual Analytics and Digital Libraries.

http://www.gris.informatik.tu-darmstadt.de/~ttekusov/

tatiana.von-landesberger@gris.tu-darmstadt.de

Zachary Wartell The University of North Carolina at Charlotte, Charlotte, USA

Zachary Wartell is an Associate Professor in the Department of Computer Science in the College of Computing and Informatics at the University of North Carolina at Charlotte. He is also the Associate Director of The Charlotte Visualization Center. Dr. Wartell received his PhD from the College of Computing at the Georgia Institute of Technology in 2001. He worked for several years at the Human Interface Technology Center at NCR. Dr. Wartell's research interests include 3D visualization and graphics and virtual/mixed reality user interfaces. Dr. Wartell has published over 30 scholarly papers and book chapters. He has received competitive research grants and contracts from NSF, ARO and DHS and various state agencies.

http://coitweb.uncc.edu/~zwartell/

Email: zwartell@uncc.edu

L.H. You National Centre for Computer Animation, Bournemouth University, Bournemouth, UK

Dr. L.H. You is currently a senior research lecturer at the National Centre for Computer Animation, Bournemouth University, UK. He received his MSc degree and PhD degree from Chongqing University, China and another PhD degree from Bournemouth University, UK. His current research interests are in computer graphics, computer animation and geometric modeling. He has produced over 160 refereed publications and is a reviewer for over 30 international journals, some international conferences and funding bodies.

Email: LYou@bournemouth.ac.uk

X.Y. You Faculty of Engineering and Computing, Coventry University, Coventry, UK

Mr. X.Y. You is currently a part-time MSc student with Coventry University, UK. He was awarded a BSc degree in computer science by the University of Warwick, UK. He is interested in the research into computer graphics.

Chapter 1
Introduction—The Best Is Yet to Come

John Dill, Rae Earnshaw, David Kasik, John Vince, and Pak Chung Wong

Abstract This book is written in honor of Jim Thomas by colleagues and friends who were inspired by his energy and enthusiasm for the fields of visual analytics and visualization. Resources that introduce these fields are provided, and these also contain bibliographies of further references. In addition, a number of organizations and institutions have provided repositories, portals, and libraries of further information that can be accessed on-line. Information is also provided on international conferences. The content of this present volume is summarized. Chapters are contributed by leading international researchers in the field with an emphasis upon exciting new aspects which are driving the field forward. It is certain that the challenges of Big Data will increase and therefore it is important to continually innovate and devise new ways of addressing these.

1.1 A Tribute

A Festschrift is normally a book honoring the contributions a notable person has made during their lifetime. A comparable volume written posthumously is termed a Gedenkschrift. This volume is neither of these, though it is written in honor of Jim Thomas by colleagues and friends who were (and still are) inspired by his energy, enthusiasm, and vision.

J. Dill
Simon Fraser University, Surrey, Canada

R. Earnshaw (✉)
University of Bradford, Bradford, UK
e-mail: R.A.Earnshaw@bradford.ac.uk

D. Kasik
The Boeing Company, Seattle, WA, USA

J. Vince
Bournemouth University, Poole, UK

P.C. Wong
Pacific Northwest National Laboratory, Richland, WA, USA

J. Dill et al. (eds.), *Expanding the Frontiers of Visual Analytics and Visualization*,
DOI 10.1007/978-1-4471-2804-5_1, © Springer-Verlag London Limited 2012

The royalties from the sale of this book go to the IEEE Jim Thomas Memorial Fund. Donations can also be made by readers as follows. To donate, make checks payable to IEEE Foundation, with "IEEE Jim Thomas Memorial Fund" noted on the check. Mail checks to the following address:

IEEE Foundation
ATTN: Karen Galuche
445 Hoes Lane
Piscataway, NJ 08854-4141
USA

On-line donations may also be made via the IEEE Foundation website.

Further information is at—http://vacommunity.org/article11

http://ewh.ieee.org/r6/richland/index.php?option=com_content&task=view&id=122&Itemid=29

Tributes have already been paid to Jim Thomas in the following publications—

"*In Memoriam: Jim Thomas 1946–2010*", IEEE Computer Graphics & Applications, Vol 30, No 6, pp 10–13, 2010

http://ieeexplore.ieee.org/stamp/stamp.jsp?tp=&arnumber=5613123

"*In Memoriam: Illuminating Our Paths—James (Jim) Joseph Thomas*," D. S. Ebert, J. Dill, and D. J. Kasik, IEEE Transactions on Visualization and Computer Graphics, Vol 16, No 6, Nov/Dec 2010, p. xxi.

http://ieeexplore.ieee.org/stamp/stamp.jsp?tp=&arnumber=5613420

"*Jim Thomas*", B. Shneiderman and P. C. Wong, Information Visualization, 9, pp 233–234, 2010.

http://ivi.sagepub.com/content/9/4/233

"*The Four Roads Less Traveled—A Tribute to Jim Thomas (1946–2010)*", P. C. Wong,

http://vgtc.org/JimThomas.html

The visual analytics community

http://vacommunity.org/article3

1.2 Background to Visual Analytics and Visualization

For readers who are new to the field of visual analytics and visualization, or who have specialized in one particular area and would like an overview of the field as whole, the following references should be useful. They also contain bibliographies of further references detailing research and development in the field, so there is no overall bibliography in this volume (though there are references at the end of each chapter). The following references are given in chronological order.

"*Visual Analytics*", P. C. Wong and J. J. Thomas (Eds), Special Issue of IEEE Computer Graphics and Applications, Vol 24, No 5, pp 20–21, 2004.

http://ieeexplore.ieee.org/stamp/stamp.jsp?tp=&arnumber=1333623&userType=inst

"*Illuminating the Path: The Research and Development Agenda for Visual Analytics*", J. J. Thomas and K. A. Cook (Eds), IEEE Computer Society Press, ISBN 0-7695-2323-4, 2005.

Free download of the book (27 MB)—http://nvac.pnl.gov/agenda.stm#book

"*Information Visualization—Design for Interaction*", R. Spence, Pearson Education Limited, 2nd edition, ISBN-13: 978-0132065504, 2007.

"*Discovering the Unexpected*", K. A. Cook, R. A. Earnshaw, and J. Stasko (Eds), Special Issue of IEEE Computer Graphics and Applications, Vol 27, No 5, 2007.

http://ieeexplore.ieee.org/stamp/stamp.jsp?tp=&arnumber=4302578

"*Foundations and Frontiers of Visual Analytics*", J. Kielman and J. Thomas, (Eds), Special Issue of Information Visualization, Vol 8, No 4, pp 239–314, 2009.

http://www.vismaster.eu/news/foundation-and-frontiers-of-visual-analytics/

(the above journal is no longer published by Palgrave and is now a Sage publication where on-line copies of articles are no longer free of charge).

"*Mastering the Information Age—Solving Problems with Visual Analytics*", D. Keim, J. Kohlhammer, G. Ellis and F. Mansmann (Eds.), pp 170, Eurographics Association, 2010.

http://www.vismaster.eu/book/

Free download of the book (23 MB)—

http://www.vismaster.eu/wp-content/uploads/2010/11/VisMaster-book-lowres.pdf

For general information on computer graphics— "*Computer Graphics: Principles and Practice*", J. F. Hughes, A. van Dam, M. McGuire, D. Sklar, J. D. Foley, S. Feiner, and K. Akeley, 3rd edition, Pearson Education, to be published May 2012.

1.3 Resources for Visual Analytics and Visualization

The following sites provide further information and resources for visual analytics and visualization—

National Visualization and Analytics Center, USA—

http://nvac.pnl.gov/about.stm

Regional Centers—

http://nvac.pnl.gov/centers.stm

Visual Analytics Benchmark Repository—

http://hcil.cs.umd.edu/localphp/hcil/vast/archive/index.php

Visual Analytics EU Portal—

http://www.visual-analytics.eu/

Related Web sites—

http://www.visual-analytics.eu/related/

The Visual Analytics Digital Library at Georgia Institute of Technology, USA—

http://vadl.cc.gatech.edu/

Vismaster—

http://www.vismaster.eu/

1.4 International Conferences

The following are the principal international conferences in the field—
IEEE Visualization (since 1990)
http://visweek.org/
http://ieeexplore.ieee.org/xpl/conhome.jsp?punumber=1000796
IEEE Information Visualization (since 1995)
http://conferences.computer.org/infovis/
IEEE Visual Analytics Science and Technology (VAST) (since 2006)
http://visweek.org/visweek/2011/info/vast-welcome/vast-welcome

1.5 This Volume

The motivation for this present volume came from the wish of the editors and the contributors to carry forward the vision of Jim Thomas, and seek to extend the frontiers as he would have done. Thus rather than reflect on many of his seminal contributions to the field, as a Festschrift volume would traditionally do, we have sought to bring together significant new material and look to the future. The aim is therefore to look forward—based on the foundations established in the past.

The volume contains the following sections—

- Evolving a Vision
- Visual Analytics and Visualization
- Interaction and User Interfaces
- Modeling and Geometry
- Architecture and Displays
- Virtual Reality and Augmented Reality
- Technology Transfer

The book begins with the dynamics of evolving a vision based on some of the principles that Jim Thomas and colleagues established and in which his leadership was evident. It is then followed by chapters in the areas of visual analytics, visualization, interaction, modeling, architecture, and virtual reality. The book concludes with the key area of technology transfer to industry. Invited authors with their co-authors have produced chapters under these general headings. Each chapter contains a summary of the paper in an Abstract. These Abstracts are also visible on the web in the electronic book corresponding to this volume.

One of Jim Thomas' favorite sayings was "*The best is yet to come*", and this volume seeks to point in the same direction. When engrossed in some of the more intractable research and development problems of the present this is not always easy to do. However, it is clearly always true. When we look back over the history of any discipline, it is clear that remarkable advances have been made over time. The important thing therefore is to recognize it to be true in the present so that those in the future may benefit. An example of this would be that today's Big Data will seem routine in the future as more effective ways are devised to analyze it. However, Big Data is sure to get even bigger and more complex, so new challenges will present themselves which will require new approaches and new innovation in order to address them. But they will be met because human ingenuity and computing resources are potentially unbounded.

Progress in scientific discovery and understanding is generally by iterative refinement of existing theories (Popper 1959, 2002). New information is discovered which is inconsistent with the current theory, which is then modified accordingly. In addition, theories can have predictive capability, which enables them to be tested by future experimentation. However, a contrary view has been expressed by Kuhn (1996) who has argued that progress is more by paradigm shifts. However, whichever side of the argument we take, progress is inevitable.

The existing structures of knowledge and information may be inadequate to cope with their future expansion. Knowledge is increasingly interdisciplinary and the traditional barriers between existing disciplines are being broken down in order to make progress. One way to begin to understand this transition, and start to address this challenge, has been set out by Wilson (2010).

In the spirit of "*The best is yet to come*" we also provide access to the following web site—

http://sites.google.com/site/introvisual1

which contains this Introduction on-line and which will be augmented with new information and resources as they become available in the future. It is therefore not a static document which will date with time, but a dynamic one that moves forward with the field. In this way, readers will have access on-line to the best and most up to date information.

We hope this volume serves its purpose, and honors the memory of a valued colleague and friend in one of the most appropriate ways possible.

References

Kuhn, T. S. (1996). *The structure of scientific revolutions* (226 pp.). Chicago: University of Chicago Press. ISBN 13: 978-0226458083 (originally published 1962). Also available as a Kindle e-book.

Popper, K. (2002). *The logic of scientific discovery* (480 pp.). London: Routledge Classics. ISBN 13: 978-0415278447 (originally published 1959). Also available as a Kindle e-book.

Wilson, A. G. (2010). *Knowledge power – interdisciplinary education in a complex world.* London: Routledge. ISBN 13: 978-0-415-55311-7 9 (paperback), ISBN 13: 978-0-203-85803-5 (electronic book). Also available as a Kindle e-book.

Part I
Evolving a Vision

Chapter 2
An Illuminated Path: The Impact of the Work of Jim Thomas

Chaomei Chen, Haiyan Hou, Zhigang Hu, and Shengbo Liu

Abstract We provide a glimpse of the impact of the most influential work of Jim Thomas on the development of visual analytics. A quantitative visual analytic approach is applied to the analysis of three datasets of scholarly publications in order to highlight the nature and profoundness of the impact in terms of the structure and dynamics of the underlying intellectual landscape. We investigate and provide intriguing evidence of the impact of the groundbreaking book in visual analytics, *Illuminating the Path*, in terms of its role in shaping the scientific literature of relevant fields. Furthermore, we analyze the intellectual structure of visual analytics in a broader context in order to set the impact of *the Illuminating the Path* in perspective.

2.1 Introduction

Visual analytics has transformed not only how we visualize complex and dynamic phenomena in the new information age, but also how we may optimize analytical reasoning and make sound decisions with incomplete and uncertain information (Keim et al. 2008). Today's widespread recognition of the indispensable value of visual analytics as a field and the rapid growth of an energetic and interdisciplinary scientific community would be simply impossible without the remarkable vision and tireless efforts of Jim Thomas, his colleagues of the National Visualization and Analytics Center (NVAC) at Pacific Northwest National Laboratory (PNNL), and the growing community in visual analytics science and technology.

James J. Thomas (March 26, 1946–August 6, 2010), an internationally recognized visionary scientist and inspirational leader in the field of visualization, motivated researchers across the world by creating and promoting the visual analytics field and by expanding the boundaries of computer graphics, user interface software,

C. Chen (✉)
College of the Information Science and Technology, Drexel University, Philadelphia, PA, USA
e-mail: cc345@drexel.edu

H. Hou · Z. Hu · S. Liu
WISELab, Dalian University of Technology, Dalian, China

J. Dill et al. (eds.), *Expanding the Frontiers of Visual Analytics and Visualization*,
DOI 10.1007/978-1-4471-2804-5_2, © Springer-Verlag London Limited 2012

and visualization (Christopher Columbus Fellowship Foundation 2009; Ebert et al. 2010).

Jim Thomas started his professional career as a computer graphics researcher and worked on computer graphics systems to support the then new computer-aided design process and rose to the top of the computer graphics community within the next decade (Ebert et al. 2010; Wong 2010). He published extensively and invented continuously. His work has inspired many generations of researchers and practitioners. His contributions to the society were recognized by international and national awards for transferring research technology to industry and universities (Christopher Columbus Fellowship Foundation 2009; Kasik et al. 2010).

Jim was a pioneer and a leader in many areas. He was the founder and the first Director of the Department of Homeland Security National Visualization and Analytics Center (NVAC). He led major technology initiatives and research programs (Christopher Columbus Fellowship Foundation 2009; Kasik et al. 2010). He led a team of PNNL scientists and developed the groundbreaking system SPIRE (Wong 2010). Its successor, IN-SPIRE, is still in use today.

In 2004, he founded NVAC and opened a new research area, visual analytics, to the world. Visual analytics is the science of analytical reasoning facilitated by visual interactive interfaces that focuses on analytical reasoning facilitated by interactive visual interfaces (Thomas and Cook 2005; Wong and Thomas 2004). Visual analytics is a multidisciplinary field. It brings together several scientific and technical communities from computer science, information visualization, cognitive and perceptual sciences, interactive design, graphic design, and social sciences. It addresses challenges involving analytical reasoning, data representations and transformations, visual representations and interaction techniques, and techniques to support production, presentation, and dissemination of the results. Although visual analytics has some overlapping goals and techniques with information visualization and scientific visualization, it is especially concerned with sense-making and reasoning and it is strongly motivated by solving problems and making sound decisions.

Visual analytics integrates new computational and theory-based tools with innovative interactive techniques and visual representations based on cognitive, design, and perceptual principles. This science of analytical reasoning is central to the analyst's task of applying human judgments to reach conclusions from a combination of evidence and assumptions (Thomas and Cook 2005). Under Jim's influence, visual analytics centers were established throughout the world, including Canada, Germany, and the United Kingdom; and universities integrated visual analytics into their core information sciences curricula which made the new field a recognized and promising outgrowth of the fields of information visualization and scientific visualization (Wong 2010).

In order to supplement the recognition of Jim's contributions by a wide variety of domain experts and leaders in science and technology, we take a unique approach and highlight patterns and trends that can be discerned computationally from the scientific literature.

In this chapter, we present several studies of three datasets, which increasingly expand the scope of our study. We begin with papers authored by Jim Thomas. Then we trace patterns found in papers that cited *Illuminating the Path*. Finally, we expand our analysis to a broader context defined by visual analytics and superimpose the impact of *Illuminating the Path* over the broader intellectual landscape.

2.2 Three Datasets

In this chapter, we analyzed three datasets: D1: 13 papers authored by Jim Thomas, D2: 135 papers that cited *the Illuminating the Path*, and D3: 2,238 papers on broadly defined visual analytics. The three datasets provide an increasingly broader view of the impact of the contributions made by Jim Thomas.

We retrieved relevant bibliographic records for D1 by using a simple topic search for publications of Jim Thomas in the Web of Science, which is the most authoritative source of scientific publications in multiple disciplines. We used the search query: AU="Thomas J*" and ZP=99352 or AU="Thomas J*" and AD="Pacific NW Natl Lab". This retrieved articles that are authored by Thomas J or Thomas JJ along with PNNL's name and zip code to ensure that this is the Jim Thomas from PNNL. According to Ebert et al. (2010), Kasik et al. (2010), PNNL was the address he used since 1976.

The topic search returned 13 papers contributed by Jim Thomas (or James Joseph Thomas), and all these papers were published after 1996. These 13 papers form the first dataset D1. The most cited one is a 2006 article entitled "A visual analytics agenda" by Thomas JJ and Cook KA. It was cited 31 times. Figure 2.1 shows a network of collaborating authors derived from the 13 papers. The network visualization was produced by CiteSpace, a freely available tool for visualizing and analyzing emerging patterns and changes in scientific literature (Chen 2004, 2006; Chen et al. 2009, 2010). Two authors are connected if they coauthored one of the 13 papers. Lines are color coded to indicate the time of collaboration. Blue lines are the earliest, followed by green, yellow, and orange. Labels in red are key phrases extracted from the titles of papers where they collaborated. For example, #1 visual analytics introduction is from the title of a paper coauthored by Jim Thomas with Joe Kielman at the Department of Homeland Security and Richard May at PNNL.

Figure 2.2 shows a network of keywords extracted from the titles and abstracts of the 13 papers. Keywords such as information visualization, visual analytics, and visualization rightly dominate the network. The labels in red characterize clusters of keywords. For example, #0 state of practice is from an article that focused on visual analytics, future, challenges, domains and applications, as well as the state of the practice.

The second dataset D2 was generated to show the impact of the book *Illuminating the Path: The Research and Development Agenda for Visual Analytics*, coauthored by Thomas and Cook (2005). It is widely known as a landmark of visual analytics. We searched for papers that cited the work in the Web of Science using a citation search for Thomas J* and Illum*. The dataset D2 contains 135 citing papers. We analyzed a variety of patterns and properties of the dataset D2. Then we used the

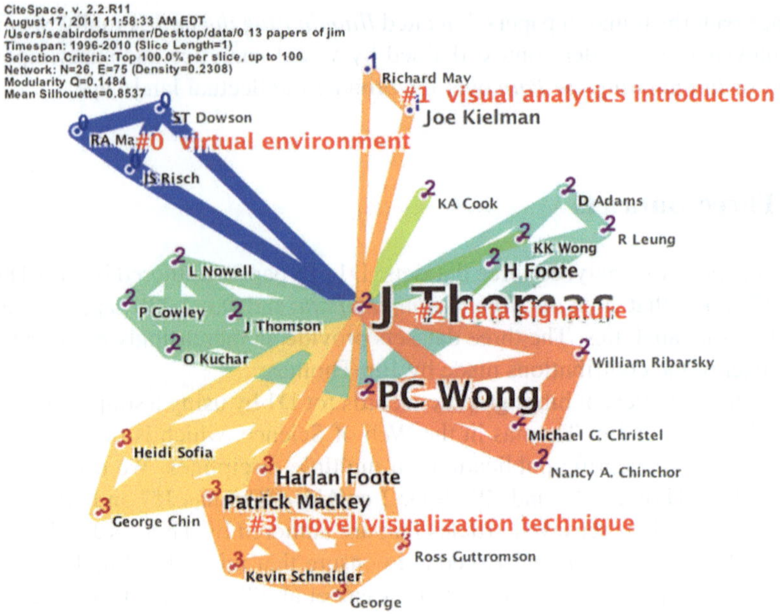

Fig. 2.1 A collaboration network of Jim Thomas

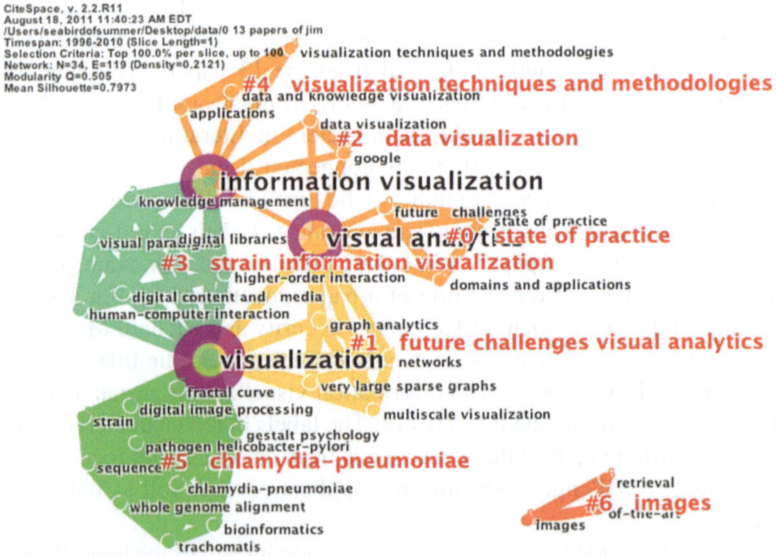

Fig. 2.2 Key topics in the 13 papers (D1)

CiteSpace software to generate a geospatial map of these authors to show countries where the impact of the book was evident. In order to obtain insights into the

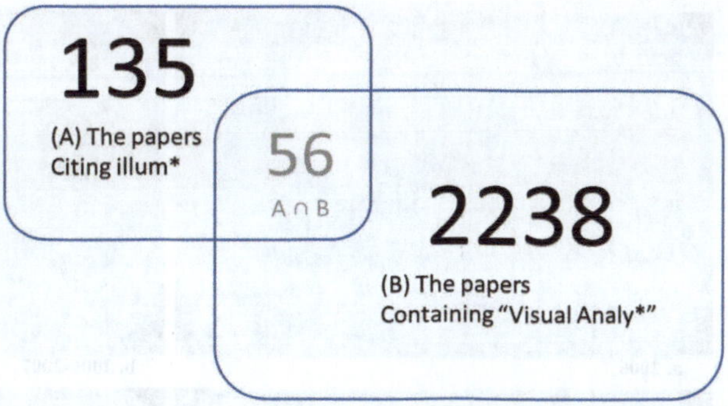

Fig. 2.3 Datasets D2 (**A**) and D3 (**B**) analyzed in this chapter

collaborative activities across institutions and countries, we generated a co-author network from the 135 citing papers. Finally, a document co-citation network was constructed and analyzed to highlight how the influence of the book evolved and spread.

In order to investigate the influence of Jim Thomas in the broader context of visual analytics, we searched for topics in the Web of Science for TS="Visual Analy*". The wildcard * was used to cover variations such as analytics, analytical, and analysis. The search resulted in 2,238 papers relevant to visual analytics. The third dataset D3 consists of these 2,238 records. As attested by the 2,238 papers, the most productive institute is PNNL! The single work that has influenced 2,238 papers is, intriguingly, the *Illuminating the Path*! The most cited author is Jim Thomas! What a remarkable tribute to Jim Thomas (Fig. 2.3).

2.3 Illuminating the Path

Jim Thomas and Kristin A. Cook co-authored "Illuminating the Path: The Research and Development Agenda for Visual Analytics". This book motivated researchers and developers to help safeguard the nation by transforming information overload into insights through visual analytics. It has provided the roadmap of visual analytics ever since: the science of analytical reasoning facilitated by interactive visual interfaces. This book had a profound impact on the course of the development of visual analytics.

2.3.1 The Spread of the Impact

The geographic map of authors and collaborative authorship were generated by CiteSpace and can be viewed interactively in Google Earth. Figure 2.4 revealed the spread of the geographic distribution of the citing papers over time. A colored disk in the map represents the location of an author. The line connecting two locations indicates that authors at the two locations collaborated on a published paper.

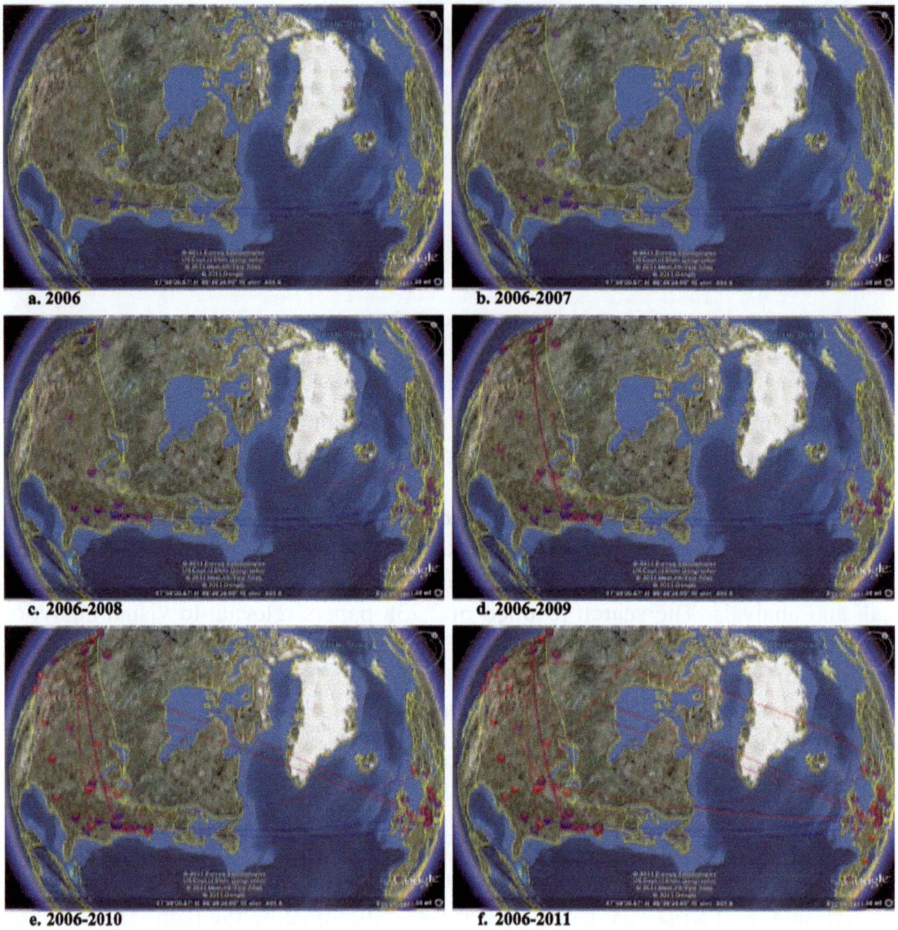

Fig. 2.4 Geographic maps of the growing influence of *Illuminating the Path*. Data source: D2

As shown in Fig. 2.4a, in 2006, this book was mainly cited on the east and west coasts of the United States, a small number of cities in European countries, such as Germany, Austria, and Netherlands. U.S.-European collaboration was evident by the blue lines across the Atlantic Ocean. In 2007, the impact of this book expanded to include more southern cities on the coast of the U.S., more European countries, and more cities in Canada (Fig. 2.4b). In the period 2008 and 2009, the influence of this book emerged in the middle of the United States with long-range collaboration links. Meanwhile, the impact of the work spread to more European cities in Sweden, Spain, England, Scotland, and Switzerland (Fig. 2.4c and 2.4d). More recently, the impact has reached more and more cities in the U.S. and other parts of the world. International collaboration increased over time with countries such as China, Israel, and some Europe countries (Fig. 2.4e and 2.4f).

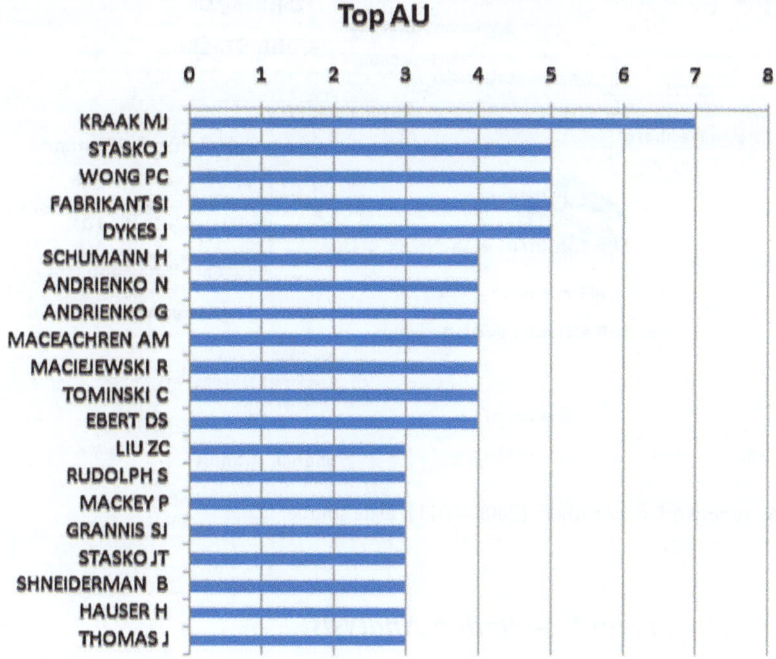

Fig. 2.5 Top 20 authors in D2 who frequently cited *Illuminating the Path*

2.3.2 The Inspired Community

There are a total of 390 citing authors in the 135 papers in dataset D2. Figure 2.5 shows the top 20 most productive authors. Menno Jan Kraak, a researcher in geographic visualization, cited *Illuminating the Path* in 7 of his papers. John Stasko, Pak Chung Wong, and a few others have cited the book in 5 of their papers.

Figure 2.6 shows a collaboration network of authors who cited *Illuminating the Path*. A group of eight authors formed in 2010, including Menno Jan Kraak, Jason Dykes, Gennady Andrienko, Natalia Andrienko, and Sara Irina Fabrikant. Most of them are known for their work in geographic visualization. They are from different institutions in different countries such as Fraunhofer Institute for Intelligent Analysis and Information Systems, Germany, the Faculty of Geo-Information Science and Earth Observation of the University of Twente, the Netherlands, and the Department of Information Science of City University London, England. They all took part in a book entitled *Exploring Geovisualization*. These authors worked together in geovisualization in 2010. Pak Chung Wong, John Stasko, and William Ribarsky are well known leaders in visual analytics among other fields of their expertise.

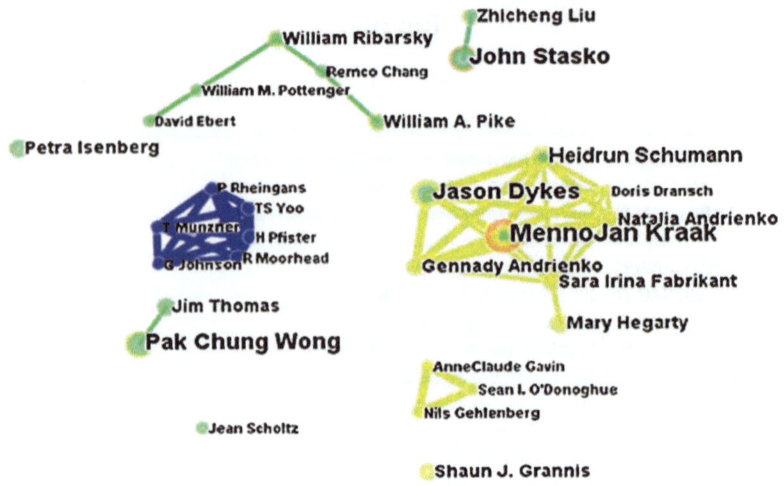

Fig. 2.6 A network of coauthors (2006–2011). Data source: D2

2.3.3 A Document Co-citation Analysis

Document co-citation analysis (DCA) is an established method to delineate the structure and dynamics of the intellectual landscape of subject areas in scientific literature. We conducted a DCA of articles that cited *Illuminating the Path* so that we could identify research topics that have been influenced by the work.

CiteSpace was used to generate the co-citation network of the citing papers. We used six one-year time slices between 2006 and 2011. The threshold was set by (c, cc, ccv) method. We set the threshold at (2, 2, 12), (3, 2, 20), (3, 2, 20). The pathfinder algorithm was used to obtain the important information on the network.

Figure 2.7 shows that the co-citation network revealed 11 topic areas with labels identified by noun phrases extracted from titles of papers that are responsible for each cluster. Labels were selected by log-likelihood ratio tests. The shaded areas highlight the boundaries of clusters. The largest node (most cited) in the visualization is *Illuminating the Path* on the upper left corner. It also has the strongest betweenness centrality, showing as a thick purple ring, which indicates its central role in the structure. It is not surprising because of the way the data was collected, but more interestingly it shows its role in forming the basis of visual analytics. And this book is direct related to cluster 0, 1, 2, 3, 4 and 10. The topic words in each cluster are listed in Table 2.1. The major topic areas are visualization, including information visualization, visualization design, and visualization model. System biology and geospatial visual analytic were also influenced by this book.

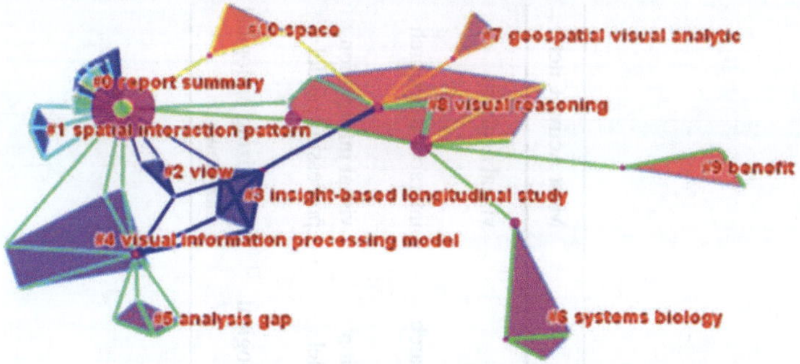

Fig. 2.7 A document co-citation network showing the impact of *Illuminating the Path*. Data source: D2

Table 2.1 Topic words of 11 topic areas influenced by *Illuminating the Path*

Cluster ID	Topic word 1	Topic word 2	Topic word 3
0	Report summary	Analysis	NIH-NSF visualization research
1	Spatial interaction pattern	Pandemic decision support	Predictive analytics approach
2	View	Visualization	Report summary
3	Insight-based longitudinal study	Function graph	Family
4	Visual information processing model	Interactive visualization environment	Visualization design
5	Analysis gap	Visual generation	Promoting insight-based evaluation
6	Systems biology	Omics data	Conjunctive visual form
7	Geospatial visual analytic	Mortality data	Construction management data visualization
8	Visual reasoning	Top-down perspective	Mental model
9	Benefit	Document collection	Co-located visual analytic
10	Space	Efficiency	Eye movement recording

2.3.4 Major Co-citation Clusters

Co-citation clusters represent codified knowledge in a field of study. The network generated from dataset D2 contains 11 co-citation clusters. These clusters are labeled by title terms from their own citers. The largest 4 clusters are summarized in Table 2.2.

The largest cluster (#0) has 21 members and a silhouette value of 0.949. It is labeled as a report summary by both LLR and TFIDF, and as visual analysis by MI.

Table 2.2 Summary of the 4 largest clusters

Cluster ID	Size	Silhouette	Label (TFIDF)	Label (LLR)	Label (MI)	Most Active Citer
0	21	0.949	(6.99) report summary	report summary (79.72, 1.0E-4)	visual analysis	visual analysis
8	13	0.809	(5.26) standards-based 3d geovisualization	visual reasoning (87.91, 1.0E-4)	interaction research	interaction research
4	6	0.673	(3.35) visual information processing model	visual information processing model (47.89, 1.0E-4)	visual information processing model	visual information processing model
6	5	0.93	(4.24) future	systems biology (39.69, 1.0E-4)	visualizing biological data-now	visualizing biological data-now

The most active citer to the cluster is *NIH-NSF visualization research challenges report summary*. The second largest cluster (#8) has 13 members and a silhouette value of 0.809. It is labeled as visual reasoning by LLR, a standards-based 3d geo-visualization by TFIDF, and interaction research by MI. The most active citer to the cluster is mental models, visual reasoning and interaction in information visualization: a top-down perspective. The third largest cluster (#4) has 6 members and a silhouette value of 0.673. It is labeled as a visual information processing model by both LLR and TFIDF, and as visual information processing model by MI. The most active citer to the cluster is a visual information processing model to characterize interactive visualization environments. The 4th largest cluster (#6) has 5 members and a silhouette value of 0.93. It is labeled as systems biology by LLR, future by TFIDF, and visualizing biological data-now by MI.

2.3.5 Landmark Papers

A number of landmark papers were co-cited with the *Illuminating the Path* in Fig. 2.7. These papers were ranked by citation counts, betweenness centrality, burst, and sigma (Chen et al. 2009, 2010).

2.3.5.1 Citation Counts

Table 2.3 lists top 10 references ranked by citation counts. The most cited one is CARD SK (1999) in Cluster #8, with a citation count of 19. This is the widely known "Readings in information visualization: using vision to think", a book of exemplar works compiled by Stuart Card, Jock Mackinlay and Ben Shneiderman. The second is SHNEIDERMAN B (1996) in Cluster #8, with a citation count of 15. The third is TUFTE E (2001) in Cluster #4, with a citation count of 10. The 4th is LARKIN JH (1987) in Cluster #10, with a citation count of 10. The 5th is Andrienko G (2007) in Cluster #7, with a citation count of 9.

2.3.5.2 Betweenness Centrality

Table 2.4 lists the top 10 ranked items by betweenness centrality. Articles with strong centrality scores are believed to be fundamental to the intellectual work of the community. The top ranked item by centrality is again CARD SK (1999) in Cluster #8, with a centrality of 0.67. The second is Mackinlay JD (2007) in Cluster #8, with a centrality of 0.53. The third is SHNEIDERMAN B (1996) in Cluster #8, with a centrality of 0.38. The 4th is MACKINLAY J (1986) in Cluster #4, with a centrality of 0.36. The 5th is Plaisant C (2008) in Cluster #6, with a centrality of 0.22.

Table 2.3 Top 10 ranked items by citation counts

Citation counts	References	Cluster #
19	CARD SK, 1999, READINGS INFORM VISU, V, P	8
15	SHNEIDERMAN B, 1996, P IEEE S VIS LANG, P336, P	8
10	TUFTE E, 2001, VISUAL DISPLAY QUANT, V, P	4
10	LARKIN JH, 1987, COGNITIVE SCI, V11, P65	10
9	Andrienko G, 2007, INT J GEOGR INF SCI, V21, P839	7
9	WARE C, 2004, INFORM VISUALIZATION, V, P	9
8	MACKINLAY J, 1986, ACM T GRAPHIC, V5, P110	4
8	Yi JS, 2007, IEEE T VIS COMPUT GR, V13, P1224	8
8	JOHNSON C, 2006, NIH NSF VISUALIZATION, V, P	4
8	PLAISANT C, 2004, P WORK C ADV VIS INT, P109, P	6

Table 2.4 Top 10 ranked items by betweenness centrality

Centrality	References	Cluster #
0.67	CARD SK, 1999, READINGS INFORM VISU, V, P	8
0.53	Mackinlay JD, 2007, IEEE T VIS COMPUT GR, V13, P1137	8
0.38	SHNEIDERMAN B, 1996, P IEEE S VIS LANG, P336, P	8
0.36	MACKINLAY J, 1986, ACM T GRAPHIC, V5, P110	4
0.22	Plaisant C, 2008, IEEE T VIS COMPUT GR, V14, P120	6
0.17	PLAISANT C, 2004, P WORK C ADV VIS INT, P109, P	6
0.16	Aigner W, 2008, IEEE T VIS COMPUT GR, V14, P47	10
0.14	WARE C, 2004, INFORMATION VISUALIZ, V, P	3
0.12	Andrienko G, 2007, INT J GEOGR INF SCI, V21, P839	7
0.12	Isenberg P, 2007, IEEE T VIS COMPUT GR, V13, P1232	9

2.3.5.3 Burst and Sigma

Articles with citation burst and sigma are regarded as having drawn a considerable amount of attention from the scientific community. There is only burst item in this network. It is WARE C (2004) in Cluster #9, with bursts of 2.38 and a sigma value 1.15.

2.3.6 Timeline View

Figure 2.8 shows a timeline visualization of the co-citation network. According to the colors of the co-citation lines, clusters #0, #1 to #5 were formed in the period 2006–2007. The co-cited papers are mostly before year 2000. They co-cited in the

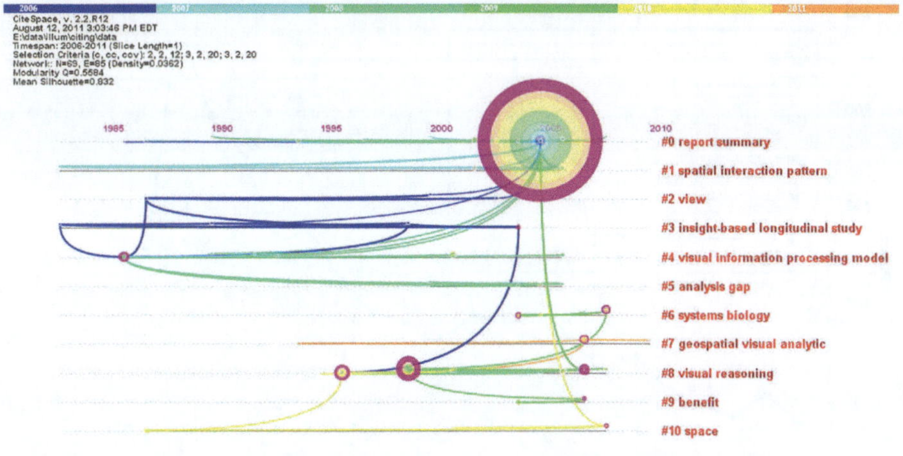

Fig. 2.8 A timeline visualization of the co-citation network. Data source: D2

field of visualization analysis and method. Clusters #6 to #10 are generated after 2007. The co-cited papers are around the year 2005. These research focii were on the application of visualization, including geospatial visual analytic, conjunctive visual form, and co-located with visual analytic.

2.4 A Broader Context

In order to set the impact of *Illuminating the Path* in a broader context, we further investigated patterns revealed by the third dataset D3, which contains 2,238 articles relevant to visual analytics. Based on this data, we identified the trend of growth, major source journals, hot topics, highly cited documents, and highly cited authors. In this way, the role of *Illuminating the Path* and the transformative impact of Jim Thomas' work can be better understood.

2.4.1 The Trend of Growth

Although the earliest article in dataset D3 dated as early as 1948, the majority of the domain began to emerge in the early 1990s. About 95 % of the articles (2,125 out of 2,238) in D3 were published after 1990. Based on the different growth rates, the overall trend since 1990 can be divided into three phases (Fig. 2.9). During the first phase (1990–1999), the number of publications per year increased from less than 50 to around 100. During the second phrase (1999–2004), the productivity per year was relatively stable, producing about 90 publications per year. During the third phase, starting from year 2005, the increase became much faster. For example,

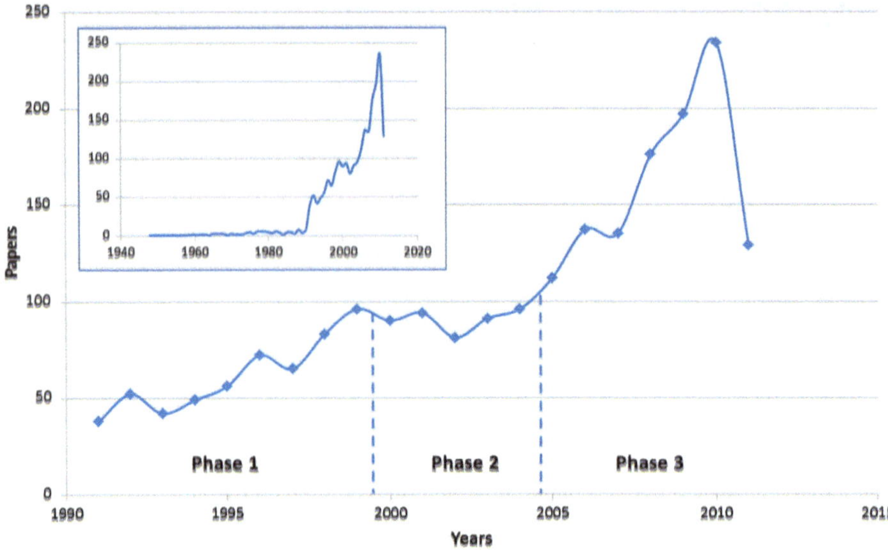

Fig. 2.9 The growth of the domain of visual analytics. Data source: D3

234 papers were published in 2010 alone, which more than doubled the number of papers published in these areas in 2004. We analyzed these three phases separately in order to characterize each phase further.

2.4.2 Major Source Journals and Hot Topics

We were interested in the following questions: what are the major intellectual works in the domain and how did Illuminating the Path transform the intellectual landscape? Articles containing the words 'visual' and 'analysis' are not necessarily relevant to today's visual analytics. Nevertheless, they provide a broader context to locate where exactly the impact of *Illuminating the Path* was.

Table 2.5 lists the top sources and the hot keywords of the 2,125 publications between 1991 and 2011. The *Journal of nuclear medicine* (*JNM*) is the major source of publication (71 papers) in this period. It is one of the top medical imaging journals worldwide with a high impact factor of 6.424 according to the newly released 2009 Journal Citation Reports. The second source journal close behind is *IEEE Transactions on Visualization and Computer Graphics* (*TVCG*). 70 papers were published in this journal. TVCG is a scholarly archival journal published monthly started in 1995. It involves subjects related to computer graphics and visualization techniques, systems, software, hardware, and user interface issues. TVCG is in computer science. Obviously, these two journals represent two quite different research fields.

Other top-ranked computer science source journals include Information Visualization, Computer Graphics Forum, and IEEE Computer Graphics and Applications.

JNM, on the other hand, belongs to Nuclear Medicine Imaging, with relevant journals such as Nuclear Medicine Communications, European Journal of Nuclear Medicine and Molecular Imaging, and Neuroimage. Is JNM a part of the modern visual analytics? Or is it connected purely by association of the words used in the query, namely visual and analy*? If it is not conceptually connected to visual analytics per se, would it be viable to consider potential connections in the future?

It should be noted that these two fields are distinct in terms of their emergence and evolution. Overall, the journals in Computer Science appeared later than the journals in the field of Medical Imaging. The latter ranked highly since 1991, while the former appeared only in the recent phase. In the top source journal TVCG for example, 67 of 71 papers in this journal were published between 2005 and 2011. Similarly, in Information Visualization and Computer Graphics Forum, all the publications sourced from them were published after 2005.

As far as the evidence from the literature is concerned, the year 2005 was a watershed for this domain even if it was probably not yet a single and conceptually integrated one. Since 2005, not only the scale of the literature expanded rapidly, but also new research directions emerged. According to the analysis of keywords, we can draw similar conclusions. Before 2005, the keywords were visual analysis, PET, SPECT, Epilepsy, and Magnetic Resonance Imaging (MRI). After 2005, the hot topics switched to Visual Analytics, Visual Analysis, Information Visualization, and Visualization. Remarkably, the new term "Visual Analytics" began to appear in 2005, and finally it became the most frequently used keyword (71 times). It is evident that *Illuminating the Path* defined, or redefined, whatever was meant by visual analysis before and after 2005.

2.4.3 Highly Cited Documents and Authors

As we know, the mission and agenda of Visual Analytics was laid down in *Illuminating the Path*. So we expect that a conceptual turning point should be detectable in the literature. To test this hypothesis, we conducted a citation analysis. A list of the top cited documents and authors are shown in Table 2.6.

In Table 2.6, Jim Thomas is the highest cited author with 82 citations according to these 2,125 publications, and *Illuminating the Path* is the most cited publication at 56 times. It confirms that *Illuminating the Path* is indeed a driving force of the emerging domain.

2.4.4 Mapping the Visual Analytics Domain

As a tool to find critical points in the development of a field or a domain, especially intellectual turning points and pivotal points, CiteSpace was used in this study to conduct a Document Co-citation Analysis (DCA) and Author Co-citation Analysis (ACA), and thus the role of Jim Thomas and his publication can be further clarified.

Table 2.5 Top source journals and hot keywords

Rank	1991–2011		1991–1999		2000–2004		2005–2011	
	Journal	Freq	Journal	Freq	Journal	Freq	Journal	Freq
1	Journal of Nuclear Medicine	71	Journal of Nuclear Medicine	31	Journal of Nuclear Medicine	17	IEEE Transactions on Visualization and Computer Graphics	69
2	IEEE Transactions on Visualization and Computer Graphics	70	Journal of The American College of Cardiology	12	Neuroimage	9	Information Visualization	38
3	Information Visualization	38	European Journal of Nuclear Medicine	10	European Journal of Nuclear Medicine and Molecular Imaging	9	Computer Graphics Forum	30
4	Nuclear Medicine Communications	35	International Journal of Remote Sensing	10	European Journal of Nuclear Medicine	9	Journal of Nuclear Medicine	23
5	Computer Graphics Forum	30	Nuclear Medicine Communications	8	Nuclear Medicine Communications	9	Nuclear Medicine Communications	18
6	European Journal of Nuclear Medicine and Molecular Imaging	24	Radiology	7	Journal of Nuclear Cardiology	7	IEEE Computer Graphics and Applications	17
7	Neuroimage	19	Epilepsia	6	Neurology	5	European Journal of Nuclear Medicine and Molecular Imaging	15
8	IEEE Computer Graphics and Applications	19	Neurology	6	Clinical Nuclear Medicine	5	BMC Bioinformatics	12
9	European Journal of Nuclear Medicine	19	Journal of Nuclear Cardiology	5	Optometry and Vision Science	5	Computers & Graphics-UK	11

Table 2.5 (*Continued*)

Rank	1991–2011		1991–1999		2000–2004		2005–2011	
	Journal	Freq	Journal	Freq	Journal	Freq	Journal	Freq
10	Journal of The American College of Cardiology	17	Electroencephalography and Clinical Neurophysiology	5	Radiology	4	International Journal of Geographical Information Science	11
	Keyword	Freq	Keyword	Freq	Keyword	Freq	Keyword	Freq
1	Visual Analytics	71	Epilepsy	16	Visual Analysis	16	Visual Analytics	71
2	Visual Analysis	66	Visual Analysis	15	Magnetic Resonance Imaging	8	Visual Analysis	35
3	Pet	42	Coronary Artery Disease	14	Myocardial Perfusion	8	Information Visualization	30
4	Information Visualization	31	PET	12	PET	8	Visualization	22
5	Positron Emission Tomography	30	SPECT	11	Positron Emission Tomography	8	PET	22
6	Epilepsy	30	Magnetic Resonance Imaging	10	Spect	7	Positron Emission Tomography	16
7	Visualization	26	Positron Emission Tomography	6	Alzheimer's Disease	6	Eeg	15
8	Spect	26	Temporal Lobe Epilepsy	6	Diagnosis	6	Fmri	12
9	Magnetic Resonance Imaging	25	Hippocampus	6	Tc-99m-Tetrofosmin	6	Breast Cancer	12
10	Coronary Artery Disease	25	Eeg	5	Coronary Artery Disease	6	Fdg	11

Table 2.6 Highly cited documents and highly cited authors

	1991–2011		1991–1999		2000–2004		2005–2011	
	Citation publication	Freq	Citation publication	Freq	Citation publication	Freq	Citation publication	Freq
1	THOMAS JJ, 2005, ILLUMINATING PATH RE	56	DEPROSPERO A, 1979, J APPL BEHAV ANAL, V12, P573	11	BONDA E, 1996, J NEUROSCI, V16, P3737	8	THOMAS JJ, 2005, ILLUMINATING PATH RE	56
2	BLAND JM, 1986, LANCET, V1, P307	41	DEPASQUALE EE, 1988, CIRCULATION, V77, P316	10	HACHAMOVITCH R, 1996, CIRCULATION, V93, P905	8	BLAND JM, 1986, LANCET, V1, P307	28
3	KAZDIN AE, 1982, SINGLE CASE RES DESI	24	KAZDIN AE, 1982, SINGLE CASE RES DESI	10	RECHTSCHAFFEN A, 1968, MANUAL STANDARDIZED	8	SHNEIDERMAN B, 1996, P IEEE S VIS LANG, P336	19
4	MATYAS TA, 1990, J APPL BEHAV ANAL, V23, P341	22	DIAMOND GA, 1979, NEW ENGL J MED, V300, P1350	9	TALAIRACH J, 1988, COPLANAR STEREOTAXIC	8	CARD SK, 1999, READINGS INFORM VISU	17
5	DEPROSPERO A, 1979, J APPL BEHAV ANAL, V12, P573	21	JACKSON GD, 1990, NEUROLOGY, V40, P1869	9	DECETY J, 1997, BRAIN, V120, P1763	7	INSELBERG A, 1985, VISUAL COMPUT, V1, P69	16
6	RECHTSCHAFFEN A, 1968, MANUAL STANDARDIZED	21	JONES RR, 1978, J APPL BEHAV ANAL, V11, P277	9	FOLSTEIN MF, 1975, J PSYCHIAT RES, V12, P189	7	KEIM DA, 2002, IEEE T VIS COMPUT GR, V8, P1	16
7	CERQUEIRA MD, 2002, CIRCULATION, V105, P539	20	CASCINO GD, 1991, ANN NEUROL, V30, P31	8	FRISTON KJ, 1995, HUMAN BRAIN MAPPING, V2, P189	7	CERQUEIRA MD, 2002, CIRCULATION, V105, P539	15
8	OLDFIELD RC, 1971, NEUROPSYCHOLOGIA, V9, P97	20	JACK CR, 1990, RADIOLOGY, V175, P423	8	HACHAMOVITCH R, 1998, CIRCULATION, V97, P535	7	ANDRIENKO G, 2007, INT J GEOGR INF SCI, V21, P839	14

Table 2.6 (*Continued*)

	1991–2011		1991–1999		2000–2004		2005–2011	
	Citation publication	Freq	Citation publication	Freq	Citation publication	Freq	Citation publication	Freq
9	SHNEIDERMAN B, 1996, P IEEE S VIS LANG, P336	19	JACK CR, 1992, ANN NEUROL, V31, P138	8	BERMAN DS, 1993, J AM COLL CARDIOL, V22, P1455	6	HAVRE S, 2002, IEEE T VIS COMPUT GR, V8, P9	12
10	TALAIRACH J, 1988, COPLANAR STEREOTAXIC	19	MATYAS TA, 1990, J APPL BEHAV ANAL, V23, P341	8	BLAND JM, 1986, LANCET, V1, P307	6	KANWISHER N, 1997, J NEUROSCI, V17, P4302	12
	Citation Author	Freq	Citation Author	Freq	Citation Author	Freq	Citation Author	Freq
1	THOMAS JJ	82	JACK CR	33	FRIED PA	34	THOMAS JJ	82
2	KEIM DA	73	ENGEL J	32	RIZZOLATTI G	26	KEIM DA	72
3	SHNEIDERMAN B	67	DOLLFUS A	30	FRISTON KJ	24	SHNEIDERMAN B	67
4	RIZZOLATTI G	65	JACKSON GD	26	BERMAN DS	24	PARKER RI	46
5	BERMAN DS	56	OTTENBACHER KJ	22	GOLDENBERG G	21	ANDRIENKO G	45
6	FRISTON KJ	55	CENDES F	22	GERMANO G	19	MACEACHREN AM	39
7	ENGEL J	54	GENTILUCCI M	22	HACHAMOVITCH R	18	HEER J	38
8	COHEN J	49	WAHL RL	21	DECETY J	17	PELPHREY KA	37
9	MACEACHREN AM	49	THEODORE WH	20	CENDES F	16	TUFTE ER	36
10	JACK CR	48	BERMAN DS	19	TALAIRACH J	16	SEO J	36

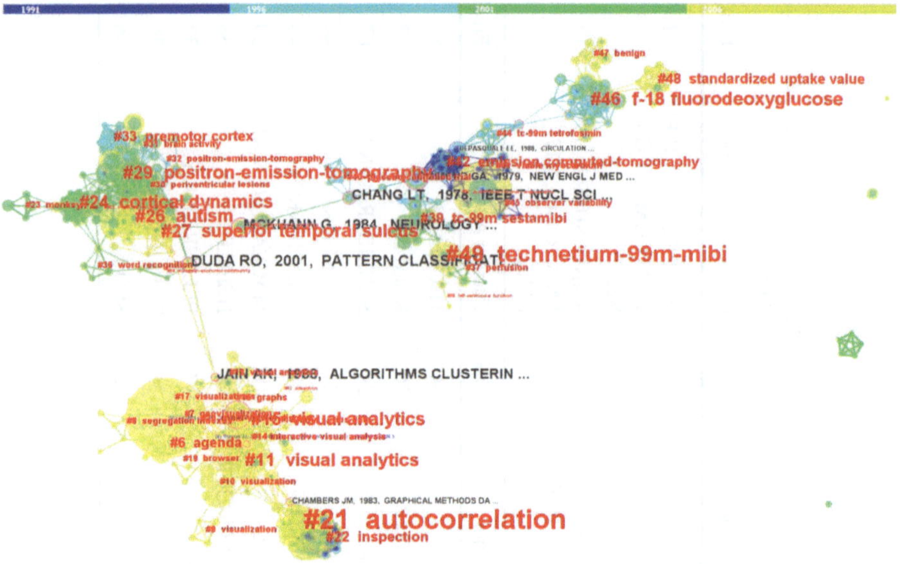

Fig. 2.10 A co-citation network showing a broader context of visual analytics, including depicting nuclear medicine imaging (*upper half*) and visual analytics (*lower half*). Data source: D3

Figure 2.10 shows a co-citation network created by CiteSpace. In this network, the top 1 % of citations for each slice (each slice equal 5 years) were chosen as the nodes. The size of the node means the number of cited times of the responding publications. The nodes are linked with each other if they were co-cited. Cluster analysis was then conducted and the label for each cluster was computationally generated by CiteSpace using an algorithm based on likelihood-ratio tests (LLR).

In Fig. 2.10, it became obvious that two separated parts emerged. The upper half corresponds to research in nuclear medicine imaging from 1991 (in blue) to 2010 (in yellow). The lower half reveals the structure of visual analytics, which is what *Illuminating the Path* promoted. Surprisingly, the two parts were still connected and it is interesting to see which ones formed the unusual bridge that connects the two distinct conceptual sub-domains. The weak connections were due to two books, *Algorithms for clustering* on the visual analytics side and *Pattern classification* on the nuclear medicine imaging side. With hindsight, this path of connection makes sense because clustering and pattern classification are essential techniques for both areas.

The role of *Illuminating the Path* can also be seen directly from the network visualization. In Fig. 2.10, the node representing *Illuminating the Path* is the largest one in size (lower left) because, as mentioned above, it is the most cited work. The betweenness centrality of each node was also calculated based on this network structure, which measures the importance in connecting the entire network together. The centrality of this node is 0.01 because it is obviously overshadowed by the two books that provided even longer-range bridges between the upper-lower boundaries.

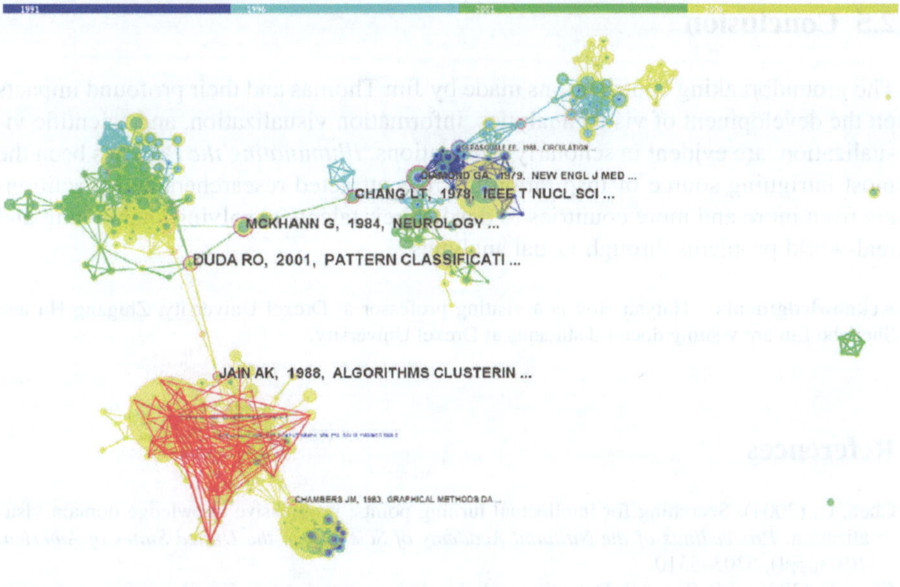

Fig. 2.11 The network overlay of the impact of *Illuminating the Path* (*red lines*) over the network of visual analysis

2.4.5 An Overlay of Network D2 in Network D3

The network shown in Fig. 2.7 was generated from the dataset D2, which consists of 135 articles that cited *Illuminating the Path*. The network shown in Fig. 2.10 was generated from dataset D3, which represents a broader context defined by over 2,200 articles relevant to visual analysis and visual analytics.

In Fig. 2.11, we superimposed the D2 network over the D3 network to highlight the network structure of citers to *Illuminating the Path* in contrast to the broader context of visual analytics. The red lines represent co-citation structures derived from the citers of Illuminating the Path. As shown in Fig. 2.11, the red sub-structure covers much of the lower half of the broader context network. The overlay network also reinforces the key position of *Illuminating the Path* in the visual analytics network.

The observed pattern from the overlay is consistent with our earlier discussion of how the domain is structured. There are two dominating areas in the domain about visual analysis. One is the domain of nuclear medicine imaging. We can see key papers in the 1970s and it evidently continues to evolve. The other is the field of visual analytics, founded by Jim Thomas and his colleagues since 2005. The overlay in Fig. 2.11 shows that currently the impact of *Illuminating the Path* is limited to the lower half of the network. Is it conceivable that the two parts will integrate more tightly in the future? Are there things that both sides could learn from each other?

2.5 Conclusion

The groundbreaking contributions made by Jim Thomas and their profound impacts on the development of visual analytics, information visualization, and scientific visualization, are evident in scholarly publications. *Illuminating the Path* has been the most intriguing source of inspiration that has attracted researchers and practitioners from more and more countries to devote their talents to solving challenging and real-world problems through visual analytics.

Acknowledgments Haiyan Hou is a visiting professor at Drexel University. Zhigang Hu and Shengbo Liu are visiting doctoral students at Drexel University.

References

Chen, C. (2004). Searching for intellectual turning points: progressive knowledge domain visualization. *Proceedings of the National Academy of Sciences of the United States of America, 101*(suppl), 5303–5310.

Chen, C. (2006). CiteSpace II: Detecting and visualizing emerging trends and transient patterns in scientific literature. *Journal of the American Society for Information Science and Technology, 57*(3), 359–377.

Chen, C., et al. (2009). Towards an explanatory and computational theory of scientific discovery. *Journal of Informetrics, 3*(3), 191–209.

Chen, C., Ibekwe-SanJuan, F., & Hou, J. (2010). The structure and dynamics of co-citation clusters: a multiple-perspective co-citation analysis. *Journal of the American Society for Information Science and Technology, 61*(7), 1386–1409.

Christopher Columbus Fellowship Foundation (2009). Homeland Security Award Columbus Scholar 2009. http://www.columbusfdn.org/homelandsecurity/2009.php.

Ebert, D. S., Dill, J., & Kasik, D. J. (2010). In memoriam: illuminating our paths—James (Jim) Joseph Thomas. In *IEEE symposium on visual analytics science and technology (VAST)* (pp. xiv–xiv).

Kasik, D., et al. (2010). Jim Thomas, 1946–2010. In memoriam. *IEEE Computer Graphics and Applications, 30*(6), 10–13.

Keim, D., et al. (2008). *Visual analytics: scope and challenges* (pp. 76–90). Visual Data Mining.

Thomas, J. J., & Cook, K. (2005). *Illuminating the path: the R&D agenda for visual analytics*. IEEE.

Wong, P. C. (2010). The four roads less traveled—a tribute to Jim Thomas (1946–2010). http://vgtc.org/JimThomas.html.

Wong, P., & Thomas, J. (2004). Visual analytics. *IEEE Computer Graphics and Applications, 24*(5), 20–21.

Chapter 3
The Evolving Leadership Path of Visual Analytics

Mike Kluse, Anthony Peurrung, and Deborah Gracio

Abstract Visual analytics has become internationally recognized as a growing research area, producing increasingly sophisticated analytic technologies. The pioneers of this multidisciplinary field blazed a leadership path, which continues to evolve as the field develops. Key leadership strategies were 1) recognizing the need for a different approach, 2) establishing the vision and concept, 3) enlisting mission-driven champions and resource providers, 4) establishing enabling structures and collaborations, and 5) developing and deploying visual analytics tools. Strategies for future growth include increasing domains and applications, improving integration within research communities, and broadening bases of support.

3.1 Leadership Lifecycle

In just a few years, a diverse group of passionate experts—including Pacific Northwest National Laboratory scientist Jim Thomas—harnessed their vision, drive, and creativity to launch visual analytics as a mainstream discipline. Today, visual analytics is internationally recognized as a growing research area, producing increasingly sophisticated analytic technologies—some of which are highlighted in this book.

The leadership path that these founders established continues to evolve, driving growth in the field and setting a vision for decades of research. Here, we take a broad look at the strategies that were used to establish the multidisciplinary field of visual analytics and how this path may evolve as the field continues to develop.

M. Kluse (✉)
Senior VP, Battelle and Laboratory Director, Pacific Northwest National Laboratory, Richland, WA, USA
e-mail: mkluse@pnl.gov

A. Peurrung
Associate Laboratory Director, National Security, Pacific Northwest National Laboratory, Richland, WA, USA

D. Gracio
Director, Computational and Statistical Analytics Division, Pacific Northwest National Laboratory, Richland, WA, USA

J. Dill et al. (eds.), *Expanding the Frontiers of Visual Analytics and Visualization*,
DOI 10.1007/978-1-4471-2804-5_3,

We are fortunate to include the perspectives of some of the world's most influential visual analytics pioneers from government, academia, and industry.

Studies on leadership typically focus on organizational management methods, or qualities that aspiring leaders should strive to develop. Case studies on the leadership required to create modern disciplines, however, are rare. One example is computer science, which created all of its foundational elements from algorithms to architecture. This creation and evolution happened over many decades, from the most rudimentary programming to scientific computing that mapped a human genome and created an interactive atlas of gene expression in the human brain.

Visual analytics blazed a somewhat different path. Many of its basic contributing disciplines already existed—such as mathematics, statistics, data visualization and computer graphics—but analytic challenges dictated that they be integrated and used in different ways.

How did visual analytics pioneers conceptualize a new way of thinking that was radically different from current practice? What was their strategy for convincing disparate, sometimes competing interests of the need for a new approach that would not subsume their existing disciplines in the process? How did they formulate research agendas that would drive the new field? How did these leaders build an infrastructure for funding and collaboration, and establish a community and venues for professional development? And perhaps most intriguing, how should the leadership strategies evolve to meet future needs?

In exploring answers to these questions, we hope to provide insights into the lifecycle of visual analytics leadership. These insights may be useful as tomorrow's leaders develop strategies for the next generation of research concepts.

For discussion purposes, we've simplified this leadership lifecycle as overlapping elements of success, from the time before visual analytics became mainstream to possible future states (Fig. 3.1). Each element and its significance are described in more detail.

3.2 Mind the Gap

Visual analytics has its roots in the information visualization community, which has existed at least since the 1980s (McCormick et al. 1987). Over the next decade, researchers from computer science fields including information retrieval, data management, human-computer interaction, and computer graphics recognized the common areas between information visualization and their fields. The subsequent loose collaboration among diverse communities laid a foundation that was ripe for the birth of visual analytics (Wong and Thomas 2009; Keim et al. 2010).

In the 1990s, a few visionary experts began recognizing a gap between data visualization capabilities and the increasingly complex analytical problems of modern society. Decision makers were faced with an increasingly staggering amount of data in databases, documents, video, imagery, audio, and sensor data. Moreover, these data often were conflicting, dynamic, and available from multiple heterogeneous

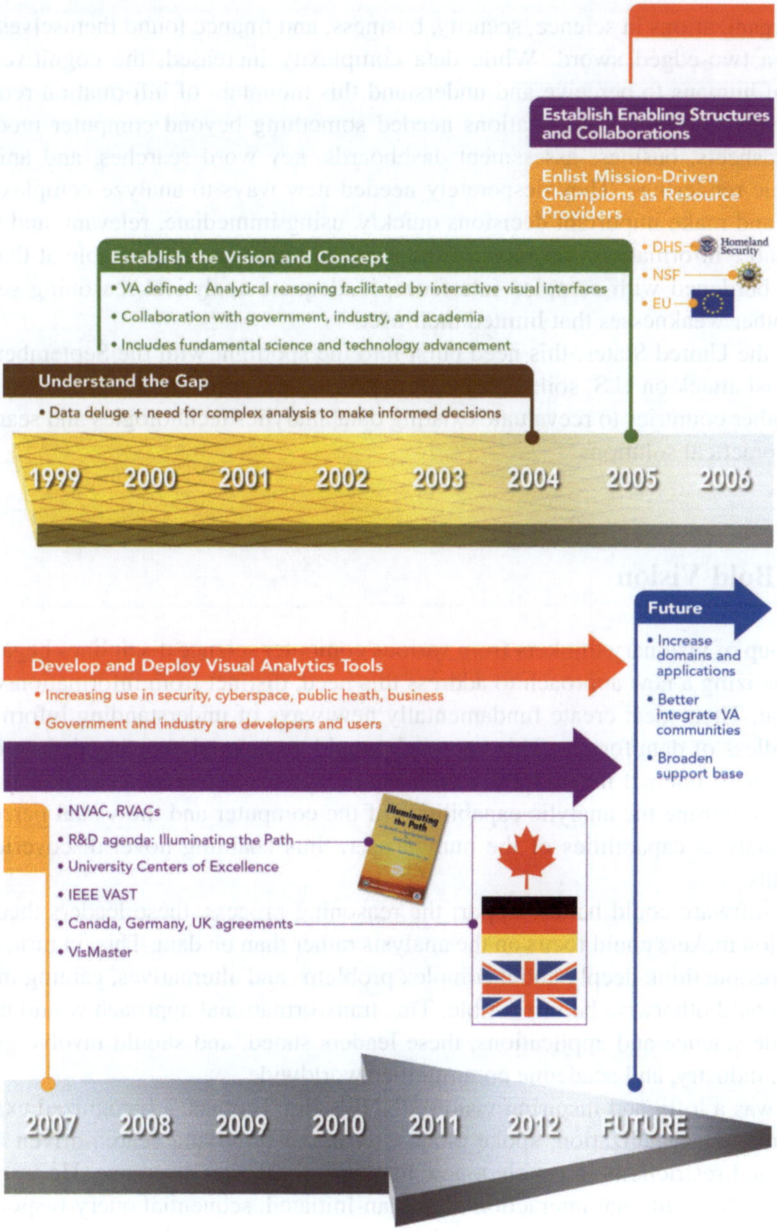

Fig. 3.1 In the visual analytics lifecycle, key strategies propel growth to the next stage along the path (note: acronyms are defined in the following sections)

sources. Yet existing methods for understanding the data were insufficient to support the level of analysis needed.

Organizations in science, security, business, and finance found themselves faced with a two-edged sword. While data complexity increased, the cognitive abilities of humans to perceive and understand this mountain of information remained relatively constant. Organizations needed something beyond computer modeling, spreadsheets, business-assessment dashboards, key word searches, and animated graphic renderings. They desperately needed new ways to analyze complex problems and make important decisions quickly, using immediate, relevant, and understandable information. Yet most of the tools and technology available at that time were burdened with complex interfaces, inadequate analytical reasoning support, and other weaknesses that limited their use.

In the United States, this need burst into the spotlight with the September 2001 terrorist attack on U.S. soil. This event motivated governments in the United States and other countries to reevaluate existing data analytics technologies and search for new, practical solutions.

3.3 Bold Vision

A group of visionary thinkers from various computer science disciplines began conceptualizing a new approach to address this need, distinct from information visualization. Their idea: create fundamentally new ways of understanding information, regardless of data format. This approach would go beyond showing data to enable the user to interact meaningfully with very large unstructured data collections. It would combine the analytic capabilities of the computer and the visual perception and analysis capabilities of the human user, thus enabling novel discoveries and insights.

If software could better support the reasoning process, these leaders theorized, decision makers could focus on the analysis rather than on data. This, in turn, would help people think deeply about complex problems and alternatives, gaining insights that would otherwise be impossible. This transformational approach would need to include science and applications, these leaders stated, and should involve government, industry, and academic communities worldwide.

It was a lofty and inspiring vision. PNNL's Jim Thomas, a recognized expert in information visualization, spoke eloquently about removing search-driven limitations and restrictions to enable a new human-information discourse. He wanted to change the traditional interaction of human-initiated, sequential query-response interaction. He envisioned a dialog, where the computer is analyzing information on its own initiative, and adapting its delivery of those data based on the user's needs. Pat Hanrahan, the Canon USA Professor of Computer Science and Electrical Engineering in the Computer Graphics Laboratory at Stanford University, described it this way: "*Visual analytics allows you to go in any direction with your thoughts while leveraging your visual perceptual system to guide you down the most useful paths*" (Hanrahan et al. 2009).

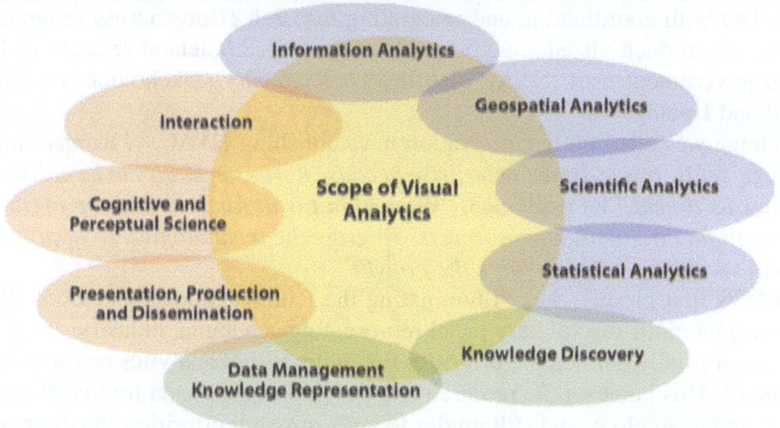

Fig. 3.2 Visual analytics integrates a number of sub-disciplines, combing aspects of visualization, data analysis, and interaction (adapted from Keim et al. 2010; used with permission). Using advanced visual interfaces, humans directly interact with the data analysis capabilities of computers, facilitating well-informed decisions in complex situations

3.4 Champions on Board

The earliest stages of visual analytics research and development relied mostly on individual efforts funded by a few government organizations in security, health, and the intelligence community, as well as some progressive commercial companies.

Now it was time to identify visionary advocates who had the resources to establish the science and technology of visual analytics on a broader, more integrated scale. In early 2000, PNNL invested internal resources in an initiative to apply visual analytics in one of its key mission areas: national security. This initiative provided the springboard for establishing a relationship with a key partner, the U.S. Department of Homeland Security (DHS).

Joseph Kielman, Science Advisor and Chief Scientist in DHS's Science and Technology Directorate, championed the new field of visual analytics as a way to address national security challenges. In 2004, with DHS support, Jim Thomas led a panel of internationally known multidisciplinary scholars to articulate the problem space and discuss the scope of the new science. This group formally defined visual analytics as "the science of analytical reasoning facilitated by interactive visual interfaces" (Thomas and Cook 2005).

Strategically, the definition was chosen to combine and build upon a wide range of established research (Fig. 3.2). One stakeholder described this definition as "*building the bridges that honored the people from various communities without threatening their realms.*" A special issue of IEEE Computer Graphics and Applications in 2004 was widely credited as the first use of the term visual analytics in the literature (Wong and Thomas 2004).

DHS and PNNL conceptualized the National Visualization and Analytics Center™ (NVAC), which DHS chartered in 2004. Under Thomas's leadership, NVAC was tasked with coordinating and integrating research efforts across programs and agencies to produce visual analytics technologies for homeland security and other federal government uses. NVAC also involved industry stakeholders such as Microsoft and Boeing.

Kielman was clear on his motivation in establishing NVAC. "*I wanted to create this large-scale, broad-based enterprise because it was necessary to establish visual analytics as a field*," he explained. "*We couldn't wait for it to develop organically, or through funding individual projects. To grow the technologies, to apply them to national security, we had to force the growth.*"

NVAC's first product was "Illuminating the Path," (Thomas and Cook 2005) a report from a multi-disciplinary panel representing academia, industry, and government that formally defined the priorities for future visual analytics research and development. This book set the research and development agenda for visual analytics science and technology and still guides today's research priorities and direction.

Soon after the book's publication, DHS funded five university-led Regional Visualization and Analytics Centers (RVACs) at Stanford University, the University of North Carolina Charlotte with Georgia Institute of Technology, Pennsylvania State University with Drexel University, Purdue University, and the University of Washington. Kielman's intent was for the university community to supply the basic research that would feed into NVAC. To diversify and broaden the academic base, DHS shifted its approach in 2009 to groups of university-led Centers of Excellence. One of these is focused on visualization sciences, comprising some 25 to 30 universities in the United States, Canada, and Germany; the other Center of Excellence targets data sciences.

The growing science focus of visual analytics attracted the attention of another important federal partner: the National Science Foundation. The agency recognized the need for multiple disciplines to apply visual analytics to large, diverse data sets—not just for homeland security, but also science, engineering, medicine, policy analysis, and commerce. "*Our agreement with DHS was that we would focus on theoretical advances that would be of value to multiple fields*," said Lawrence Rosenblum, NSF's Program Director for Graphics and Visualization.

In 2008, NSF and DHS launched the jointly funded program known as Foundations of Data and Visual Analytics, a five-year effort to develop the basic mathematics and computational science needed to grow the field. "*It's brought people from the math and computational fields, many of whom hadn't heard of visual analytics, to look at high-dimensional, complex data*," Rosenblum said. "*The goal is to develop methods to reduce the dimensionality of the data while maintaining the information content in order to assure that future visual analytics systems will be able to handle the ever-expanding data flow.*"

The European Union came on board as an advocate and sponsor to strengthen its member nations' visual analytics community. In 2008, a European Union Coordination Action Project financed VisMaster, a two-year collaboration among 11 countries. The project was designed to advance European academic and industrial research and development from several individual disciplines. In 2010, the group published its own research roadmap, "Master the Information Age—Solving Problems with Visual Analytics" (Keim et al. 2010).

These three organizations and their champions were instrumental in transforming visual analytics from concept to mainstream reality. Without the substantial financial sponsorship and advocacy to create these centralized focal areas and the resulting shared science and technology base, the discipline of visual analytics would likely have had a much slower and less synergistic evolution.

3.5 Structures and Collaborations

An important element in catalyzing the identity and direction for visual analytics was to establish formal structures as channels for research, technology development, application, and collaboration. The formation of NVAC and the university partnerships, along with the research and development agendas, marked the beginning of these structures.

The visual analytics pioneers began working to build professional venues where participants could be recognized, rewarded, and challenged. Special issues of magazines and journals provided early outlets for emerging research and applications within visual analytics (Kielman et al. 2009).

In 2005, NVAC began hosting semi-annual consortium meetings to bring academia, industry, and national laboratories together with end users, government sponsors, and international partners to advance this new field of research. In just five years after the inception of NVAC, the organization and its partner universities had published more than 200 peer-reviewed papers, adding to those published by other research teams worldwide.

In 2006, IEEE launched the Symposium on Visual Analytics Science and Technology (VAST), the first international symposium dedicated to visual analytics science and technology. This included an annual competition known as the VAST challenge, a contest that supplied datasets generated by NVAC's Threat Stream Generator project team and challenged researchers to find the ground truth despite false trails. The VAST challenge continues to stimulate researchers and students and led to a repository of large heterogeneous datasets that are used now by researchers and in education (Visual Analytics Benchmark Repository 2012). An increasing number of workshops and other events around the world have been held on related topics as diverse as financial analytics and mathematical foundations.

In parallel to U.S. efforts, individual research groups around the world were establishing visual analytics centers and hosting conferences, such as EuroVA, with visual analytics as a topic of interest. Starting in 2008, DHS signed a series of joint research agreements with Canada, Germany, and the United Kingdom that include visual analytics as one area of collaboration. Through these mechanisms and others, such as VisMaster and Germany's Deutsche Forschungsgemeinschaft Schwerpunktprogramm Scalable Visual Analytics programs, rapid developments and contributions from around the world spurred the growth of the new discipline.

European collaborations broadened the research base and brought new resources to the mix. For example, European and Canadian researchers focus many of their visual analytics projects in domains other than security, including engineering, biomedical, and geospatial applications—thus expanding the reach of applications.

3.6 Technology Deployment

As the following anecdote demonstrates, the evidence of a truly transformational field is user adoption of its results.

Soon after NVAC was established in 2004, Thomas gave an invited talk to high-level Canadian officials representing that country's law enforcement and intelligence communities. As John Dill, a professor in the School for Interactive Arts & Technology, Simon Fraser University, British Columbia, tells it, the officials were skeptical that "a group of academics" would have much to offer their fields. Then, Thomas showed an example of a visual analytics tool and the resulting security-related documents of interest. Seeing was believing. The officials immediately grasped the astounding new potential this kind of tool represented for their domains. Since then, Defence R&D Canada has embraced visual analytics as a viable method to help increase decision-maker awareness for defeating threats, protecting critical infrastructure, and implementing emergency management (Defence Research and Development Canada 2006).

The science, engineering, and industrial communities are gradually delivering scientific research and technologies for end users in the field. Today, visual analytics technology is used in applications including the security of international wire transactions and wire fraud detection, improving the effectiveness of law enforcement personnel, exploring the security of government cyber networks, and improving public health surveillance and response.

More commercial software vendors are selling visual analytics products and consulting services to industry customers. Larger companies are developing the capabilities themselves, as well as acquiring smaller software developers to position themselves as expert providers of these tools. A certain class of nimble companies is discovering that visual analytics delivers more value from their data so they can respond to a rapidly changing market faster than their competitors do. For example, Apple, Pfizer, Microsoft, Coca Cola, Google, Cornell University, Progressive Insurance, Amazon, Georgetown University, the Veteran's Administration, and Blue Cross Blue Shield are using visual analytics applications in their business (Hanrahan et al. 2009). They are using these tools to analyze competitors, improve product quality and features, and assess their internal processes, making their businesses more productive and cost effective.

Procter & Gamble, for example, uses visual analytics tools to search for patterns in patent filings and to identify problems in its supply chain (Totty 2006). The Boeing Company is using visual analytics to assess bird strike impacts. The results have affected aircraft design decisions. Boeing is also using visual analytics to evaluate industrial safety to get a full picture of activities that result in repetitive stress injuries (Kasik 2011). Pharmaceutical and bioinformatics companies are increasingly using visual analytics for drug discovery and improvement (Saffer et al. 2004; Saraiya et al. 2005).

Technology adoption challenges remain. For example, institutional inhibitors make it difficult to obtain and share real data to conduct research and create domain-specific prototypes. Data may be proprietary, contain personally identifiable information, or reveal problems that organizations don't want to expose to others. Even within an organization, data "silos" make it difficult to share data with other parts of the organization.

3.7 Strategies for Future Growth

Researchers and developers have made significant progress on parts of the original R&D agenda. Thomas and Kielman (2009) described ten of the now-common approaches and features that support analysis and reasoning, from relationship discovery to temporal interactions, capturing of analytical processes, and results for reporting.

Other parts of the path are clearly still under construction and present significant challenges. Thomas and Kielman (2009) described technical aspirations that include untethered interaction, the use of indefinite data, lower transaction costs, and trust—both in the validity of the data, as well as security and privacy for data access and interaction. Scholtz et al. (2009) described the needs that must be met to better transition the technology into widespread use. These technical and transition challenges will take many years to address fully.

To sustain and grow the field, some of today's top leaders recommend the following essential strategies.

3.7.1 Increase Domains and Applications

Because homeland security was the initial domain driving the development of visual analytics, some of the first technologies deployed were for public safety and emergency response. But it has always been part of the vision to expand into other domains that require complex analysis and the need to communicate analytical outcomes simply and clearly.

Kielman et al. (2009) described opportunities to expand visual analytics further into the fields of security, health, energy, environment, commerce, transportation, food/agriculture, and cyber security. Daniel Keim, Chair of Information Processing at the University of Konstanz, Germany, points to molecular biology as an emerging area, "because there's no fully automated way to accomplish essential tasks such as understanding gene function and conducting drug discovery."

Applications also must scale better from a single user to a collaborative, multi-user environment, such as operating an electrical grid or a national emergency management center, according to David Ebert, professor at Purdue's Visualization and Analytics Center and lead for DHS's Center of Excellence in visual analytics. Applications must support the decision making processes in complex situations involving collaborations at the same time, at different levels of an organization, and in different organizations.

3.7.2 Better Integrate the Communities Within Visual Analytics

The visualization and data analysis fields, essential components of visual analytics, must continue to integrate. Keim, of the University of Konstanz, makes the point that fields such as machine learning, artificial intelligence, and data mining still work largely by automation, without the benefit of visualization.

One of the challenges to adoption is demonstrating the value to the data community, Keim believes. "*Where data analysts might typically measure the efficiency of algorithms, or click-through times, articulating the benefits of the entire visual analytics process is more complex*," he said. Keim and others believe research into the value of visual analytics will spur user adoption.

Many of today's leaders are looking to the cognitive sciences communities for the next wave of integration. These experts can help design improved user interfaces, methods, and tools for perception-driven, multimodal interaction techniques.

3.7.3 Broaden the Base of Support

"*We're coming to the time when government needs to move out of this area and the participants look to other sources of funding and application spaces where visual analytics will grow*," said DHS's Kielman. He postulates an industry-research institution model, such as the global consortium called Semiconductor Manufacturing Technology, or SEMATECH, which "*worked wonders for creating a microelectronics capability in the United States*." Commercial companies in the finance, medical, and business intelligence fields, who are at the forefront of analysis in their industries, may be among the most promising supporters.

In Europe, to implement the vision in its research roadmap (Keim et al. 2010), members of the VisMaster project suggested the establishment of a "proactive topic" within the European Union's Information and Communication Technologies "theme." This enterprise would fund and coordinate projects in visual analytics.

At the same time, a broader support base must take care not to become fragmented, with overlapping work focused on specific domains. Funding and sharing of open-source tools, data sets, results, and guidelines must be coordinated at some level for optimal impact.

3.8 The Path Ahead

Visual analytics has seen unprecedented growth in its first years of mainstream existence. The field of study is fundamentally changing how humans interact, analyze, report, and act on information from law enforcement, health organizations, intelligence agencies, and other sectors.

At PNNL, visual analytics and related disciplines are an important base for collaborative science that addresses grand challenges. Through the pioneering work of Jim Thomas and many others at PNNL, we are privileged to be recognized internationally in advanced scientific computing, information visualization and analysis, visual analytics, and data-intensive computing. We continue to make significant internal research and capability investments in new approaches for interacting with complex, heterogeneous data and information from distributed sources. We are collaborating with DOE's Office of Science and others on problems in extreme-scale visual analytics, addressing issues in the transformation and representation of extremely high-dimensional data. And, through our commitment to the professional development of our staff, we are continuing to nurture leaders like Jim who inspire others and transform their worlds for the better.

Jim and other visual analytics pioneers believed that visual analytics must not only evolve in science and technology, but also in leadership. The field is now at a critical juncture, similar to a startup company that transitions to a more complex operational team as it matures. Students who were beginning their Ph.D. studies when this field started are now leaders in their universities, well-positioned to advance the science. More champions have risen up in government, industry, and national laboratories. The growth process described here must continue evolving to one that includes a wide variety of leadership roles, crossing into more domains.

Will visual analytics maintain its current form? Some think it will continue to grow as a vibrant, sustainable research field with its own identity. Others think it will evolve into a general science of problem solving and interactive discovery. Still others think it will gradually merge back into the broader realm of computer science, serving as an enabling capability to address analytical challenges. Regardless of the direction visual analytics takes, we hope the insights presented here will inspire emerging and potential leaders to continue transforming the field, in whatever direction that may be.

The illuminated path that began years ago is brighter in some places, and longer in others, but just as full of opportunity. Jim's catchphrase is still true: "*The best is yet to come*."

Acknowledgments We are deeply grateful to the following experts who contributed their insights for this chapter: Joseph Kielman, U.S. Department of Homeland Security Science & Technology Directorate; Lawrence Rosenblum, National Science Foundation; John Dill, Simon Fraser University, British Columbia, Canada; David Ebert, Purdue University Visualization and Analytics Center; Daniel Keim, University of Konstanz, Germany; David Kasik, Visualization and Interactive Techniques, The Boeing Company; and Richard May and Kris Cook, PNNL. Rich Quadrel, Pak Wong, Julie Fisher, and Andrea McMakin, all from PNNL, provided valuable reviews and assistance. Rosenblum's remarks in this article represent his own opinions and are not official positions of the National Science Foundation. Pacific Northwest National Laboratory is managed for the U.S. Department of Energy by Battelle under Contract DE-AC05-76RLO1830. PNNL-SA-82406.

References

Defence Research and Development Canada (2006). *Defence S&T strategy: science and technology for a secure Canada*. Ottawa: Government of Canada Publications.

Hanrahan, P., Stolte, C., & Mackinlay, J. (2009). Selecting a visual analytics application. Tableau software white paper. http://www.tableausoftware.com/whitepapers/selecting-visual-analytics-application. Accessed on 22 August 2011.

Kasik, D. (2011). Acquiring information from diverse industrial processes using visual analytics. In: D. Caivano et al. (Eds.), *Lecture notes in computer science: Vol. 6759. Product-focused software process improvement, 12th international conference, PROFES 2011*, Torre Canne, Italy, June 20–22, 2011 (p. 2). Berlin: Springer. doi:10.1007/978-3-642-21843-9_2.

Keim, D., Kohlhammer, J., Ellis, G., & Mansmann, F. (Eds.) (2010). *Mastering the information age—solving problems with visual analytics*. Germany: Konstanz.

Kielman, J., Thomas, J. J., & May, R. (2009). Foundations and frontiers in visual analytics. *Information Visualization*, *8*(4), 239–246. Special issue: foundations and frontiers of visual analytics.

McCormick, B. H., DeFanti, T. A., & Brown, M. D. (Eds.) (1987). Visualization in scientific computing. *ACM SIGGRAPH Computer Graphics*, *21*(6), 1–14.

Saffer, J. D., Burnett, V. L., Chen, G., & van der Spek, P. (2004). Visual analytics in the pharmaceutical industry. *IEEE Computer Graphics and Applications*, *24*(5), 10–15.

Saraiya, P., North, C., & Duca, K. (2005). An insight-based methodology for evaluating bioinformatics visualizations. *IEEE Transactions on Visualization and Computer Graphics*, *11*(4), 443–456.

Scholtz, J., Cook, K. A., Whiting, M. A., Lemon, D., & Greenblatt, H. (2009). Visual analytics technology transition progress. *Information Visualization*, *8*(4), 294–301. Special issue: foundations and frontiers of visual analytics.

Thomas, J. J., & Cook, K. A. (Eds.) (2005). *Illuminating the path: the research and development agenda for visual analytics*. Los Alamitos: IEEE Computer Society Press.

Thomas, J. J., & Kielman, J. (2009). Challenges for visual analytics. *Information Visualization*, *8*(4), 309–314. Special issue: foundations and frontiers of visual analytics.

Totty, M. (2006). A new look for number crunching. *The Wall Street Journal Online*, *April 3*, R6.

Visual Analytics Benchmark Repository (2012). http://hcil.cs.umd.edu/localphp/hcil/vast/archive/index.php.

Wong, P. C., & Thomas, J. (2004). Visual analytics. *IEEE Computer Graphics and Applications*, *24*(5), 20–21.

Wong, P. C., & Thomas, J. J. (2009). Visual analytics: building a vibrant and resilient national science. *Information Visualization*, *8*(4), 302–308. Special issue: foundations and frontiers of visual analytics.

Part II
Visual Analytics and Visualization

Chapter 4
Visual Search and Analysis in Complex Information Spaces—Approaches and Research Challenges

T. von Landesberger, T. Schreck, D.W. Fellner, and J. Kohlhammer

Abstract One of the central motivations for visual analytics research is the so-called information overload—implying the challenge for human users in understanding and making decisions in presence of too much information (Yang et al. in Decision Support Systems 35(1):89–102, 2003). Visual-interactive systems, integrated with automatic data analysis techniques, can help in making use of such large data sets (Thomas and Cook, Illuminating the path: The research and development agenda for visual analytics, 2005). Visual Analytics solutions not only need to cope with data volumes that are large on the nominal scale, but also with data that show high *complexity*. Important characteristics of complex data are that the data items are difficult to compare in a meaningful way based on the raw data. Also, the data items may be composed of different base data types, giving rise to multiple analytical perspectives. Example data types include research data compound of several base data types, multimedia data composed of different media modalities, etc.

In this paper, we discuss the role of data complexity for visual analysis and search, and identify implications for designing respective visual analytics applications. We first introduce a data complexity model, and present current example visual analysis approaches based on it, for a selected number of complex data types. We also outline important research challenges for visual search and analysis.

T. von Landesberger (✉) · D.W. Fellner
Technische Universität Darmstadt, Darmstadt, Germany
e-mail: ttekusov@gris.tu-darmstadt.de

D.W. Fellner
e-mail: d.fellner@gris.tu-darmstadt.de

T. Schreck
Universität Konstanz, Konstanz, Germany
e-mail: tobias.schreck@uni-konstanz.de

D.W. Fellner
TU Graz, Graz, Austria

J. Kohlhammer
Fraunhofer IGD, Darmstadt, Germany
e-mail: joern.kohlhammer@igd.fraunhofer.de

J. Dill et al. (eds.), *Expanding the Frontiers of Visual Analytics and Visualization*,
DOI 10.1007/978-1-4471-2804-5_4, © Springer-Verlag London Limited 2012

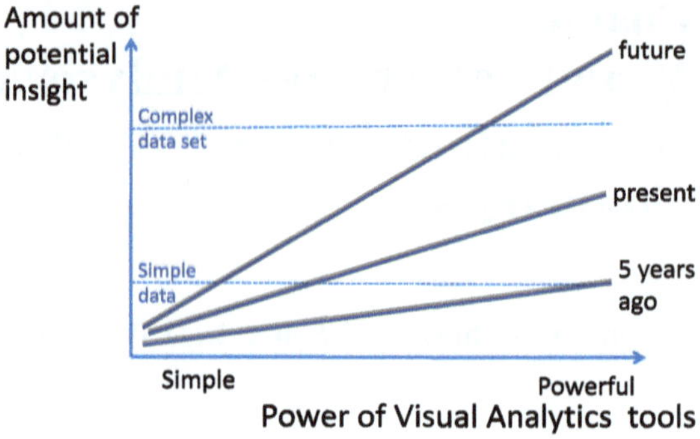

Fig. 4.1 Supposed functional dependency between sophistication of Visual Analytics tools and potential insight achievable, for data of different complexity. Research in Visual Analytics for complex data aims at increasing the slope of the assumed functional dependency

4.1 Introduction

Visual-interactive techniques, combined with intelligent data analysis methods, can be valuable tools for obtaining useful insights and actionable findings from *large* and *complex* data sources (Thomas and Cook 2005). They are used in many application areas including biology, medicine, engineering and manufacturing, finance, and scientific research, just to name a few. While data size relates to the nominal quantity of data under concern (such as the number of objects), complexity is related to inherent properties of the data.

The **need for visual analysis of large and complex data** stems from the general assumption that the analysis of larger and more complex data may lead to more insight (i.e., discoveries of new previously unknown knowledge). This assumption holds if the tools for analyzing these data enable the user to discover all included insights. However, creating tools scaling up with data size and data complexity is still a key challenge in the Visual Analytics area (Keim et al. 2010; Thomas and Cook 2005).

While no generally acknowledged **definition for complexity** exists, we associate with it (a) the data items being difficult to compare based on raw data, and / or (b) data compound of several base data types. An example of complex data difficult to compare is multimedia data. Two raster (pixel) images typically cannot be meaningfully compared based only on the raster representations, but rather, content-based descriptions need to be extracted beforehand for this purpose. An example for a compound-complex data set is earth-observation research data, which may comprise remote sensing image data, annotated by textual meta data, and connected to time series of environmental observation parameters such as temperatures, radiation levels, humidity, or the like.

Complexity properties affect the data processing throughout the whole **analytical workflow**. Both the Visual Analytics reference model (Keim et al. 2008) and the Information Visualization reference model (Card et al. 1999) suggest to transform input data for mapping them to visual representations. For complex data, this transformation is often difficult and ambiguous. Usually, domain- and data-specific transformation steps need to be applied, to make the data available for visual mapping and aggregation. Moreover, user interaction methods, visual displays and further automatic data analysis methods need to be adapted to the complexity characteristics of data.

Given several different notions of data complexity and their implications for the Visual Analysis workflow, there is a need to more explicitly consider the role of data complexity in Visual Analytics. We here examine two important key **user tasks** in Visual Analysis systems for complex data: *Searching* for data items of interest, and *analyzing* for relationships among and between sets of data items. Searching and analyzing are very related, and often, a sequence of searching tasks is conducted that leads to findings on the global analysis level.

Progress in data acquisition, storage, and transmission leads to data repositories integrating different data modalities. To date, many visual analysis systems focus on data sets of given complexity, mostly addressing a single complex data type. The amount of potential insight obtained from data of a given complexity can be raised by the degree of sophistication of the visual analysis system. A visual analysis tool of given technological development status will provide increasing insight potential, as data gets more complex. However, the relation between sophistication of the visual analysis solutions and the complexity of the data is limited by the technological state of the art of the tools. We expect that by systematically researching and improving visual analysis technology, the slope of the relationships between tool sophistication and data complexity with respect to potential insight can be increased. Figure 4.1 sketches the basic functional dependencies as we assume them. By pushing the limit in visual analysis tool support for complex data, the slope of the functional relationships between the two variables can be made more steep. Focusing on improved approaches for addressing data complexity in visual analysis tools, we hope to be able to push the limits. In the following, we give a definition of complex data sets, provide an overview of approaches to visual search and analysis therein, and identify future research challenges. We state that if the raised challenges are addressed appropriately, future visual analysis tools will be able to derive more potential insight from a given type of complex data.

The remainder of this paper is structured as follows. In Sect. 4.2, we identify two main sources for complexity, and discuss their role in relationship to Visual Analytics applications. In Sect. 4.3, we discuss tasks and problems when dealing with complex data. Section 4.4 then provides proposed Visual Analytics solutions to a number of example problems from various data and application domains. Based on this, in Sect. 4.5, we identify a number research challenges considered important and interesting. Finally, Sect. 4.6 concludes.

4.2 Definition of Complex Data Sets

The term complex data is often used in a loosely defined way. In our view, data complexity can be attributed to two fundamental dimensions. Complexity may stem (a) from intrinsic properties of a given single kind of data (type complexity), or (b) from the data being structured based on a mix of different types, either simple or

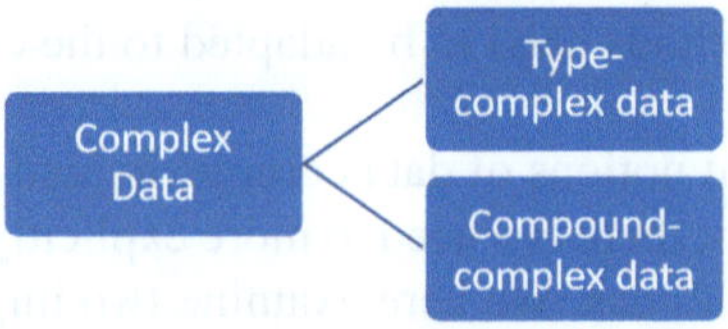

Fig. 4.2 Categorization of complex data. In our definition, we distinguish between complexity stemming from inherit properties of a given single data type (type-complex data), or from the data being compound of multiple base data types (compound-complex data)

complex in turn (compound complexity) (see Fig. 4.2). Both dimensions impact the difficulty of algorithmic and visual processing of the data. For searching and analyzing, a key fundamental data operation involves calculation of similarity properties among data items.

In the first type of complex data (**type-complex data**) the specific properties of a single given data type incurs difficulty to algorithmically process the data for similarity in a straightforward way. In particular, for these data types it is difficult to measure similarity meaningfully between data instances based on the raw data representation. For example, image data, audio data, video data, biochemical molecule data, 3D object data, or graph data are data types of this category. In all cases, the raw data needs to be transformed by specialized preprocessing steps for further algorithmic and visual analysis. The difficulty can be explained in the following example showing the difference between multivariate numeric data (considered simple here) and image data (considered complex here). For multivariate data, we can usually compute the similarity of data records based on forming sums of absolute differences of the respective field values in the records. In contrast, consider the task of comparing a query and a candidate image. For most practical purposes, it is not possible to calculate the similarity based on the raw image pixel arrays. Rather, a preprocessing step which extracts relevant information from the images, such as the presence of specific object types, or color and texture patterns, is needed. Then, query processing can take place on this extracted information (Rüger 2010).

In the second type of complex data (**compound-complex data**) the data items are aggregated from multiple "base" data types, each of which could be complex or non-complex in turn. Again here, it is difficult to calculate similarities, because it is a priori not clear how to aggregate the similarities between the individual data components. Depending on the application context, either one of the base data types could be the relevant perspective, or also, a combination thereof. Moreover, the data components may be complex themselves, raising the complexity by the number of involved base data types. As an example, consider research data from the earth observation domain. Here, measurement data can be comprised of several complex data types. A realistic example includes multivariate time-dependent measurements of environmental parameters. Additionally, geo-locations, trajectories, and image data may be available for the specific data. Even further, the particular experiments which lead to the acquisition of this data may be described in a research paper, which is relevant to understanding the data. An earth observation scientist might be interested in searching and analyzing each of these aspects simultaneously. Nowadays, large repositories of such data are set up and made publicly available. While access to the data per se is given, in absence of appropriate search and analysis tools, these repositories are often not easily accessible. Earth observation data is just one example for compound-complex data. Others include compound graphs, biologic experimental data, spatio-temporal data, intelligence data compound by textual reports, intelligence findings and image documentation, and so on and so forth.

4.3 Tasks and Problems of Visual Search and Analysis in Complex Data

We next describe two fundamental user tasks in visual analysis systems—searching and analyzing. We then outline the key problems of supporting these tasks in presence of complex data.

4.3.1 Visual Search and Analysis

Searching and analyzing are key user tasks in information systems. Searching relates to finding information entities of interest to a user on a more local level, based on specific query formulation. Analyzing, in its generic sense, can be defined as finding structures and abstractions on the set level, adding to the understanding of a data set as a whole.

Search is an inherent part of the data analysis process and can take several **forms**. Although it may not be seen at the first sight, search tasks are comparable to the basic information visualization tasks defined by Shneiderman (1996). Search includes, e.g., identification of the data needed for the analysis, searching for similar data items among a set of items, detection for recurring motifs in a sequence or network, or discovery of outliers or exceptional events. For visual support of these tasks, appropriate user interfaces are needed. These interfaces need to include visual means of query specification and results presentation.

By *analysis* we understand tasks related to identification of global relationships and structures in the data. Questions of interest relate to the number of groups existing in the data, the similarities and differences between them, and how they relate to each other. Cluster analysis and association rule mining are two examples of analysis methods. Visual support for analysis tasks require the appropriate visual steering of the analysis algorithms, and expressive visual displays to present the output of the analysis methods. Also, navigation facilities to allow overview and details-on-demand are important ingredients in respective systems.

Searching and analyzing are often interrelated through cycles of corresponding activities. For example, evidence for a hypothesis may be collected by issuing a series of queries, which select subsets of the data for some aggregation purpose. Often, sets of searching subtasks, each of relative short duration, are nested within longer-running, overarching analysis processes.

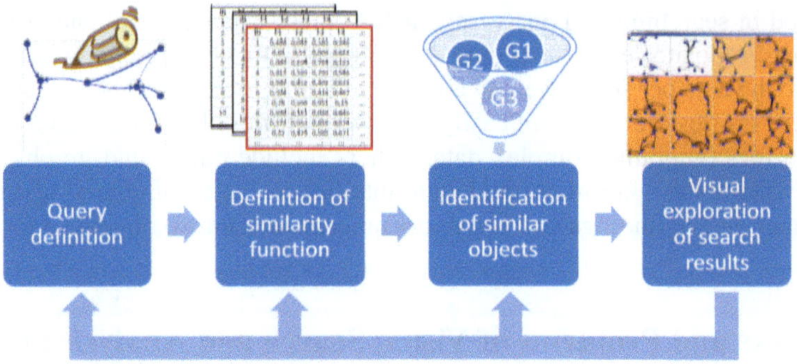

Fig. 4.3 Visual search process. By means of a visually specified query, and relying on a selected descriptor, similar objects are retrieved and visualized, often in context of the whole data repository

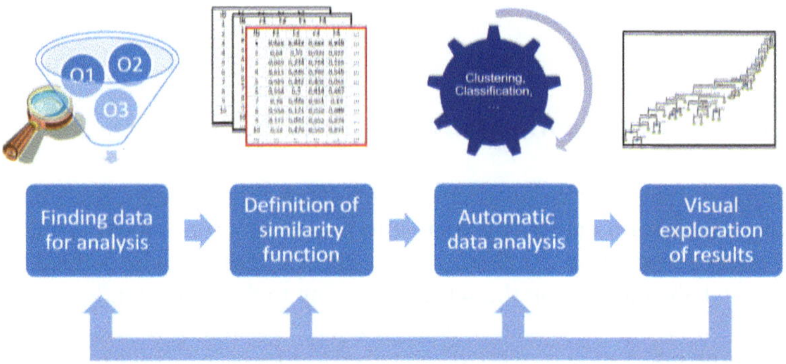

Fig. 4.4 Visual analysis process. After specification of the data for the analysis and their similarity function, the selected analysis function is executed and the results are visually inspected

4.3.2 Problems in Presence of Complex Data

Complex data imply specific problems for visual search and analysis. These problems depend both on the task (searching vs. analyzing) and on the type of data complexity. For searching, Fig. 4.3 illustrates a process model of visual search in complex data. Based on visual query specification, and by means of appropriately selected and configured descriptors, similar objects to the query are identified. Visual overview displays are useful for showing search results in context of the whole data set. In our model of the analysis process (see Fig. 4.4), first the suitable data set needs to be found for further processing. After determining the appropriate similarity function and selecting an analysis method, the results are visually inspected. This process includes several feedback loops creating an incremental process. In both cases, each process step poses problems for developing visual analysis methods.

For *type-complex data*, sophisticated data transformation needs to be applied before data items can be queried, compared, grouped, and visualized. Typically, custom similarity functions, for example, based on descriptors (or feature vectors) need to be defined. However, for many type-complex data sets, multiple alternating descriptors are possible, and it typically is not clear which one suites the current task best. Furthermore, descriptor extraction is a non-trivial, parameterized process, and analysts are often not aware of its implications. On the other hand, meaningful analysis (interpretable results) requires the user to understand the specific notions of similarity which lead to search results or object groupings. Also, query specification is difficult if descriptors cannot be easily interpreted—direct numeric feature specification is typically not useful for average users. How can querying be visually supported, visually representing the relevant similarity concepts and thresholds for which objects are considered similar by the system? How sensitive are query and analysis results with respect to parameterizations of the similarity function? Such questions need to be addressed by ideal visual analysis systems.

These problems are potentially multiplied for *compound-complex data*. In these data, searching and analyzing tasks need to be based on a joint similarity function which appropriately reflects similarity concepts for each included base data type. All base types have possibly different similarity functions. These similarity notions need to be both configured individually and appropriately aggregated. Consider the example of compound-complex research data from our example of earth observation research, where an exemplary task is to analyze for similar observations. Similarity can be constituted by similarity of respective measurement series, but also, geographic location, measurement method applied, or researchers involved. How can an aggregate similarity function be defined for searching in such data? How can such data be clustered? Clearly, the user needs to be given appropriate visual query formulation tools which allow to select and weight the involved data perspectives, and specify a query in all of these relevant perspectives.

We summarize key design problems for visual search and analysis systems for complex data as follows. As can be seen from the respective processes, there are many parallels between the two tasks (search and analysis) but they also have several specifics.

4.3.2.1 Visual Search

- *Query formulation.* The user needs to be enabled to specify the query visually and interactively. The design problem is to derive visual representations for the query properties of interest. In case the data has a visual representation, so-called *query by sketch* is possible, where the user outlines a draft shape to be searched for. A problem to address is the level of abstraction, by which the query is specified. In case of compound-complex data, the query specification is potentially multiplied by each involved data modality.
- *Similarity function.* The similarity function to use for evaluating the query needs to be selected and parameterized. For the user to make an informed selection, the system should visually represent the implications of the selected similarity function for the result to be expected. While for type-complex data a single similarity

function needs to be specified, for compound-complex data, possibly for each base data type one similarity function needs to be selected, and a combination needs to be found.

- *Visual result presentation.* The visual search systems needs to present the sequence of found results and their potential relevance to the query. Each object needs to be shown by a visual representation. In case of data with visual representation, thumbnail views are common. Visualizing result sets for compound-complex data involves finding appropriate visual representations for the combined data perspectives, and how each of the base data instance for each data type relates to the issued compound query.
- *User feedback.* Effective search systems require the user to quickly converge to a satisfying result, only using a few iterations of query adaptation and result inspection. Therefore, it is crucial that the system offers ways for the user to understand why the found results relate to the user query, both in terms of the query specification and descriptor selected.

4.3.2.2 Visual Analysis

- *Similarity function.* Like in searching, many analysis algorithms rely on a similarity function to be defined for the data objects (e.g., clustering). This should be also supported by involving the user in an interactive process of defining similarity and evaluating analysis results. It again often involves selection of an appropriate descriptor, and specification of combinations of descriptors, in case of compound-complex data.
- *Selection of analysis method.* The user needs to interactively select an appropriate analysis algorithm to apply. This involves selecting the type of analysis algorithm (e.g., cluster analysis, association rule mining, classification analysis, etc.) as well as its configuration. This is not an easy task as not all analysis methods can deal with complex data sets and therefore specific analysis methods need to be applied or developed.
- *Visual result presentation.* Presentation of analysis results, similar to presentation of search results, requires finding an appropriate visual abstraction. While in search, the level of interest is on the object level, on the other hand in analysis, often aggregates (e.g., clusters) or abstractions (e.g., hierarchies) are found. These need to be visualized, reflecting possible visual representations of the single of compound base data types.
- *User feedback.* In analysis algorithms, user feedback again plays an important role. We expect that to arrive at satisfying results, several analysis iterations need to be performed. Comparison of search results is rather straightforward, as ranked lists need to be compared. In case of analysis, the problem may become more difficult, as aggregate and abstract analysis outputs need to be compared, for the user to understand the differences between the choices. For example, an appropriate visualization should allow the user to effectively compare two clusterings obtained from two difference compound similarity functions.

4.4 Approaches

In this section, we discuss selected examples of visual search and analysis systems, which illustrate the variability of the problem. In Sect. 4.4.1, we will illustrate key principles by means of classic example systems from the field. In Sect. 4.4.2, we will discuss some approaches for type-complex data, and in Sect. 4.4.3, we will present examples for support of compound-complex data.

4.4.1 Generic Examples for Visual Search and Analysis Systems

Generic approaches to visual search and analysis date back as early as to the beginning of Information Visualization as a field. Shneiderman in his Visual Information Seeking Mantra (Shneiderman 1996) proposed to support the search and analysis process by visual-interactive tools. He and Ahlberg proposed the FilmFinder system (Ahlberg and Shneiderman 1994a), which supported a new way of interactive search (see Fig. 4.5(a)). In this concept, visual overviews allow to analyze the data set at an abstract level, with interactive query interfaces allowing drill-down queries to arrive at details-on-demand. Visual-interactive displays for searching and analyzing aim to provide intuitive access and navigation. Leveraging the human visual perceptual system, they are supposed to provide a high bandwidth interface, encourage explorative analysis and creative processes in the users mind.

Another generic example of an exploratory system for complex data is the well-known INSPIRE system for exploration of document collections proposed by Wise et al. (1995) (see Fig. 4.5(b)). Text is type-complex data as it cannot be meaningfully compared based on the raw data, but it needs to be, preprocessed e.g., using word frequency vectors. INSPIRE relies on projection of high-dimensional document vectors to a 2D display to provide an overview of document corpora for similarity of topics and for exploration. An appropriate visual design shows documents in a landscape metaphor which can be readily navigated by the user.

We can learn from examples such as these, that complexity is often dealt with by **simplification**: Complex data is transformed to feature vectors; dimensionality reduction is applied to project data to interactive displays, and large data sets are sampled to provide overviews. In case of compound-data, projection to a selected data perspective of interest is a pragmatic approach. However, such approaches often incur a loss in formation. Visualization also applies a simplification by mapping only selected dimensions to visual variables, or visually aggregating many data samples (such as many documents in INSPIRE) to a landscape, where height indicates groups of data and position their relationships.

There are general principles that help the user working with complex data. These include **consistency** and **user guidance**. Consistency means the same way of working with similar data in various environments. This is especially needed when dealing with compound-complex data in multiple perspectives. There, each perspective should use the same interaction means and mappings, if possible. User guidance

(a) Film Finder (b) Inspire

Fig. 4.5 *Left*: The FilmFinder system (Ahlberg and Shneiderman 1994b) is an example for visual search in multivariate data (Figure ©1994 ACM, Inc. Included here by permission). *Right*: The Inspire system (Wise et al. 1995) is an example of an analysis system, which allows to relate and compare subsets of elements in a visual way (Figure ©1995 IEEE)

helps the user in the search and analysis process providing her with a set of steps to follow, or recommendations for suitable parameters in algorithmic analysis.

4.4.2 Example Approaches to Visual Search and Analysis of Type-Complex Data

In the next section, we consider examples for visual search and analysis in type-complex data including 3D object data, graph data, and biochemical data.

4.4.2.1 Visual Search in 3D Object Data

Many multimedia data types are of type complexity or compound complexity. An example of type-complexity is the area of 3D model data. By specific data structures, the shape and other properties of 3D objects can be modeled with applications in computer-aided manufacturing, architecture, and simulation, just to name a few. A widely used data structure to encode the shape of 3D models are polygonal meshes. While simple in terms of data structure, two mesh models cannot be meaningfully compared based on their polygons. However, a wealth of description extraction methods has been proposed to date (Tangelder and Veltkamp 2008). The idea is to extract descriptor from mesh models, which allow for meaningful comparison. In the project PROBADO, we have considered visual search methods to help architects query in 3D building models. The idea is to allow the users to quickly

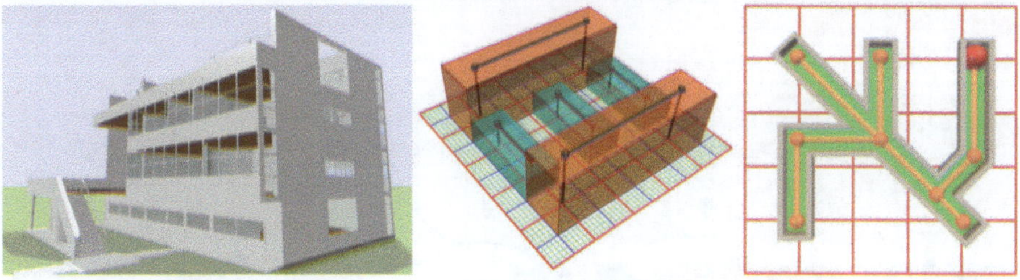

(a) 3D building model (b) Volume sketch (c) Floor plan sketch

Fig. 4.6 Example visual search modalities for querying in 3D architectural object data

specify properties of interest in a building. To this end, we considered two query modalities: Querying by global 3D shape, and querying for room connectivity structure (Berndt et al. 2009). Querying by global building shape is supported by the user sketching the coarse outline of a building by a simple 3D block editor. Having entered a 3D sketch, any global 3D descriptor (Tangelder and Veltkamp 2008) can be used to retrieve similar objects. A more specialized query modality suggested by architects included the querying for the structure of rooms in a building (floor plan). To this end, we devised a method to extract a room connectivity graph from each building in the repository. The user then enters a query structure by means of a simple graph editor, and again, the system finds similar objects based on a graph matching strategy. Figure 4.6 illustrates a sample 3D building model, and the two query editors.

From this example, we see that often, many generic descriptors already exist for a given complex data type. However, not always do the existing descriptors support all possible domain-specific search modalities. For example, the room connectivity structure was of interest to architect users, so it needed to be developed anew.

4.4.2.2 Visual Search in Graphs—Visual Query Definition

Graphs are used in various application areas such as chemical, social or shareholder network analysis. Finding relevant graphs in large graph databases is thereby an important problem. Such search starts with the definition of the query object. Defining the query graph quickly and effectively so that it matches meaningful data in the database is difficult. In Landesberger et al. (2010), we introduced a system that guides the user through the process of query graph building. We proposed three ways of defining the query graph, which support the user with intelligent, data dependent recommendations. In this way, the query graph is defined more quickly and corresponds better to the underlying data set.

1. Smart Choice of Data Samples

The first approach employs a query-by-example technique, where one existing graph is used as a query object. For the choice of query object, we offer a suitable selection of example graphs from the database. The proposed selection provides

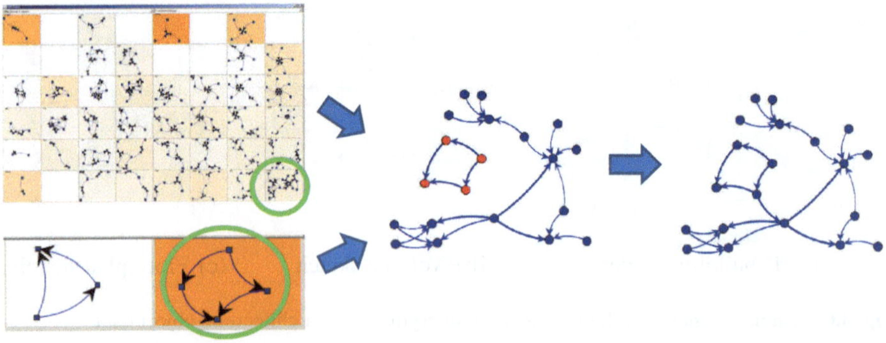

(a) The choice of graph sample from the SOM result and a selection of graph building blocks

(b) Using graph sample and a building block for graph definition

(c) Query graph created by combining graph sample and a building block

Fig. 4.7 Combining smart sketching with data samples for leveraging the advantages of both techniques. (**a**) The proposal for graph samples using SOM clustering and graph building blocks with frequency indication. (**b**) The selection of a graph sample and a building block for creating the query graph. The selected sample and the building block are highlighted with *green circles* in the proposal view. (**c**) The final query graph combining both graph samples and building blocks with sketched edges

an overview of the available graphs. It is based on the result of clustering by Self Organizing Map (SOM) algorithm (Kohonen 2001) as introduced in Landesberger et al. (2009) (see Fig. 4.7 left top).

2. Graph Sketching Supported by Data-Dependent Graph Building Blocks Another approach to query definition is query-by-sketch—creating the query object itself. Graph editing from scratch by adding individual nodes and edges one by one can be very time consuming for large graphs. Therefore, we extended graph editing by adding multiple nodes and edges at once—using the so called graph building blocks. The building blocks are small sub-graphs that occur often in graphs (i.e., motifs). These blocks are interactively combined so they support fast creation of graphs. Moreover, we analyze the underlying data space to present to the user additional guidance, in particular, information on frequency of occurrence of these blocks in the database (see Fig. 4.7 left bottom).

3. Combination of Sketching and Examples As sketching may be time consuming and examples may not provide enough flexibility, we combined both approaches. The query definition starts from an existing object chosen from the proposed set. This object can be modified by adding and deleting of edges and nodes or adding building blocks. Combination of these techniques provides a fast definition of a specific and meaningful query object (see Fig. 4.7).

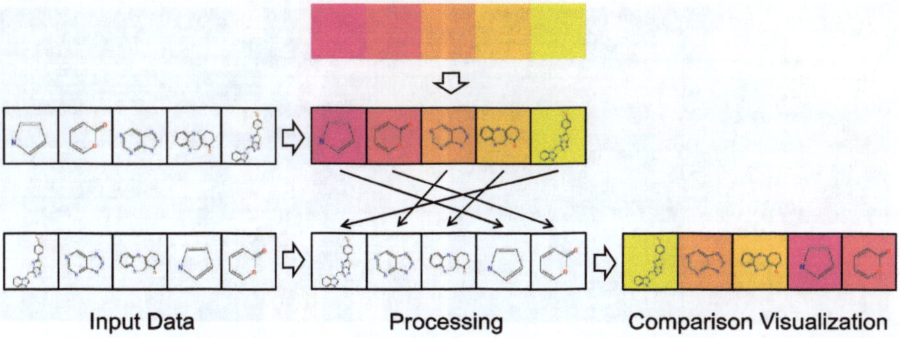

Fig. 4.8 Two meaningful data descriptors of biochemical data and their comparison. Descriptors: atom resp. nitrogen count. *Left*: The input data is sorted according to each descriptor. *Center*: Color is mapped to the first ordering. The sorting is compared using connectors. *Right*: Compact comparison view based on object identity reveals descriptor correspondence

4.4.2.3 Visual Search and Analysis of Biochemical Data—Similarity Function Definition Using Visual Comparison of Descriptors

The analysis of biologic and chemical data is gaining importance in the Visual Analytics community. Biologic and chemical data can be regarded type-complex data types. For example, chemical compounds cannot be analyzed directly but need to be described by their properties such as size, charge, solubility, atom connectivity, etc. The selection of these properties is used to define similarity between objects. The employed description is heavily use case dependent, therefore, user knowledge is very important for the evaluation of the selections. This evaluation is however difficult, if different representations of the whole dataset are presented to the user. For example, in the analysis of high throughput screening (HTS), an overview and comparison of thousands of molecules is needed.

In Bremm et al. (2011a), we presented a novel visual analysis approach for determining data descriptions suitable for the task at hand. We developed dedicated visualizations for comparison of sets of multi-dimensional data descriptors. These techniques are based on low-dimensional data presentation using color for comparison of groupings resulting in the different descriptor spaces (see Fig. 4.8). For large data sets, we employ adaptive grids with clustering properties (Self-Organizing Maps, Kohonen 2001). These views allow for spotting overall similar descriptors and locally similar object groups in heterogeneous data sets. The finding of potentially interesting descriptors is supported by an interactive pipeline, which guides the user through the analysis process. The result of initial automatic data analysis provides recommendations and offers the user the possibility to interactively refine the results. These refinements are supported in visual-interactive way.

As an application example, 18 commonly used chemical descriptors for 9989 molecules with 773 dimensions in total were examined. The comparison of two descriptors in Fig. 4.9 shows a very homogeneous color gradient representing the descriptors for weight and number of atoms of the molecules. This validates an

Fig. 4.9 *Left*: Comparison of the weight to an atom count descriptor. The homogeneous color gradient validates the expected correlation of the descriptors. *Right*: The 1-D WienerNumber descriptor shows a high separability for molecules which are all in one cell in the SOM of the 26-D ExtendendFingerprint

expectation of the coherence between weight and size. Looking at the comparison of the ExtendendFingerprint with the WienerNumber descriptor, we see that many cells are homogeneously colored (Fig. 4.9 right). All of the purple molecules in the WienerNumber SOM are located in one cell of the ExtendendFingerprint SOM. If the pharmacologist is interested in these molecules, the WienerNumber descriptor is preferable. It leads to a higher diversity of the concerned molecules at a lower dimensionality (1 vs. 26).

4.4.3 Example Approaches to Visual Search and Analysis of Compound-Complex Data

We next discuss example systems for search and analysis in compound-complex data. Examples span research data, geo-temporal event data, and security-related data.

4.4.3.1 Visual Search in Research Data—Visual Query Definition and Visualization of Search Results

Science as a domain heavily depends on the timely availability of appropriate information. Recently, the need for persistent storage of data produced in public research has been recognized by data producers, researchers, and public funding agencies alike. For example, in the earth observation sciences, massive amounts of data are collected by sensor networks, or by data acquisition campaigns. Currently, large data repositories, such as the *PANGAEA Publishing Network for Geoscientific and Environmental Data* (PANGAEA 2012), are being built. Persistent availability and sharing of such data among the research community can foster scientific progress,

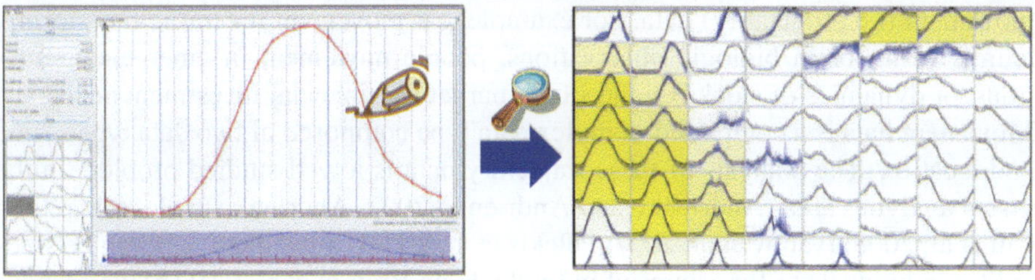

Fig. 4.10 Visual query specification (*left*) and result visualization (*right*) for searching in time-oriented research data

allow results to be reproduced, and document present states of the environment for future research.

Visual search and analysis facilities in such data are highly desirable to enable researchers to access the data (Ahmed et al. 2011). The data under concern typically is complex in that it consists for multiple base data types which together form the observation data. For example, earth observation data can consist of time-dependent multi parameter measurements for environment factors, in addition to images of multi spectral satellite analysis and X-ray images of sediment cores, extracted from the area of measurement. Typically, researchers want to search for content of the data, to compare or formulate hypotheses. To this end, the research data needs to be indexed by an array of different descriptors; and appropriate visual search interfaces need to be provided. In Bernard et al. (2010), we have described an early prototype system which allows a multi-faceted search in earth observation data. Content-based search is supported by allowing the user to specify the draft shape of a time series of a given observation parameter (cf. Fig. 4.10 (left)). Based on curve descriptors, the most similar curves can be retrieved, and further filtering of result sets based on geo-location, seasonal and other meta data attributes are possible. The search results and refinements thereof are visualized in context of an overview of a larger data set, e.g., the given data repository (cf. Fig. 4.10 (right)). To this end, a visual cluster analysis of the overall data set is performed, and search results are highlighted in their context.

In this system, we have explored the tight integration of searching and analyzing. A visual catalog is the central visual element of the system, showing an overview over the most important time series patterns. Search results can be shown in context of the overview. Also, curves from the overview can be selected and adapted in the query editor, for an adjusted search. While the system also allows to query for the other involved compound data aspects (textual meta data, geo-location, etc.) currently the system is oriented towards search in the time series shape space.

4.4.3.2 Visual Search and Analysis of Spatio-temporal Data—Identification of Interesting Events

The analysis of spatio-temporal data plays a prominent role in many applications such as transportation, meteorology, finance or biology. One area is the analysis of movement (i.e., trajectory) data. For example, car movement for traffic monitoring, animal behavior in biologic observations, people movement in emergency situations, or dynamics of stocks on the stock market for financial investment decisions. Movement data is a compound-complex data type composed of two data types: time and location. The analysis of these trajectory data is a well studied problem in the visual analytics area (Andrienko and Andrienko 2007; Andrienko et al. 2007, 2009; Cui et al. 2008; Ivanov et al. 2007; Pelekis et al. 2007). Movement data can be studied for individuals or for groups of individuals. In Bremm et al. (2011b) we propose an approach that addresses the analysis of grouped spatio-temporal data. It is based on the notion of Parallel Sets (Kosara et al. 2006), extended for automatic identification of interesting points in time that are suggested to the user for inspection.

Generally, the groupings data may be pre-defined (e.g., by identification of animal herds in biology), or may be a result of previous analysis (e.g., clustering). When the group membership changes over time, it is necessary to examine these aspects (e.g., which herds change members and when).

As the number of analyzed time moments may be very large, the group changes cannot be manually inspected in each time point. Therefore, a good selection of the points in time for a detailed analysis is important. It should represent the data well—reveal important movements or outliers. It should highlight overall trends and identify time periods of high activity (shorter intervals). Moreover, detection of outliers provides a set of moments with extraordinary group-change events.

As an application example, we can regard the analysis of people movements in the case of an emergency. As a basis for respective research, the VAST Challenge 2008 data (Grinstein et al. 2008) includes the movement data for 82 subjects in a building over 837 points in time. The grouping is based on areas in the building (Fig. 4.11 top left). It assigns subjects into groups according to their location in every time moment. In this scenario, at a specific time, a bomb detonated and afterwards people die or start to move towards the exits (turquoise and purple areas).

The automatic analysis of group changes identifies interesting time moments for detailed analysis. The result puts more emphasis on time periods of high movements (after the explosion) and identifies behavior of people who move differently from the rest or in an unexpected way (away from exits). Tracking these people reveals that despite their odd routing, the majority reaches the exits (Fig. 4.11 bottom).

4.4.3.3 Visual Analytics for Security

Starting from the NVAC initiative (National Visualization and Analytics Center) in the US and its visual analytics research agenda (Thomas and Cook 2005), a number of research programs and initiatives evolved in the direction of visual analytics for security. While in the United States there has always been an applicable emphasis on homeland security among other fields, there was no such strong focus in Europe where a large number of application areas offered a wide range of opportunities (Keim et al. 2006).

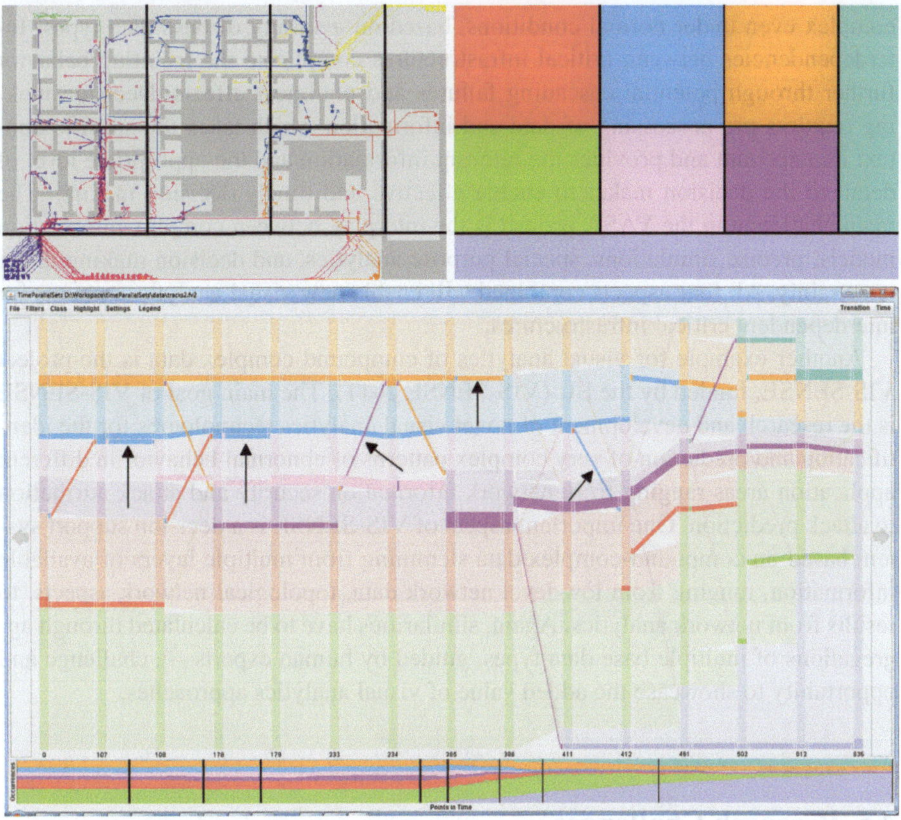

Fig. 4.11 *Top*: The example of emergency evacuation analysis using dataset from the VAST challenge 2008 (Grinstein et al. 2008). *Left*: Trajectory based visualization of the movement of the people (Andrienko and Andrienko 2010) with partitioning of the building into 8 areas. *Right*: Coloring of the areas. *Bottom*: Analysis of group changes and unexpected movements showing automatically selected time movements. Tracking of surprising movements reveals that surprisingly most of these people reach the exit in time

Partly initiated by Jim Thomas and after different transatlantic initiatives and joint workshops, Germany and the U.S. have jointly started the project VASA (Visual Analytics for Security Applications) to develop tools that will aid in the protection, security, and resiliency of U.S. and German critical infrastructures in 2010 (VASA 2011). The goal of VASA is to apply visual analytics to disaster prevention and crisis response, with a focus on critical infrastructures in logistics, transportation, food safety, digital networks and power grids at the national levels.

VASA works on a fundamental challenge in the analysis of compound-complex data. After all, critical infrastructures are complex socio-technical systems with components and sub-systems that are characterized by specific behaviors which result from the applied rules of physics, from technical specifications, and the established control regime. Such behaviors of single critical infrastructures are quite complex even under normal conditions, based on a variety of base data types. Interdependencies between critical infrastructures complicate the resulting behavior further through potential cascading failures and nonlinear effects. Decision making requires pre-processing of data and information which takes the specific context into account and provides the relevant information and the appropriate level of detail to the decision maker to enable effective and timely decision making. The main challenge in the VASA project is the interplay between complex information models, precise simulations, special purpose analytics, and decision making under uncertainty. All four aspects combined will enable new visual analytics systems for interdependent critical infrastructures.

Another example for visual analytics of compound-complex data is the project VIS-SENSE, funded by the EU (VIS-SENSE 2011). The main goal of VIS-SENSE is the research and development of novel visual analytics technologies for the identification and prediction of very complex patterns of abnormal behavior in different application areas ranging from network information security and attack attribution to attack prediction. One important aspect of VIS-SENSE is a decision support system based on compound-complex data stemming from multiple layers of available information, ranging from low-level network data, topological network aspects, to results from network analytics. Again, similarities have to be calculated through aggregations of multiple base data types, guided by human experts—a challenge and opportunity to showcase the added value of visual analytics approaches.

4.5 Research Challenges

The previous examples served to illustrate the breadth and with of the problem of visual search and analysis of complex data. We believe that in accordance with increasing volumes of data, complexity of data poses new challenges to the development of visual analytics tools. These challenges are strengthened by the emergence of new application areas such as biology, medicine, architecture, and emergency management. Integrated search and analysis, in a cross-domain, cross-data-type and cross-data-repository environment will become more and more important, and will thereby require new appropriate solutions.

As an example, the definition of similarity functions for complex data can be considered. To date, already many data transformation methods are available, which allow to extract descriptors for complex data, and make them comparable in this way. Visual search and analysis systems should rely on these established methods where possible. However, it is typically difficult for a user to chose for the appropriate descriptor, either because there are too many available, or that the similarity notion required is not covered by the existing descriptors.

We next summarize a number of research challenges we deem interesting and critical, in the context of the discussed problems and application examples.

4.5.1 Infrastructures

Visual Analytics is a multi-disciplinary discipline, which incorporates research from various fields. Practitioners in visual analytics have started to implement ad-hoc systems, such as in-memory databases or user-steerable algorithms. However, these are still quite isolated attempts and not sustainable solutions in the long term. The community lacks an infrastructure to allow a flexible interoperability of components that might be specialized for certain type-complex or compound-complex data (Keim et al. 2010). The goal is to allow practitioners from different fields of research to benefit more from each other's work.

This corresponds to the challenging task to design a common language, a collection of accepted practices and an architectural model that can be agreed upon by different fields of research related to data analysis. Current research in data analysis is dispersed and sometimes virtually isolated in their respective domain. In several analytics technologies, database researchers, machine-learning and data analysis researchers, as well as visualization researchers focus on specific aspects. However, visualization approaches, data management procedures, and data mining methods all have to work together in newly orchestrated ways, leading to a new definition of interoperable visual analytics building blocks that allow the coherent creation of visual analytics systems.

4.5.2 New Data Types

Once the building blocks of visual analytics systems are well understood, more research on data typing is needed. For example, exposing the semantic type of data in databases is essential in order to know what kind of analysis can be applied and what kind of visualization is meaningful. Today's data classifications (like nominal or quantitative) are rich enough for most statistical approaches, but it is not sufficient for visualization. The semantic web is an example of an application domain where sophisticated data types are being defined, but there are other initiatives and it is not clear yet how they will converge and how the field of visual analytics will benefit from it.

4.5.3 Search Problem and Comparative Visualization

Searching and analyzing in complex data require the user to make a number of profound decisions regarding query specification, descriptor selection, algorithm configuration, and combining of different data perspectives. Arriving at satisfying search and analysis results requires also to solve a meta search problem for these search and analysis parameters. Only visual systems which provide fast response times and can cope with high data complexity and sizeability allow this process to be effective. This puts high requirements with respect to scalability of the implementations.

Furthermore, appropriate visual representations are needed to show the user the implications of specific choices. How do the search result lists differ, if the descriptor is changed? How does a clustering result change with respect to the algorithm parameters set? Comparative (or delta) visualization tools could be helpful as a meta visualization.

4.5.4 User Guidance in the Visual Analysis Process

In the field of information and multimedia retrieval, relevance feedback (Rüger 2010) is a standard technique to help users indirectly to configure search parameters, e.g., choice of descriptors and similarity functions. Based on the user providing relevance votes to candidate results, an optimization problem is solved for weighing features. We believe the relevance feedback approach is a promising tool to help the user in an intuitive, indirect way to solve the descriptor and parameter choice problem. However, to be applicable to the visual search and analysis problem in complex data, we believe it needs to be adapted to reflect different data structures. Most importantly, choice of descriptors, and weighing of individual similarity functions for compound-complex data need to be optimized. To this end, the relevance feedback problem needs to be reformulated. Also, it needs to be considered what is the right level of relevance feedback judgments. Possibly, new interaction techniques need to be devised as well. While a difficult problem for visual search, relevance feedback for visual analysis is expected to be an even harder problem. A formal model for the analysis process in complex data is needed to discuss where relevance feedback for visual analysis can be installed.

4.5.5 Benchmarking

Benchmarking and evaluation play an important role in devising effective visual search and analysis systems. In the area of multimedia retrieval, benchmark data sets are available mainly for standard and type-complex data such as multivariate data (Frank and Asuncion 2010), 3D models (Shilane et al. 2004) or images (Datta et al. 2008; Deselaers et al. 2008). To our knowledge, there are no established benchmarks for compound-complex data available, up to the TREC-Video data set (Smeaton et al. 2006). Measuring the effectivity of visual search systems requires extended benchmark data sets, which together with user-oriented evaluation approaches are useful to compare new system designs. Benchmark data sets of general analysis problems are however expensive and difficult to obtain. The VAST analytic challenges (Grinstein et al. 2008) are a promising starting point to compare visual analysis systems. A deeper understanding and modeling of the analysis process could be expected to lead to more analysis benchmarks being devised in the future.

4.6 Conclusions

Visual search and analysis are important key tasks in making use of data. Besides nominal data volumes, data complexity is a scalability limit for existing solutions. We discussed two views on complexity in this article. One is based on the inherent complexity properties of a given data type (type-complexity), while the other stems from data being composed of several base data types (compound-complex data). Supporting visual search and analysis in this data raises several problems, including choice of data descriptors, parameterization and weighting of similarity function, visual query specification and result visualization. We aimed at illustrating the breadth and width of the problem by considering a variety of application scenarios from domains such as 3D object data, network data, scientific research data, and biochemical data. The presented solutions are just individual solutions in a large problem space. We believe that approaching a number of identified research challenges, especially in comparative visualization, user feedback, benchmarking, and infrastructure will foster further development of new solutions. Given the emergence of data in ever growing volumes and in increasing complexity, the community requires such novel approaches and solutions to access and exploit today's information spaces.

Acknowledgments This work has been supported by the following research programs and projects: The projects Visual Feature Space Analysis and Visual Analytics Methods for Modeling in Medical Imaging, funded by the German Research Foundation (DFG) within the Strategic Research Initiative on Scalable Visual Analytics (SPP 1335); the project VIS-SENSE funded by the European Commission's Seventh Framework Programme (FP7 2007-2013) under grant agreement Nr. 257495; the THESEUS Programm funded by the German Federal Ministry of Economics and Technology; the German part of the project VASA funded by the German Federal Ministry of Education and Research; the PROBADO project funded by the German Research Foundation (DFG Leistungszentrum für Forschungsinformation); and the project VisInfo funded by the Leibniz Association (WGL). We are grateful for helpful collaboration with Prof. Kay Hamacher and other colleagues within research projects.

References

Ahlberg, C., & Shneiderman, B. (1994a). Visual information seeking using the FilmFinder. In *Conference companion on human factors in computing systems* (pp. 433–434). New York: ACM.

Ahlberg, C., & Shneiderman, B. (1994b). Visual information seeking: tight coupling of dynamic query filters with starfield displays. In *Proc. SIGCHI conference on human factors in computing systems* (pp. 313–317). New York: ACM.

Ahmed, Z., Yost, P., McGovern, A., & Weaver, C. (2011). Steerable clustering for visual analysis of ecosystems. In *EuroVA international workshop on visual analytics*.

Andrienko, N., & Andrienko, G. (2007). Designing visual analytics methods for massive collections of movement data. *Cartographica*, *42*(2), 117–138.

Andrienko, G., & Andrienko, N. (2010). Interactive cluster analysis of diverse types of spatio-temporal data. *ACM Special Interest Group on Knowledge Discovery and Data Mining (SIGKDD) Explorations*, *11*, 19–28.

Andrienko, G., Andrienko, N., & Wrobel, S. (2007). Visual analytics tools for analysis of movement data. *ACM Special Interest Group on Knowledge Discovery and Data Mining (SIGKDD) Explorations*, *9*(2), 38–46.

Andrienko, G., Andrienko, N., Rinzivillo, S., Nanni, M., Pedreschi, D., & Giannotti, F. (2009). Interactive visual clustering of large collections of trajectories. In *Proceedings of IEEE symposium on visual analytics science and technology* (pp. 3–10).

Bernard, J., Brase, J., Fellner, D., Koepler, O., Kohlhammer, J., Ruppert, T., Schreck, T., & Sens, I. (2010). A visual digital library approach for time-oriented scientific primary data. In *Research and advanced technology for digital libraries* (pp. 352–363).

Berndt, R., Blümel, I., Krottmaier, H., Wessel, R., & Schreck, T. (2009). Demonstration of user interfaces for querying in 3D architectural content in PROBADO3D. In *Lecture notes in computer science: Vol. 5714. European conference on digital libraries* (pp. 491–492). Berlin: Springer.

Bremm, S., Landesberger, T. V., Bernard, J., & Schreck, T. (2011a). Assisted descriptor selection based on visual comparative data analysis. *Computer Graphics Forum, 30*(3), 891–900.

Bremm, S., von Landesberger, T., Andrienko, G., & Andrienko, N. (2011b). Interactive analysis of object group changes over time. In *EuroVA international workshop on visual analytics*.

Card, S. C., Mackinlay, J., & Shneiderman, B. (1999). *Readings in information visualization: Using vision to think*. San Mateo: Morgan Kaufmann Publishers.

Cui, W., Zhou, H., Qu, H., Wong, P. C., & Li, X. (2008). Geometry-based edge clustering for graph visualization. *IEEE Transactions on Visualization and Computer Graphics, 14*(6), 1277–1284.

Datta, R., Joshi, D., Li, J., & Wang, J. (2008). Image retrieval: Ideas, influences, and trends of the new age. *ACM Computing Surveys (CSUR), 40*(2), 5.

Deselaers, T., Keysers, D., & Ney, H. (2008). Features for image retrieval: An experimental comparison. *Information Retrieval, 11*(2), 77–107.

Frank, A., & Asuncion, A. (2010). UCI machine learning repository. http://archive.ics.uci.edu/ml.

Grinstein, G., Plaisant, C., Laskowski, S., O'connell, T., Scholtz, J., & Whiting, M. (2008). VAST 2008 challenge: Introducing mini-challenges. In *IEEE symposium on visual analytics science and technology* (pp. 195–196).

Ivanov, Y., Wren, C., Sorokin, A., & Kaur, I. (2007). Visualizing the history of living spaces. *IEEE Transactions on Visualization and Computer Graphics, 13*(6), 1153–1160.

Keim, D., Kohlhammer, J., May, T., & Tomas, J. (2006). Event summary of the workshop on visual analytics. *Computers & Graphics, 30*(2), 284–286.

Keim, D. A., Mansmann, F., Schneidewind, J., Thomas, J., & Ziegler, H. (2008). Visual analytics: scope and challenges. In S. Simoff, M. H. Boehlen, & A. Mazeika (Eds.) *Lecture notes in computer science (LNCS). Visual data mining: Theory, techniques and tools for visual analytics*. Berlin: Springer.

Keim, D., Kohlhammer, J., Ellis, G., & Mansmann, F. (Eds.) (2010). *Mastering the information age – solving problems with visual analytics*. Eurographics.

Kohonen, T. (2001). *Self-organizing maps* (3rd edn.). Berlin: Springer.

Kosara, R., Bendix, F., & Hauser, H. (2006). Parallel sets: Interactive exploration and visual analysis of categorical data. In *IEEE transactions on visualization and computer graphics* (pp. 558–568).

Landesberger, T. V., Bremm, S., Bernard, J., & Schreck, T. (2010). Smart query definition for content-based search in large sets of graphs. In *EuroVAST 2010* (pp. 7–12). Goslar: European Association for Computer Graphics (Eurographics), Eurographics Association.

PANGAEA Publishing Network for Geoscientific & Environmental Data (2012). http://www.pangaea.de/.

Pelekis, N., Kopanakis, I., Marketos, G., Ntoutsi, I., Andrienko, G., & Theodoridis, Y. (2007). Similarity search in trajectory databases. In *Proceedings of international symposium on temporal representation and reasoning* (pp. 129–140).

Rüger, S. (2010). *Multimedia information retrieval. Synthesis lectures on information concepts, retrieval and services*. Morgan & Claypool Publishers.

Shilane, P., Min, P., Kazhdan, M., & Funkhouser, T. (2004). The Princeton shape benchmark. In *Shape modeling applications proceedings* (pp. 167–178). IEEE.

Shneiderman, B. (1996). The eyes have it: A task by data type taxonomy for information visualizations. In *IEEE visual languages* (pp. 336–343).

Smeaton, A. F., Over, P., & Kraaij, W. (2006). Evaluation campaigns and trecvid. In *Proc. ACM international workshop on multimedia information retrieval* (pp. 321–330). New York: ACM Press.

Tangelder, J. W. H., & Veltkamp, R. C. (2008). A survey of content based 3d shape retrieval methods. *Multimedia Tools and Applications*, *39*(3), 441–471.

Thomas, J., & Cook, K. (2005). *Illuminating the path: The research and development agenda for visual analytics*. Los Alamitos: IEEE Computer Society.

VASA Addresses Cascading Effects Across Critical Infrastructures (2011). http://www.theivac.org/content/vasa-addresses-cascading-effects-across-critical-infrastructures. Last accessed on Aug. 11, 2011.

VIS-SENSE: Visual Analytic Representation of Large Datasets for Enhancing Network Security (2011). http://www.vis-sense.eu. Last accessed on Aug. 11, 2011.

von Landesberger, T., Goerner, M., & Schreck, T. (2009). Visual analysis of graphs with multiple connected components. In *Proceedings of IEEE symposium on visual analytics science and technology*.

Wise, J. A., Thomas, J. J., Pennock, K., Lantrip, D., Pottier, M., Schur, A., & Crow, V. (1995). Visualizing the non-visual: Spatial analysis and interaction with information from text documents. In *Proceedings of IEEE symposium on information visualization* (pp. 51–58).

Yang, C., Chen, H., & Honga, K. (2003). Visualization of large category map for internet browsing. *Decision Support Systems*, *35*(1), 89–102.

Chapter 5
Dynamic Visual Analytics—Facing the Real-Time Challenge

Florian Mansmann, Fabian Fischer, and Daniel A. Keim

Abstract Modern communication infrastructures enable more and more information to be available in real-time. While this has proven to be useful for very targeted pieces of information, the human capability to process larger quantities of mostly textual information is definitely limited. Dynamic visual analytics has the potential to circumvent this real-time information overload by combining incremental analysis algorithms and visualizations to facilitate data stream analysis and provide situational awareness. In this book chapter we will thus define dynamic visual analytics, discuss its key requirements and present a pipeline focusing on the integration of human analysts in real-time applications. To validate this pipeline, we will demonstrate its applicability in a real-time monitoring scenario of server logs.

5.1 Introduction

Real-time analysis is a challenging and important field, motivated through both the potential to gain value from up-to-date information as demonstrated in the financial sector, and the thread of damage to be caused if timely assessments are unavailable as, for example, in emergency situations, air traffic control or network monitoring scenarios. In many such cases, it has been shown that automated solutions alone are insufficient since the severity of consequences often requires humans to be in the loop for making adequate decisions. Therefore, applying visual analytics for real-time analysis appears to be a rewarding undertaking.

Since most analysis and visualization methods focus on static data sets, adding a dynamic component to the data source results in major challenges for both the automated and visual analysis methods. Besides typical technical challenges such as

F. Mansmann (✉) · F. Fischer · D.A. Keim
University of Konstanz, Konstanz, Germany
e-mail: Florian.Mansmann@uni-konstanz.de

F. Fischer
e-mail: Fabian.Fischer@uni-konstanz.de

D.A. Keim
e-mail: Daniel.Keim@uni-konstanz.de
url: http://infovis.uni-konstanz.de

J. Dill et al. (eds.), *Expanding the Frontiers of Visual Analytics and Visualization*,
DOI 10.1007/978-1-4471-2804-5_5, © Springer-Verlag London Limited 2012

unpredictable data volumes, unexpected data features and unforeseen extreme values, a major challenge is the capability of analysis methods to work incrementally. In the essence this means that current results need to build upon previous results, which applies both to knowledge discovery methods such as clustering as well as visualization methods. Adding a node and several edges in a force-directed graph visualization, for example, will result in significant visual changes, whereas adding a data point to a scatter plot only triggers one small visual change. Therefore, certain methods are more suitable than others to be used in an incremental fashion.

The field of visual analytics has developed significantly over the last years with more and more methods solving challenging application problems. While Thomas and Cook (2005) defined the purpose of visual analytics tools to "provide timely, defensible, and understandable assessments", to date little research has focused on the timely aspects of visual analytics, and—in particular—its applicability for real-time analysis. We therefore hope that this book chapter inspires and triggers developments in this area.

Real-time analysis task can be as diverse as monitoring (i.e., timely detection of changes or trends), getting an overview, retrieval of past data items, prediction of a future status or making decisions. Despite this diversity of tasks, common to most real-time analysis tasks is the need to provide situational awareness. Ensley describes what he calls "situation awareness" as "the perception of the elements in the environment within a volume of time and space, the comprehension of their meaning, and the projection of their status in the near future" (Endsley 1995). In particular, this definition includes Ensley's three levels of situation awareness, which are 1) the perception of elements in current situation, 2) the comprehension of the current situation, and 3) the projection of the future status.

Based on these two ground-breaking works we define dynamic visual analytics as follows:

Definition 5.1 Dynamic Visual Analytics is the process of integrating knowledge discovery and interactive visual interfaces to facilitate data stream analysis and provide situational awareness in real-time.

The goal of dynamic visual analytics is thus to provide situational awareness by minimizing the time between happening and assessment of critical events and enabling a prediction of the future status.

Besides defining dynamic visual analytics, the core contribution of this book chapter is to develop an abstract model for dynamic visual analytics, which will then be applied to the application scenario of server monitoring. The remainder of this paper is structured as follows: We will discuss previous work in relation to dynamic visual analytics in Sect. 5.2, thoroughly analyze the user's role and key requirements for dynamic visual analytics methods in Sect. 5.3 and apply our model for dynamic visual analytics to a system log analysis scenario in Sect. 5.4. The last section summarizes our contributions.

5.2 Background

5.2.1 Visual Analytics

In 2005 Thomas and Cook from the National Visualization and Analytics Center coined the term *visual analytics* in their research and development agenda (Thomas and Cook 2005). This document explicitly stated "the need for analysis techniques for streaming data" (recommendation 3.13, p. 91) to deal with the problems of situational awareness, change assessment and information fusion.

Likewise, the recently published book *Mastering the Information Age: Solving Problems with Visual Analytics* (Keim et al. 2010) identifies data streaming as one of the major challenges for visual analytics: "Streaming data presents many challenges—coping with very large amounts of data arriving in bursts or continuously (...), tackling the difficulties of indexing and aggregation in real-time, identifying trends and detecting unexpected behavior when the dataset is changing dynamically."

In contrast to these two fundamental theoretical publications, we exclusively focus on the real-time aspects of dynamic visual analytics for data streams in this book chapter by defining dynamic visual analytics, listing technical requirements and describing the user's role in this interactive real-time analysis process.

5.2.2 Data Streams: Management and Automated Analysis

From an infrastructural point of view data in streaming applications are difficult to manage in comparison to occasionally updated data sets. As stated in Chaudhry et al. (2005), a number of key characteristics change when moving from traditional database management systems (DBMS) towards streaming applications. First, one-time queries are replaced by continuous queries that not only once evaluate the query against the database, but also stay active and continuously produce results. Second, traditional DBMSs do not necessarily possess a notion of time since an update of an attribute overwrites the previous value, whereas streaming applications might issue continuous queries such as the average speed of cars over the last 5 minutes. Third, the unbounded nature of streams can lead to changes during query execution against such an unbounded data set. Fourth, while data reliability is assumed for a traditional DBMS, failures or delays of sensors might introduce unreliability into streaming applications since records might be reported out-of-order. Lastly, the monitoring nature of streams requires streaming application to have a reactive capability whereas traditional DBMS only passively react to human-issued queries.

A recent review of currently methods and systems can be found in the book *Data Stream Management* by Golab and Özsu (2010). Besides data stream management systems, storing and accessing both historic and real-time data in streaming data warehouses are the core topics of their book.

Not only has data management of streams become an active area of research, but deriving valuable information from data streams through knowledge discovery has also emerged. Besides applying traditional data mining techniques such as clustering, classification, frequent pattern mining and forecasting to data streams, stream-specific topics such as sliding-window computations, stream indexing and querying are emerging and discussed in detail in Aggarwal (2007). In many cases, the unbounded and high-frequency characteristics of data streams pose additional challenges for the analysis from an algorithmic and computational point of view: Evolving data over time might require changes in the derived models. As a result of high data volumes, it might no longer be possible to process the data efficiently more than once. In addition to this book, Gama's comprehensive book (Gama 2010) focuses on a number of stream mining solutions based on *adaptive learning algorithms*. Thereby the set of examples is not only incremented for a given learning algorithm, but also outdated examples are forgotten. Gama furthermore argues that machine learning algorithms have to work with limited rationality, which he describes as the fact that rational decisions might not be feasible due to the finite computational resources available for making them.

Dynamic visual analytics needs to build upon the emerging infrastructure technology to query and store data streams. Furthermore, knowledge discovery from data streams can also be considered a relatively young research field. As a result of the technology's immaturity, intensive training to application-specific solutions and continuous adaption to still changing concepts are currently characteristic to data streaming since off-the-shelve solutions are for most application fields not yet available.

5.2.3 Time Series Visualization

So far, the most common field to include real-time visualization was *time series visualization* as surveyed in the recently published book *Visualization of Time-oriented Data* (Aigner et al. 2011). While there is a large body of work about interactive visualization and exploration of static time series (e.g., the TimeSearcher, Hochheiser and Shneiderman 2004), further research aspects in this field include the combination of knowledge discovery and visualization techniques as, for example, demonstrated in the classical paper *Cluster and calendar based visualization of time series data* by Van Wijk and Van Selow (1999). Yet another interesting work is VizTree (Lin et al. 2004), a system that can be used to mine and monitor frequently occurring patterns in time series through a data abstraction and pattern frequency tree visualization.

Some more recent publications explicitly focus on the real-time analysis and visualization aspects of time series: The work of Kasetty et al. (2008) focuses on real-time classification of streaming sensor data. The authors use Symbolic Aggregate Approximation (SAX) (Lin et al. 2003) to transform the time series data and then show how time series bitmaps representing pattern frequencies can be updated in constant time for classifying high-rate data streams. Hao et al. (2008) investigate the use of cell-based time series for monitoring data streams to reveal root causes of anomalies. In this work they focus on circular overlay displays, which start overwriting the screen once full, and variable resolution density displays, which adaptively increase the resolution of the display once more data is available. The LiveRAC system (McLachlan et al. 2008) follows a reorderable matrix of charts approach with semantic zoom to monitor a large number of network devices in real-time.

In contrast to these dynamic time series visualizations, a number of domain-specific real-time visualization systems exist. The VisAlert system (Foresti et al. 2006), for example, aims at establishing situational awareness in the field of network security. A circular layout is used to visualize the relationships between where (w.r.t. the network infrastructure), what (type of alert) and when network security alerts occurred. While real-time aspects were not explicitly considered in this work, the system of Best et al. (2010) puts its focus there. Using a high-throughput processing platform, the authors base their network monitoring work on the above mentioned SAX technique to model behavior of actors in the network in real-time and visualize these through a glyph representation. In addition to that, they use LiveRAC and a spiral pixel visualization to interactively investigate streamed network traffic. Other domain-specific work focuses on near real-time visualization of online news (Krstajic et al. 2010). The technique merges several articles into threads and uses categories to display the threads in a temporal colored line visualization.

As shown in this review of related work, combining knowledge discovery and visualization methods for real-time analysis remains challenging and therefore only little work about dynamic visual analytics exists to date. The purpose of this publication is thus to establish a link between the worlds of data stream management, real-time knowledge discovery and interactive dynamic visualization to tackle extremely challenging data analysis problems in streaming applications in the near future.

5.3 Dynamic Visual Analytics

Dynamic visual analytics applications are different from traditional visual analytics systems because a number of requirements from the perspective of data management, knowledge discovery and visualization need to adhere to the incremental nature of streams. Furthermore, the user's role changes since his focus on exploration is extended to include real-time monitoring tasks.

5.3.1 Requirements for Dynamic Visual Analytics Methods

When dealing with massive data streams requirements especially from the data management perspective need to be fulfilled before knowledge discovery or interactive

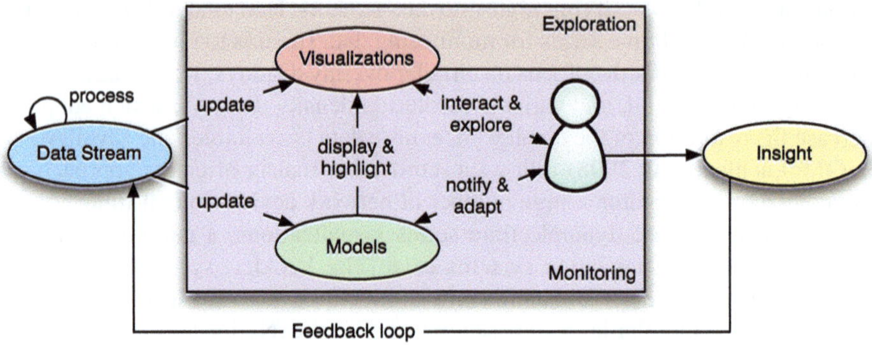

Fig. 5.1 The dynamic visual analytics pipeline

visualization methods can be applied. In particular, this means that (distributed) data gathering & processing in real-time, stream query languages, methods to deal with uncertainty (e.g. error bounds in sensor networks) and reactive capabilities of the database management system are readily available. Furthermore, many applications might not only require querying the stream itself, but also need to access to historic records stored in streaming data warehouses.

Knowledge discovery methods then need to deal with the output of the processed data streams. One key requirement thereby are incremental algorithms that can deal with limited computational resources on the one side and the unbound and possible uncertain nature of the streams on the other side. Again, depending on the application, both the notion of uncertainty as well as the one of real-time might be considerably different.

The set of suitable visualization methods is also dramatically reduced for streaming applications since not all visualizations are designed in a way to accommodate for changes. By nature, time plays an important role in dynamic visualizations and should thus be treated in a way that the age of both historic and recent data items on the screen can be easily distinguished. One prominent way of realizing this is to use the x-position for time, either by shifting historic items to one side in order to make space for new arriving data, by removing and aggregating old data, or by rotating and overwriting old data. However, many more options exist and should be investigated with respect to the specifics of the stream application. In addition to time, visualizations for dynamic visual analytics should be capable of enhancing currently displayed items based on the continuously arriving results of employed online knowledge discovery methods. This could, for example, be done by using a color scales to express the abnormality of an event in a system monitoring scenario. Note that the unbounded nature of streams could lead to the need to make changes to data elements which are already displayed, for example, when a cluster emerges in the stream that extends over both recent and historic items.

After considering these data management, knowledge discovery and visualization requirements for dynamic visual analytics, we will now discuss what role the user plays in interactive streaming applications.

5.3.2 The Role of the User in Dynamic Visual Analytics

Besides different methods, the core difference between automated streaming solutions and dynamic visual analytics is the role of the user. In the essence, background knowledge and decision making capabilities of humans are key to maintain situational awareness by monitoring and exploring data streams. Therefore, we adapted the visual analytics process model of Keim et al. (2008) to match the interactive analysis of data streams.

Figure 5.1 shows the *dynamic visual analytics pipeline*. The nature of data streams differs from static data sets in so far that dynamic updates in the subsequent models and visualizations will be automatically triggered. Likewise, traditional preprocessing will not only be conducted once, but will also be applied to new incoming data on the fly. Visualization or modeling of raw data is an extremely rare and in many application areas unrealistic. Transformation of this raw data into meaningful aggregates or assignment of relevance scores are thus usually the first steps of the analysis. Note that we discard the details of stream data management in our model due to the fact that we focus on the interactive component of streaming applications. Therefore, we consider stream data management as a one-time setup with only rare changes through the user. However, such changes are implicitly modeled through the feedback loop.

Classical stream monitoring applications are built in a way that the incoming data is continuously matched with one or several models. The analyst is then notified about unexpected results and will assess how relevant these are. If exploited near real-time, the gained insight is the outcome that will translate into value for his company. As an example, a company could make money using this information through fast trading on the stock exchange. However, fine-tuning these real-time models is difficult because nobody knows what the future will bring in such a dynamic scenario. Therefore, in critical situations the system might either not pass the relevant notifications or it will trigger an abundance of irrelevant notifications to the user.

Dynamic visualizations can be used to give more control over the data stream into the hands of the analyst. These visualization can either be updated through processed results from the data stream itself, or from derived results from the dynamic models that display the essence of what is going on and highlight supposedly important parts of the data. It is then up to the user to interact with and explore the visualizations to verify his hypotheses and to come up with new ones. Note that our dynamic visual analytics pipeline does not contain an explicit arrow from visualizations to models. However, the two double arrows connecting to the user implicitly allow for adaption of the dynamic knowledge discovery models based on the findings in the visualizations.

Probably the largest part in most dynamic visual analytics application scenarios is devoted to the task of monitoring data streams, which includes both methods from knowledge discovery and visualization. Analysts therefore watch trends, wait for certain events to occur or make projections of future states. Exploration on the other side is a mostly visual process that in most cases will work on a static snapshot of the data. Normally, elements that capture the attention of the analyst might be investigated in detail to assess their relevance with respect to the application dependent analysis goals. Visual methods for exploration of dynamically changing scenarios are so far the exception, but might obtain a more important role for specialized purposes in the near future.

Due to the central role of the user in dynamic visual analytics, human factors play an important role. Individual factors, such as the analyst's long term memory capability, the degree of automaticity for the tasks that he routinely performs and his individual information processing capabilities will influence the analysis results. In particular, the degree of situational awareness, decisions and subsequent actions are strongly influenced by these individual factors. Besides having different preconceptions and expectations, the goals and objectives might vary between analysts. In addition, there might be a variance of the attention capabilities among the analysts, which can also influence the final results.

5.4 Server Log Monitoring Application Example

In this section we describe how to visually analyze a large-scale real-time event data stream, which is based on log entries of several servers. In particular, this application example represents a prototypical implementation of the proposed dynamic visual analytics pipeline as discussed above.

System administration and *log analysis* is a typical domain in which experts have to analyze and react to such data streams. Moreover many tasks discussed in the previous sections are relevant in this domain. Large computer networks with all their servers and devices, produce a vast amount of status, error and debug messages or alerts. Not only do the server's operating systems produce this continuous flow of information, but the software, the processes and services running on those machines also generate even more log data (e.g. access log data). The amount of this data is unbounded and is heavily affected by the utilization of the services. A busy web server will produce a higher number of error and status messages than an idle server system. This makes it obvious that the data stream is unpredictable with peaks and bursts, which need to be processed by the analysis system. Fully automated systems, which try to cluster and extract relevant or unusual events out of this data streams, are often not sufficient for further analysis, because the context is not preserved and the analyst is not able to gain an overview of these potentially critical events.

Closely monitoring the events in its context can help to minimize possible downtimes by reacting to and pro-actively solving issues as early as possible. Implementing a dynamic visual analytics approach helps to minimize expenses or prevent compensations. In particular, such an approach provides situational awareness and enhances both monitoring and exploration through visualization techniques.

In the following we explain how the dynamic visual analytics pipeline, sketched in Fig. 5.1, influenced the implementation of the prototype framework. The visual user interface, which is presented to the analyst, is shown in Fig. 5.2.

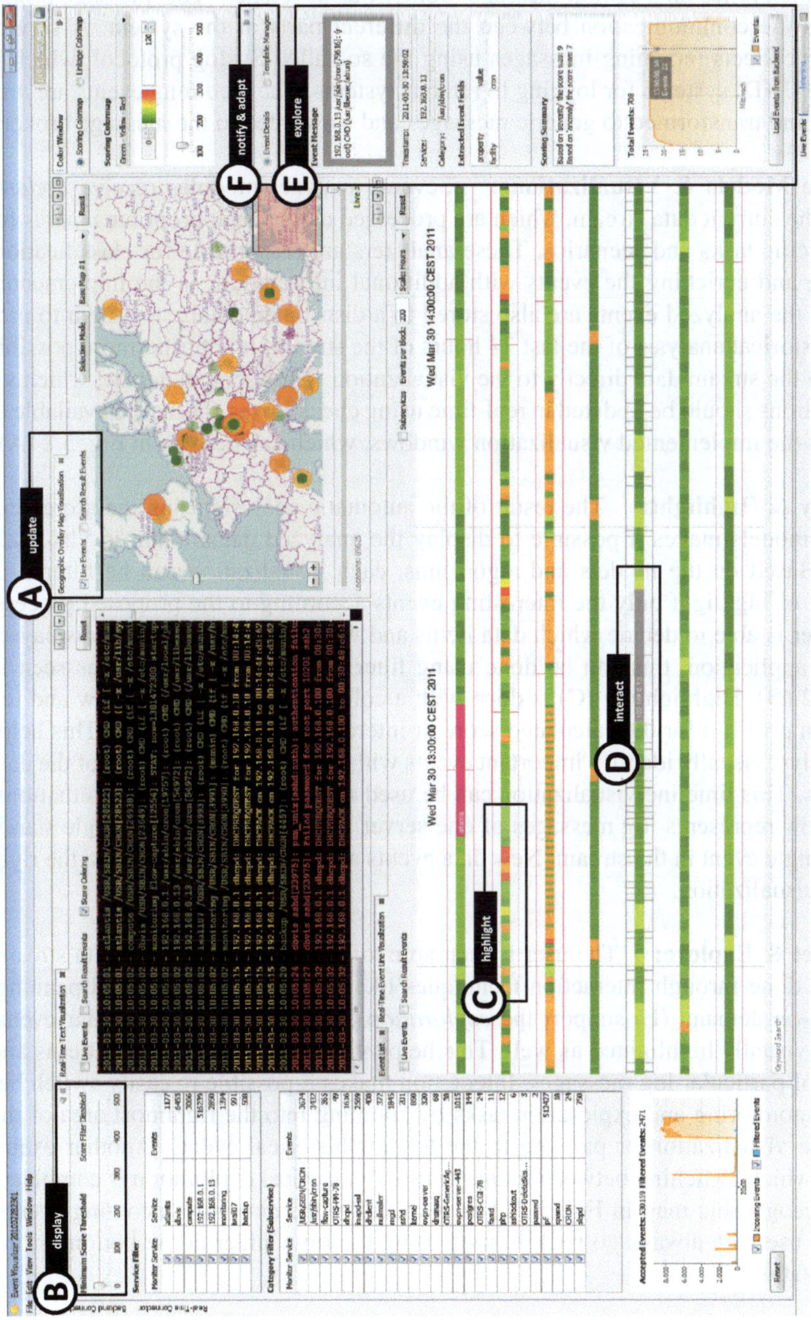

Fig. 5.2 A modular dynamic visual analytics software to visually monitor and explore event data streams in real-time

Processing: To support the needed functionality a robust distributed backend system, which relies on a central message broker, was developed. This message broker handles the communication between the different parts of the system. A service module collects incoming messages using the so-called Syslog protocol, which is used in UNIX systems for logging to remote systems. The incoming events are *processed* and transformed to generic messages and forwarded to the message broker.

Update Models & Visualizations: Several analyzer modules receive *updates* about the current data stream, which are processed using the appropriate *models* for the specific tasks and scenarios. These analyzers are responsible for classification, scoring and enriching the events with additional information. In the implemented system the analyzed events are also stored to a distributed database system to provide historical analysis of the last 24 hours of the stream. It is furthermore possible to push the stream data directly to the visualization. The user can decide, which visualizations should be updated in real-time using check boxes. These are available in each of the implemented visualization windows, which can be seen in Fig. 5.2 (A).

Display & Highlight: The result of the automatic analysis using the aforementioned models makes it possible to display the analyzed data stream in visualizations. Based on the models and algorithms, each visualization can be filtered to display or highlight only the interesting events according to the proposed process. The user is able to decide which data items and which stream should be displayed. In our application, this can be done using filter and threshold sliders, as seen in Fig. 5.2 (B). Highlighting (C) is done with a color scheme (green for low and red for high priority) for the calculated score or interestingness of the event. This helps the analyst visually identify important events within the temporal context of the data streams. This timeline visualization can be used in real-time monitoring situations. Each row represents log messages of one server and each colored rectangle stands for a single event in the stream. New data events are continuously added to the right of the visualization.

Interact & Explore: The user is then able to *interact* (D) with the data stream. This is done through interaction techniques like selecting, zooming and panning. Details-on-demand (E) support the *exploration* of selected events. Similar events can be visually highlighted as well. This helps visually identify event patterns and bursts of particular log messages. Interaction makes it possible to easily switch between monitoring and exploration tasks by zooming into the rightmost area of the timeline visualization or panning to the left for historical events. Another example, in which switching between monitoring and historical exploration is combined, is the geographic map in Fig. 5.2. The map shows the currently incoming events, but the user can always go back in time using the time slider at the bottom of the visualization.

Notify & Adapt: Switching to the template manager in Fig. 5.2 (F) allows the user to *adapt* the used models and rules according to his specifications. Applying score modifiers for particular event types or defining regular expressions, which are proposed by the system based on the currently selected events, influence the classification process. In a production version of the system, the usage of special alerting templates could be integrated to directly *notify* the user over different reliable communication channels about events, which need immediate response.

Feedback Loop: Adapting and influencing the models and processing algorithms through the user, is one implementation for a feedback loop. Such changes are directly forwarded to the message broker and automatically distributed to collecting services and available analyzers. This makes it possible to push background knowledge or insights formulated as rules, parameters and score modifiers to the algorithmic processes. As a result, gained insights are not lost, but pushed back to the system's backend to improve future classification or to support other analysts by presenting the corresponding annotations in the user interface.

5.5 Conclusions

This book chapter discussed dynamic visual analytics. In particular, we defined it as the process of integrating knowledge discovery and interactive visual interfaces. Its purpose is to facilitate interactive data stream analysis and provide situational awareness in real-time.

The core of this chapter was the discussion of requirements and the user's role in dynamic visual analytics. In contrast to automated streaming solutions, the presented dynamic visual analytics pipeline accentuates that the analyst's background knowledge and intuition is integrated in the stream analysis process through continuously updated visual interfaces and interaction. Furthermore, automated analysis methods could retrieve continuous user feedback through a notification and adaptation loop between the employed models and the user.

As an example of how the model can be applied in practice, we discussed a dynamic visual analytics application for real-time analysis of log entries from multiple servers. Besides depicting dynamic visual analytics in a demonstrative scenario, it made clear how visualization and user interaction could be used to foster insight and provide situational awareness in time-critical situations.

References

Aggarwal, C. C. (2007). *Data streams: models and algorithms*. New York: Springer.

Aigner, W., Miksch, S., Schumann, H., & Tominski, C. (2011). *Visualization of time-oriented data. Human-computer interaction series*. New York: Springer.

Best, D., Bohn, S., Love, D., Wynne, A., & Pike, W. (2010). Real-time visualization of network behaviors for situational awareness. *Proceedings of the seventh international symposium on visualization for cyber security* (pp. 79–90). New York: ACM.

Chaudhry, N., Shaw, K., & Abdelguerfi, M. (2005). *Stream data management* (Vol. 30). Berlin: Springer.
Endsley, M. (1995). Toward a theory of situation awareness in dynamic systems. *Human Factors: The Journal of the Human Factors and Ergonomics Society*, *37*(1), 32–64.
Foresti, S., Agutter, J., Livnat, Y., Moon, S., & Erbacher, R. (2006). Visual correlation of network alerts. *IEEE Computer Graphics and Applications*, *26*, 48–59.
Gama, J. (2010). *Knowledge discovery from data streams. Data mining and knowledge discovery series*. Boca Raton: Chapman & Hall, CRC Press.
Golab, L., & Özsu, M. (2010). *Data stream management*. Morgan & Claypool Publishers.
Hao, M. C., Keim, D. A., Dayal, U., Oelke, D., & Tremblay, C. (2008). Density displays for data stream monitoring. *Computer Graphics Forum*, *27*(3), 895–902.
Hochheiser, H., & Shneiderman, B. (2004). Dynamic query tools for time series data sets: timebox widgets for interactive exploration. *Information Visualization*, *3*(1), 1.
Kasetty, S., Stafford, C., Walker, G., Wang, X., & Keogh, E. (2008). Real-time classification of streaming sensor data. In *Tools with artificial intelligence, 2008. ICTAI'08. 20th IEEE international conference* (Vol. 1, pp. 149–156). IEEE.
Keim, D. A., Mansmann, F., Schneidewind, J., Thomas, J., & Ziegler, H. (2008). Visual analytics: scope and challenges. In S. Simoff, M. H. Boehlen & A. Mazeika (Eds.), *Lecture notes in computer science (LNCS). Visual data mining: theory, techniques and tools for visual analytics*. Berlin: Springer.
Keim, D. A., Kohlhammer, J., Ellis, G., & Mansmann, F. (Eds.) (2010). *Mastering the information age—solving problems with visual analytics*. Eurographics.
Krstajic, M., Bertini, E., Mansmann, F., & Keim, D. A. (2010). Visual analysis of news streams with article threads. In *StreamKDD '10: proceedings of the first international workshop on novel data stream pattern mining techniques* (pp. 39–46). New York: ACM.
Lin, J., Keogh, E., Lonardi, S., & Chiu, B. (2003). A symbolic representation of time series, with implications for streaming algorithms. In *Proceedings of the 8th ACM SIGMOD workshop on research issues in data mining and knowledge discovery* (p. 11). New York: ACM.
Lin, J., Keogh, E., Lonardi, S., Lankford, J., & Nystrom, D. (2004). VizTree: a tool for visually mining and monitoring massive time series databases. In *Proceedings of the thirtieth international conference on very large data bases* (Vol. 30, pp. 1269–1272). VLDB Endowment.
McLachlan, P., Munzner, T., Koutsofios, E., & North, S. (2008). Liverac: interactive visual exploration of system management time-series data. In *Proceedings of the twenty-sixth annual SIGCHI conference on human factors in computing systems* (pp. 1483–1492). New York: ACM.
Thomas, J., & Cook, K. (2005). *Illuminating the path: the research and development agenda for visual analytics*. Los Alamitos: IEEE Computer Society.
Van Wijk, J., & Van Selow, E. (1999). Cluster and calendar based visualization of time series data. In *Infovis*. Los Alamitos: IEEE Computer Society.

Chapter 6
A Review of Uncertainty in Data Visualization

Ken Brodlie, Rodolfo Allendes Osorio, and Adriano Lopes

Abstract Most visualization techniques have been designed on the assumption that the data to be represented are free from uncertainty. Yet this is rarely the case. Recently the visualization community has risen to the challenge of incorporating an indication of uncertainty into visual representations, and in this article we review their work. We place the work in the context of a reference model for data visualization, that sees data pass through a pipeline of processes. This allows us to distinguish the *visualization of uncertainty*—which considers how we depict uncertainty specified with the data—and the *uncertainty of visualization*—which considers how much inaccuracy occurs as we process data through the pipeline. It has taken some time for uncertain visualization methods to be developed, and we explore why uncertainty visualization is hard—one explanation is that we typically need to find another display dimension and we may have used these up already! To organize the material we return to a typology developed by one of us in the early days of visualization, and make use of this to present a catalog of visualization techniques describing the research that has been done to extend each method to handle uncertainty. Finally we note the responsibility on us all to incorporate any known uncertainty into a visualization, so that integrity of the discipline is maintained.

6.1 Introduction

Understanding uncertainty is one of the great scientific challenges of our time. It impacts on many crucial issues facing the world today—from climate change

K. Brodlie (✉)
University of Leeds, Leeds LS2 9JT, UK
e-mail: k.w.brodlie@leeds.ac.uk

R. Allendes Osorio
Depto. de Ciencias de la Computación, Fac. de Ingeneria, Universidad de Talca, Talca, Chile
e-mail: rallendes@utalca.cl

A. Lopes
CITI / Depto. Informática, FCT, Universidade Nova de Lisboa, Lisbon, Portugal
e-mail: alopes@fct.unl.pt

J. Dill et al. (eds.), *Expanding the Frontiers of Visual Analytics and Visualization*,
DOI 10.1007/978-1-4471-2804-5_6,

prediction, to economic modeling, to interpretation of medical data. Visualization is now well accepted as a powerful means to allow scientists to explore large datasets, and to present their results to a wider audience. Yet most visualization techniques make the assumption that the data they are displaying are *exact*. We may encounter error bars on graphs, but we rarely see the equivalent on contour maps or isosurfaces. Indeed the very crispness of an isosurface gives an impression of confidence that is frankly often an illusion. This is a major issue when visualizations are used in decision making—such as planning evacuations based on a visualization of the predicted hurricane path. Indeed as computation power and capability continue to increase we see a rise in *ensemble computing*, where many simulations of a phenomenon are carried out for different initial conditions, or different settings of unknown parameters—leading not to a unique data value, but to a set of values—so-called multivalue data. There is a growing awareness of the uncertainty problem within the visualization community, and many traditional techniques are being extended to represent not only the data, but also the uncertainty information associated with the data. We call this *visualization of uncertainty*. In addition it is important to realize that, even if there is certainty about the data, errors can occur in the process of turning the data into a picture. We call this *uncertainty of visualization*. In this paper we aim to review the current state of the art in uncertainty in scientific visualization, looking at both of these aspects.

There are a growing number of application areas where uncertainty visualization is being put to good effect. Here is a brief list, together with relevant citations: agriculture (Juang et al. 2004); astrophysics (Li et al. 2007); biology (Cumming et al. 2007); climate studies (Pöthkow et al. 2011; Potter et al. 2009); fluid flow (Botchen et al. 2005; Hlawatsch et al. 2011; Otto et al. 2010; Wittenbrink et al. 1996; Zuk et al. 2008); geography (Aerts et al. 2003; Davis and Keller 1997; Ehlschlaeger et al. 1997; Goodchild et al. 1994; Hengl 2003; Love et al. 2005; MacEachren 1992; MacEachren et al. 2005); geophysics (Zehner et al. 2010); medicine (Kniss et al. 2005; Lundstrom et al. 2007; Prabni et al. 2010); meteorology (Boller et al. 2010; Luo et al. 2003; Sanyal et al. 2010); oceanography (Allendes Osorio and Brodlie 2008; Bingham and Haines 2006; Djurcilov et al. 2002); underground assets (Boukhelifa and Duke 2007); visual analytics (Correa et al. 2009).

Historically the geovisualization community were perhaps the first to realize the importance of uncertainty. This community have long been concerned with issues of data quality so that the limitations of the data are understood when looking at maps. Buttenfield and Beard (1994) suggested that:

> Computer generated maps, a standard output of GIS, generally imply an accuracy not warranted by the data.

The paper by Goodchild et al. (1994) presents a view of the 1994 state of art in visualizing data validity, while MacEachren et al. (2005) provides a view of the field in 2005. Interest within the scientific visualization community developed rather later: the paper by Pang et al. (1997) provides possibly the first significant review of the field. Important subsequent reviews include the papers by Griethe and Schumann (2006) and by Zuk and Carpendale (2006) (who look at the area from the perspective

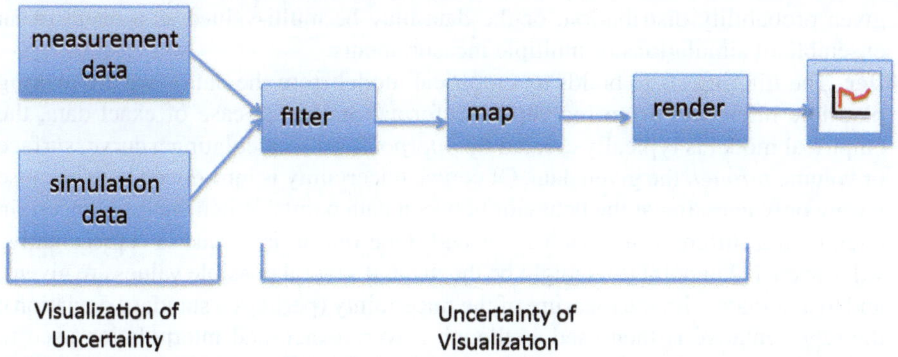

Fig. 6.1 Haber and McNabb model: visualization of uncertainty and uncertainty of visualization

of perceptual theory and in particular the work of Bertin, Tufte and Ware), while important awareness-raising papers are Johnson and Sanderson (2003) and Johnson (2004) who includes the representation of error and uncertainty as one of his top ten research problems. Recent theses include those of Allendes Osorio (2010) and Zuk (2008).

The structure of our review is as follows. We begin in Sect. 6.2 with a reference model for uncertainty visualization that can help us understand where uncertainty occurs in visualization. We then reflect in Sect. 6.3 on why visualization of uncertainty, and uncertainty of visualization, are hard problems. We then organize the main body of the review under a classification similar to that introduced by Brodlie et al. (1992) and used and extended by Pang et al. (1997) in their review. Section 6.4 introduces the notation and is followed by two sections: Sect. 6.5 focuses on visualization of uncertain data, where most of the research has been done; and Sect. 6.6 looks at the uncertainty of visualization.

6.2 Uncertainty Reference Model

We can understand the different sources of uncertainty by re-visiting the visualization reference model presented by Haber and McNabb (1990). In Fig. 6.1, we show the traditional model of data passing through a pipeline. The first step is to filter, or reconstruct through interpolation or approximation, creating a model of the entity underlying the data. This model is then passed to a mapping stage, where a visualization algorithm produces geometry. Finally this geometry is rendered as an image. Uncertainty occurs at all stages—visualization of uncertainty focuses on the data stage, while the uncertainty of visualization begins at the filter stage and passes through to the render stage.

data The source of the data may be measurement or simulation. In either case, the data may have associated uncertainty information—this may be in the form of a known range of error; or the data may be described as a random variate with a given probability distribution; or the data may be multi-valued as a result of an ensemble of simulations or multiple measurements.

filter The filtering stage builds an empirical model from the data—we are making plausible inferences from incomplete information. In the case of exact data, the empirical model is typically created by *interpolation*—calculating a curve, surface or volume *through* the given data. Of course uncertainty is introduced here because we are only guessing at the behavior between data points. When we have uncertain data, then a different approach is needed. One option is to take a representative value at each datapoint (this might be the mean if several possible values are given), and to associate with it a measure of the uncertainty (perhaps a standard deviation); the representative is then used as though it were exact, and interpolation used to create an empirical model, but with the associated uncertainty model attached to it. A variation of this is to estimate the distribution at a datapoint as a Probability Density Function (PDF), and build an empirical model as an interpolation of these PDFs. A different option, if we have prior knowledge of the form of the model, is to fit a parameterized form of the model to the data forming in some sense a best *approximation*—for example, if the model is linear, then linear regression would be appropriate; more generally, spline data-fitting using least-squares will enable a useful approximation to be constructed. The $E02$ chapter of the NAG Library is a good source of software for data fitting (www.nag.co.uk). This second option of data fitting has not been the focus of the recent uncertainty visualization research, and so we shall not discuss it further here—but it remains a very important practical approach.

map The map process, or visualization algorithm, where a geometric model is created, may involve computation that is subject to error—for example the approximation of curved surfaces by polygons, or the creation of streamlines by numerical solution of ordinary differential equations.

render The render process which rasterizes the geometry involves a discretization step that may hide information—for example if the resolution of the output image is of a lower order of magnitude than the resolution of the data. Here focus and context ideas might usefully be employed to overcome this difficulty.

Other authors have similarly used the Haber and McNabb model as a reference for uncertainty, including Pang et al. (1997), Griethe and Schumann (2006), Lopes and Brodlie (1999), Correa et al. (2009).

We tend to see the pipeline as a left-to-right output process, with uncertainty accumulating as data passes through. In interactive work, we also traverse the model from right-to-left, and uncertainty needs to be borne in mind as we pass back along the pipeline.

6.3 Why Is Uncertainty so Hard?

Most visualization techniques have been developed, and used, under an assumption that the given data are exact—and any uncertainty information is not included in the picture. While this situation is changing, it has taken a long time. Why is uncertainty a hard topic in visualization? Here are some possible explanations:

Uncertainty is complex Uncertainty, by its very nature, is a difficult subject. Indeed as Davis and Keller (1997) note, even the terminology is often unhelpful:

> The self-referential problem of uncertainty about uncertainty terminology has been a notable stumbling block in this avenue of inquiry.

A useful step forward here is the typology for uncertainty in geospatially referenced information presented by Thomson et al. (2005) (building on earlier work in standardization bodies—see USGS 1977). They distinguish nine categories in their typology: accuracy/error (these are often confusing, and used interchangeably to refer to difference between observed and true or modeled values, but in this typology are sensibly combined as a single category), precision (exactness of measurement), and a number of more qualitative categories—completeness, consistency, currency/timing, credibility, subjectiveness and interrelatedness. A final category, lineage, covers the provenance information associated with a dataset. Although this typology is specific to geovisualization, it would be a useful exercise to extend it to the wider area of scientific data visualization—looking perhaps at further issues introduced by the multiple simulations of ensemble computing.

Uncertainty information is presented in different ways In scientific visualization, we are normally presented with a dataset (assuming scalar data for simplicity) $f_i(x_1, \ldots, x_n)$, $i = 1, 2, \ldots, m$, being unique values at a given set of m points in n-dimensional space. The additional uncertainty information may be supplied in different ways:

as a PDF Rather than a unique value f, statistical analysis may have resulted in data at each point being provided as a random variate, F say, with Probability Density Function (PDF), $g(F)$, where

$$Pr(a \leq F \leq b) = \int_a^b g(f)df$$

as multivalue data If the data results from several simulations as in ensemble computing, or from several physical measurements of the same entity, then we will have many values at each datapoint. That is, we will have p values at each point:

$$f_i^j(x_1, \ldots, x_n), \quad j = 1, 2, \ldots, p$$

This data can then be passed for visualization as a multivalued dataset, or a PDF can be estimated from the data (in which case we generate a PDF, and we have the case above).

as bounded data Sometimes the data may be given simply as falling within finite bounds. Olston and Mackinlay (2002) refer to this as bounded uncertainty to contrast with statistical uncertainty, where we do not know bounds but we know the probability distribution, typically normal with mean and standard deviation (i.e. the PDF case above).

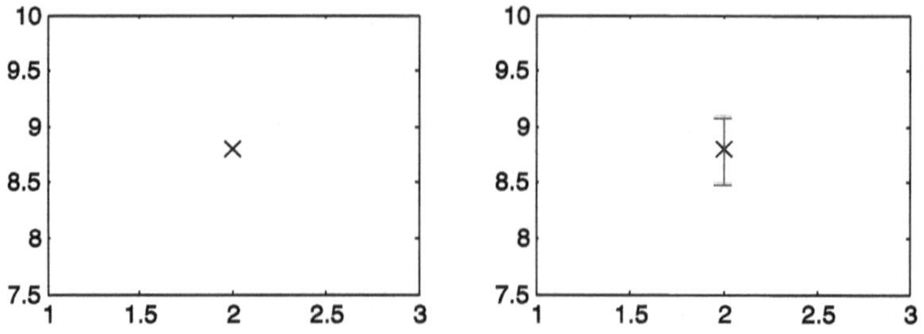

Fig. 6.2 Error bars add a dimension: the point becomes a line

Uncertainty propagates When we calculate with uncertain data, we propagate the uncertainty. In the pipeline of Fig. 6.1, the original data goes through a number of transformations before an image is created. We need to understand how to propagate uncertainty in the data, through to uncertainty in the image. Careful mathematics and statistics are required, and a good primer is the NPL report by Cox and Harris (2004). The propagation problem can be stated formally as follows: given a model $Y = g(X)$ where $X = (X_1, \ldots, X_n)^T$, and the Probability Density Functions $f_{X_i}(x_i)$ for the input quantities X_i, with $i = 1, \ldots, n$, determine the PDF $f_Y(y)$ for the output quantity Y. Occasionally this can be solved analytically, but often a Monte Carlo approach is required.

In the context of visual analytics, Correa et al. (2009) describe uncertainty propagation for two common data analysis operations: Principal Components Analysis and clustering using k-means.

Uncertainty adds a dimension to the visualization The most elementary example will illustrate this. A single data point (2, 8.8) is plotted in Fig. 6.2—the marker is zero-dimensional, i.e. a point. But if there is uncertainty in the y-value, say 8.8 ± 0.3, then adding an error bar increases the dimension by one, as the marker becomes a line. (The *dimension of the data* remains the same—i.e. zero—but we have required an extra dimension *in the visualization* to display the additional uncertainty variable.) Similarly we shall see that isolines with uncertainty become areas, and isosurfaces become volumes. For lower dimensions this poses little problem—but on a two-dimensional display surface, we have enough problems visualizing exact 3D or higher dimensional data without introducing another dimension for uncertainty.

Even if we do not increase the spatial dimension, we still need to find a 'dimension' from somewhere. Various ideas have been tried with varying degrees of success:

juxtaposition A common approach is to provide a visualization of the uncertainty in a separate picture, alongside a standard representation (perhaps showing a standard deviation plot alongside a mean value plot). See for example Aerts et al. (2003).

animation A number of authors have used animation, making use of time as an extra dimension. A simple example is to replace the above juxtaposition approach with a toggle facility, where the user can swap between the normal view and a view of the associated uncertainty. Experiments by Aerts et al. (2003) showed that in fact juxtaposition was better than toggling. Another use of animation is to display a sequence of different possible realizations of a model. For example, looking at uncertainty in Digital Elevation Models (DEMs), Ehlschlaeger et al. (1997) create a sequence of different realizations of a given DEM, and then generate in-between frames in order to produce a smooth animation showing the range of possibilities. Animation must be used carefully—Brown (2004) gives a good overview of the pitfalls, and suggests a useful 'vibration' technique, again illustrated on DEMs. In medical visualization, animation has been used by Lundstrom et al. (2007).

overlay With some visualizations, it is possible to overlay a visualization of uncertainty on top of the normal visualization. For example, Bingham and Haines (2006) overlay a contour map of an error field on top of a heatmap of the mean value of a multivalue dataset.

sound There were a number of early attempts to use sound to encode uncertainty—see Lodha et al. (1996a) and Fisher (1994). A difficulty is that sound is essentially a local feature (you get feedback on uncertainty at a point), whereas images give a global view—perhaps this explains why there seems to have been little recent work on using sound.

colour A number of authors have experimented with use of the hue, saturation, value components of color to encode uncertainty. See for example MacEachren (1992), and Hengl (2003) who adds white to indicate degree of uncertainty.

Uncertainty tends to dominate certainty In most natural visual representations of uncertainty, the greatest emphasis is placed on data of greatest uncertainty. Consider error bars: long bars correspond to high uncertainty. However as Hlawatsch et al. (2011) note in the context of fluid flow, it is sometimes areas of *certainty* that are more important.

Uncertainty adds another discipline Some of the best visualizations have been created by multidisciplinary teams, bringing together domain scientists, numerical analysts, visualization scientists and artists. See for example the storm cloud visualizations from NCSA (access.ncsa.illinois.edu/Stories/supertwister/index.htm). There is a further discipline to be added now: statistics is the branch of mathematics that deals with uncertainty, and we need increasing collaborations with statisticians in order to improve the rigor of uncertainty visualization.

The above reasons help to explain why visualization of uncertainty is hard. But the area of uncertainty of visualization is difficult too, perhaps for the following reason:

Linearity adds uncertainty Computer graphics hardware—from early graph plotters to current graphics cards—encourages the approximation of curves and surfaces by straight lines and triangles, inevitably introducing error.

6.4 Notation

In this section we re-visit an early attempt to classify scientific visualization algorithms by Brodlie et al. (1992). This work saw data as discrete items being sampled from some underlying entity, and visualization as the process of viewing a continuous empirical model built from the data. The classification was based on the dimensions of the independent variable (often spatial or temporal), and the type of dependent variable—point, scalar, vector or tensor. The classification has since been extended by a number of authors, notably Tory and Moeller (2004) who have extended the work to information visualization, and Pang et al. (1997) who used it for uncertainty visualization classification.

An E notation was introduced in the 1992 paper, with a subscript indicating the number of independent variables and a superscript indicating the type of dependent variable. Thus:

$$E_1^S$$

represented a model of a scalar function of one variable, such as temperature measured over time. In the case of multifield data, where there are several variables at a datapoint, the notation extends to, for example:

$$E_1^{kS}$$

for k variables, such as temperature, pressure, ... In the original work, the character E had no real meaning (other than underlying Entity) and was redundant. With serendipity, we now interpret it as 'Exact', to act as a notation for *certain* data. For *uncertain* data, we simply replace E by U.

Table 6.1 organizes the main visualization algorithms according to this classification. We subdivide the scalar class into three distinct approaches: *embed*, where we place the visualization into a higher dimensional display space (e.g. a surface view where we view a 2D data set in a 3D space); *dense*, where we view the data at every point in the domain; and *sparse*, where we extract an important feature such as a contour line. For vector visualization, we follow the subdivision suggested by Post et al. (2003): *direct*, *dense*, *geometric* and *feature-based*. The table is not complete—there are many more visualization techniques to include—but it acts as a roadmap for the techniques that have been enhanced to include uncertainty and are discussed in this article.

6.5 Visualization of Uncertainty

6.5.1 Introduction

In this section we review the efforts that have been made to extend existing 'exact' visualization techniques to cater for uncertainty information. To organize this large body of research, we use the U notation of the previous section.

Table 6.1 Classification of techniques—key: SP = Scatter Plot; PC = Parallel Coordinates; CSV = Colored Surface View

Dim	Point E/U^P	Scalar E/U^S			Multifield kE/U^S	Vector E/U^V			
		embed	dense	sparse		direct	dense	geometric	feature
E/U_0		Point			SP & PC				
E/U_1	Markers	Graph	Col Line						
E/U_2		Surface view	Heatmap	Contour	CSV	Glyphs	LIC	Particles	Topology
E/U_3			Vol Render	Isosurface			IBFV	Streamlines	

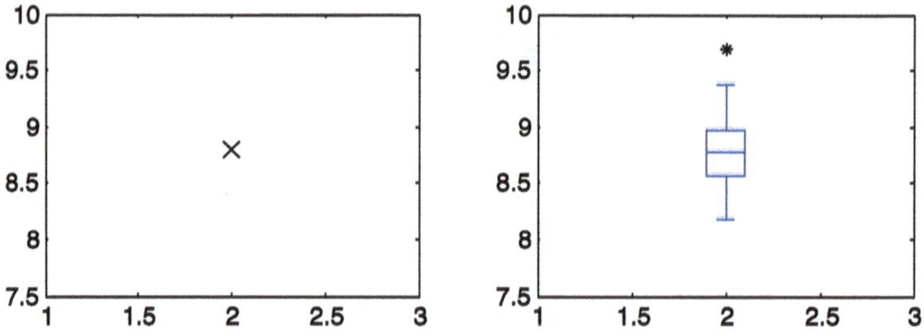

Fig. 6.3 Tukey box plot—*on left*, a single point represents the exact observation; *on right*, the uncertainty of multiple observations is summarized as rectangle, line and outlier point, an increase of display dimension

6.5.2 Point Data U^P

Occasionally the underlying entity is simply a collection of points in nD space, with no dependent variable associated with the points. An example in 3D would be the positions of stars in the universe, which are typically described in terms of a distance component (along line of sight from earth) and equatorial coordinates (RA, Dec) to describe the direction. Li et al. (2007) consider this very problem: uncertainty in distance is much greater than in RA/Dec, and so error bars on the line of sight are possible, or an ellipsoid centered on the star if the RA/Dec component is important.

6.5.3 Scalar Data U^S

6.5.3.1 Zero Dimensional Data U_0^S

This is the very simple case: with exact data, we are just plotting one point! In the uncertain case, we are typically presented with many observations of a single scalar variable. A standard uncertainty visualization is the boxplot proposed by Tukey (1977), showing the five summary statistics of upper and lower bounds, upper and lower quartiles and median. See Fig. 6.3 which takes the data point of Fig. 6.2 and assumes now that a large number of measurements have been made—notice the dimensionality increase in the visualization as uncertainty is added—rectangle, lines and outlier point rather than just a point (arguably the rectangle is only 1D as its width is not significant). There have since been many extensions and modifications (see Potter et al. 2010 for a review, and suggestion of a summary plot which incorporates further descriptive statistics such as skew and kurtosis). Cumming et al. (2007) provide important guidelines for the use and interpretation of error bars.

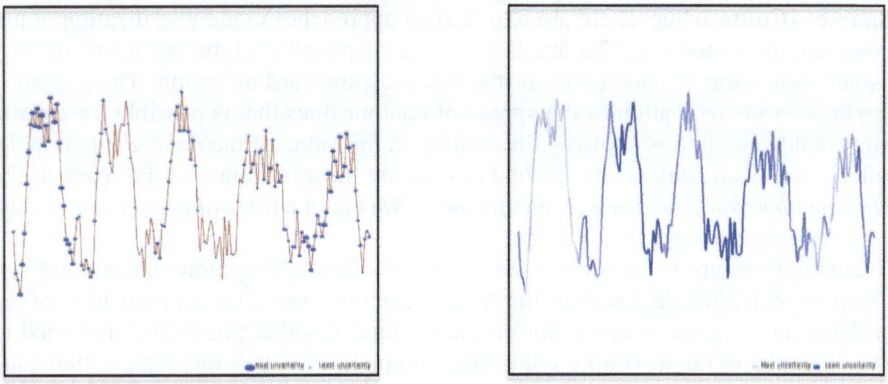

(a) (b)

Fig. 6.4 Examples from Sanyal et al. (2009) user study: (**a**) glyph size; (**b**) graph color. Images kindly created for this article by J. Sanyal and R.J. Moorhead

6.5.3.2 One Dimensional Data U_1^S

Embed—Graph This is the ubiquitous one-dimensional graph—probably the most common of all visualizations. There are a variety of ways that an indication of uncertainty can be added: error bars can be added to the data point markers, or the markers themselves can encode the uncertainty through size or color of the glyph. A continuous model of uncertainty can be provided by color coding the graph itself, using an uncertainty color map. Sanyal et al. (2009) compare different approaches: their user study found different methods were best depending on whether the task was to locate least uncertainty (glyph size best) or highest uncertainty (color best). Figure 6.4 shows two examples from their study: showing uncertainty by glyph size and by graph color, in the latter case using different levels of saturation of blue following the early suggestion of MacEachren (1992).

6.5.3.3 Two Dimensional Data U_2^S

Embed—Surface Views When surface views are used, the third space dimension is used for the visualization itself, and so another 'dimension' is needed for uncertainty. The time dimension is commonly used and animated effects are described by Ehlschlaeger et al. (1997) and Brown (2004).

Sanyal et al. (2009) do a similar study as for 1D graphs mentioned above. They examine adding glyphs at the data points on the surface, varying size and color; adding error bars to the surface; and color mapping the surface with an uncertainty measure. Here surface color worked well, except for counting of uncertainty features—where possibly perception of the shape of the mean surface was affected by the uncertainty color mapping.

Sparse—Contouring There are two distinct approaches to the visualization of uncertainty in contouring. The first is to draw a crisp isoline of the mean, and overlay some indication of uncertainty of the data, say standard deviation. The second is to draw some indication of the spread of contour lines that is possible for a given threshold. The first is showing uncertainty in the value of the *dependent* variable, along the mean contour; the second is showing the uncertainty in the space of the *independent* variable, for a given threshold. We call the first *value uncertainty*, and the second *positional uncertainty*.

Value uncertainty is explored in Sanyal et al. (2010). They draw uncertainty ribbons in which the thickness of the 'mean' contour lines gives an indication of the relative uncertainty at that point on the contour. Another possibility (not tried to our knowledge) is to simply color the contour lines with a measure of the value uncertainty.

Positional uncertainty has been studied by a number of researchers. The standard approach of meteorologists for example is to draw a spaghetti plot, in which a contour line is drawn for each model in an ensemble. Sanyal et al. (2010) and Potter et al. (2009) describe the use of spaghetti plots—the former comparing spaghetti plots with uncertainty ribbons, and discussing the merits of value and positional uncertainty visualization. Juang et al. (2004) use juxtaposition to look at contour plots from different realizations of a model.

Allendes Osorio and Brodlie (2008) take an image-based approach to positional uncertainty, identifying pixels where the probability of a value close to the contour threshold is sufficiently high. This gives a contour band—an area rather than a line, showing again the dimension increase that comes with uncertainty visualization. In contrast to the uncertainty ribbons in Sanyal et al. (2010), the width of the band indicates positional rather than value uncertainty. In a further variation, by mapping the probability to intensity, a fuzzy contour effect is produced, with high intensity indicating high probability of a contour passing through the pixel.

Pöthkow and Hege (2010) describe a similar method: from a set of gridded data, defined as random variates with associated PDF, they interpolate to gain a PDF defined continuously over the domain; at any point, they calculate the probability of taking two samples from the distribution, and having one sample greater than the contour threshold, and the other less. This too gives a fuzzy contour effect. The method depends on the assumption that the data at grid points is independent. This is rarely the case: in an ensemble situation, if the value from one model at a data point is greater than the ensemble mean, then it is likely that the model will similarly be above the mean at adjacent datapoints. Therefore in a subsequent paper Pöthkow et al. (2011) take the spatial correlation of the data into account; the effect is to sharpen the areas of uncertainty.

There is one further method which does not fall neatly into either category. Love et al. (2005) consider the situation where it makes sense to regard not just the data as a random variate, but also the threshold. They look for the greatest similarity between the distributions of data and the distribution of threshold. These give edge intersections which are linked as in normal contouring.

In order to illustrate some of these ideas, we make use of an oceanography case study, described by Bingham and Haines (2006). The study of Ocean Dynamic

Fig. 6.5 Contour band: This shows the extent of the 95 % confidence interval for the zero contour, with the zero contour for the average data at each point shown for comparison

Topography (ODT), the height of the sea surface above its rest state (the geoid), is of importance to oceanographers, as it allows them to understand the circulation patterns of oceans and the associate surface currents, one of the main players in the regulation of the Earth's climate. Calculation of the ODT is difficult and so scientists focus on computation of the associated Mean Dynamic Topography (MDT). Several models for calculation of the MDT exist; Bingham and Haines collected data from eight such models, allowing them to calculate an average value, together with a formal estimate of the error. In their paper they use an overlay approach, in which the contours of the average MDT are overlaid on a heatmap of an error field. We shall use a simple method for positional uncertainty, and apply it to this problem, working directly with the ensemble data rather than estimating PDFs. Since we can interpolate each model, we assume we have values for each model everywhere in the domain. At any point, we will wish to test the null hypothesis that the data comes from a distribution whose mean value equals the contour threshold, say zero: i.e.

$$H_0 : m = 0$$

The alternative hypothesis is non-directional:

$$H_1 : m \neq 0$$

A t-test is applied to test the hypothesis and leads to two uncertain contour representations: a contour band, similar to that of Allendes Osorio and Brodlie (2008), where the 95 % confidence interval is displayed, that is, all points where the null hypothesis would not normally be rejected (see Fig. 6.5); and a fuzzy contour, where the value of the t-statistic is mapped to a color scale between sea-blue and black, giving an inky effect (see Fig. 6.6). For comparison, Fig. 6.7 shows a spaghetti plot of all eight models. (Note that we only do the calculation at points where we have data from all eight models—hence the 'unusual' geography in places!)

Finally note that it would be possible to combine both positional and value uncertainty in a single representation—for example by modifying the contour band

Fig. 6.6 Fuzzy contour: This shows the value of the t-statistic from the hypothesis test with a color mapping from sea-blue to black based on the size of the t-statistic

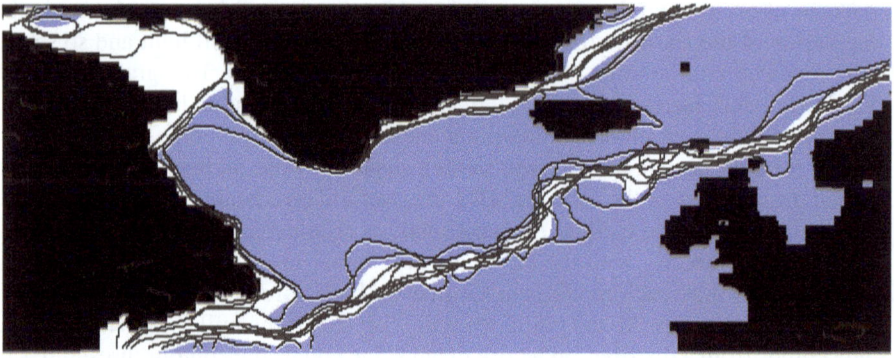

Fig. 6.7 Spaghetti plot: zero contours from each of the eight individual models, superimposed on 95 % confidence band

shown in white in Fig. 6.5 so that a measure of the value error (say, standard deviation) was color mapped on to the band.

Dense—Heatmap A heatmap uses color mapping (sometimes called pseudocoloring) to visualize a scalar function over a 2D region. Various approaches have been suggested for uncertainty: a straightforward idea is to map uncertain data to a derived scalar such as mean or standard deviation (see for example Love et al. 2005); Hengl (2003) suggests addition of whiteness in areas of uncertainty; Cedilnik and Rheingans (2000) superimpose a grid where the grid lines are subtly modified to indicate uncertainty (for example, through mapping uncertainty to an intensity/width combination); Coninx et al. (2011) add Perlin noise effects.

6.5.3.4 Three Dimensional Data U_3^S

The problem gets harder! The three space dimensions are already in use for the normal, 'certain', visualization, either by isosurfacing or volume rendering, and so the uncertainty problem becomes challenging. Embedding is no longer an option.

Sparse—Isosurface The approaches here mirror those for contouring. Again there is a choice between visualization of value uncertainty (mean isosurface with indication of uncertainty in data), or positional uncertainty (indication of the spread of isosurfaces possible for the defined threshold).

For value uncertainty, the 'mean' isosurface can be enhanced with an indication of uncertainty, either through color (Rhodes et al. 2003) or glyphs (Newman and Lee 2004). Grigoryan and Rheingans (2004) displace surface points in the direction of the surface normal, by a distance proportional to the uncertainty.

Positional uncertainty of isosurfaces has been addressed by the same researchers who studied positional uncertainty in contouring, as the extensions are straightforward: see the thesis of Allendes Osorio (2010), and the papers by Pöthkow and Hege (2010) and Pöthkow et al. (2011), the second incorporating spatial correlation. The fuzzy contours from the 2D case become fuzzy regions in 3D. Perception gets harder as the dimensionality increases, and the addition of a crisp, opaque isosurface of the mean of the data is necessary. Figure 6.8 shows uncertain isosurfaces using the methods of Pöthkow and Hege (2010) and Pöthkow et al. (2011): in (a) the isosurface is drawn without taking spatial correlation into account, while in (b) the use of spatial correlation gives a more localized spatial distribution of the uncertain isosurface.

Zehner et al. (2010) look at both value and positional approaches: in their value method, they extend Hengl (2003) idea of saturation mapping to indicate standard deviation; in their positional method, they construct three isosurfaces (mean, upper and lower bounds of a confidence interval), drawing the mean isosurface plus rays emanating from this to the upper and lower surfaces. Finally Love et al. (2005) extend their contour method that matches a target distribution for the threshold with the distribution of the data.

Dense—Volume Render This is a rather difficult technique to extend, since it already uses all three space dimensions plus color and opacity. Early work by Djurcilov et al. (2002) explored two approaches: first, the transfer function used in volume rendering was modified to map data to color and uncertainty to opacity; second, a post-processing step was added to incorporate special effects (holes, noise, texture) in areas of uncertainty.

Not surprisingly, the time dimension has also been exploited, for example by Lundstrom et al. (2007). Their application is to medical visualization where they note different transfer functions (used because the classifications are uncertain) may give different indications of how wide a vessel might be. Clinicians will generally try different preset transfer functions in order to make a decision on the stenosis. Lundstrom et al work from a probabilistic classification model, where explicit material probabilities are assigned to each CT value. An animation is then produced where areas of confident tissue classification appear static, while uncertain parts

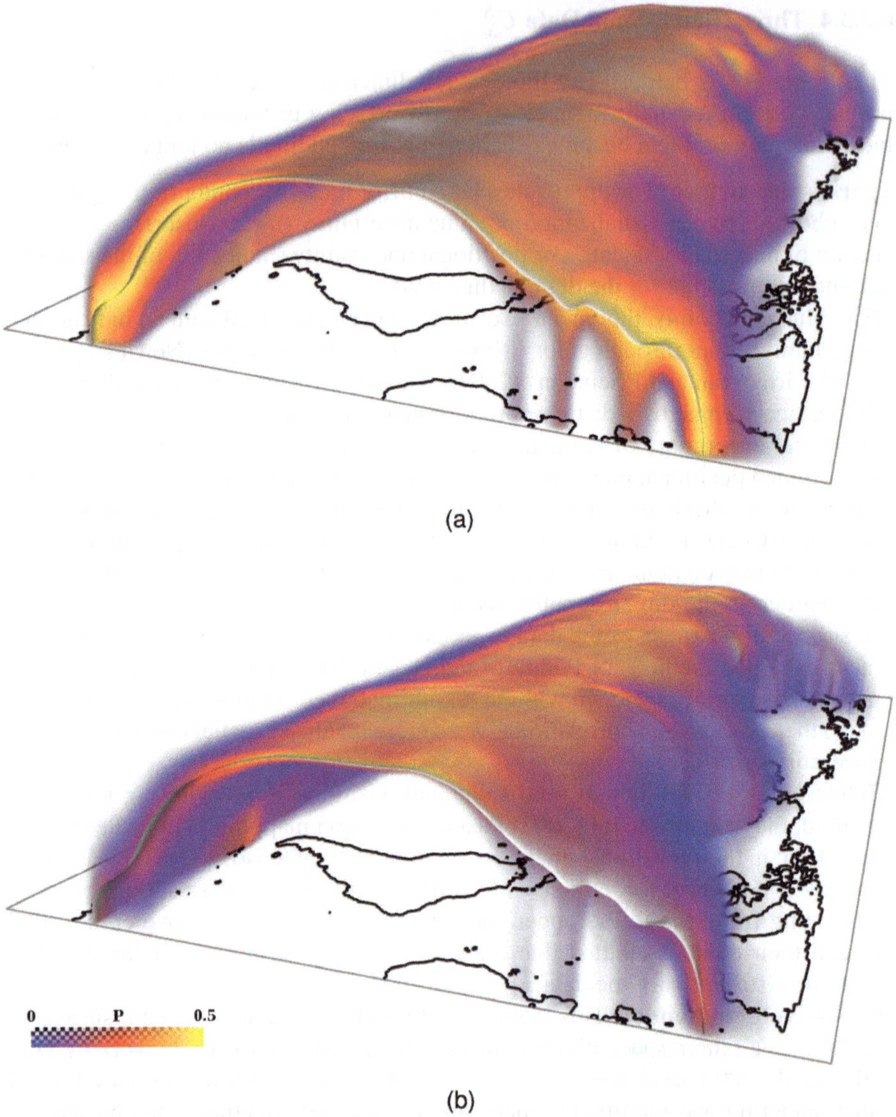

Fig. 6.8 Uncertain isosurfaces: these are drawn using the methods of Pöthkow and Hege (2010) and Pöthkow et al. (2011): in (**a**) the isosurface is drawn without taking spatial correlation into account, while in (**b**) the use of spatial correlation gives a more localized spatial distribution of the uncertain isosurface. We are grateful to the authors for permission to use this picture which first appeared in Pöthkow et al. (2011)

change with time. In a user trial, radiologists came close to performing as well with the single animation, as with lengthy experimentation with different transfer functions.

Segmentation uncertainty is also considered in Kniss et al. (2005) and Prabni et al. (2010).

6.5.4 Multifield Scalar Data kU^S

6.5.4.1 Zero Dimensional Data U_0^{kS}

This is the case of multivariate data where we have measurements of a set of variables, but no specific dependency on space, time or anything else. It is often visualized as a scatter plot, but is essentially a different datatype to U^P. Parallel coordinates is another popular technique. Uncertainty has been incorporated into scatter plots and parallel coordinates by Xie et al. (2006) who compare different visual encodings such as hue, and by Feng et al. (2010), who use density plots based on representing the data as PDFs.

6.5.4.2 Higher Dimensional Data $U_{>0}^{kS}$

There is increasing interest in the visualization of multifield data defined over 2D and 3D domains, sometimes with time as an additional dimension—see for example, Jänicke et al. (2007). It is not easy to find visualizations that represent sensibly in a single picture a number of separate variables.The addition of uncertainty makes the problem even harder. Consider for example one of the simplest cases of multifield visualization, where we use a surface view to depict a 2D dataset, with height representing one variable and color representing another. The use of color for the second variable prohibits us using color for uncertainty information about the first variable, as mentioned earlier in Sect. 6.5.3.3. This is an interesting challenge. Advances in multifield visualization may help uncertainty visualization (because an uncertainty measure such as standard deviation can be treated as an extra variable), and vice versa.

6.5.5 Vector Data U^V

6.5.5.1 Two Dimensional Data U_2^V

Direct—Glyphs Glyphs in the form of arrows provide a simple 2D vector visualization technique, especially for steady flows. Wittenbrink et al. (1996) consider carefully the design of uncertainty glyphs, proposing an arrow shape that widens to indicate uncertainty in bearing, with extra arrow heads for uncertainty in magnitude. Zuk et al. (2008) re-visit the topic for dense, bi-directional fields.

For unsteady flow, glyphs can be animated but the load placed on the human memory is considerable, and certainly challenging when uncertainty is added.

Hlawatsch et al. (2011) suggest a static glyph representation for unsteady flow: a glyph in the form of a small curve is traced out in polar coordinates at each data point, with the direction mapped to angle, θ, and time mapped to radius, r. For uncertainty, curves can be drawn for the upper and lower bounds of the sequence of angles over time, and the area between the curves shaded to give an indication of the range of directions at each data point.

Geometric—Particle Advection and Streamlines Euler's equation gives a very simple (but not always accurate) means of calculating particle paths in a flow field:

$$x_{n+1} = x_n + v(x_n) * \Delta t \tag{6.1}$$

where x_n is position at time step n, $v(x)$ is the velocity at x and Δt is the time-step. With uncertain data, we can think of $v(x)$ as a random variate with associated PDF (perhaps estimated from multivalue data). Luo et al. (2003) and Love et al. (2005) suggest a number of approaches:

1. a representative scalar can be used at each step, for example the mean of the distribution, and the particle path constructed as normal, without any indication of uncertainty
2. a set of paths (e.g. corresponding to the multiple values in case of multivalue data) are followed from the seed-point for the first time-step; then the centroid of the resulting end-points is calculated and used to initiate another set of paths, and so on
3. Equation (6.1) is interpreted directly in terms of PDFs, and generates a result at each time step which is a PDF—a simple means of adding two PDFs is suggested.

Although Euler's method is used here for simplicity, it would be straightforward to extend to, say, Runge-Kutta.

Dense—Texture-Based Approaches A number of important approaches use textures to give a visual impression of the flow field: either as a dense, noise-like pattern or as a sparse effect produced from a simulation of injecting dye. A leading method is Line Integral Convolution, or LIC, in which a dense texture is created by considering a random noise pattern, and integrating the noise forwards and backwards along streamlines through a pixel. The effect for surface velocity in the ocean example of Sect. 6.5.3.3 is studied in Allendes Osorio and Brodlie (2009). They explore different ways of encoding uncertainty within LIC: by varying the frequency of the noise pattern (low frequency—giving blur—is used for high uncertainty); with color, by assigning hue to uncertainty, and lightness to normal LIC; and by adding fog to indicate uncertainty. Figure 6.9 shows the effect of coloring the LIC.

Another popular texture approach is based on semi-Lagrangian texture advection. An example is Image-Based Flow Visualization (IBFV), in which texture is advected by the flow field and a visualization created by blending successive frames to show flow lines. Allendes Osorio (2010) explores the use of multiple frequencies (as in LIC); he also connects the opacity used in blending with the level of uncertainty in order to blur flow lines in areas of high uncertainty. Similarly, Botchen et

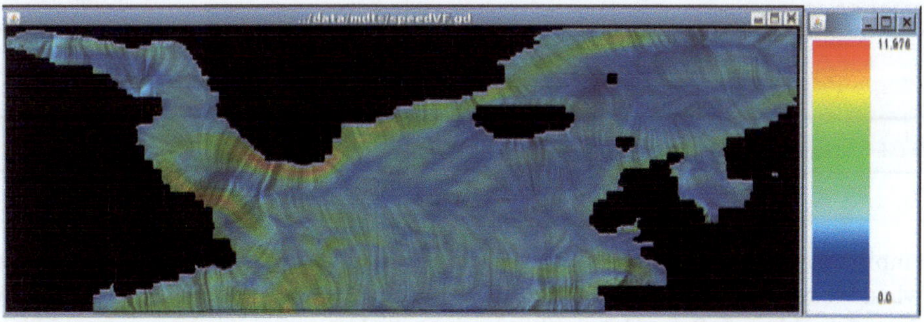

Fig. 6.9 Uncertain LIC: here hue is used to encode the uncertainty while lightness is used to represent the LIC computation

al. (2005) explore the incorporation of uncertainty into semi-Lagrangian methods: in two of their methods, they apply a post-processing step which has a smearing effect proportional to the uncertainty—either by adding an advection perpendicular to the flow, or by diffusing in all directions; in a final method, pre-rather than post-processing, they also use multi-frequency noise. An advantage of the post-processing methods is that they work both for dense and sparse texture effects.

Feature—Topology-Based Methods An increasingly important set of methods focus on identifying the topological characteristics of the flow field. This enables a global view to be taken, in which critical points (zero velocity) are identified and the domain is segmented into regions with common flow behavior. Otto et al. (2010) have extended the topological analysis to the case of uncertain flow data. Faced with the particle advection difficulty of uncertain velocities in Eq. (6.1), they consider streamline integration not in terms of a single particle at point (x, y) but rather a particle density function defined over the whole domain. This density function is then advected in the flow. With an initial distribution concentrated at a seed point, the integration will typically converge to a 'critical point distribution'.

6.5.5.2 Three Dimensional Data U_3^V

The work on uncertain 2D flow visualization largely carries forward into 3D. So for example, Otto et al. (2011) extend their 2D topological analysis to the 3D case. The trajectory of stars is studied by Li et al. (2007) where cones are used to visualize the range of possible trajectories—over 50,000 years!

6.6 Uncertainty of Visualization

Even when we are certain about the data, we may introduce uncertainty when we generate a visualization. We take a brief look at this area now. There are two aspects: at the filter stage, we incur error when we build an interpolant from the data as an

Table 6.2 Oxygen in flue gas

	x (time in mins)						
	0	2	4	10	28	30	32
y (% of oxygen)	20.8	8.8	4.2	0.5	3.9	6.2	9.6

empirical model of the true entity; and in the map and render stages, we incur error when we represent the model in a visualization. Again we use the classification of Sect. 6.4, although Point Data in this case is trivial so we omit it.

6.6.1 Scalar Data E^S

6.6.1.1 One Dimensional Data E_1^S

Interpolation plays a major role in scalar visualization—it lets us see not only the data but also suggests the behavior where there is no data. A simple 1D example (used before—see Brodlie 1993—but still relevant) highlights this. Consider coal burning in a furnace, with the percentage of oxygen measured in the flue gas. Data is collected at intervals of time, as shown in Table 6.2. The perils are illustrated in Fig. 6.10. The top left image shows just the data; top right is a piecewise linear interpolant—but do we really believe the rate of change of oxygen jumps dramatically at each data point?; bottom left shows a smoothly changing model, using cubic spline interpolation—but how can we have a negative percentage of oxygen?; bottom right is more credible—but still just an estimate.

6.6.1.2 Two Dimensional Data E_2^S

In 2D, bilinear interpolation dominates for rectangular gridded data. For contour drawing, this gives contour lines that are hyperbolas. Graphics systems tend to work in straight lines and so an approximation to the hyperbola is made, often very crudely by joining the intersections of the contour lines with cell edges. Lopes and Brodlie (1998) show the sort of error that can occur. The calculation of edge intersections can itself be a difficult task numerically: if the values at the end points of an edge are close to each other, and close to the threshold, the intersection calculation is ill-conditioned, as Pöthkow and Hege (2010) demonstrate.

Higher order interpolation can be used—Preusser (1989) provides a bicubic contouring routine.

If the grid is triangular, linear interpolation can be used—resulting in straight line contours.

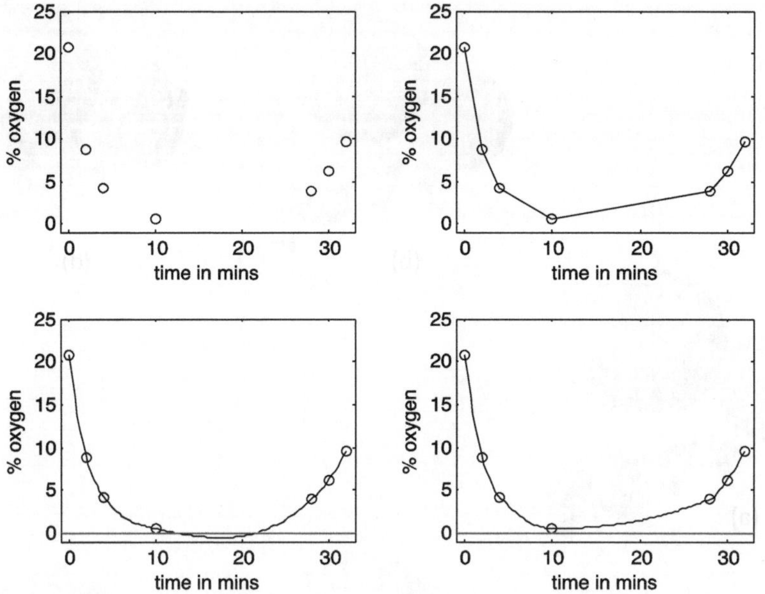

Fig. 6.10 Perils of interpolation: oxygen burning in furnace—*top left* is data; *top right* is piecewise linear (with sharp changes in slope); *bottom left* is smooth spline, but how can a percentage be negative?; *bottom right* is a monotonic curve, credible because positive, but is minimum at 10 minutes exactly?

6.6.1.3 Three Dimensional Data E_3^S

In isosurfacing, the normal practice is to use trilinear interpolation to build an empirical model inside each cell of a rectilinear grid. This again causes difficulty further down the pipeline: the shape of an isosurface is complex and hard to represent consistently using the triangular facets required by typical graphics systems such as OpenGL (see, for example, Lopes and Brodlie 2003) who also explore issues of robustness—for example, how sensitive the representation of the isosurface is to small changes in the threshold).

Again, tetrahedral grids allow linear interpolation and triangular facet isosurfaces. Thus for rectilinear grids, it is tempting to split each cell into a set of tetrahedra in order to simplify the isosurface construction. Beware! Carr et al. (2006) nicely demonstrate the different results obtained when various different tetrahedral decompositions are used. Figure 6.11 shows the visual artifacts created from isosurfacing a test dataset; the data is sampled from a sum of nine Gaussians with most of the peaks aligned in a zig-zag pattern along the grid, the 'ground truth' isosurface being a set of spheres. Subimage (a) shows a marching cubes visualization—piecewise linear approximation to trilinear interpolation on rectangular cells; subimages (b) and (c) both show piecewise linear interpolants after cell subdivision into five tetrahedra, but doing the subdivision in two, different, equally plausible ways; subimages (d) and (e) show piecewise linear interpolants after cell subdivision into six tetrahedra,

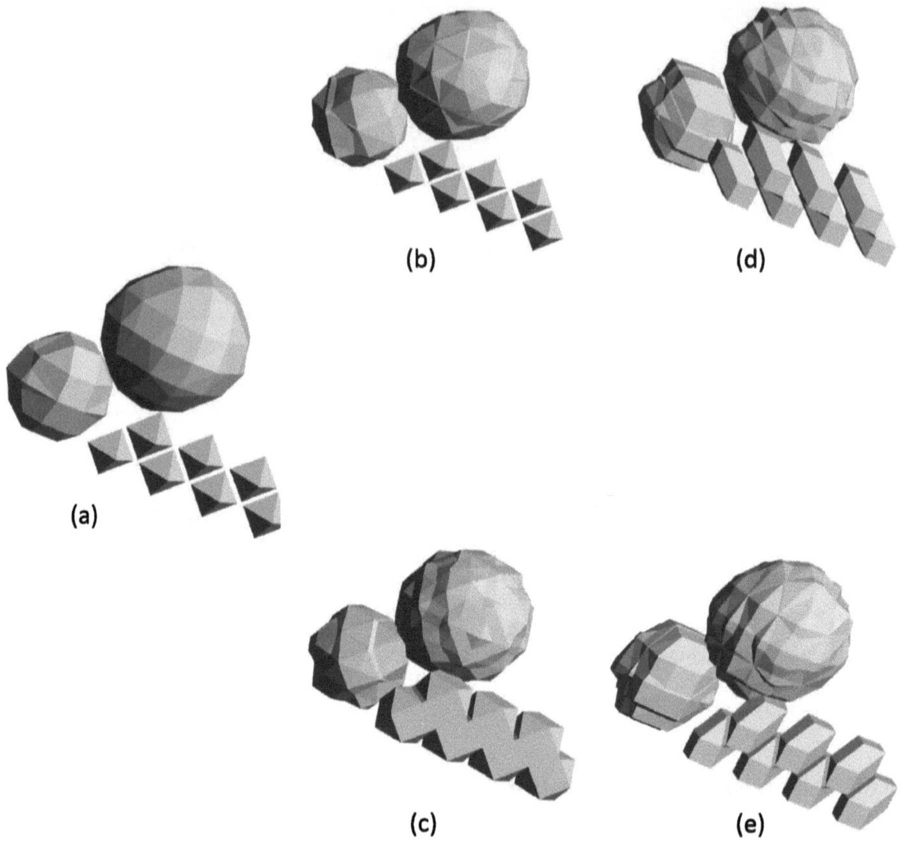

Fig. 6.11 Effect of simplicial subdivision on isosurfaces: subimage (**a**) shows a marching cubes visualization—piecewise linear approximation to trilinear interpolation on rectangular cells; subimages (**b**) and (**c**) both show piecewise linear interpolants after cell subdivision into five tetrahedra, but doing the subdivision in two, different, equally plausible ways—notice the different topologies that result; subimages (**d**) and (**e**) show piecewise linear interpolants after cell subdivision into six tetrahedra, but using different major diagonals of the cell to do the split. Images kindly created for this article by H. Carr

but using different major diagonals of the cell to do the split. Each image (b)–(e) in Fig. 6.11 uses the same data, uses the same interpolation (piecewise linear), but shows quite different results. Further subdivisions, illustrating further artifacts, are included in the paper.

It can be frustrating for scientists who carry out simulations using higher order approximations, to find that linear approximations are required in order to visualize their results—with consequent loss of accuracy. Thus there is growing interest in being able to pass the higher order data through the visualization pipeline. For example, Nelson and Kirby (2006) show how isosurfaces can be drawn by direct ray-tracing of high order finite element data. The cost is a loss of interactivity compared with sampling on a 'fairly well-spaced' mesh and using marching cubes with its piecewise trilinear interpolation. However Nelson and Kirby show that for high accuracy it is better to ray trace the high order data directly, than to run marching cubes on a very finely sampled mesh. Subsequent work by the authors (Nelson et al. 2011) demonstrates interactivity is possible for cut surfaces (i.e. E_2^S) extracted from high order finite element data, and visualized using GPU hardware; however, accurate and interactive isosurface rendering of high order data remains a challenging topic.

6.6.2 Multifield Scalar Data kE^S

Interpolation is important in design studies, where there are a number of parameters as independent variables, and a number of values that are calculated and used in multiobjective optimization. Visualization can be used to guide the optimization process by showing models of the objective functions, interpolated from sample values. Often however the calculation of a sample can be a major task, and so the data points have to be chosen with care. Wright et al. (2000) show how visualization can help steer the selection of good sample points. Berger et al. (2011) use statistical learning techniques to improve the process, and provide sensitivity analysis.

6.6.3 Vector Data E^V

For vector data, we again require interpolation. In some applications involving flow, interpolation error is a long standing issue. For example, in meteorology, Kahl and Sampson (1986) describe how substantial errors in spatial and to a lesser extent temporal interpolation can lead to false conclusions about air pollution. More recently, Boller et al. (2010) perform a study in which they aim to bound the interpolation error in each grid cell and visualize the resulting uncertainty as ribbons of varying thickness around the estimated path.

For particle advection methods, there is the additional step of numerical integration in order to calculate the path over time. Lodha et al. (1996b) explore a number of approaches to visualizing the error in the integration, such as creating a ribbon between a pair of streamlines generated by different integration methods (Euler and Runge-Kutta). Similarly, Lopes and Brodlie (1999) use the error estimates provided by NAG Library ODE solvers to provide indications of trajectory errors; Fig. 6.12 shows an envelope of trajectories formed by re-integrating with a smaller tolerance.

As in the scalar case, there is a very useful simplification for triangular or tetrahedral meshes. If we use linear interpolation in such cells, it is possible to solve the ODE analytically, removing the need for numerical integration. This idea is due to Nielson and Jung (1999), and has been further developed by Kipfer et al. (2003) and by Bhatia et al. (2011).

Accurate particle advection for high order data has been studied by Coppola et al. (2001).

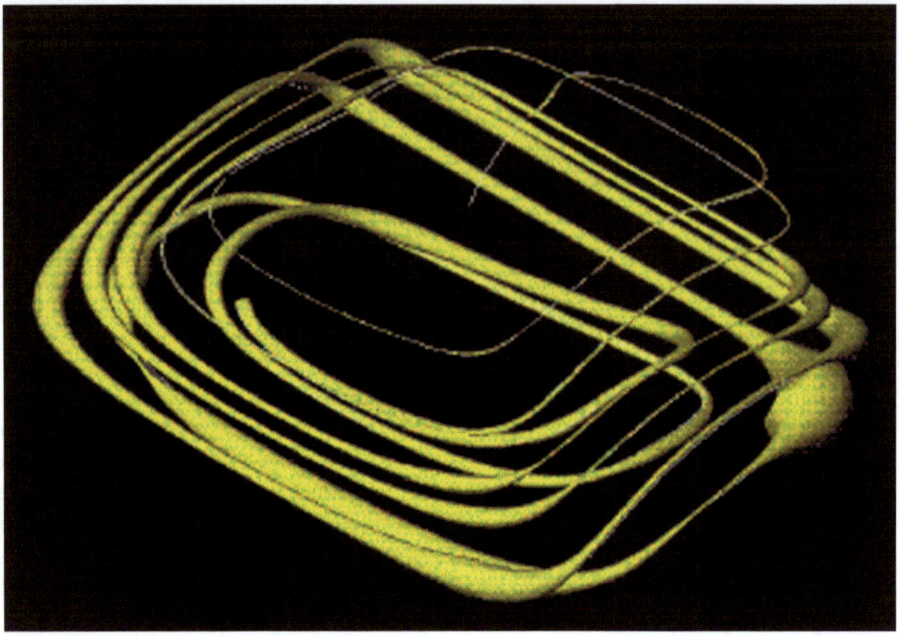

Fig. 6.12 Uncertainty of Particle Advection: the *yellow tube* indicates an envelope within which the exact path might lie, based on integrating with different tolerances

6.7 Conclusions

We have reviewed the state of the art in uncertainty visualization, looking at both the visualization of uncertainty of data and also the uncertainty of the visualization process itself. We have seen that the visualization research community has enthusiastically taken up the challenge of uncertainty and most of the popular visualization techniques have been extended in some way to handle uncertain data. There is some way to go however before these techniques are standard facilities in visualization software toolkits.

A measure of the increasing interest in uncertainty visualization is that another state-of-the-art paper is underway, following discussions at a Dagstuhl seminar in 2011 (Bonneau et al. 2012); it will act as a companion paper to this review.

There remain significant research challenges ahead. While incorporation of uncertainty into 1D and 2D visualization, both scalar and vector, is relatively straightforward, there are difficult perceptual issues in adding an indication of uncertainty in 3D. There is also work to be done in linking uncertainty and risk: Daradkeh et al. (2010) for example look at the influence of uncertainty associated with the input variables of a model, on the risk associated with decision-making. In this review we have looked separately at visualization of uncertainty, and uncertainty of visualization: we need to study how both can be incorporated in a single representation.

We have mentioned that uncertainty is hard. But it is simple to ignore. Fred Brooks, in a keynote address to the IEEE Visualization conference in 1993, reminded the audience of the need to present data honestly—while in some areas, such as realistic rendering, there is a ground truth against which the correctness of an image may be judged, in visualization we rely on the integrity of the visualization scientist. This gives us the responsibility to include in our visualizations an indication of the reliance we may place on the picture we have drawn.

Acknowledgments We have many people to thank: Alan McKinnon of Lincoln University, NZ, who helped us during his sabbatical at Leeds in 2009; Roger Payne, of VSNi Ltd, showed us how t-tests could help draw uncertain contours; Rory Bingham and Keith Haines who lent us the ocean data we have used in most of our uncertainty studies; Christian Hege who gave permission for us to use Fig. 6.8; Robert Moorhead, Jibonananda Sanyal and Hamish Carr who created images especially for this article; and members past and present of the VVR group at University of Leeds.

References

Aerts, J. C. J. H., Clarke, K. C., & Keuper, A. D. (2003). Testing popular visualization techniques for representing model uncertainty. *Cartography and Geographic Information Science*, *30*(3), 249–261.

Allendes Osorio, R. S. (2010). *Visualization of uncertainty in scientific data*. PhD thesis, University of Leeds.

Allendes Osorio, R. S., & Brodlie, K. W. (2008). Contouring with uncertainty. In I. S. Lim, & W. Tang (Eds.), *Proceedings 6th theory & practice of computer graphics conference (TP.CG.08)*. Eurographics Association.

Allendes Osorio, R. S., & Brodlie, K. W. (2009). Uncertain flow visualization using LIC. In W. Tang, & J. Collomosse (Eds.), *Theory and practice of computer graphics—Eurographics UK chapter proceedings* (pp. 215–222).

Berger, W., Piringer, H., Filzmoser, P., & Gröller, E. (2011). Uncertainty-aware exploration of continuous parameter spaces using multivariate prediction. *Computer Graphics Forum*, *30*(3), 911–920.

Bhatia, H., Jadhav, S., Bremer, P.-T., Chen, G., Levine, J. A., Nonato, L. G., & Pascucci, V. (2011). Edge maps: representing flow with bounded error. In *Proceedings of IEEE Pacific visualization symposium 2011*, March 2011 (pp. 75–82).

Bingham, R. J., & Haines, K. (2006). Mean dynamic topography: intercomparisons and errors. *Philosophical Transactions of the Royal Society A*, 903–916.

Boller, R. A., Braun, S. A., Miles, J., & Laidlaw, D. H. (2010). Application of uncertainty visualization methods to meteorological trajectories. *Earth Science Informatics*, *3*, 119–126.

Bonneau, G. P., Kindlmann, G., Hege, H. C., Johnson, C. R., Oliveira, M., Potter, K., & Rheinghans, P. (2012, in preparation). Overview and state-of-the-art of uncertainty visualization. In M. Chen, H. Hagen, C. Hansen, C. Johnson, & A. Kaufmann (Eds.), *Scientific visualization: challenges for the future*.

Botchen, R. P., Weiskopf, D., & Ertl, T. (2005). Texture-based visualization of uncertainty in flow fields. In *Proceedings of IEEE visualization 2005* (pp. 647–654).

Boukhelifa, N., & Duke, D. J. (2007). The uncertain reality of underground assets. In *Proceedings of ISPRS/ICA/DGfK joint workshop on visualization and exploration of geospatial data*. ISPRS.

Brodlie, K. (1993). A classification scheme for scientific visualization. In R. A. Earnshaw, & D. Watson (Eds.), *Animation and scientific visualization* (pp. 125–140). San Diego: Academic Press.

Brodlie, K. W., Carpenter, L. A., Earnshaw, R. A., Gallop, J. R., Hubbold, R. J., Mumford, A. M., Osland, C. D., & Quarendon, P. (Eds.) (1992). *Scientific visualization—techniques and applications*. Berlin: Springer.

Brown, R. A. (2004). Animated visual vibrations as an uncertainty visualisation technique. In *International conference on computer graphics and interactive techniques in Australasia and South East Asia* (pp. 84–89).

Buttenfield, B., & Beard, M. K. (1994). Graphical and geographical components of data quality. In H. M. Hearnshaw, & D. J. Unwin (Eds.), *Visualization in graphical information systems* (pp. 150–157). New York: Wiley.

Carr, H., Moller, T., & Snoeyink, J. (2006). Artifacts caused by simplicial subdivision. *IEEE Transactions on Visualization and Computer Graphics*, *12*(2), 231–242.

Cedilnik, A., & Rheingans, P. (2000). Procedural annotation of uncertain information. In *Proceedings of visualization 2000* (pp. 77–84). Los Alamitos: IEEE Computer Society Press.

Coninx, A., Bonneau, G.-P., Droulez, J., & Thibault, G. (2011). Visualization of uncertain scalar data fields using color scales and perceptually adapted noise. In *Applied perception in graphics and visualization*. Toulouse, France.

Coppola, G., Sherwin, S. J., & Peiro, J. (2001). Nonlinear particle tracking for high-order elements. *Journal of Computational Physics*, *172*(1), 356–386.

Correa, C. D., Chan, Y.-H., & Ma, K.-L. (2009). A framework for uncertainty-aware visual analytics. In *Proceedings of IEEE symposium on visual analytics science and technology VAST 09*.

Cox, M. G., & Harris, P. M. (2004). *Uncertainty evaluation* (Technical Report). National Physical Laboratory, March 2004. Software Support for Metrology. Best Practice Guide No. 6.

Cumming, G., Fidler, F., & Vaux, D. L. (2007). Error bars in experimental biology. *The Journal of Cell Biology*, *177*(1), 7–11.

Daradkeh, M., McKinnon, A., & Churcher, C. (2010). Visualisation tools for exploring the uncertainty-risk relationship in the decision-making process: a preliminary empirical evaluation. In *Proceedings of the eleventh Australasian conference on user interface, Auic '10* (Vol. 106, pp. 42–51). Darlinghurst: Australian Computer Society

Davis, T. J., & Keller, C. P. (1997). Modelling and visualizing multiple spatial uncertainties. *Computers and Geosciences*, *23*(4), 397–408. Exploratory Cartographic Visualisation.

Djurcilov, S., Kim, K., Lermusiaux, P., & Pang, A. (2002). Visualizing scalar volumetric data with uncertainty. *Computers & Graphics*, *26*, 239–248.

Ehlschlaeger, C. R., Shortridge, A. M., & Goodchild, M. F. (1997). Visualizing spatial data uncertainty using animation. *Computers and Geosciences*, *23*(4), 387–395.

Feng, D., Kwock, L., Lee, Y., & Taylor, R. M. (2010). Matching visual saliency to confidence in plots of uncertain data. *IEEE Transactions on Visualization and Computer Graphics*, *16*(6), 980–989.

Fisher, P. (1994). Animation and sound for the visualization of uncertain spatial information. In *Visualization in graphical information systems* (pp. 181–185). New York: Wiley.

Goodchild, M., Buttenfield, B., & Wood, J. (1994). Introduction to visualizing data validity. In H. M. Hearnshaw, & D. J. Unwin (Eds.), *Visualization in graphical information systems* (pp. 141–149). New York: Wiley.

Griethe, H., & Schumann, H. (2006). The visualization of uncertain data: methods and problems. In *Proceedings of the 17th simulation and visualization conference*.

Grigoryan, G., & Rheingans, P. (2004). Point-based probabilistic surfaces to show surface uncertainty. *IEEE Transactions on Visualization and Computer Graphics*, *10*(5), 564–573.

Haber, R. B., & McNabb, D. A. (1990). Visualization idioms: a conceptual model for scientific visualization systems. In B. Shriver, G. M. Nielson, & L. J. Rosenblum (Eds.), *Visualization in scientific computing* (pp. 74–93). IEEE.

Hengl, T. (2003). Visualisation of uncertainty using the hsi colour model: computation with colours. In *Proceedings of the 7th international conference on geocomputation* (pp. 8–17). Southampton, United Kingdom.

Hlawatsch, M., Leube, P., Nowak, W., & Weiskopf, D. (2011). Flow radar glyphs—static visualization of unsteady flow with uncertainty. *IEEE Transactions on Visualization and Computer Graphics*, *17*(12), 1949–1958.

Jänicke, H., Wiebel, A., Scheuermann, G., & Kollmann, W. (2007). Multifield visualization using local statistical complexity. *IEEE Transactions on Visualization and Computer Graphics*, *13*(6), 1384–1391.

Johnson, C. (2004). Top scientific visualization research problems. *IEEE Computer Graphics and Applications*, *July/August*, 13–17.

Johnson, C. R., & Sanderson, A. R. (2003). A next step: visualizing errors and uncertainties. *IEEE Computer Graphics and Applications*, 6–10.

Juang, K.-W., Chen, Y.-S., & Lee, D.-Y. (2004). Using sequential indicator simulation to assess the uncertainty of delineating heavy-metal contaminated soils. *Environmental Pollution*, *127*, 229–238.

Kahl, J. D., & Sampson, P. J. (1986). Uncertainty in trajectory calculations due to low resolution meteorological data. *Journal of Climate and Applied Meteorology*, *25*, 1816–1831.

Kipfer, P., Reck, F., & Greiner, G. (2003). Local exact particle tracing on unstructured grids. *Computer Graphics Forum*, *22*, 133–142.

Kniss, J. M., Uitert, R. V., Stephens, A., Li, G.-S., Tasdizen, T., & Hansen, C. (2005). Statistically quantitative volume visualization. In *IEEE visualization 2005*.

Li, H., Fu, C.-W., Li, Y., & Hanson, A. J. (2007). Visualizing large-scale uncertainty in astrophysical data. *IEEE Transactions on Visualization and Computer Graphics*, *13*(6), 1640–1647.

Lodha, S. K., Wilson, C. M., & Sheehan, R. E. (1996a). LISTEN: sounding uncertainty visualization. In *Proceedings of visualization 96* (pp. 189–195).

Lodha, S. K., Pang, A., Sheehan, R. E., & Wittenbrink, C. M. (1996b). UFLOW: visualizing uncertainty in fluid flow. In R. Yagel, & G. M. Nielson (Eds.), *IEEE visualization '96* (pp. 249–254).

Lopes, A., & Brodlie, K. (1998). Accuracy in contour drawing. In *Proceedings of Eurographics* (pp. 301–312).

Lopes, A., & Brodlie, K. (1999). Accuracy in 3D particle tracing. In H. C. Hege, & K. Polthier (Eds.), *Mathematical visualization: algorithms, applications and numerics* (pp. 329–341). Berlin: Springer.

Lopes, A., & Brodlie, K. (2003). Improving the robustness and accuracy of the marching cubes algorithm for isosurfacing. *IEEE Transactions on Visualization and Computer Graphics*, *9*, 16–29.

Love, A. L., Pang, A. T., & Kao, D. L. (2005). Visualizing spatial multivalue data. *IEEE Computer Graphics and Applications*, 69–79.

Lundstrom, C., Ljung, P., Persson, A., & Ynnerman, A. (2007). Uncertainty visualization in medical volume rendering using probabilistic animation. *IEEE Transactions on Visualization and Computer Graphics*, *13*(6), 1648–1655.

Luo, A., Kao, D., & Pang, A. (2003). Visualizing spatial distribution data sets. In *Proceedings of VISSYM '03—Eurographics and IEEE TVCG symposium on visualization* (pp. 29–38). Eurographics Association.

MacEachren, A. M. (1992). Visualizing uncertain information. *Cartographic Perspective*, *Fall 13*, 10–19.

MacEachren, A. M., Robinson, A., Hopper, S., Gardner, S., Murray, R., Gahegan, M., & Hetzler, E. (2005). Visualizing geospatial information uncertainty: what we know and what we need to know. *Cartography and Geographic Information Science*, *32*(8), 139–160.

Nelson, B., & Kirby, R. M. (2006). Ray-tracing polymorphic multidomain spectral/hp elements for isosurface rendering. *IEEE Transactions on Visualization and Computer Graphics*, *12*(1), 114–126.

Nelson, B., Kirby, R. M., & Haimes, R. (2011). Gpu-based interactive cut-surface extraction from high-order finite element fields. *IEEE Transactions on Visualization and Computer Graphics*, *17*(12), 1803–1811.

Newman, T. S., & Lee, W. (2004). On visualizing uncertainty in volumetric data: techniques and their evaluation. *Journal of Visual Languages and Computing*, *15*, 463–491.

Nielson, G. M., & Jung, I.-H. (1999). Tools for computing tangent curves for linearly varying vector fields over tetrahedral domains. *IEEE Transactions on Visualization and Computer Graphics*, *5*(4), 360–372.

Olston, C., & Mackinlay, J. D. (2002). Visualizing data with bounded uncertainty. In *INFOVIS* (p. 37).
Otto, M., Germer, T., Hege, H.-C., & Theisel, H. (2010). Uncertain 2d vector field topology. *Computer Graphics Forum*, *29*(2), 347–356.
Otto, M., Germer, T., & Theisel, H. (2011). Uncertain topology of 3d vector fields. In *Visualization symposium* (pp. 67–74). IEEE Pacific.
Pang, A. T., Wittenbrink, C. M., & Lodha, S. K. (1997). Approaches to uncertainty visualization. *The Visual Computer*, *13*(8), 370–390.
Post, F. H., Vrolijk, B., Hauser, H., Laramee, R. S., & Doleisch, H. (2003). The state of the art in flow visualisation: feature extraction and tracking. *Computer Graphics Forum*, *22*(4), 775–792.
Pöthkow, K., & Hege, H.-C. (2010). Positional uncertainty of isocontours: condition analysis and probabilistic measures. *IEEE Transactions on Visualization and Computer Graphics*.
Pöthkow, K., Weber, B., & Hege, H.-C. (2011). Probabilistic marching cubes. *Computer Graphics Forum*, *30*(3), 931–940.
Potter, K., Wilson, A., Bremer, P.-T., Williams, D., Doutriaux, C., Pascucci, V., & Johnson, C. R. (2009). Ensemble-vis: a framework for the statistical visualization of ensemble data. In *Proceedings of the 2009 IEEE international conference on data mining workshops* (pp. 233–240). Los Alamitos: IEEE Computer Society.
Potter, K., Kniss, J., Riesenfeld, R., & Johnson, C. R. (2010). Visualizing summary statistics and uncertainty. *Computer Graphics Forum*, *29*(3), 823–831.
Prabni, J.-S., Ropinski, T., & Hinrichs, K. (2010). Uncertainty-aware guided volume segmentation. *IEEE Transactions on Visualization and Computer Graphics*, *16*(6), 1358–1365.
Preusser, A. (1989). Algorithm 671: Farb-e-2d: fill area with bicubics on rectangles—a contour plot program. *ACM Transactions on Mathematical Software*, *15*, 79–89.
Rhodes, P. J., Laramee, R. S., Bergeron, R. D., & Sparr, T. M. (2003). Uncertainty visualization methods in isosurface rendering. In M. Chover, H. Hagen, & D. Tost (Eds.), *Proceedings of Eurographics*. The Eurographics Association.
Sanyal, J., Zhang, S., Bhattacharya, G., Amburn, P., & Moorhead, R. J. (2009). A user study to compare four uncertainty visualization methods for 1D and 2D datasets. *IEEE Transactions on Visualization and Computer Graphics*, *15*(6), 1209–1218.
Sanyal, J., Zhang, S., Dyer, J., Mercer, A., Amburn, P., & Moorhead, R. J. (2010). Noodles: a tool for visualization of numerical weather model ensemble uncertainty. *IEEE Transactions on Visualization and Computer Graphics*, *16*(6), 1421–1430.
Thomson, J., Hetzler, B., MacEachren, A., Gahegan, M., & Pavel, M. (2005). A typology for visualizing uncertainty. In *Proceedings of the SPIE, visualization and data analysis* (pp. 146–157).
Tory, M., & Moeller, T. (2004). Rethinking visualization: a high-level taxonomy. In *Proceedings of IEEE symposium on information visualization* (pp. 151–158).
Tukey, J. W. (1977). *Exploratory data analysis*. Reading: Addison-Wesley.
USGS (1977). *Spatial data transfer standard (SDTS): logical specifications*.
Wittenbrink, C. M., Pang, A. T., & Lodha, S. K. (1996). Glyphs for visualizing uncertainty in vector fields. *IEEE Transactions on Visualization and Computer Graphics*, *2*, 266–279.
Wright, H., Brodlie, K., & David, T. (2000). Navigating high-dimensional spaces to support design steering. In *Proceedings of IEEE visualization 2000* (pp. 291–296).
Xie, Z., Huang, S., Ward, M. O., & Rundensteiner, E. A. (2006). Exploratory visualization of multivariate data with variable quality. In *IEEE symposium on visual analytics science and technology* (pp. 183–190).
Zehner, B., Watanabe, N., & Kolditz, O. (2010). Visualization of gridded scalar data with uncertainty in geosciences. *Computers and Geosciences*, *36*(10), 1268–1275.
Zuk, T. (2008). *Visualizing uncertainty*. PhD thesis, Department of Computer Science, University of Calgary.
Zuk, T., & Carpendale, S. (2006). Theoretical analysis of uncertainty visualizations. In *Visualization and data analysis*.

Zuk, T., Downton, J., Gray, D., Carpendale, S., & Liang, J. D. (2008). Exploration of uncertainty in bidirectional vector fields. In K. Börner, M. T. Grönh, J. Park, & J. C. Roberts (Eds.), *Visualization and data analysis 2008, proceedings of SPIE-IS&T electronic imaging*. Bellingham: SPIE and IS&T.

Chapter 7
How to Draw a Graph, Revisited

Peter Eades and Seok-Hee Hong

Abstract W. T. Tutte published a paper in 1963 entitled "How to Draw a Graph". Tutte's motivation was mathematical, and his paper can be seen as a contribution to the long tradition of geometric representations of combinatorial objects. Over the following 40 odd years, the motivation for creating visual representations of graphs has changed from mathematical curiosity to Visual Analytics. Current demand for Graph Drawing methods is now high, because of the potential for more human-comprehensible visual forms in industries as diverse as Biotechnology, Homeland Security, and Sensor Networks. Many new methods have been proposed, tested, implemented, and found their way into commercial tools. This paper describes two strands of this history: the force directed approach, and the planarity approach. Both approaches originate in Tutte's paper.

7.1 Introduction

Graph Drawing has a long history (see Kruja et al. 2002), but one can argue that the first Graph Drawing *algorithm* was published in 1963, with the paper entitled "How to draw a graph" by the celebrated mathematician W. T. Tutte.

Tutte's paper was preceded by a long tradition of investigations into geometric representations of planar graphs, that is, graphs that can be drawn without edge crossings. A beautiful and classical result, known as *Fáry's Theorem*, asserts that every planar topological graph has a planar drawing with straight-line segments as edges (see Fáry 1948; Wagner 1936, and Stein 1951). From the mathematician's point of view, Tutte's paper is a chapter in this long tradition. However, the preceding work did not describe any implementable algorithms. From the perspective of Computer Science, Tutte's paper marks the beginning of research into algorithms for making visual representations of graphs. The algorithm in his paper can be seen

P. Eades (✉) · S.-H. Hong
University of Sydney, Sydney, Australia
e-mail: peter.eades@sydney.edu.au

S.-H. Hong
e-mail: seokhee.hong@sydney.edu.au

J. Dill et al. (eds.), *Expanding the Frontiers of Visual Analytics and Visualization*,
DOI 10.1007/978-1-4471-2804-5_7,

in two disparate ways: as a force-directed method, and as a planarity-based method. In this paper we review these two strands in Graph Drawing.

The next section described Tutte's algorithm. The following two sections review the two strands of Graph Drawing that originate in Tutte's paper. In the final section we evaluate the progress in these two strands since Tutte's paper, and make some suggestions for further research.

7.2 The Barycenter Algorithm

Some graph theoretic terminology is helpful in understanding Tutte's approach. Suppose that $G = (V, E)$ is a graph with vertex set V and edge set E. If $v \in V$ then $N(v)$ denotes the *neighborhood* of v, that is, $N(v) = \{u : (u, v) \in E\}$, and $deg(v)$ denotes the *degree* of v, that is $deg(v) = |N(v)|$.

A *drawing* p, q of G consists of a *vertex mapping* p that assigns a position $p(v) = (x_v, y_v)$ to each vertex $v \in V$, and an *edge mapping* q that assigns an open curve $q(u, v)$ in the plane to each edge $(u, v) \in E$ such that the endpoints of $q(u, v)$ are $p(u)$ and $p(v)$. The drawing is a *straight-line drawing* if each curve $q(u, v)$ is a straight-line segment. In this paper we restrict our attention to straight-line drawings, and as such there is no need to specify the edge mapping q.

Two edges *cross* if they have a point in common. The point in common is a *crossing*. To avoid some pathological cases, some constraints apply: (i) An edge does not contain a vertex; (ii) No edge crosses itself; (iii) Edges must not meet tangentially; (iv) No three edges share a crossing.

A drawing p of a graph is *planar* if it has no edge crossings; a graph is *planar* if it has a planar drawing. A planar drawing divides the plane into regions called *faces*. The drawing is a *convex drawing* if each face (including the outside face) is a convex polygon.

A graph is *k-connected* if there is no set of k vertices whose removal would disconnect the graph.

7.2.1 *Tutte's General Approach*

The general approach of Tutte's algorithm is quite straightforward. The input consists of a graph $G = (V, E)$, subset A of V with $3 \le |A| \le |V|$, and a position $p_0(a)$ in the plane for each $a \in A$. The output is a straight-line drawing p of G with $p(a) = p_0(a)$ for each vertex $a \in A$, and for each vertex $b \in B = V - A$,

$$p(b) = \frac{1}{deg(b)} \sum_{u \in N(b)} p(u). \tag{7.1}$$

Equations (7.1) place each $b \in B$ at the *barycenter*, or average position, of its neighbors. For this reason, the method is often called the "barycenter algorithm".

Fig. 7.1 A planar graph drawn using the barycenter algorithm

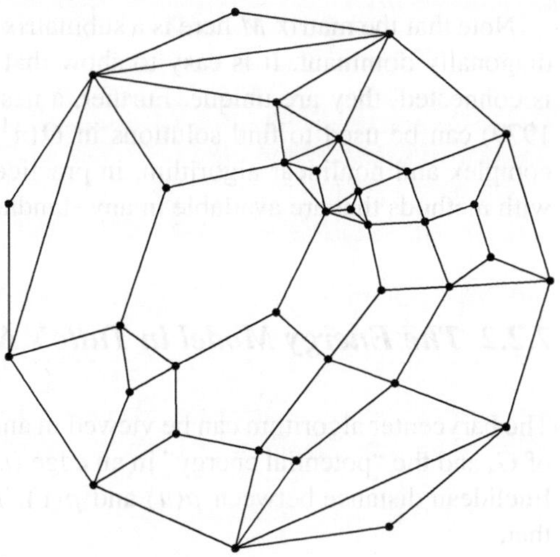

Fig. 7.2 A nonplanar graph drawn using the barycenter algorithm

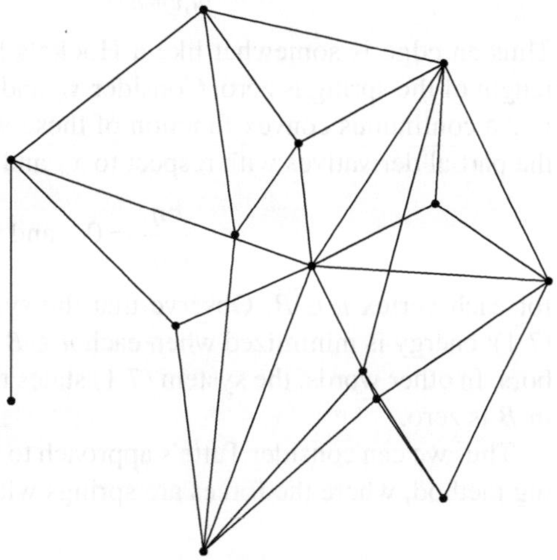

Examples of output of the barycenter algorithm are in Figs. 7.1 and 7.2.

There are several ways to choose A and p_0. For the examples in Figs. 7.1 and 7.2, the vertices of A are placed by p_0 at the vertices of a regular polygon.

The algorithm involves solving the linear equations (7.1). Note that there are two equations for each $b \in B$, one for x_b and one for y_b. Thus we can write (7.1) as two sets of equations:

$$M\mathbf{x} = \alpha \quad \text{and} \quad M\mathbf{y} = \beta, \tag{7.2}$$

where $\mathbf{x}$ (respectively $\mathbf{y}$) is a vector of the variables x_b (resp. y_b) for $b \in B$, and α (respectively β) is a vector of the values $\sum_{a \in A \cap N(b)} x_a$ (resp. $\sum_{a \in A \cap N(b)} y_a$).

Note that the matrix M here is a submatrix of the Laplacian of G, and it is strictly diagonally dominant. It is easy to show that the solutions exist and, as long as G is connected, they are unique. Further, a nested dissection approach (Lipton et al. 1979) can be used to find solutions in $O(n^{1.5})$ time. While nested dissection is a complex and nonlinear algorithm, in practice solutions can be obtained efficiently with methods that are available in any standard numerical linear algebra system.

7.2.2 The Energy Model in Tutte's Algorithm

The barycenter algorithm can be viewed in another way. Suppose that p is a drawing of G, and the "potential energy" in an edge (u, v) in the drawing is the square of the Euclidean distance between $p(u)$ and $p(v)$. The total potential energy $\eta(p)$ in p is then

$$\eta(p) = \sum_{(u,v)\in E} (x_u - x_v)^2 + (y_u - y_v)^2. \tag{7.3}$$

Thus an edge is somewhat like a Hooke's law spring, with energy zero when the length of the spring is zero. Consider x_u and y_u for all $u \in B$ as variables. Note that η is a continuous convex function of these variables. It has a minimum point when the partial derivatives with respect to x_u and y_u of η are zero, that is, when

$$\frac{\partial \eta}{\partial x_u} = 0 \quad \text{and} \quad \frac{\partial \eta}{\partial y_u} = 0 \tag{7.4}$$

for each vertex $u \in B$. Observe that the system (7.4) of equations is the same as (7.1); energy is minimized when each $u \in B$ is placed at the barycenter of its neighbors. In other words, the system (7.1) states that the sum of the forces on each vertex in B is zero.

Thus we can consider Tutte's approach to be the first "force directed" graph drawing method, where the forces are springs with natural length zero.

7.2.3 Tutte's Algorithm for Planar Graphs

Tutte was mainly concerned with the theories of planarity and connectivity for graphs.

From a well-known theorem of Whitney (1932), every planar drawing of a 3-connected planar graph has the same set of faces; for this reason, we can talk about *the* faces of a 3-connected planar graph.

Tutte's original barycenter algorithm was applied to 3-connected planar graphs. The input consists of a planar 3-connected graph $G = (V, E)$, a face A of G, a convex polygon P_0 with the same number of vertices as A, and a one-to-one mapping p_0 from the vertices of A to the vertices of P_0. The output is a straight-line drawing

p of G with $p(a) = p_0(a)$ for each $a \in A$, and $p(b)$ at the barycenter of the neighbors of b for each $b \in B = V - A$. Tutte proved a remarkable theorem about this algorithm.

Theorem 7.1 (Tutte 1963) *Suppose that p is a straight-line drawing of a 3-connected planar graph $G = (V, E)$. Suppose that*

1. *A is a set of vertices that induces a face of G,*
2. *The drawing of A (that is, $\{p_0(a) : a \in A\}$) forms a convex polygon, and*
3. *For each $b \in V - A$, $p(b) = \frac{1}{deg(b)} \sum_{u \in N(b)} p(u)$.*

Then p is planar and convex.

Tomassen (2004) gives a relatively simple proof of Theorem 7.1, and shows that the theorem holds even when the edges are weighted and Eq. (7.1) is replaced by a weighted version.

From the Mathematical point of view, Theorem 7.1 provides another proof of Fáry's theorem; further, it adds the property that as long as the input is 3-connected, we can demand that the drawing be convex. The next section discusses the significance of Tutte's algorithm from the visualization point of view.

7.2.4 Tutte's Algorithm as a Visualization Method

About twenty years after Tutte's paper, increased awareness of the capability of Computer Graphics began to drive investigations into making visual representations of graphs. The aim was to help humans understand complex relational structures, such as large software systems, large biological systems, and social networks. The challenge was to create algorithms that produce pictures that are easy to read, easy to remember, and beautiful. Tutte's elegant barycenter algorithm was an immediate contender for such an algorithm. Planarity is a much admired property of good visualizations (see Purchase 1997), and so Theorem 7.1 promises at least some degree of human understandability.

Although no human experiments have validated the importance of convex faces, it is an intuitive aim. This is especially important if for "dual representations", where the faces of the graph represent information, as in Fig. 7.3.

Further, it is not difficult to show that the barycenter algorithm produces symmetric drawings for graphs that have appropriate combinatorial symmetry (Eades and Lin 1999).

However, in general the effectiveness of the barycenter algorithm is poor. The main problem is that the *vertex resolution* can be very low, that is, vertices can be placed very close to each other. For example, Fig. 7.4 shows a Tutte drawing in which two vertices are very close together; one can show that if this example is generalized to have k vertices in B, then the barycenter algorithm will place some vertices so that the distance between them is $O(\frac{1}{2^k})$. Worse still, many practical real world graphs exhibit poor resolution when drawn with the barycenter algorithm.

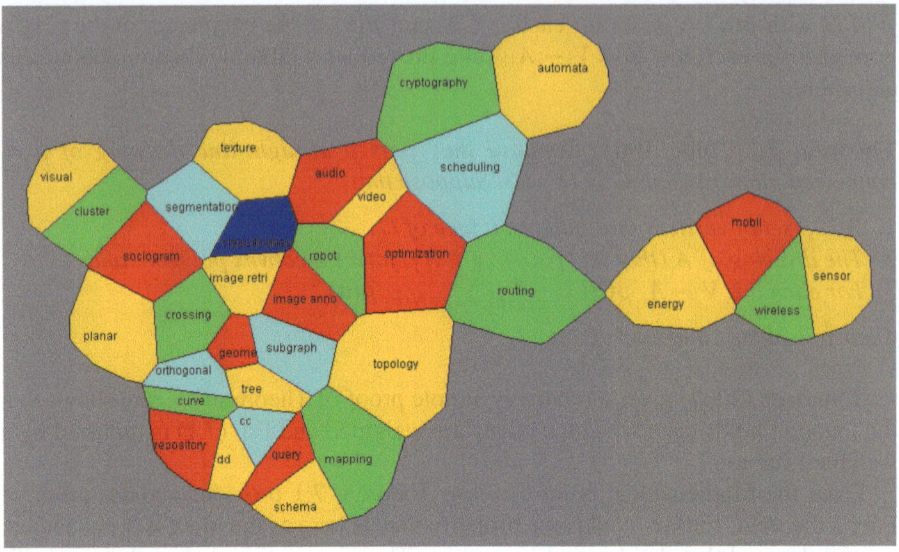

Fig. 7.3 A "dual representation" (from Liu 2011; see also Gansner et al. 2010). Here the entities are research fields, represented by the faces of a planar graph. The relationships between the entities are shown by sharing borders between faces, that is, two research fields are related if they share a common boundary

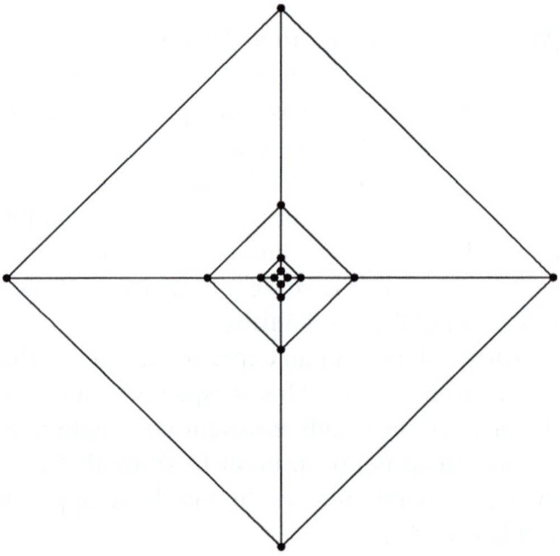

Fig. 7.4 A planar graph, drawn using the barycenter algorithm. This drawing has poor vertex resolution: the vertices near the center are exponentially close together

Further, to obtain a planar drawing, the input graph should be planar and 3-connected. Real world graphs are seldom so well structured.

Nevertheless, Tutte's paper inspired two disparate strands of research in Graph Visualization: force directed algorithms, and planarity based algorithms. The next two sections review these strands.

7.3 The Force Directed Approach

The most obvious way to repair the resolution problem in the barycenter algorithm is to use some kind of repulsion forces between vertices. One can vary Tutte's spring forces to springs with a nonzero natural length, that is, the potential energy in the edge (u, v) is proportional to $(d(p(u), p(v)) - \ell_{uv})^2$, where $d(p(u), p(v))$ is Euclidean distance between u and v, and ℓ_{uv} is the (constant) natural length of the spring between u and v. From the visualization point of view, the constant ℓ_{uv} specifies the desirable distance between u and v. The force exerted by this spring is proportional to $d(p(u), p(v)) - \ell_{uv}$. One also needs a force between nonadjacent vertices to prevent them from coming too close to each other; an inverse square law force is appropriate.

This gives a system of equations as follows. For every vertex u:

$$\sum_{v \in N(u)} \big(d\big(p(u), p(v)\big) - \ell_{uv}\big)\boldsymbol{\iota_{uv}} + \sum_{w \in V - N(u)} \frac{1}{d(p(u), p(w))^2}\boldsymbol{\iota_{uw}} = \mathbf{0}, \tag{7.5}$$

where $\boldsymbol{\iota_{uv}}$ is a unit vector in the direction of the edge (u, v). In terms of the x and y coordinates, this becomes

$$\sum_{v \in N(u)} \left(1 - \frac{\ell_{uv}}{((x_u - x_v)^2 + (y_u - y_v)^2)^{\frac{1}{2}}}\right)(x_u - x_v) + \sum_{w \in V - N(u)} \frac{1}{((x_u - x_w)^2 + (y_u - y_w)^2)^{\frac{3}{2}}}(x_u - x_w) = 0,$$

and

$$\sum_{v \in N(u)} \left(1 - \frac{\ell_{uv}}{((x_u - x_v)^2 + (y_u - y_v)^2)^{\frac{1}{2}}}\right)(y_u - y_v) + \sum_{w \in V - N(u)} \frac{1}{((x_u - x_w)^2 + (y_u - y_w)^2)^{\frac{3}{2}}}(y_u - y_w) = 0. \tag{7.6}$$

An example drawing obtained with the spring model in Eqs. (7.6) is in Fig. 7.5. This is the same graph as in Fig. 7.4. Note that Theorem 7.1 no longer holds: the drawing in Fig. 7.5 is not planar. However, Fig. 7.5 has better vertex resolution than Fig. 7.4. In general the spring model of Eqs. (7.6) gives better results than the barycenter algorithm.

Many other force models have been published (see Brandes 2001 and Kobourov 2011 for surveys). Most of these models result in similar drawings.

The main problem with equations such as (7.6) is that they are much more complex than the barycenter equations (7.2), and solutions are more difficult to compute. In general, the solutions for (7.6) are not unique; this reflects the fact that the associated energy function may have a number of local minima.

A simple iterative algorithm to solve Eqs. (7.6) is acceptable for a small number of vertices (Eades 1984); but as the data size grows, this naive approach takes a long time to converge. Fortunately, equations of this type are well studied in other

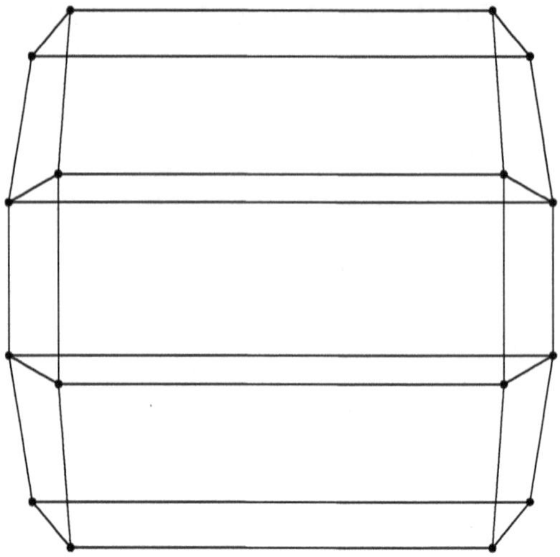

Fig. 7.5 A planar graph, drawn using the force-directed model in Eqs. (7.6). This is the same graph as in Fig. 7.4, but it has better vertex resolution. Note, however, that it is not planar

fields, and visualization algorithms can borrow from a number of theories. For example, the FADE algorithm (Quigley and Eades 2000; Tunkelang 1999) borrows from methods in astronomy to give speed ups by several orders of magnitude. Many *multiscale methods* (Pavliotis and Stuart 2008) have been used (for example, Hachul and Juenger 2004; Harel and Koren 2002; Walshaw 2003). Multidimensional scaling can efficiently produce results that are very similar to force directed methods (see, for example, de Fraysseix 1999; Koren et al. 2002).

Using such methods, force-based algorithms can run very fast in practice. However, quality issues remain; all force directed methods give poor results on graphs with a moderately large numbers of vertices and edges. See Fig. 7.6 for an example.

7.4 The Planarity Approach

The barycenter algorithm described in Sect. 7.2 has some shortcomings: it does not run in linear time, it has poor vertex resolution, and its effectiveness is restricted to planar graphs. In this section we review attempts to address these shortcomings. To understand the planarity approach, one needs the concept of "topological embedding" (sometimes called "plane graph", or "topological graph"). This concept sits between a combinatorial graph and a drawing of the graph. Mathematically, a topological embedding is an equivalence class of drawings under homeomorphism. More intuitively, a topological embedding specifies the incidence relationships between vertices, edges, and faces, but does not specify the locations of vertices or the routes of edges.

Methods for drawing planar graphs mostly involve two algorithms. The first takes the graph as input and constructs a topological embedding. The second constructs a drawing of the topological embedding. Further details can be found in di Battista et al. (1999). In this paper we consider the second step.

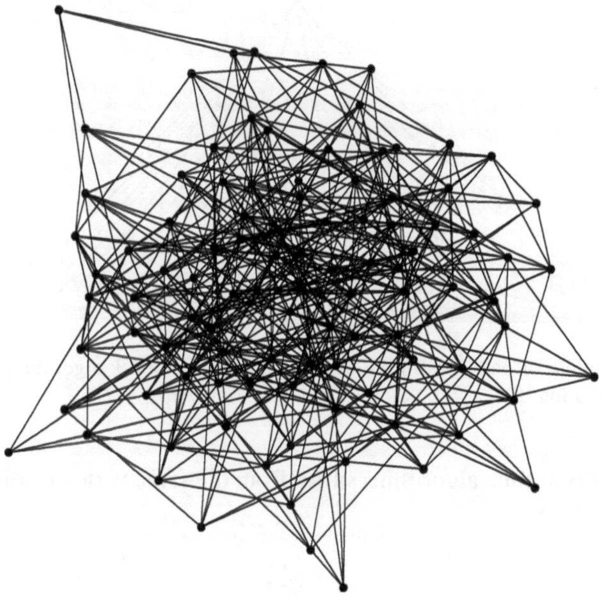

Fig. 7.6 A typical poor quality force directed graph drawing

7.4.1 Linear Time Algorithms for Planar Graphs

In the 1970s, the mathematician R. C. Read began developing a graph visualization system (Read 1978), aimed at assisting graph theorists to prove theorems. He needed a module to draw planar graphs with straight-line edges, and subsequently developed a linear-time algorithm (Read 1987).

Read's algorithm assumes that the input is a *triangulated* plane graph, that is, each inner face of G is a triangle. This seems to be not overly restrictive: if the graph is not triangulated, then we can triangulate it in linear time, by adding dummy edges to each non-triangular face.

The algorithm first chooses a vertex v of low degree from the input graph G (the sparsity of planar graphs ensures that there is at least one vertex of degree at most 5). The vertex v and all edges incident to v are then deleted. Deletion of v creates a face f that might not be a triangle; but we can triangulate f by adding a set D of dummy edges, to form a graph G'. Next G' is drawn recursively. Then the set D of dummy edges is removed from the drawing, and v is placed in f. Read describes data structures that enable the whole algorithm to run in linear time.

Chiba et al. (1984) describe another linear time algorithm, effectively implementing a theorem of Thomassen (1984) in linear time. Like Tutte's algorithm, the input consists of a graph G, a set A of vertices of G, and location $p_0(v) \in R^2$ for each $a \in A$. The output of their algorithm is a straight-line convex planar drawing p of G with $p(a) = p_0(a)$ for each $a \in A$. The algorithm relaxes the requirement that the input be 3-connected, but has a slightly weaker connectivity assumption.

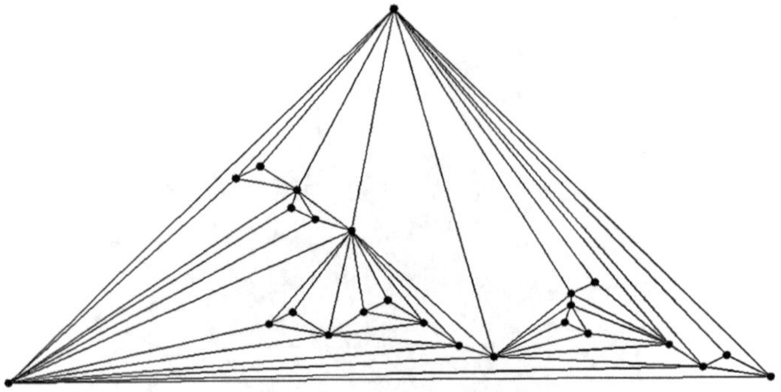

Fig. 7.7 An example of output from the de Fraysseix-Pach-Pollack algorithm. Note that it has poor angular resolution

Both these linear time algorithms suffer from the same vertex resolution problem as Tutte's algorithm.

7.4.2 Planar Drawings with Good Vertex Resolution

In 1990, de Fraysseix et al. (1990) presented an algorithm that constructs planar drawings with (asymptotically) optimal vertex resolution. The algorithm takes a planar graph as input and produces a straight-line planar drawing such that each vertex has integer coordinates, and the whole drawing fits inside a $(2n-4)\times(n-2)$ rectangle. Effectively this means that on a screen of size $w \times h$, the separation between two vertices is at least $\frac{\min(w,h)}{2n-4}$.

The algorithm begins by placing two vertices on the x axis, and then places the other vertices one by one, increasing the y coordinate by one for each vertex. The vertices must be added in a special order, called the "canonical" order. At each step of the algorithm, a subgraph of the current drawing is shifted sideways, in order to guarantee that edges do not cross. Chrobak and Payne (1995) showed how to implement the algorithm in linear time. An output from this algorithm is in Fig. 7.7.

Using a different approach, Schnyder (1990) independently gave an algorithm that constructs a straight-line planar drawing on a $(n-2)\times(n-2)$ integer grid in linear time.

The vertex resolution achieved by these algorithms is asymptotically optimal, since there are graphs that require quadratic area when drawn on the integer grid (Valiant 1981). However, several researchers have improved the original algorithm by a constant, using refinements of the approach of de Fraysseix et al. (for examples, see Chrobak and Payne 1995, Kant 1996, Zhang and He 2005).

The algorithms of de Fraysseix et al. and Schnyder solved the vertex resolution problem, but the resulting drawings still have some problems. First, the algorithms are designed for triangulations. Of course, it is true that any planar graph can be

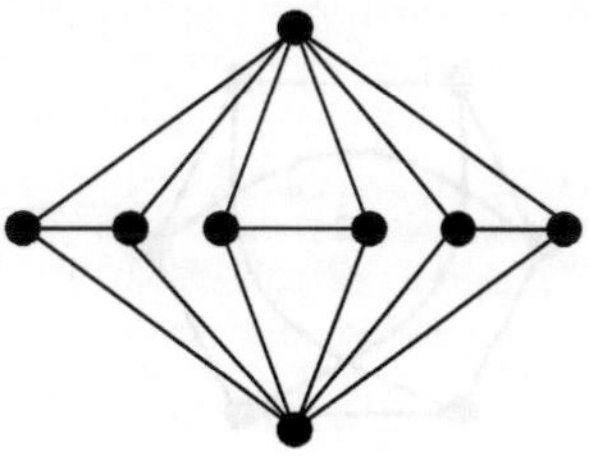

Fig. 7.8 A star-shaped drawing. Two of the internal faces here are star-shaped but not convex

augmented to a triangulation by adding dummy edges; but the quality of the resulting drawing depends critically on which edges are used to augment the graph. Second, the output drawings tend to have poor *angular resolution*, that is, the angles formed where edges meet at a vertex can be very small. There have been a number of attempts to address these problems; however to date there are no good solutions.

7.4.3 Drawing Planar Graphs with Star-Shaped Faces

The output of Tutte's original algorithm is a convex drawing, and a number of subsequent planar graph drawing algorithms also aimed for convexity. However, as shown by Tomassen (2004), convexity requires the graph to satisfy some relatively strong connectivity conditions.

The concept of "star-shaped" is a generalization of convexity. A simple polygon P is *star-shaped* if it contains a point q such that q can "see" every vertex of P, that is, for every vertex p of P, the straight-line segment between p and q does not cross the boundary of P. In a convex polygon, every internal angle at a vertex is at most π. This is not true for a star-shaped polygon; however, the number of vertices of a star-shaped polygon with internal angles greater than π gives a measure of how "convex" the polygon is.

A *star-shaped drawing* is a straight-line planar drawing such that each inner facial cycle is drawn as a star-shaped polygon, and the outer facial cycle is drawn as a convex polygon. Hong and Nagamochi (2008, 2010a,b) recently showed how to extend convex drawings to star-shaped drawings. Their algorithm minimizes the number of concave corners, and runs in linear time. A variation of the algorithm can be used to specify which corners are allowed to be concave. An example of a star-shaped drawing with the minimum number of concave corners is in Fig. 7.8.

7.4.4 Drawing Nonplanar Graphs Using Planarity Based Methods

One of the major problems with planarity-based methods is that most graphs that arise in practice are not planar. Because of this, a method for "planarizing" an input graph $G = (V, E)$ has been used (see di Battista et al. 1999). The method takes 4 steps to draw an input graph $G = (V, E)$:

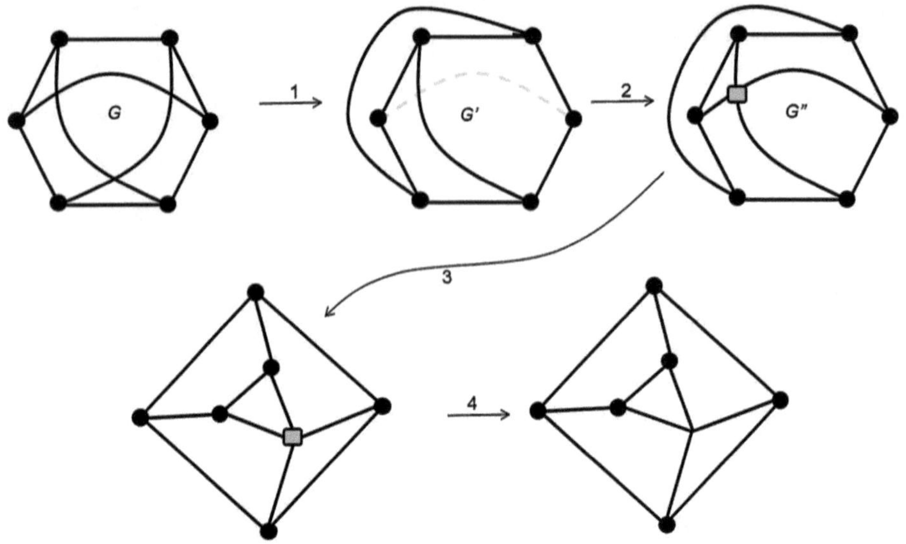

Fig. 7.9 The four steps of the planarization method: (**1**) Find a large planar subgraph. (**2**) Find a route for each edge that is not in the planar subgraph, placing a dummy vertex at each crossing. (**3**) Draw the resulting graph. (**4**) remove the dummy vertices

1. Find a large planar subgraph $G' = (V, E')$ of G and a topological embedding of G'.
2. For each edge $(u, v) \in E - E'$, find a path from u to v that crosses a small number of edges. Add a dummy vertex on each edge that this path crosses, giving a planar topological embedding G''.
3. Using a planar graph drawing algorithm, draw G''.
4. Remove the dummy vertices from G'' to give a drawing of G.

The planarization method is illustrated in Fig. 7.9. Implementation of each of the steps involves a number of NP-hard problems; however, a range of effective heuristics are available. For orthogonal drawings, planarization works well and has been adopted into Graph Drawing systems (for example, see Chimani et al. 2011). However, as seen in Fig. 7.9, it does badly for straight-line drawings since edges bend at the crossing points.

Recently, researchers have investigated a planarization approach for graphs that are "almost" planar, in some sense. An interesting example is the class of *1-planar* graphs, that is, graphs that can be drawn with at most one crossing per edge. This class of graphs has been extensively investigated by Mathematicians (see Pach 1999, Pach and Toth 1997). It is a larger class than planar graphs, and perhaps covers more of the "real world" graphs. An example of a 1-planar graph is in Fig. 7.10.

The approach is to firstly find an appropriate 1-planar topological embedding G' of the input graph G, and secondly find a good drawing of G'. The first step here seems difficult (Korzhik and Mohar 2009). However, some progress has been made on the second step. Fundamentally, there are only two 1-planar topological graphs

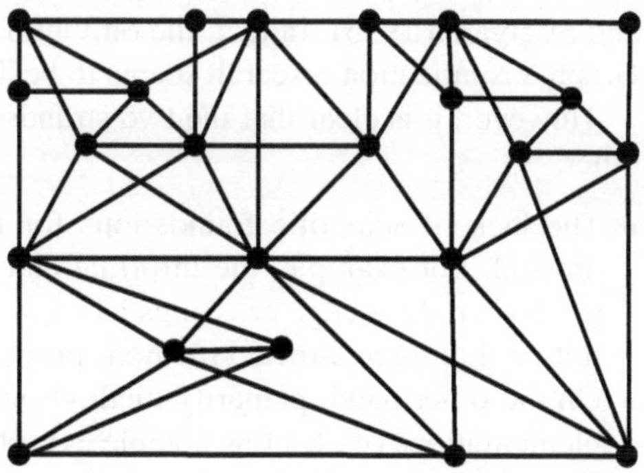

Fig. 7.10 A one-planar graph

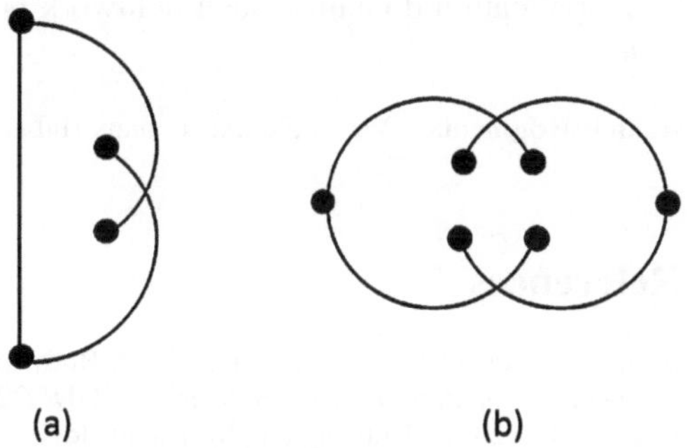

Fig. 7.11 (**a**) The bulgari graph; (**b**) the gucci graph. If a topological 1-planar embedding does not have either of these two subgraphs, then it has a 1-plane drawing with straight-line edges

(called the *bulgari graph* and the *gucci graph*) that cannot be drawn with straight-line edges, illustrated in Fig. 7.11. Further, there is a linear time algorithm that takes a 1-planar topological graph without these two forbidden substructures as input, and computes a straight-line drawing (see Eades et al. 2011).

This research is in its infancy and there are many unsolved problems.

7.5 Remarks

Tutte's 1963 paper inspired two separate strands in Graph Drawing research: the force directed approach, and the planarity approach. These strands differ in many ways. The planarity approach has been primarily scientific, while research in force directed methods has been primarily engineering. The planarity approach is based on mathematical certainty backed up by scientific experiments (Purchase 1997), whereas the force directed approach is mostly based on intuition rather than proven metrics. Many algorithms in the planarity approach are complex and difficult to code; many force directed algorithms are simple and can be coded by undergraduate students. The planarity approach is seldom seen outside University laboratories, while every software provider in Graph Visualization includes at least one force directed approach in their toolkit. We could not find one patent for a planarity-based algorithm, while there is a plethora of patents on force directed variants (for example, see Adachi et al. 2009, Han and Byun 2004, Lauther et al. 2002, Misue and Sugiyama 1995). In fact, the only unifying element between the two strands of Graph Visualization research seems to be Theorem 7.1.

However, it is clear that the two strands of research can become learn from each other.

- The lack of scientific foundations for force-directed methods needs to be addressed. For example, the informal claim of Kamada (1989) that force directed methods reduce edge crossings has never been validated mathematically. The intuition that force directed methods produce visual clusters has not been validated.
- On the other hand, planarity methods suffer from a lack of well-engineered implementations (with a few notable exceptions Chimani et al. 2011; Yworks 2012). Fieldwork research is needed evaluate the suitability of planarity-based methods in application domains. Such fieldwork is needed to guide future theoretical research.

Acknowledgments We would like to thank Hui Liu for creating the pictures in this paper.

References

Adachi, N., Kananaka, S., Matsumoto, Y., & Rudy, R. (2009). *Apparatus and method for supporting document data search*. US Patent US2009/03272779 A1.

Brandes, U. (2001). Drawing on physical analogies. In Kaufmann, & Wagner (Eds.), *LNCS tutorial: Vol. 2025. Drawing graphs: methods and models* (pp. 71–86). Berlin: Springer.

Chiba, N., Yamanouchi, T., & Nishizeki, T. (1984). Linear algorithms for convex drawings of planar graphs. In Bondy (Ed.), *Progress in graph theory* (pp. 153–173). San Diego: Academic Press.

Chimani, M., Gutwenger, C., Juenger, M., Klau, G., Klein, K., & Mutzel, P. (2011). The open graph drawing framework (OGDF). http://www.cs.brown.edu/~rt/gdhandbook/chapters/ogdf.pdf.

Chrobak, M., & Payne, T. (1995). A linear-time algorithm for drawing a planar graph on a grid. *Information Processing Letters*, *54*, 241–246.

de Fraysseix, H. (1999). An heuristic for graph symmetry detection. In *Graph drawing 1999* (pp. 276–285).

de Fraysseix, H., Pach, J., & Pollack, R. (1990). How to draw a planar graph on a grid. *Combinatorica*, *10*(1), 41–51.

di Battista, G., Eades, P., Tamassia, R., & Tollis, I. (1999). *Graph drawing: algorithms for the visualization of graphs*. New York: Prentice-Hall.

Eades, P. (1984). A heuristic for graph drawing. *Congressus Numerantium*, *42*, 149–160.

Eades, P., & Lin, X. (1999). Spring algorithms and symmetry. *Theoretical Computer Science*, *240*, 379–405.

Eades, P., Hong, S., & Liotta, G. (2011). Straight-line drawings of 1-planar graphs. Submitted.

Fáry, I. (1948). On straight line representations of planar graphs. *Acta Scientiarum Mathematicarum Szeged*, *11*, 229–233.

Gansner, E., Hu, Y., & Kobourov, S. (2010). GMap: visualizing graphs and clusters as maps. In *Pacific Vis 2010* (pp. 201–208).

Hachul, S., & Juenger, M. (2004). Drawing large graphs with a potential-field-based multilevel algorithm. In *Lecture notes in computer science: Vol. 3383. GD2004* (pp. 285–295).

Han, K., & Byun, Y. (2004). *Method for partitioned layout of protein interaction networks*. US Patent US2004/0059522 A1.

Harel, D., & Koren, Y. (2002). A fast multi-scale method for drawing large graphs. *Journal of Graph Algorithms and Applications*, *6*(3), 179–202.

Hong, S., & Nagamochi, H. (2008). Star-shaped drawings of graphs with fixed embedding and concave corner constraints. In *Lecture notes in computer science: Vol. 5092. Proc. of COCOON 2008* (pp. 405–414).
Hong, S., & Nagamochi, H. (2010a). An algorithm for constructing star-shaped drawings of plane graphs. *Computational Geometry*, *43*(2), 191–206.
Hong, S., & Nagamochi, H. (2010b). A linear time algorithm for star-shaped drawings of planar graphs with the minimum number of concave corners. *Algorithmica*. To appear.
Kamada, T. (1989). *Visualizing abstract objects and relations*. Singapore: World Scientific.
Kant, G. (1996). Drawing planar graphs using the canonical ordering. *Algorithmica*, *16*(1), 4–32.
Kobourov, S. (2011). Force directed drawing algorithms. www.cs.brown.edu/~rt/gdhandbook/chapters/force-directed.pdf.
Koren, Y., Carmel, L., & Harel, D. (2002). ACE: A fast multiscale eigenvectors computation for drawing huge graphs. In *INFOVIS 2002* (pp. 137–144).
Korzhik, V., & Mohar, B. (2009). Minimal obstructions for 1-immersions and hardness of 1-planarity testing. In *Proc. of graph drawing 2008* (pp. 302–312).
Kruja, E., Marks, J., Blair, A., & Waters, R. (2002). A short note on the history of graph drawing. In S. Kobourov, & M. Goodrich (Eds.), *Lecture notes in computer science: Vol. 2265. Graph drawing* (pp. 602–606).
Lauther, U., Stubinger, A., Malisch, F., & Dostert, P. (2002). *Method for producing diagrammatic network plans*. US Patent US2004/0199759.
Lipton, R., Rose, D., & Tarjan, R. (1979). Generalized nested dissection. *SIAM Journal on Numerical Analysis*, *16*(2), 346–358.
Liu, H. (2011). *Dynamic concept cartography for social networks*. Masters thesis, University of Sydney.
Misue, K., & Sugiyama, K. (1995). *Automatic graph layout apparatus and methods determining and using a stable state of a physical model*. US Patent US005764239.
Pach, J. (1999). Geometric graph theory. In Lamb, & Preece (Eds.), *London mathematical society lecture notes: Vol. 267. Surveys in combinatorics* (pp. 167–200). Cambridge: Cambridge University Press.
Pach, J., & Toth, G. (1997). Graphs drawn with few crossings per edge. *Combinatorica*, *17*(3), 427–439.
Pavliotis, G., & Stuart, A. (2008.) *Multiscale methods: averaging and homogenization. Texts in applied mathematics: Vol. 53*. Berlin: Springer.
Purchase, H. (1997). Which aesthetic has the greatest effect on human understanding? *Graph Drawing*, *1997*, 248–261.
Quigley, A., & Eades, P. (2000). FADE: graph drawing, clustering, and visual abstraction. In *GD2000* (pp. 197–210).
Read, R. (1978). Some applications of computers in graph theory. In Beincke, & Wilson (Eds.), *Selected topics in graph theory* (pp. 417–444). San Diego: Academic Press.
Read, R. (1987). A new method for drawing a planar graph given the cyclic order of the edges at each vertex. *Congressus Numerantium*, *56*, 31–44.
Schnyder, W. (1990). Embedding planar graphs on the grid. In *Proc. of SODA* (pp. 138–148).
Stein, K. (1951). Convex maps. *Proceedings of the American Mathematical Society*, *2*, 464–466.
Thomassen, C. (1984). Plane representations of graphs. In Bondy, & Murty (Eds.), *Progress in graph theory* (pp. 43–69). San Diego: Academic Press.
Tomassen, C. (2004). Tutte's spring theorem. *Journal of Graph Theory*, *45*, 275–280.
Tutte, W. (1963). How to draw a graph. *Proceedings of the London Mathematical Society*, *13*, 743–767.
Tunkelang, D. (1999). *A numerical optimization approach to general graph drawing*. PhD thesis, Carnegie Mellon University.
Valiant, L. (1981). Universality considerations in VLSI circuits. *IEEE Transactions on Computers*, *30*(2), 135–140.
Wagner, K. (1936). Bemerkungen zum Vierfarbenproblem. *Jahresbericht der Deutschen Mathematiker-Vereinigung*, *46*, 26–32.

Walshaw, C. (2003). A multilevel algorithm for force-directed graph drawing. *Journal of Graph Algorithms and Applications*, *7*(3), 253–285.

Whitney, H. (1932). Non-separable and planar graphs. *Transactions of the American Mathematical Society*, *34*, 339–362.

Yworks (2012). http://www.yworks.com/en/index.html.

Zhang, H., & He, X. (2005). Canonical ordering trees and their applications in graph drawing. *Discrete & Computational Geometry*, *33*, 321–344.

Chapter 8
Using Extruded Volumes to Visualize Time-Series Datasets

Nick Schultz and Mike Bailey

Abstract Time-series datasets are used to construct simulations for alternative future scenarios. They support the identification of patterns and trends over time. This allows effective interactions between the various actors involved in decision-making processes, such as planners and policy makers, whilst considering the environmental implications of any plan.

8.1 Introduction

Viewing time-series datasets gives users a unique perspective and allows them to identify patterns and trends over time. This chapter demonstrates a visualization technique that involves a process of time-extrusion to view an "animation" over time in a single image.

This project's goals were to visualize simulation data created by the Envision software (Bolte et al. 2007). Envision is a software tool to project the impacts of land-use decisions into the future. To show how the simulation progressed, snapshots were presented of the landscape side by side which allowed the viewer to compare the images. Figure 8.1 is a visualization showing a 50 year simulation in 10 year increments using this side-by-side technique.

Viewing the changes between these snapshots proved to be a difficult task. While individual times can be observed, recognizing trends between the time-slices is problematic. We found that we could use a crossed-eye fusion technique to detect changes between two images. However, the extent of the technique was limited as only two images can be crossed at a time.

We also developed a visualization tool to display animations that blended between various years. This worked well when comparing a short series, say 2 to 5 years, as the viewer could see regions of the dataset fading from one color to another.

N. Schultz (✉) · M. Bailey
Oregon State University, Corvallis, USA
e-mail: nick.schultz@live.com

M. Bailey
e-mail: mjb@cs.oregonstate.edu

J. Dill et al. (eds.), *Expanding the Frontiers of Visual Analytics and Visualization*,
DOI 10.1007/978-1-4471-2804-5_8,

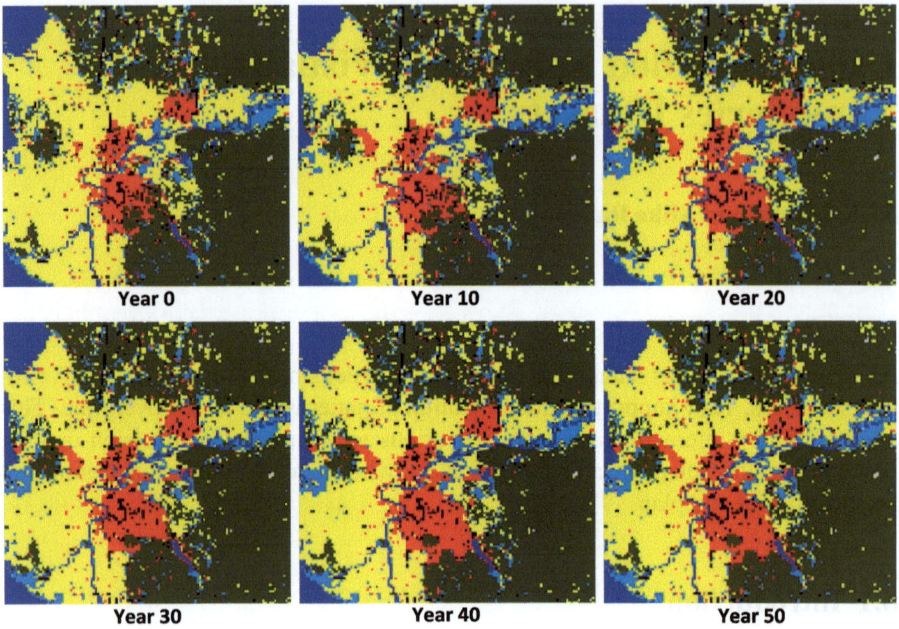

Fig. 8.1 Sequential 10-year snapshots. Source: Envision Skagit 2060 Project

However, as the duration of the visualization increased, it became more challenging to compare the current frame with the entire animation. Thus, discerning patterns over time becomes a difficult task.

8.2 Project Description

8.2.1 Envision

Envision is a software framework for constructing alternative future scenario simulations, and is the main source of data used for the visualizations. Envision allows users to simulate the interactions between Actors (decision-makers, such as county officials, city planners), Policies (descriptions of the constraints on the Actors, such as laws and/or usage goals), and the Landscape (environment metrics). Users are typically concerned with the resulting Landscape and shape Policies to try to conform to an ideal environment, such as increased wetlands.

The data is typically composed of polygons with associated attributes describing the Landscape. To visualize this data, the user can rasterize the polygons with the relevant environment metrics (Land Use/Land Cover, Population Density) perform a color transfer function to produce a 2D image. These images can then be compiled into an animation to show the changes of the Landscape as the simulation progresses.

Simulation data from the Envision Skagit 2060 Project was used as a testing dataset (Envision Skagit 2060 2011). The project's purpose is to develop and implement a 50-year plan to protect and enhance the Skagit and Samish watersheds' (located in northern Washington) environments. Envision will be used to simulate four different alternative future scenarios. The outcome of these simulations will help shape recommendations to the county government's comprehensive plans and policies addressing land use planning, economic development, environment protection and natural resource conservation.

8.2.2 Tools Used

Data preparation was scripted in Perl, utilizing shape file rasterization utilities from the Geospatial Data Abstraction Library (GDAL 2011). The volume visualization software's user interface is based on GLUI 2.01 and has a custom range slider control developed by Mike Bailey and John Rapp. The range slider allows the user to define the width of a selection range and use the slider to drag it. The Open Source project, FreeImage Library, is used to support importing multiple image types (FreeImage 2011). For the sake of simplicity, the OpenGL Mathematics (Riccio 2011) library provided mathematical classes and functions similar to those provided by OpenGL Shading Language (GLSL).

8.2.3 Methodology

The derivation of the term "time-extruded volumes" comes from the fact that the features created within these volumes look similar to extruded objects. Stacking each sequential slice of time from a time-series dataset on top of each other creates a volume. Data that does not change over time creates time-extruded columns within the volume. If the data changes, it results in either a growing, shrinking, or disappearing column. Viewing these columns in a 3D environment provides an intuitive visualization of the trends in a dataset.

This visualization of time-series data involved three major steps: (1) data extraction and preparation into a 3D data volume, (2) rendering the volume, and (3) implementation of user interface tools for data manipulation.

8.2.4 Data Extraction and Preparation

To gather simulation data, the scenario was first run in Envision. Envision offers the ability to export a snapshot of the Landscape in yearly increments. The exported polygonal data are in ESRI shape files (.shp).

To ease development, the decision was made to rasterize the shape files as a pre-process to the visualization. Adding a pre-process simplified the importation process of the program. A Perl script was developed that utilized the GDAL utility "gdal_rasterize" to create TIFF images rasterized with the raw attribute values. To take advantage of the multiple cores in modern machines, calls were made to the utility in parallel. After rasterizing the shape files, images were then cropped to 256×256 or 512×512.

To import the image layers, the FreeImage library was used to load the images into a 3D array. Each layer in the X–Y plane of the array represented a yearly time slice of the data. The entire dataset was then loaded into the graphics card as a 3D texture. Since the images had been rasterized into raw data values, the 3D texture was filled with floating point data instead of color values. This gave greater flexibility as color transfer functions could be applied on the fly within the fragment shader.

Envision creates essentially two types of data: categorical (discrete) and continuous data. Categorical data can be thought of as storing labels instead of continuous scalar values. Interpolating labels does not have a meaning. Therefore, categorical data must be interpolated using nearest interpolation, selecting the label closest to the sampling point.

8.2.5 Rendering Techniques

The volume rendering was implemented using texture mapping on parallel planes. Quad slicing, the drawing of 2D quads with texture coordinates that are within the volume texture, provided a way to sample the volume. The appearance of a volume was reproduced by stacking these slices together. Alpha blending was used to provide a translucent effect and gave the ability to peer into the volume. Due to depth testing, the slices needed to be drawn in a back-to-front fashion to avoid being z-culled and to make blending work.

A single 3D texture was used to hold the data. This allowed us to use any number of slices and gave us the ability to trilinearly interpolate sample points between voxels. Drawing the slices such that they were perpendicular to the viewing direction eliminated artifacts that would have been created with axis-aligned slices.

The quads were generated on the fly with a geometry shader that accepted GL_POINTS as inputs and then output sets of two GL_TRIANGLE_STRIPs to create quads. The geometry shader created a view-aligned quad centered at the incoming point. Performing the quad calculation in the shader program moved the calculation onto the more powerful graphics hardware. This also reduced the number of vertex coordinates needed to transfer to the graphics hardware.

Figure 8.2a shows the effect of the geometry shader. First, a set of points on the view vector are submitted to the graphics pipeline in a back to front order. Figure 8.2b then shows the result of the geometry shader with texture mapping turned off. Finally, Fig. 8.2c shows the final result with texture mapping turned on.

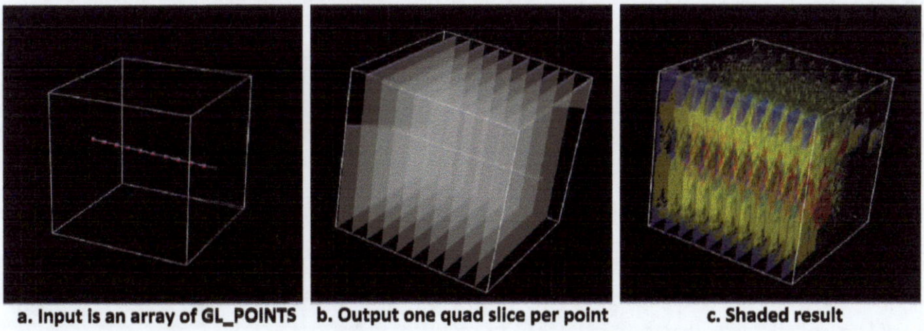

Fig. 8.2 An example visualizing the programmable graphic shader. In this example, 11 points were submitted to the graphics pipeline

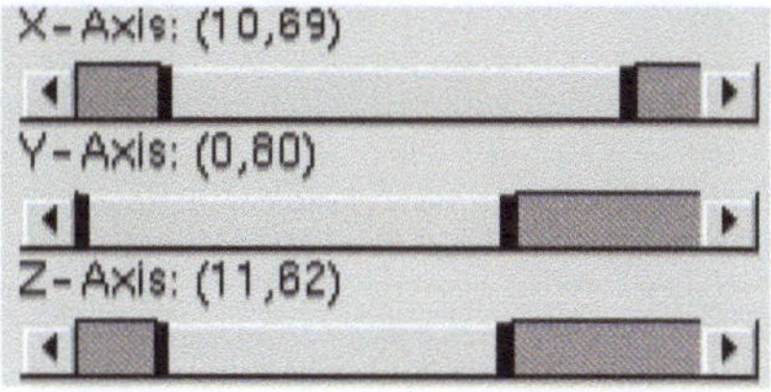

Fig. 8.3 Slicing Tool interface

When the cube dimensions were made the same as the texture dimension (1.0 × 1.0 × 1.0), both the vertex and texture coordinates occupied the same space. This simplified the calculations and eliminated the need to send any texture coordinates to the graphics card. Instead they were computed in the geometry shader. User-defined clip planes were used to slice into the volume to view surfaces within the volume.

8.2.6 Visualization User Interface

Having the ability to manipulate and filter the volumetric data empowers users with the ability to visualize and explore their data effectively. Initially, several types of visualization tools were implemented to assist users with what they were seeking to accomplish.

8.2.6.1 Slicing Tool

Figure 8.3 shows a simple set of range slider tools used to control the clipping planes. The clipping plane controls are double-ended and allowed the ability to control the slicing on either side of the volume's axis. With these sliders, the user can narrow the scope of the visualization. As the user adjusts the sliders, the labels are updated with the selected viewing ranges.

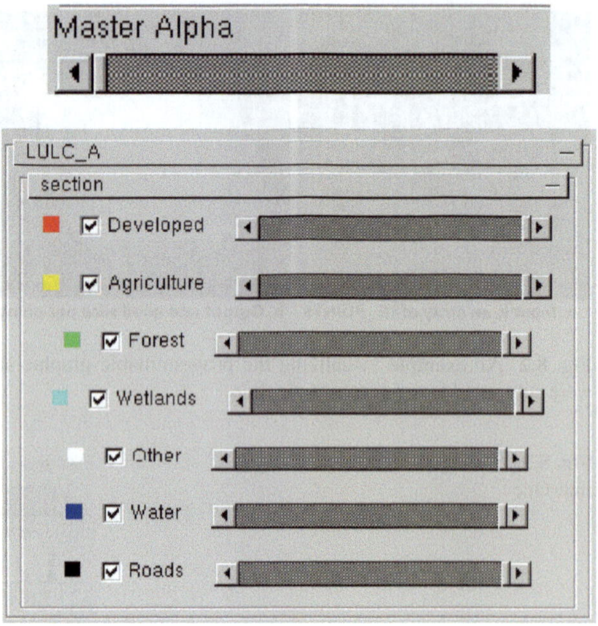

Fig. 8.4 Master Alpha slider (*top*) and Category Alpha slider (*bottom*) interfaces

Slicing within the Z-axis range slider reveals a new time slice and can be used to determine at what time events occur in the time-series. Slicing with either the X or Y axis range sliders traverses spatially through the dataset in the respective directions.

8.2.6.2 Alpha Control Tools

The alpha controls are a set of sliders that control the transparency values of the voxels. Figure 8.4 shows an example of the Master Alpha and Category Alpha sliders. The Master Alpha slider allows the user to change the overall opacity of the entire volume, allowing the viewer to look through the volume with varying degrees of transparency.

The Category sliders are then used to control the alpha values of individual categories of data. This allows users to individually adjust the opacity of categories such that only their data of interest strongly appears in the volume. The independent slider feature was only implemented for Categorical data.

Additionally, the checkboxes allow the quick enabling or disabling of features within the volume. Colored boxes were also implemented in GLUI to give a data legend for the user.

Fig. 8.5 Highlighter Tool interface

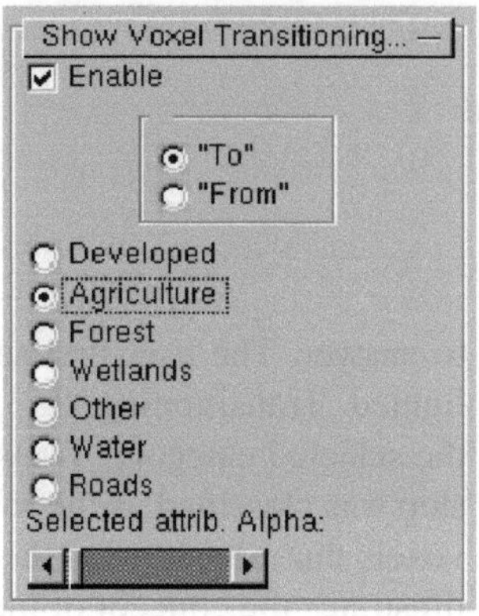

Fig. 8.6 Transitioning Tool interface

8.2.6.3 Highlighter Tool

The Highlighter Tool allows the user to quickly highlight a specific data category as an opaque white. A picture of the user interface is shown in Fig. 8.5. Used in conjunction with the Master Alpha slider, the user can shade the volume as transparent and then use the highlighter to quickly visualize various categories in the volume.

The advantage to using an opaque white is that it gives the user an obvious indication of the highlighted voxels and reduces the error of misinterpreting blended colors. The user also has the option of either viewing the rest of the volume in the original color transfer function, or in the monochrome equivalent. The latter produces visualizations similar to an X-ray image.

8.2.6.4 Transitioning Tool

The Transitioning Tool allows the user to see when, where, and to what value, the data is changing. Figure 8.6 shows an example of the tool's interface. The interface is formulated in a way that allowed the user to specify a question for the visualization

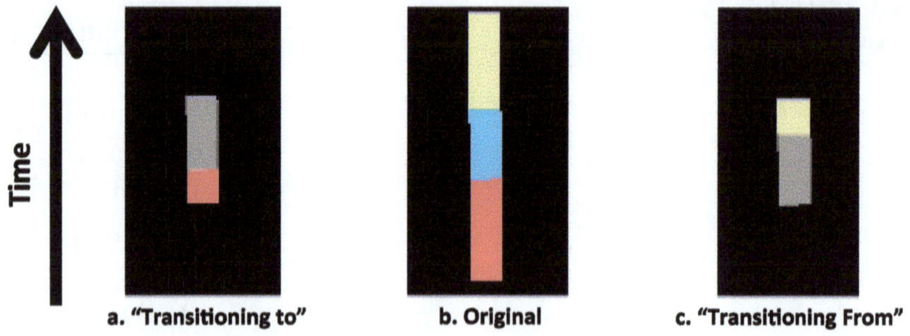

Fig. 8.7 Example describing the applications of Transitioning Tool

Fig. 8.8 The Orienteer

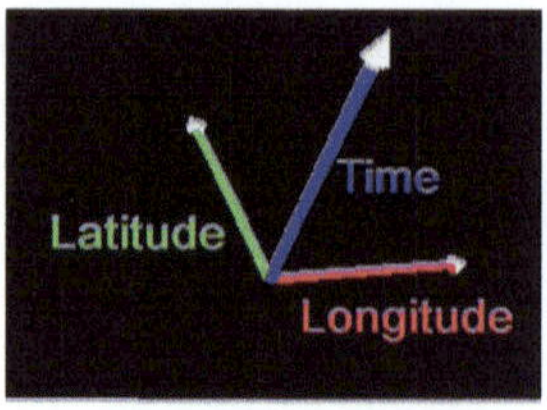

to answer. The user first selects which direction they want the voxels to be highlighted. Transitioning "to" shows the voxels whose next time-step transitions into the selected category. Transitioning "from" shows the voxels whose previous time-step was classified as the selected category. For example, Fig. 8.6 asks to "Show the voxels that transition to the Agriculture category at the next time-slice." Figure 8.7 illustrates the concept of the Transitioning tool.

Figure 8.7b shows the original voxel data with three data values. Figure 8.7a shows the "voxel transitioning to the blue value." As shown, the blue value is now highlighted as a translucent white and the last voxel that transitioned-to-the "blue value" is colored fully opaque. Alternatively, Fig. 8.8c displays "voxel transitioning from the blue value." The "blue value" is still a translucent white; however the first voxel that has transitioned-from-the selected value is colored fully opaque.

Applying this visualization technique across the entire volume essentially gives the effect of a 3D scatter plot. Viewing the highlighted voxels gives insight into the dataset, in particular to what the voxels are changing into.

8.2.6.5 Orienteer Tool

To orient the user as to where they are viewing the volume, an "XYZ" axis is drawn as an overlay to show from which angle the user is viewing the data. Figure 8.8 shows an example of the Orienteer. The blue axis represents time, whereas the green and red axes represent the 2D spatial coordinate system (usually latitude and longitude, respectively). The arrows of the orienteer point in the positive direction. For example, time increases in the direction of the blue arrow.

8.3 Test Setup

To show the usability of this project, two actual datasets from recent simulation studies were used. The first dataset was generated from Envision and focused on Skagit County in the state of Washington. The "Plan Trend" scenario was used, which simulates the current trends and activities within the region. The simulation begins in 2007 and continues through the year 2060. For the purpose of this study, visualization of the LULC_A attribute will be used. LULC stands for "Land use/Land Cover" and is used to classify sections of land into types. Major land types used in this study included Developed, Agriculture, and Forest, and Wetlands.

The second dataset was generated from a MC1 simulation and focused on the Apache-Sitgreaves National Forest in Arizona. The vegetation maps were generated by Dr. David Conklin for a project funded by the Western Wildland Environmental Threat Assessment Center, USDA Forest Service Joint Venture Agreements PNW 09-JV-11261900-003 (Conklin 2011). The data values represent the potential vegetation type produced by MC1 for cells on a 30 arc-second grid. This particular output came from a run for the years 2009–2100, using future climate data from the MIROC general circulation model under the A2 emissions scenario, as produced for the Fourth Assessment Report of the Intergovernmental Panel on Climate Change.

The difference between these two datasets allowed testing of the visualizer with two different levels of complexity. The Envision Skagit 2060 Project contained data with few (seven) categories and a relatively small amount of change between time-slices. The Apache-Sitgreaves Study had a total of 26 categories, all of which transition at a rate higher than the first dataset.

8.4 Results and Discussion

The following images were rendered on a Dell XPS L502x laptop with an Intel Core i7 2720QM @ 2.20 GHz, 8 GB of DDR3 memory, and an NVIDIA GeForce GT 540M graphics card. At a rendering resolution of 600 × 60 pixels, 400 volume slices displayed at a rate of 40 frames per second. With 1700 slices, the display rate was nine frames per second.

8.4.1 Skagit Study Area: LULC_A

Figure 8.9a shows the time-series data represented in a volume without any slicing or filtering. As shown, viewing the data in a volume is the 3D equivalent of the 2D images as previously available. Instead of viewing a single slice of time, there are three planes: X–Y plane, X–Z plane, and Y–Z plane, where X and Y represents the latitude and longitude respectively and the Z axis represents time. Therefore, images parallel to the X–Y plane show the original 2D images. The X–Z and Y–Z planes show the values of a particular point over time. These viewing planes

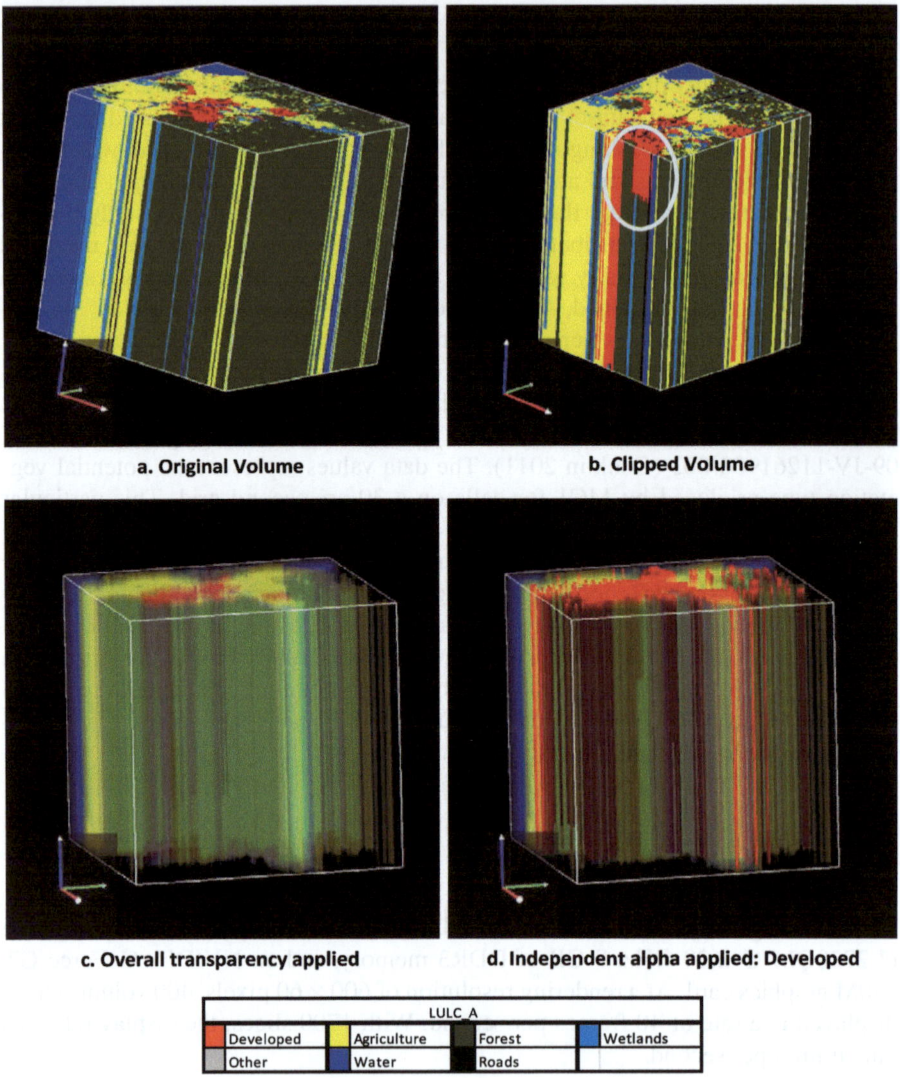

Fig. 8.9 Snapshots of the time-extruded volume. Source: Envision Skagit 2060 Project

made it possible to visualize any trends or patterns over time in the simulation. If a particular spatial location does not change over time, a column is extruded through the visualization.

By using clipping planes, the volume can be sliced to reveal new surfaces. Using the range sliders to manipulate the clipping planes achieves the effect of animating through various 2D slices as we have previously done. Traversing through the volume, we can look for slices that show trends in the data. For example, in Fig. 8.9b,

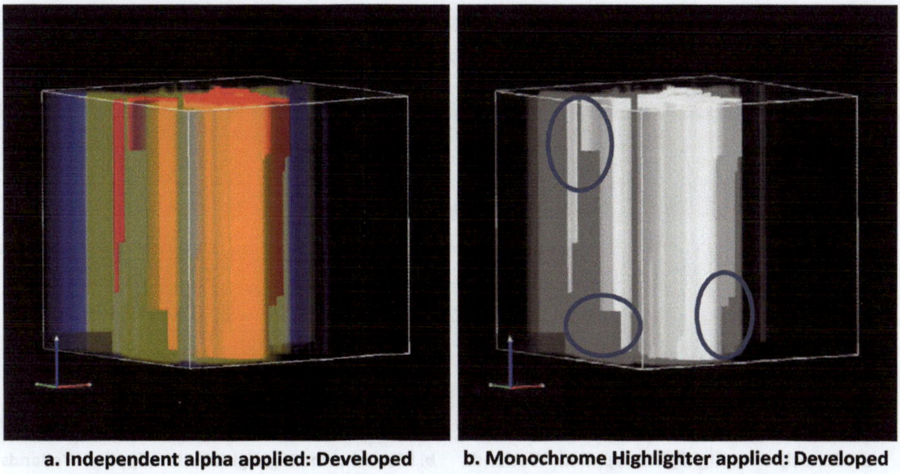

Fig. 8.10 Viewing the volume with interest of the Developed category. Source: Envision Skagit 2060 Project

it was easy to locate a fairly widespread creation of the Developed category towards the end of the simulation.

However, just this technique alone still lacks the ability to show what the previous frame looked like. Therefore, any trends or patterns perpendicular to the slicing planes are not easily recognized. In order to view inside the volume, the transparency of the volume was adjusted by using the Alpha Controls. Figure 8.9c shows a uniform transparency added to all categories in the volume. Since the volume is now translucent, the time-extruded columns are no longer two dimensional but appear to have depth.

Viewing into the volume gives the user a context of the data. This allows the entire set of three dimensional columns to be viewed and be able to spatially compare them with other columns within the volume. By increasing the opacity of the Developed land voxels as shown in Fig. 8.9d, the user had a better view of the extruded columns.

Figure 8.10 shows a transparent time-extruded volume with the Developed voxels rendered opaque. Figure 8.10b shows the volume with the Monochrome Highlighter Tool enabled. The circled areas of the screenshot highlight the areas where development has been introduced. The visualization shows that as time progresses large sections of the screen shot change to developed lands and stay developed for the duration of the study.

The highlighter function was then used to color the selected category to an opaque white. Figure 8.11a highlights the wetlands in a monochrome coloring scheme. As shown in this figure, the majority of the wetlands are maintained throughout the simulation, as the three dimensional columns stretch over the entire volume. Columns that terminate within the volume represent wetlands that have been converted into another land type. The two columns marked in the figure indicate that a wetland has been eliminated.

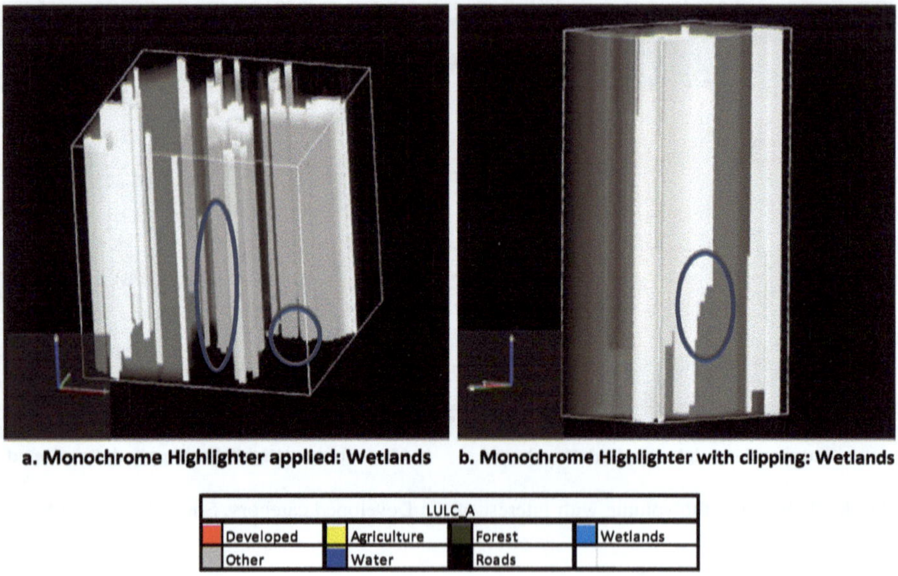

Fig. 8.11 Viewing the volume with interest of the Wetlands category. Source: Envision Skagit 2060 Project

Figure 8.11b shows the same volume, however from a different viewing angle and cropped to show the western region of the study. This view shows wetlands were created fairly early in the simulation as they did not exist at the bottom of the volume. These areas are highlighted with a circle. The visualization also shows that once created, the wetlands continued to exist to the end of the study. Additionally, as the simulation progressed, the volume of the columns grew, indicating a growing trend.

Figure 8.12 shows the Transitioning Tool in action. Specifically it shows the "from" transitioning of selected categories. These visualizations can be thought of as the loss of a particular category to the voxel shown. For example, the loss of Agriculture to wetlands or the loss of forest to developed land. This ability to show the loss of one category to another is important when attempting to find patterns and trends over an increased period of time.

Figure 8.12a shows all voxels that have previously transitioned from an Agriculture land type. With this tool, the user is quickly able to determine spatially where, at what time in the simulation, and to what type the Agriculture voxels transition to. With the transitioning tool enabled, we are able to see that Agriculture voxels had mostly transitioned into either Wetlands or Developed voxels.

Figure 8.12b shows voxels that have transitioned from Forest. In this example, we can see that the majority of transitioned Forest voxels have turned into the Developed type. The three circled areas represent short periods of time where the majority of the voxels transitioned.

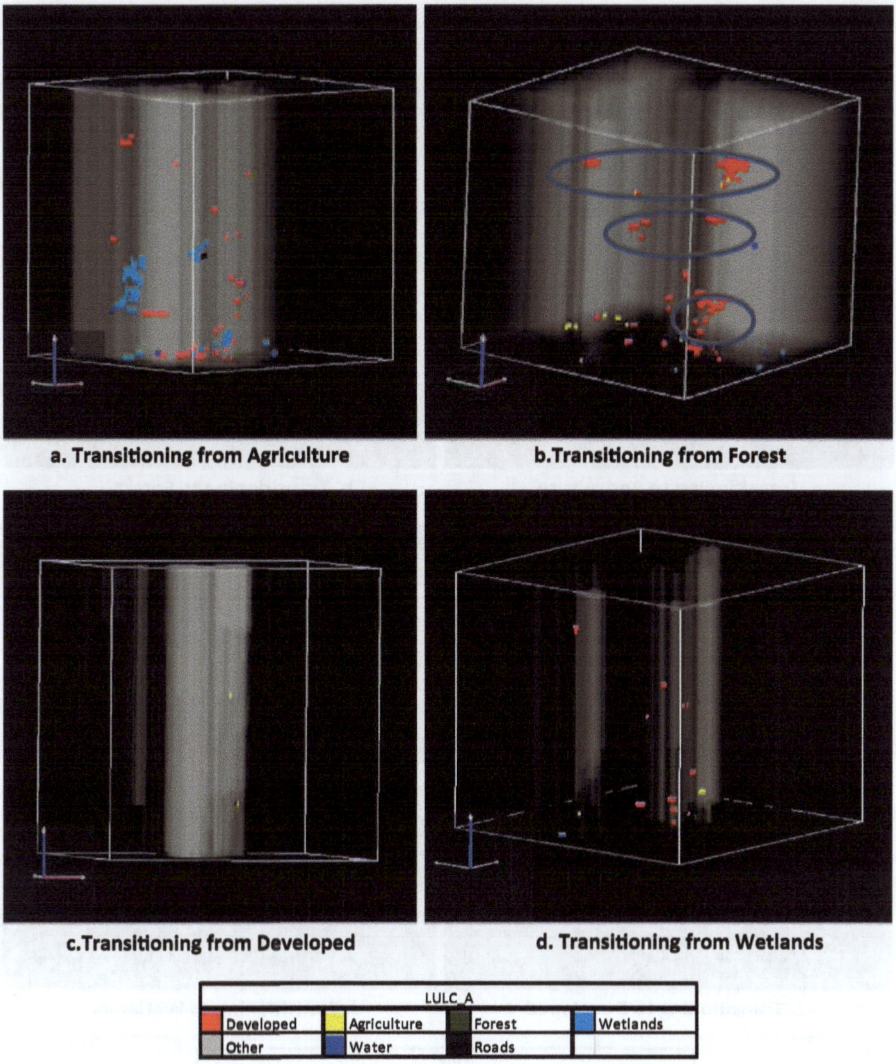

Fig. 8.12 Transitioning Tool applying "from" transitioning. The transparent white voxels represent the selected category. The opaque colored voxels represent voxels whose next time-step transitioned to the selected category. Source: Envision Skagit 2060 Project

Figure 8.12c is slightly different then 8.12a and 8.12b. When Fig. 8.12c is viewed with the Transitioning tool, the lack of colored voxels indicated that the selected data category rarely transitions. This distinguishes this screen shot from the others by its ability to either help validate the dataset or raise questions for concern. Figure 8.12c indicates that developed land rarely tends to transition. This sounds reasonable as it is expected that Developed regions will remain Developed. However, interestingly enough the few small voxels that made a transition changed from Developed land

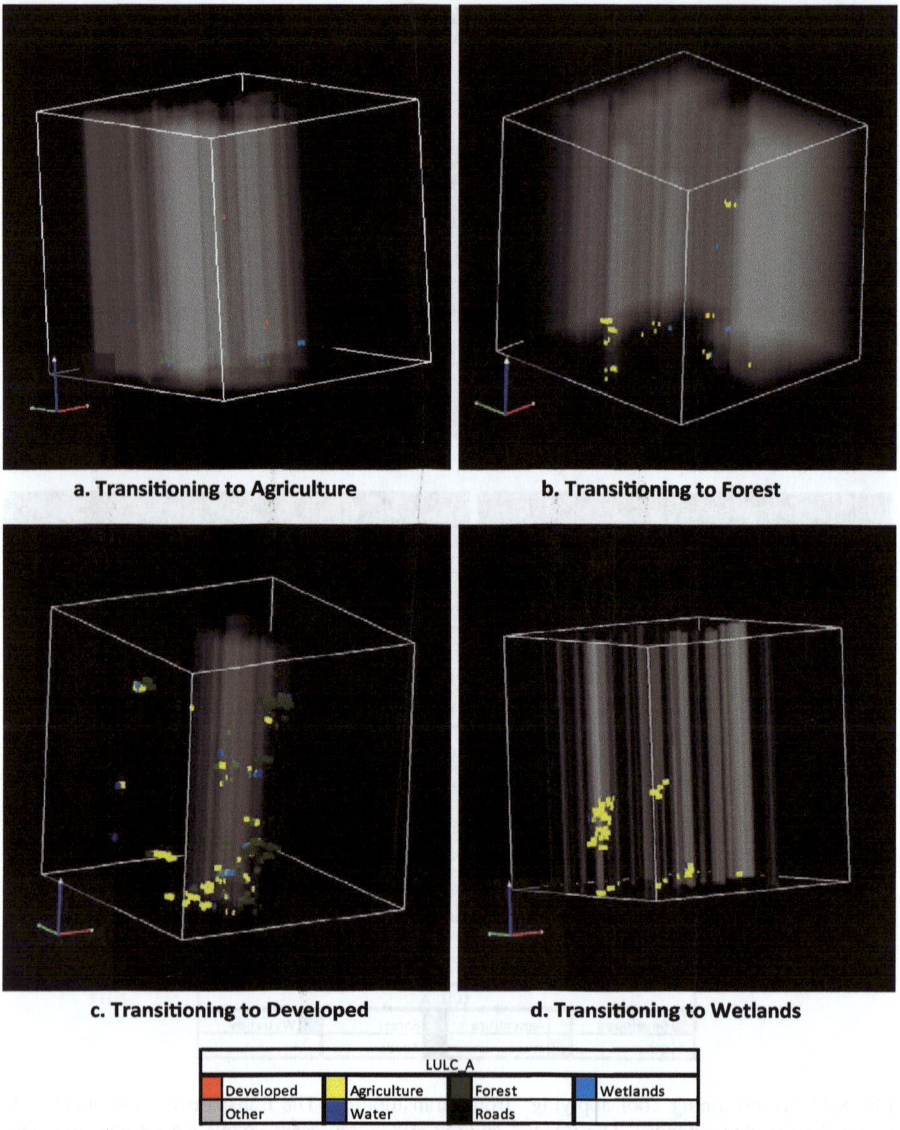

Fig. 8.13 Transitioning Tool applying "to" transitioning. The opaque colored voxels represent voxels whose previous time-step transitioned to the selected category. Source: Envision Skagit 2060 Project

to Agriculture. This could possibly represent an error in the data, as this transition contradicts current data, trends, and intuition.

Figure 8.12d shows voxels transitioning from Wetlands to different land categories. The primary transition is of Wetlands to Developed land. However, also shown in the visualization are a few areas of Wetland to Agriculture, Wetlands to Forest and one area of Wetlands to Water.

The next figure, Fig. 8.13, also displays the Transitioning Tool in action, however instead of representing the "from" transition, the "to" transition is shown. These visualizations can be thought of as the gain of the selected category, rather than the loss shown in the previous example (Fig. 8.12). For instance, the transition of Agriculture to Forest is shown as well as Wetlands to Developed land. Data displayed in this new visualization not only show the addition of types of land, but also give the viewer a clear representation of when the transition was made and where, a tool that was not previously available.

In Fig. 8.13a only a small amount of data is shown transitioning to agriculture. The few colored voxels that are represented are transitioning from forest to Agriculture and wetlands to Agriculture. Although on first glance there appears to be little information in this screen shot, the lack of information could raise concerns or questions as to why there appears to be a limited transition to agricultural land in the time period shown in this data set.

Figure 8.13b also contains only a selected amount of information. The few colored voxels shown made a transition from agricultural lands to Forest. Also noticeable is the lack of transition represented later in the simulation. Only a few voxels transition to forest from Agriculture, compared to many more in the beginning of the simulation.

Figure 8.13c is different from the previous two by containing more data. The transitions made were from agricultural lands to Developed as well as Forest land to Developed. Perhaps the most interesting aspect of this particular frame is the diversification over time. At the beginning of the visualization a mix of Agriculture and forest are shown transitioning to Developed lands, however towards the end of the simulation, the majority of land changing to Developed is Forest, not Agriculture.

The final Fig. 8.13d shows the transition of the voxels to Wetlands. As stated before, wetlands have been a particular focus in this study and are extremely important to show throughout the visualization. Figure 8.13d shows an almost exclusive transition from Agriculture to Wetlands. Although there are a few small areas with a transition from Forest to Agriculture, the major trend shown is a loss of Agriculture to Wetlands.

8.4.2 Apache-Sitgreaves National Forest Study Area: Vegetation Type

Figure 8.14a shows the time-series data represented in a volume without any slicing or filtering. The viewing angle in Fig. 8.14a shows that the majority of the vegetation ultimately transitioned to C4 Grassland. The second most prevalent vegetation type shown was temperate shrub land. At the bottom of the volume, the viewer sees a prevalent area of subalpine forest. Rotating the volume as shown in Fig. 8.14b

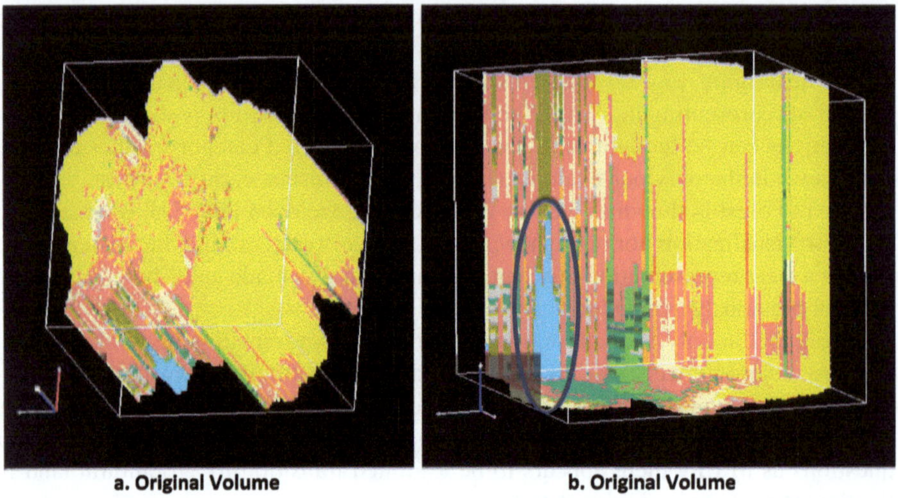

Fig. 8.14 Source: Dave Conklin

gives the viewer a new perspective of the entire duration of the simulation. The circled region in Fig. 8.14b visualized the eradication of the subalpine forest vegetation type. Figure 8.15 represents the volume with an overall transparency applied. Figure 8.15a shows a uniform transparency. On the right side of the simulation, a large region is shown to primarily contain one vegetation type. Although other vegetation types are visible in a few columns, C4 Grassland dominates the right side of the volume. Alternatively, the left side shows a diverse array of vegetation types. A large green region toward the bottom left is viewable and represents a patch of forest type. Additionally as time progresses, the forest type gradually disappears into what appears to be Coniferous Xeromorphic Woodland.

Figure 8.15b shows an independent alpha applied to the temperate needleleaf forest category, shading it opaque. Decreasing the transparency of the selected category gives the viewer a clear view of one particular vegetation type. In this example, the Temperate Needleleaf Forest type has been chosen, and presents a new perspective on the same data viewed not only in Fig. 8.15a, but Figs. 8.14a and 8.14b as well. In Fig. 8.15a, the right side of the volume appears to be dominated by C4 Grassland. However, when the Temperate Needleleaf Forest type is made opaque, the visualization changes and the C4 Grassland vegetation type is not viewed as a continuous block, as much of the area also contains Temperate Needleleaf Forest. This ability to highlight one vegetation type is important because it allows the viewer to see the same material from a variety of viewpoints.

Additionally, a portion of Fig. 8.15b is highlighted by a circle in the bottom right. This circle shows an intriguing aspect of the simulation where the temperate needleleaf forest vegetation type exists for several years and then completely disappears only to reappear and continue for the rest of the simulation. This sudden fluctuation is interesting and could contain important information about the changes taking place during that time period.

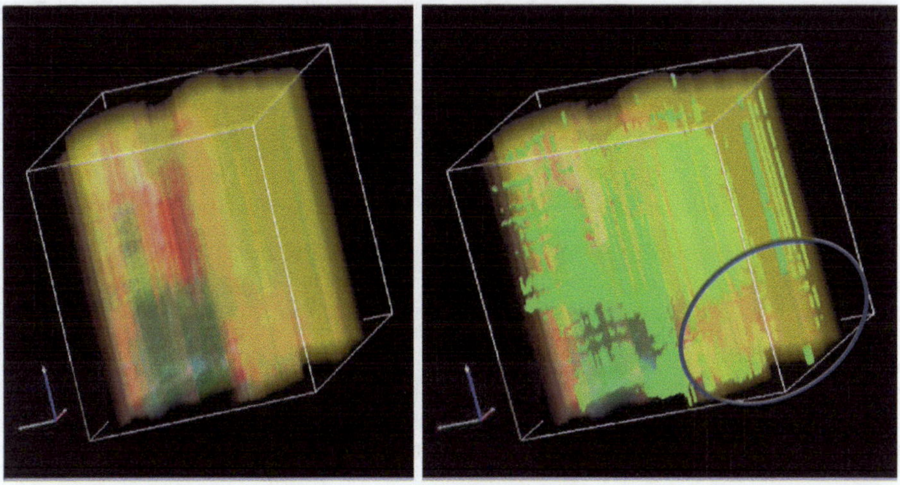

a. Overall transparency applied

b. Independent Alpha applied: Temperate Needleaf Forest

Vegetation Type			
ice aka barren	temperate warm mixed forest	temperate desert	coniferous xeromorphic woodland
tundra aka alpine	temperate needleleaf woodland	subtropical needleleaf forest	
subalpine forest	temperate deciduous broadleaf woodland	subtropical shrubland	subalpine meadow
maritime needleleaf forest	temperate cool mixed woodland	C4 grassland	water
temperate needleleaf forest	temperate warm mixed woodland	subtropical	natural barren
temperate deciduous broadleaf forest	temperate shrubland	tropical	developed
temperate cool mixed forest	C3 grassland	cool needleleaf forest	

Fig. 8.15 Source: Dave Conklin

Figures 8.16's and 8.17's focus is primarily on the vegetation type C4 Grassland, an attribute considered important by the study group. Figure 8.16 is similar to Fig. 8.14 in that it highlights a specific vegetation type and creates an opaque shading. Figure 8.16a applies an independent Alpha to C4 Grassland presented to the viewer in bright yellow. As seen in Fig. 8.16, C4 Grassland is prevalent throughout the volume; however with the application of an opaque shading to the vegetation type, C4 is shown as even more of a dominant vegetation type, especially towards the end of the study.

In Fig. 8.16b a monochrome highlighter was applied. This eliminates all color blending of the visualization making the selected attribute more pronounced. Additionally, a section at the bottom left is highlighted with a circle. A region of C4 Grassland appears and begins the growing trend of an increased amount of C4 Grassland vegetation.

Figure 8.17 is similar to Figs. 8.12 and 8.13 where a transition "to" and "from" a certain land or vegetation type is shown. In this visualization C3 Grassland and temperate shrubland made a transition to C4 Grassland. However, this figure shows

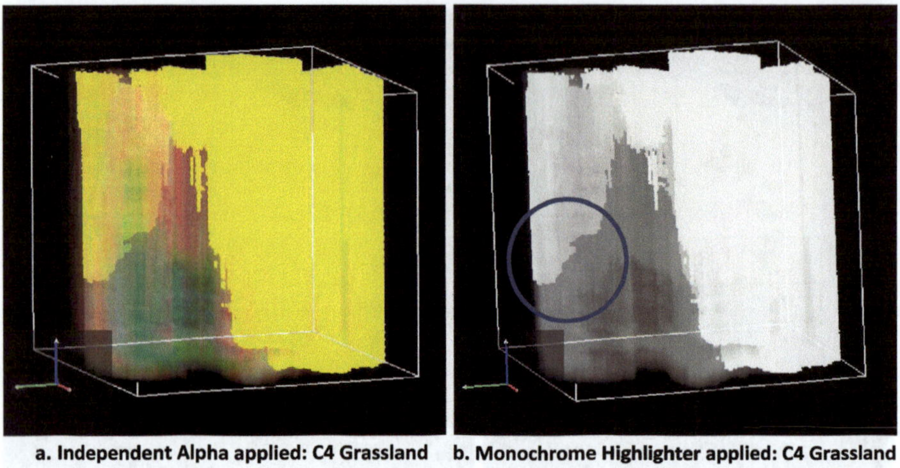

Fig. 8.16 Time-extruded volumes with C4 Grassland as the focus. Source: Dave Conklin

that the frequency of transitions is much higher in this data set than as shown in Fig. 8.13. With a high rate of transitions to C4 Grassland, the visualization appears as a 3D scatter plot showing the voxels that have transitions to C4 Grassland. In Fig. 8.17a, a circled section of C4 Grassland appeared abruptly and starts the trend of C4 Grassland prevalence. This new volume in Fig. 8.17b shows that C4 Grassland was not making a transition from multiple vegetation types, but was transitioning only from C3 Grassland in that area.

Figure 8.18a shows the voxels transitioning to the Coniferous Xeromorphic Woodland category from temperate shrubland as well as Temperate Needleleaf Woodland. Although the transition to Coniferous Xeromorphic Woodland is shown throughout the data set the majority of the transitions take place towards the end of the simulation.

Figure 8.18b shows the voxels transitioning from the Coniferous Xeromorphic Woodland to Temperate Needleleaf Woodland and C4 Grassland, as well as Temperate Shrubland. The transitions happen at different points in the data set. At the beginning of the simulation, the majority of transitions from Coniferous Xeromorphic Woodland is to Temperate Shrubland, however later in the visualization it appears to be transforming to C4 Grassland and Temperate Shrubland.

Figure 8.19a represents the voxels transitioning to C3 Grassland from Temperate Shrubland and Temperate Needleleaf Woodland. The data appears to show that roughly ever y five years the C3 Grassland transitions into Temperate Shrubland and then transitions back to C3 Grassland. This episodic feature lasts throughout the entire simulation as seen by the horizontal grouping of voxels along the same time plane.

Figure 8.19b shows the voxels transitioning from C3 Grassland. The data shows that the transition is primarily taking place from temperate scrubland and C4 Grassland. This volume reemphasizes the episodic nature of the C3 Grassland transitioning in and out with temperate shrubland. When compared, Figs. 8.19a and 8.19b

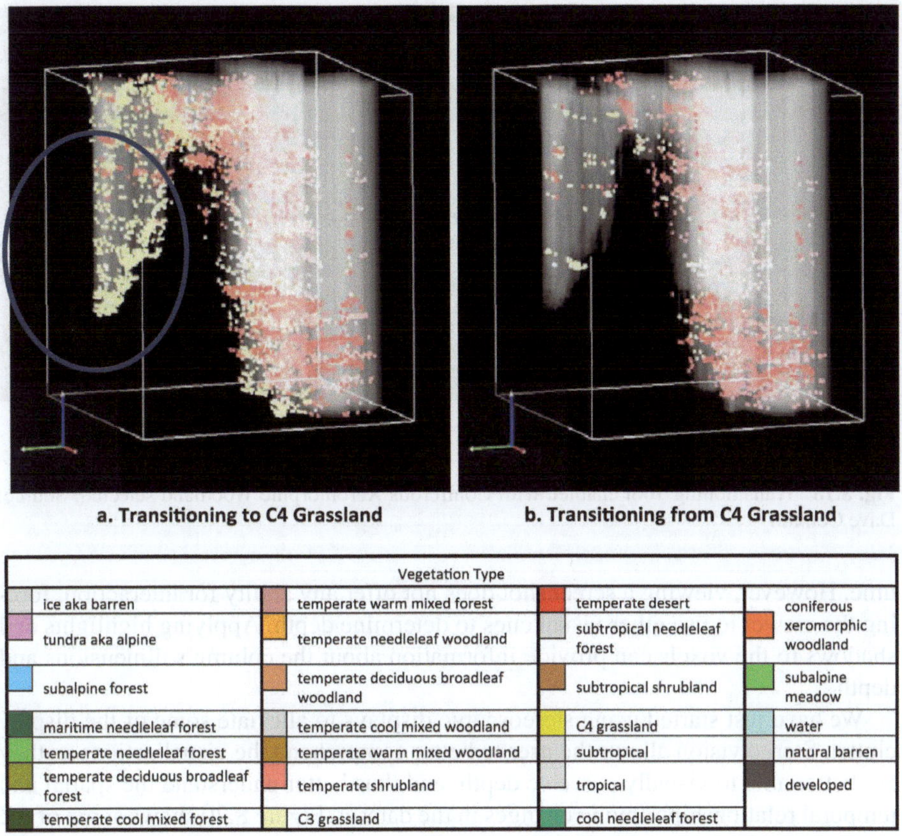

Fig. 8.17 Transitioning Tool enabled with C4 Grassland selected. Source: Dave Conklin

show that more C3 Grassland is transitioning to C4 Grassland than C4 Grassland to C3 Grassland. This occurrence demonstrates that once the transition to C4 Grassland is made, the transition is more likely to be permanent.

8.5 Future Work

For this project, the major type of data was Categorical. Thus, the tools created were oriented more towards Categorical data and less towards Continuous data. Tools such as the Highlighter and Transitioning Tools have yet to be implemented for continuous data. Completing these tools will require further research on setting threshold values, as well as implementing a user interface. In the meantime, Continuous data can be converted into Categorical data by utilizing multiple RangedBins.

When viewers are able to freely rotate the volume, giving them a sense of depth, they can then determine where various columns/voxels are located within the vol-

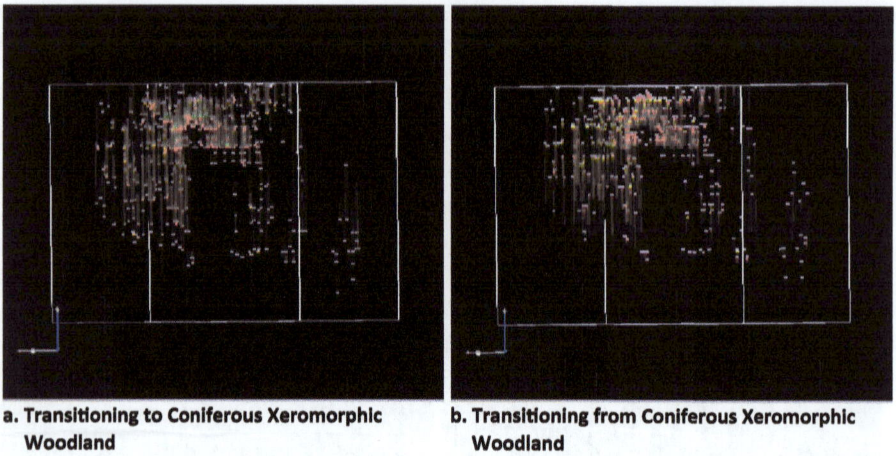

Fig. 8.18 Transitioning Tool enabled with Coniferous Xeromorphic Woodland selected. Source: Dave Conklin

ume. However, viewing a screenshot does not offer any ability for interaction, forcing the viewer to use other visual cues to determine depth. Applying highlights and shadows to the voxels can provide information about the column's dimensions and depth.

We have just started using stereoscopic displays to alleviate some of the display clutter. Stereo vision allows the user to better comprehend the visualizations as they are better able to visually perceive depth, and thus better understand the spatial and temporal relationships among changes in the dataset. Figure 8.20 shows some of the preliminary results.

For continuous data, the gradient computed at a specific voxel can be used as the normal vector for a light shading algorithm. However, deriving a gradient from Categorical Data does not result in a useful normal vector—an alternative method of deriving the normal vectors will need to be developed. One approach would be to create isosurfaces from the volume data and extract the normal vectors from the generated triangular geometry. This visual cue might give the viewer a better sense of depth of the highlighted regions. Therefore, the user would have a better estimation of the location of the columns within the volume and a better understanding of a screenshot.

8.6 Conclusion

This work presented a technique for visualizing time-series data through the process of time-extrusion. With this technique, the visualization of time-series datasets is given to users in a unique perspective that allows for the identification of patterns and trends over time. However, this technique is dependent on the accompanying tools such as the Transitioning Tool and Highlighting tool. Empowering users with

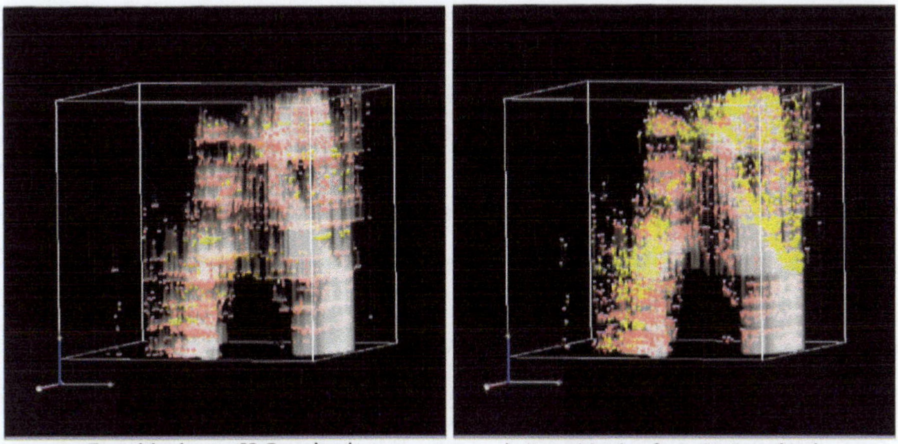

Vegetation Type			
ice aka barren	temperate warm mixed forest	temperate desert	coniferous xeromorphic woodland
tundra aka alpine	temperate needleleaf woodland	subtropical needleleaf forest	
subalpine forest	temperate deciduous broadleaf woodland	subtropical shrubland	subalpine meadow
maritime needleleaf forest	temperate cool mixed woodland	C4 grassland	water
temperate needleleaf forest	temperate warm mixed woodland	subtropical	natural barren
temperate deciduous broadleaf forest	temperate shrubland	tropical	developed
temperate cool mixed forest	C3 grassland	cool needleleaf forest	

Fig. 8.19 Transitioning Tool enabled with C3 Grasslands selected. Source: Dave Conklin

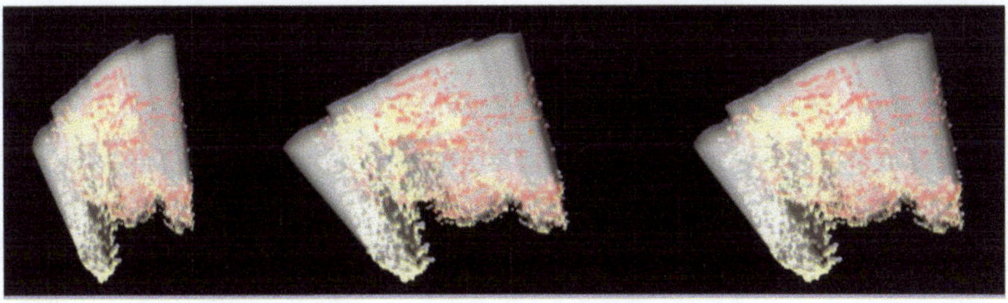

Fig. 8.20 Stereo views. If you can free (i.e., parallel) view, look at the left two images. If you are better at crossing your eyes, look at the right two

these tools gives them the ability to explore their data in a way not available before. Continuation in the direction of improving the screenshot aspect of this work should be considered, as providing intuitive visualizations without depth is difficult.

References

Bolte, J. P., et al. (2007). Modeling biocomplexity—actors, landscapes and alternative futures. *Environmental Modelling & Software*, *22*(5), 570–579.

Conklin, D. (2011). Personal communication (Dataset). Corvallis: Conservation Biology Institute.

FreeImage Open Source Image Library 3.15.0 (2011). Software library. The FreeImage project. http://freeimage.sourceforge.net/.

GDAL—Geospatial Data Abstraction Library 1.8.0 (2011). Software library. Open source geospatial foundation. http://www.gdal.org/.

Envision Skagit 2060 (2011). Department of Biological & Ecological Engineering, Oregon State University (Online). Cited: May 11, 2011. http://envision.bioe.orst.edu/StudyAreas/Skagit/Skagit.html.

Riccio, C. (2011). OpenGL Mathematics 0.9.1.0. Software library. G-Truc Creation. http://glm.g-truc.net/.

Chapter 9
Event Structuring as a General Approach to Building Knowledge in Time-Based Collections

William Ribarsky, Zachary Wartell, and Wenwen Dou

Abstract Many kinds of data collections are time-based or can be collected in a temporal manner. There has been a desire in the geography and geospatial communities to put temporal behavior on the same footing as spatial structure and to develop a comprehensive geo-temporal information system. In many cases, temporal information refers to sequences of happenings in the world. To efficiently represent such temporal information, we present event structuring as a general approach to build knowledge in time-based collections. In this case, an event is defined as a meaningful occurrence that has substantial impact on subsequent developments. A properly organized event sequence forms a narrative, or story. Such stories are powerful mechanisms for human understanding; not only are they in a form that make them easier to recall, but they also lead to mental models that can be intuited, examined, and joined together into larger models. In this paper, the proposed event structuring methods are not limited to geospatial data, but apply to any type of time-based collection such as text corpora. We first provide the definition of event structuring, and then describe detailed examples of event structures built upon different kinds of data. Last, we raise the need for an event descriptive language in order to generate, organize, and compare event structures.

9.1 Introduction

There are many kinds of data collections that are time-based. These include many types of physical data, either from simulations or observations, text collections with temporal information embedded, and multimedia collections with time stamps, embedded temporal information, or references to events in times. In many cases, this temporal information refers to happenings in the world, whether real, simulated, or imagined. An example of physical data is the result from simulating a hurricane, where a storm surge forms that, depending on the direction and wind fields of the hurricane, is followed by inundation of barrier islands and coastal areas, after which

W. Ribarsky (✉) · Z. Wartell · W. Dou
The University of North Carolina at Charlotte, Charlotte, USA
e-mail: ribarsky@uncc.edu

J. Dill et al. (eds.), *Expanding the Frontiers of Visual Analytics and Visualization*,
DOI 10.1007/978-1-4471-2804-5_9,

there is flooding, rain squalls, and damaging winds. This sequence of events forms a narrative, or story, of the hurricane. An example of a text collection is a set of histories and/or reports. Embedded in the text are dates, names, places, and occurrences that can be organized as events in time. For a particular geographical region, there could be social, political, military, weather, and other events that when brought together in an overall organization would reveal relationships among the events and thus among the histories. An example of a multimedia collection is online news pages aggregated over time. When properly organized along the time dimension, the stories extracted from these pages can be aggregated into topic clusters, which typically show a burst of related stories after a motivating event (e.g., the tsunami in Japan) (Luo et al. 2010). For a large event there is an ebb and flow of related stories and many sub-topic clusters.

Central to all these types of data is the idea of an event, which we define here as a meaningful occurrence in time. In this paper, we demonstrate that an event is a powerful organizing concept, giving meaning and structure to temporal information. When properly organized, a sequence of events with associated topics could indicate a cause and effect relationship and a sequence with similar topics would indicate a trend. A hierarchical event structure could emerge with larger events encompassing distributions of smaller events. Additional meanings would emerge from the event sequencing and structuring itself. A properly organized sequence would tell a story, as in the hurricane example above. These stories are powerful mechanisms for human understanding; not only are they in a form that make them easier to recall, but they lead to mental models that can be intuited, examined, and joined together into larger models.

To the extent that a data collection refers to happenings in the world, there is often a geographical reference. A GIS can be used to organize and make queries of the geographical references, but there is then the question of how to include the time structure. Time is a dimension, like the three spatial dimensions, and this fact can be used to provide a similar organization as in the 3D GIS. But time is also different, as will be discussed further below. Events, here with the expanded definition of meaningful occurrences in time and space, provide the additional organization that will lead to a full 4D GIS.

9.2 Defining Events, Creating Event Structures, Organizing the Time Dimension

To organize the time dimension in a way similar to the spatial dimensions, we employ the events defined above. Since the unstructured time dimension is unbounded, the events provide a scale. Time units can be centuries, decades, years, months, days, hours, seconds, and nanoseconds. Seasonal weather events have a scale of hours to days whereas climate events have a scale of decades to centuries. The scale is determined by the event category.

The idea of a motivating event provides further structuring. The motivating event for the Japanese tsunami and nuclear meltdown was the tsunami itself. The motivating event for the Israeli incursion into Lebanon in 2006 was the firing of rockets at Israeli border towns by Hezbollah. All sorts of sub-events, reactions, and responses flowed from this motivating event. In cases such as the latter case, there may be some dispute about the motivating event and when it occurred. However, topic-temporal analysis and/or spatial temporal analysis will find the strongest clusters of events and their associated motivating event(s). We have shown this to be the case for broadcast news story analysis (Luo et al. 2006, 2010). Since, for example, visual analysis tools that use this structure are exploratory, one does not expect to be given the single right description of a story but rather the main thread and associated relevant information from which one can make his own interpretation. There are other examples demonstrating that these event structures can generally be generated automatically or semi-automatically. For example, we have shown that storm surge, hurricane wind field, and atmospheric events associated with air quality can be generated by identifying and tracking 2D and 3D features of interest in simulations or observational data (Yu et al. 2010). Events associated with the development of new research themes and ideas can be identified in large collections of proposals or research papers using a combination of temporal and topic modeling (Dou et al. 2011), though in this case information from outside the collections must be used to describe the events in detail (e.g., information about when a new NSF program was launched that led to the development of the new ideas).

The motivating events provide a hierarchical structure. A main motivating event can encompass subordinate motivating events. (In the case of the tsunami, these subordinate events would be the breakdown of cooling systems that led to successive core meltdowns, evacuations, emergency maintenance, and so on.) In addition, we use the fact that all these time structures have a beginning and an end. To this we apply a "narrative imperative", where we assume a story is told between the beginning and the end. As much as possible, we apply a shaping based on the event clustering (including spatial-temporal and topical modeling) and make an interpretation that brings out the story, since this will provide the most meaningful structure in time. We have found that this hierarchical structuring and narrative shape emerge in a variety of different types of temporal data; we posit that this is a general phenomenon. However, the best, most meaningful structuring cannot be done entirely automatically, though our experience is that much of it can be. Here the user's knowledge and reasoning can be inserted. One goal of a visual analytics interface would be to guide the user to do this at just the right point in the time structure. Because of the hierarchical structure, this can be done quickly at higher levels.

9.3 Events in Space: 4D GIS

Since Einstein, it has been realized that time stands on an equal footing with the spatial dimensions in the physical world. Although this equivalence is apparent at, say, the scale of the universe, time takes on a different character than the other dimensions at our earth-centered scale. Most significantly, time is unbounded at this scale whereas the other 3 dimensions are bounded. (The spatial dimensions are also unbounded at the scale of the expanding universe, but this is not the relevant scale for an earth-centered focus.) Thus, the spatial dimensions latitude, longitude, and altitude are bound to the surface of the earth (and thin shells above and below the surface) since that is where almost all earth-focused detail lies. (The thin shell above the earth's surface extends, say, through the stratosphere, and that below the earth's surface to the deepest mines.) But unlike the spatial dimensions, time keeps unspooling, starting with the primordial earth and unfolding inexorably as the present becomes the past. One thing is for sure; each passing instant adds to the time dimension.

This temporal behavior has the effect of endless "stacking up" of occurrences over spatial regions. In fact, the GeoTime papers take advantage of this metaphor to provide a rich visualization of events over geography.

9.4 Events in a Narrative Structure

According to a report published by the International Data Corporation, information that was either created or replicated in digital form in 2007 alone was 281 exabytes, and the projected compound annual growth rate between 2008 and 2011 was almost 60 %. Without a doubt, such information contains valuable knowledge regarding every aspect of our lives, such as history, social behavior, new scientific inventions, etc. However, given the overwhelming amount of information, it is nearly impossible to manually sanitize, extract meaningful events, organize, and analyze these digital collections. Although organizing such information based on content or meaning is important, creating event structures along time allows us to discover the historic evolution of the events, themes, and even ideas. One can construct narratives and stories that effectively summarize and make coherent large amount of information. Lawrence Stone (1979) defines narrative as: "the organization of material in a chronologically sequential order and the focusing of the content into a single coherent story, albeit with subplots. Narratives are analytic constructs that unify a number of past of contemporaneous actions and happenings, which might otherwise have been viewed as discrete or disparate, into a coherent relational whole that gives meaning to and explains each of its elements and is, at the same time, constituted by them (McCullagh 1978). Narrative permits a form of sequential causation that allows for twisting, varied, and heterogeneous time paths to a particular outcome" (Griffin 1993). Our process of event structuring is similar to narrative in that it's not just temporally aligned incidents; it is centered on events that signal the beginning of multiple thematically related incidents. And the structure of the events makes the connections and relationships between incidents easily inferable. Organizing unstructured information into an event structure allows one to grasp the gist of massive amount of information. For example, an event structure constructed based on everyday news could clearly represent what is/was happening and how each event progresses throughout time. An event structure built upon social media such as tweets could provide an up-to-the-minute of what everyone is talking about around us and across the globe. However, with 140 million new tweets per day, constructing an efficient analysis has become a highly challenging problem.

9.4.1 Human-Computer Generated Linear Narrative

Ideally, the event-based narrative structures should be general enough so that their general aspects can be widely applied to different kinds of data sources, be it GIS or non-geospatial data. In addition, the narrative should be human-computer generated, since without automation it will not be scalable and without human input it will not be fully meaningful.

For a human-computer generated narrative, we have the following goals.

1. Create an interactive analysis program, *ING* ("InteractiveNarrativeGenerator") such that a human user, *P* ("Person"), using program *ING* can interactively compute a digital narrative, N, from an arbitrary dataset D.
2. Create a program, *NC* ("NarrativeComparator"), that can autonomously compare and cluster large sets of these digital narratives generated via interactive computation using the *ING* tool.

Below we give our operational definition of narrative and show how our goals above have a perhaps not entirely superficial similarity to several fundamental theorems in computer science.

A digital narrative is a narrative encoded in digital media (whether it is encoded as data or a program is an independent issue). A human generated digital narrative is a narrative generated by a person, but without using a software tool that explicitly aims to semi-automate the creation of the final narrative structure. (So a narrative created by a person using a word processor, or electronic search and analysis tool such as Matlab, is still called a human generated narrative.) In contrast, a human-computer generated narrative is a digital narrative generated by a software tool that explicitly extracts events in and/or helps the user interactively structure the digital narrative. Referring to our above, we desire to make an InteractiveNarrative-Generator program that helps people generate human-computed generated narratives for arbitrary digital datasets.

At present, we limit ourselves to human-computer generated linear narratives rather than branching or recursive narratives. We briefly discuss some intuitive reasons here. Following Occam's Razor, one should generate the simplest narrative which explains the temporal dataset unless one can trade simplicity for greater explanatory power. We further take the following stance. When comparing two otherwise similar narratives of roughly the same length, a person will generally find linear narratives easier to understand than branching narratives or recursive narratives. This is consistent with the observation that introductory computer science students are typically introduced to imperative programming constructs starting with sequential statements, then branching, then loops and finally recursion. A major caveat is that narrative length is important as well. One can imagine two narratives (which happen to be proper algorithms) that have equivalent interpretations, but where the first one is linear and 100 sentences long and the second one is iterative using a loop construct and only 3 sentences long. The former would be easier to understand for a person with imperative programming knowledge. However, we contend that generating a short linear narrative whose sentences use a high-level of abstraction is more desirable than generating a more precise (i.e. using less abstraction) branching or recursive narrative.

9.5 Events in Non-geographic Information Spaces

There is much time-dependent information that is not spatial or not strongly spatial (e.g., text or multimedia collections). The event structuring described above can be pulled out from the spatial dimensions and used alone for these types of data. It appears that the ideas developed for geographic time will apply as well to these time-dependent information spaces.

Take document collections as an example: similar to the 4D GIS, document collections contain bounded dimensions plus the unbounded time dimension. The words, for example, are bounded by a finite vocabulary (though it may slowly grow over time), and the organization of the words is bounded by a set of explicit rules—grammar. Eventually copying all documents, from the beginning of writing on paper, to digital space from a paper-centric should bring tremendous benefits. However, the growth of digital information is exponential, as described above.

Visual Representation and Analysis of Temporal Structures. Certain types of visualizations, such as ThemeRiver (Havre et al. 2000), are particularly appropriate for representing temporal information. ThemeRiver is initially designed to visualize thematic variations over time within a large collection of documents (Havre et al. 2000). ThemeRiver provides a macro-view of thematic changes in a corpus of documents over a serial dimension. It is designed to facilitate the identification of trends, patterns, and unexpected occurrence or non-occurrence of themes or topics. Figure 9.1 shows an instance of ThemeRiver constructed based on microblogs. Although the x-axis displays time in a linear manner, according to studies on perception (Kohler 1947), attention is usually drawn to the sudden increase and decrease of "currents" within the river. Therefore, significant patterns such as "bursty themes" are easily discovered by users through exploring the ThemeRiver.

Let's take a look at a concrete example of how ThemeRiver can facilitate identifying the beginning of an epidemic spread. The data are provided by the VAST challenge 2011 committee. The goal of the VAST challenge is to push the forefront of visual analytics tools using benchmark data sets and establishing a forum to advance visual analytics evaluation methods (IEEE VAST Challenge 2011). One of the tasks in the 2011 challenge is to characterize an epidemic spread in a metropolitan

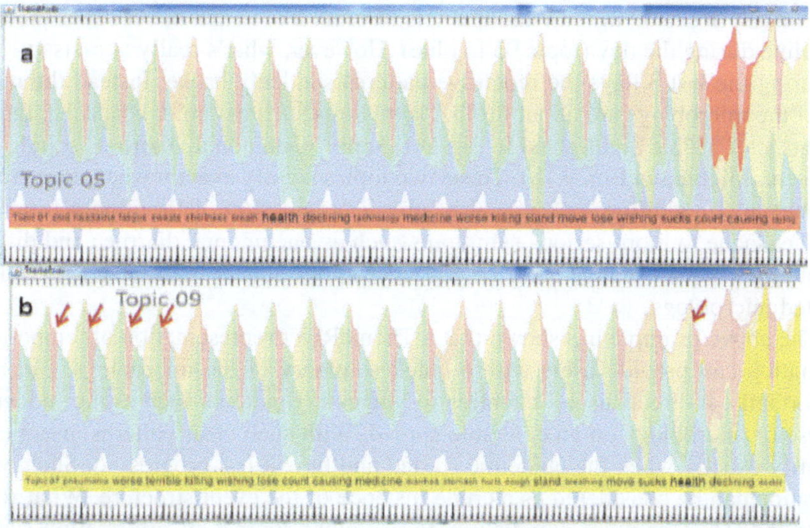

Fig. 9.1 Two salient topical trends in the ThemeRiver regarding the epidemic spread. (**a**) Microblogs about flu-like symptoms such as "cold, sweats, headache". (**b**) More severe symptoms such as "pneumonia, diarrhea" started appearing

area. One of the datasets for this task is the microblog messages collected from users in that region. The question is when and where the outbreak started and whether it is contained. With more than 1 million microblog messages in the data set, it is impossible to manually sift through all the messages, not to mention that lots of noise (random microblogs) exists in the data. An event structure constructed based on the microblogs can provide both a summary of all messages and insights regarding specific events such as the epidemic spread that the city officials worry about.

In order to construct the temporal event structure, we first processed all microblogs and extracted 10 thematically meaningful topics using Latent Dirichlet Allocation (LDA). LDA is a generative model that represents the content of words and documents with probabilistic topics (Blei et al. 2003). The LDA has several advantages comparing to the previous vector space models (VSM) widely used for text analysis, one of which is that each topic now is individually interpretable, providing a probability distribution over words that picks out a coherent cluster of correlated terms (Blei et al. 2010). Among the 10 extracted topics, two of them (Fig. 9.1) are highly relevant to illness, in particular flu-like symptoms. Having the topical summary of all microblog messages, we further visualize the topical trend in ThemeRiver to reveal temporal patterns and events. In Fig. 9.2, each "current" represents a topic with the color schema connecting the topical trend and the actual content of the topic. The x-axis is time, with each interval denoting 4 hours in a day. In this case, we are portraying the topical trends of the microblog data between April 29th and May 19th.

Given the ThemeRiver view, one can easily discover that there are repetitive patterns among several topics, such as users blogging about TV shows and commercials every night (topic 09 in red), and that lots of users like to talk about songs they love any time during the day (topic 05 in blue). However, what's really attracts attention is during the last 3 days the repetitive patterns suddenly broke. Instead the majority of the microblogs are about flu-like symptoms such as "cold, headache, fatigue, sweats, etc." (topic highlighted in Fig. 9.1a) and "pneumonia, diarrhea, cough, etc." (topic highlighted in Fig. 9.1b). These two topics signify exactly when the outbreak has begun. In addition, one can also infer a progression of the illness from cold and headache to more serious symptoms such as pneumonia, diarrhea and difficult breathing since all orange topic related microblogs appear before the yellow topic related microblogs.

The above example has shown that a ThemeRiver representation of temporal information can provide users with a quick summary of the microblogs. But more importantly, it directs users' attention to interesting patterns such as the sudden increase of microblogs on an epidemic spread. With such clear patterns, users could identify exactly when the epidemic started and how it has progressed. Such representation can be considered as a crude instance of the event structure. What would make the structure more complete is to use other sources of information such as news to label the ThemeRiver with motivating events, so that users could infer causal relationship between the news and people's reaction reflected in their microblogs. A powerful further advance would be to arrange the motivating events and important sub-events into a linear narrative, using the ideas described above. The whole arc of the epidemic could then be described in a coherent fashion. These considerations apply to all event-based temporal analyses.

Another data set provided by the 2011 VAST challenge committee is a text corpus containing new reports. If the ThemeRiver is properly labeled with relevant news information, the origin of the epidemic could be accurately discovered. We also applied the same topic modeling method to the news corpus and then filtered based on region and time to look for local news that might be related to the outbreak. Through our analysis, the most relevant incident we have found took place on May 17th, 2011, a news report of a truck accident on the interstate 610 bridge in the evening. The bridge leads over the main river in the metropolitan area and, as a result of the accident, the truck's cargo, probably containing some sort of chemicals, was spilled into the river. Tracing a few days back, on May 15th, a dangerous suspect who is member of the terrorist group "Paramurderers of Chaos" was arrested for trespassing near the loading docks at a food preparation plant in southwest part of the metropolitan area. Following this lead, we further discovered from the news data that the terrorist group had been planning a bioterrorism attack on the metropolitan area, which includes robbing equipment from a local university to manufacture dangerous microbes. As shown in Fig. 9.2, with proper news events labeled on the microblogs data, one can infer causal relationship between an event and reactions to the event and begin to make an overall narrative.

Through combining different sources of information to augment each other, one can construct an effective event structure, which not only summarizes "what happened" but also allows inference of causal relationship between an event and subsequent outcomes. Above we used news reports to label information gathered from

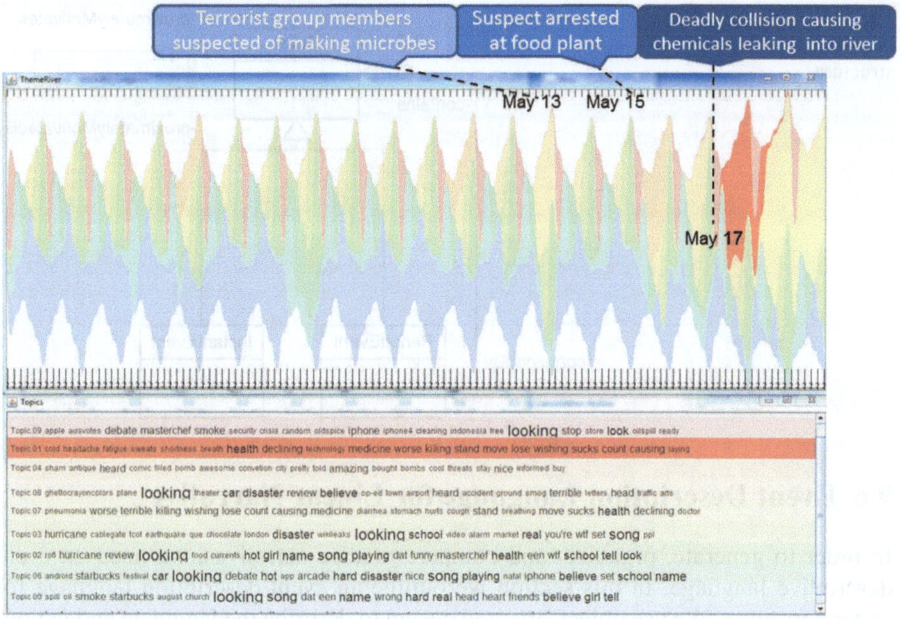

Fig. 9.2 The microblog topical trends labeled with news information. On May 17th, right after a deadly collision involving a food truck that leaked chemicals into the major river in the city, people start showing flu-like symptoms. Following this lead, one can discover from the news that members of a terrorist group were manufacturing dangerous microbes and poisoned a local food plant. Through combing the microblogs with the news information, not only one can discover "what happened" with respect to the epidemic spread, but also what caused it

social media (how people react to certain news reports). Such structure could allow one to immediately identify what have caused the reaction and infer why people have reacted in a certain way. Similar ideas could be applied to the field of scientific research. For example, when visualizing the topical trends of scientific publications, other sources of information such as grant awards could be used to label the trends. Therefore one can infer the impact of the grant award on the evolution of scientific fields. The temporal scale of such analysis might be significantly different from analyzing a news corpus, which is more instantaneous, causing immediate splash in social media. The lag between the time one scientific proposal has been awarded and the time that similar topics are seen in the form of publications could be more than a full year. Therefore, when constructing event structures, proper time scale should be carefully chosen. But, as we have noted above, this scale can be found from analysis of event patterns for a given category of events. In the case of scientific themes, for example, application of topic modeling to proposal and scientific paper collections would, upon analysis, reveal the spacing between an idea introduced in a proposal and subsequent development of that idea in papers.

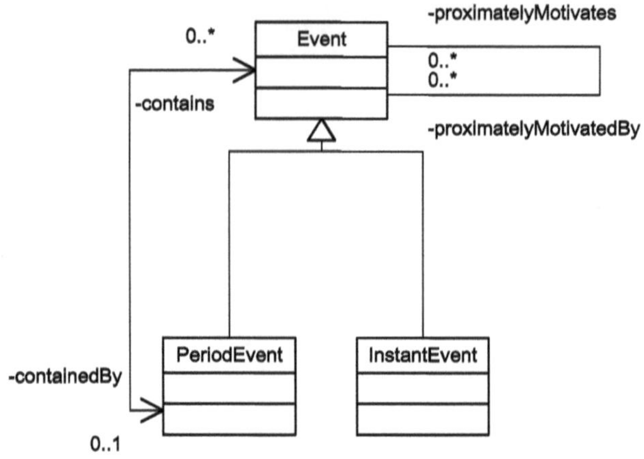

Fig. 9.3 Abbreviated class hierarchy for our event structure

9.6 Event Description Language for Linear Narrative

In order to generate, organize, and compare precise narratives, we need an event descriptive language. In this section we outline an event description language for linear narratives. We use object-oriented design to describe the language and temporal database terminology (Zaniolo et al. 1997). We are continuing to investigate the literature on temporal logic (Øhrstrøm and Hasle 1995), trace theory (Mazurkiewicz 1995), structural equation modeling (Pearl 2002), discrete-event modeling and simulation (Wainer 2009) and narratology (Jahn 2005). There is significant overlap between these domains and our goals.

We briefly review temporal database terminology. An instant is a single number, a 1-dimensional point in time. A period is a pair of instants. An interval is a single number, a 1-dimensional vector representing the displacement between two instants. Valid time is the historical time period during which a database fact is true. Transaction time is the period of time when a fact was entered into the database. Temporal databases and TAMs may support valid-time only, transaction-time only, or both. The latter is called a bi-temporal database. Decades of real-world usage indicate that bi-temporal databases should be provided because as temporal facts are gathered, changes, corrections, and filling in of omissions are inevitable and end-users inevitably want the ability to rollback the database to see the history of these change operations.

In our class hierarchy, an instant has a numeric value, a unit of measure, a calendar and a confidence descriptor. The latter three may be stored in an instant's tuple or computed. The calendar is a 1D temporal coordinate system. The confidence descriptor may indicate a confidence interval, a probability density function, or special value indicating either no error or that confidence information is not available. An instant's numeric value may be +infinite. For example, a database fact with an associated period (0, +infinite) is interpreted as holding true from instant 0 through the rest of time.

Next we define our event classes. A schematic of the class hierarchy is shown in Fig. 9.3. An Event is an abstract class with 0 or 1 parent PeriodEvent objects (a forward declared class). PeriodEvent is an abstract class that has a valid time period and transaction time period. An InstantEvent is an abstract class that has a valid time instant and transaction time period. For example consider a sample from a digital thermometer such as (60°, 12:00PM 8/19/2011). This indicates a temperature of 60° was recorded at the given instant. A PeriodEvent also has a list of child Event objects. This parent-child structure defines a navigatable 1-to-N binary relation called TemporalContainment. The TemporalContainment relation induces a forest of tree structures on Event objects. There is a second bi-directional, navigatable N-to-N binary relation called the ProximatelyMotivates relation defined on the Event class. If Event A proximately motivates Event B, then A is an Event as a proximate cause of B. We restrict the proximatelyMotivates induced graph to be a directed-acyclic graph (DAG). Further, an Event A is said to "motivate" an event C if there is a path through the proximately motivates graph from A to C.

Various constraints must be maintained between the proximately motivates and temporal containment relations to avoid semantic inconsistencies. For example, a PeriodEvent's valid time period must contain the valid time periods of all child PeriodEvent's and the instant of all child InstantEvent's.

The structure of the temporal DAG can be created from an analysis of the motivating events and relevant sub-events, which can be derived from a variety of temporal feature analysis methods, as described above. The duration of events and their children (sub-events), appearance and disappearance of objects, cause-effect relations, and other temporal features can be described in the rich narrative descriptor language.

9.7 Towards a GTIS and TIS

For some time, there has been a desire in the geography and geospatial communities to put temporal behavior on the same footing as spatial structure and to develop a comprehensive geo-temporal information system. This need has become more acute because of the explosion in the number of compact, relatively inexpensive devices that make possible widespread, repeated measurement in the environment over time. (Repeated collection of airborne LIDAR data over wide areas is just one example.) That geo-temporal structuring is still an open problem is reflected in the recent report outlining important challenges from the National Academy of Sciences (NAS 2010).

Thinking in terms of a 4D GIS, as mentioned at the beginning of this paper, is one way of approaching this problem. However, as indicated above, time is different than the spatial dimensions, and therefore it is more accurate to speak about a *geo-temporal information system* (GTIS). Events can then be derived for each category of data in the system (e.g., geologic, climate, human history, weather, etc.) and the distribution of events over time provide the relevant scale and the periods for each category. Each of these event categories will have its own hierarchical structure and its own forest of trees, to which can be applied the human-computer narrative organization described above. GIS concepts can then be brought into the GTIS structure.

For example, the idea of layers can be introduced. Each category could be a GTIS layer, which could be turned on or off as desired. A weather event layer could be overlaid on a human activity layer. One would then see the correlation, spatial and temporal, of these categories. There might be interesting cause-effect relations revealed between events in different categories. To encode these would require some interconnections of the originally independent categorical forests of trees. It would also be good to replicate in the temporal domain some of the GIS symbology and data organization. Of course, much of this grew out of hundreds of years of cartographic tradition. Road and political boundary vectors, for example, came from cartography and from the ongoing need to depict and use this information efficiently. Not nearly as much work has been done for the temporal dimension nor is there a generally agreed upon set of symbols and data needs. The framework we have described here can be the basis for developing these things. For example, timelines annotated with key events are widely used to give an overview of history, military events, geologic events, key cultural moments, and so on. Having a structure within the GTIS to efficiently produce these would be a powerful thing.

To show the flexibility of such an approach, we recently described how the whole story of a city might be aggregated in a collection of hierarchical temporal event structures connected to a GIS structure (Ribarsky et al. 2012). We chose Rome because of its 2500 year history as a major center of Western civilization. One can then consider architectural, military, political, cultural, ethnographic, weather/climate, disease spread, and other histories, each with its own event hierarchy embedded at certain levels in the overall GIS structure. For Rome there are massive amounts of documentation, including texts and images, for this collection of histories. Moreover, there is a substantial and growing digital archive. But all this detail has never been brought together into an integrated, whole story of Rome. It is clear that new causes, effects, and relationships would be discovered if this were done. We described in this paper how interactive timelines could be set up for these overlapping histories, so that major historical events could be unfolded into their sub-events and so that selection of any events on the timeline would reveal the details of the geographic extent (or how something like urban demographics, for example, developed over time). When considering two or more histories together, key points and patterns of correlation become evident. The event and narrative structuring described in this paper provide a rich, meaningful, and effective organization for comprehensive histories like this.

As discussed in previous sections of the paper, there are many information sources that are richly temporal without having a strong spatial component. Document collections which are augmented over time (such as proposal, research paper, and report collections) often fall into this category. For these collections, a *temporal information system* (TIS) would be appropriate and very useful. It seems to us that the event structuring and narrative approach we have described here can be brought to these types of information. Of course, the nature of the narratives and time scales of the events might be different. We have already started doing this in our studies of research paper and proposal collections (Dou et al. 2011).

Although work has been done that shows that data-driven, semi-automatic event discovery and narrative structuring can be developed for a variety of data

(Luo et al. 2006, 2010; Yu et al. 2010), much work remains to be done. In particular, we must remember that the ultimate goal is to make events and narratives meaningful so that people can gather insights, develop actionable knowledge, and create powerful hypotheses and models. More work on automated processing to extract more meaningful results is needed. But we must keep in mind that the human is the final agent that reasons and attaches meaning. Thus improved interactive visualization techniques, especially ones that insert human intelligence at exactly the right points, are absolutely necessary.

References

Blei, D., Ng, A., & Jordan, M. (2003). Latent Dirichlet allocation. *Journal of Machine Learning Research, 3*, 993–1022.

Blei, D., Carin, L., & Dunson, D. (2010). Probabilistic topic models. *Signal Processing Magazine, IEEE, 27*(6), 55–65.

Dou, W., Chang, R., Wang, X., & Ribarsky, W. (2011). ParallelTopics: a probabilistic approach to exploring document collections. In *IEEE visual analytics science and technology (VAST)*, 23–28 October (pp. 231–240). http://dx.doi.org/10.1109/VAST.2011.6102461.

Griffin, L. (1993). Narrative, event-structure analysis, and causal interpretation in historical sociology. *American Journal of Sociology, 98*, 1094–1133.

Havre, S., Hetzler, B., & Nowell, L. (2000). ThemeRiver: visualizing theme changes over time. In *Proc. IEEE symposium on information visualization* (pp. 115–123).

IEEE VAST Challenge (2011). http://hcil.cs.umd.edu/localphp/hcil/vast11. Accessed 1 September 2011.

Jahn, M. (2005). Narratology: a guide to the theory of narrative (Version 1.8). English Department, University of Cologne. http://www.uni-koeln.de/~ame02/pppn.htm. Accessed 1 September 2011.

Kohler, W. (1947). *Gestalt psychology*. New York: Liveright.

Luo, H., Fan, J., Yang, J., Ribarsky, W., & Sato, S. (2006). Exploring large-scale video news via interactive visualization. In *IEEE VAST* (pp. 75–82).

Luo, D., Yang, J., Krstajic, M., Fan, J., Ribarsky, W., & Keim, D. (2010). EventRiver: interactive visual exploration of constantly evolving text collections. *IEEE Transactions on Visualization and Computer Graphics*. doi:ieeecomputersociety.org/10.1109/TVCG.2010.225.

Mazurkiewicz, A. (1995). Introduction to trace theory. In G. Diekert, & Rozenberg (Eds.), *The book of traces V* (pp. 3–67). Singapore: World Scientific.

McCullagh, C. B. (1978). Colligation and classification in history. *History and Theory, 13*, 267–284.

NAS (National Academy of Sciences) Workshop (2010). *New research directions for the National Geospatial Intelligence Agency*. May 2010, Washington, DC.

Øhrstrøm, P., & Hasle, P. (1995). *Temporal logic: from ancient ideas to artificial intelligence*. Berlin: Springer.

Pearl, J. (2002). Causality: models, reasoning, and inference. *IIE Transactions, 34*(6), 583–589.

Ribarsky, W., Sauda, E., Balmer, J., & Wartell, Z. (2012) The whole story: building the computer history of a place. In *Hawaii international conference on systems science (HICSS)*. Accepted for publication.

Wainer, G. (2009). *Discrete-event modeling and simulation a practitioner's approach* (pp. 3–33). Boca Raton: CRC Press.

Yu, L., Lu, A., Ribarsky, W., & Chen, W. (2010). Digital storytelling: automatic animation for time-varying data visualization. *Computer Graphics Forum*, *29*(7), 2271–2280.

Zaniolo, C., Ceri, S., Faloutsos, C., Snodgrass, R. T., Subrahmanian, V. S., & Zicari, R. (1997). *Advanced database systems. The Morgan Kaufmann series in data management systems.*

Chapter 10
A Visual Analytics Approach for Protein Disorder Prediction

Jaegul Choo, Fuxin Li, Keehyoung Joo, and Haesun Park

Abstract In this chapter, we present a case study of performing visual analytics to the protein disorder prediction problem. Protein disorder is one of the most important characteristics in understanding many biological functions and interactions. Due to the high cost to perform lab experiments, machine learning algorithms such as neural networks and support vector machines have been used for its identification. Rather than applying these generic methods, we show in this chapter that more insights can be found using visual analytics. Visualizations using linear discriminant analysis reveal that the disorder within each protein is usually well separated linearly. However, if various proteins are integrated together, there does not exist a clear linear separation rule in general. Based on this observation, we perform another visualization on the linear discriminant vector for each protein and confirm that the proteins are clearly clustered into several groups. Inspired by such findings, we apply k-means clustering on the proteins and construct a different classifier on each group, which leads us to a significant improvement of disorder prediction performance. Moreover, within the identified protein subgroups, the separation accuracy topped 99 %, a clear indicator for further biological investigations on these subgroups.

J. Choo (✉) · F. Li · H. Park
Computational Science and Engineering, Georgia Institute of Technology, Atlanta, USA
e-mail: jaegul.choo@cc.gatech.edu

F. Li
e-mail: fli@cc.gatech.edu

H. Park
e-mail: hpark@cc.gatech.edu

K. Joo
Center for Advanced Computation, Korea Institute for Advanced Study, Seoul, Korea
e-mail: newton@kias.re.kr

J. Dill et al. (eds.), *Expanding the Frontiers of Visual Analytics and Visualization*,
DOI 10.1007/978-1-4471-2804-5_10,

10.1 Introduction

Today's internet era has bombarded analysts in many research fields with an excess amount of information. Extremely complicated structures in data have unearthed new challenges to the statistics and machine learning field. In the past 50 years, many excellent methods have been architected to handle *flat* data—data with simple problem structures. Good examples are the traditional classification and regression problems: given some training input and output, attempt to build a predictive model for the data that can accurately predict future inputs (Hastie et al. 2001). However, real-life data are often not flat, requiring that a certain structure unique to each problem be utilized in order to obtain good results. Since the structure may differ so much among the datasets, it is extremely hard to design automated methods to capture each and every one of the particular problem structures.

Because of this difficulty, visual analytics has drawn a lot of interest. Humans are much better than computers in gaining structural insights. However, a significant portion of their analytic ability comes visually, whereas even the fastest computers have yet to achieve a human's capability to quickly summarize fairly complicated pictures and plots. Certainly it would be extremely beneficial to combine the strengths of both humans and computers in order to make better sense of our data reservoir, but the question is exactly how this can be practically done. Solving practical problems of interest tends to be much more difficult than boasting about the accomplishments of theoretical principles.

The diverse nature of data indicates that there exists no simple answer. In general, pattern recognition techniques can be utilized to reduce the data into a form people can read and look at. Nonetheless, people can handle a limited number of objects (Bishop and Tipping 1998): it is well-known that usually a human can simultaneously handle at most a handful of objects (Baddeley 1994; Miller 1956), an embarrassingly small number given that the data may contain millions of instances that contain thousands of features (dimensions). It is hard to believe that there exists any panacean algorithm that can reduce every kind of data to a much smaller number of objects of interest.

Therefore, in visual analytics, a lot of creativity and interaction with data are needed to analyze a problem. This does not necessarily mean producing beautiful renderings and eye-catching animations, but putting more problem-specific efforts to reveal the underlying structure in the data. We argue that in the current stage of visual analytics research, having a lot of use cases of applying visual analytics to a variety of problems is important, since these solid advices can potentially help people to draw more general guidelines in the future. Therefore, this chapter focuses on just one particular problem and shows how we apply visual analytic principles, combined with simple classic pattern recognition methods, to obtain some structural insights and enhance our knowledge and predictive ability about the problem. It is our hope that our analysis described in this chapter can give some inspiration to more and better visual analytics use cases in the future.

The rest of this chapter is organized as follows. Section 10.2 introduces the problem of protein disorder prediction and describes the dataset and features. Section 10.3 briefly discusses the variant of discriminant analysis algorithm that we use to visualize the data. Section 10.4 presents the details of our visual analysis. Section 10.5 shows the experimental results of our visualization-driven approach. Finally, Sect. 10.6 draws conclusions and suggests possible future work.

10.2 Protein Disorder Prediction

Proteins are fundamental biochemical compounds in which a linear chain of amino acids (or residues) are formed via polypeptide bonds and folded into complex three-dimensional structures. In most cases, the complex structures of proteins are stable, but some proteins may contain some unstable sub-sequences within its amino acid chains, which we call intrinsically disordered regions.

These intrinsically disordered regions play important biological roles by facilitating flexible couplings and bindings with other proteins. Thus, the identification of disorder regions has been a crucial task within biology domains (Dunker et al. 2002). This problem has also continuously been one of the main focuses in the biannual world-wide experiment called critical assessment of methods of protein structure prediction, i.e., CASP (Protein Structure Prediction Center 2012).

This task is typically done by experimental methods such as X-ray scattering and nuclear magnetic resonance spectroscopy, which cost nontrivial amounts of time and money. Alternatively, a lot of effort has been spent in developing computational methods that statistically predict the disorder region of a given protein using a set of training proteins whose disorder labels are known. From a computational perspective, protein disorder prediction can be viewed as a binary classification problem, which determines whether each amino acid in a given protein is disordered or not. Until recently, numerous methods have been proposed (Ferron et al. 2006), and some of them adopt popular classification techniques such as neural network (Cheng et al. 2005; Hecker et al. 2008) and support vector machines (SVM) (Rangwala et al. 2009; Ward et al. 2004).

The protein disorder prediction data in this study is a standard database (Cheng 2004). It contains the amino acid sequences of 723 proteins, which has, in total, 215,612 residues as well as their labels that describe whether or not a residue is disordered. Approximately 6.4 % of them are classified as disordered.

To apply classification techniques to the dataset, the data items that need to be classified are typically encoded as high-dimensional vectors. We have used one of the standard encoding schemes to represent each residue in a particular protein, which takes into account the neighborhood residues within a particular window size (Kim and Park 2003, 2004). To be specific, for a window size of $(2w + 1)$, a residue is encoded using itself as well as the previous w and the next w residues. For these $(2w + 1)$ residues, their PSI-BLAST profiles (Altschul et al. 1997), the secondary structure, the solvent accessibility, and the hydrophobicity features are concatenated as a high-dimensional vector to represent the residue at the center. The details of these features are as follows.

PSI-BLAST profile In the first part of the features, each of the $(2w+1)$ residues in the window is represented as a 20-dimensional PSI-BLAST vector. This 20-dimensional vector is then normalized so that it sums up to one. However, the first and the last w residues at N- or C-termini do not have all the valid $(2w+1)$ residues in their windows. In order to allow a window to extend over N- and C-termini, an additional 21st dimension is appended. For those positions that extend out of the protein, no amino acid exists in which case the 20-dimensional vector is set to all zero, but the 21st dimensional value is set to one. Otherwise, the 21st dimensional value stays zero. Additionally, we put another dimension representing the entropy value of a PSI-BLAST vector. In the end, the PSI-BLAST profile takes up $22 \times (2w+1)$ dimensions.

Secondary structure profile The secondary structure of a protein refers to certain types of the three-dimensional local structure. Although it originally has 8 different types, we use a simpler categorization of three states of helix, sheet, and coil. To obtain the secondary structure profile, we utilize one of the popular secondary structure prediction methods called PSIPRED (Bryson et al. 2005; Jones 1999). Assigning one dimension for the resulting probability or likelihood of each state, the secondary structure of each residue is encoded as a three-dimensional vector, which has $3 \times (2w+1)$ dimensions in total.

Solvent accessibility profile The solvent accessibility is another important characteristic associated with residues in a protein. For this profile, we use a recent method based on the k-nearest neighbor classifier by Joo et al. (2012) and encode it as a scalar value for each residue. Additionally, we add another dimension to represent the average solvent accessibility within the window. Thus, $(2w+1)+1$ dimensions are used in total.

Hydrophobicity profile The hydrophobicity also plays an important role in disorder prediction, and in practice, hydrophilic residues are frequently shown in disorder regions. We encode the hydrophobicity of each residue as a scalar value by using the Kyte-Doolittle hydrophobicity values (Kyte and Doolittle 1982), and similar to the solvent accessibility profile, we include an additional dimension of its average value within the window. Furthermore, considering its significant influence on prediction, we put another additional dimension of the average hydrophobicity throughout the entire residue sequence within a certain protein. Finally, $(2w+1)+1+1$ dimensions are used for this profile.

In our experiments, we set w to 7 since it resulted in providing a higher classification performance in a reasonable computation time. Finally, the total number of dimensions in the data is 408.

10.3 Discriminant Analysis for Visualization

Discriminant analysis transforms high-dimensional data into a low-dimensional space so that different classes of data are well separated from each other. One of the most popular methods is linear discriminant analysis (LDA) (Fukunaga 1990), and it has been successfully applied to the visualization of clustered high-dimensional data by reducing the data dimension to two or three (Choo et al. 2009, 2010).

Let us briefly describe LDA by introducing the notion of scatter matrices used to define the cluster quality and the criteria of LDA. Suppose a given data matrix $A = [a_1, a_2, \ldots, a_n] \in \mathbb{R}^{m \times n}$ whose columns are data items and let $\mathcal{N}_i$ denote the set of data item indices belonging to class i. Assuming that the number of classes is r, the within-class scatter matrix S_w and the between-class scatter matrix S_b are defined, respectively, as

$$S_w = \sum_{i=1}^{r} \sum_{j \in \mathcal{N}_i} (a_j - c^{(i)})(a_j - c^{(i)})^T \quad \text{and}$$

$$S_b = \sum_{i=1}^{r} |\mathcal{N}_i| (c^{(i)} - c)(c^{(i)} - c)^T,$$

where $c^{(i)}$ is the centroid of class i, and c is the global centroid. The traces of these matrices are expressed as

$$\text{trace}(S_w) = \sum_{i=1}^{r} \sum_{j \in \mathcal{N}_i} \|a_j - c^{(i)}\|^2 \quad \text{and}$$

$$\text{trace}(S_b) = \sum_{i=1}^{r} \| |\mathcal{N}_i| (c^{(i)} - c) \|^2,$$

respectively. A large trace(S_w) and a small trace(S_w) corresponds to a stronger discrimination between classes.

In the reduced dimensional space generated by a linear transformation $G^T \in \mathbb{R}^{l \times m}$ ($m > l$), a data item a_j is represented as $G^T a_j$, and accordingly, the scatter matrices S_w and S_b become $G^T S_w G$ and $G^T S_b G$, respectively. LDA solves G such that it maximizes trace($G^T S_b G$) while minimizing trace($G^T S_w G$) by solving a single approximated criterion,

$$\max_G \text{trace}\big((G^T S_w G)^{-1} (G^T S_b G)\big),$$

whose solution is obtained by generalized eigendecomposition (Fukunaga 1990) or generalized singular value decomposition (Howland and Park 2004).

In this vanilla version of LDA, the rank of G is at most $k - 1$ due to the rank of S_b, and in the current binary classification problem only one-dimensional output can be generated, which is too restricted for visualization. To avoid this issue, we modify the centroid terms used in S_w and S_b to nearest neighbor points (Fukunaga and Mantock 1983; Wang et al. 2009) such that

$$S_w^{NN} = \sum_{j=1}^{n} \sum_{k=1}^{K} (a_j - NN_w(a_j, k))(a_j - NN_w(a_j, k))^T \quad \text{and}$$

$$S_b^{NN} = \sum_{j=1}^{n} \sum_{k=1}^{K} (a_j - NN_b(a_j, k))(a_j - NN_b(a_j, k))^T,$$

where $NN_w(a_j, k)$ is the k-th nearest neighbor point of a_j among the data in the same class of a_j, and $NN_b(a_j, k)$ is the one among the data that belongs to a class different than that of a_j. With such modifications, the rank of the matrix G is no longer restricted to the number of classes k, and one can visualize the data by using the two or three most significant dimensions of the solution obtained from generalized eigendecomposition/singular value decomposition.

10.4 Visualization of Protein Disorder Data

Although the protein disorder prediction problem can be described as a *flat* binary classification problem of individual amino acids, there is one more layer in its structure—the protein level. If this structure is used, each amino acid would not be treated separately, but rather grouped together by their respective proteins and some protein-level clue would be used. This is no longer trivial and needs both a motivation why it is needed, and a strategy to perform it. We will detail our visual approach in this section that gives both a motivation and a strategy.

10.4.1 Knowledge Discovery from Visualization

The first idea is to visualize a simpler subproblem: the amino acids within each protein. By using the neighborhood-based discriminant analysis described in Sect. 10.3, we have generated the 2D scatter plot of residues along with their disorder labels using different colors. Figure 10.1 shows several visualizations of different proteins. As can be seen in Fig. 10.1(a)–(c), the two classes are clearly separated from each other in almost all the proteins. Especially, the non-disorder amino acids almost form a Gaussian distribution in every protein, hinting that discriminant analysis methods are suitable for this problem (LDA is the optimal classifier when both classes are from Gaussians with equal covariance. If the covariance is not equal, quadratic discriminant analysis (QDA) generates the optimal classifier, Duda et al. 2001).

Knowing that within each protein, linear separability is achievable, a natural next question is whether this extends when multiple proteins are analyzed together. Interestingly though, only a few proteins need to be put together to lose the separability: when performing discriminant analysis on residues from several proteins, the two classes almost always have significant overlap (Fig. 10.1(d)). The structural knowledge we have gained through this visualization is that the non-disorder amino acids approximate a Gaussian distribution within each protein, but these Gaussians differ for different proteins.

These structural observations motivate us to carefully design the disorder predictor depending on the proteins. To this end, instead of visualizing individual residues,

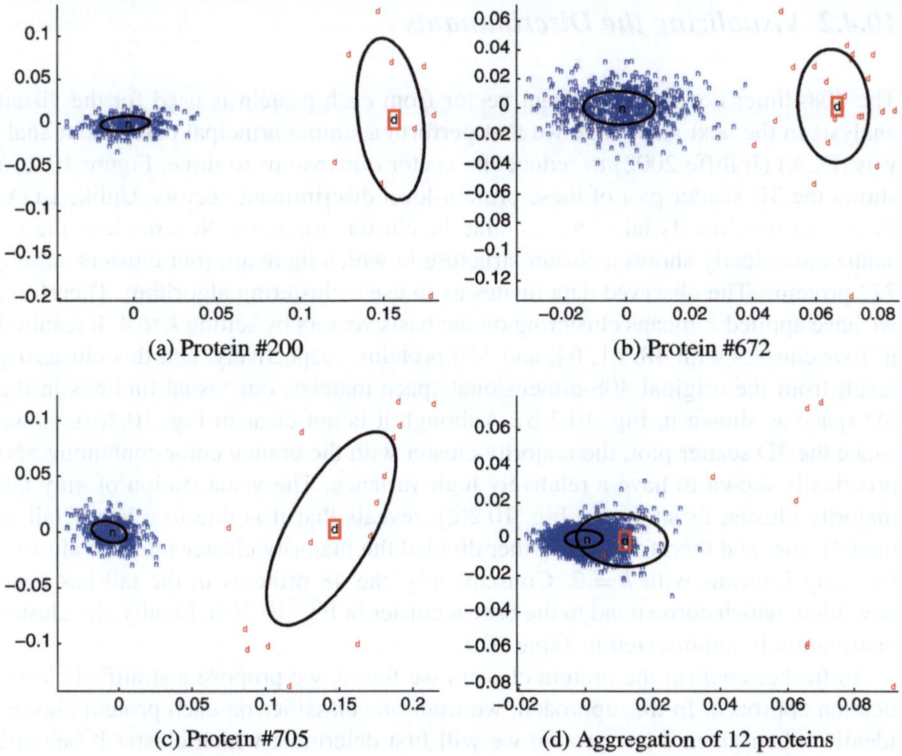

Fig. 10.1 Visualization examples of randomly chosen proteins from the 723 proteins database (Cheng 2004). (**a**)–(**c**) are for individual proteins, and (**d**) for 12 proteins including the proteins used in (**a**)–(**c**). The *blue* and *red* color correspond to the non-disorder and the disorder clusters, respectively. The sample mean and covariance for each cluster are also shown as a letter in a *rectangle* and a *black ellipse*, respectively

we now visualize the proteins as individual data items. For this case, however, we need a high-dimensional vector representation for each protein. Our second important idea in the paper is to use the first basis (or discriminant) vector computed from discriminant analysis to represent each protein.

The justification of using it is as follows. As shown in Fig. 10.1, in most of the proteins, the discrimination between the two clusters are achieved in the first dimension, i.e., along the horizontal axis, and in this sense, using the first basis vector is sufficient to characterize how the two clusters are separated in each protein. In addition, since discriminant vectors differ among proteins, visualizing them could reveal if some proteins have similar discriminant vectors, or if there is no special patterns there.

10.4.2 Visualizing the Discriminants

The 408-dimensional discriminant vector from each protein is used for the visual analysis in the next step. Here we first perform a simple principal component analysis (PCA) (Jolliffe 2002) to reduce the vector dimensions to three. Figure 10.2(a) shows the 3D scatter plot of these protein-level discriminant vectors. Unlike LDA, PCA does not directly take into account the cluster structures. Nevertheless, the visualization clearly shows a cluster structure in which there are four clusters among 723 proteins. The observed data invites us to use a clustering algorithm. Therefore, we have applied k-means clustering on the basis vectors by setting k to 4. It resulted in four clusters with 48, 61, 64, and 550 proteins, respectively, and this clustering result from the original 408-dimensional space matches our visual findings in the 3D space as shown in Fig. 10.2(b). Although it is not clear in Fig. 10.2(b), as we rotate the 3D scatter plot, the majority cluster with the orange color containing 550 proteins is shown to have a relatively high variance. The visualization of only the majority cluster, as shown in Fig. 10.2(c), reveals that it is due to a heavy tail at the left side, and therefore, we further divided the majority cluster into two clusters by using k-means with $k = 2$. Consequently, the 48 proteins in the tail has been identified, which correspond to the brown cluster in Fig. 10.2(d). Finally, the cluster distribution is summarized in Table 10.1.

To further confirm the protein clusters we found, we propose a stratified classification approach. In this approach, we train one classifier on each protein cluster. Ideally, when given a test protein we will first determine which cluster it belongs to and then use the respective classifier to predict its disorder regions. A Bayesian approach can also be taken such that the final decision is made by

$$\Pr(P_a \text{ is disordered}) = \sum_i \Pr(P \in G_i)\Pr(P_a \text{ is disordered}|G_i)$$

where $P_a \in P$ is an amino acid in protein P, and G_i defines the protein groups found from the cluster analysis. This equation marks a difference from previous approaches: here we factorize the desired probability that an amino acid a is disordered into two distinctive parts. The first is the probability that the protein P belongs to a specific protein subgroup. Then, given this subgroup and the amino acid, the final decision is made.

In this chapter we will train the classifier to give $\Pr(\text{disorder}|a, G_i)$ and leave the protein grouping as a future research topic. Solving the protein grouping problem would require the support of biologists, who already have a variety of tools and databases to select homologous proteins and similar proteins.

10.5 Classification Evaluation and Discussion

To evaluate disorder prediction performance, we adopt a standard procedure, K-fold cross-validation, where K is set to 10. The five different random cross-validation

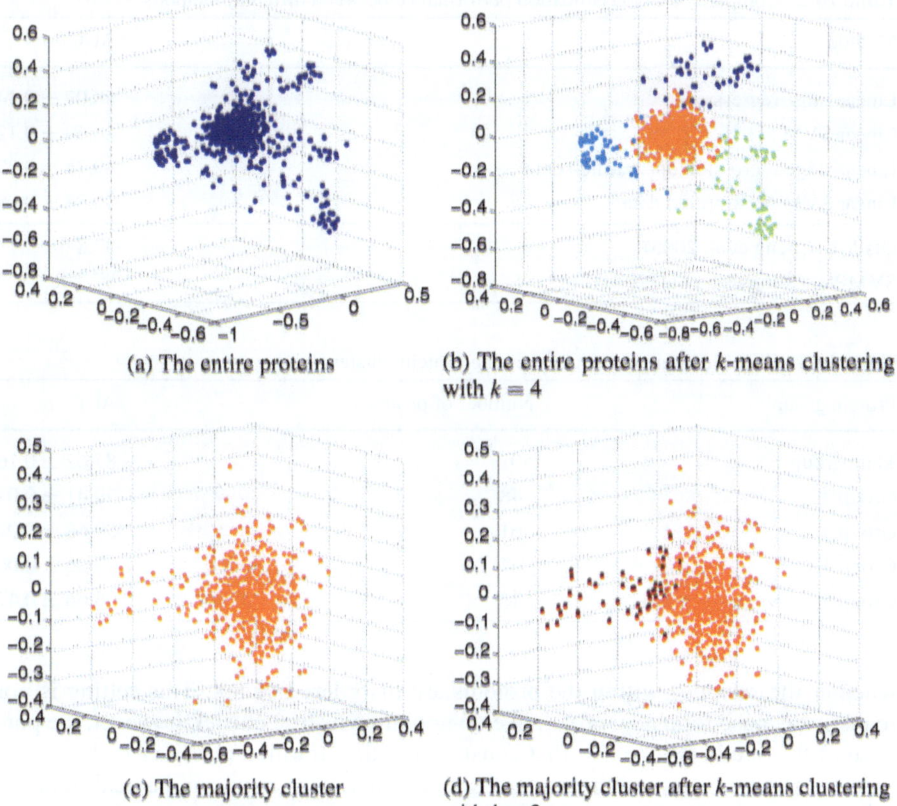

(a) The entire proteins

(b) The entire proteins after k-means clustering with $k = 4$

(c) The majority cluster

(d) The majority cluster after k-means clustering with $k = 2$

Fig. 10.2 3D scatter plots of the first bases of discriminant analysis applied to each of the 723 proteins. PCA has been used to generated the scatter plots, and the different colors indicate the cluster labels obtained from k-means clustering

Table 10.1 Cluster distribution of 723 proteins shown in Figs. 10.2(b) and (d)

Main group	Group 2	Group 3	Group 4	Group 5
Orange	Dark blue	Light blue	Green	Brown
502	48	61	64	48

splits are used to assess the standard deviation of the methods. The split is done on the proteins so that each time the test prediction is performed on the protein data points that are not part of the training set. It is also independent of the stratification, which means we do not control the number of training proteins for each protein cluster. For stratified classification, we initially put the training proteins into their correspondent clusters and train one classifier per each cluster. Then for the test proteins, we identify their clusters and apply the corresponding classifier to predict

Table 10.2 Comparison of classification performance between different methods

Method	AUC
Linear ridge regression	88.07 ± 0.14
Linear SVM	88.59 ± 0.12
Linear ridge regression on stratified data	89.74 ± 0.07
Linear SVM on stratified data	90.88 ± 0.08
DisProt (Cheng et al. 2005)	87.8
SVMPrat (Rangwala et al. 2009)	87.7

Table 10.3 Classification performance on the protein clusters

Protein group	Number of proteins	AUC
Main group	502	87.62 ± 0.16
Group 2	48	99.41 ± 0.07
Group 3	61	99.68 ± 0.07
Group 4	64	99.06 ± 0.06
Group 5	48	95.66 ± 0.47

whether the residues within the proteins are disordered or not. This setting is not realistic because for a new protein we do not know its true cluster, however, the purpose of this study is to verify that constructing the stratified classifier makes sense and improves the prediction accuracy significantly. This issue can be dealt with by learning another classifier that classifies the test protein into its proper cluster in the future research.

We compare the results from both literature and standard algorithms such as linear ridge regression and linear SVM applied to our feature representation described in Sect. 10.2. Linear SVM is computed with the LIBLINEAR package (Lin 2012) with an L_2-loss and L_2-regularization. The ridge parameter of ridge regression is fixed as 500 and the linear SVM C parameter is fixed as 5. Area under ROC curve (AUC) is used as a performance measure since the dataset is highly imbalanced. The results are shown in Table 10.2. It can be seen that the performance greatly increases for stratified classifiers. With linear SVM, the performance shows the highest results, 91 %, which are significantly better than the best known result on the dataset.

Moreover, depending on the identified protein clusters, the performance can be extremely good as shown in Table 10.3. On each of the protein groups 2, 3, and 4, the performances are more than 99 %, which is almost perfect. Even on group 5, the performance is better, e.g., 95.66 %, than the main group. In other words, if one determines that the protein is different from the main group, a very confident prediction of the protein disorder can be made. This finding makes the identification of protein groups a very interesting problem and should also shed some light on the biological side.

We want to re-emphasize again that this finding is a direct result of the visual analytics approach we take. Previous studies on this dataset have mostly emphasized performance improvements without careful investigation of the data themselves. Contrary to the previous studies, our study, which employed visualization techniques, has been able to pinpoint the structure in the protein disorder problem: 1) In each protein, ordered and disordered residues are well separated, but the separation rule is different for each protein. 2) Separation rules of each protein can be naturally clustered among various proteins. These two transitions are important for obtaining deep insight into the problem, further opening up an interesting direction in the biology and bioinformatics domains.

10.6 Conclusion

In this chapter, we have studied the application of visual analysis principles in the protein disorder prediction problem. With simple techniques such as linear discriminant analysis and k-means clustering, we were able to unveil the special structure within the data that the disorder in each protein can be linearly separated while the separation rule is different between the proteins. Based on this visual observation, we grouped the proteins into five different groups and learned classifiers on each group. This turns out to perform better than many existing methods which have grouped all the proteins together. Especially, in three subgroups, we were able to obtain more than 99 % accuracy, urging biological studies in these groups.

Of course, the reason we are obtaining some degree of success is because the structure in the data is still relatively simple. Instead of the linear structure, in bigger and more complicated datasets the inherent structure may be nonlinear manifolds, which are much harder to identify. Extension to such areas would be interesting for the future work.

Acknowledgments This research is partially supported by NSF grant CCF-0808863. Any opinions, findings and conclusions or recommendations expressed in this material are those of the authors and do not necessarily reflect the views of the National Science Foundation.

References

Altschul, S. F., Madden, T. L., Schaffer, A. A., Zhang, J., Zhang, Z., Miller, W., & Lipman, D. J. (1997). Gapped blast and psi-blast: a new generation of protein database search programs. *Nucleic Acids Research*, *25*(17), 3389–3402.

Baddeley, A. (1994). The magical number seven: still magic after all these years? *The Psychological Review*, *101*, 353–356.

Bishop, C. M., & Tipping, M. E. (1998). A hierarchical latent variable model for data visualization. *IEEE Transactions on Pattern Analysis and Machine Intelligence*, *20*, 281–293.

Bryson, K., McGuffin, L. J., Marsden, R. L., Ward, J. J., Sodhi, J. S., & Jones, D. T. (2005). Protein structure prediction servers at University College London. *Nucleic Acids Research*, *33*(suppl 2), W36–W38.

Cheng, J. (2004). Protein disorder dataset: Disorder723. http://casp.rnet.missouri.edu/download/disorder.dataset.

Cheng, J., Sweredoski, M., & Baldi, P. (2005). Accurate prediction of protein disordered regions by mining protein structure data. *Data Mining and Knowledge Discovery*, *11*, 213–222. doi:10.1007/s10618-005-0001-y.

Choo, J., Bohn, S., & Park, H. (2009). Two-stage framework for visualization of clustered high dimensional data. In *IEEE symposium on visual analytics science and technology, 2009. VAST 2009* (pp. 67–74).

Choo, J., Lee, H., Kihm, J., & Park, H. (2010). iVisClassifier: an interactive visual analytics system for classification based on supervised dimension reduction. In *2010 IEEE conference on visual analytics science and technology (VAST)* (pp. 27–34).

Duda, R. O., Hart, P. E., & Stork, D. G. (2001). *Pattern classification* (2nd edn.). New York: Wiley-Interscience.

Dunker, A. K., Brown, C. J., Lawson, J. D., Iakoucheva, L. M., & Obradovic, Z. (2002). Intrinsic disorder and protein function. *Biochemistry*, *41*(21), 6573–6582. doi:10.1021/bi012159+. PMID: 12022860.

Ferron, F., Longhi, S., Canard, B., & Karlin, D. (2006). A practical overview of protein disorder prediction methods. *Proteins: Structure, Function, and Bioinformatics*, *65*(1), 1–14.

Fukunaga, K. (1990). *Introduction to statistical pattern recognition* (2nd edn.). Boston: Academic Press.

Fukunaga, K., & Mantock, J. M. (1983). Nonparametric discriminant analysis. *IEEE Transactions on Pattern Analysis and Machine Intelligence*, *5*, 671–678.

Hastie, T., Tibshirani, R., & Friedman, J. (2001). *The elements of statistical learning: data mining, inference, and prediction*. Berlin: Springer.

Hecker, J., Yang, J., & Cheng, J. (2008). Protein disorder prediction at multiple levels of sensitivity and specificity. *BMC Genomics*, *9*(suppl 1), 9.

Howland, P., & Park, H. (2004). Generalizing discriminant analysis using the generalized singular value decomposition. *IEEE Transactions on Pattern Analysis and Machine Intelligence*, *26*(8), 995–1006.

Jolliffe, I. T. (2002). *Principal component analysis*. Berlin: Springer.

Jones, D. T. (1999). Protein secondary structure prediction based on position-specific scoring matrices. *Journal of Molecular Biology*, *292*(2), 195–202.

Joo, K., Lee, S. J., & Lee, J. (2012). Sann: Solvent accessibility prediction of proteins by nearest neighbor method. *Proteins—Structure, Function, Bioinformatics*. Wiley, published online. doi:10.1002/prot.24074. http://onlinelibrary.wiley.com/doi/10.1002/prot.24074/pdf.

Kim, H., & Park, H. (2003). Protein secondary structure prediction based on an improved support vector machines approach. *Protein Engineering*, *16*(8), 553–560.

Kim, H., & Park, H. (2004). Prediction of protein relative solvent accessibility with support vector machines and long-range interaction 3D local descriptor. *Proteins: Structure, Function, and Bioinformatics*, *54*(3), 557–562.

Kyte, J., & Doolittle, R. F. (1982). A simple method for displaying the hydropathic character of a protein. *Journal of Molecular Biology*, *157*(1), 105–132.

Lin, C.-J. (2012). Liblinear—a library for large linear classification. http://www.csie.ntu.edu.tw/~cjlin/liblinear/.

Miller, G. A. (1956). The magical number seven, plus or minus two: some limits on our capacity for processing information. *The Psychological Review*, *63*, 81–97.

Protein Structure Prediction Center (2012). http://predictioncenter.org/.

Rangwala, H., Kauffman, C., & Karypis, G. (2009). svmprat: Svm-based protein residue annotation toolkit. *BMC Bioinformatics*, *10*(1), 439.

Wang, F., Sun, J., Li, T., & Anerousis, N. (2009). Two heads better than one: metric+active learning and its applications for it service classification. In *ICDM '09. Ninth IEEE international conference on data mining, 2009* (pp. 1022–1027).

Ward, J. J., Sodhi, J. S., McGuffin, L. J., Buxton, B. F., & Jones, D. T. (2004). Prediction and functional analysis of native disorder in proteins from the three kingdoms of life. *Journal of Molecular Biology*, *337*(3), 635–645.

Chapter 11
Visual Storytelling in Education Applied to Spatial-Temporal Multivariate Statistics Data

Patrik Lundblad and Mikael Jern

Abstract The paper focuses on an ancient social ritual: "visual storytelling"—exemplified through telling stories about a country's development over time that shape its economic growth and well-being. Discoveries are made that draw the user into reflecting on how life is lived—and may be improved—from one region to another. In addition, the user can interactively participate in the web-based process which is important to the education and dissemination of public statistics. A toolkit GAV Flash (geoanalytics visualization) is constructed which is programmed in Adobe's ActionScript. This is the basis for the statistics information visualization application "World eXplorer". This uses integrated storytelling and is based on multiple linked views and an integrated database link to the public World dataBank. This has more than 400 performance indicators for the time period 1960–2010. An interactive visual story mechanism assists teachers to improve a student's knowledge through reflections on how life is lived by using a variety of demographics, such as healthcare, environment, and educational and economic indicators. Educators can develop interactive teaching material based on this storytelling mechanism. Integrated snapshots can be captured at any time during an explorative data analysis process and they become an important component of the analytical reasoning process. Students can access geovisual applications and explore statistical relations on their own guided by the stories prepared by the teachers. With the associated science of perception and cognition in relation to the use of multivariate spatio-temporal statistical data, this paper contributes to the growing interest in geovisual statistics analytics in education.

P. Lundblad (✉) · M. Jern
Media and Information Technology, National Centre for Visual Analytics, Linköping University, Linköping, Sweden
e-mail: patrik.lundblad@liu.se

M. Jern
e-mail: mikael.jern@liu.se

J. Dill et al. (eds.), *Expanding the Frontiers of Visual Analytics and Visualization*,
DOI 10.1007/978-1-4471-2804-5_11, © Springer-Verlag London Limited 2012

11.1 Introduction

The "participative web" is increasingly utilized by intelligent web services which empower developers to customize web-enabled visualization applications that contribute to collaboration and communicate visual content (Fig. 11.1). In this context, we introduce a collaborative geovisual analytics framework for official statistics based on dynamic visual user interfaces and its increasing role in worldwide collaboration and communication. International comparisons of economies and societies tend to be undertaken at the national level. Statistics refer to gross national product, for example, while health and education levels tend to be measured and debated in national terms. However, economic performance and social indicators can vary within countries as much as between countries. In recent years regional (sub-national) differences in economic output, labor productivity, job creation, labor force participation and education within countries have been at least twice as great as those among countries. Understanding the variety in regional economic structures and performance is essential knowledge for initiating developments which could improve regional competitiveness and in turn increase national growth. The results from our research make these variations more visible, providing region-by region indicators in the form of motion graphs and maps that could lead to better identification of areas that are outperforming or lagging behind. Patterns of growth and the persistence of inequalities are analyzed over time, highlighting the factors responsible for them. How can such significant knowledge about these statistical facts be brought together and published to analysts and citizens?

The paper introduces geovisual analytics tools for integrated statistics analysis. The collaboration and publication process facilitates storytelling aimed at producing statistical news content in support of an automatic authoring process. The author simply presses a button to publish the knowledge gained from a visual interactive discovery process. Storytelling, in our context, is about telling a story on the statistics data and the related analytics reasoning processes on how knowledge was obtained. Storytelling within an interactive web context could more engagingly draw the user into reflections and sometimes change a perspective altogether. The story is placed in the hands of those who need it, e.g. policy and decision makers, teachers and also informed citizens. This dynamic visual storytelling is a way of telling stories through interactive web-enabled visualization with integrated snapshots highlighting important discoveries. Stories enable a leap in understanding by the user in order to grasp how statistical indicators may influence society.

The web-enabled application World eXplorer [http://www.ncomva.se/v4/world/] is utilized for exploring, presentation, communicating and publishing national statistics data. A novel storytelling mechanism is introduced for the analyst and author to:

(1) import statistical data through Excel or World Databank;
(2) explore and make discoveries through trends and patterns and derive insight
(3) create a story
(4) share the story with colleagues and reach consensus and trust. Visual discoveries are captured into snapshots together with descriptive metadata and hyperlinks

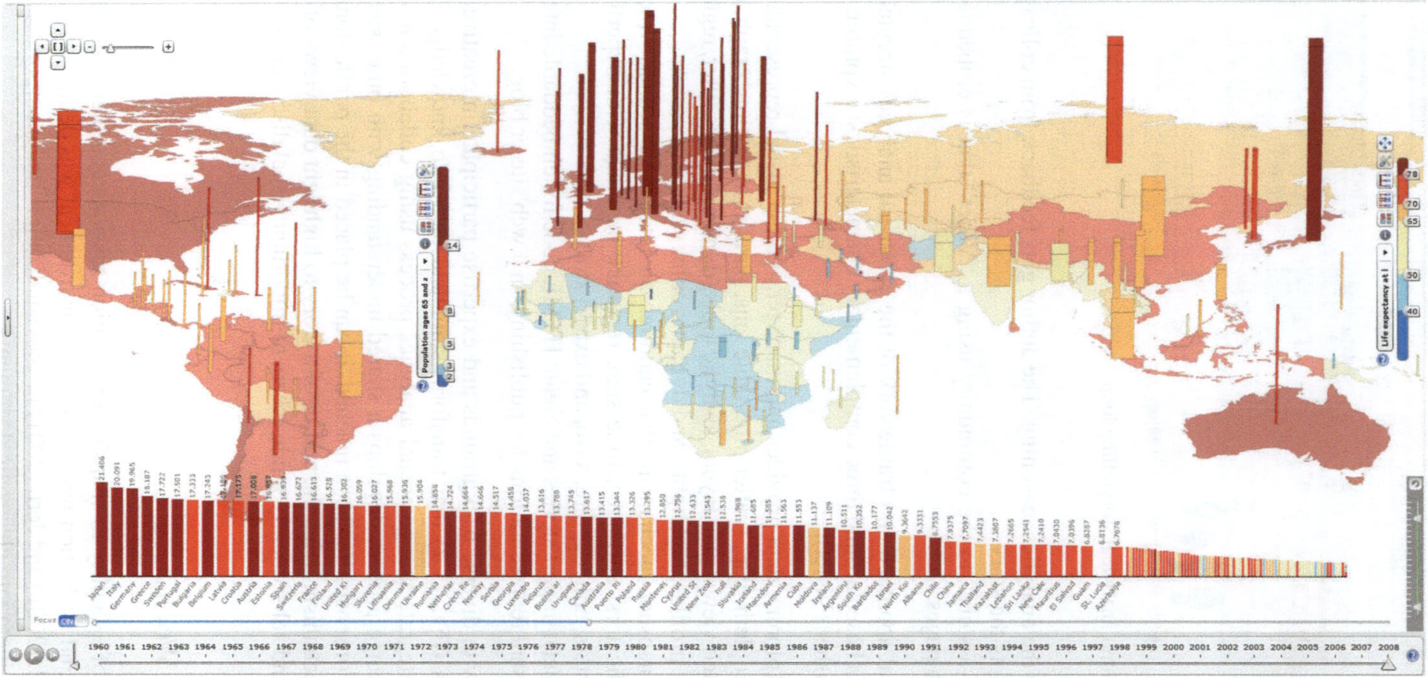

Fig. 11.1 Web-enabled 3D view of the world animating statistical indicators from the World Databank simultaneously in two linked views for 1960–2010. The map and histogram color representing Life expectancy is displayed in the choropleth map; the height of the 3D bars shows percentage of age group 65+ and bar width represents the total population. http://www.ncomva.se/flash/projects/3d/Thesis3D_world.html. The dynamic histogram implemented with traditional fish eye technique allows all countries to be analyzed together

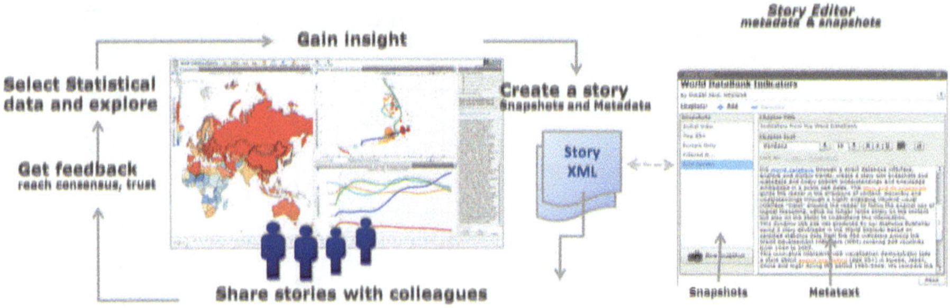

Fig. 11.2 The eXplorer analytical storytelling loop

in relation to the analytics reasoning. The author gets feedback from colleagues and then adapts the story

(5) publish "tell-a-story" to the community using a "Vislet" that is embedded in blogs or Web pages.

The conceptual approach and framework of the geovisual analytics storytelling implementation is based around three complementary characteristics: eXplorer, tell-a-story and Publisher (Vislet):

- Authoring (eXplorer): data provider and manager, motion visual representations including choropleth map, scatter plot, table lens, parallel axes, time graph, data grid, coordinated views, map layers, analytic tools (dynamic query, filter, regional categorization, profiles, highlight), and dynamic color scale.
- Tell-a-story: snapshot mechanism that captures an interactive scenario (active views and indicators, attributes, time step, regions), metadata with hyperlinks, story and chapters, edit, capture, save, and export story.
- Publisher (Vislet): import stories and create HTML code for embeddable interactive motion visual representations for publishing on a web site or blog.

Statisticians with diverse backgrounds and expertise participate in creative discovery processes (Fig. 11.2) that transform statistical data into knowledge. Storytelling tools integrate this geovisual analytics process using collaboration. This knowledge exchange process develops a shared understanding with other statisticians and, after consensus has been reached, it can be placed in the public domain. The snapshot mechanism helps the author of a story to highlight data views of particular interest, and subsequently guide others to important visual discoveries.

11.2 Related Work

The importance of a facility to snapshot exploration sessions and then reuse them for presentation and evaluation within the same environment was demonstrated by MacEachren et al. (2001) and Jern (2001) in geovisualization, and incorporated features to integrate them into electronic documents.

A variety of software is now available for creating snapshots. One of these is CCMaps (Carr et al. 2005) which is a conditioned choropleth mapping tool where the user can create snapshots of events and then reuse them for presentation. Another method is called "Re-Visualization" (Robinson 2006) and is used in the tool ReVise which captures the analysis sessions and allows them to be reused. A further toolkit is the Visual Inquiry Toolkit (Guo et al. 2006) that allows users to place pertinent clusters into a "pattern-basket" to be reused in the visualization process. In the research area of volume visualization Wohlfart and Hauser (2007) describes a storytelling approach which combines interactive volume visualization with annotated animation. With regard to sense-making, Keel (2006) describes a visual analytics system of computational agents that supports the exchange of task-relevant information and the incremental discoveries of relationships and knowledge among team members. The Web-based Analysis and Visualization Environment (Weave) (Baumann 2011) is a Framework that uses session states and stores them on a server for later reuse. Another application that uses a similar approach where the user stores the data on-line is Many Eyes (Viégas et al. 2007), which is a public website where novice users can upload their own data, create dynamic visualizations and participate in discussions. But Many Eyes seems limited to showing only one visualization at a time and has no animation facilities for time sequences.

For many of these systems the snapshot has be to loaded into the same application environment as the one that created it. This puts a restriction on usage and sharing if the application requires a software license. Such applications may not be easily accessible to team members without installing external software (Jern et al. 2008). Security considerations could also act as further constraints. In this context, we introduce a web compliant layered component toolkit with a snapshot mechanism that captures, re-uses and shares active properties for individual functional components. We have demonstrated (OECD 2012) that such an implementation could provide a more open and collaborative GeoAnalytics framework for public use.

Collaborative geovisual analytics tools have been proved to work well with statistics data (Jern 2010a), but so far little attention has been directed to using geovisual analytics tools and statistics data within a school environment. However, initial tests have shown significant potential (Jern 2010b; Stenliden and Jern 2010) when making them accessible to educators and their students. Research on multi external representational tools (MERs) (Ainsworth 2006) has shown that when learners can interact with an appropriate representation their performance is enhanced, especially if the circumstances are good (Goldman et al. 1989). With the availability of current web enabled geovisual analytics tools it is appropriate to explore the possibilities of using these tools within schools and allow educators to use these tools in different application areas (Kinzel and Wright 2008). There is significant future potential for educators to present and explore scientific data sets together with students.

11.3 System Implementation

11.3.1 GAV Flash Framework

The conceptual model and framework for the toolkit GAV Flash (GeoAnalytics Visualization) was developed based on a recommendation from the visual analytics (VA) research program (Thomas and Cook 2005) to "*support seamless integration of tools so that data requests, visual analysis, note-taking, presentation composition and dissemination all take place within a cohesive environment*". This addresses the need for integrated exploratory, analytical reasoning, communicative and publishing tools. Common geovisualization and information visualization components are included that support interactive features such as tooltips, brushing, highlight, visual inquiry, conditioned filter mechanisms that can discover outliers, and methods supporting time-linked multiple views. Tools also support data analysis algorithms, connect the components to each other, and support data providers that can load data from various sources (Fig. 11.3).

The GAV Flash architecture, programmed in Adobe's object-oriented language ActionScript, allows new or existing components/classes to be included with existing components. Means are also provided for a developer to extend and further customize the popular information visualization methods using the lower-level "atomic" components that are the foundation for the "functional" high level components, with integrated user interactions and controls.

The core philosophy of GAV Flash is modularity, in order to allow application developers to select from a wide range of visualizations, data providers and data transforms, and combine them in various ways. This puts a high priority for each component of the framework to be generalized so it can receive and communicate data with other components, but also be self-contained so that the advanced functionality is always present, irrespective of which components are combined. This generalization is achieved through the definition of interfaces, which detail only the required functions and properties in assets shared by components. An example of this is the data set, whose interface is limited to functions that supply data and metadata; all other functionality is encapsulated in the implementation. As the components are only aware of the interfaces, the data set can easily be replaced with some other structure, for example a direct database connection, without re-implementing any visualizations or data processors. Apart from the data sets, GAV Flash applications are built using a combination of visualization components and linked modules that control selection, filtering, color and animation. Other components handle application level events such as menus, and a module for the snapshot mechanism. The abstraction into interfaces also allows other users to extend the framework with new functionality, such as new visualizations or data providers. The framework definitions can then be followed with regard to accessing data and shared assets in order to produce new implementations. For more information see: http://ncomva.se/flash/prototypes/devguide/.

The generalization of components coupled with advanced features can make it difficult to encompass all data scenarios in a component. Data could be a large multivariate dataset or a highly dense temporal set. These two types of datasets often

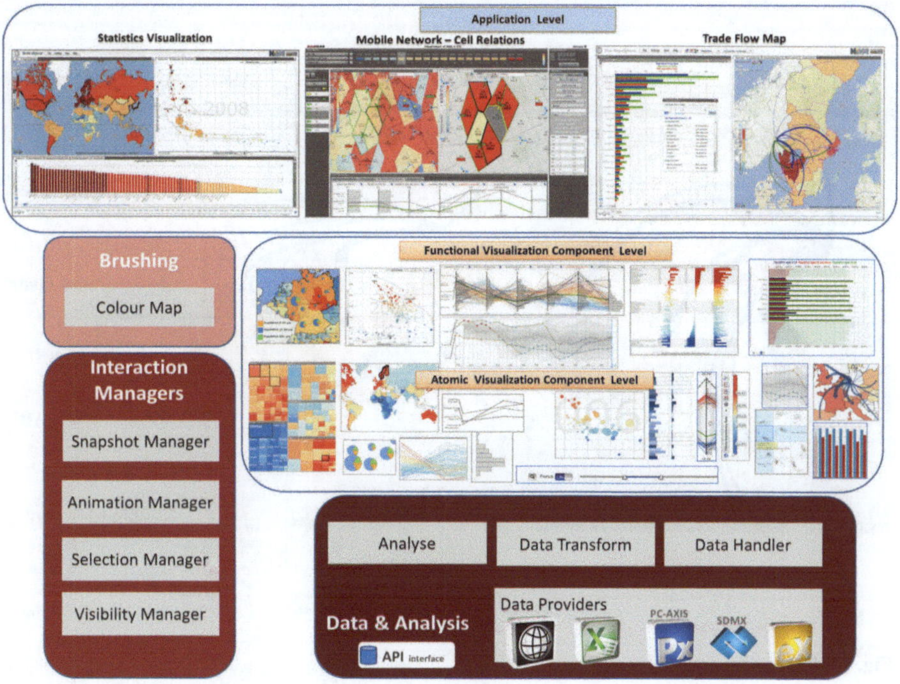

Fig. 11.3 The GAV Flash framework

require different solutions in terms of the data processing, the element drawing, and also the end user experience of the visualization. To facilitate the need for dynamic components we break them down into small blocks called atomic components (Fig. 11.3). These can be combined to form a fully functional component but they are not dependent on each other. This concept can take many forms depending on the parent component, the simplest example being how the map uses different layers to display different levels of data presented below (Fig. 11.4). The same concept is used in other components.

The combination of a component base with one or more atomic parts forms a functional component. They are generally encapsulated together with the required GUI elements needed to control the visualization so that only the combined properties of all atomic parts are visible to the surrounding application. The atomic parts allow the creation of customized functional components that can differ significantly depending on the end users' needs. A number of atomic parts can be reused in several components. For example, a range filter can be used in both the parallel coordinates and the color legend. The functional components can in turn be used by application developers and linked to each other through the use of linking components such as a selection manager, a visibility manager, and an animation controller to create quick prototypes and provide a first look at the data. The first prototype can then determine the direction the visualization needs to go, and whether some kind of special atomic and/or functional component is required.

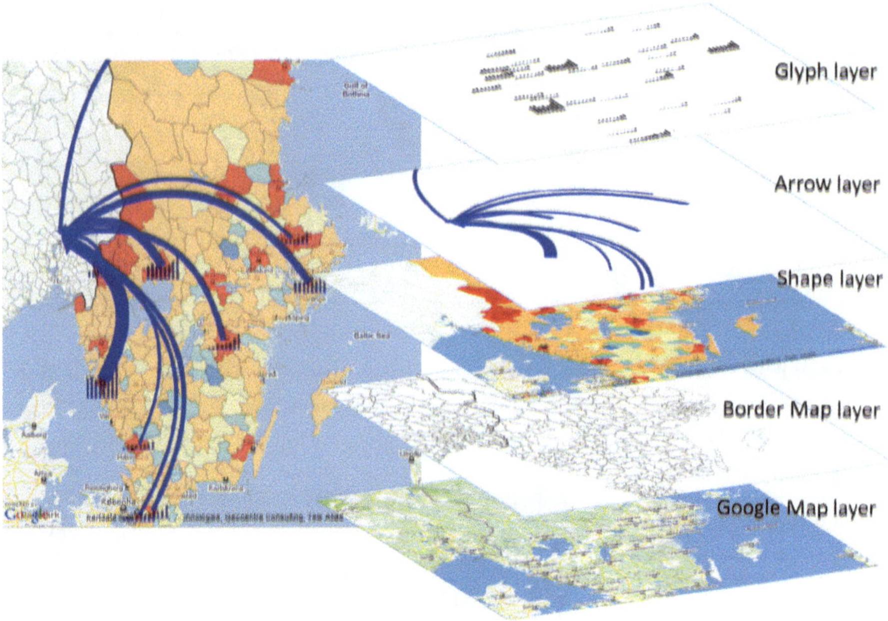

Fig. 11.4 Map layers

Interactive controls in the functional components enable the user to enter a visual dialog with the data and Shneiderman's information seeking rule (Shneiderman 1996) is used (overview first, zoom and filter, details-on-demand) with Keim's later modification (Keim et al. 2006) (analyze first, show the important, zoom, filter and analyze further, details-on-demand). The functional components also provide the foundation for using linked and coordinated views (Roberts 2007; Ward 1994) and are applied together with combinations of brushes. Over the past fifteen years a technique has emerged for the analysis of complex relations in spatio-temporal multivariate data which has demonstrated its utility, and which also realizes the overall concept of a GAV framework. This uses multiple linked views (Figs. 11.3 and 11.7) to simultaneously present, explore, and analyze different aspects of multivariate data. The views are used adjacent to each other and include map, scatter plot, histogram, time graph, parallel coordinates etc. Interesting subsets of the data are interactively selected and brushed, and the relations are investigated in all the linked views. A data-of-interest method is used in all linked views to visually separate interesting data features from the rest of the data. To accomplish this the framework uses focus + context visualization (Doleisch et al. 2003; Muigg et al. 2008) such as the fish eye technique (Furnas 1986) in histograms (Fig. 11.1) and dynamic queries (Ahlberg et al. 1992) in parallel coordinates (Fig. 11.3), table lens and an attached color legend extending the analysis capabilities to scenarios with larger data sets.

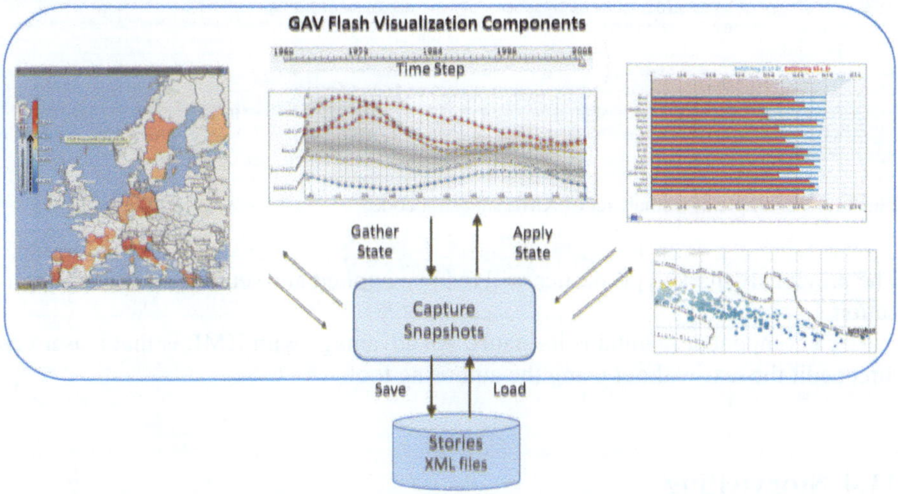

Fig. 11.5 The snapshot system scans through all active views to gather and apply states

11.3.2 Integrated Snapshot Mechanism

GAV Flash is not only an exploration and discovery tool, but also a means of collecting snapshots and writing associated stories to support a social style in the use of visual analytics. Storytelling (Jern 2001; MacEachren et al. 2001) is achieved through a mechanism in GAV Flash that supports the storage of interactive events in an analytical reasoning process through "memorized interactive visualization views" or "snapshots" that can be captured at any time during an explorative data analysis process. This is an important part of the analytical reasoning process.

When exploring and making sense of comprehensive statistics data, we need a coherent cognitive workspace to hold discoveries for organizational and navigational purposes. In GAV Flash capturing, saving and packaging the results of an eXplorer "gain insight" process in a series of "snapshots" helps the analyst highlight views of particular interest, and subsequently guide other analysts to identify important discoveries (Fig. 11.5). The snapshot tool creates a single, or a continuous series (story) of, visualization captures during the exploration process. In a typical scenario the analyst has selected relevant indicators, time series, color class values, range filter conditions for selected indicators and highlights the discoveries in simultaneously linked views.

The analyst requests a snapshot with the Capture function that results in a snapshot class operation scanning through all the connected GAV Flash components for the properties that are to be captured. Each of these properties will then be parsed into XML and stored. The final XML story file normally includes the selected indicator data and the references to the geographical regions that were applied. When a snapshot is activated, the saved state of the snapshot class will be read from the XML file (Fig. 11.6) and parse its nodes back into the component properties again.

```
<component name="floatingColorLegend" type="colorLegend">
    <axis min="0" max="1"/>
</component>
<component name="scatterPlot" type="scatterPlot2D" showTrails="true">
    <axis id="x" indicator="4" min="0.11807817589576547" max="0.979885993485342"/>
    <axis id="y" indicator="0" min="28.03571428571428" max="92.85714285714286"/>
    <axis id="size" indicator="0" scale="55"/>
</component>
```

Fig. 11.6 Example of a small set of XML snapshot code

The previously marked properties will then be applied and set the state of the application.

Each component maintains its status. An advantage with XML is that a user can direct edit the text without using the authoring tool.

11.4 Storytelling

The use of innovative geovisual analytics tools helps to communicate statistics to non-expert users. A tool provides the capability to create order in the user experiences, combining and reading data through its basic elements (words and text for the natural language, images and graphs for the visual aspects). However, it prevents the users from considering other specific issues. For example, it is impossible to extract a synthetic snapshot from texts in natural languages, or to highlight single events in a choropleth map at a glance.

A method is needed for the visualization of spatio-temporal data and the ability to link free texts to such models, which are also shareable with other users. This represents a meaningful step in turning data into knowledge. Visual storytelling is a way of telling stories through interactive web-enabled visualization, and facilitates a leap in understanding by the public enabling them to appreciate how statistical indicators may influence our society.

Statisticians with diverse background and expertise participate in creative discovery processes (Fig. 11.2) that transform statistical data into knowledge. Storytelling tools integrate this geovisual analytics process, and through collaboration shared understanding is developed with other statisticians. After a consensus has been reached, the results can be published. The snapshot mechanism helps the author of a story to highlight data views of particular interest and subsequently guide others to significant visual discoveries.

The author creates a single or discrete series of captures during the explorative process by selecting relevant indicators, regions-of-interest, color schema, filter conditions focusing on the data-of-interest, or a time step for temporal statistics. Associated explanatory text provides a richer functionality than simple metatext by allowing the reader to click on key words and learn about topics in the story. A story hyperlink is a reference in the story metatext that links to an external URL web site or a captured snapshot. To insert a hyperlink in the metatext the text is selected and a button "Link" is made visible and two options appear: a) new capture (snapshot) or b) link to an external URL (Fig. 11.7).

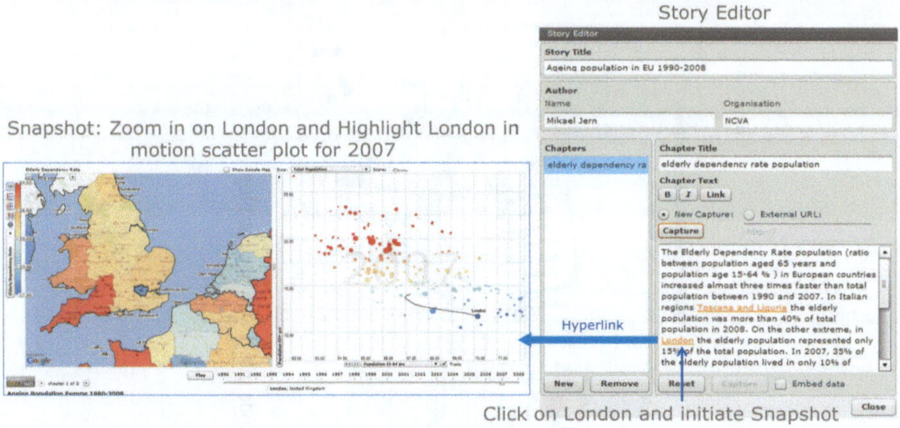

Fig. 11.7 Example of a use of the Snapshot mechanism in GAV Flash

Before the actual capture is done, the user navigates the map view to a particular country, select indicator, select indicators for the scatter plot, and select time step. A "Capture" is made and all preferred states are saved. When the story is read subsequently, hyperlinks can be initiated and eXplorer will display the state-of-the-snapshots. Hyperlinks that instantiate a state in the eXplorer application are a central feature of the storytelling mechanism, with associated descriptive text that can guide the reader. A few words and a snapshot can provide the difference between a pretty picture and understanding.

11.4.1 Publisher and Vislets

A Vislet is a standalone Flash application (widget) assembled from low-level GAV Flash components in a class library and Adobe Flex GUI tools. This may be represented by a composite time-linked histogram and scatter plot view (Fig. 11.8). A Vislet facilitates the translation of selected detailed statistics data into heterogeneous and communicative sense-making news. It also integrates metadata and dynamic embedded animated visualizations that can engage the user. Publisher is the server tool that imports a story and generates the HTML code that represents the Vislet and metadata. First, the user selects an appropriate visual representation for the Vislet e.g. map, scatter plot, parallel axes, table lens or time graph. Then the size of the Vislet window with metadata is set and Publisher generates the HTML code. This code is manually copied and embedded into a web page. The Vislet can then be opened in the user's Web browser and dynamically communicate the story (Fig. 11.9). A Publisher server maintains the Vislet flash (swf) files with a story repository, statistical data and, if required, regional shape maps. The Vislets run locally in the client's Flash Player and can therefore achieve dynamic interactive performance.

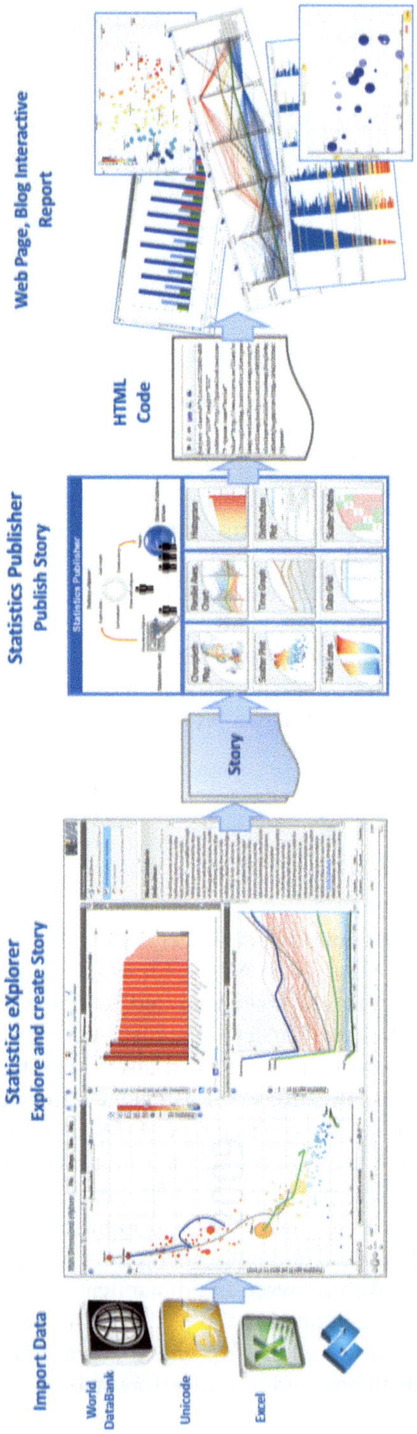

Fig. 11.8 From importing data, exploring and creating a story, to publishing and finally embedding the HTML code into a web page or blog

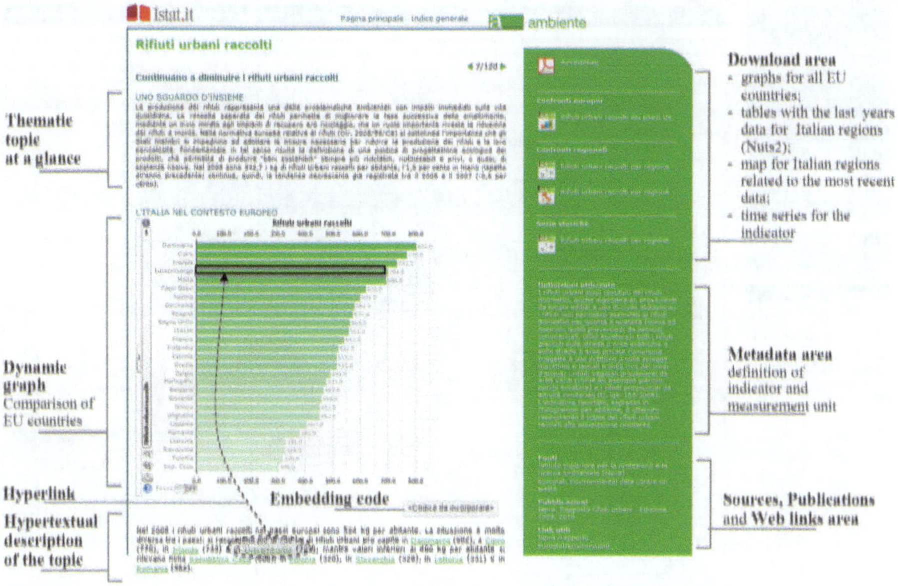

Fig. 11.9 Example of a Vislet implementation by Italian national statistics ISTAT http://noi-italia.istat.it/

Interactive features in a Vislet are available to all visualizations including tooltips, brushing, highlight, and filters that can discover outliers and dynamic multiple-linked views. Several specialist color legend tasks are supported e.g. show outliers based on 5th and 95th percentiles in certain colors, or dynamic sliders that control class values.

11.5 Interactive Documents

The code of practice for European statistics with regard to dissemination, states that "*European Statistics should be presented in a clear and understandable form, disseminated in a suitable and convenient manner, available and accessible on an impartial basis with supporting metadata and guidance*". This is a principle of accessibility and clarity. To comply with this, OECD in collaboration with the authors have developed the interactive Web document "Regions-at-a-Glance" presenting statistical indicators ranging from economic, social, demographic and environmental fields for more than 2000 local OECD regions from all over the world (http://www.oecd.org/regional/regionsataglance). The result represents an innovative solution from the statistical point of view, and offers a dynamic and interactive method for the visualization of spatio-temporal regional data, and the ability to link metatext to such a model.

An interactive document is based on interactive "vislets" embedded into the document instead of static images. This makes the diagrams interactive so that the user

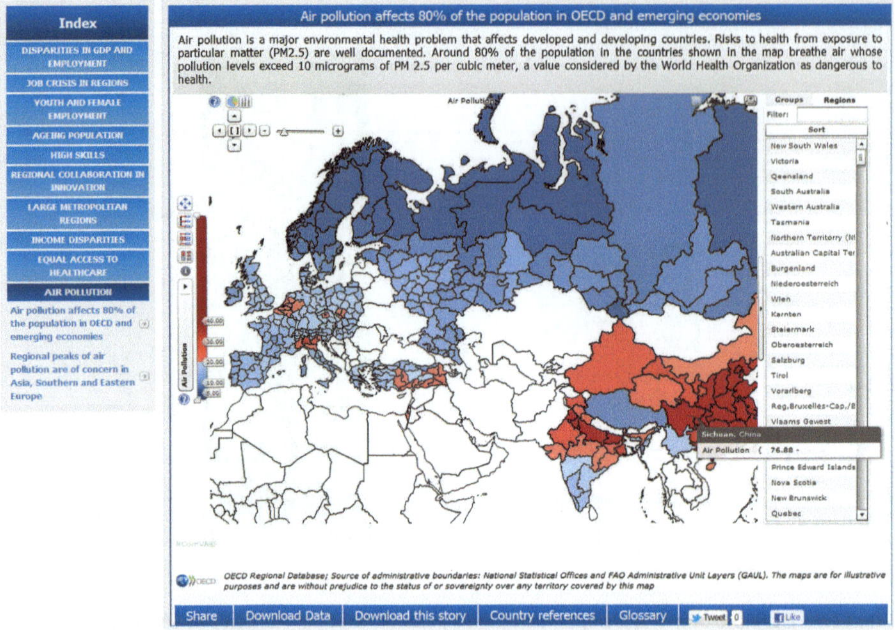

Fig. 11.10 Dynamic document OECD Region-at-a-Glance http://www.oecd.org/regional/regionsataglance

can change the indicators, and also view how the data changes over time using the animation facilities available.

One of the interactive documents created is the regions at a glance document published by OECD (Fig. 11.10). For the interactive documents, the analysts at OECD created snapshots for the regions at a glance data dividing them into different chapters and sections within the chapters. From these snapshots the visualizations were chosen and vislets were created. Some of the vislets only have one visualization component per chapter while others have multiple components and chapters with links embedded into the hypertext. These vislets are then stored with the text for the chapter in an XML file that has been divided into sections.

The interactive document platform is based on php and xsl transformations. When the web page is accessed the platform loads all the XML files available and creates the interactive document with an index page as the start page. For each chapter the user visits they see the text regarding that chapter, the vislet connected to the text, and also the hyperlinks in the text linking to other snapshots. JavaScript is also used to link to the previous and next chapter/section so that the user can navigate through the interactive document in the same way as a person turns the pages of a book.

For the interactive documents, some extra features have been added for each chapter. The user can download the data that is used in the visualization by clicking on the download data button and accessing the data in Excel format. The text from

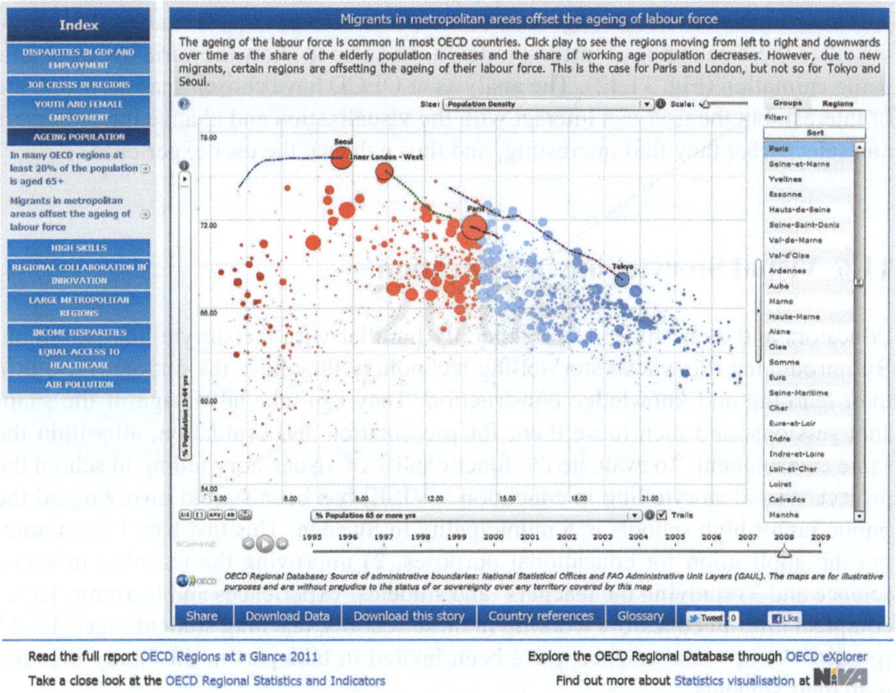

Fig. 11.11 The OECD Regions at a Glance interactive edition Chap. 8 equal access to healthcare

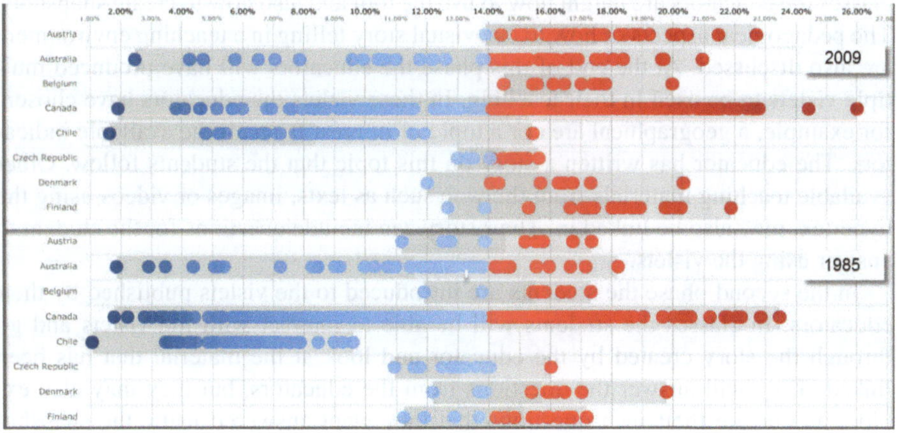

Fig. 11.12 Example of an interesting change in the distribution visualization over time

the printed document is also available for each chapter so that the user can download and read the chapter as a pdf. To make it easier to share the vislet a button has been added that displays the code for the vislet. The user may select a vislet that is interesting and copy it to a web page or blog and share it (Fig. 11.11).

The main benefit of making the document interactive is that it enables the user to visualize the data that is of interest to them, and also to show the variation over time using animation (Fig. 11.12). The analysts at OECD have chosen snapshots that are of interest, but the user can interact with the visualization and change the indicators and select what they find interesting, and thus enhance the user experience.

11.6 Visual Storytelling in Education

Educators and their students are generally familiar with the storytelling paradigm. By introducing this visual storytelling technology they have the option to use it in their learning and knowledge construction. They can take advantage of the snapshot sessions, and then reuse them for presentation and evaluation, all within the same environment. To evaluate the functionality of visual story telling in school the project "visual storytelling in education" (VISE) has been started involving all the public junior high schools in a municipality in Sweden. This involves 1) customizing the application for educational purposes, 2) improving the teaching in social science and 3) studying the teachers' and students' experiences and learning. To accomplish this, all educators working in these schools, teaching students aged 13–15 (grade 6–9) in social science, have been invited to take part in this study together with their students.

The project has been divided into a number of phases. In phase one the teachers are introduced to World eXplorer and the concepts of visual storytelling. During classes the educators are taught how to use the tool and also how to create snapshots. The pedagogical aspects of how to use visual story telling in a teaching environment are also discussed. At the end of this phase the educators will have produced multiple vislets to be used in their teaching. In these vislets the educators have chosen, for example, a geographical area or a topic of interest from all the available indicators. The educator has written a story on this topic that the students follow. Other available teaching materials from the web such as texts, images or videos using the hypertext may also be linked in. Their story can include questions for the student to answer using the vislets.

In the second phase the students are introduced to the vislets published by their educators. In classes the students will be able to interact with the vislets and go through the story created by the educator and look at the material that has been linked. They will answer the questions from the educators, but they may also explore and create their own questions that they want answered using the snapshot mechanism. At the end of the lesson the educator can use the vislet to go through what has been learned and the students can show their own snapshots and discuss in groups what they have found. Examples of questions that have been raised during a pre-study for this project have been "Where in the world do people live?". For this question the students have compared the population in different geographical areas. Then they have used extra indicators to look at both geographical as well as socio-political indicators to see how living standards are different around the world.

Together with extra material linked in, such as topology maps, the students have gained a better understanding of birth rates, how long people live, and how access to fresh water can change the population within an area.

The last phase is for the educators to teach other educators. When the project ends the aim is that visual storytelling will be available for use in social science education and that educators will be able to continue their work teaching their colleagues how to use visual storytelling in school.

Our aim with this project is that visual storytelling will give educators innovative tools that can make national and regional statistics interactive and visually understandable and usable to the student. It will also challenge the students to investigate new theories and then communicate them visually.

11.7 Conclusions and Future Development

Traditional practices for geovisual analytics methods applied to official statistics have required tools for greater user participation and an improved user experience. The approach set out in this paper allows the analyst (teacher) to communicate with interested readers (students) through visual discoveries captured in snapshots with descriptive text. Selected indicators and visual representations can be published with their metadata, thus facilitating the comprehension of statistical information by non-expert readers. This advanced storytelling technology can be very useful for educational purposes. At the same time, the Vislet technique applied to World eXplorer can help in developing immediate on-line publications, which draw attention to recent trends in data.

The integrated statistics exploration, collaboration and publication process addresses editorial storytelling aimed at producing statistical news content supported by an automatic authoring process. HTML code representing insight and knowledge is embedded into a web page or blog and communicates statistical data using dynamic visualization. Storytelling technology is introduced with the goal of advancing research on statistical collaboration. It also delivers these facilities in a web-enabled toolkit. At the same time, it encourages the use of more advanced, collaborative geovisual analytics technologies because of its accessibility. It can import any regional statistical data from national statistics to statistics from a neighborhood. It can also enable the users to take a more active role in the discovery process. For example, users can identify those areas that outperform other regions of their country. The tool increases the interest in, and knowledge of, regional structures and development patterns among specialist as well as non-specialist users.

Reviews from the partners OECD, Sweden and Denmark Statistics, Eurostat, Italy Statistics, Goteborg City and many others who have evaluated the platform and toolkit highlight the following features:

- eXplorer can easily be customized by a statistics organization—it requires only regional boundaries (shape file) and associate indicator data;

- eXplorer is a comprehensive tool for advanced users—the Vislet approach is also regarded as an easy to use and attractive approach for the public;
- Encourages collaboration between statistics analysts and users of statistics;
- Capturing, saving and opening discoveries (snapshots) with associated analytics reasoning metadata e.g. Storytelling;
- IT expertise is not required to publish interactive visualization embedded in blogs or web pages;
- Strategic tool for news media to publish statistics news on the web;
- Easy to import external statistical data into eXplorer;
- Ability to have dynamic time-link views and see the multi-dimensionality of regional development;
- Increased expectations in terms of user experience;
- Will encourage greater educational use of official statistics.

Acknowledgments This applied research case study was carried out by NCVA and a spin-off company NComVA, in close collaboration with OECD who supplied data and a comprehensive evaluation of the application. The research is supported in part by funding from the "Visualization Program" coordinated by the Swedish Knowledge Foundation. The authors thank Tobias Åström at the National Centre for Visual Analytics (NCVA) at MIT, Linkoping University.

References

Ahlberg, C., Williamson, C., & Shneiderman, B. (1992). Dynamic queries for information exploration: An implementation and evaluation. In *Proc. ACM CHI'92: Human factors in computing systems* (pp. 619–626). Link to HCIL TR 92-01.

Ainsworth, S. (2006). DeFT: A conceptual framework for considering learning with multiple representations. *Learning and Instruction*, *16*(3), 183–198.

Baumann, A. (2011). *The design and implementation of weave: A session state driven, web-based visualization framework*. University of Massachusetts Lowell.

Carr, D., White, D., & MacEachren, A. M. (2005). Conditioned choropleth maps and hypothesis generation. *Annals of the Association of American Geographers*, *95*(1).

Doleisch, H., Gasser, M., & Hauser, H. (2003). Interactive feature specification for focus + context visualization of complex simulation data. In *Proc. symposium on visualization (VisSym)* (pp. 239–248).

Furnas, G. W. (1986). Generalized fisheye views. In *Proc. human factors in computing systems (CHI '86)* (pp. 16–23).

Goldman, S. R., L Mertz, D., & Pellegrino, J. W. (1989). Individual differences in extended practice functions and solution strategies for basic addition facts. *Journal of Educational Psychology*, *81*(4), 481–496.

Guo, D., Chen, J., MacEachren, A. M., & Liao, K. (2006). A visualization system for space-time and multivariate patterns. *IEEE Visualization and Computer Graphics*, *12*(6).

Jern, M. (2001). Smart documents for web-enabled collaboration. In J. A. Vince, & R. A. Earnshaw (Eds.), *Digital content creation*. Berlin: Springer.

Jern, M. (2010a). Collaborative Educational GeoAnalytics applied to large statistics temporal data. In *Reviewed proceedings, CSEDU 2010, conference on computer supported education*, Valencia, April 2010.

Jern, M. (2010b). Educating students in official statistics using embedded geovisual analytics storytelling methods. In *Reviewed proceedings in Eurographics*, Norrköping, May 2010.

Jern, M., Rogstadius, J., Åström, T., & Ynnerman, A. (2008). Visual analytics presentation tools applied in HTML documents. In *Reviewed proceedings, IV08*, London, July 2008. Los Alamitos: IEEE Computer Society.

Keel, P. (2006). Collaborative visual analytics: Inferring from the spatial organisation and collaborative use of information. In *VAST 2006* (pp. 137–144). IEEE.

Keim, D., Mansmann, F., Schneidewind, J., & Ziegler, H. (2006). Challenges in visual data analysis. In *Proc. international conference on information visualization (IV '06)* (pp. 9–16).

Kinzel, M., & Wright, D. (2008). Using geovisualizations in the curriculum: Do multimedia tools enhance geography education? In *Environmental systems research institute education user's conference*. Paper Number 1290.

MacEachren, A. M., Brewer, I., et al. (2001). Geovisualization to mediate collaborative work: Tools to support different-place knowledge construction and decision-making. In *20th international cartographic conference*, Beijing, China.

Muigg, P., Kehrer, J., Oeltze, S., Piringer, H., Doleisch, H., Preim, B., & Hauser, H. (2008). A four-level focus + context approach to interactive visual analysis of temporal features in large scientific data. *Computer Graphics Forum*, *27*(3), 775–782.

OECD web site (2012). http://www.oecd.org/GOV/regionaldevelopment.

Roberts, J. C. (2007). State of the art: Coordinated & multiple views in exploratory visualization. In *Proc. coordinated & multiple views in exploratory visualization* (pp. 61–71).

Robinson, A. (2006). Re-Visualization: Interactive visualization of the progress of visual analysis. In *Workshop proceedings, VASDS*.

Shneiderman, B. (1996). The eyes have it: A task by data type taxonomy for information visualizations. In *Proc. IEEE symposium on visual languages* (pp. 336–343).

Stenliden, L., & Jern, M. (2010. Educating official statistics using geovisual analytics storytelling methods. In *Reviewed proceedings, international technology, education and development conference, INTED*, Valencia, 2010.

Thomas, J., & Cook, K. (2005). Illuminating the path: The research and development agenda for visual analytics.

Viégas, F. B., Wattenberg, M., Ham, F. V., Kriss, J., & McKeon, M. (2007). Many eyes: A site for visualization at Internet scale. *IEEE Transactions on Visualization and Computer Graphics*, *13*(6), 1121–1128.

Ward, M. (1994). XmdvTool: Integrating multiple methods for visualizing multivariate data. In *Proc. IEEE visualization* (pp. 326–336).

Wohlfart, M., & Hauser, H. (2007). Story telling for presentation in volume visualization. In *EuroVis2007*.

Part III
Interaction and User Interfaces

Chapter 12
Top Ten Interaction Challenges in Extreme-Scale Visual Analytics

Pak Chung Wong, Han-Wei Shen, and Chaomei Chen

Abstract The chapter presents ten selected user interface and interaction challenges in extreme-scale visual analytics. The study of visual analytics is often referred to as "the science of analytical reasoning facilitated by interactive visual interfaces" in the literature. The discussion focuses on applying visual analytics technologies to extreme-scale scientific and non-scientific data ranging from petabyte to exabyte in sizes. The ten challenges are: in situ interactive analysis, user-driven data reduction, scalability and multi-level hierarchy, representation of evidence and uncertainty, heterogeneous data fusion, data summarization and triage for interactive query, analytics of temporally evolving features, the human bottleneck, design and engineering development, and the Renaissance of conventional wisdom. The discussion addresses concerns that arise from the different areas of hardware, software, computation, algorithms, and human factors. The chapter also evaluates the likelihood of success in meeting these challenges in the near future.

12.1 Introduction

Extreme-scale visual analytics, generally speaking, is about applying visual analytics to extreme-scale data. Thomas and Cook (2005) define visual analytics (VA) as "*the science of analytical reasoning facilitated by interactive visual interfaces.*" By extreme-scale data, we are referring to both scientific and non-scientific data of a petabyte (10^{15}) today to the magnitude of exabyte (10^{18}) in the next five years.

P.C. Wong (✉)
Pacific Northwest National Laboratory, Richland, WA, USA
e-mail: pak.wong@pnnl.gov

H.-W. Shen
The Ohio State University, Columbus, OH, USA
e-mail: hwshen@cse.ohio-state.edu

C. Chen
Drexel University, Philadelphia, PA, USA
e-mail: chaomei.chen@drexel.edu

J. Dill et al. (eds.), *Expanding the Frontiers of Visual Analytics and Visualization*,
DOI 10.1007/978-1-4471-2804-5_12,

When the VA research and development (R&D) agenda (Thomas and Cook 2005) was published in 2005, the focus of the R&D community was largely on non-scientific data analytics and their applications. The agenda was not intended to be a static, final document but rather an evolutionary recommendation that guides the community based on its needs and priorities. In the years since the agenda was published, the VA community has continued to evolve and new requirements have emerged.

For example, the National Science Foundation (NSF)'s Foundations of Data and Visual Analytics (FODAVA) (FODAVA 2012) program has taken a particular interest in, among others, the mathematical foundations that enable and support data and visual analytics. The U.S. Department of Energy (DOE)'s Advanced Scientific Computing Research (ASCR) program (DOE 2010) has set a goal to address the exabyte data problem with a vision of future exascale computer systems comprising as many as a billion cores. Visual Analysis of Extreme-Scale Scientific Data is one of the six major R&D areas formally identified by DOE.

Size does count. When data size reaches the magnitude of an exabyte, it creates a significant set of unsolved and potentially unsolvable problems that challenges the conventional wisdom and assumptions in computing, computational reasoning, visualization, etc. In fact, some domain and computation scientists have already suggested that everything ranging from hardware to software must adapt and change, and change quickly (Ahern et al. 2011; Ahrens et al. 2010), to fully address the extreme-scale data challenges looming on the horizon.

Because we want to accelerate the pace of progress towards addressing the extreme-scale visual analytics challenges, we present a set of hard problems in this chapter and invite the readers to consider the challenges from different technical and intellectual viewpoints. These hard problems are presented as a list of top *interface and interaction design* challenges of extreme-scale visual analytics. The list was created based on what we have learned from our work and extensive discussion with domain experts in the community. We intend to continue to identify and rank additional top-problem lists in areas such as hardware and computation as related to extreme-scale visual analytics.

The chapter presents related work in extreme-scale data analytics in Sect. 12.2, describes what an extreme-scale visual analytics problem should be in Sect. 12.3, and identifies and ranks a list of top interface and interaction design problems in extreme-scale visual analytics in Sect. 12.4. We evaluate the likelihood of success of the selected challenges in Sect. 12.5 and conclude our discussion in Sect. 12.6.

12.2 Related Work

We highlight some of today's extreme-scale data problems found in scientific and technological communities, describe recent R&D efforts to address some of the extreme-scale challenges, and present three top-ten problem lists reported in modern data visualization and visual interface literature.

12.2.1 Some Well-Known Extreme-Scale Data Problems Today

The problem of managing extreme-scale datasets is real and growing more serious every year. In 2007, *The Wall Street Journal* (Swanson 2007) published an article on *Exaflood* information transmitted over the internet. Multiple datasets have since been identified in the literature that either have reached, or have the potential to reach, multi-exabyte in size. These datasets include the world's digital content (500 exabytes in 2009) (Wray 2009), broadcasted information (1900 exabytes compressed in 2007) (Hilbert and Lopez 2011), and telecommunication (projected to be two exabytes per month by 2013) (Cisco Network Index 2012).

12.2.2 Extreme-Scale Data Visualization and Management

There are a number of recent U.S. Department of Energy (DOE)-sponsored workshop reports that discuss the mission and R&D opportunities in exascale data management and visualization (Ahern et al. 2011; Ahrens et al. 2010). Within the scientific visualization community, both VACET (2012) and Institute for Ultra-Scale Visualization (2012) have continuously developed new and innovative visualization technologies for petabyte data applications.

In his keynote speech at the ACM SIGMOD/PODS Conference in 2008, Ben Shneiderman (2008) discussed the challenges of visualizing extreme-scale datasets with a limited number of display pixels. Most of the examples discussed are related to non-scientific data visualization applications.

12.2.3 Top-Ten Visualization and Visual Interface Challenges in Literature

A number of top-ten problem lists have been presented in the visualization and visual interface literature. Hibbard (1999) presents perhaps the first ever top-ten list of problems in visualization, which includes topics from virtual reality to direct data manipulation with visualization, and focuses mainly on early scientific visualization problems found in the 1990s.

In 2002, Chen and Börner (2002) presented their top-ten list in visual interface to digital libraries. Although the topic area is somewhat similar to the Hibbard list, the Chen and Börner list has a wider topic scope that emphasizes information analytics.

Finally, Chen (2005) presented a bona fide list of unsolved problems in information visualization. The list, which was published just before Thomas and Cook (2005), contains modern analytical topics from prediction to quality measure studies that align well with the visual analytics R&D agenda presented in Thomas and Cook (2005).

12.3 Three Fundamental Elements of Extreme-Scale Visual Analytics

During the preparation of this chapter, we attempted to define extreme-scale visual analytics among ourselves by looking at the underlying data (scientific, non-scientific, social, etc.), the analytical techniques (mathematical, cognitive, immersive, etc.), and the ultimate goals (presentation, reasoning, sensemaking, etc.) of the problem. In the end, instead of providing an elegant definition of the emerging area, we suggest three fundamental elements that characterize an extreme-scale visual analytics problem to facilitate the rest of the discussion, and leave the formal definition open for others to contribute to and elaborate further.

The first element, of course, is the *size* of the underlying data. The reason we emphasize size is that the traditional *post-mortem* approach of storing data on disk and visualizing it later is going to break down at the petascale and will undoubtedly have to change for exascale (Ahern et al. 2011; Ahrens et al. 2010). Extreme data size is the root of many computational and analytical difficulties. However, it also provides the broadest possible opportunity for R&D in the area.

The second element is the inclusion of both visual and analytical means in the solution of the problem. Following the recommendations in Thomas and Cook (2005), a visual analytics process normally involves a combination of visual representation, data transformation, interactive manipulation, and sensemaking. In other words, visualizing an extreme-scale dataset as a static display or a video is not visual analytics. Such visualizations are sometimes referred to as *presentation visualization* in the literature.

The third and final element is the active involvement of a human being in reasoning and sensemaking during the visual analytics process. To borrow a term from the data mining community, visual analytics is indeed a *supervised data analysis* process that involves active interactions between the computer and human being. The interaction element as implemented on a parallel high-performance computer (HPC) has subsequently become a top challenge in our discussion in Sect. 12.4.

12.4 Imminent Challenges of Interface and Interaction Design

We present ten selected *interface*-focused and *interaction design*-focused challenges for extreme-scale visual analytics. The order of the challenges does not reflect relative importance, but rather the content correlation among individual challenges.

12.4.1 In Situ Interactive Analysis

We mentioned earlier that the traditional post-mortem approach of storing extreme-scale data on disk and then analyzing it later may not be possible beyond petascale in the near future. Instead, the *in situ* visual analytics approach attempts to perform as much analysis as possible while the data are still in memory. This approach can greatly reduce the cost of I/O and maximize the ratio of data use to disk access.

However, today's HPC architectures generally do not support or promote *interactive* operations. Even though an interactive operation is technically possible, the time spent waiting for user responses in an interactive operation will quickly increase the cost of the computation to a prohibitive level. Thus, one of the major challenges is how do we optimally share the cores within the hardware execution units and alleviate the overall disruption of the workflow brought by the human-computer interactions.

12.4.2 User-Driven Data Reduction

While many agree that more aggressive data reduction needs to be done for extreme-scale applications, it is not clear where and how such data reduction should take place. Traditionally, data reduction is often performed via compression. However, given that the size of data is overwhelmingly large, and many datasets have single or double precision, the effectiveness of compression will be extremely limited.

Several other data reduction mechanisms are possible. For example, data can be stored at a much lower resolution if little or no interesting features exist. The definition of features can be geometrical, topological, or statistical. Because different applications will have different requirements, it is risky to perform data reduction without involving the humans that produce the data. Thus, the challenge of data reduction for extreme-scale application is to develop a flexible mechanism that can be easily controlled by users based on their needs. It is likely such a customized mechanism will be multi-level (data level, feature level, and application level), and all levels will need to work seamlessly together. Furthermore, unnecessary details such as the lower level storage and I/O also need to be encapsulated and hidden from the user.

12.4.3 Scalability and Multi-level Hierarchy

Scalability has been a continual challenge for any big data problems. Whether it is algorithmic, visualization, or display scalability issues, the multi-level approach has always played a vital role in the computation, analysis, and final outcomes. We discuss the multi-level concept and different mechanisms for user-driven data reduction in the last section. But no matter what mechanism is applied to the dataset, the corresponding hierarchical outcomes will often result in additional challenge to the rest of the visual analytics tasks.

Given a big dataset G, a prevailing multiresolution approach is to generate an increasingly coarsened hierarchy $G_0, G_1 \ldots G_i \ldots G_n$ such that the fine levels provide local details and the coarsened levels give the overall structures for both computation and visualization. The multi-level concept has addressed the big data problem for years when the data size remains in the terabyte range. When the data size increases further, the number of hierarchical levels can quickly escalate. For example, if we generate a multi-level hierarchy from an exabyte dataset using a dyadic approach, there will be as many as 60 levels between the coarsest and finest levels. Navigating such a *deep* hierarchy, and searching for the optimal resolution (and details) at the same time, has become one of the major challenges for scalable analysis.

12.4.4 Representation of Evidence and Uncertainty

Evidence synthesis and uncertainty quantification are two fundamental data analytics problems in their own right. Evidence and uncertainty often both supplement each other and underscore each other's inferiority. In a visual analytics environment, this information is frequently united by visual representation for further reasoning and sensemaking.

The issue of evidence representation is that the interpretation of evidence is subject to the person doing the interpretation. The process often depends on prior knowledge, subjective settings, and the analyst's viewpoint (Chen 2008). As data size grows, the problem becomes more complicated and more human decisions are involved. Uncertainty quantification attempts to model the consequences of various machine and human decisions based on the presented evidence and to predict the qualities of the corresponding outcomes. The primary challenge is how to represent the evidence and uncertainty information of extreme-scale data clearly and *without bias* through visualization.

Additionally, humans are cognitively vulnerable, especially when dealing with large-scale data visualization. A secondary challenge is how to help humans to be aware of cognitive biases and pitfalls that could potentially alter what they believe they are seeing. As one can lie with statistics, one can also lie with perceptual illusions and cognitive patterns, whether it is intended or not.

12.4.5 Heterogeneous Data Fusion

We seldom see fully homogeneous datasets at extreme-scales in real life. Most of the known extreme data problems today are highly heterogeneous and proper attention must be paid to analyzing the interrelationships among the heterogeneous data objects or entities. As the size and complexity of a heterogeneous dataset continue to grow, extracting the data semantics and interactively fusing them together for visual analytics will significantly add additional burdens to both computation and complexity of the problems.

For example, we used to harvest multimedia data—such as text, images, audio, and video—and then analyze them independently. As multimedia becomes increasingly digital and connected, knowledge is potentially embedded in data of all types/sources and in the aggregate. Extracting knowledge may require mining the entire dataset in order to measure and assess the relative relevance of the information. Thus, the data size directly, and in many cases non-linearly, affects the dimensionality and scope of the underlying analytical problem. Similar challenges can also be found in scientific computing domains such as climate modeling, where scalar fields meet flow fields referenced by both geographic coordinates and topological structures. Overall, the data heterogeneity problem makes the extreme-scale visual analytics challenge even more formidable.

12.4.6 Data Summarization and Triage for Interactive Query

As the size of data exceeds petabytes, it becomes very difficult, if not impossible, to examine the complete dataset all at once. Instead, the model of visual analytics and data analysis for extreme-scale datasets will be more like database queries—that is, the user requests data with particular characteristics, and only the corresponding results are presented.

One key to support interactive data query is effective data summarization. The goal of data summarization is to organize the data based on the presence and the type of features, which can be defined by certain general criteria as well as domain-specific input. For scientific data, features can be roughly classified as geometrical, topological, and statistical. For non-scientific datasets, features are often related to the semantic or syntactic components of the data. Extraction of meaningful features can be a major challenge. As the dimensionality of features can be high, it is necessary to reduce the dimensionality of feature descriptors to a manageable space that allows efficient exploration by the users. Finally, after data summarization is completed, the data needs to be stored and indexed in an I/O efficient format that allows rapid runtime retrieval. One technical challenge is to make the underlying I/O components work hand in hand with the data summarization and triage results, which together facilitate interactive query of the extreme-scale data.

12.4.7 Analytics of Temporally Evolving Features

We live in a dynamic world, and hence data generated from most applications will evolve with time. For example, the topics of interest in Twitter messages can change daily, if not hourly. The evolution of data characteristics often contains important information about the underlying problem and therefore should be a focus of data analysis and visual analytics.

Several challenges exist when analyzing temporally evolving extreme-scale data. One is that the size of data is often quite large, which makes lengthy calculation or preprocessing impractical for daily use. Another challenge is that when the features occur at different spatial and temporal scales, traditional visualization methods such as animations, or displaying small multiples, often fail. The key challenge for analyzing extreme-scale temporal data is to develop effective visual analytics techniques that are computationally practical and that can take advantage of humans' unique cognitive ability to track moving objects.

12.4.8 The Human Bottleneck

HPC experts have recently predicted that all major components related to computational science—from power, memory, storage, I/O bandwidth, to total concurrency, etc.—will improve by a factor of three to 4444 times by 2018 (Ashby et al. 2010). Human cognitive capabilities, however, will undoubtedly remain constant. The human is rapidly becoming the bottleneck in extreme-scale visual analytics.

We know that humans are not good at visually detecting patterns in a large amount of data. When data grows to a certain size, patterns within the data tend to become white noise. Human cognitive biases also tend to distort or inhibit understanding of data patterns in large data. Researchers have used large, tiled displays to increase the visualization space and alleviate the big data visualization problem, but there is a visual acuity limitation (Yost et al. 2007) that potentially hinders the effectiveness of the large screen approach. There is no Moore's Law for any cognitive activities. The human bottleneck problem in extreme-scale visual analytics will stay relevant for a long time.

12.4.9 Design and Engineering Development

The HPC community has offered little to motivate the adoption of API and framework standards for general user interface development on HPCs. Much of today's large scale data analytics interface development is implemented and executed on desktop-based environments such as a desktop computer. It is nevertheless a feasible, and often the only, solution for today's large-scale visualization and visual analytics efforts. In other words, community-wide API and framework support on an HPC platform is still not an option today.

Beside the hardware challenges, software support for user interaction development is also a major problem today. Programs will need to be compiled using a 64-bit compiler to allow access to a much larger memory address space. Unfortunately, some of the prevailing user-interface frameworks such as Qt (Qt Framework 2012) still do not fully support 64-bit Windows OS, which allows much greater memory space and thus larger datasets. Additional compatibility challenges also come from programming languages, operating system platforms, customized domain software, and threading programming problems on today's desktop computers. This will remain a problem until either there is a massively parallel desktop computer or a new HPC that addresses some of the above-mentioned challenges.

12.4.10 The Renaissance of Conventional Wisdom

Throughout the years, our community has acquired nuggets of wisdom that are widely adopted by both researchers and practitioners when working on information analytics problems. Many of these once seemingly infallible nuggets will inevitably be confronted by the above challenges when dealing with extreme-scale data. Among the well-known controversies, for example, is Ben Shneiderman's "*overview first, zoom and filter, then details-on-demands*" mantra for navigating or viewing big data.

We agree that full-blown interactive analytics on HPC will be possible eventually but probably not any time soon. For now, we will need a secondary machine such as a desktop computer to support post-mortem visualization. But writing such an extreme amount of data on disks is also not likely to happen soon. All these, plus *the-human-bottleneck* challenge, work against Shneiderman's mantra that requires effective access to all information at one time and in one place. So our final, and perhaps most important challenge, is to spark the Renaissance of conventional wisdom in visual analytics as applied to extreme-scale data. Successfully bringing back the conventional wisdom will most likely foster solutions to many of the problems described in the chapter.

12.5 Evaluation and Likelihood of Success

The *In-Situ Interactive Analysis* challenge could theoretically be solved even today. The potential solution would require a radical change in the operation, regulation, and policy of the HPC-wide community as well as the system and engineering support of the commercial hardware vendors.

The *User-Driven Data Reduction* and *Scalability and Multi-Level* challenges are both related to the size of the extreme-scale data. As HPC is becoming increasingly mainstream, many problems with respect to these challenges can potentially be addressed, or at least alleviated, by building more powerful machines and developing more advanced data and computation algorithms.

The *Representation of Evidence and Uncertainty* challenge is a hard problem to solve because it often involves human bias in the process, which may not be fully addressed by machine-based automated systems. The problem also coexists with two other difficult, non-visual problems (evidence synthesis and uncertainty quantification), which further exacerbates the challenge.

With a wider range of applications and stronger demand in growth for the HPC community, the *Heterogeneous Data Fusion* and *Data Summarization and Triage* challenges for many database-oriented problems can potentially be addressed in the near future. The increasing availability of low-cost, high-performance data warehouse appliances such as Netezza Data Warehouse (2012) also offers alternative solutions to the data challenges.

Both *Analytics of Temporally Evolving Features* and *The Human Bottleneck* challenges push the human performance to the limit. These challenges are not meant to be solved entirely. Remedies that alleviate some of the problems may potentially come from a combination of better computation hardware and more advanced human-computer interaction hardware devices and interfaces.

The *Design and Engineering Development* challenge will be addressed when the demand rises for HPC-based user interface and interaction science and technology and outweighs the cost of development. The success of this challenge also lies in the availability of solutions that meet the *In-Situ Interactive Analysis* challenge above.

As for the *Renaissance of Conventional Wisdom* challenge, we fully expect that it will eventually happen as the high-performance computer is becoming increasingly popular and will be the norm of everyday computation in the future.

12.6 Conclusions

This chapter discusses the emerging area of extreme-scale visual analytics and presents some of the top user interface and interaction design challenges facing the current and future research and development of the area. Much of the discussion is drawn from the experience of our ongoing work, as well as the experiences of our colleagues in the exabyte data visualization and management areas. While the scientists and researchers of the extreme-scale data analytics community may have a different priority on these and other challenges, solving some of these challenges can certainly lead to very desirable outcomes for scientific discoveries and advances in technology for the society.

Like Thomas and Cook (2005), the discussion of this chapter is not meant to be a static, final document. It will most likely evolve as both hardware and software technologies advance in the future. We hope the discussion of these important issues can inspire enthusiasm and creative solutions to the challenges, and ultimately lead to a vibrant and engaged community for extreme-scale analytics.

Acknowledgments This work has been supported in part by the U.S. Department of Energy Office of Science Advanced Scientific Computing Research under award number 59172, program manager Lucy Nowell; the National Science Foundation; the U.S. Department of Homeland Security, Science and Technology Directorate; the National Visualization and Analytics Center™ at the Pacific Northwest National Laboratory; and the Pfizer Corporation.

The Pacific Northwest National Laboratory is managed for the U.S. Department of Energy by Battelle Memorial Institute under Contract DE-AC05-76RL01830.

Special thanks to Jim Thomas for his support and friendship through the years—he is missed.

References

Ahern, S., Shoshani, A., Ma, K.-L., Choudhary, A., Critchlow, T., Klasky, S., Pascucci, V., Ahrens, J., Bethel, W., Childs, H., Huang, J., Joy, K., Koziol, Q., Lofstead, G., Meredith, J., Moreland, K., Ostrouchov, G., Papka, M., Vishwanath, V., Wolf, M., Wright, N., & Wu, K. (2011). Scientific discovery at the exascale: report from the DOE ASCR 2011 workshop on exascale data management, analysis, and visualization. http://www.olcf.ornl.gov/wp-content/uploads/2011/01/Exascale-ASCR-Analysis.pdf.

Ahrens, J., Rogers, D., Springmeyer, B., Brugger, E., Crossno, P., Jiang, M., Harrison, C., Monroe, L., Tomlinson, B., Pavlakos, D., Childs, H., Klasky, S., & Ma, K.-L. (2010). *Visualization and data analysis at the exascale—a white paper for the National Nuclear Security Administration (NNSA) Accelerated Strategic Computing (ASC) exascale environment planning process* (Lawrence Livermore National Laboratory Technical Report LLNL-TR-474731). https://asc.llnl.gov/exascale/exascale-vdaWG.pdf.

Ashby, S., Beckman, P., Chen, J., Colella, P., Collins, B., Crawford, D., Dongarra, J., Kothe, D., Lusk, R., Messina, P., Mezzacappa, T., Moin, P., Norman, M., Rosner, R., Sarkar, V., Siegel, A., Streitz, F., White, A., & Wright, M. (2010). The opportunities and challenges of exascale computing—summary report of the advanced scientific computing advisory committee (ASCAC) subcommittee. US Department of Energy Office of Science. http://science.energy.gov/~/media/ascr/ascac/pdf/reports/Exascale_subcommittee_report.pdf.

Chen, C. (2005). Top 10 unsolved information visualization problems. *IEEE Computer Graphics and Applications*, *25*(4), 12–16.

Chen, C. (2008). An information-theoretic view of visual analytics. *IEEE Computer Graphics and Applications*, *28*(1), 18–23.

Chen, C., & Börner, K. (2002). Top ten problems in visual interfaces to digital libraries. In *LNCS: Vol. 2539. Visual interfaces to digital libraries* (pp. 225–231). Berlin: Springer.

Cisco Network Index (Cisco VNI) (2012). http://www.cisco.com/en/US/netsol/ns827/networking_solutions_sub_solution.html.

U.S. Department of Energy (DOE) Office of Science (SC) (2010). Scientific data management and analysis at extreme-scale. http://science.energy.gov/~/media/ascr/pdf/funding/notices/Lab_10_256.pdf.

Foundations of Data and Visual Analytics (FODAVA) (2012). http://nvac.pnl.gov/nsf.stm, http://fodava.gatech.edu/node/3.

Hibbard, B. (1999). Top ten visualization problems. *ACM SIGGRAPH Newsletter*, *33*(2).

Hilbert, M., & Lopez, P. (2011). The world's technology capacity to store, communicate, and computer information. *Science*, *332*(6025), 60–65. http://www.sciencemag.org/content/332/6025/60.full.

Institute for Ultra-Scale Visualization (2012). http://ultravis.ucdavis.edu/.

Netezza Data Warehouse (2012). http://www.netezza.com.

Qt Framework (2012). http://en.wikipedia.org/wiki/Qt_framework, http://qt.nokia.com/products/.

Shneiderman, B. (2008). Extreme visualization: squeezing a billion records into a million pixels. In *Proceedings of the 2008 ACM SIGMOD international conference on management of data*, Vancouver, Canada (pp. 3–12).

Swanson, B. (2007). The coming exaflood. *The Wall Street Journal*. http://www.discovery.org/a/3869.

Thomas, J. J., & Cook, K. A. (Eds.) (2005). *Illuminating the path—the research and development agenda for visual analytics*. Los Alamitos: IEEE Computer Society Press.

VACET (2012). http://www.vacet.org/.

Wray, R. (2009). Internet data heads for 500 bn gigabytes. *The Guardian*. http://www.guardian.co.uk/business/2009/may/18/digital-content-expansion.

Yost, B., Haciahmetoglu, Y., & North, C. (2007). Beyond visual acuity: the perceptual scalability of information visualizations for large displays. In *Proceedings of SIGCHI conference on human factors in computing (CHI '07)* (pp. 101–110). New York: ACM.

Chapter 13
GUI 4D—The Role and the Impact of Visual, Multimedia and Multilingual User Interfaces in ICT Applications and Services for Users Coming from the Bottom of the Pyramid—First Concepts, Prototypes and Experiences

G. Baduza, J.H.P. Eloff, D. Kok, J. Encarnação, C. Merz, and M. Przewloka

Abstract Graphical User Interfaces (GUI) are discussed in the context of being used by users coming from the "bottom of the pyramid" to interact with and to run ICT (Information and Communication Technologies) applications for real life usage in their developing world. These interfaces are called "GUI 4D" (Graphical User Interfaces for Development). GUI 4D methodologies are a key aspect in enabling the users in the bottom of the pyramid to become part—within their own needs and capabilities—of integrated value/business chains, and also in finally closing both the digital and the social gap. They are presented and discussed here first from a technical and from an implementation point of view and considerations are also given on how the corresponding requirements, constraints and specifications are developed and used for GUI 4D implementations. Several examples, case studies and use cases from ongoing research projects, from existing pilots and prototypes and from related initiatives in Africa are presented. Some analysis of system adoption and the perceived benefits from using GUI 4D's are then given and discussed. The chapter concludes with a brief consideration of target applications and markets for GUI 4D's in the developing world, taking into consideration the dependencies and

G. Baduza (✉) · J.H.P. Eloff · D. Kok · C. Merz · M. Przewloka
SAP Research Internet Applications & Services, Pretoria, South Africa
e-mail: gugulethu.baduza@sap.com

J.H.P. Eloff
e-mail: jan.eloff@sap.com

D. Kok
e-mail: danie.kok@sap.com

C. Merz
e-mail: christian.merz@sap.com

M. Przewloka
e-mail: martin.przewloka@sap.com

J. Encarnação
TU Darmstadt, Darmstadt, Germany
e-mail: jle@gris.informatik.tu-darmstadt.de

J. Dill et al. (eds.), *Expanding the Frontiers of Visual Analytics and Visualization*, DOI 10.1007/978-1-4471-2804-5_13,

needs between the established and the informal economy in these countries. An extensive set of references used or related to the subject is given at the end of the chapter.

13.1 Introduction

User-Interfaces are in the ICT (Information and Communication Technologies) world the key-factor for the usability of applications, for user acceptance and for the performance of users and applications in a given context and environment. They are therefore extremely important and a very prominent area of research worldwide.

Putting these GUI's in the context of their "what ?" and "what for ?", we then have to consider the GUI in relation to the application and to the user for which it has to be designed, implemented and used (see Fig. 13.1).

Looking at the user, we have to consider two classes of users: the standard user, as we find it in the developed world, and the user coming from the "bottom of the pyramid", as we find it in the developing world. This classification helps in considering two types of GUI's, the standard, classical GUI and the GUI 4D (Graphical User Interface for Development), in which we consider a User with low or no literacy and computer knowledge and experience. In this chapter we address these considerations and use them to develop the requirements, constraints and specifications for the implementation of GUI 4D's for the different application domains and usage considerations, as well as for the different user constituencies.

This classification in two types of user interfaces, in GUI's and in GUI 4D's, is done to achieve a conceptual clarity and also to get some simplicity into the approach of defining the requirements and specifications for the implementation of a given user interface, for a certain user constituency and in a specific-application context. This distinction cannot be seen as absolutely clear and sharp; in reality both interface types (GUI and GUI 4D) are different instances or development stages in a continuum specified by various elements such as, the context of application, user, and environment. The final deployment of a user interface in a real-life environment will always be "something in-between", customized and dedicated to the existing context.

Several examples, pilots, case studies and use cases will be introduced and used to show the impact and reality of GUI 4D's in real life usage for ICT applications in the developing world. They form the basis to develop the needs and considerations for target applications and markets, especially in the context of the emerging economies that you find in the developing world.

13.2 Scope, Definitions and Classification

The focus of this chapter is to elaborate on graphical user interfaces suitable for facilitating the adoption of ICT applications in the developing world, in short referred

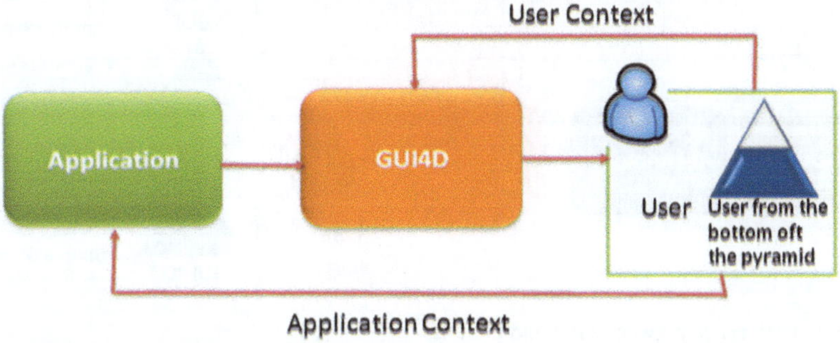

Fig. 13.1 Context considerations in a GUI 4D

to as GUI 4D. To avoid misunderstandings, the difference between GUI 4D and graphical user interfaces (GUI), in general, requires to be highlighted.

According to the Linux Information Project (2004), a GUI enables a user of a computer system to present the information in visual form and to interact with the system through visual objects such as icons. Furthermore a GUI includes all relevant information and different actions that the user can use to accomplish a task. GUI 4D is a term frequently referred to in formal and informal discussions on GUI matters within the context of the developing world. However, the existing literature lacks a proper definition for GUI 4D. The authors of this chapter postulate that GUI 4D focuses on the impact of visual, multi-media and multilingual user interfaces in ICT applications and services for users at the bottom of the pyramid. According to the IBM Research Lab in India (2006), users at the bottom of the pyramid are not IT literate and cannot afford to acquire ICT infrastructure such as PC's, laptops and servers. Furthermore, these users are highly mobile and will mainly interact via mobile devices. In short, GUI 4D focuses on the bottom of the pyramid. Access to ICT infrastructure and facilities in urban areas is higher than in rural areas. People in urban areas most typically have access to email, with a high percentage having mobile phones, households have at least one PC or laptop, therefore they have more access to ICT's (Gillwald and Esselaar 2005).

Information and Communication Technologies (ICT's) have become a means for people to communicate worldwide. In the context of the bottom of the pyramid and specifically in African countries, it has also changed the way people interact with each other, while also affecting cultures and communities (Blake and Tucker 2005; Chetty 2005; Emmanuel and Muyingi 2008). However, ICT's cannot be applied appropriately when 'what is appropriate' is not known. Whatever these goals, it is possible that ICT can provide a cost-effective way of reaching some of those goals, if the technology made available to the bottom of the pyramid addresses the unique requirements of GUI 4D. This is depicted in Fig. 13.2 which highlights the important differences between GUI and GUI 4D.

As shown in Fig. 13.2, the three main system components from a user's perspective are the application, the technology being used and the GUI. It is important to note that currently available GUI's, mostly designed and implemented in the developed world, are mainly technology driven as shown in the top right triangle. When

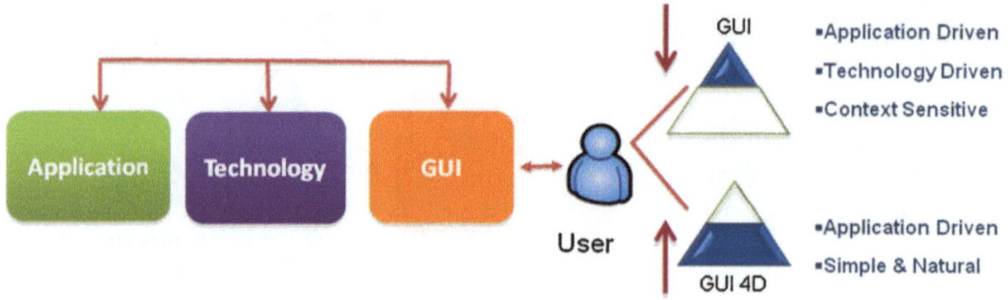

Fig. 13.2 Difference between GUI and GUI 4D

considering GUI 4D, the focus shifts from the technology perspective to interfaces that are, from inception, designed to be simple and natural. Furthermore GUI 4D should also focus on the user experience (UX) by facilitating interaction with applications that are designed to reflect the requirements of the developing world and therefore be useful in the local context.

In summary, we may say that the classical GUI's are application and technology driven, and also context-sensitive, while GUI 4D's are mainly application driven and more forced to be simple and natural on the interaction level. This implies that GUI's often use the latest and most advanced technologies, whereas GUI 4D's, on the other hand, have to quite often "hide" as much as possible of the underlying technology.

GUI 4D has significant potential to contribute in narrowing the digital divide between the users at the bottom of the pyramid and the rest of the world. The phenomenal spread of mobile phones in rural communities is gradually narrowing down the Digital Divide and promoting information accessibility in rural areas (Chetty 2005). The Digital Divide refers to the growing gap between individuals who have access to the Information and Communication Technologies and those who do not have such access for various reasons such as: illiteracy; personal handicaps; applications and contents are catering for specific cultural groups; digital infrastructure is poor; or appropriate computer equipment is lacking (Blake and Tucker 2005). The contribution that GUI 4D can make in narrowing the digital divide are twofold: firstly, the characteristics of the bottom of the pyramid users, such as no or low IT literacy levels, should be addressed by harnessing the benefits from multi-medial, multi-modal and multi-language approaches in GUI design; secondly, GUI 4D can enable a simple and natural interaction experience by creating environments that are adaptive, intelligent and highly visual. This dual role of GUI 4D is depicted in Fig. 13.3.

As already mentioned a GUI 4D should enable a natural yet simple experience for the user. However, this is not possible if aspects such as localization and appropriateness are overlooked. For the authors of this chapter the aspect of localization is of particular importance. For the purpose of this work localization refers to "What?" and "Where?". It is within this context that cognizance should be taken of whether the user interface is designed for people living in urban areas, or people living in rural areas.

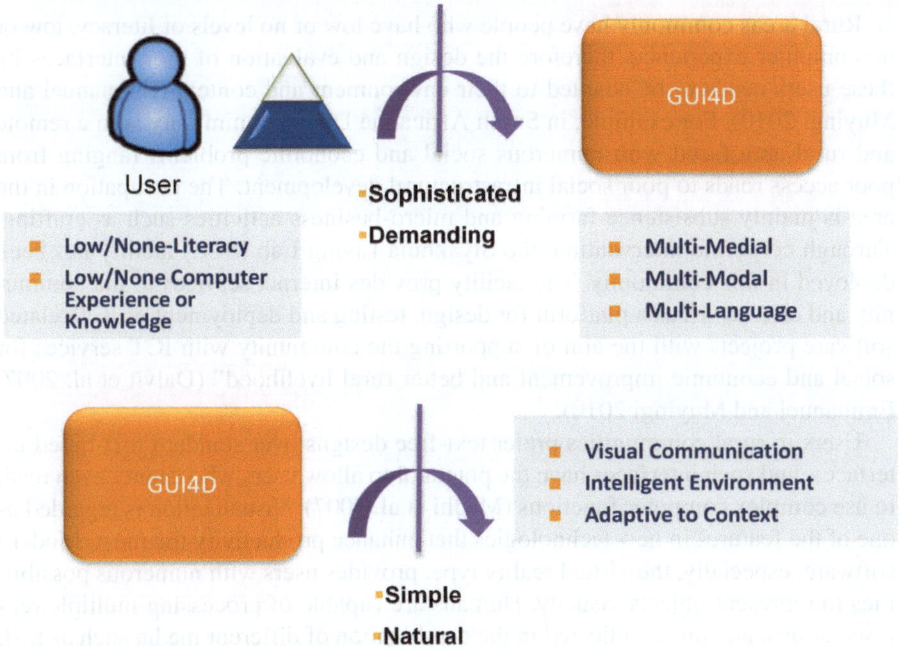

Fig. 13.3 Narrowing the digital divide

In urban areas the health and education opportunities are often better than in rural areas, but because of poverty other problems are worse. Examples include: overcrowding, unhygienic conditions, pollution, and unsafe houses. In rural areas poor education and health services, lack of infrastructure and many other services, poverty and low levels of literacy may prevail, but people usually live in healthier and safer environments (UNISA 2011).

GUI 4D focuses on addressing the unique requirements of users in the bottom of the pyramid. But "Who is the user in the bottom of the pyramid?" "These are the citizens who inhabit the Fourth World that sits beneath the Third World; some dozens of countries that, in the words of economist Paul Collier *are falling behind, and often falling apart*" (Collier 2008). Heeks (2009) stated that users in the bottom of the pyramid are non-IT literate. However he says that the situation is changing. When one looks at statistics it appears alarmingly low when it is noted that only 3 out of 100 people in the bottom of the pyramid have Internet access. The important point made by Heeks, which is often overlooked, is the fact that IT in the Fourth World should be seen as a communal as opposed to an individual resource. For example, it is common practice in the rural areas in South Africa to have a communal mobile phone for the whole village thereby providing Internet connectivity in reach of the users in the bottom of the pyramid. "Internet connectivity is also growing fast: by 42 % per annum in the bottom of the pyramid, compared to 18 % in Europe" (Heeks 2009).

Rural areas commonly have people who have low or no levels of literacy, low or no computer experience, therefore the design and evaluation of user interfaces by these users needs to be adapted to their environment and context (Emmanuel and Muyingi 2010). For example, in South Africa the Dwesa community is in a remote and rural area faced with numerous social and economic problems ranging from poor access roads to poor social infrastructural development. The occupation in the area is mainly subsistence farming and micro-business activities such as crafting. Through corporate intervention, the Siyakhula Living Lab (SLL) facility has been deployed in this community. The facility provides Internet services to the community and also serves as a platform for design, testing and deployment of ICT related software projects with the aim of supporting the community with ICT services for social and economic improvement and better rural livelihood" (Dalvit et al. 2007; Emmanuel and Muyingi 2010).

Users in rural communities prefer text-free designs over standard text-based interfaces, and such interfaces have the potential to allow users who cannot even read, to use complex computer functions (Medhi et al. 2007). Visualization is regarded as one of the features in new technologies that enhance productivity the most. Modern software, especially, the virtual reality type, provides users with numerous possibilities to represent objects visually. Humans are capable of processing multiple representations, and this is reflected in the combination of different media such as text, graphics, sound, and animation (Ligorio 2001). Visual communication is a simple way of interacting hence the use of GUI.

13.3 Design and Implementation

GUI 4D presents very unique challenges from a design and implementation point of view.

The design of a user interface is directly related to the amount of effort a future user of the system has to put in, in order to use the system productively. There are many methodologies currently available giving guidelines on the design of user interfaces.

Living Labs can also be considered as an important approach for supporting and facilitating the implementation of GUI 4D. SAP Research Internet Applications & Services Africa has very successfully used the Living Lab approach for obtaining direct user involvement in projects. Living Lab methodologies require the formalization of partnerships, thereby contributing to a collaborative design and implementation environment. One of the projects that benefited from this approach in our lab is the Overture project. The objective of Overture was to deliver mobile business services to Very Small Enterprises (VSEs). In this project the following partners played a vital role in designing user interfaces for real end-users: VSEs, suppliers of goods to VSEs, associations representing industry and non-governmental organizations, government representatives and tele-communications providers. These partners formed an ecosystem not only from a technology point of view but also an economic-socio perspective. Within a Living Lab it is common to use User Centered Design.

User Centered Design (UCD) is one of the more well-known methodologies that focus on user involvement from the beginning. Most researchers in South Africa (Emmanuel and Muyingi 2008, 2010; European Commission 2009; Horan 2005; Mulder et al. 2008) agree on using the User-Centered Design Approach in designing user interfaces for the rural communities, as the involvement of the user will be vital in determining what the user prefers. We believe a user-centered approach is most appropriate for GUI 4D.

When UCD is used in the design phase it claims to achieve, amongst other things, visibility and accessibility. This is done through the use of metaphors such as Persona, Scenario and Use Case (Blake and Tucker 2005; Chetty 2005; Emmanuel and Muyingi 2010; Gelderblom et al. 2011; Horan 2005). User personas have proved to be an invaluable tool within the context of GUI 4D. It is interesting to note that some publications regard the design of GUI's based on user personas as more important than the functional features of the application. They argue that users will not know what is possible but rather participate in testing out what they themselves have designed (Chetty 2005). It is vital to know the user's age, gender, culture, language, education level, physical limitations, computer experience, motivation and attitude, social context, relationships and communication patterns as well as the roles users are expected to play, in order to avoid the stereotype trap. At SAP Research Internet Applications & Services Africa (SAP Research IA&S Africa) we have used Persona very successfully on the Rustica project. The Rustica project implemented a prototype for eProcurement for Very Small Enterprises (VSEs) in rural and remote environments. Personas were developed for the owners of these VSEs and leaders in the community. GUI 4D examples for the Rustica project are discussed later on in this work.

Emmanuel and Muyingi (2010) proposes that a designer for UI in the developing world has to know the background of the user very well and suggested that ethnographic methods can be used to investigate the social background as well as the context. Ethnographic methods also enable user interface designers to be exposed to vast amounts of data which proved to be useful in developing the interface. Another advantage of ethnographic studies is the support for developing trust relationships with the users in order to prevent the user from feeling intimidated by their lack of experience in technology and computer literacy. Ethnographic approaches will also expose UI designers to being more aware of the environment which would also inform them of issues that are not evident at first sight. One very common approach whilst using ethnographic methods is contextual inquiry. This is based on the concept of apprenticeship, where the UI designer works as an apprentice to the user, one distinct outcome of this is a communication flow model which is very important in developing the UI's (Chetty 2005; Crabtree 1998).

Another view in the design of GUI's 4D is to design according to the culture of the community. A culture-sensitive user interface makes the users believe that the artifact belongs to them and also promotes technology acceptance (Emmanuel and Muyingi 2008). User interfaces that are culture-sensitive for a target group will

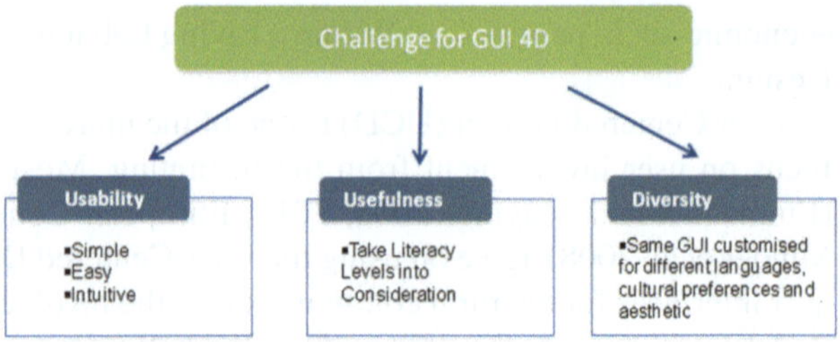

Fig. 13.4 Design and implementation challenges for GUI 4D

reflect aspects such as the language and cultural conventions of the people. When the cultural identities of a specific target group are considered during design, together with the required intuition and simplicity of a user interface, then the users' experience will be enhanced (Emmanuel and Muyingi 2008).

The design and implementation challenges for GUI 4D are summarized in Fig. 13.4.

A user and environment analysis has to be conducted in order to identify who the application is being designed for Emmanuel and Muyingi (2010). In the context of GUI 4D, the users are generally communities or target groups within community such as small traders, youth, and school children (European Commission 2009; Gelderblom et al. 2011; Palmer 2010). It is also advisable to know more about the users of the GUI 4D. Understanding their needs, the dreams and drives of the community and users, will enable the creation of a GUI that is in synchronization with their lives and aspirations (Mulder et al. 2008). The factors listed above will enable the creation of GUI's that adapt to the current situation and state of mind of the user, but also a GUI that can be used timelessly when the user has more knowledge of ICT's and GUI's.

13.4 Requirements and Constraints—Implementation Framework

The requirements and constraints for designing and implementing GUI 4D are summarized below:

1. Ensure that there is "Added-value" for the user within the context of the developing world. The objective should be to provide useful applications that reflect local requirements and culture. "Less" can be more—if the user sees the added value, he/she will accept the GUI 4D.
2. Special consideration should be given to ensure that there is a low level of intimidation by the technology. The aim should be to design the GUI 4D for novice users, namely users without prior knowledge (Chetty 2005).
3. Simplicity is a required design feature allowing, amongst other things, people to interact with a system with minimum training. The GUI should be easy to use i.e. being natural and intuitive.

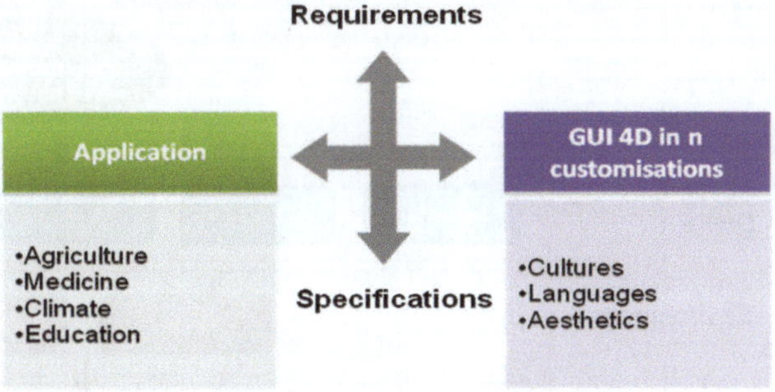

Fig. 13.5 $(1 \times n)$—implementability

4. Provide suitable input and output channels for illiteracy (Chetty 2005). For example, avoid input of text especially when mobile phones are used as the end devices (Parikh and Lazowska 2006).
5. Use visual displays such as icons (Chetty 2005; Emmanuel and Muyingi 2008; Parikh and Lazowska 2006).
6. A user interface for a specific culture group will reflect the language, text, layout of for example menus and labels, colors, metaphors, sounds and the look and feel as well as the social context of the culture. Other aspects such as time, dates, currency, number format, address format, dialogs, error messages, and navigation will also reflect the local culture of the target users. Localization enhances information accessibility, understanding and usability for the users. Localization provides a natural sense of interaction and an easy to use interface (Emmanuel and Muyingi 2008; Parikh and Lazowska 2006).
7. Focus should be on the community rather than the individual regarding access and ownership of infrastructure; and human-mediated access rather than direct access to hardware, network and information; visual, and interactive formats rather than text-intensive formats (Sood 2002).

Figures 13.5, 13.6, 13.7 depict how the requirements and constraints regarding GUI 4D all contribute to an implementation framework for GUI 4D's. The implementation framework clearly indicates the bottom of the pyramid user and his/her interaction with the application is the most important component.

The following highlights some of the aspects discussed in the implementation framework:

- Usefulness (Functional Requirements) refers to the value that is added for the user. For example, an eProcurement system that supports a cost effective way for delivering stock to very small enterprises in remote and rural areas which is normally not serviced by wholesalers.
- Performance (Evaluation Levels) can focus on multiple aspects including: (1) the usability of the user interface; and (2) the online/offline availability, especially in the situation where mobile applications are used in remote and rural areas. Mobile and Telecommunications involves operators as well as synchronization aspects between front ends (mobile phones) and back-ends which require special consideration.

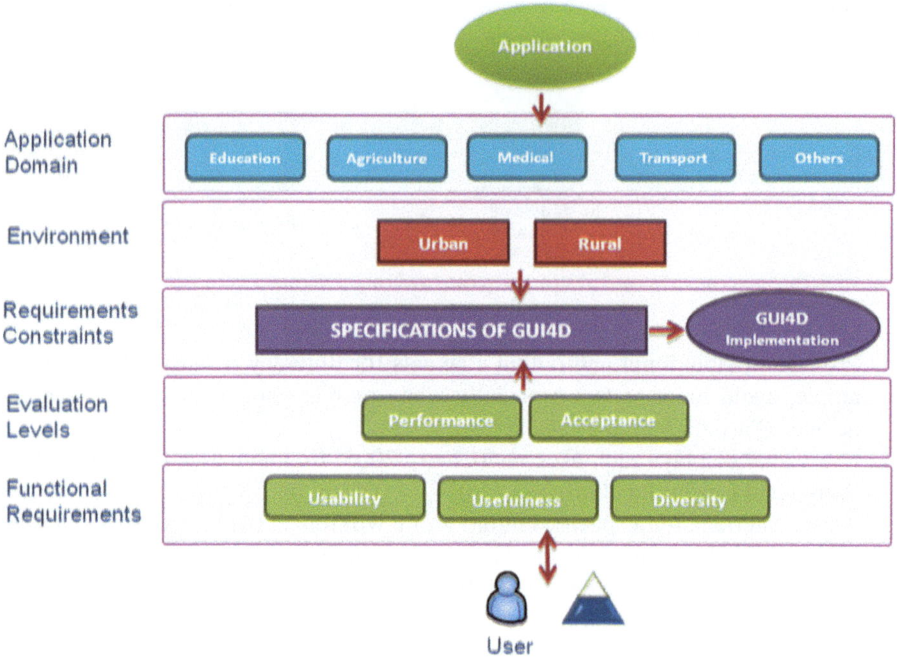

Fig. 13.6 Requirements and constraints for a GUI 4D

Fig. 13.7 Implementation framework for a GUI 4D

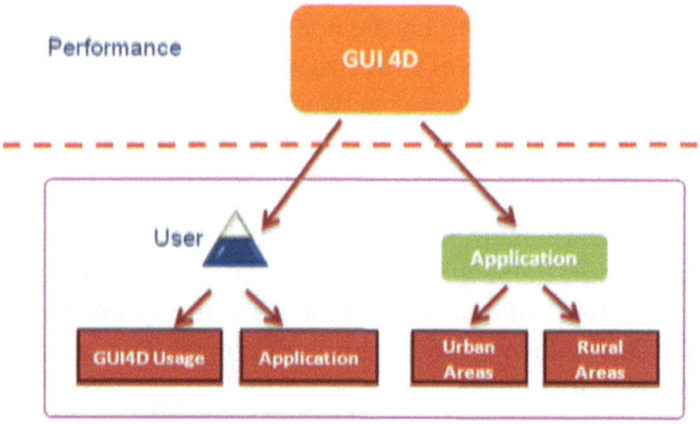

- GUI 4D Implementation (Requirements & Constraints) can be facilitated by adopting a Living Lab approach with real-life participants.
- Rural communities (Environment) present unique challenges to GUI 4D. Aspects such as social, trust, language and accessibility needs to be taken in consideration.
- Application Domains within the context of the developing world might be different from that of the developed world.

The Evaluation aspect (see Figs. 13.6 and 13.7) of the GUI 4D implementation framework requires further elaboration. Evaluation in this context can benefit from currently available usability evaluation methodologies which present several advantages and disadvantages depending on their application and context of use. SAP Research IA&S Africa has conducted usability evaluation projects on different mobile web applications using a variety of different methods. One of the methods used is an eye tracking methodology. This has contributed to an improved understanding of how the users actually perceive interface elements while trying to complete a task. The eye tracking methodology and tools used for evaluating the application on a mobile device in a controlled environment has the advantage of identifying specific usability issues without taking into account environmental factors and just concentrating on the core application.

Figure 13.7 indicates that there are two different perspectives on performance when designing and specifying GUI 4D: firstly the performance of the user with regard to the GUI 4D and the application, and secondly, the performance of the application for the user. The performance of the application for the user is dependent on how the application reflects the needs of urban versus rural users.

13.5 The SAP Strategy and Vision on GUI 4D's

13.5.1 Target Groups

Modern ICT technology penetrates more and more to the bottom of the pyramid and includes above all the capabilities of mobile devices, especially smart-phones. This leads to the conclusion that the affinity with using mobile devices is extremely high, and therefore mobility has to be a key topic of the research activities and projects at SAP. In this context, SAP decided to set a focus of the research projects in emerging economies on very small enterprises (VSEs) as well as on the end-users as target groups.

The decision to make the requirements of VSEs and end-users a guiding theme of current research activities assumes that we have to ensure that these requirements are equally economically and socially relevant.

From a research perspective, mobile enterprise applications help us to determine the following:

- Analysis of mobile application usage scenarios in emerging economies
- Analysis of contextual environment, user requirements, user behavior and user acceptance
- Transaction costs minimization in a high volume environment supported by high scalable and cost-effective IT-architectures
- Analysis and creation of new business models and business cases taking financial and social key figures into account
- Fullest possible integration of the end users and all stakeholders into the economic value chains and into the supply chains
- Analysis of security, trust and privacy for mobile business solutions

According to the standardized model ISO/IEC 9126, which was replaced by ISO IEC 25000 (2005), regarding the development of quality software [ISO1995], we are aligning our research projects within the development and pilot phase of software applications for the bottom of the pyramid in answering the following questions:

Functionality:

- Do the mobile application and the business software comply with the users' functional demands?
- To what extent does the software have to be fitted exclusively to the use case, or can the application cover several use cases, providing an elevated scope of operation and thus a higher universality?

Usability:

- How quick can our solution portfolio be introduced and used successfully by the end user?
- Which are the differences between GUI 4D and user interfaces for developed markets? What do they have in common, or how big is the necessary factor of differentiation?
- How intuitive is the solution, and do the end users use the solution efficiently?
- To what extent should we use concepts, which come from user interfaces that can be configured for the end user or from adaptive user interfaces?
- Which role does documentation still have for the end user?

Reliability:

- How reliable and fault-tolerant is the software regarding the technical and infrastructural edge conditions and regarding the end user's abilities?
- Are type or input errors from end users treated in a fault-tolerant way so that they do not affect the system stability?

Flexibility:

- How can a sensible and efficient maintenance concept be created? Which 'pull' or 'push' principles should be applied in the case of release changes and patch inputs?
- How flexible is the software regarding the adaption to other or changing use cases? What does this imply, especially for the user interfaces (GUI 4D)?
- To what extent does the software have to be modularized in such a way that as many components as possible can be re-used again? How easily can these components be assembled to create a new or different solution, or application, that can be applied as quickly and efficiently as possible ('time to market')?
- To what extent does the software have to be deployed? Which introduction and distribution concepts do we have to use, considering the fact that in the field of mobile applications we are confronted with a large number of technologically different and constantly changing devices?

Total Cost of Ownership (TCO):

- Which are the significant cost drivers for the different use cases?

- How can direct and indirect (software) costs be in a sensible relationship regarding the benefit? What volume and what diffusion (for the end-users) do we have to ensure to achieve the objectives with cost-benefit-considerations for the different parties ('win-win')?
- To what extent can modern architecture models (e.g. cloud computing) be adapted, thus leading to a sustainable decrease of the total costs?

The answers to most of these questions are very much related to, and dependent on, the quality, functionality and performance of the User-Interfaces (GUI's).

Thus the core research areas for SAP Research in this context are:

- Solutions that support (new) business models for VSEs (e.g. shop owners, service technicians)
- Domain and use cases in the area of eEnergy—optimal use of (household) energy resources/Internet of Energy
- Solutions that support small farm holders (the African Cashew Initiative—ACI)
- Domain and use cases in the area of Education and Learning

There is much analysis and research regarding user behavior in emerging economies as well as about particular user behavior of VSEs (see for example (EDI 2010) (Edim Azom and Muyingi 2010). This was discussed in Sect. 13.2. Likewise a number of publications have been written proposing recommendations and guidelines for cultural sensitive interfaces (see for example Hofstede 1997; Yeo 1996). Moreover, we have to keep the local technical boundary conditions in mind that we often find for users of mobile applications in rural areas such as the following:

- Poor and unsteady connections and mostly low bandwidth
- Applications are required to offer offline operations ensuring consistent data storage and—processing in offline and online mode
- Many different end-user devices and peripherals (manufacturer-wise, operating-systems, interfaces)
- User interfaces failing to meet the important requirements, expectations and needs of the target groups, leading to a rapid failure of the projects or which are counterproductive (Lalji and Good 2008). "One size fits all" simply does not work.

These issues were presented and detailed in Sects. 13.3 and 13.4 and will be illustrated by some examples and case studies in Sect. 13.7.

13.5.2 Motivation and Mission of SAP Research Internet Applications and Services Africa (Pretoria, South Africa)

The establishment of a SAP Research Centre in Pretoria, South Africa in 2005 was preceded by an applied research journey starting in 2002. During this period every effort was made to transfer and introduce first world technology solutions into the education and training sector in South Africa—to provide under-serviced and disadvantaged communities and learners with access to quality and affordable education and training from which they were previously deprived. Many lessons were learned but most critically were the re-discovery that first world technologies, including software, are not necessarily appropriate and relevant to the needs of emerging or developing regions. Although it is clear that there are large differences in assumptions related to the cost, power, and usage, there has been little work on how technology needs in developing regions differ from those of industrialized nations. We argue that Western market forces will continue to meet the needs of developing regions accidentally at best (the case for Technology in Developing Regions, Perspectives, Published by the IEEE Computer Society, June 2005, Brewer 2005).

Little is known about the needs of emerging economies and developing nations and prescribing first world solutions rather than collaborating on understanding the developing context and developing appropriate solutions to match the context (needs and opportunities in these economies) will not result in the expected outcomes. It holds true for both business and social development objectives. In the cases of "indiscriminate" development aid and the unconsidered utilization of first world ICT to solve developmental challenges and to grasp business opportunities in developing economies, both causes may be lost.

The importance of emerging economies to business software companies such as SAP should not be underestimated. The GDP of BRICS countries (representing emerging economies) will equal that of rich countries by 2020. In 2007, BRICS had a population of 2,829 bn, a combined GDP of $14,370 bn (= trillion) with ICT spend in 2011 estimated at $140 bn.

The facts and sentiments expressed above were part of the motivation for the establishment of an SAP Research Centre in the developing world—in Pretoria, South Africa in 2005. From its inception the research focus was on the *Technologies for Emerging Economies*. In very practical terms the Research Centre made every effort to understand the developing and emerging economy context, identify challenges, needs and opportunities where ICT could be utilized, whilst identifying business opportunities for SAP—opportunities leading to the development of appropriate business software and service solutions and its commercialization in the emerging world.

13.5.3 Examples and Case Studies from SAP Research Internet Applications and Services Africa (Pretoria)

SAP Research Internet Applications & Services in Africa focus on the inception, design and implementation of Technologies for Emerging Economies. The research agenda aims to conduct research and delivering proof-of-concepts that can make an economic and social intervention within the African context. Application domains that are of current interest are: business services for very small enterprises; education and energy. The following projects are discussed in this chapter to demonstrate work done in this lab on GUI 4D:

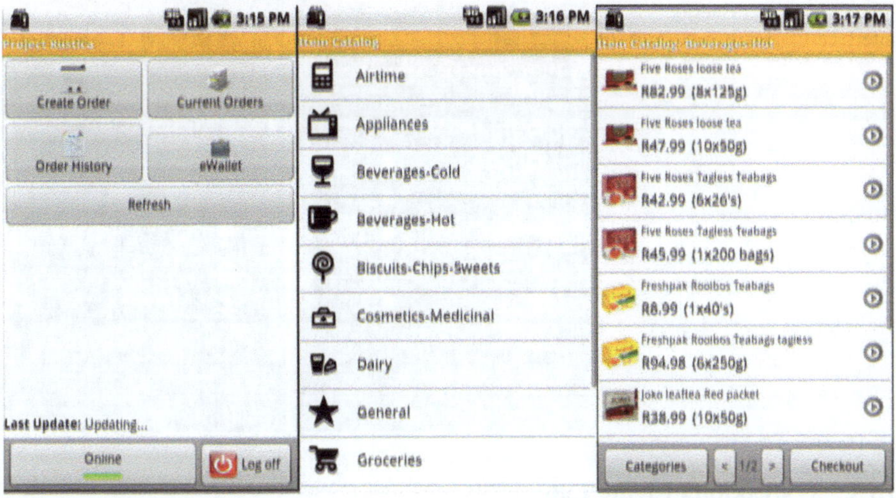

Fig. 13.8 Rustica interface

- Rustica
- Smart Energy
- Siyakhula Living Lab

13.5.3.1 Rustica

The Rustica Catalogue component on a mobile phone front end allows very small enterprises to order stock from a supplier which is then delivered to the VSE in the local community. In designing the interface familiar icons which were identified during interactions with the local community, have been used to illustrate what is being purchased. To confirm what is to be bought, exact pictures of the products are also displayed. The pictures represent the products that they are familiar with as well as the locally known brand names. All textual descriptions on the interface were provided by the local community (Fig. 13.8).

13.5.3.2 Smart Energy

The Smart Energy project is concerned with the detection of energy usage patterns by local rural households in order to determine the possibility of moving households to a smart grid. Whilst developing the UI for this project, common names and icons are also used that the households in the specific local remote community are familiar with. Simple and common words have been used that are known and used by the rural community. On the application layer the user is able to add stock (energy resources) that they use in their house as the application is customized to reflect their household profile. Users can view how much they spend on the different energy sources they purchase and also view their consumption (Fig. 13.9).

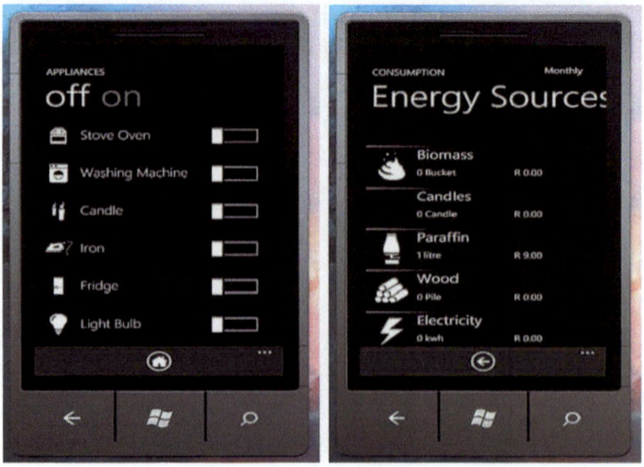

Fig. 13.9 Smart Energy interface

13.5.3.3 Siyakhula Living Lab

Cultural requirements were used to design the prototype of the Siyakhula Living Lab. The user interface is shown in Fig. 13.10, whilst the customer home page in Fig. 13.10a while Fig. 13.10b displays the products in an online shop for the customer. Figure 13.10c depicts the shop-owner main menu showing the tasks to perform and Fig. 13.10d the input screens for updating an item in a shop. The application allows rural micro-entrepreneurs to open online shops where customers from outside the community are able to access these items for purchase. Different interfaces are designed for the customers and the shop owners in order to accommodate the shops' owners who are usually community members with low literacy levels. The customer is able to login, browse products and place an order using the mobile phone. The shop-owner is able to manage their online shop using the mobile user interface on their mobile phone. The shop-owner tasks include monitoring orders, adding/removing artifacts, performing updates, adding new online shops, and other management activities (Emmanuel and Muyingi 2008).

13.6 Ongoing Projects and R&D Activities in GUI 4D's in Africa

13.6.1 Case Study—The African Cashew Initiative

13.6.1.1 Objectives

The African Cashew Initiative (ACi) is one of several multi-million dollar initiatives co-funded by the Bill & Melinda Gates Foundation and the German Federal Ministry for Economic Cooperation and Development to incubate and leverage the income of small holder farmers in developing countries (ACi 2010; Gates Foundation Pledge 2009). ACi focuses on organizing and supporting cashew producers in five African project countries—Benin, Burkina Faso, Côte d'Ivoire, Ghana

Fig. 13.10 Siyakhula prototype interface

and Mozambique—in order to enable them to increase their yields and the quality of their products, to improve business linkages with the medium and large scale processing industry, brokers and traders and develop advanced marketing strategies (including quality management). The initiative is currently in the third year of its project lifetime.

13.6.1.2 Use Cases

SAP in close cooperation with ACi partners explores how mobile business applications support small holder cashew farmers and processors in an African rural context. Through the introduction of Smartphone and geo-ERP (Enterprise Resource Planning) applications farmer cooperatives are enabled to run their business in a structured, effective and efficient way. The main interventions comprise applications to support the governance of farmer cooperatives (e.g. memberships, financials), operative business process support (e.g. bulk selling of raw cashew to buyers), analytics and certification (e.g. for fair-trade specialty markets). Essentially farmers get access to profitable markets that allow them to increase their income.

Established players like local processors, buyers and multinationals profit from enhanced transparency and reliability when doing business with farmer cooperatives. Such enterprises also include existing SAP customers. They are enabled to plan and forecast accurately. Ultimately, previously existing economic activities with farmer groups are sustained. This not only boosts local economic activity but could in a very direct way also improve the socio-economic situation for a vast number of under-serviced rural inhabitants.

Fig. 13.11 Smartphone usage at cashew buying stations

13.6.1.3 Piloting—Real Life Usage

Business and technology related interventions are guided by the so called Living Lab methodology (Niitamo et al. 2006; Schaffers et al. 2010; Van Greunen et al. 2009) comprising holistic efforts including business process innovations, added value propositions for each stakeholder, conceptual revenue models, organizational capacity building, scalable system design, development and real life roll-out as well as a close and regular interaction with end-users having diverse cultural and social backgrounds.

Agile development in an adapted SCRUM (Schwaber 2004) mode considers extended end user co-participation. in particular on use case design (before the system is deployed) and human computer interaction (once the prototypical system is deployed for the first time).

The pilot activities roll-out solutions that make use of advanced, reusable technical concepts and components. These components are part of a toolset that builds upon a so called Bottom Billion Architecture which is compliant to open standards and relies on an Open Source Design and Runtime (Dörflinger and Gross 2011).

Real life piloting took place during the cashew season 2011 (March till early June) in Brong-Ahafo, Ghana and concentrated on a digitally supported cashew buying and collection process (SAP TV, Video 2011). In detail the following use cases have been implemented at the Wenchi Cooperative Cashew Farming/Marketing Society Ltd:

- cooperative membership management
- cashew buying
- coordination of cashew collection
- digital tracing of primary produce
- specialty market certification support [e.g. Fairtrade]
- agricultural market information
- geo-analytics

The Union was constituted a number of years ago and represents more than 1000 cashew farmers in the region. It sources its raw cashew nut (RCN) from 11 buying stations, which are organized as independent farmer associations.

With the start of the cashew season in March 2011, the Union piloted the newly developed applications both at its secretariat and at 5 of its buying stations (~380 farmers). While the secretary was equipped with a GIS-based management system

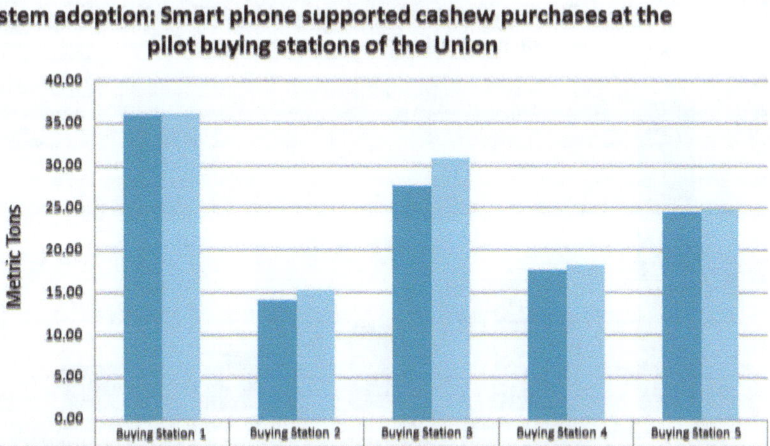

	Buying Station 1	Buying Station 2	Buying Station 3	Buying Station 4	Buying Station 5
Total smart phone purchases	35,95	14,03	27,51	17,62	24,45
Total purchases according to Union's books	36,13	15,30	30,86	18,28	24,82

Fig. 13.12 System adoption—comparison between Smartphone supported cashew purchases versus purchases according to the Union's books

on a laptop, the buying stations were equipped with robust Smartphones, allowing them to process cashew purchases as well as cashew movement (see Fig. 13.11). The system used barcodes to identify farmers and the cashew jute sacks are also traced via a barcode tagging system. Data synchronization is utilizing a combination of SMS and GPRS channels.

13.6.1.4 Results

The results of the system piloting have exceeded initial expectations. Within the cashew season 2011 close to 120 metric tons of cashew purchases have been recorded by the system, amounting to more than 1600 single buying transactions. System usability has proven to be very satisfactory and through the introduction of an incentive model for zonal facilitators an adoption rate of 96 % has been achieved (see Fig. 13.12).

The collected data allows very interesting analytics to gain insight knowledge about the cashew supply chain at the bottom of the economic pyramid (farmer and cooperative level). Roughly 60 % (205 out of 380) of the registered farmers sold to the union agents. Although this leaves room for speculation, a possible interpretation could be that the remaining farmers are selling their produce to other buyers. It remains to be seen whether the system's ability to document all sales on a farmer batch level (thus guaranteeing farmers their fair share of a fair trade premium) can serve as value proposition to farmers to increasingly sell their produce to the Union in future.

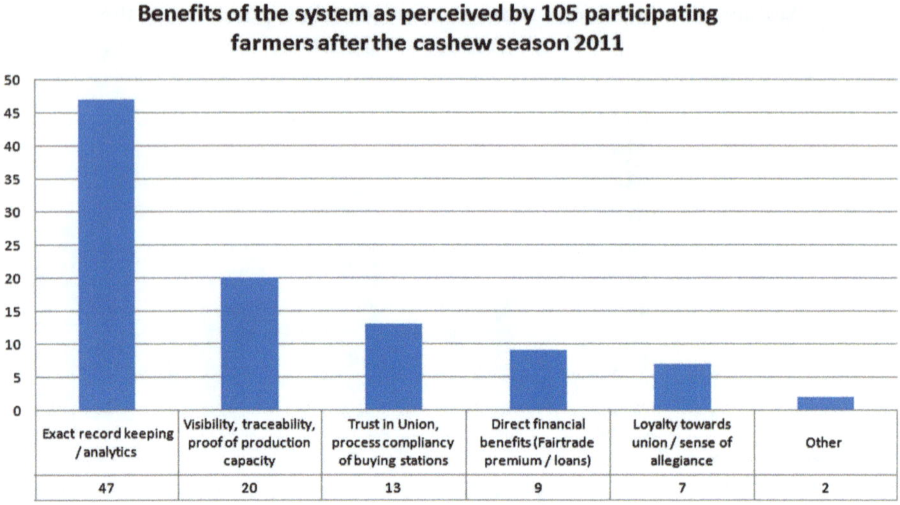

Fig. 13.13 Perceived benefits for participating farmers

The top supplier sold 18 times as much (>4700 kg) as the farmer with the lowest supply. It can also be observed that a small percentage of farmers are producing a significant amount of the total cashew volumes. 85 % of the produce is sold by 40 % of the farmers. By analyzing the transactional data it is also easy to identify typical business incidents such as changes in buying price or gaps in pre-finance available to the buying stations.

For the first time the reliably collected data allows interpretations that could steer further interventions to the benefit of farmers, cooperative and buyers (e.g. loyalty packages, target specific training, loan offerings, extension services, closing gaps in the pre-finance provided by contractual buyer etc.). Acting on such simple system statistics could potentially have a huge impact on the overall performance of the cashew Union.

Very good feedback has been received regarding the piloting results from various stakeholders including the participating farmers. After the season 2011, farmers were given individual statements of their total production and a quick survey has been conducted amongst 105 farmers. All of the farmers replied that they like the system. Roughly 85 % provided a motivation for their answer, see Fig. 13.13.

In summary, system adoption and the according statistics of transactional data are very promising. The remaining project life time will be used to gather more detailed statistics in order to derive a detailed business case for commercialization, and stabilizing and enriching the current applications in the field.

13.6.2 Other Interesting GUI 4D Research and Development Activities in Africa

The digital doorway project is one of the ongoing projects in South Africa which is a joint undertaking by the Department of Science and Technology as well as the Council for Scientific and Industrial Research. The project seeks to verify that children possess the cognitive ability to acquire functional computer skills without formal training. The project entails providing access to a multi-terminal multimedia computer system, which provides access to various applications and information (CSIR & DST 2011). It could also suggest another pathway towards building human capacity in support of the advancement of the Information Society in South Africa and its nearby regions. The typical infrastructure of this multimedia system contains a keyboard, an LCD screen, webcam and speakers (CSIR & DST 2011).

Another interesting project in Africa that can be classified in the GUI 4D category is the Macha Works project in Zambia. Comprehensive coverage on this project is available at http://www.machaworks.org. This project has as one of its objectives accessibility to the Internet for rural communities and it is a very good example of a situation where the needs of the local community are considered in providing value to the community and in reflecting the local culture. Young people from the rural communities in Zambia are the project team members of the Macha project. These young people identify and develop applications that reflect not only the social structures of villages but also local needs.

13.6.3 Conclusions for GUI 4D

Regarding the GUI 4D, our use cases focus strongly on the ‘classic’/traditional human-machine-interfaces, which are textual, mouse-, button- and touch-based inputs as well as visualization/response via monitor/display. We can consider what that situation would be with alternative technologies (speech input and output, control with gestures, multimedia connection etc.). The answer should lead to gradually approaching the adoption of new technologies. Another argument is that we want and need to build robust, fault-tolerant systems and it is the well-tried techniques that are suitable for this, in the first approach. Finally, we also pay special attention to the business plausibility and the investigation of the processes and process chains and we want to connect these with GUI 4D, instead of privileging the adaption of disruptive communication technologies.

13.7 Target Applications and Markets

13.7.1 The Informal Sector in the "Bottom of the Pyramid"

Agricultural employment and non-agricultural informal employment together constitute the biggest part of all economic activities in the developing world. The agricultural work force in developing countries is estimated at 1.3 billion people, making up 51 percent of those countries' total labor force (Food and Agricultural Organization, FAO 2009). A considerable amount of the remaining work force in developing countries is employed in the informal sector representing 53 percent of non-agricultural employment in sub-Saharan Africa, 44 percent in Latin America and 32 percent in Asia (Horan 2005; ILO 2002). It is also important to note that a significant proportion of this activity is conducted in rural areas, with almost 60 percent of the population in developing countries living in rural areas. Both sectors employ people at the very bottom of the global income pyramid and both sectors suffer from a serious disconnect to the more formal markets typically associated with higher incomes and established structures.

Roughly 98 percent of all agricultural workers are living in developing countries. These include subsistence farmers, self-employed small scale-farmers and landless hired agricultural labor (seasonal workers) among others. For many workers, agricultural production represents the only possible source of income and their living environment is typically characterized by socio-economic underdevelopment, lack of agricultural knowledge and training, as well as various infrastructural impediments, specifically with regard to transportation and logistics. Beyond that, the sector suffers from non-transparent and complex value chains, both nationally and globally. Consequently, farmers typically receive only a very small share of the final product's profit since formal processors, producers and retailers have more favorable market positions. On the other hand, these formal participants are increasingly under market pressures to comply with quality standards as well social standards at the very bottom of the entire agricultural value chain. It is thus fair to say, that all value-adding participants of the value chain suffer from information deficits, inefficiencies, lack of long term business relations and a general disconnect between farmers at the bottom of the income pyramid and formal business partners at higher levels in the supply chain.

13.7.1.1 Dependencies and Needs Between the Established Economy and Informal Economy

The gap between the formal and informal economic sectors both in national and global value chains can most appropriately be described as a combination of:

- market distortions and imperfections in the economic value chain (e.g. monopolies in the informal sector, lack of knowledge about market conditions in the informal sector)

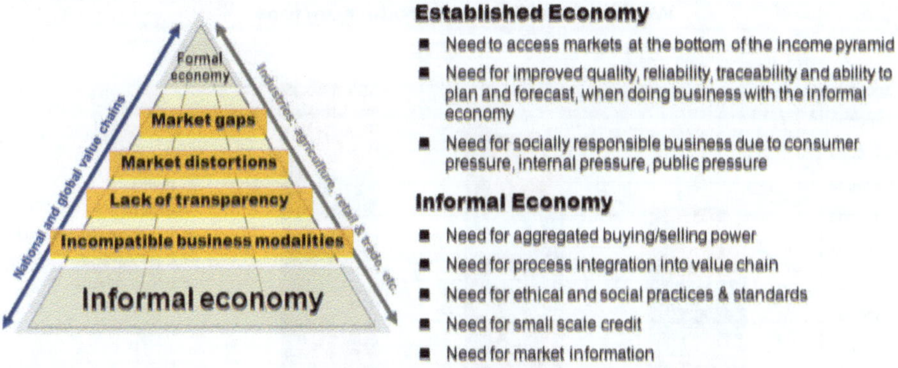

Fig. 13.14 Needs and dependencies of the established and informal economy

- incompatible business modalities (e.g. regarding volumes, financial securities, formalities such as having to provide an official physical address)
- lack of transparency (e.g. non-value-adding middlemen, no direct contact between partners at the bottom and at the top of the value chain)

As a result, business relations between the two sectors are either hampered through ineffectiveness and inefficiencies or they do not exist at all. Figure 13.14 illustrates the situation in terms of a global income pyramid, describing the different needs and requirements of the formal and informal sectors. With regard to the formal sector, there are many examples of a clear business need to engage with the informal sector. Large retail corporations need to access new and growing markets, and many processors of agricultural inputs are relying on agricultural produce supply chains out of Africa, Asia and Latin America. The latter are also increasingly facing the challenge to provide their consumers with a clear audit trail of the source of all inputs while at the same time having to train their suppliers in quality assurance and having to proactively enforce ethical and social standards in a very non-transparent sector. This calls for long-term and reliable business agreements between value-chain participants, which are a significant challenge.

The informal economy on the other hand is hampered by a number of challenges such as the lack of bargaining power, in inadequate direct access to the value chain and the lack of access to resources (credit agreements, pre-finance, loans), as well as market information.

At the same time, economic value chains have undergone an unprecedented globalization in recent years, consequently creating stronger interdependencies between different actors in the value chain. For both the informal and formal sector there are sound economic incentives to develop stronger relationships. Projects like the African Cashew Initiative (see above) intend to provide the enabling mechanisms.

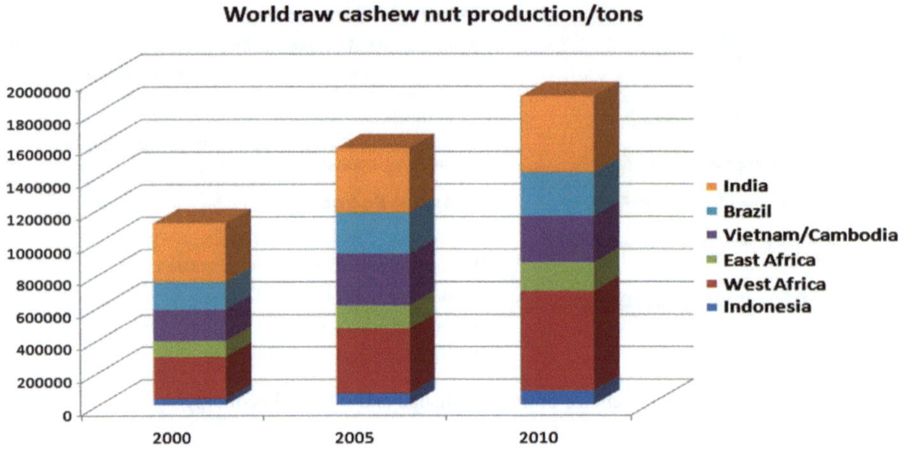

Fig. 13.15 Raw cashew nut production in 2000, 2005 and 2010 in metric tons

13.7.2 Global Agricultural Supply Chains—The Cashew Market as an Example

The cashew sector in Africa is characterized by an estimated 2.5 million cashew farmers of whom 90 % can be considered as rural poor with 0.5 to 4 hectares of cultivation area with diversified cropping systems. Considering that the USD 1.5 to 2.0 billion global market for processed cashew kernel is growing by 2 to 5 % per annum, and that African raw cashew nut (RCN) production constitutes 40 % of global market, the cashew market presents a significant potential opportunity to improve the lives of these farmers and their families, see Fig. 13.15.

Though global supply and demand have stabilized in recent years, the distribution of value in the market does not currently benefit local small holder farmers in Africa to the greatest extent possible. The low competitiveness of smallholders in the cashew value chain is attributable to poor agricultural practices, limited technical knowledge, weak research support, missing access to extension services and poor organization of farmer groups. These impediments are reflected in unstructured and non-standardized business processes and missing common business modalities (e.g. regarding volumes, financial securities, formalities) between distinctive stakeholders along the supply chain. In addition, poor quality and uncertain supply discourage food companies, retailers, and processors from seriously investing in the sector.

Cashew production and processing are seen as economic key sectors that provide an income for many of (West) Africa's inhabitants. Cashew farming receives high attention and is considered as a predestined lighthouse topic for restructured and optimized supply chains for the benefit of small holder farmers up to the consumer, typically located in the US and Western Europe.

13.7.3 Market Potential

Projects like the African Cashew Initiative fully subscribe to the bottom of the pyramid (BOP) approach prominently described by Prahalad (2004), who considers business actors in the informal economy to have the potential to be reliable and profitable partners in an economically sustainable business relationship with established business.

Private sector interests can promote development in certain sectors of developing societies. Accordingly, GUI 4D projects engage in the development of specific solutions which leverage the power and efficiency of private market forces to support a sustainable socio-economic development. Typically, such solutions are based on innovations both in the areas of technology as well as business models.

There could be a significant value proposition for multinationals in the BOP markets. Some of Europe's technology providers have a large customer base within the formal economy in developing countries and can provide appropriate technologies and mechanisms. On the other hand, there are significant risks for established industries who do not fully understand the exact nature of their value chain relationship into the informal economy. This has been convincingly described by Friedman relating to the case of Nike and its subcontractors in South-East Asia (Friedman 2005).

Additionally, the significant market share increase of Fair-Trade products in developed countries will provide international and local players with an incentive to invest in technologies supporting such fair trade (Stiglitz and Charlton 2005). Again this project offers the unique opportunity to showcase the supporting role of ICT.

Business software for the bottom of the billion end users from the developing world differs in most cases to the products and services in advanced markets. The majority of consumers in emerging markets live in semi-urban and rural areas. GUI 4D projects can only leverage the growth potential of this market segment with locally relevant and contextualized solutions according to the Pareto distribution (Anderson 2006).

Limited buying power, and the perceived added value of ICT in particular in the informal sector, require a dedicated long term strategy which approaches research and development from a different engineering target point of view. A co-innovative setup like Living Labs methodologies help to achieve market oriented results. The use of participatory methods for active involvement of all end users and stakeholders, and the planned real life experimentation with several hundred end users, will inform partners on sustainable business options beyond their existing markets.

13.8 Future Research and Work to Be Done

Future research activities in GUI 4D at SAP Research IA&S Africa will focus firstly on the interaction of the user with the GUI 4D and the application, and secondly, on how applications can provide a useful experience within the developing world context. The following are some areas for future research:

- The design and development of a framework which facilitates the alignment of community needs, especially those of rural and urban communities, with living lab strategies and methodologies.
- Usability evaluation methodologies for GUI 4D requires new and novel approaches. We are specifically interested in the usability aspects of mobile phone GUI 4D's and applications.
- Research on employing new and interesting technologies such as eye tracking tools for the improvement and advancement of GUI 4D.
- Conducting advanced field studies with actual users who use mobile phones as the main interaction device connecting to applications in a cloud computing architecture.
- How GUI 4D can be employed in providing remote assistance on mobile phones for example in the health sector. Ideas to be explored will include the use of avatars on mobile phones delivering specialized medical advice, such as physiotherapy, to remote and rural communities.
- Research of a more technical nature where the emphasis is on synchronization aspects of GUI 4D's with applications in hybrid object based clouds with special reference to virtualization.

13.9 Conclusions and Summary

This chapter describes and discusses GUI 4D's, showing the differences to standard, classical GUI's due to the type of User (coming from the "bottom of the pyramid") and the type of ICT applications (for and in establish and informal economies) for which they have to be designed. These GUI 4D's have to be simple, natural and application driven, and are designed for a very special type of user. As such, they help and contribute in narrowing the Digital Divide and in increasing information accessibility in the developing world.

The issues on how to develop the GUI 4D related requirements, constraints and specifications and on what framework to base the implementation, are the next topics to be addressed, including the considerations guaranteeing that these implementations are successful in the field: acceptance, usability, usefulness, diversity and performance.

SAP Research, with Headquarters in Walldorf, Germany, is strongly involved and committed to research and to develop experience in GUI 4D's, especially in its SAP Research Internet Applications & Services Africa lab in Pretoria, South Africa, to support and promote the development in the developing world. The vision and strategy for this approach is also presented. Several examples, pilots, case studies and use cases are finally presented and analyzed; they have helped through a "learning curve" for the area, in learning about the important issues and challenges and how to solve them, and in developing realistic concepts and strategies for the future. They have already proven usability and acceptance in most cases.

This work is published in a book devoted to the memory of Jim Thomas, a very distinguished peer and expert in ICT, with a very high international reputation in this area, especially in the context of information visualization and user-centered interaction. He was also extremely interested in, and significant promoter of, innovation and technology transfer in general, and strongly believed in their potential to support global development, especially in the developing world. Therefore we believe that the area of this work—the Graphical User Interfaces for Development (GUI 4D)—very well suits and serves the purpose and vision of the book, edited and published in his memory.

Acknowledgments The support of SAP Research Internet Applications & Services and SAP Meraka UTD (CSIR) towards this research is hereby acknowledged. In particular, the authors would like to express their gratitude to the following persons and entities for their contributions in preparing this chapter: Edna Chelule; Akash Singh; Jhani de Bruin; The Rustica Project team members; The Smart Energy Project team members and the members of the Siyakhula Living Lab. Opinions expressed and conclusions arrived at are those of the authors and are not necessarily to be attributed to the persons or to the companies mentioned in this acknowledgment.

The results of the African Cashew Initiative discussed in this work have been elaborated by a team of SAP researchers located in Karlsruhe, Germany. We would like to thank in particular Jörg Dörflinger, Carsten Friedland and Tirdad Rahmani for their valuable contributions.

References

ACi (2010). The African Cashew Initiative. Public website. http://www.aci.africancashewalliance.com. Accessed 15th August 2011.

Anderson, Ch. (2006). *The long tail: why the future of business is selling less of more*. New York: Hyperion. ISBN 1-4013-0237-8.

Blake, E. B., & Tucker, W. D. (2005). User interfaces for communication bridges across the digital divide. *AI & Society*, *20*(2), 232–242. doi:10.1007/s00146-005-0018-1.

Brewer, E. (2005). The case for technology in developing regions. *Computer*, *38*(6), 531–538.

Chetty, M. (2005). *Developing locally relevant applications for rural South Africa: a telemedicine example*. Cape Town: University of Cape Town.

Collier, B. P. (2008). The bottom billion. *The Electronic Journal of Sustainable Development*, *1*(2), 3–4.

Crabtree, A. (1998). Ethnography in participatory design. In *Participatory design conference*, Seattle, Washington (pp. 93–105).

CSIR, & DST (2011). The digital doorway. Retrieved from http://www.digitaldoorway.org.za/index_main.php?do=concept.

Dalvit, L., Thinyane, M., Muyingi, H., & Terzoli, A. (2007). The deployment of an e-commerce platform and related projects in a rural area in South Africa. *International Journal of Computing and ICT Research*, *1*(1), 9–18.

Dörflinger, J., & Gross, T. (2011). Bottom billion architecture—a generic software architecture for ICTD use case scenarios. In *MobileHCI 2011*, Aug 30–Sept 2, 2011, Stockholm, Sweden.

Edim Azom, E., & Muyingi, H. N. (2010). A user interface for micro-entrepreneurs in a rural community. *EJISDC*, *43*(2), 1–19.

Emmanuel, E. A., & Muyingi, H. N. (2008). A cultural user interface for a rural community in South Africa. In *Proceedings of SATNAC*. www.satnac.org.za/proceedings.

Emmanuel, E. A., & Muyingi, H. N. (2010). A user interface for micro-entrepreneurs in a rural community. *The Electronic Journal on Information Systems in Developing Countries*, *43*(2), 1–19.

European Commission (2009). Living Labs for user-driven open innovation. In *Facilities* (pp. 1–64). Belgium: European Commission, Information Society and Media.

Food and Agricultural Organization (FAO) (2009). Summary of world food and agricultural statistics. http://www.fao.org/fileadmin/templates/ess/documents/publications_studies/publications/sumfas_en_web_2009.pdf. Accessed 9th April 2010.

Friedman, Th. (2005). *The world is flat: a brief history of the twenty-first century*. Farrar, Straus and Giroux.

Gates Foundation Pledge (2009). Gates Foundation, partners pledge $90 million to boost incomes of small farmers in Africa. Public announcement of the Bill & Melinda Gates Foundation. http://www.gatesfoundation.org/press-releases/Pages/african-cocoa-and-cashew-farmers-090218.aspx. Accessed 9th April 2010.

Gelderblom, H., De Bruin, J. D. E., & Singh, A. (2011). Three methods for evaluating mobile phone applications aimed users in a developing environment: a comparative case study. *Building*.

Gillwald, A., & Esselaar, S. (2005). A comparative analysis of ICT access and usage in 19 African countries. In A. Gillwald (Ed.), *Towards an African e-index: ICT access and usage*, Johannesburg, South Africa. http://link.wits.ac.za/papers/e-index-front.pdf. Accessed 03 April 2012.

Heeks, R. (2009). ICTs and the world's bottom billion. Policy. Manchester. http://www.sed.manchester.ac.uk/idpm/research/publications/wp/di/short/di_sp10.pdf.

Hofstede, G. (1997). *Cultures and organizations: software of the mind, intercultural cooperation and its importance for survival*. New York: McGraw-Hill.

Horan, T. A. (2005). A design theory approach to community informatics: community-centered development and action research testing of online social networking prototype. *The Journal of Community Informatics*, *3*(1), 2007.

International Labour Organization (ILO) (2002). Women and men in the informal economy: a statistical picture. Geneva. Employment sector. Retrieved from http://www.ilo.org/public/english/region/ampro/cinterfor/temas/gender/doc/wminfor.htm. Last accessed on 9 April 2010.

ISO/IEC 25000 (2005). Software engineering—Software product Quality Requirements and Evaluation (SQuaRE)—Guide to SQuaRE. In *ISO/IEC 2005*.

Lalji, Z., & Good, J. (2008). Designing new technologies for illiterate populations: a study in mobile phone interface design. *Interacting with Computers*, *20*, 574–586.

Ligorio, M. (2001). Integrating communication formats: synchronous versus asynchronous and text-based versus visual. *Computers & Education*, *37*(2), 103–125. doi:10.1016/S0360-1315(01)00039-2.

Medhi, I., Sagar, A., & Toyama, K. (2007). Text-free user interfaces for illiterate and semiliterate users. *Information Technologies and International Development*, *4*(1), 37–50. doi:10.1162/itid.2007.4.1.37.

Mulder, I., Bohle, W., Boshomane, S., Morris, C., & Tempelman, H. (2008). Real-world innovation in rural South Africa. *The Electronic Journal for Virtual Organizations and Networks, 10*, Special Issue on Living Labs.

Niitamo, V.-P., Kulkki, S., Eriksson, M., & Hribernik, K. A. (2006). State of the art and good practice in the field of living labs. In K. D. Thoben, et al. (Eds.), *Proceedings of the 12th international conference on concurrent enterprising* (pp. 341–348).

Palmer, R. (2010). ICT4D and the Siyakhula Living Lab: an anthropological contribution to digital development. *Anthropology Southern Africa*, *33*(1&2), 19–32.

Parikh, T. S., & Lazowska, E. D. (2006). Designing an architecture for delivering mobile information services to the rural developing world. In *WWW '06. Proceedings of the 15th international conference on world wide web*. New York: ACM. ISBN 1-59593-323-9. doi:10.1145/1135777.1135897.

Prahalad, C. K. (2004). *The fortune at the bottom of the pyramid: eradicating poverty through profits*. Englewood Cliffs: Prentice Hall International. ISBN-10: 0131467506.

SAP TV, Video (2011). Software for developing countries. http://www.sap-tv.com/7313. Accessed 15th August 2011.

Schaffers, H., Guzmán, J. G., Navarro de la Cruz M., & Merz, Ch. (Eds.) (2010). *Living labs for rural development—results from the C@R integrated project, TRAGSA*. ISBN-13: 978-84-693-0040-4.

Schwaber, K. (2004). *Agile project management with scrum* (163 pp). Microsoft Press. ISBN 0-7356-1993-X.

Sood, A. D. (2002). Domesticating the desktop. In *Development by design (dyd02)*. Bangalore. http://www.cks.in/html/cks_pdfs/domesticatingdeskt.

Stiglitz, J. E., & Charlton, A. (2005). *Fair trade for all: how trade can promote development*. Oxford: Oxford University Press.

UNISA (2011). Understanding poverty and development. http://www.etu.org.za/toolbox/docs/development/poverty.html.

Van Greunen, D., De Louw, R., Dörflinger, J., Friedland, C., & Merz, Ch. (2009). Sekhukhune Living Lab: lessons learnt from end user community building and interaction. In *Proceedings of the IST Africa 2009*, Kampala, Uganda, 06–08 May 2009.

Yeo, A. (1996). World-wide CHI: cultural user interfaces, a silver lining in cultural diversity. *SIGCHI Bulletin*, *28*, 4–7.

Chapter 14
Emotion in Human-Computer Interaction

Christian Peter and Bodo Urban

Abstract Affect and emotion are probably the most important facets of our lives. They make our lives worth living by enabling us to enjoy experiences, to value the behavior of others and helping us to make decisions more easily. They enforce or fade out the memory of distinct events and make some of them unique in the sequence of episodes that we undergo each day. But also, they function as a modulator of information when interacting with other people and play an essential role in fine-tuning our communication. The ability to express and understand emotional signs can hence be considered vital for interacting with human beings. Leveraging the power of emotion recognition to enhance technology seems obligatory when designing technology for people. This chapter introduces the physiological background of emotion recognition, describes the general approach to detecting emotion using physiological sensors, and gives two examples of affective applications.

14.1 Introduction

Affect and emotion play an important role in our lives. They are present in most of our activities, often without us being aware of them. Particularly when interacting with other people, emotions affect our thinking and activities. Emotional signs are emitted through our voice, the face, and the whole body, carrying important information for our interaction partner. Unconsciously we rely on this affective information being received and properly decoded. Observing the other's face and posture and listening to the tone of the voice that carries the responsive information, we look for subtle yet important hints on how our information has been perceived. If the reaction differs from our expectations, we quickly send corrective signs to drive the interaction in the desired direction. But what if the interaction partner does not

C. Peter (✉) · B. Urban
Fraunhofer IGD, Joachim-Jungius-Str. 11, 18059 Rostock, Germany
e-mail: christian.peter@igd-r.fraunhofer.de

B. Urban
e-mail: bodo.urban@igd-r.fraunhofer.de

J. Dill et al. (eds.), *Expanding the Frontiers of Visual Analytics and Visualization*, DOI 10.1007/978-1-4471-2804-5_14, © Springer-Verlag London Limited 2012

respond to our affective hints? What if the other side doesn't seem to care if we are angry, upset or frustrated about the encountered interaction? What, if the other side reacts like ... a machine?

As humans, we enjoy interaction. We prefer inter-actions to pure actions because they give us feedback on what we do. That feedback might cheer us up, encourage us, or bring us down to earth in case we get too enthusiastic. In other words, what we enjoy when communicating with other humans is the affective feedback on our doing, the giving, taking and sharing of emotional experiences. Communicating affective information is a very important aspect of human interaction.

Machines are considered being different. As tools, they don't need to show us their perception of the current situation, and in fact we would consider a hammer that tells us about the joy it feels each time we hit those nails on their head somewhat weird. But what if the hammer would reflect our joy of having hit properly, and later of having done the job? What if it would encourage us to keep on hitting when we are just about to quit? Wouldn't that be different? What if the machines we use had an idea what their current action is doing with us? What if they would adjust their behavior so that we are pleased? Or if they would give us a helpful hint when they realize that we are completely stranded? Wouldn't that be a step in the right direction?

With computers being the most interactive tools humans have developed, it seems obligatory they also use the affective channel to convey and receive information. As Affective Computing pioneer Rosalind Picard wrote more than ten years ago: "Computers do not need affective abilities for the fanciful goal of becoming humanoids, they need them for a meeker and more practical goal: to function with intelligence and sensitivity towards humans" (Picard 1997, p. 247). With sensor technology now being small and powerful enough to be included in every day devices, it is time to enable them to do so. While solutions for speech and facial features are worked on steadily and an impressive body of knowledge has been created over the last years (ACII 2005, 2007, 2009, 2011; IEEE Transactions on Affective Computing 2012; Peter and Beale 2008; Tao and Tan 2009), this chapter will focus on physiology-based affective sensing.

The first part of this chapter starts with a brief introduction to the physiological background of emotions and concludes with challenges of and requirements for emotion-related human-computer interaction. It continues describing a common emotion recognition pipeline for physiological affective data, as it is applied in many affective computing projects. The second part of the chapter introduces the Fraunhofer EREC system for emotion recognition. It is a well-functioning implementation of the previously described emotion recognition pipeline and has been used in several industrial and research projects. Two of these projects are described in the Applications section of this chapter. A concluding discussion of further prospects closes this chapter.

14.2 Emotion Recognition

14.2.1 Physiological Background

Emotions are manifested in physiological changes controlled by the autonomous nervous system (ANS). Those changes can be observed in facial expressions, gestures, body movements, as well as in the voice. Besides these directly observable expressive channels, physiological changes can also occur in parameters such as blood pressure, heart rate, or electro-dermal activity that are not directly recognized by human observers.

These physiological changes can be attributed to the following physiological processes (Cacioppo et al. 2000; Schwartz and Andrasik 2003):

1. Muscle tension;
2. Peripheral vasoconstriction i.e. changes in blood flow; and
3. Sweat gland activity.

These three processes are well recognized as being deeply involved in emotional arousal and there is increased agreement of them being associated with valence, i.e. the degree of perceived pleasantness of an event. In the following we will briefly describe these processes, ways to measure them, and derive issues to bear in mind in the HCI context. The physiological information is mainly taken from Cacioppo et al. (2000) and Schwartz and Andrasik (2003), for more details please refer to these sources.

Muscle tension can most easily be observed in postural changes, body movements and gestures. The most common way to infer muscle tension is measuring changes in the electrical potentials actuating the muscle fibers, which are accessible through surface electrodes attached to the skin above the muscle. This principle is called surface electromyography (sEMG), or just EMG. The measurement value is usually provided in micro Volts (mV). While EMG provides information on very fine muscle movements, EMG measurements are affected by voluntary movements of the body part.

Another way to infer muscle tension is to monitor the human with a video-based camera system to capture specific movement parameters. Using the captured data, sophisticated algorithms are applied to distinguish specific body movements (gestures) or even subtle changes in the person's face. Ekman and various colleagues have distinguished specific patterns of facial muscle activity related to emotions (Ekman and Davidson 1994; Ekman and Friesen 1976; Ekman et al. 1983). They define 46 specific regions in the face plus 25 head- and eye movement codes, so called "action units" which, according to them, can be used to decode certain affective states (Ekman and Friesen 1978). An "action unit", or AU, can be seen as a single region in the face that is moved by muscles, encoding a certain affect-related expression, or parts thereof. Examples for action units are AU 7 decoding the lid tightener, AU 9 decoding the nose wrinkle, or AU 43 decoding that the eyes are closed. For more information on video-based emotion detection (Wimmer 2007) and (Tao and Tan 2009) be suggested for further reading.

Peripheral vasoconstriction refers to a decrease in the diameter of blood vessels. Since it is not yet possible to non-invasively measure the diameter of blood vessels (or the muscle activity that cause this) directly, correlates of it have to be used. Most commonly used methods for this are measurements of the peripheral (i.e. skin) temperature, and photo transmission.

Another way to indirectly infer the amount of peripheral blood flow is by light. Most common techniques use special light sources and receptors for this, usually in the red/infra-red spectrum, benefiting from the fact that light absorption in these frequency bands change significantly with the oxy/deoxyhemoglobin levels of the blood. The light source (usually a light emitting diode LED) transmits light into a finger, for example, and a nearby light receptor measures the amount of light reaching the other side of the finger or being reflected off the bone. The amount of light that reaches the receptor changes with the volume of blood to be passed by the light.

The advantage of this method is that it can be used to infer several different physiological changes that are associated with changes in affect. For example, by choosing the right frequencies of light, heart rate can be assessed, or the amount of hemoglobin within the blood can be detected and used as a measure of blood oxygenation.

The disadvantage of this method is that the measurements are quite sensitive to movements that occur thereby affecting the quality of the captured data. Artifacts are mostly caused by movements of either the body part, or the sensing element against the body part. For example, movements of a body part, such as a hand, cause more or less blood flowing into the extremities due to centrifugal forces. While these changes are too fast to be detected by temperature sensors due to their relatively long response time, photo transmission devices are well able to observe them. These changes can be of similar amplitude and frequency as those caused by ANS activity and hence pose significant problems in non-lab settings. Movement of the sensing elements against the body part causes a change in the path of light, resulting in measurement changes. It also may cause day light to enter the path of light, resulting in more photons reaching the receiving part.

Sweat gland activity is not directly measurable. Therefore, glandular activity is commonly inferred by measuring changes in electrical conductivity of the skin. Since sweat contains a number of electrically conductive minerals, increased conductivity is associated with a higher activity of the glands.

To measure electro-dermal activity, a small voltage is applied on an area with a high concentration of sweat glands (e.g. palms of the hand, the foot). The measured electrical current between the two electrodes correlates with the sweat glands' activity. Usually, measurements are given as conductance level, since conductance increases linearly with sweat glands' activity. Some studies, however, work with the resistance values, with electric resistance being reciprocal to electric conductivity. Skin conductance is measured in μS (micro Siemens), skin resistance in $k\Omega$ (kilo Ohms).

The tonic level (SCL—skin conductance level, SRL—skin resistance level) effectively represents a baseline, or resting, level. It usually changes very slowly and represents the relative level of sympathetic arousal of a person. The phasic changes (SCR—skin conductance response, SRR—skin resistance response) are short episodes of increased glands activity caused by increased sympathetic arousal, generated by a stimulus. SCR reactions on a stimulus appear about 1–2 seconds after the stimulus, stay on a certain level depending on the intensity of the stimulating event and how long it lasts and then falls back to the tonic level.

It is important to bear in mind that a phasic change might lead to an elevated baseline if the person's sympathetic system does not completely recover from the triggering event. Conversely, when the person's sympathetic system "relaxes" over time, the tonic level might decrease over time. The important point is, for affective computing applications, phasic changes as well as changes to the tonic level are of interest. However, this can only be taken into account when measurements are taken permanently at the same location. Temporarily detached electrodes or changing electrode positions may result in different absolute values, wrongly suggesting a change in the tonic skin conductance level.

As a technical challenge, baseline changes caused by sympathetic reactions are difficult to distinguish from measurement drifts caused by internal processes in the sensing electronics. If the device requires electrode gel to be used, chemical reactions within the gel over time can lead to measurement drifts which have to be considered as well.

14.2.2 Measuring Emotional Signs

There are three main approaches to observe emotional signs: speech analysis[1]; visual observation of gestures, body posture or facial features; and measuring physiological parameters through sensors with direct body contact. Both approaches observe changes to physiological processes related to emotional states, and each of them has its advantages and drawbacks.

Visual observation has the advantage of being only minimally intrusive. While a camera is being considered an intrusion into privacy, people are inclined to accept and forget about it once they get used to it and see a value in the service provided through this device.

The disadvantage of the visual approach is that it requires the person being in the view field (and possibly the focus area) of the camera. Further, certain lighting conditions must be met, and the body parts or facial features to be observed must be in view of the camera i.e. not hidden by clothing or accessories like glasses or baseball hats.

[1] Speech analysis is also successfully used to conclude on emotional processes in a user. The emotional coloring of the voice happens through ANS controlled changes of the tension of the muscles of the vocal tract. As speech analysis can only be performed when the person is talking, it is a rather sporadic source of information and will not discussed here any further. Please refer Peter and Beale (2008) and Tao and Tan (2009).

While some of the technical drawbacks might be overcome in the near future, there is the problem that some of the features usually observed with cameras are barely present in HCI settings. For instance, people tend not to show much facial expressions when interacting with technical systems. Display of emotional states through the face is a deeply social means of human-to-human interaction, acquired through evolution to facilitate better communication and influential actions through this additional, subtle channel. Since machines do not (yet) respond to emotional expressions, humans have not yet learned to use this channel when communicating with technology. Hence, observation of affective facial expressions and other visually observable signs of emotions are restricted to either staged (exaggerated) expressions or strong emotions in real life.

Physiological readings have the advantage of being present all the time. Further, people usually don't mask their physiological parameters to influence their communication partner as they do with e.g. facial features. Hence, physiological readings may provide much more realistic data on the ongoing emotional processes than visually expressive channels, such as facial expressions, can provide. Another advantage of this channel is the relative simplicity of the data. Parameters like heart rate, skin temperature, and skin conductivity are very simple one-dimensional data that are easily processed and analyzed.

The drawback of working with physiological readings is the personal access required to measure them. Direct contact to the person's body is needed to access most parameters. This requires first the acceptance and willingness of the person to wear the device and second the person actually wearing it the right way, i.e. the person being able and willing to use the device. As with visual observation, the cooperation of the user is required. Wearable sensors have to meet various usability and technological requirements (reliability, robustness, availability and quality of data) which are often very difficult to match.

There are projects running (e.g. Poh et al. 2010) that try to read physiological parameters contactless via cameras, with promising results. Since cameras are used here, some of the disadvantages of visual observation apply, such as the need of a clear facial view of the person.

At Fraunhofer IGD, we investigate in affective sensing using physiological sensors. We believe that, if devices are designed properly, physiological sensors can provide much better information on the affective state of a person than is possible by other means due to the advantages mentioned above. The direct access to ANS triggered processes, together with their relatively simple nature and consequent fast processing make physiological data an ideal information source for affective systems.

In the following, we identify major challenges that have to be addressed when applying physiological sensing in affective computing scenarios and conclude with major requirements on physiological sensor systems.

14.2.2.1 Challenges

Several challenges can be identified relating to sensing affective states in human-computer interaction scenarios.

For affective sensors to be used in real-world settings, it is essential that they are accepted (and also used) by the users. This implies that aspects of intrusiveness, usefulness, usability, and user experience must be considered. Since affective sensors need either physical contact or a good camera view of the person, it is essential that this person allows this to happen. The challenge is to design affective sensors in such a way that people will use and engage with them and so that they are fully operational and can provide affective information in sufficiently good quality.

Technology in real-world HCI scenarios often has to operate in adverse conditions. It cannot be assumed that it will be treated with care by the user nor can users be expected to follow certain restrictive directives to allow the device to operate properly. Further, there is the problem that no single sensor is able to permanently provide affective information of users in everyday life. Visual sensors will lose view of the person; physiological sensors might not be worn or might suffer from movement artifacts or other interferences. It therefore seems advisable to tap more than one modality and find suitable ways to merge results. It also seems to be mandatory to provide information on the reliability of the data provided. The challenge here is to design device sufficiently robustly and to provide information on the reliability of the sensor data in real-time along with the data.

For applications that aim to react sensibly to the detected affective state it is important to know how reliable the provided information is. Given that no single sensor is able to provide reliable information permanently (see above), provision of reliability information is essential. Another challenge is to find suitable ways to fuse sensor data that come from different modalities and are of a totally different nature in terms of complexity, time behavior and accuracy.

14.2.2.2 Requirements

Real life HCI applications have special requirements on physiological sensors. They differ from medical applications in that they need to be easy to use, non-obtrusive, flexible in providing their data, and being accurate and precise while being operated outside controlled lab conditions. A number of requirements on affective system can be identified.

The device should be tolerant against movements of any kind. A user cannot be assumed to behave in a particular way just to allow the system to operate properly. Hence, the system should be able to recognize movements and detect movement artifacts or blurred sections in the sensor data. This information should permanently be available as reliability information along with the actual data.

A system should not irritate the users in any way. It should operate without the need of users' attention and not be in the users' way at any of their activities. For wearable sensors this also implies a comfortable fit, no visible wires, and wireless data transmission. A small form factor and light weight are also beneficial as is integration in clothing that the user is familiar with wearing.

It seems obvious that, in order to be accepted by users, a system must not require them to run through lengthy installation and calibration routines or learn and adhere to complicated operation instructions. There should be no need for the user to connect different components in a pre-described fashion to get the system running, or to place electrodes at specific body parts using tape or Velcro fastener, or to configure and adjust software prior to collecting data. Also, energy consumption should be low, to allow for a long operation time without the need of changing or recharging batteries.

Data should be immediately available. For studies, the experimenter should get permanent and in-real-time feedback on the subject's performance. For affective applications, permanent provision of actual data is a prerequisite to allow for continuous adaptation of the system to an ever-changing user state.

There should always be sensible data available to speed up data processing and ease analysis. Error-handling should be done within the device, freeing the developer from caring about lost connections, transmission errors, badly fitted electrodes, and other technical side aspects. Ideally, data should be provided in an open format.

Being also an aspect of ease of integration, data should be made available in engineering units. This avoids inclusion of sensor-specific conversion formulae into applications, increases flexibility, and eliminates the risk of conversion errors.

These identified requirements are the core features necessary for a physiological sensor system to be used and accepted as an affective input device. Obviously, these requirements are of varying importance in different scenarios, and each scenario might add further specific requirements to the list.

14.2.3 The Emotion Recognition Pipeline

Many projects apply various methods to pre-process, analyze and classify physiological data with the final goal to identify the emotional state of a person. Throughout the projects, recognition rates vary, but most rates reported in projects are similar to those achieved with other modalities like speech and facial feature analysis (between 60 and 80 %), which is close to the recognition rate achieved by humans, cf. (Picard et al. 2001).

The general approach to infer an emotional state from physiological signals is shown in Fig. 14.1. Physiological signals are first pre-processed, and, if more than one sensor is involved, synchronized before passed on to the next stage. The now cleaned and possibly enhanced data are analyzed for characteristic attributes, or features (feature extraction), which involves statistical analyses. The calculated features then are classified according to a pre-defined model using neural nets, fuzzy logic or other classifiers, and the likely emotion is calculated and finally provided for further processing.

When comparing the approaches for feature extraction and emotion classification used in different projects, it becomes obvious that no single, or best, algorithm

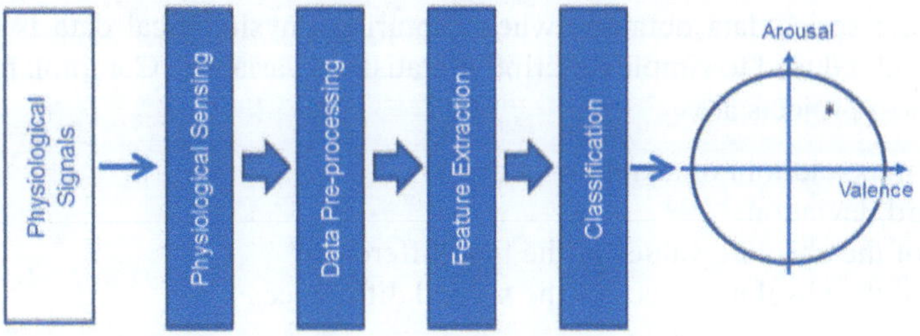

Fig. 14.1 Emotion recognition pipeline for physiological signals

exists (cf. e.g. Kim and André 2008, King et al. 1995, Nasoz et al. 2004). Various algorithms have been tried for the different stages, and many have been found to be suitable in their specific use case. Obviously, environmental factors, behavior patterns, cognitive processes as well as social aspects have a considerable impact on physiological parameters related to emotion, cf. van den Broek (2009), Knapp et al. (2011).

For further reference, a good and concise introductory review is given in Picard (1997), advance discussions can be found in Nasoz et al. (2004) and Petta (2011).

14.2.3.1 Data Pre-processing

Physiological data are difficult to access, and are usually measured indirectly. Pre-processing of physiological data usually includes

- Validation of data, i.e. check if measurements are in a sensible range
- Smoothing, i.e. treat glitches and obvious artifacts
- Normalization, i.e. convert data into a range that is easy to process
- Synchronization/discretization, i.e. put the data into a useful timely order, possibly in relation to other data

14.2.3.2 Feature Extraction

Feature extraction usually refers to the process of generating specific features of signals used to distinguish different characteristics within the signal. These features either describe the nature of the signal, like (quasi-) periodicity of a heart rate or respiration signal, or statistical values like mean values or standard deviations. Obviously, features themselves can be combined again, so as to describe another characteristic, resulting in another feature.

Note that some approaches skip the step of feature extraction, applying the classifying algorithm directly on the pre-processed data. Fuzzy logic approaches (Mandryk and Atkins 2007) and neural nets (Haag et al. 2004; Yoo et al. 2005) are examples.

The time series data obtained when capturing physiological data is often discretized and reduced to simple descriptive statistical variables. Common parameters used in most projects are

- Mean, max and min of absolute values
- Standard deviation
- Mean of the absolute values of the first differences
- Mean of the absolute values of the second differences

Further, the following features have been shown to yield good results:

- Median
- Mean rise duration
- Number of peaks within a defined window, i.e. sequence of samples
- Inter beat interval, incl. LF/HF ratio

In some projects, the same algorithms are applied to both, the raw signal and the normalized signal. The output must be split into separate features.

14.2.3.3 Classification

Pattern recognition methods used to classify physiological data usually apply either statistical classification techniques or template matching schemes to the generated features. For different application scenarios, environmental conditions, and specific variant of emotional signs different classification methods have been used (King et al. 1995; Nasoz et al. 2004). Among the most popular are

- k-Nearest Neighbor
- Regression tree
- Bayesian Networks
- Support Vector Machines
- Fuzzy Logic
- Artificial Neural Networks

For more detailed explanations of the described methods, and many more, Bishop (2006) and Hastie et al. (2009) are suggested as good references.

14.3 The EREC Emotion Recognition System

14.3.1 The EREC Sensor System

At Fraunhofer IGD we developed a sensor system that allows to measure emotion-related physiological parameters. Other than commercially available sensor systems, the focus of our work was on usability and acceptability of the device. Aiming at systems that are able to respond sensibly to their user's perception of a situation, we identified the following important aspects:

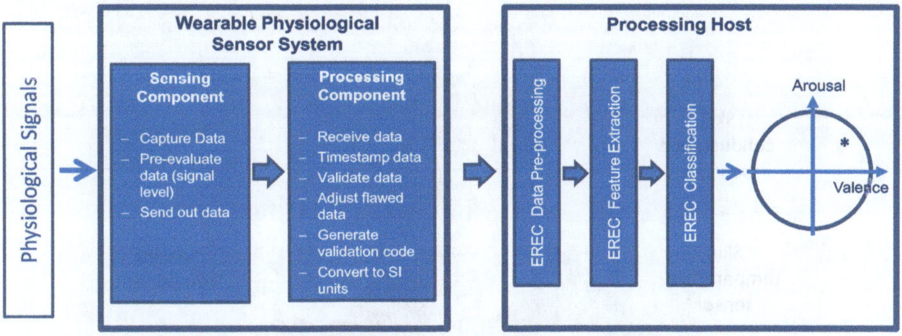

Fig. 14.2 Distributed architecture of the EREC emotion recognition system

- Robustness;
- Non-obtrusiveness;
- Easy usage/usability;
- User experience;
- Immediate access to data;
- Ease of integration;
- Standard conformance.

For a system to meet the criteria above, we decided for a distributed architecture with wirelessly connected components. This allows design of small and robust distributed components while avoiding wires to communicate the data.

The complete system consists of a wearable physiological sensor system for sensing and low-level pre-procession of the data, and a processing host implementing high-level pre-procession, feature extraction, classification and emotion representation, and finally hosts the affective application (see Fig. 14.2).

The EREC sensor system has been developed that measures skin conductivity, heart rate, skin temperature and, as auxiliary information, ambient air temperature (Peter et al. 2005, 2007). The system comprises three units: a glove hosting the sensing elements for skin conductance and skin temperature as well as a receiver for heart rate data; a wrist pocket containing the sensing component's electronics; and a unit containing the processing component, see Fig. 14.3. As an alternative to the chest belt, an optical sensor for heart rate can be used that also provides further information like blood oxygen saturation (S_PO_2).

The **sensor glove** is of light mesh fabric which is comfortable to wear even for longer periods of time. Sensing elements for skin conductance and skin temperature are placed on the fingers of the glove and additionally the thenar (skin conductance only). On the back of the glove resides the receiver for heart rate data which are provided by a commercial chest belt. The wires from the sensing elements are woven into the mesh fabric of the glove, nearly invisible for the user. A connection connects the glove with the sensing component. The connection is designed resembling more a security cable than an electronic connection, increasing acceptance with users.

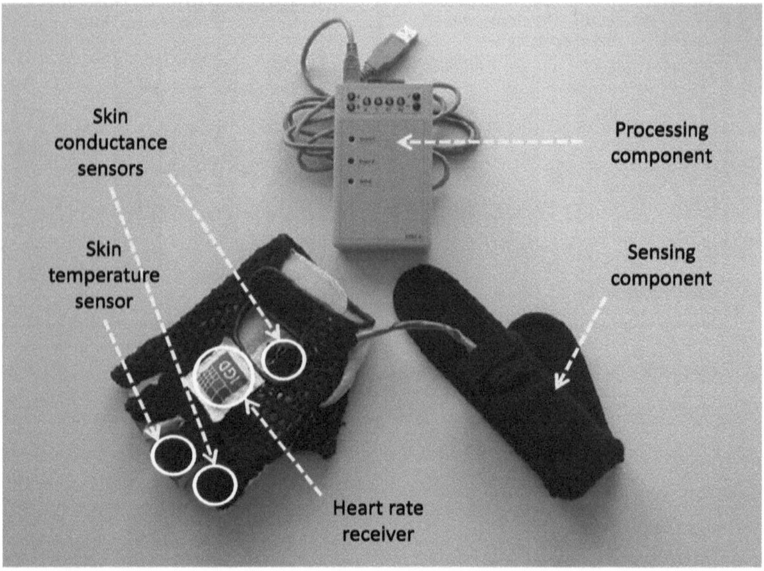

Fig. 14.3 The EREC sensor system

The main task of the **sensing component** is to capture the data and to perform basic pre-evaluations, such as detecting measurement errors or sensor failures. If errors occur, the data need to be treated and appropriate action can be initiated, like re-adjustment of the sensing elements, calibration of electronic components, or notification to the processing component for further treatment. The sensing component is hidden in a wrist pocket so that no electronics or wires can be seen. The different sensing elements are sampled permanently at a rate of 20 Hz, i.e. every 50 milliseconds. The data then are evaluated on the signal level (e.g. for sensor failure) and equipped with reliability information. The data are then wrapped in an appropriate transmission protocol and equipped with a checksum before they are sent to the processing component.

On the **processing component**, data are equipped with a time stamp to allow for synchronizing data from different sensors (e.g. skin temperature and environmental temperature), as well as for allowing correlation of sensor data with application specific events. In a next step, data can be evaluated for sensibility, based on stored information on typical values, measurement history, physical laws, and possibly under consideration of data from other sensors. For instance, when all sensors don't send sensible data, it is likely that the sensing component is not attached properly to the user. When just one sensor reports unusual data, there might be a problem with that sensor, or a single sensing element might not be properly attached. In case of a general sensor error, the sensing component could, for instance, be reset. In case a bad attachment of the sensing component is assumed, the user could be notified and asked for assistance. Each measurement value is such evaluated and equipped with data validation information. In the next step, output data can be prepared taking into account information of the validation of the input data. Finally, the measurement values are converted to SI units. With this done, the data is stored on a memory card as well as provided via USB to be read out in real-time for to be processed by feature extraction and classification algorithms.

An important aspect is **validation** of the measured data. Data should be validated at different levels on their way from entering the system as raw measurands to finally being provided as reliable measurement values to processing applications. First, at the raw sensing level, data should be evaluated if the measurands obtained represent sensible data. For instance, a skin conductance value dropping to zero can only mean the sensor not being attached to the skin, which should be treated accordingly. Second, the data should be evaluated at a higher processing level, combining all sensor data, including auxiliary information, and evaluating the different measurands in relation to each other and in context of the process that is being observed. For example, if a wearable device hosts both a skin conductance sensor and a skin temperature sensor at nearby locations (e.g. the same finger) and the skin conductance is very low, the skin temperature value should be treated with care as it is likely that the sensing elements have no proper contact to the person's skin.

A very good procedure to validate sensor data at this level is proposed by the standard for self-validating sensors (SEVA), (Henry and Clarke 1993) which has been developed at Oxford University and has been adopted as a British standard (British Standards Institution 2004). The basic idea behind SEVA is that an intelligent sensor should provide more useful information than the measurand and a device-specific error code. SEVA devices monitor their own performance, validate the quality of the data, and provide a standard-formatted quality index for each measurement value they pass on. If an error occurs its impact on the measurement is assessed, the measurement value—if necessary—corrected, and the quality index set accordingly.

By moving the validation task from the application level to the sensor itself it is possible to perform process- and sensor specific validations in-situ and to apply possible corrective measures directly to the sensor. No process- or sensor specific knowledge is needed at application level and the communication from sensor to application is reduced to a minimum, i.e. only sensible data are sent to the processing domain. SEVA also suggests pre-processing the data in the sensor system so far so that measurement values are already provided in engineering units. This step keeps all low-level sensor specific parameters and conversion algorithms within the sensor system, making integration of such sensor systems simple and straightforward.

Further, introducing a quality index keeps analyzing the process data simpler, and thanks to the device-independent standard format of the quality information, the software at the system level becomes independent from the chosen hardware, which allows a more flexible planning and changing of hardware components. As a side effect, the data processing algorithms can be made simpler, since a permanent flow of guaranteed useful data is provided and the assessment of the reliability of the data is already done by the sensor in a standardized way.

14.3.2 Data Interpretation

For data pre-processing, feature extraction and classification, we developed the OmniRoute framework (Mader et al. 2004). OmniRoute allows simple system configuration for heterogeneous data types. The particular advantage of OmniRoute is that it allows connecting different sensor sources (i.e. the different physiological data channels) with processing components that perform the dedicated processing steps such as smoothing, feature extraction, and finally classification.

14.3.2.1 Data Pre-processing

EREC provides physiological data that are already pre-processed on the signal level, i.e. glitches, gaps in sensor data and unrealistic data are already dealt with. Pre-processing of the collected data at this level can usually be confined to normalizing the data of each channel (heart rate, skin temperature and EDA). For some applications, pre-processing might also include further smoothing of the data such as applying a moving average window.

14.3.2.2 Feature Extraction and Classification

From the pre-processed data, characteristic features are extracted before they are classified. As a basic feature set the collection from Picard et al. (2001) can be suggested, i.e. the mean, standard deviation, mean of the absolute values of the first differences, and mean of the absolute values of the second differences, each applied to the raw data as well as the normalized values. These features allow for a good estimate of the emotional state of a person in many standard scenarios, as has been shown in many projects (Barreto et al. 2007; Kim et al. 2004; Lichtenstein et al. 2008; Magjarevic et al. 2009; Picard et al. 2001; Rigas et al. 2009; Verhoef et al. 2009).

For classification, different approaches have been used at IGD. The classifier has to be chosen depending on the scenario. For fast processing, decisions trees are often used with acceptable results by Barreto et al. (2007) and Rani et al. (2006). Fuzzy logic approaches as e.g. described by Mandryk and Atkins (2007) have also been used successfully at IGD. More accurate results can usually be obtained with support vector machines (SVM) (Barreto et al. 2007; Kim et al. 2004; Rani et al. 2006) and Bayesian networks (Rani et al. 2006; Verhoef et al. 2009), at the cost of longer processing times.

14.4 Applications

The EREC System has been used in various applications ranging from simple visualization of the emotional state, via utilization of emotion recognition as part of usability analysis, to an affective e-learning application.

For all applications the EREC system was used for providing data on valence and arousal of a person. Based on the values representing the actual affective state of the user, the application's performance can be adapted. Three principle types of system responses to affective changes in the user can be defined: First, feeding back the classified emotion information e.g. by visualization of an icon or the arousal-valence diagram makes the users aware of their emotions, delegating emotion regulation to the users. Second, application independent actions can be applied. Motivating verbal feedback or stimulating mini-games are examples here. Third, application dependent actions take into account the application domain and available functionality. As an example, an e-learning application can adjust the course of a session to the current state of the person, e.g. by choosing more or less challenging task.

In the following, two of these applications are described briefly.

14.4.1 Affective Usability Evaluation Tool

Usability test systems usually collect a huge amount of various data. Screen recording, gaze tracking, mouse and keyboard input are just basic components of data streams usually generated by nowadays usability programs. Further data sources like audio data and face monitors add to the ever growing wealth of data to be processed, and even newer technologies like emotion detection and human performance monitoring emerge and promise to add to the quality and value of usability studies.

Processing and analyzing those data is very expensive in time and human resources, even if good tools for visualization and analysis of the data are available. The reason for this is that common tools have no means of automatically identifying interesting sections in the test data, such as episodes in which the subject experienced high mental load or prominent emotions. The common procedure is that after the test, the usability expert browses manually to supposedly critical positions in the test data for analysis. However, critical spots not envisioned by the expert may be missed if the expert does not watch the whole sequence of data.

The goal of the work described here is to apply automatic analysis algorithms for identifying ongoing emotions and high cognitive load in the user to speed up the analysis process and to spot critical situations in the data stream more easily. We will show that enhancing a usability test system with affect recognition techniques can help to automatically detect critical situations in usability studies by use of novel sensors and knowledge discovery techniques.

14.4.1.1 The RealEYES Framework

The RealEYES framework is a usability test framework that combines a number of tools to support the entire process of a usability study, from preparation, execution, and analysis to communicating test setup data, measurement data and test results in an efficient manner.

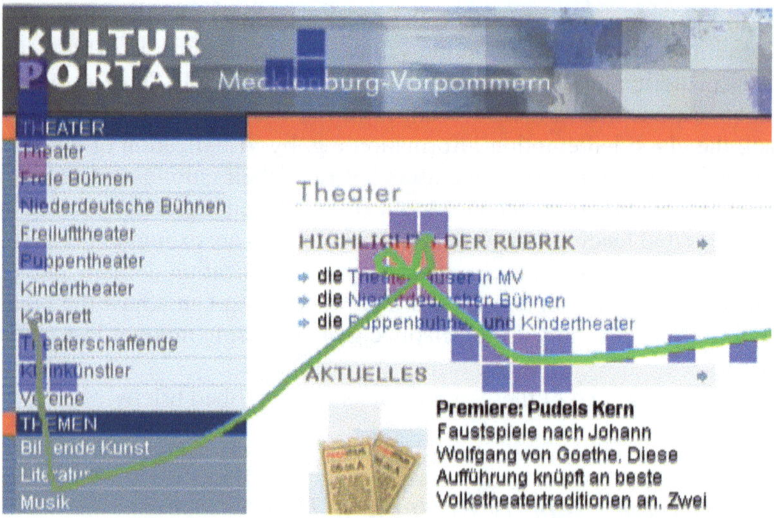

Fig. 14.4 Common visualization with the RealEYES Analyzer with eye gaze and mouse pointer information

The standard version of the framework supports a multitude of data types in its data backbone: meta data on the test, screen-shot videos and video capture of the user, audio data, gaze and mouse pointer positions, and application—and test—specific events. The data is collected and synchronized in a single data stream per subject. After recording, the test data of the subjects may be visualized or analyzed in various ways including playback and statistical analyses.

The most important tools in the RealEYES framework are the RealEYES Recorder and RealEYES Analyzer. The RealEYES Recorder manages the recording of all data. It requests the meta data, captures, synchronizes and compresses the test data and writes it to a single AVI file per session. The RealEYES Analyzer is the main analyzing application that replays the video streams and visualizes the collected meta data. Many standard and advanced visualizations of the screen video are available along with the gaze and mouse data. The adjustable visualizations offer detailed insights into the actual user interactions with the tested product (Fig. 14.4).

The RealEYES Analyzer is a tool for offline analysis of the collected test data and supports navigation using standard video player controls as well as event marks. Event marks may be inserted automatically by the Recorder, manually by the usability expert during the test and the analysis phase, or semi-automatically using scripts written in JavaScript that run in the Analyzer's script engine during offline analysis. Regions of interest may be defined and simple statistical calculations can be performed on them. The regions may not only be defined geometrically but can also be bound in time or to certain tasks. Other tools of the framework may resort to these regions. To improve the ability to test web-applications that often do not fit completely on the screen, both Recorder and Analyzer support and obey a scrolling region in all their features.

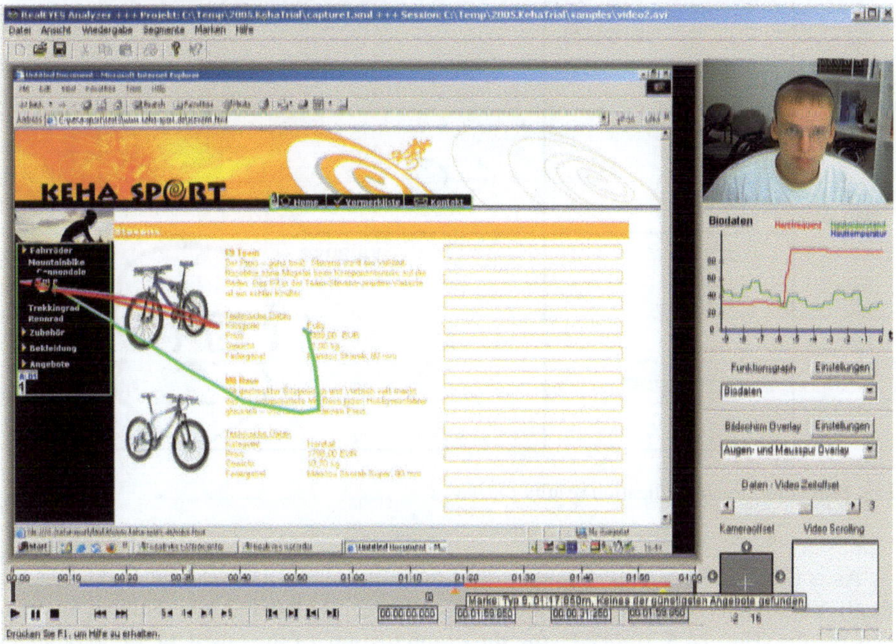

Fig. 14.5 Extended RealEYES Analyzer window. Note the time line with added event marks at the bottom

Further components of the RealEYES framework are RealEYES Statistics and RealEYES Questioning. The Statistics tool allows for complex statistical analyses to be accomplished on the acquired data. Furthermore, the Statistics tool is able to analyze and visualize data from all sessions of a study, i.e. to perform analyses over data of different users of a study. To illustrate, the Statistics tool can answer questions like "Did the majority of the subjects see the navigation buttons" or "What's the average time users looked at the advertisement". The Questioning tool allows the usability expert to create and utilize online questionnaires. The data gathered from the questionnaires can directly be processed by the Statistics tool.

14.4.1.2 Affective Extension to the RealEYES Framework

As user experience is closely coupled with emotions and cognitive load, we investigated in adding affect detection techniques to the framework to provide further, user- and usage specific information for analysis.

With the EREC system being a readily available sensor system for measuring emotion-related physiological parameters, we incorporated the system into the RealEYES framework. With EREC providing its already validated data in engineering units, integrating the system into the framework proved to be relatively easy.

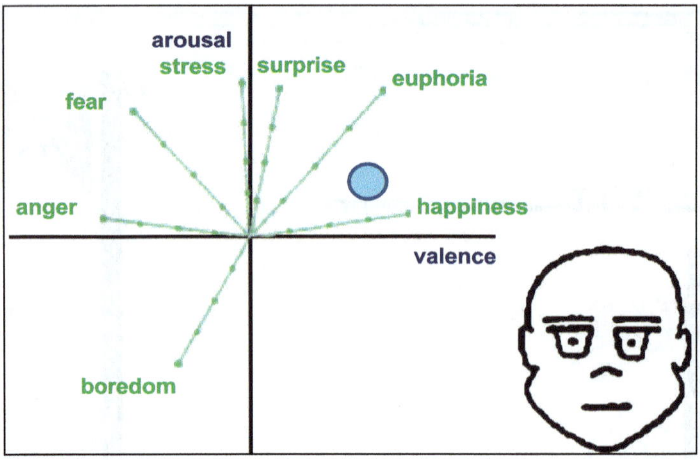

Fig. 14.6 Emotion classification results

As a first measure, we visualize the emotion-related physiological data in the RealEYES Analyzer along with the captured screen video and other statistical analysis results (Fig. 14.5, right). Using the graph display of the raw data, rapid changes in the physiological data (e.g. skin resistance) hint that stress may be discovered easily by the usability expert.

In another step, automatic data analysis is applied to the data to insert event marks in the data stream. We analyze the data for rapid changes in some attributes and generate event marks for the complete test session. These emotion-related event-marks make it easy for the experimenter to navigate to supposedly critical sections in the test. Nevertheless, we plan to integrate a visualization of the raw data in graph form in the Statistics tool. Here we could calculate and display values for a complete session and even for all test subjects from all sessions of the test at once.

14.4.1.3 Visualizing Classification Results

For visualizing emotion classification, results were already created in the context of our EmoTetris study (see Rani et al. 2006). In an attempt to map categorical basic emotions to the dimensional space of valence and arousal, we showed classification results of classifiers for the seven states happiness, euphoria, surprise, stress, anger, fear, and boredom in a star plot diagram mapped onto the valence/arousal diagram. As an additional visualization, we displayed a comic face representing the most prominent state as detected by the classifiers (see Fig. 14.6). In the future, we plan to integrate a graph display similar to the one for physiological data into the Analyzer and the Statistics tools. Similar to the script that detects rapid changes in physiological data, event marks will be inserted when a classifier detects a high stress level, or another affective measure.

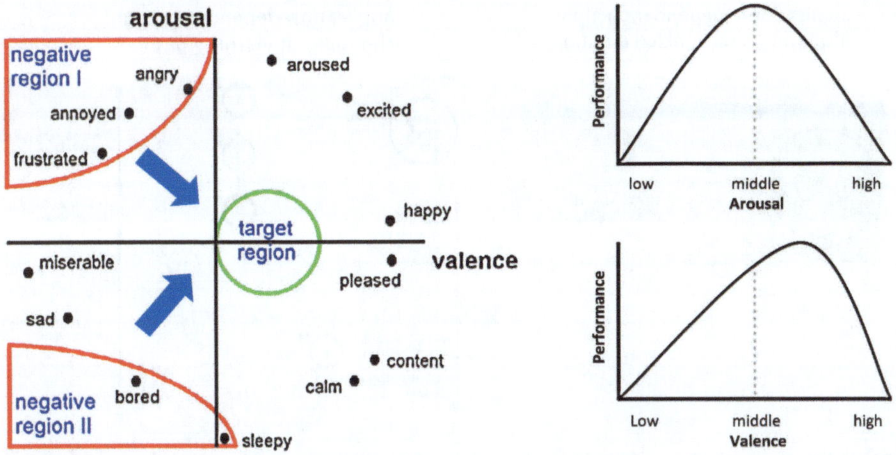

Fig. 14.7 Emotions in learning applications

Extending the RealEYES framework with affective sensors and related analysis algorithms allows automatically detecting critical incidents in usability studies. We found that our approach is not only applicable but opens new perspectives in usability studies. Further work will focus on improving the detection rates using more physiological parameters (breathing activity, blood oxygen level) and improved knowledge discovery algorithms. We will also investigate in new means to detect certain mental processes such as cognitive overload, tiredness or disorientation.

14.4.2 Affective E-Learning Environment

E-learning has become a well-recognized method for acquiring knowledge, be it for studies, further education, or work-related on-the-job training. Although e-learning environments support tutoring and cooperation, an essential part of learning here is self-contained with the learner communicating mainly with an electronic system. This requires more discipline and self-motivation due to lack of human communication which usually functions as motivator in traditional learning scenarios. An adaptive system that reacts to unfavorable affective states of the learner could improve not only the learning experience of the person, but also the overall learning results.

The Yerkes-Dodson law (Yerkes and Dodson 1908) demonstrates an empirical relationship between arousal and performance with a bell-shaped curve. It dictates that performance increases with cognitive arousal but only to a certain point: when levels of arousal become too high, performance will decrease. A corollary is that there is an optimal level of arousal for a given task. In contrast, a slight positive valence seems to be the optimum for performing a task.

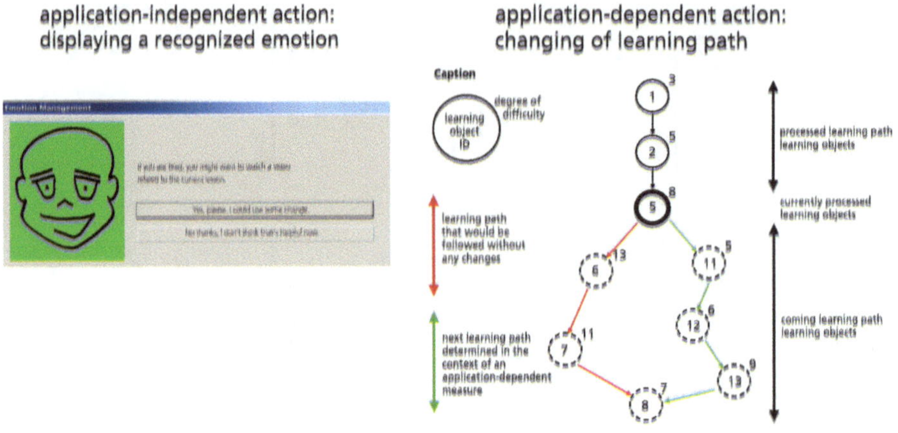

Fig. 14.8 Examples for application-independent and application dependent actions

Based on this we can identify areas of negative emotions for learning, that should be avoided and a target region for optimal learning in the arousal-valence diagram (Fig. 14.7). Region 1 with negative valence and positive arousal stands for emotions like frustration and angriness. Emotions like boredom and sleepiness are represented by region 2, characterized by negative valence and negative arousal. The target region for emotion, specified by a slight positive valence and neutral arousal, provides a maximum of efficiency and factual knowledge respectively.

An affective e-learning system has to invoke action depending on the learner's affective state to move his emotion from the negative regions towards the target region.

We have implemented an extension of an e-learning environment with following components: (1) an emotion recognition module (EREC System); (2) a catalog of actions to reply negative emotions; (3) a module for selection of appropriate actions; (4) a module for execution of these actions.

The e-learning environment and the affective component are connected via a special communication channel and represented by one user interface the learners are interacting with.

The catalog of actions contains application-independent and application-dependent actions. Examples for application-independent actions are motivational statements, the possibility to express displeasure, the suggestion of a short break or even a way to treat the computer with hammer, flamethrower and chain saw to reduce stress and frustration.

Application-dependent actions, bound to the given e-learning system or at least to the application domain, are mainly changes of lessons or of manner to present the subject (e.g. an animation instead of pure text) or the start of a questionnaire to check the learners learn progress (Fig. 14.8).

Selected actions are proposed to the learner and may be confirmed or rejected. The selection itself depends on the availability of actions: while application-independent actions can be continuously offered application-dependent actions have to consider constraints of application and relations between actions as well.

A field study proved that the fun factor of the course was rated higher, that a greater learning success was achieved, and that actions of the affective extension did not hinder the learning or exploring process.

14.5 Conclusion and Further Prospects

We have motivated the consideration of emotions in human-computer interaction and after a discussion of principles of emotion recognition we have presented an emotion recognition system—the EREC System. This system has been proved in several applications and by means of some selected applications we demonstrated the potential of affective systems.

Affect and emotion have influence on cognition and attention (e.g. Bush et al. 2000; Lane 2000). Research during the last years has shed some light on the underlying neural processes of, for example, erroneous behavior and visual attention (e.g. Posner 2004) and the impact of other, non-visual factors including emotional or affective prominence. There is also consensus that emotional response to erroneous behavior is accessible to current brain imaging technology like functional magnetic resonance imaging (fMRI) and electrical brain imaging with electroencephalography (EEG) (Olofsson et al. 2008; Vuilleumier and Driver 2007). Recent results document that such measurements are also possible with less intrusive sensor technology like sensors for measuring the electrocardiogram (ECG), galvanic skin response (GSR) and skin temperature.

Large display environments for visualization of simulations deliver simultaneously a huge amount of data in high detail and variety. Since processing capabilities are limited, the focus of visual attention and the information reception by the user should be considered. There exist several methods to attract the user's attention, but only less objective and technical supported methods to identify the focus of attention (see Horvitz et al. 2003) or recognize the impact of these methods on the user. Methods for recognizing the attentional state and the information reception as well as the emotional state and cognitive load are especially relevant for large high-resolution display environments. Recognition of affect and cognitive load creates a basis for both better usability analysis of applications in large high-resolution display environments and adaptive visualization and interaction. We will address this challenge in an application scenario for presentation of interactive simulation data on large high-resolution display environments.

References

ACII (2005). *1st international conference on affective computing and intelligent interaction.* Beijing, 2005. Berlin: Springer ISBN 3-540-29621-2.

ACII (2007). *2nd international conference on affective computing and intelligent interaction*. Lisbon, Portugal.

ACII (2009). *3rd international conference on affective computing and intelligent interaction*. Amsterdam. The Netherlands.

ACII (2011). *4th international conference on affective computing and intelligent interaction*. Memphis, USA.

Barreto, A., Zhai, J., & Adjouadi, M. (2007). Non-intrusive physiological monitoring for automated stress detection in human-computer interaction. In M. Lew, N. Sebe, T. S. Huang, & E. M. Bakker (Eds.), *LNCS: Vol. 4796. HCI 2007* (pp. 29–38). Heidelberg: Springer.

Bishop, C. M. (2006). *Pattern recognition and machine learning*. London: Springer. ISBN 978-0-387-31073-2.

British Standards Institution (2004). BS 7986: Industrial process measurement and control – Data quality metrics. Available from BSI Customer Services email: orders@bsi-global.com.

Bush, G., Luu, P., & Posner, M. I. (2000). Cognitive and emotional influences in anterior cingulate cortex. *Trends in Cognitive Sciences*, *4*(6), 215–222.

Cacioppo, J. T., Tassinary, L. G., & Berntson, G. G. (Eds.) (2000). *Handbook of psychophysiology* (2nd edn.). Cambridge: Cambridge University Press. ISBN 0-521-62634-X

Ekman, P., & Davidson, R. J. (Eds.) (1994). *The nature of emotion: fundamental questions*. New York: Oxford University Press.

Ekman, P., & Friesen, W. (1976) *Pictures of facial affect*. Palo Alto: Consulting Psychologists Press.

Ekman, P., & Friesen, W. (1978). *Facial action coding system: a technique for the mea-surement of facial movement*. Palo Alto: Consulting Psychologists Press.

Ekman, P., Levenson, R. W., & Friesen, W. (1983). Autonomic nervous system activity distinguishes among emotions. *Science*, *221*. The American Association for Advancement of Science.

Haag, A., Goronzy, S., Schaich, P., & Williams, J. (2004). Emotion recognition using bio-sensors: first steps towards an automatic system. In André, et al. (Eds.), *Lecture notes in computer science: Vol. 3068. Affective dialogue systems, proceedings of the Kloster Irsee tutorial and research workshop on affective dialogue systems* (pp. 36–48). Berlin: Springer.

Hastie, T., Tibshirani, R., & Friedman, J. (2009). *The elements of statistical learning: data mining, inference, and prediction. Springer series in statistics* (2nd edn.). Corr. 3rd printing, 5th Printing, 2009. ISBN 978-0-387-84857-0.

Henry, M. P., & Clarke, D. W. (1993). The self-validating sensor: rationale, definitions and examples. *Control Engineering Practice*, *1*, 585.

Horvitz, E., Kadie, C., Paek, T., & Hovel, D. (2003). Models of attention in computing and communication: from principles to applications. *Communications of the ACM*, *46*(3), 52–59.

IEEE Transactions on Affective Computing (2012). http://www.computer.org/portal/web/tac. ISSN: 1949-3045.

Kim, J., & André, E. (2008). Emotion recognition based on physiological changes in music listening. *IEEE Transactions on Pattern Analysis and Machine Intelligence*, *30*(12), 2067–2083.

Kim, K. H., Bang, S. W., & Kim, S. R. (2004). Emotion recognition system using shortterm monitoring of physiological signals. *Medical and Biological Engineering and Computing*, *42*(2004), 419–427.

King, R. D., Feng, C., & Sutherland, A. (1995). Statlog: comparison of classification algorithms on large real-world problems. *Applied Artificial Intelligence*, *9*(3), 289–333

Knapp, R. B., Kim, J., & André, E. (2011). Physiological signals and their use in augmenting emotion recognition for human-machine interaction. In P. Petta, C. Pelachaud, & R. Cowie (Eds.), *Emotion-oriented systems: the humaine handbook*. Berlin: Springer.

Lane, R. (2000). *Cognitive neuroscience of emotion*. New York: Oxford University Press.

Lichtenstein, A., Oehme, A., Kupschick, S., & Jürgensohn, T. (2008). Comparing two emotion models for deriving affective states from physiological data. In C. Peter, & R. Beale (Eds.), *LNCS: Vol. 4868. Affect and emotion in human-computer interaction*. Heidelberg: Springer. ISBN 978-3-540-85098-4.

Mader, S., Peter, C., Göcke, R., Schultz, R., Voskamp, J., & Urban, B. (2004). A freely configurable, multi-modal sensor system for affective computing. In André, et al. (Eds.), *Affective dialogue systems: tutorial and research workshop* (pp. 313–318). Berlin: Springer.

Magjarevic, M., Gao, Y., Barreto, A., & Adjouadi, M. (2009). Comparative analysis of noninvasively monitored biosignals for affective assessment of a computer user. In A. J. McGoron, C.-Z. Li, & W.-C. Lin (Eds.), *IFMBE proceedings: Vol. 24. 25th southern biomedical engineering conference 2009*, 15–17 May 2009, Miami, Florida, USA (pp. 255–260). Berlin: Springer. doi:10.1007/978-3-642-01697-4_90.

Mandryk, R. L., & Atkins, M. S. (2007). A fuzzy physiological approach for continuously modeling emotion during interaction with play technologies. *International Journal of Human-Computer Studies*, *65*, 329–347.

Nasoz, F., Alvarez, K., Lisetti, C.L., & Finkelstein, N. (2004). Emotion recognition from physiological signals using wireless sensors for presence technologies. *International Journal of Cognition, Technology, and Work—Special Issue on Presence, 6*.

Olofsson, J. K., Nordin, S., Sequeira, H., & Polich, J. (2008). Affective picture processing: An integrative review of ERP findings. *Biological Psychology*, *77*(3), 247–265.

Peter, C., & Beale, R. (Eds.) (2008). *Affect and emotion in human-computer interaction. LNCS: Vol. 4868*. Heidelberg: Springer, ISBN 978-3-540-85098-4

Peter, C., Ebert, E., & Beikirch, H. (2005). A wearable multi-sensor system for mobile acquisition of emotion-related physiological data. In *Proceedings of the 1st international conference on affective computing and intelligent interaction*, Beijing, 2005. Berlin: Springer.

Peter, C., Schultz, R., Voskamp, J., Urban, B., Nowack, N., Janik, H., Kraft, K., & Göcke, R. (2007). EREC-II in use—studies on usability and suitability of a sensor system for affect detection and human performance monitoring. In J. Jacko (Ed.), *LNCS: Vol. 4552. Human-computer interaction, part III, HCII 2007* (pp. 465–474). Berlin: Springer.

Petta, P., Pelachaud C., & Cowie, R. (Eds.) (2011). *Emotion-oriented systems: the humaine handbook*. Berlin: Springer.

Picard, R. W. (1997). *Affective computing*. Cambridge: M.I.T. Press

Picard, R. W., Vyzas, E., & Healey, J. (2001). Toward machine emotional intelligence – analysis of affective physiological state. *IEEE Transactions on Pattern Analysis and Machine Intelligence*, *23*(10), 1175–1191.

Poh, M.-Z., McDuff, D. J., & Picard, R. W. (2010). Non-contact, automated cardiac pulse measurements using video imaging and blind source separation. *Optics Express*, *18*(10(c)), 10763–10774.

Posner, M. (2004). *Cognitive neuroscience of attention*. New York: Guilford Press.

Rani, P., Liu, C., Sarkar, N., & Vanman, E. (2006). An empirical study of machine learning techniques for affect recognition in human–robot interaction. *Pattern Analysis & Applications*, *9*(1).

Rigas, G., Katsis, C., Ganiatsas, G., & Fotiadis, D. (2009). A user independent, biosignal based, emotion recognition method. In C. Conati, K. McCoy, & G. Paliouras (Eds.), *Lecture notes in computer science: Vol. 4511. User modeling 2007*. (pp. 314–318). Berlin: Springer. doi:10.1007/978-3-540-73078-1_36

Schwartz, M. S., & Andrasik, F. (2003). *Biofeedback: a practitioner's guide* (3rd edn.). New York: Guilford Press. ISBN 1-57230-845-1

Tao, J., & Tan, T. (Eds.) (2009). *Affective information processing*. London: Springer. ISBN 978-1-84800-305–978-1-84800-7.

van den Broek, E. L., Janssen, J. H., Westerink, J. H. D. M., & Healey, J. A. (2009). Prerequisites for affective signal processing (ASP). In *International conference on bio-inspired systems and signal processing, biosignals*, 14–17 Jan 2009, Porto, Portugal.

Verhoef, T., Lisetti, C., Barreto, A., Ortega, F., van der Zant, T., & Cnossen, F. (2009). Bio-sensing for emotional characterization without word labels. In J. A. Jacko (Ed.), *LNCS: Vol. 5612. Human-computer interaction, Part III, ambient, ubiquitous and intelligent interaction* (pp. 693–702). Berlin: Springer.

Vuilleumier, P., & Driver, J. (2007). Modulation of visual processing by attention and emotion: windows on causal interactions between human brain regions. *Philosophical Transactions of the Royal Society B: Biological Sciences*, *362*(1481), 837–855.
Wimmer, M. (2007). *Model-based image interpretation with application to facial expression recognition.* Ph.D. Thesis, Technische Universitat München, Institute for Informatics.
Yerkes, R. M., & Dodson, J. D. (1908). The relation of strength of stimulus to rapidity of habit-formation. *Journal of Comparative Neurology and Psychology*, *18*, 459–482.
Yoo, S. K., Lee, C. K., Park, Y. J., Kim, N. H., Lee, B. C., & Jeong, K. S. (2005). Neural network based emotion estimation using heart rate variability and skin resistance. In L. Wang, K. Chen, & Y. S. Ong (Eds.), *Lecture notes in computer science: vol. 3610. Advances in natural computation* (pp. 818–824). Berlin: Springer.

Chapter 15
Applying Artistic Color Theories to Visualization

Theresa-Marie Rhyne

Abstract We explore practical approaches to applying color theory to creating and examining visualizations and digital media. Our paper highlights general background on color theory as well as various color models and color spaces developed by painters, printers and scientists over the centuries. We review the color wheel as well as the hue, saturation and brightness (HSL) and hue, saturation and value (HSV) models targeted at addressing color display monitors and digital media. Finally, we discuss color schemes and show how these concepts can be applied to creating color maps for visualizations. We explore color analysis methods using online systems such as Adobe's Kuler and Color Scheme Designer tools.

15.1 Introduction

Color Theory includes the practical knowledge on the mixing of colors as well as the visual impact of specific color combinations. This paper explores practical approaches to applying color theory to creating and examining visualizations and digital media. We begin by providing some background on color theory including its application to computer graphics and digital media. We highlight various color models and color spaces established by painters, printers and scientists over the centuries. Next, we review the color wheel and how it is assembled. From there, we highlight the hue, saturation and brightness (HSL) and hue, saturation and value (HSV) models targeted at addressing color display monitors and digital media. Color schemes and their relationships to the color wheel follow.

With these color theory concepts, we explore analyzing the colors in digital imagery. We show how online systems such as Adobe's Kuler and Color Scheme Designer tools can aid us in this color assessment process. From there, we apply color scheme concepts to creating visualizations. We show a step by step process for building individual color maps for two data visualization examples. Finally, we provided a detailed bibliography of historical writings on color theory and listing of selected color and visualization tools we have used.

T.-M. Rhyne (✉)
Durham, NC 27713, USA
e-mail: theresamarierhyne@gmail.com

J. Dill et al. (eds.), *Expanding the Frontiers of Visual Analytics and Visualization*,
DOI 10.1007/978-1-4471-2804-5_15,

Fig. 15.1 The Artistic or Painter's primary color model of Red, Yellow and Blue (RYB)

Fig. 15.2 Additive primary color model of Red, Yellow and Blue (RGB) lights associated with color display devices and photography

15.2 Some Background on Color Theory

Writings on color theory can be traced back to Renaissance times and include entries in the notebooks of Leonardo da Vinci in the 1490s. It was not until the 1660s when Isaac Newton and others developed color optics and the notion of primary colors that "color theory" evolved formally as a body of knowledge. Although there are many scientific theories based on color perception and vision science, our discussion here focuses on artistic notions of color theories.

Color Theory was originally defined in terms of three "primitive" or "primary" colors, Red, Yellow and Blue (RYB). It was thought that various combinations or mixtures of Red, Yellow and Blue yielded all other colors. This color mixing behavior was recognized and applied by printers, dyers and painters. The two founding documents on Color Theory appeared in the 1800s. The first was produced in 1810 by Johann Wolfgang von Goethe and entitled "Theory of Colours". The second writing, produced in 1839, was prepared by Michel Eugene Chevreul and entitled "The Law of Simultaneous Color Contrast" (Fig. 15.1).

In the late 1800s, English and German scientists established color perception principals based on a different set of primary colors. These Red, Green and Blue (RGB) primary colors were based on an additive mixture of monochromatic lights. Further research of different responses to light in the retina of the eye established three (Red, Green and Blue) types of color receptors or cones in the retina. Hermann von Helmholtz's publication, The Handbook of Psychological Optics, articulated these concepts in the 1850s and 1860s. The usage of RGB as a primary set of colors was thus solidified. In the early 1900s, with the use of the RBG primary set of colors along with a series of encompassing models of color space and color perception (Fig. 15.2).

Fig. 15.3 Subtractive primary color model of Cyan, Magenta, Yellow and Key Black (CYMK) for color printing

The industrial chemical production of lightfast synthetic pigments for improved saturation of color mixtures also evolved in the early 1900s. This paved the way for the evolution of color photography and color printing. The concepts of three color printing along with artists notions of color theory were adapted to support primary colors most effective in inks or photographic dyes. These three primary colors include Cyan, Magenta and Yellow (CMY). For color printing, dark colors are supplemented by black ink to allow for the production of stable and readable typography. This results in the Cyan, Magenta, Yellow and Key Black (CMYK) color system (Fig. 15.3).

The CMY primary colors were shown to be a subtractive method for producing printed colors that could be reconciled with the Red, Green and Blue (RGB) additive color system for lights. This reconciliation resulted in each of the CMY colors absorbing only one of the RGB retinal colors. As a result, Cyan absorbed only Red, Magenta absorbed only Green and Yellow absorbed only Blue Violet colors. The CMYK color system produced an economical way for facilitating color printing. However, CMYK was shown to be deficient in producing oranges, greens and purples. This resulted in the addition of other colors to the printing process.

Color Theory expanded to include the RGB and the CMY primary color concepts. In the early 1900s, Albert Munsell developed a color atlas to support these concepts that was published in his 1905 "Color Notation" book. A more robust discussion of the color atlas was published in his 1915 book entitled "Atlas of the Munsell Color System". The Munsell Color System obtained international acceptance and served as the foundation for many other color order systems.

After Munsell published his color system, scientists in color perception conducted experiments on human eye sight. The experiments provided the foundation for the International Commission on Illumination (CIE) 1931 standard entitled CIE 1931 XYZ color space. In 1976, an update CIE 1976 color space or CIELUV color space was released to establish improved perceptual uniformity.

As abstract art began to evolve in the 1900s, many artists wrote on the foundation of forms and color harmony. In 1911, Wassily Kandinsky published "On the Spiritual Nature of Art" that defined colors in terms of emotions. He observed that yellow tends to depict warmth while blue tends to depict cold. He also defined clarity in terms of white and obscurity in terms of black. The Warm and Cool color concept continues to be frequently used for building color schemes.

In the 1919 to 1931 timeframe, there were major advances in color theory made by artists teaching at or associated with the German Bauhaus. The Bauhaus was a school in Germany that combined the fine arts and crafts. The school was well known for its approach to design that it publicized and taught. Paul Klee, Wassily Kandinsky, Johannes Itten and Josef Albers specifically developed color theory writings and demonstration based studies of color design principles for the courses they taught at the Bauhaus. Many of their writings either began before or evolved further after the artists left the Bauhaus.

The writings of Itten and Albers solidified after their Bauhaus years. "The Art of Color: The Subjective Experience and Objective Rationale of Color" was first published in Germany in 1961 by Johannes Itten and later published in the United State by John Wiley and Sons in 1974. In 1963, Josef Albers' first published his book, entitled "The Interaction of Color", with Yale University Press in 1963. In 2009, Yale University Press published a new complete edition of Albers' book that provides a robust portfolio of the color examples that Albers' developed.

Contemporary color theory has expanded to include digital media methods and print management systems. In the 1970s, the computer graphics community developed the concepts of Hue, Saturation and Value (HSV) and Hue, Saturation and Brightness (HSL) to build color models targeted at televisions, computer displays and projectors. These devices produce colors based on Red, Green, and Blue lights or the RGB additive primary colors model. The resulting mixtures of light produced a wide variety of colors called a gamut. The resulting colors can be very different from colors derived from the subtractive color mixing of Cyan, Magenta and Yellow (CMY) for printing or the traditional painterly subtractive color space of Red, Yellow and Blue (RYB). In 1978, Alvy Ray Smith published a landmark computer graphics paper that defined the hue, saturation and value (HSV) color model and the hue, saturation and brightness (HSL) color model. The HSV and HSL color models are used in color pickers and color modification tools for digital imaging and computer graphics systems.

In 2003, A.K. Peters published Maureen Stone's book, "A Field Guide to Digital Color", that provides an excellent overview of this subject. There are also a number of web sites and online tools dealing with color management. Janet Lynn Ford has developed an robust color theory tutorial on her Worqx Web site available online at http://www.worqx.com/color/index.htm. There are also numerous color mapping tools. We will highlight a few of these tools in our following discussion on applying color theory to visualization.

15.3 The Color Wheel for the RYB Painterly Set of Primary Colors

The Color Wheel is a diagram that organizes color hues around a circle to depict primary, secondary, complementary and adjacent color relationships. Using the Red, Yellow and Blue (RYB) painterly primary colors as our color model, we begin building a color wheel by first positioning the primary hues Red, Yellow and

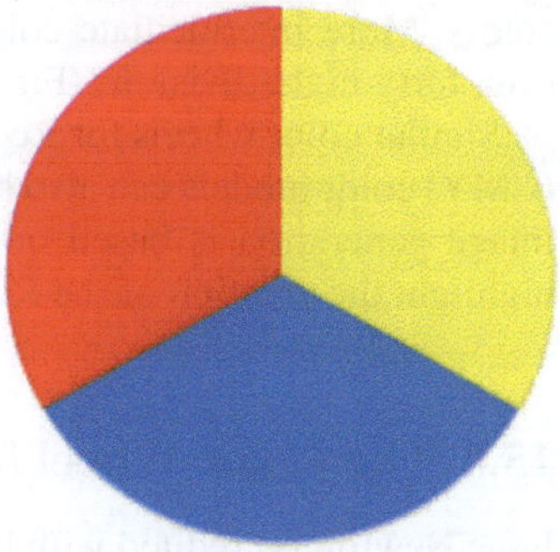

Fig. 15.4 Step 1 for a Painter's Color Wheel—laying out the Red, Yellow and Blue (RYB) primary colors

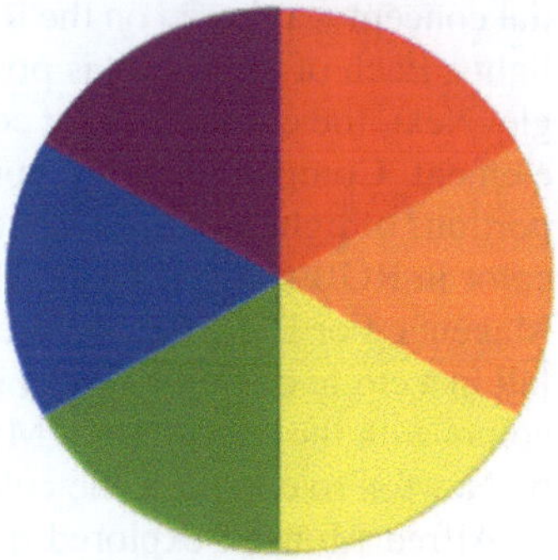

Fig. 15.5 Step 2 for a Painter's Color Wheel—inserting the secondary colors of Orange, Green and Purple in between the Red, Yellow and Blue (RYB) primary colors

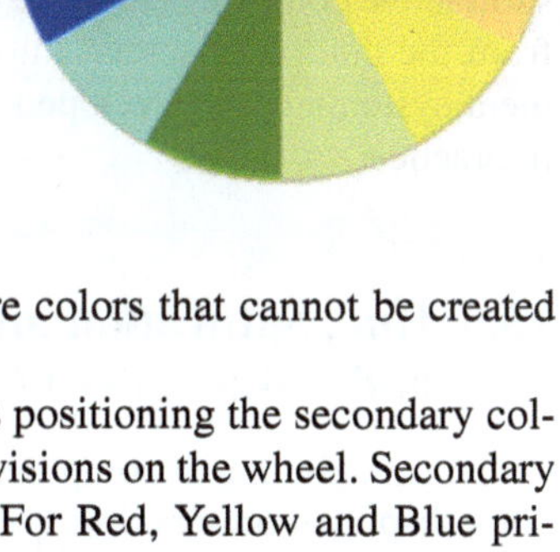

Fig. 15.6 Step 3 for a Painter's Color Wheel—inserting the tertiary colors of Yellow-Orange, Red-Orange, Red-Purple, Purple-Blue, Blue-Green, and Green-Yellow

Blue equidistant from each other. Primary colors are colors that cannot be created by mixing secondary colors (Fig. 15.4).

The next step in creating a Color Wheel involves positioning the secondary colors between the primary set of colors to create six divisions on the wheel. Secondary colors are obtained by mixing two primary colors. For Red, Yellow and Blue primary colors, the secondary colors are Orange, Green and Purple (Fig. 15.5).

The placing of tertiary colors adds twelve divisions to the Color Wheel. Tertiary colors are obtained by mixing and primary and secondary hues. Yellow-Orange, Red-Orange, Red-Purple, Purple-Blue, Blue-Green, and Green-Yellow are tertiary colors. More intermediate colors can be added to obtain twenty-four divisions or even forty-eight divisions (Fig. 15.6).

Similar color wheels for Red, Green, Blue (RGB) and Cyan, Magenta and Yellow (CMY) color models can also be developed. In computer graphics and visualization, image generation is based on the display of a computer screen. As a result, we highlight the creation of the RGB Color Wheel in the next section of our paper.

15.4 The Color Wheel for the RGB Model

Issac Newton is credited with having developed the first color circle or Color Wheel by joining the red and violet ends of the color visual spectrum into a circle. His initial concept was based on the Red, Green and Blue (RGB) additive primary colors of lights. Each of the colors is positioned equidistant from each other to create a triangle. Next, the corresponding complementary color is placed across from each RGB element. Complementary colors are pairs of colors that when mixed in equal proportions of light produce a neutral color (usually gray). For Red, the complementary color in RGB space is Cyan. For Green, the complementary color in RGB space is Magenta. For Blue, the complementary color in RGB space is Yellow. These colors fall in a circle or Color Wheel in the order of wavelengths of corresponding spectral colors with the exception of Magenta. Magenta is not a spectral color but was added by Newton to complete the color circle.

Alfred Munsell explored quantifying the circumference of the Color Wheel in terms of Hue and the radius of the Color Wheel in terms of Saturation. This resulted in the development of a formal color system and color atlas entitled the Munsell System. Our Color Theory background section discussion further highlighted Alfred Munsell's contribution to color theory,

As we further explore the complements of RGB space, we discover the RGB complements to be Cyan, Magenta and Yellow (CYM). The CYM joined with key black becomes the subtractive model for color printing known as CYMK. So, there is a clear inverse relationship between the additive RGB color space and the CYM subtractive color space that we can apply when converting our visualization imagery from the computer screen into print. Adobe Photoshop and other Color Management systems have developed algorithms for effectively applying this relationship in practice.

15.5 Hue, Saturation and Brightness (HSL) & Hue, Saturation and Value (HSV) Models

With the beginning of computer graphics, there became a desire for digital control of color display monitors. In a color monitor, the red, green and blue (RGB) electronic guns excite respective phosphors to create digital imagery. The range of colors created with this process is called the RGB monitor gamut. Each display has its own RGB gamut profile or range. Color printers or other type of digital output device also has a color gamut.

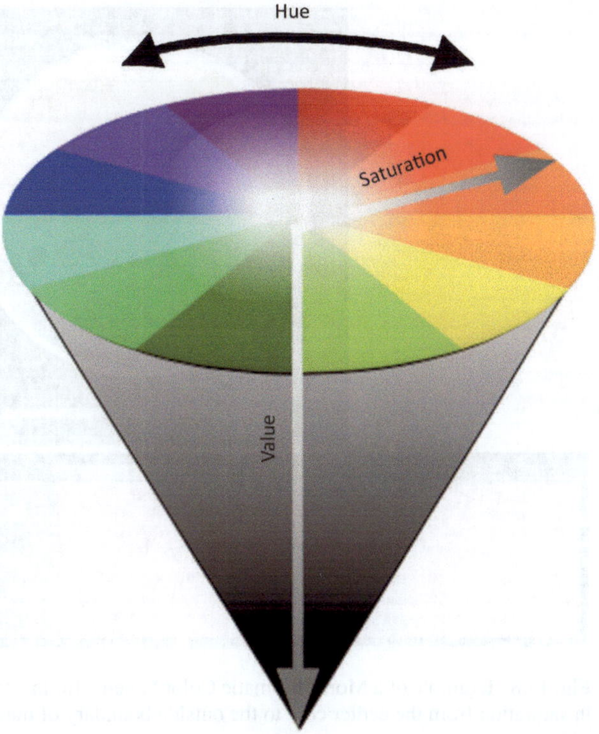

Fig. 15.7 Three dimensional cone representation of the Hue, Saturation and Value (HSV) color model for color display devices

The additive RGB additive color model along with the CMY and RYB subtractive colors models do not define color relationships in the same manner that the human eye does. The Hue Saturation and Brightness (HSL) as well as the Hue Saturation and Value (HSV) models attempt to improve upon the RGB color model in regard to human perception. Our discussion below will focus on describing the HSV color model.

Hue is used to define a particular color selection. It is more specifically described in terms of a wavelength dimension given to a specific color. The Color Wheel provides the reference frame for diagramming hues for the HSV color model. The change of a given color can be described with two key parameters: The lightness or darkness of a color is expressed in terms of Value. The overall intensity or strength of the spectral light is described by Value. For the HSV color model, Value is the linear axis running through the middle of the Color Wheel. Saturation refers to the dominance of hue in a color. At the outer edge of the Color Wheel, color hues are "pure" or dominant with the HSV color model. Moving toward the central linear axis, color hues decrease in Saturation. Along the central axis, desaturation results and a grayscale forms. The grayscale runs from white to black with all of the immediate grays in between. The HSV color model thus is a three dimensional cone representation. Our explorations of color theory, including the HSV color model for computer graphics, demonstrate the importance of the Color Wheel as a basic reference frame for diagramming color relationships (Fig. 15.7).

Fig. 15.8 Example of a Monochromatic Color Scheme for the color Magenta. The color hues vary in saturation from the center core to the outside boundary of the color wheel

Fig. 15.9 Example of a Complementary Color Scheme of Orange and Cyan. The colors oppose each other on the Color Wheel

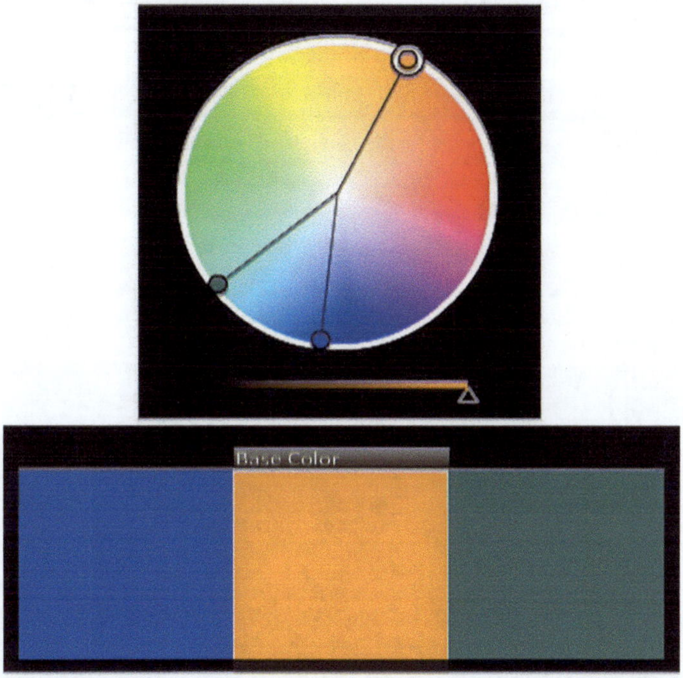

Fig. 15.10 Example of a Split Complementary Color Scheme with Blue and Blue Green being the split complementary colors to Orange on the Color Wheel

15.6 Color Schemes

With our Color Wheel as a guide, we can next develop color schemes that guide in combining various hues together in a graphic design or visualization. A color scheme that combines values of a single hue, mixing various color saturations from almost white to very dark is called a monochromatic color scheme (Fig. 15.8).

We can increase in color scheme complexity by combining two colors together. Two hues that are opposite from each other on the Color Wheel form a complementary color scheme (Fig. 15.9).

A split complementary color scheme combines a color with two colors that are adjacent on either side of its complementary color. This steps up to a color scheme with three hues (Fig. 15.10).

An analogous color scheme frequently includes three colors that are adjacent to each other on the color wheel. With the analogous color scheme, often one color is the dominant color with adjacent hues used to enhance the color scheme (Fig. 15.11).

The triadic color scheme includes three colors that are equally space around the color wheel. Red, Yellow and Blue (RYB), the painterly primary colors, as well as Orange, Green and Purple, the painterly secondary colors, are examples of triadic color schemes. Red, Green and Blue (RGB), the additive primary colors of light,

Fig. 15.11 Example of an Analogous Color Scheme of Red Purple, Purple and Blue Purple—three colors adjacent to each other on the Color Wheel

and Cyan, Yellow and Magenta (CYM), the subtractive colors associated with color printing, are other examples of triadic color schemes (Fig. 15.12).

A tetradic color scheme uses four colors. A popular tetradic scheme includes combining two complementary color pairs. Red and Green combined with Orange and Blur, complementary color pairs from the RYB painterly color space, produces a tetradic color scheme. These color schemes are optimized when one of the four colors dominates the composition (Fig. 15.13).

Another tetradic color scheme is the Accented Analogous Color Scheme. Accented Analogous Color Schemes include three analogous colors and the middle analogous color's complementary element. On a RYB Color Wheel, the Purple, Red and Orange analogous color elements combined with Red's Complementary Color (Green) form an Accented Analogous Color Scheme (Fig. 15.14).

A neutral color scheme includes colors that are not on the Color Wheel such as beige, brown, gray, black and white. When a neutral color scheme expands to include colors on the Color Wheel, it is termed an Accented Neutral Color Scheme (Fig. 15.15).

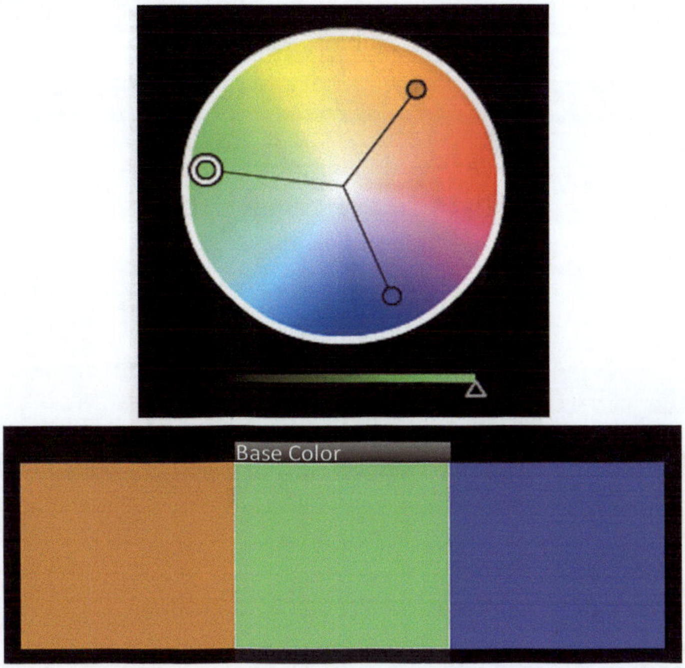

Fig. 15.12 Example of a Triadic Color Scheme of Orange, Green and Purple—three colors equally spaced from each other on the Color Wheel

15.7 Color Wheel and Color Scheme Software Tools

Software like Adobe Photoshop allows for creating digital imagery with the color concepts we have previously discussed in this paper. There are also many online or mobile application tools that allow for color scheme analysis and creation.

Adobe has developed an online tool entitled Kuler that allows for establishing a color scheme from an existing color digital image. This tool is available at http://kuler.adobe.com/. Color Scheme Designer, another online tool, assists with creating and evaluating color schemes. Color Scheme Designer is available at http://colorschemedesigner.com/. Pantone has developed an application for the iPhone, iPod or iPad that helps with color selections entitled "myPANTONE". myPANTONE is available from Apple's itunes site at http://itunes.apple.com/us/app/mypantone/id329515634?mt=8.

There are numerous other color palette tools for online and mobile applications that can be found by searching the Web. Two online listings include sitepoint.com's listing at http://blogs.sitepoint.com/21-stimulating-color-palette-tools-for-designers/ and instantshift.com's listing at http://www.instantshift.com/2011/02/04/effective-color-palette-and-color-scheme-generators/.

ColorBrewer is another excellent online system targeted at cartographic visualization efforts. In 2001 and 2002, Cynthia Brewer and Mark Harrower of Pennsylvania State University originally created their "color advice for maps tool" with

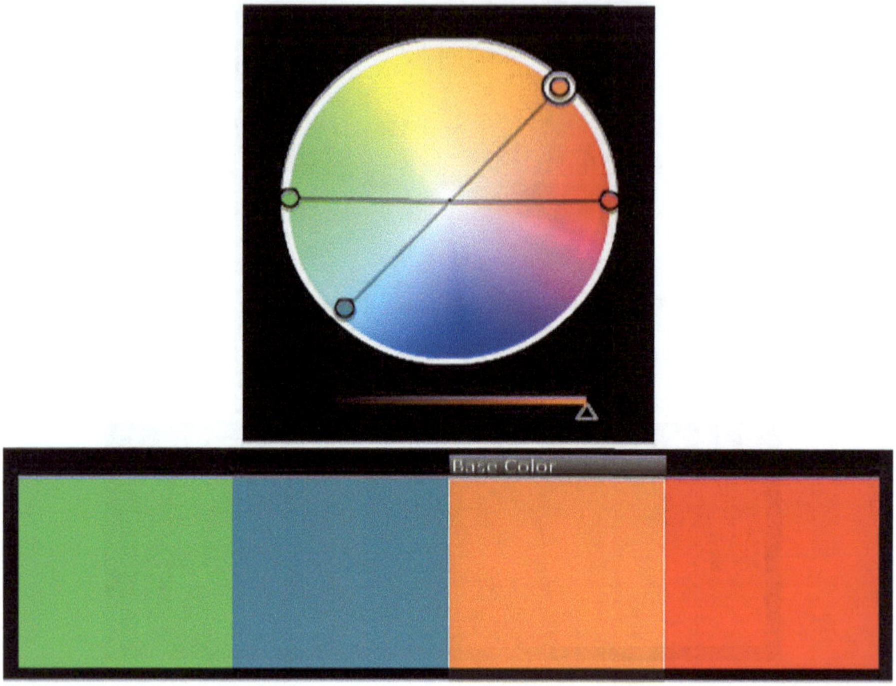

Fig. 15.13 Example of a Tetradic Color Scheme on the Color Wheel. This example depicts two complimentary pairs of colors: Red and Green with Cyan and Orange

funding from the United States of America's National Science Foundation (NSF), http://www.personal.psu.edu/cab38/ColorBrewer/ColorBrewer.html.

An upgraded version, ColorBrewer 2.0, was developed in 2009 with funding from Axis Maps. LLC, http://colorbrewer2.org/.

Our future sections on creating and analyzing digital color schemes for visualization will focus on the use of Adobe's Kuler tool as well as the use of Color Scheme Designer. Other color palette tools can also be used for this purpose.

15.8 Analyzing Digital Images with the Color Wheel and Color Schemes

One way to explore color hue relationships is to work with a basic object or image of an object. Josef Albers studied color relationships in his Homage to a Square set of paintings created over a twenty-five year period. In these abstract paintings, Albers depicted many variations of the color schemes we described in the previous section of this paper.

In my own color analysis work, I am partial to taking digital imagery of roses and analyzing the associated hue, saturation and value parameters. For the color

Fig. 15.14 Example of an Accented Analogous Color Scheme with the three analogous colors of Red Purple, Purple and Blue Purple combined with the Green Yellow (Lime Green) complementary color on the Color Wheel

analysis work, I use Adobe's Kuler tool to import a JPEG version of my digital image for initial hue analysis. Next, I use the online tool, "Color Scheme Designer", to diagram the color relationships or schemes on a Color Wheel. Below, we show a digital image of a rose with magenta, orange and white hues (Fig. 15.16).

For our color analysis, we will focus on the magenta and orange colors. We can use Adobe's Kuler tool (http://kuler.adobe.com/) to precisely examine the color elements in the digital image of our rose. With the Kuler tool, we are able to examine five points on a digital image to establish an actual color scheme. If we have more than five basic color elements, we can repeat the use of the Kuler tool until we capture the fundamental color scheme. For our rose image, five color elements will suffice. We present the actual color elements evaluation below (Fig. 15.17).

We can now use the Color Scheme Designer tool (http://colorschemedesigner.com/) to analyze our rose's color scheme. As we examine the color wheel, we notice the magenta and orange are in close proximity to each other. Color Scheme designer allows us to select an analogous color relationship to discover that magenta, red and orange are adjacent hues on the Color Wheel. So, we have an almost analogous color scheme that includes Magenta and Orange with the neutral hue of White serving as a bridge color (Fig. 15.18).

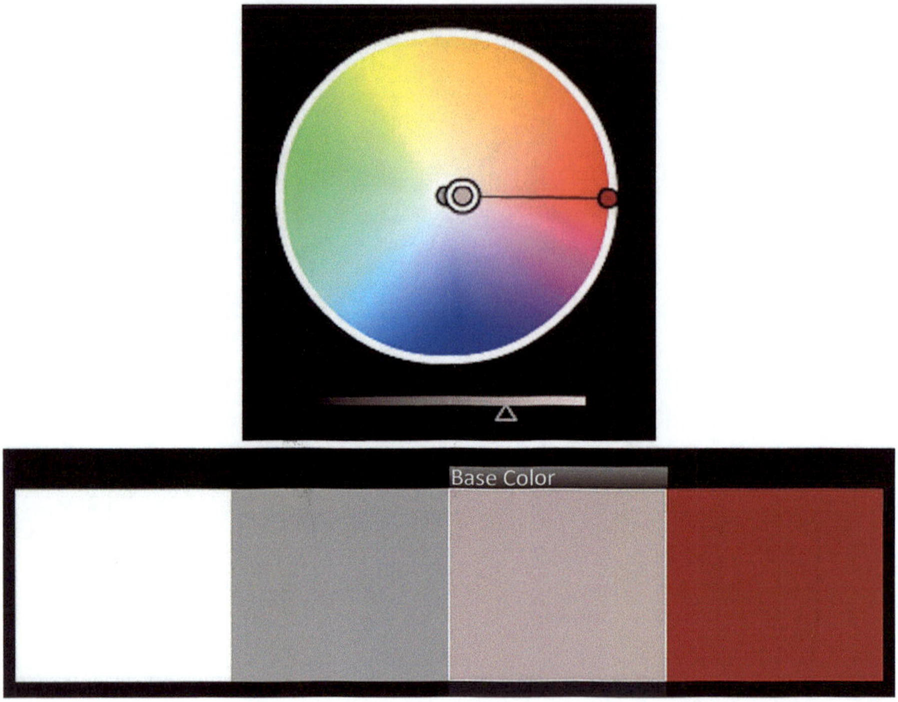

Fig. 15.15 Example of an Accented Neutral Color Scheme with the three neutral colors of White, Gray and Gray Brown combined with a Red accent color on the Color Wheel

15.9 Applying Color Scheme Concepts to Creating Visualizations

We can apply color scheme concepts in developing visualizations. Below, we show a three dimensional object that is a derived from a computational physics model of a Supernova or dying star. To emphasize data value changes, we use an analogous color scheme of Yellow, Green and Blue. Color Scheme Designer helps us locate the digital values of these hues (Fig. 15.19).

For our visualization, we chose Yellow as our dominant color for the analogous scheme with Green and Blue emphasizing additional numeric changes. The highest data values of the Supernova visualization actually appear around the edge of our three dimensional object. We emphasize these changes by applying a complementary color scheme. With Color Scheme Designer, we determine the complementary color to yellow to be blue-purple. We show both the analogous and complementary color schemes using Color Scheme Designer below (Fig. 15.20).

Using the color values from Color Scheme Designer, we transferred these color selections into CEI's Ensight software tool to build initial color maps (Fig. 15.21).

Below, we show a detailed analysis of the color elements of our actual Supernova visualization, using Adobe's Kuler tool below.

Fig. 15.16 Digital Image of a Rose with Magenta, Orange and White Hues. We will use this image for further color analyses

Fig. 15.17 Color Analysis of the Magenta and Orange Hue elements in the digital image of our rose. Our Color Analysis was performed with Adobe's Kuler tool: http://kuler.adobe.com

Fig. 15.18 Color Scheme Evaluation of the Magenta and Orange Hue elements in the digital image of our rose. An analogous color scheme is shown using the Color Scheme Designer online tool available at http://colorschemedesigner.com

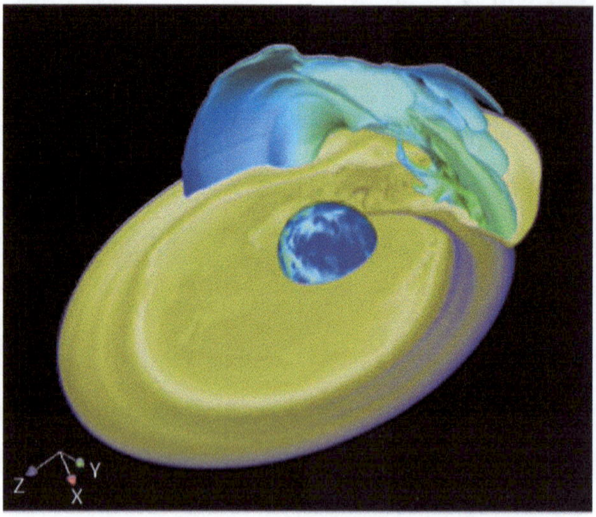

Fig. 15.19 Visualization of a three dimensional object derived from a computational physics model of a Supernova or dying star. The visualization was done with CEI's Insight software tool, see: http://www.ensight.com/

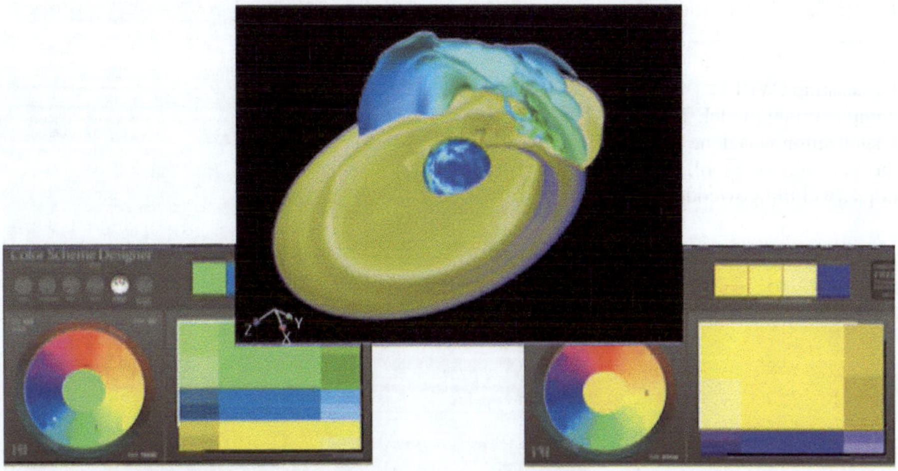

Fig. 15.20 Two color schemes were applied in designing this Supernova visualization. An analogous color scheme of Yellow, Green and Blue was applied to depict the data values across the three dimensional object. A complementary color scheme of Yellow and Purple was selected to emphasize the data values at edge of the Supernova visualization. We depict these color schemes using the Color Scheme Designer online tool available at http://colorschemedesigner.com

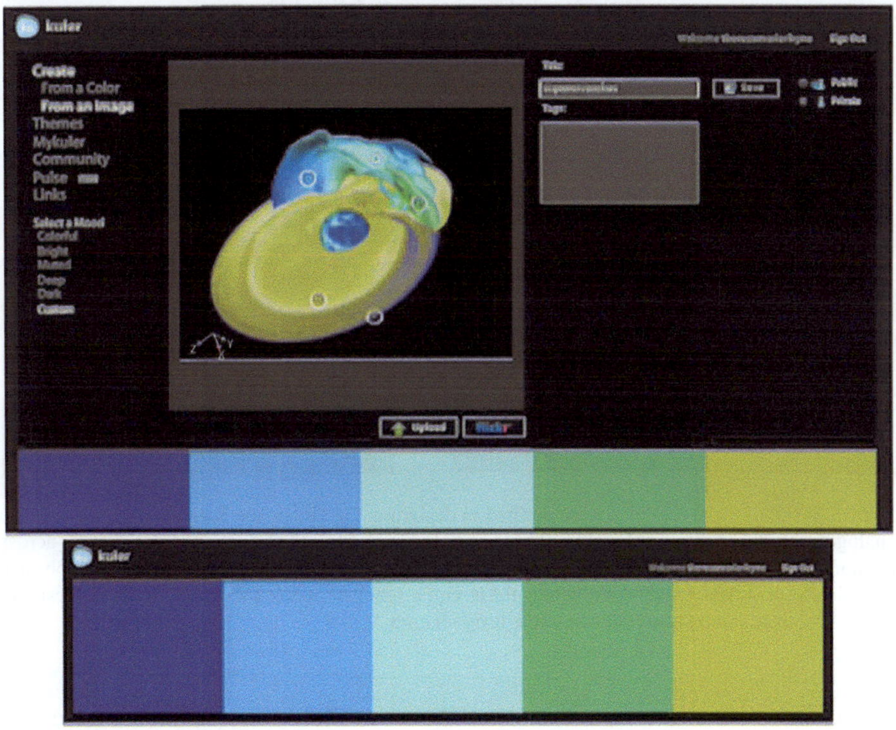

Fig. 15.21 Using Adobe's Kuler tool: http://kuler.adobe.com, the color hues across our Supernova Visualization are examined in detail. We can modify our color options further if we so desire

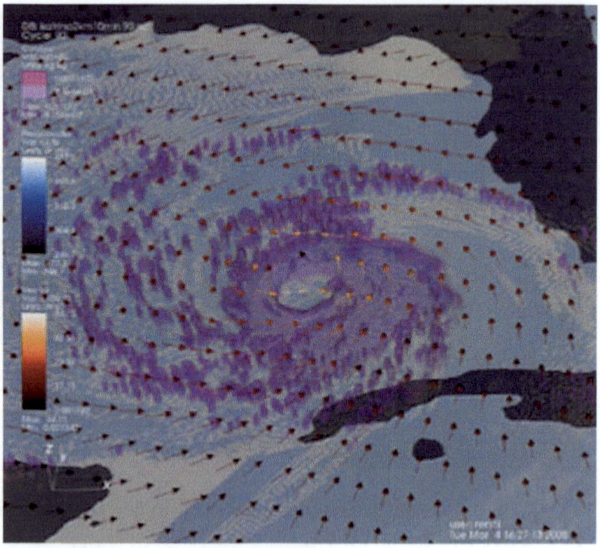

Fig. 15.22 Visualization of Hurricane Katrina data from the Weather Research Forecasting (WRF) computational model. The visualization was done with the VisIt software tool, see: https://wci.llnl.gov/codes/visit/

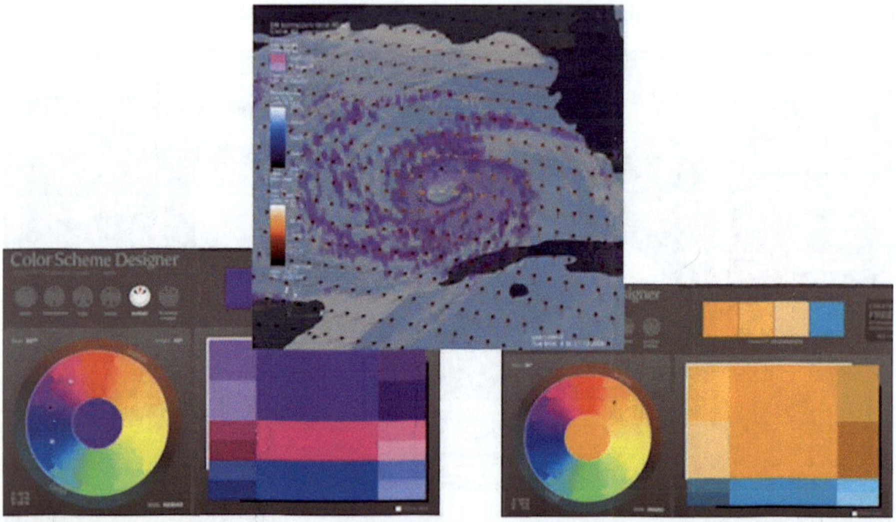

Fig. 15.23 Two color schemes were applied in designing the Hurricane Katrina visualization. An analogous color scheme of Magenta, Purple and Blue was applied to depict the data values across the hurricane data. A complementary color scheme of Orange and Blue was selected to emphasize the wind vector data values. We depict these color schemes using the Color Scheme Designer online tool available at http://colorschemedesigner.com

For a second example, we show a Hurricane Katrina visualization based on the execution of a Weather Research Forecasting (WRF) computational model (Fig. 15.22).

We also use Color Scheme Designer to show our color scheme selections. To depict the hurricane, we used an analogous color scheme of "Magenta", "Purple" and "Blue". Our dominant colors in this analogous color scheme are the Blue hues. This allows use to use Magenta and Purple hues to emphasize the formation of the modeled hurricane in our time series animation. To depict the wind vectors, we used a complementary color scheme based on the dominant Blue hues. Orange tones form this complementary color range. Using the color values from Color Scheme Designer, we transferred these color selections into the VisIt software tool to build initial color maps. An iterative process of color tweaking resulted until we obtained our desired final color maps for the visualization (Fig. 15.23).

15.10 Conclusion

In this paper, we have discussed a few artistic concepts of color theory and shown how to apply these notions to designing visualizations. Additionally, we have provided some historical background on color theory. Color models, color wheel and color scheme concepts have been introduced. We then used these concepts to examine digital images as well as building color maps for specific data visualization examples. In our discussions, we used Adobe's Kuler tool (http://kuler.adobe.com) and Color Scheme Designer (http://colorschemedesigner.com/).

Color tools and visualization software:
Adobe's Kuler Tool: http://kuler.adobe.com
Color Scheme Designer: http://colorschemedesigner.com/
ColorBrewer 2.0: http://colorbrewer2.org/
Color Stream: http://colorstreamapp.com/
CEI's Ensight Visualization Tool: http://www.ensight.com/
VisIt Tool: https://wci.llnl.gov/codes/visit/.

References

Albers, J. (1963). *Interaction of color*. New Haven: Yale University Press. A complete edition with full color plates was published by Yale University Press in 2009: http://yalepress.yale.edu/book.asp?isbn=9780300146936. Earlier Version is available as a Google Book: http://books.google.com/books?id=wN9o0OULXjIC&printsec=frontcover&dq=interaction+of+color+josef+albers&source=bl&ots=KYf8sqh372&sig=NmF4LLjaHFp7x-D2EK_n3dFLgBo&hl=en&ei=qWC1TZCjM9GWtweMz4HqDg&sa=X&oi=book_result&ct=result&resnum=16&ved=0CGsQ6AEwDw#v=onepage&q&f=false.

Bergdoll, B., & Diekerman, L. (2009a). *Buahaus 1919–1933 workshops in modernity (exhibition catalog)*. New York: Museum of Modern Art. Available as a Google Book: http://books.google.com/books?id=VEmZRkK2aDoC&lpg=PT111&ots=ax3GiaaRfx&dq=bauhaus%20workshop%20on%20modernity&pg=PA1#v=onepage&q=ba&f=false.

Bergdoll, B., & Diekerman, L. (2009b). *Buahaus 1919–1933 workshops in modernity (exhibition web site).* New York: Museum of Modern Art. http://www.moma.org/interactives/exhibitions/2009/bauhaus/.

Brewer, C. A., Hatchard, G. A., & Harrower, M. A. (2003). ColorBrewer in print: a catalog of color schemes for maps. *Cartography and Geographic Information Science*, *30*(1), 5–32.

Broadbent, A. D. (2004). A critical review of the development of the CIE 1931 RGB color-matching functions. *Color Research & Applications*, *29*(4), 267–272.

Chevreul, M. E. (1857). *The laws of contrast of colour: and their application to the arts* (translated from French by John Spanton). New York: G. Routledge & Co. Available as a Google Book: http://books.google.com/books?id=yHNN4H8qchIC&printsec=frontcover&dq=chevreul+the+law+of+simultaneous+color+contrast&source=bl&ots=HgQ1lg9PA3&sig=ZVtFRe-UnsGcpLQddfbmIdqhsVs&hl=en&ei=BsmuTdK3GoS3twec-IndAw&sa=X&oi=book_result&ct=result&resnum=2&ved=0CCQQ6AEwATgK#v=onepage&q&f=false.

Ford, J. L. (1998–2009). Color theory: overview. Worqx.com web site. http://www.worqx.com/color/index.htm.

Gatter, M. (2004). *Getting it right in print: digital pre-press for graphic designers.* London: Laurence King Publishing. Available as a Google Book: http://books.google.com/books?id=Pva2EkbmBYEC&pg=PA31&lpg=PA31&ots=OcF8Gm RhUr&sig=4jL0kGyhFXbohJ7rznXl1QHfNhQ#v=onepage&q&f=false.

Gregory, A. (2009). 21 stimulating color palette tools for designers. sitepoint.com. http://blogs.sitepoint.com/21-stimulating-color-palette-tools-for-designers/.

Itten, J. (1961). *Kunst der Farbe* (translated into English and published in the United States of America as The Art of Color: The Subjective Experience and Objective Rationale of Color, 1974). New York: John Wiley & Sons. Available as a Google Book: http://books.google.com/books?id=D-skaDZAumIC&printsec=frontcover&source=gbs_ge_summary_r&cad=0#v=onepage&q&f=false.

Kandinsky, W. (1911). *Über das Geistige in der Kunst* (translated into English by M.T.H. Sadler as "The Art of Spiritual Harmony" and published in 1914). New York: MFA Publications. Available from The Project Gutenberg EBook of Concerning the Spiritual in Art. http://www.gutenberg.org/cache/epub/5321/pg5321.html.

Klee, P. (1956). *Das bildnerische Denken* (translated into English by R. Manhiem as The Thinking Eye—The Notebooks of Paul Klee). London: Lund Humphries.

Klee, P., & Klee, Felix (1968). *The Diaries of Paul Klee, 1898–1919.* Berkeley: University of California Press. Available as a Google Book: http://books.google.com/books?id=YnntZEk8VTEC&pg=PR7&lpg=PR7&dq=diaries+of+paul+klee&source=bl&ots=44l6e1J6RX&sig=UyW1ovDuH1B9iIZGRVI1ju93Im4&hl=en&ei=GN-yTfOKAsS_tgeInOTpDg&sa=X&oi=book_result&ct=result&resnum=10&ved=0CGIQ6AEwCQ#v=onepage&q&f=false.

Kumar, S. (2011). Effective color palette and color scheme generators. instanshift.com. http://www.instantshift.com/2011/02/04/effective-color-palette-and-color-scheme-generators/.

Lang, H. (1987). Color vision theories in nineteenth century Germany between idealism and empiricism. *Color Research & Application*, *12*(5), 270–281. Online abstract available at: http://onlinelibrary.wiley.com/doi/10.1002/col.5080120509/abstract.

Lupton, E., & Miller, J. A. (1996). *The ABC's of Bauhaus, the Bauhaus and design theory.* Princeton: Princeton Architectural Press.

Munsell, A. H. (1905). *A color notation.* Boston: G. H. Eillis Co. Available as a Google Book: http://books.google.com/books?id=PgcCAAAAYAAJ&printsec=frontcover#v=onepage&q&f=false.

Munsell, A. H. (1915). *Atlas of the Munsell color system*, Wadsworth: Howland & Co.

Newton, I. (1704). *Opticks: or, a treatise of the reflexions, refractions, inflexions and colours of light. Also two treatises of the species and magnituder of curvilinear figures.* London: Samuel Smith and Benjamin Walford. Available from The Project Gutenberg EBook of Opticks: http://www.gutenberg.org/files/33504/33504-h/33504-h.htm.

Nickerson, D. (1940). History of the Munsell color system and its scientific application. *Journal of the Optical Society of America (JOSA)*, *30*(1), 575–586. Online abstract available at: http://www.opticsinfobase.org/josa/abstract.cfm?URI=josa-30-12-575.

Shevell, S. K. (Ed.) (2003). *The science of color* (2nd edn.). Oxford: Optical Society of America, Elsevier. Available as a Google Book: http://books.google.com/books?id=-fNJZ0xmTFIC&printsec=frontcover&dq=the+Science+of+color&source=bll&ots=rYjDxSe_RM&sig=coPoBKk901oQxFbjQQGplWnHcGg&hl=en&ei=u8G-TcqTOI6gtwfR9LTQBQ&sa=X&oi=book_result&ct=result&resnum=11&ved=0CGQQ6AEwCg#v=onepage&q&f=false.

Smith, A. R. (1978). Color gamut transform pairs. *Computer Graphics (SIGGRAPH '78 Conference Proceedings)*, *12*(3), 12–19. http://alvyray.com/Papers/color78.pdf.

Stone, M. C. (2003). *A field guide to digital color*. Natick: A.K. Peters. Available as a Google Book: http://books.google.com/books?id=k8IsqEF8FgQC&printsec=frontcover&dq=maureen+stone+field+guide+to+digital+color&source=bl&ots=Az6C1Jel6e&sig=iRQ6WTGqOwt4qAN6FTGLhIy4p4w&hl=en&ei=kcWyTdHnGNGatwel87HpDg&sa=X&oi=book_result&ct=result&resnum=3&ved=0CCwQ6AEwAg#v=onepage&q&f=false.

von Goethe, J. W. (1840). *Theory of colours* (translated from German by Charles Locke Eastlake). London: John Murray. Available as a Google Book: http://books.google.com/books?id=OIoIAAAAMAAJ&printsec=frontcover&source=gbs_ge_summary_r&cad=0#v=onepage&q&f=false.

von Helmhotz, H. (1924–25). *Handbuch der physiologischen Optik* (2 vols., 1856, 1867, translated into English by J. P. C. Southall as Handbook of Physiological Optics). New York: Dover Publications.

Chapter 16
e-Culture and m-Culture: The Way that Electronic, Computing and Mobile Devices are Changing the Nature of Art, Design and Culture

Stuart Cunningham and Peter S. Excell

Abstract We are now becoming used to the notion that electronic devices and communications systems are creating new categories of art forms, such as television programs, computer-generated special effects in movies and electronically enhanced music. However, we need to be aware that this process is accelerating and is likely to have an even larger significance in the future than has already been the case. Computer games, for example, while apparently being just an ephemeral way to use a little spare time, are actually an embryonic new art form, since they require detailed design and creative input analogous to computer-generated movies and special effects, but with the great difference that many different options must be available, depending on the choices of the user. They can thus be seen as a new type of interactive art form which can also be interpreted from the technological standpoint as a very rich form of interaction between the human being and a relatively powerful computer. Just as, in their early days, movie films, still photographs and television programs were originally seen as trivial and ephemeral, but were later recognized as having long-term artistic merit, the same will surely apply to computer games and to other forms of human interaction with computers. This can be termed 'e-culture'.

Although these fields have evolved relatively rapidly on the desktop computer, another major change is now occurring, in that mobile devices, particularly advanced mobile phones (smartphones) are now acquiring the ability to do many of the things that the desktop or laptop computer can do. While they have the obvious disadvantages that the screen size is much smaller and the input interface is very restricted (typically, fewer keys and a touchscreen or other imprecise navigation control, rather than a mouse), they have the major positive aspects that they are carried more or less permanently on the person by a high proportion of people in developed societies and a rapidly increasing proportion in developing societies as well. In this respect, they appear to represent one of the most radically transforming technologies the world has ever seen, with over half the population of the world now having a mobile device of some sort. This proportion is rapidly rising, as are the abilities of the devices.

S. Cunningham (✉) · P.S. Excell
Glyndwr University, Wrexham, Wales, UK
e-mail: s.cunningham@glyndwr.ac.uk

J. Dill et al. (eds.), *Expanding the Frontiers of Visual Analytics and Visualization*, DOI 10.1007/978-1-4471-2804-5_16, © Springer-Verlag London Limited 2012

This new mobile aspect can be termed 'm-culture' and we are only just beginning to think expansively about its implications. Experience indicates that it can only be properly addressed and understood by taking a very comprehensive view of all of the interlinked aspects, taken together:

- The aesthetic design of the device
- The design of content to be displayed on the screen
- The design of the software to implement particular functions within the device
- The electronic engineering design of the hardware functions within the device
- The business model that ensures sufficient revenue to fund the design and development of advancing devices.

Young people are the most important users of such devices and their experience and insights are of immense importance in advancing designs and trying to determine the probable path of development: it is important to seek the opinions of them and to involve them actively in these matters.

16.1 The Development of Esteem for Cultural Product Creators

There is a fundamental human mission to feel that one is doing something worthwhile: for people doing creative work (including both arts and technologies) their products are either 'throw-away' (ephemeral), or else they might hope they will be remembered and maybe become part of 'Culture'.

Throughout recent history, new and enriched modes of communication (in the widest sense) have at first been seen by 'the establishment' as superficial and ephemeral. When they have established themselves as being significant in society, they are adopted by the (evolved) establishment as being part of 'Culture with a Capital C' and 'Art with a Capital A'. This has been seen this with photography, cinema, TV and rock music, to quote the most salient examples. Now new, computer-based, communication art forms are emerging, e.g. computer graphics, Web design and computer games, which might be expected to evolve in esteem in the same way.

There are strong grounds for expecting that mobile forms are the next big thing. People entering these fields now have a good chance of becoming influential, analogously to the people who entered the film and TV industries in the past. Young people are major users of, and major innovators in, these new technologies: their comments and suggestions are of critical significance.

Curiously, Googling for 'Culture' yielded a "comprehensive" solution (Fig. 16.1). It is pertinent to observe that Google and eBay are now arguably part of e-culture.

More formally, the American Heritage English Dictionary (Houghton Mifflin 2006) says that culture is:

"The totality of socially transmitted behavior patterns, arts, beliefs, institutions, and all other products of human work and thought."

The influential pioneer of cultural studies Raymond Williams stated:

Fig. 16.1 Top 'AdWords' sidebar result associated with a Google search for the word 'culture', circa 2006 (N.b. no longer current)

"[Culture is] the general state of intellectual development, in a society as a whole... The general body of the arts... A whole way of life, material, intellectual and spiritual" (Williams 1983).

The key concepts in these quotations are: 'totality'; 'socially transmitted'; 'general state' and 'whole way of life', implying the need for consensus within a significant social group. This in turn explains the inertia in elevation of new forms of creative work to the status of "Culture with a capital C".

16.2 Evolving Culture, with a Capital 'C'

This was laid down in 'The Canon': e.g. classical architecture; representational art; Shakespeare; classical music; ballet and opera, but then things started to change:

- The invention of photography significantly undermined two-dimensional representational art. More than undermining its traditional market, however, it also can be argued to have democratized it by placing a form of instant creativity in the hands of the masses. High-quality photography then gradually became accepted as part of 'culture'.
- Similarly, the invention of the phonograph undermined live music performance, but again it placed a wide range of musical choice in the hands of the masses at modest cost.
- Music was divided between "classical" for the elite and largely ephemeral folk forms, but then Jazz (which started as a folk form) led the way in bridging the divide, based on the availability of cheap recording technology.
- The advancement of schooling meant that more people were able to read and hence mass production of cheap books became a viable industry: at first these were ephemeral "Penny dreadfuls", but in the 1930s they rose to the cultural high ground through the launch of the Penguin paperback imprint.
- Cinema was also initially an ephemeral entertainment medium. Now recognized as a legitimate artform, at least in its "serious" manifestations, this transition might predominantly be associated with the post-Second World War Italian art cinema movement.

The "old" Arts had to become highly innovative:

- Competition from photography led intellectual artists increasingly down the pathway of non-representational painting, e.g. Cubism, Surrealism, and specific exemplars such as Jackson Pollock.

- Despite there being no direct competition from technology or the mass market, three-dimensional art (sculpture) also became increasingly non-representational, e.g. Henry Moore and Barbara Hepworth. This appears to have been driven by the general change in two-dimensional art, rather than as a result of specific technological competition.
- Intellectual drama became much more abstract: the plays of Beckett are particular exemplars.
- "Serious" new music became increasingly abstract, e.g. Stockhausen.

However, these innovations tended to address an increasingly isolated minority, specialist, audience. The majority however chose other forms of 'new arts':

- In cinema, early efforts that were originally seen as ephemeral entertainment, e.g. Chaplin, later became respected as part of "culture".
- Popular music was, if anything, regarded as being even more ephemeral, led fundamentally by various forms of music of black origin (long before "MOBO" was coined), e.g. jazz, rock 'n' roll, many white artists aping black models and then the emergence of black artists in the mainstream. This was very much driven by the availability of cheap recording and playback technology and, again, has been accepted into the mainstream of "culture". In particular, when Bob Dylan was first discussed on BBC Radio 3, a line had been crossed and it was clear that the definition of 'culture' had changed substantially.
- Television programs were necessarily predominantly ephemeral while recording technology was costly, but as those who enjoyed certain programs when they were young grew up to become leaders of thought and acceptance that the best programs were also "culture" began to emerge: illustrated, for example, by the Edinburgh International Television Festival.

Thus, popular ephemeral forms slowly became 'art with a capital A' and 'culture with a capital C'. Was this a new phenomenon? No. Even centuries ago, a degree of popular choice ultimately emerged to define culture: in Europe, music was originally confined to austere forms for monks, but then more polyphonic forms for the masses started to be permitted. Theater was suppressed by religious authorities, but then 'Mystery Plays' opened a breach in this policy. Mass production of books opened up literature and knowledge: printing, pioneered by Gutenberg, is recognized as the first media technology revolution (McLuhan 1962).

16.3 Technological Influences

Much of the evolution of culture in the 20th century was driven by new technologies, such as photography, cinematography, sound recording, radio and television: it is of course true that the first three of the these started in the 19th century, but it can be said that they only had a major impact on the mass market in the 20th century.

However, insertion of computers into the systems introduced many new opportunities. They were originally seen as costly devices that were only justified in high-value applications, but commoditisation, driven by Moore's Law (Moore 1965), has enabled microcomputers to become a low-cost quasi-intelligent component that has transformed many categories of device.

Moore's prediction (as slightly refined over time), that the achievable density of components on a microelectronic chip doubles about every 18 months, has, remarkably, held true for over 40 years. This increase in power, combined with accelerating demand and hence increasing efficiency of mass production, has led to the phenomenon of commoditisation, in which mass production is taken to such a high level that the products become too cheap to be worth maintaining or reselling when used, similar to commodities like foodstuffs and fuels. Their cost then becomes negligible compared with the cost of production of the products in which they are embedded and hence the inclusion of digital technology in a wide range of product becomes the norm rather than a costly exception.

The inclusion of what may be described (as a shorthand term) as "intelligence" in products, especially media technology products can now be seen to created a transformed situation where both the concept of a computer and the concepts of all media technology devices has been radically changed, almost out of recognition in some cases. But many errors were made on this journey. Electronic computers emerged about 65 years ago but were initially seen as almost exclusively mathematical devices and this viewpoint was a great hindrance on the road to their commoditisation. Ironically, there was the germ of an alternative view at the beginning, where the computer could have been clearly envisioned as a communications device, if only this interpretation had been applied to the British Colossus code-breaking computer (now recreated at Bletchley Park).

Computer communications were also at first only for 'serious' uses and the early PC uses were also 'serious'. The result was that the PC business almost died and was predicted to be approaching stagnation (Basalla 1989), but then the Cold War ended and the business model had to change radically: the mass market had to be pleased. Consumer applications (initially surprisingly) threw up worthwhile new challenges and the transformed situation that we see in the modern world emerged. Perhaps we would have made more rapid progress if we had broken with the 'serious' uses sooner and paid more attention to the mass market and consumer applications? The lessons of this phase should be borne in mind as we experience future technological evolutions and revolutions.

A major, closely linked, revolution that is still in progress is that in communications. Here, the huge capacity of optical fibers is leading to a phenomenon similar to commoditisation in fixed network capacity, but, again, commoditised processing chips have been essential in facilitating packetised messages—the basis of the Internet. The transformation in wireless systems has been even more striking: the spectacular success of the digital mobile phone system that evolved from the GSM standard is delivering a numerical rate of growth in bandwidth per user which surpasses Moore's law. Figure 16.2 shows an approximate graph of the nominal capacity of the mobile handset evolving through the GSM upgrade path from second to fourth generation. Unlike computer processor chips, which have had to switch strategy to multicore, with attendant programming problems, in order to maintain adherence to Moore's Law, mobile communications bandwidth continues to grow at

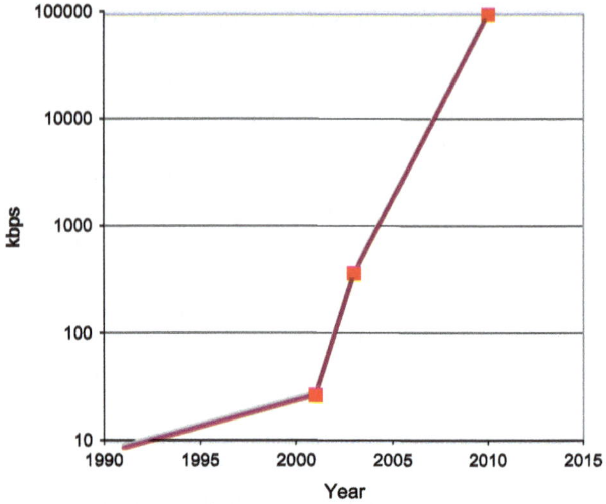

Fig. 16.2 Nominal data capacity of mobile handsets evolving through the GSM upgrade path from second to fourth generation

an average rate that approximates to doubling every year. Already, plans are being laid for the fifth generation which might be expected to deliver as much as 100 Gbps in around 2020.

This graph illustrates the seminal influence of the mobile phone: already it has more processing power than recent personal computers; it has a degree of Internet ability and hence all it needs to supplant the PC is improved storage and better HCI (human-computer interface). Even this is beginning to emerge in concepts like the iPad although this lacks the portability of a phone and some of the flexibility of a PC, but it is probable that these deficiencies will soon be overcome.

16.4 Connecting with the User—The CU in Culture

As we discuss elsewhere in this chapter, interaction with electronic and mobile devices has traditionally been very limited to simple hand and finger movements, small screen displays (albeit potentially well designed) and limited auditory feedback, particularly leading to 'heads-down interaction' (Brewster 2009). Furthermore, it can be argued that for a truly personalized and personally representative experience, technologies can be utilized to derive key pieces of information about the user, and their environment, that can lead to highly personalized, effective information and processing.

These key pieces of information, we feel are crucial to achieving personalized and adaptive user experiences are those of the user's *context*, *emotional state*, and the *content* of whatever media they might be creatively working with at the time. A particular example of this that we have considered is the use of this information in compiling music playlists for mobile devices and MP3 players. The data is used to tailor a computer-generated playlist to better match the user's needs and expectations, based upon information that can be extracted *a priori* and that which is available in real-time. For example, the mobile music device is able to recommend appropriate music for a user who is exercising with up-tempo, rhythmic music or for a user who is relaxing in the evening, with slower, less complex music (Cunningham et al. 2010).

Taking this concept further, we can imagine how such active awareness of the user and their circumstances might be applied in other creative disciplines. Music composition can be aided by the emotional state and physical state of the music, laying down foundations for speed and styles of rhythm and the scales and harmonic progressions to be used in composition, for example. Artists and animators can inform their work by incorporating elements of their own physical experience of a stimulant by mapping their biometric data to colors, intensities, patterns, frequency of object occurrence, etc. The dawn of integrating the user's environment and experience has already taken its first steps in the gaming field, by adapting in-game events to data captured from the real world, such as the level of light intensity, volume of sounds, matching of music tempo to heart rate, and so on. The entertainment and creative potential is immense.

This type of data is also of interest to creative businesses that can capture this response and environmental information and use it to tailor media to their audiences. This has been used for traditional television and can be exploited much more in the future, especially to understand what "works" for individual users on mobile devices. Such user-tailored marketing and advertising is already undertaken by the majority of popular online retailers such as Amazon, eBay and also Google. Their algorithms have gone beyond the use of traditional automated collaborative filtering systems, and now begin to consider user context (Earnshaw et al. 2011). More context- and user-aware algorithms can take into account the geographic location, time of day, mood or emotion of the user, biometric characteristics, to target the advertisement of products and services.

The interactive elements afforded by viewing of film and television through computers and mobile devices, also means that product placement takes on a new dimension. A viewer could easily pause a sequence of video and click on an item in the frame where they are then taken to the site of an online retailer where they can purchase that particular item, for example. Product placement advertising has been viewed with disfavor in the past, but it could easily be expanded to cover any kind of web browsing and hence has the potential to become a form of recommend a system, especially for reluctant users of Internet resources.

16.5 Mobile Paradigms Transforming Journalism

The spread of sophisticated mobile devices means that a large proportion of the population are able to not only make emotive and creative contributions to culture, but that they are able to record and report events going on in the world around them, either through personal blogs and social networking, but also by contributing to national and international news providers' news repositories. Everyone can now be a

Fig. 16.3 Sky News iPhone App

journalist and news and media organizations have access to local and community-level news being reported upon as well as different perspectives and insights into international news and events of the day. This leads us to *citizen journalism* (Robison et al. 2009).

Although the creative and cultural value of this development may not be immediately obvious, it does afford users a degree of journalistic freedom of expression with the potential to be the source and producer of media content that could endure for a number of years. Although television is a relative newcomer in relative terms, images depicting significant historical events have become part of the culture that defines a year, a decade, and the people who lived in that time. Consider the powerful images showing the fall of the Berlin wall, Richard Nixon's resignation, the marriage of Prince Charles to Lady Diana Spencer, or the Tiananmen Square protests. A number of the historical events of the future are very likely be produced on mobile devices by those not simply observing the event, but participating in it.

An example of a straightforward, existing method for the wannabe Pulitzer Prize winning mobile user to contribute to the national and international news is shown in Fig. 16.3; the iPhone app from Sky News. This app allows mobile users to quickly and concisely send their own news stories, with pictures, from their mobile device.

It is not unusual to now see image, sound and video footage from mobile devices to appear on prime-time news on the UK national TV network and in other countries around the world. Although the quality of the footage falls far below the expected level of quality normally experienced, the ability to report important events far outweighs the quality issues. Indeed, it can be argued that shaky, noisy, fuzzy video footage adds extra realism and grit to the report. Technical limitations such as low resolution, restricted depth-of-field, lack of image stabilization, and lossy audio/video compression currently pose some problems, but these do not seem to be considered a major setback by TV producers. The quality issues will soon disappear in any case, as the cameras on mobile device become more advanced and bandwidth increases on mobile networks with 4G and beyond.

16.6 Narrative

The concept of narrative is particularly important in the traditional arts and humanities. Whether this is the subtlety of a hidden narrative within a picture, story or poem, or a more outward, clear statement of experience, emotion or intent. Artists are influenced and inspired by their lives and the world around them. This is one of the key factors in any creative field. Very few people create exclusively in a vacuum. The rule holds fast in electronic forms of creativity too. The notions of e-culture and m-culture already hold large amounts of potential for creativity that can be both ephemeral and enduring.

In terms of e-culture, narrative has played an important role in the development of computer games, graphics and web design. Furthermore, the ability to express narrative has been enhanced through electronic metaphors from the real-world, such as online blogs and photo journals. Thanks to the (relatively) recent, widespread uptake of social media communication tools, real-time narrative has evolved. Users are now but a tweet or Facebook status update away from being able to share their feelings, thoughts, and more, to an audience whose constitution can be as small or as large as they wish. If anyone is in doubt about the cultural contribution and relevance of these contemporary, seemingly ephemeral tools, they need only search the web for an "*I Facebooked your Mum*" t-shirt and wear it proudly as a culturally defunct artifact.

M-culture too has pounced upon the social media and narrative bandwagon. Mobile users can update their blogs, statuses, photo stream, and more from anywhere in the world, using a mobile device. The introduction of geographical mapping and GPS technology now means that users can notify their world of exactly where on earth they are, who they are with (hyperlinked of course) and what they are doing. For those with the time and inclination, real-time narrative is now entirely possible. Perhaps an interesting cultural issue will further arise from the difference between those who are 'watchers' and those who are the 'contributors'.

Couple this theory of narrative with some of the technologies and mobile interfaces we discuss in this paper and you are presented with a series of intriguing innovations that are already realizable. Facebook and Twitter updates in future could include things like a user's blood pressure, heart rate, ambient temperature, samples of ambient noise to accompany photo updates, galvanic skin response, blood alcohol content, voice stress analysis, and many other, potentially intimate, pieces of information to share and compare with the user's audience. Equally, consider the outputs and ways of presenting this information that could be available. Imagine being able to tune-in to sonified heart rate beats of friends and loved ones, 3D images of the surrounding environments, or even smell-o-vision, to enhance they portrayal of that extra tasty meal.

16.7 Growing Pains in Mobile Technology

Mobile technology has evolved rapidly to the point where mobile phones and devices have large amounts of processing power, data storage capacity, connectivity (including Bluetooth and Wi-Fi), and memory. Modern devices are effectively miniaturized computers, with many functioning with operating systems that are cut-down versions of those traditionally only seen on the personal computer market. In the last 4 or 5 years, the ability to download applications (or 'apps') has seen phenomenal uptake, allowing the devices to be used for a variety of business, educational, and personal tasks (The Economist 2010). In order to harness this power and fully utilize the resource of the device itself, user interfaces have developed to permit greater interaction. Fully QWERTY keyboards replaced alpha-numeric keypads, and touch-screen is gradually replacing the physical keyboard. Screen size has increased too, allowing a larger viewable space with higher resolution. However, there is a difficulty in providing more and more sophisticated software while keeping the physical size of the device within mobile confines, and being able to interact with the device properly. On the whole, devices are currently limited by not having sufficiently rich channels for input and output, without sacrificing mobility. The design challenges here are to provide new ways that information can be exchanged.

Potential solutions can be split by their input of output function. Examples of technological advances that help increase usability, but retain mobility are:

Input: Voice recognition, handwriting recognition, folding/miniaturized keyboards, projected keyboards, gesture recognition, context awareness, accelerometers and gyroscopes.

Output: Larger video displays in phones, unfurlable screens, 'head-up' display devices, mini-projectors, surround sound/spatial audio output, text-to-speech feedback, vibratory feedback.

Notable changes in the media as a result of mobile technology, and indicative of e-culture and m-culture, is the use of acronyms and abbreviations that were traditionally found on internet chat forums and in text messages, where restrictions on number of characters and/or bandwidth, resulted in users coming up with *de facto* standards to shorten frequently used terms. This, coupled with the use of emoticons, or smileys, have found themselves now almost universally understood. Specific examples of these, now engrained in broad Western culture, would include (capitals are optional):

lol	:-(	FTW!
lmao	rofl	;-)
:-)	w00t!	omg

This kind of integration with culture and community is widely recognized, and although it is not generally perceived to be derogatory, it has certainly allowed new ways to allow communication, particularly where language may be a barrier (Soffer 2010).

16.8 Technology, Communities and 'Culture'

The impact of the Internet and mobile technologies has gone beyond commonplace and finds itself engrained within popular culture such that it is increasingly becoming a ubiquitous part of everyday life. Web 2.0 technologies such as MySpace, Facebook, Bebo, Twitter and the immersive Second Life and World of Warcraft have become fashionable and contributed greatly to the development of real-life culture and virtual culture and communities. Indeed, there are many communities and cultures established around common stereotypes and subject interests.

In particular, a technology-related culture has emerged in recent years that popularizes the role of the geek and nerd. A no doubt contributory factor to this phenomenon is that technology enthusiasts are exceptionally useful to general society, in this technology-rich age. They have skills and interests that are now deeply valued by a large amount of the general population, now that technology proliferates in so much of their personal and work lives. An interesting tongue-in-cheek snapshot of the level of sub-culture is provided by Randall Munroe's online comic entitled *xkcd—A webcomic of romance, sarcasm, math, and language*,[1] which addresses many of the stereotypes of self-proclaimed geek culture.

Television too has made reactionary responses to the popularization of technology's influence upon the culture of modern society. Early, mainly unsuccessful incarnations before the advent of Web 2.0 include Warner Bros'. 1995's *Dweebs*, which ran only for one season. More recently as Web 2.0 and social networking tools have become more accepted a stronger presence has been felt with the airing of Talkback Thames' *The IT Crowd* (since 2006) and *The* Big Bang Theory (since 2007) from CBS, with the appropriate tagline "*Smart Is the New Sexy*".

Other TV shows known for their particular assimilation of cultural elements and witty satire to have made regular geek quips of note include *The Simpsons*, *Family Guy*, and *The Office*. Inevitably however, these shows attempt to bridge the gap between the sitcom and the technology-specific subject material, which is reflective of how common technology is perceived in society at present; a social mechanism around which personal relationships, work practices, business, and education are becoming attached. The main source to draw amusement from in media expressions

[1] http://www.xkcd.com.

of geek culture is not normally afforded by recognition of Internet applications or physical devices themselves, but by the putative social inadequacy and quirks of the characters that chose to embrace these technologies as part of their lifestyle.

16.9 Where Next?

The growing penetration of computer mediation into increasing aspects of human activity, particularly those which might be defined as "culture", is an irreversible phenomenon. Although controversial, the ideas of Raymond Kurzweil on this merit consideration since they are based on plausible science and substantial relevant experience (Kurzweil 2005). Kurzweil speculates that computer-based systems will surpass human intelligence around the middle of this century, leading to a total transformation in the way in which ideas about the future are formulated (the "Kurzweil Singularity"). While this concept may not come to fruition in quite the way in which he envisages it, the principle of the insertion of increasing amounts of computer "intelligence" into many aspects of life seems unavoidable and hence those who do not wish to be left behind by the future need to ensure that they have soundly based visionary views of the way that their fields of activity are evolving. "Culture" is an important such field and hence it can be argued that digital mediation of it will be a crucial and defining aspect.

In our existing conceptions of media, computer-facilitation will continue to see incremental improvements. Thus, computer animation (CGI) and computer-mediated special effects will grow in importance in filmmaking and television, to the extent that they may well become dominating technologies: it is certain that they will transform the creative options for these media. Similarly, in popular music, computer-generated sounds have become increasingly adopted, although they currently still tend to sit in the background behind the "stars": but will this continue to be the case in the future? The 'star' system gives a frame of reference for society and so there may still need to be identifiable virtual stars, even if human ones decline in significance.

In a technical sense, the digital transformation is already complete since most television and an increasing amount of audio is already delivered in digital form. However, this is a mechanistic modification of the transmission medium which has not directly influenced the content, although there has certainly been significant indirect influence due to the sudden availability of vastly more channels. However, digitally-mediated transmission of video is only the first step on much longer road and it is certain that greatly enriched interactivity will soon become the norm, either through IPTV or some other modality. This offers both opportunities and pitfalls. It is very probable that traditional audiences do not have an appetite for "too much" interactivity, but a certain amount will be welcomed and it has been suggested (Earnshaw et al. 2011) that this could become much more than simply a way of responding to advertisements and voting within reality shows: it could become an alternative mode of interaction with the World Wide Web that might be more appealing to a certain type of audience than the use of traditional web browsers. Further, programs chosen by the users could act as the basis of a “recommender system” that would indicate the type of web content that would be of interest.

These considerations point to the probability of a significant transformation of television media content and a partial closing the gap between television/video and computer games (which represent video content with the very high level of interactivity). Combined with the usefulness and social significance of the interactivity, this suggests that these new media forms will have an even larger ”cultural” significance than is ascribed to traditional television at present.

Another major new development that is emerging in television and video content is that of three-dimensional displays. At present, several technologies are vying for leadership, with those requiring special spectacles currently in the lead, although most users regard such spectacles as an encumbrance and unsightly. It is thus likely that systems that do not require spectacles, such as lenticular screens or holographic displays, will ultimately dominate. The holographic versions would appear to be superior and work on these is developing within a number of groups. This development will also change the nature of the content and, again, appears to add to the blurring of the line between video media and computer games.

16.10 Wearable Computing and Communications

Mobile communications can be argued to be the most transformative technology that there has ever been, since it potentially enables everyone in the world, even the very poorest, to link to the global digital knowledge system (actually, the proportion is currently only around 60–70 %, but it will be virtually 100 %, excepting digital refuseniks, within a very few years). In addition to digitally enfranchising the poor, the system has also enabled women to become far more integrated with such technological opportunities than before. However, as suggested by Fig. 16.2, the potential of the system is growing faster than the ability of application developers to imagine effective ways to exploit its potential richness. Already, it is clear that the bandwidth of 3G is not being used effectively to increase the richness of communication and there is little evidence of imaginative ideas to exploit the vastly greater bandwidths of 4G and 5G I the near- or medium-term futures.

The greatest bottleneck now is the human interface to the mobile device, and this is overdue for radical transformation. The success of the Apple iPad shows the need for a large screen on a mobile device, but it is suggested that the tablet solution is non-optimal and we need to break away from the integrated rectangular box solution for mobile devices. Since the mobile is carried semi-permanently on the person, integration with garments or garment accessories is the obvious way forward.

The integration of mobile technologies and wearables, such as in garments and jewelery, is a field that is expanding quickly. There have been many attempts, for a number of years, to integrate new technologies with everyday objects and clothes,

Fig. 16.4 Responsive ring with light sensor and LEDs (Alonso and Edwards 2011)

to attempt to realize ubiquitous communications and information systems. One major stumbling block, until relatively recently however, has been the lack of input from fashion and product designers. This has resulted in wearable technologies designed by scientists and engineers. The outcome is, unsurprisingly, garments and accessories that are distinctly un-cool and unattractive in the market place and to the general public.

Recently, designers have become more and more interested in embedding technology in their work. The advent of very small microprocessors, LEDs, sensors, and power cells, means it is now easier to discreetly implant technology in everyday items. Coupled with the ability to integrate communication mechanisms through Bluetooth, RFID (Near Field Communications—NFC), ZigBee and even Wi-Fi (and hopefully ultrawideband in the future), a new set of interactive, responsive and reactive garments and accessories is now within reach.

Some recent work at Glyndŵr University has been focused upon integrating such technologies with items of jewelery. This has employed RFID, Arduino and other technologies to produce attractive, well-designed objects, capable of carrying out communication functions, as well as responding to actions of the wearer. One limitation that still exists for these designers is that of managing to supply the energy-dependent items with power. Power cells still require reasonable physical space, leading to investigations into self-generating mechanisms, such as can be seen in kinetically charged watches. Two areas have been focused on:

- Responsive jewelery. The responsive ring features LED emitters that change intensity depending upon movement in the hand, detected using an optical resistor: this is shown in Fig. 16.4.
- Embedding of narrative information in jewelery. Their projects to date have included necklaces and lockets containing small RFID tags that can be used to trigger narrative information, for example, information about the owner and/or the meaning or significance of the item of jewelery. (Alonso and Edwards 2010).

Work with others has extended into garments using communication tools and input and output devices to engage with the wearer. In particular, a project entitled

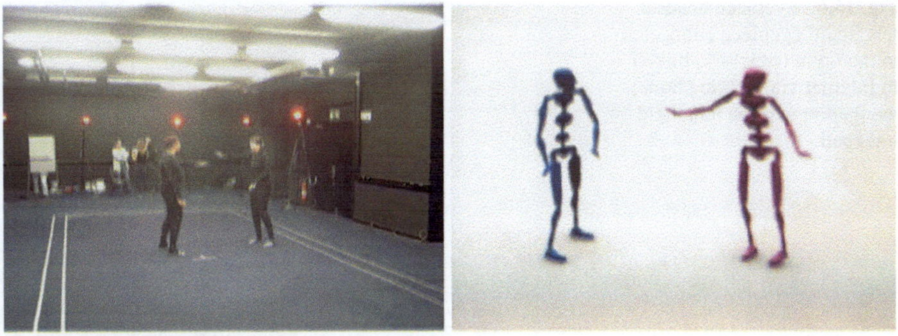

Fig. 16.5 The 'Emotional Wardrobe' project: exploration of social interaction using a motion capture facility (Bradford University)

'The Emotional Wardrobe' (in which one of the present authors was a collaborator) investigated how intelligent garments should be designed and evaluated. This focused upon the need to integrate high-quality design and market appeal with rich communication and interactive technologies. The project laid a foundation by way of methodologies and design principles, to integrate affective computing into smart garments (Baurley 2011). An example of an exploration of social interaction within this project, using a motion capture facility, is shown in Fig. 16.5.

Commercial products are now emerging that attempt to combine sensors and technology in an engaging and, ideally, interactive way. Simple examples include the '*T*-Qualizer' a t-shirt that employs LEDs to light-up a chest panel in a t-shirt, in response to sound input. Whilst the item itself is relatively low priced, aesthetically pleasing, and functional, it requires the wearer to accommodate a battery pack and adjust to the slight weight increase that the lighted chest panel brings.

A notable, more advanced, example that is now available for purchase is that of *The Hug Shirt* by CuteCircuit (2011), described most accurately by its creators:

> "*The Hug Shirt™ is a shirt that makes people send hugs over distance! The HugShirt was invented by Francesca Rosella and Ryan Genz the co-founders of CuteCircuit, the London based award-winning design company. Embedded in the shirt there are sensors that feel the strength of the touch, the skin warmth and the heartbeat rate of the sender and actuators that recreate the sensation of touch, warmth and emotion of the hug to the shirt of the distant loved one.*" (CuteCircuit, 2011)

The shirt is triggered by SMS messages, sent to the mobile phone of the wearer. The mobile then sends the required signals and data to the sensors and actuators in the shirt via Bluetooth transmission. The garment itself is fashionable and does not externally look significantly different from garments that do not contain any form of embedded technology. This concept is similar to some of the basic objectives of the Emotional Wardrobe, but without the specifics of affective computing technology. Such concepts illustrate the opportunities that exist to broaden the richness of human communications, which are currently highly asymmetric (HD stereoscopic video and stereo audio inputs vs. low-quality monaural audio output); hence any concepts that enrich the human output channels would be of great value.

Fig. 16.6 Eyepiece headset test: Icuiti eyepiece connected to laptop in backpack, linked to Internet via mobile phone; navigation was via handheld trackball

More conventional enriching technologies include the established haptic glove and the eyepiece (or head-up) display. The latter has been established for some time in the concept of the wearable computer and also in military applications, but its failure to penetrate the mainstream thus far is surprising. Such devices can display a full-size computer screen in a very compact structure which is far more portable than a tablet computer and also consumes far less power, giving longer battery life and/or lighter weight. The view has been expressed by some that the device is socially unacceptable (Fig. 16.6), but similar arguments were advanced when earpieces were introduced for general use (e.g. with the Sony Walkman) and yet they have become socially acceptable.

What was abundantly clear from the experiment depicted in Fig. 16.6 was that entirely different content would be needed with such a device. 'Surfing the Web' in the traditional manner is of little use in such a scenario and it would be far more beneficial to overlay data on the real-world scene seen by the user, as in augmented reality, but further enriched with metadata and fixed to the external scene by (for instance) gyroscopic sensing of head movement.

As mentioned above, 4th and 5th generation mobile technologies will deliver vastly more bandwidth than heretofore and radical innovations to exploit this are urgently needed. The eyepiece or head-up display appears to be a strong candidate to facilitate this, but new content software will be needed and when this is bedded down into social acceptability it will inherently become a part of our digital culture.

16.11 Some Conclusions

Examining the historical record, it can be seen that new media technologies that enable content that seems ephemeral at first can become embedded in the collective consciousness of what is valuable and hence accepted as 'culture'. Those who recognize this ahead of the cultural establishment can become dominant influencers of society, with a profound stake in their respective futures.

Microcomputer commoditisation has transformed most media technologies, particularly in allowing interactivity, but also in profoundly changing business models. Many of the interaction formats currently used with personal computers will almost inevitably be recognized as part of the culture of our times in the future. However, the PC is changing and seems likely to be overtaken by mobile paradigms in the near future: mobile technology has huge potential because it digitally enfranchises the whole world, opening up vast opportunities for content creation, much with cultural significance. This is especially highlighted by the emerging 4G–5G evolution path which offers massive unexplored potential that creatives and entrepreneurs should be exploring now.

To come back to the theme of the ephemeral, it seems clear that the throw-away (commoditised) and historically unimportant elements will be the technological hardware and devices themselves. Though they may be remembered as revolutionary technologies, history has shown us that it is the content and creativity achieved with a tool that is ultimately important and lasting. Very few people are interested in the detail of the paintbrush Leonardo used to paint the Mona Lisa or the ropes and pulleys the Egyptians used to help build the pyramids. This brings us back to a useful reminder; that without creativity and purpose, technology alone is able to achieve very little.

References

Alonso, C., & Edwards, E. (2010). Externalisation and mediation of memories. Integration of digital memories within hand-made objects. In A. Mousoutzanis, & D. Riha (Eds.), *New media and the politics of online communities* (pp. 183–190). Oxford: Interdisciplinary Press. ISBN 978-1-84888-032-0.

Alonso, C., & Edwards, E. (2011). Responsive jewellery. Convergent design. http://www.convergentdesign.org/wordpress/?p=10. Accessed 14th September 2011.

Basalla, G. (1989). *The evolution of technology. Studies in the history of science*. Cambridge: Cambridge University Press. ISBN 9780521296816.

Baurley, S. (2011). The role of design in facilitating multi-disciplinary collaboration in wearable technology. In Westerink, et al. (Eds.), *Philips research book series: Vol. 12. Sensing emotions* (pp. 181–195).

Brewster, S. (2009). 'Head up' interaction: can we break our addiction to the screen and keyboard? In *Keynote address, third international conference on internet technologies & applications*, Wrexham, UK, 8th–11th September, 2009.

Cunningham, S., Grout, V., & Picking, R. (2010). Emotion, content & context in sound and music. In M. Grimshaw (Ed.), *Game sound technology and player interaction: concepts and developments*. IGI Global Publishing.

Earnshaw, R. A., Robison, D., Al Sheik Salem, O., & Excell, P. S (2011). Implementation of mobile television environments with new forms of content and commercial advertising. In *Fourth international conference on internet technologies & applications*, Wrexham, UK, 6th–9th September, 2011.

Houghton Mifflin (2006). *The American heritage dictionary of the English language*. Boston: Houghton Mifflin Company.

Kurzweil, R. (2005). *The singularity is near*. London: Duckworth.

McLuhan, M. (1962). *The Gutenberg galaxy: the making of typographic man*. Toronto: University of Toronto Press. ISBN 978-0802060412.

Moore, G. E. (1965). Cramming more components onto integrated circuits. *Electronics*, *38*(8), 114–117.
Munroe, R. (2008). A better idea. xkcd—a webcomic of romance, sarcasm, math, and language. http://xkcd.com/422/. Accessed 13 September 2011.
Robison, D., Palmer, I. J., Excell, P. S., Earnshaw, R. A., & Salem, O. A.-S. (2009). Multi-platform human computer interaction in converged media spaces. In *Proceedings of the international conference on CyberWorlds*, Bradford, UK, 7–11 Sept., 2009 (pp. 279–286).
Soffer, O. (2010). Silent orality: toward a conceptualization of the digital oral features in CMC and SMS texts. *Communication Theory*, *20*, 387–404. doi:10.1111/j.1468-2885.2010.01368.x.
The Economist (2010). Apps and downs. *The Economist, 17th June 2010*. The Economist Newspaper Limited, London.
T-Qualizer (2011). The T-qualizer store T-qualizer shirts/equalizer T-shirts T-qualizer—raver, The T-qualizer store. http://www.tqualizer.com/tqualizer/t-qualizer-flashing-equalizer-shirt-raver.html. Accessed 14/9/2011.
Williams, R. (1983). *Culture and society 1780–1950*. New York: Columbia University Press.

Part IV
Modeling and Geometry

Chapter 17
Shape Identification in Temporal Data Sets

Machon Gregory and Ben Shneiderman

Abstract Shapes are a concise way to describe temporal variable behaviors. Some commonly used shapes are spikes, sinks, rises, and drops. A spike describes a set of variable values that rapidly increase, then immediately rapidly decrease. The variable may be the value of a stock or a person's blood sugar levels. Shapes are abstract. Details such as the height of spike or its rate increase, are lost in the abstraction. These hidden details make it difficult to define shapes and compare one to another. For example, what attributes of a spike determine its "spikiness"? The ability to define and compare shapes is important because it allows shapes to be identified and ranked, according to an attribute of interest. Work has been done in the area of shape identification through pattern matching and other data mining techniques, but ideas combining the identification and comparison of shapes have received less attention. This paper fills the gap by presenting a set of shapes and the attributes by which they can identified, compared, and ranked. Neither the set of shapes, nor their attributes presented in this paper are exhaustive, but it provides an example of how a shape's attributes can be used for identification and comparison. The intention of this paper is not to replace any particular mathematical method of identifying a particular behavior, but to provide a toolset for knowledge discovery and an intuitive method of data mining for novices. Spikes, sinks, rises, drops, lines, plateaus, valleys, and gaps are the shapes presented in this paper. Several attributes for each shape are defined. These attributes will be the basis for constructing definitions that allow the shapes to be identified and ranked. The second contribution is an information visualization tool, TimeSearcher: Shape Search Edition (SSE), which allows users to explore data sets using the identification and ranking ideas in this paper.

M. Gregory (✉)
University of Maryland, College Park, MD 20742, USA
e-mail: machon.gregory@gmail.com

B. Shneiderman
Dept of Computer Science & Human and Computer Interaction Lab, University of Maryland, College Park, MD 20742, USA
e-mail: ben@cs.umd.edu

J. Dill et al. (eds.), *Expanding the Frontiers of Visual Analytics and Visualization*,
DOI 10.1007/978-1-4471-2804-5_17, © Springer-Verlag London Limited 2012

17.1 What Are Shapes?

Shapes are a succinct way of describing the behavior of a temporal variable. For instance, a spike describes a sharp increase followed by a shape decrease. A shape describes a behavior abstractly. Therefore, the rate a spike increases or the height of the peak, as well as other details about the variable's behavior are lost. The absence of these details makes it difficult to compare one shape to another. For example, given a spike, how can it be described or compared to another spike? A lot of work has been done identifying a particular shape in a specific data set, but little work has been done to examine individual shapes and generalize their use.

Shapes such as spikes, drops and increasing lines are used by professionals in many different fields to describe the behavior of temporal variables. Stock market analysts use shapes to describe changes in stock prices. Published research results offer concrete evidence of the usefulness of shape identification. For example, spikes were used by Balog et al. to understand the mood of bloggers in relation to world events (Balog et al. 2006), by Dettki and Erisson to analyze the seasonal migration patterns of moose (Dettki and Ericsson 2008), and Shamma et al. to model microblog conversations (Shamma et al. 2011). These shapes are obvious in a visual representation to the informed observer, but they are often hard to describe precisely and compare to other shapes of the same type. The ability to identify and rank shapes of interest in a visualization of temporal data sets can be helpful to novice analyst and in knowledge discovery.

This paper examines eight simple shapes: lines, spikes, sinks, rises, drops, plateaus, valleys, and gaps. A spike is defined as a significant increase in value followed by a significant decrease in value in a set of sequential points. A sink is a significant decrease in value followed by a significant increase in value in a set of sequential points. A line is a set of sequential points with the same general behavior. A rise is a sustained increase in value in a set of sequential points. A drop is a sustained decrease in value in a set of sequential points. A plateau is a temporary increase in value in a set of sequential points. A valley is a temporary decrease in value in a set of sequential points. A gap is a specific type of valley where the values temporarily decrease to zero.

Each shape will be assessed by a set of measurable attributes. For example, a line shape's primary attributes are its endpoints and slope. An attribute, such as the "spikiness" of a spike, may be manifested as one or more measurements of the shape's attributes. Each measurement or set of measurements represents a different behavior. The attributes are used to define a shape's behavior and compare and rank the shapes. A shape definition consists of one or more constrained attributes. For instance, a line with the slope constrained to be positive defines an increasing line. A shape can have many definitions that identify different behaviors of interest. A ranking metric is one or more attributes by which a shape is compared to other shapes of the same definition and ranked. A ranking metric results from one or more calculations performed over values associated with a particular variable. The shapes that will be discussed are not an exhaustive set of shapes, nor are the attributes. This paper presents the idea of identifying behaviors of interest through shape identification, then ranking the shapes according a set of attributes.

The shapes and attributes that will be discussed are simple, as are the measurements of the attributes. This work is not a replacement for pattern mining techniques, used to identify a unique behavior in a data set. But the work presents a way of thinking about an identified behavior of interest and how it is defined and can be compared to other behaviors.

A subset of the shapes with multiple definitions for each are incorporated into TimeSearcher: Shape Search Edition (SSE), an information visualization tool. SSE is built upon TimeSearcher 1 (Keogh et al. 2002), and allows for the exploration of temporal data sets by identifying shapes of interest and ranking them according to a ranking metric. SSE visualizes shapes and provides a numerical ranking metric, which allows the shapes to be compared. SSE can identify shapes like increasing, decreasing, and volatile lines, as well as spike, sinks, rises, and drops. SSE has several definitions for each of the shapes to identify different types of behaviors.

17.2 Background

A lot of research has been done to understand how to define shapes. Some of the research, such as Agrawal et al.'s shape definition language (SDL) (Agrawal et al. 1995) and Hochheiser, et al.'s timeboxes (Hochheiser 2002), focuses on allowing users to define a shape of interest and then identify them in a data set. Research in the area of pattern discovery has focused less on the definition of the pattern and more on the value of the identified pattern. Many of the papers on pattern discovery start to answer the question "How significant or interesting is the identified pattern?" Much of the work in this area takes an automated approach, examining sets of values in a data set and determining their value based on some function. The idea that patterns can be evaluated to estimate their value to the user is one of the ideas presented in this paper.

17.2.1 Shape Definition

Providing an expressive language for identifying and comparing shapes is one goal of this paper. Agrawal et al. and Hochheiser et al. present two distinct methods of defining shapes. Both are expressive, but for different reasons. Agrawal et al.'s SDL provides a language consisting of an alphabet and a set of operators to define a shape; Hochheiser et al.'s research has focused on visual widgets as the method of defining shapes.

SDL provides a simple alphabet to describe point to point transitions in time series data. For example, the user defined symbol "Up" may indicate a significant increase in a stock price from one time point to the next. Using the symbols and the operators users can define an alphabet to describe any shape. The symbols define the amount of variation from point to point and the operator describe the relationship between the symbols.

TimeSearcher 1, an information visualization tool for exploring time series data, provides different techniques for defining shapes. The TimeSearcher 1 uses timeboxes and several other types of queries to allow users to visually define shapes. Timeboxes facilitate shape definition by allowing users to visually specify a range of values for the x and y coordinates of the data points within a shape. In addition to the timeboxes, TimeSearcher 1, includes an angular query widget. The angular query widget allows users to define a range of slope values. The timeboxes are a fairly course-grained approach to defining shapes, the angular queries provide a much more granular approach.

QuerySketch (Wattenberg 2001) allows the user to define shapes of interest using freehand sketches. Similarly, QueryLines provides a structured method of creating shapes using a series of line segments. QueryLines (Ryall et al. 2005) combines the point-to-point expressiveness of SDL and the dynamic visual query language of TimeSearcher 1. QueryLines is an information visualization tool that incorporates visual shape definition and user defined rankings to identify shapes of interest in temporal and ordered data sets. QueryLines, like TimeSearcher, can be bound by the x or y values, or both. QueryLines also allows the user to specify a set of contiguous line segments that define a shape; identified shapes are ranked according to their similarity to the user defined shape.

SDL, TimeSearcher 1, and QueryLines enable users to define shapes of interest and locate their occurrences within a data set. SDL is an expressive solution that can be tailored to the needs of its users, but it could be hard to use effectively by common users. On the other hand, TimeSearcher 1, is less expressive, but provide the users with the ability to define shapes in terms they understand (what they can see visually see). Keogh et al. extended timeboxes create variable time timeboxes (VTT) to increase their expressiveness (Keogh et al. 2002). VTT allows users to define a shape and then locate it over a range of values. Other research offers expressive ways of defining shapes over categorical data, such as temporal logic (Padmanabhan and Tuzhilin 1996) and regular expressions (Garofalakis et al. 1999), but the techniques do not easily transfer to temporal data sets. QueryLines has the expressiveness of SDL in visual query tool, but it is unable to express higher level behaviors, like anomalous spikes.

17.2.2 Shape Evaluation

In SDL and TimeSearcher 1, the significance of a shape is based strictly on whether the shape conforms to the definition or not. Although, the values used by the angular query widget could be used to define the significance of the identified shape, it is not an inherent capability in the tool. Because all shapes have the same significance they cannot be compared to one another. However, research in the area of pattern discovery (Guralnik and Srivastava 1999; Han et al. 1998) focuses on evaluating the significance of identified shapes. The ability to evaluate the significance of a shape implies that the identified shapes are comparable by some measurable attribute. For example, Dubinko et al.'s research in visualizing the evolution of social network tags, defines "interestingness" as the likelihood of a tag occurring during a particular period of time (Dubinko et al. 2006). The definition of "interestingness" provides a measurable attribute, frequency of tags occurrence during a particular period of time, by which tags can be compared. Similarly, clustering techniques are used to identify patterns of interest. In this technique, similar patterns are grouped together into a cluster (Das et al. 1998; Fu et al. 2001). Patterns identified using this technique can be compared based on the size of the cluster, the larger the cluster the more interesting the pattern. Yang et al.'s STAMP algorithm uses statistics to measure the importance of identified patterns (Yang et al. 2003). Each of these techniques provides a metric by which an identified pattern can be compared to another pattern. Unfortunately, these techniques are primarily associated with pattern discovery techniques and offer users little control over what patterns are identified.

Garofalakis et al. recognized the "lack of user controlled focus in the pattern mining process" and introduce a set of algorithms deemed SPIRIT, Sequential Pattern Mining with Regular Expression Constraints (Garofalakis et al. 1999). This research combines the ability to identify significance by using some measurable attributes, frequency, and an expressive definition language, regular expressions. The regular expressions provide users with the ability to constrain the results returned by the pattern mining algorithm to just the patterns of interest to the users. This paper goals are to provide capabilities similar to the SPIRIT algorithms, shape identification and ranking techniques using a user defined shape definition. Going beyond the SPIRIT algorithms this paper presents techniques that allow users to define what is "interesting" in terms that are familiar to them.

In addition to assisting users in defining shapes this paper presents attributes by which shapes can be ranked. There are many novel techniques for identifying similar patterns, but few offer users the ability to direct the ranking of the results. The idea of ranking data according to user-specific feature is not new, Seo and Shneiderman's created the rank-by-feature framework to assist users in selecting a feature that may interest them (Seo and Shneiderman 2004).

17.3 Shape Definitions

There are an infinite number of shapes; many of them are too complex to describe succinctly or create mathematical definitions to identify them. But there are a set of simple shapes that are commonly used to describe a particular behavior. In the following sections several shapes will be described, as well as their attributes. These attributes will be used to provide examples of shape definitions and ranking metrics. Additionally, examples explaining how the shapes, their definitions and ranking metric may be used to answer different types of queries will be given. Line, spike, sink, rise, drop, plateau, valley and gap shapes will be discussed.

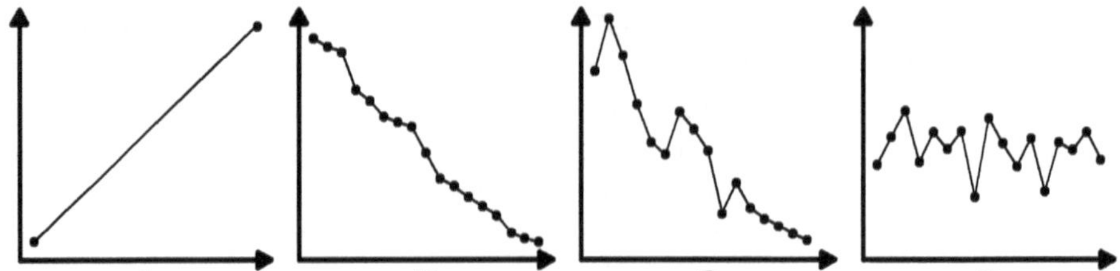

Fig. 17.1 Graphs *A* through *D* show examples of line shapes. *A* shows a 2-point increasing line and *B* a multi-point constantly decreasing line. *C* is an example of a multi-point decreasing line that could be identified by a linear regression calculated using the values that compose it. The last graph, *D*, is an example of a volatile line, where volatility is a measure of the standard deviation of the values in the line

17.3.1 Line Shapes

The simplest shape, a line, is defined as one or more line segments created by a set of contiguous time points. In a 2D Cartesian plane, a geometric line can be defined using the equation, $y = mx + b$, where m is the slope, b is the y-intercept, and x is an independent variable. A line segment is a portion of a line defined by its endpoints. Line shapes are interesting because they can be used to describe any other shape, but they are most useful in describing consistent behaviors, such as generally increasing, decreasing, stable, or volatile periods. For instance, a stock that consistently rises over a period of time can be described by an increasing line shape. Depending on how its attributes are constrained, a line shape can be used to generalize the behavior of a set of time points or identify a specific behavior, that is characterized by limited range of value changes between time points. For example, a linear regression identifies a relationship between a set of variables, that generalizes their behavior, but calculating the slope of each individual line segment can identify a specific behavior.

The attributes associated with line shapes are the length, slope, and volatility. The length attribute is the number of time points in the shape. The slope attribute is a measure of the rate at which the line shape is changing. The slope definition varies depending on whether the goal is to identify a particular behavior in the time series or to generalize the behavior of a set of time points. To identify a specific behavior, slope can be defined as the change in value between two time points. This definition is identical to the definition of slope for a geometric line. Using this definition of slope any constraint applied to the slope must be consistent across every line segment in the line shape. For example, if one line segment is increasing, all line segments in the line shape must be increasing. On the other hand, if the goal is to generalize the behavior of a set of time points, the slope definition should consider all of the points together. For example, the slope of a line shape may be defined as:

- amount of change between two time points that may or may not be contiguous
- the sum of the change of between all contiguous time points in the line shape

- the geometric slope of a linear regression computed over the time points in the shape.

These are examples of ways of calculating slopes. Figure 17.1C shows a line that could be identified using a linear regression, the set of values in the line have a decreasing trend. Each of these definitions describes a different behavior that may be of interest. Using different definitions for slope will result in different slope calculations for line shapes, therefore identifying different behaviors.

The term volatility can refer to the relative rate at which a stock increases and decreases. The same definition will be used to describe the volatility attribute of a line shape. The standard deviation of the values within a line shape can be used as a measure of a line's volatility. Figure 17.1D is an example of a volatile line. Other calculations may be more appropriate for measuring the volatility of line shape depending on the behavior of interest.

The slope, length, and volatility are attributes by which line shapes can be defined and ranked. Constraining the slope of a line shape to be a positive or negative value creates two definitions of line shapes, increasing and decreasing, respectively. According to the slope definition, an increasing line shape will characterize different behaviors. Constraining each individual line segment in a line shape to be negative creates a monotonically decreasing line, like the line shape in Fig. 17.1B. In addition to constraining the slope of the line, the number of time points can also be constrained. Figure 17.1A is an example of a 2-point line shape; Figs. 17.1B, 17.1C and 17.1D are examples of multiple point line shapes.

17.3.2 Spike and Sink Shapes

Spikes and sinks describe a temporal behavior in which a variable has a significant change over a period of time in one direction and then a significant change in the opposite direction. The point at which this change in direction occurs is the peak point. A spike, specifically, is a significant increase followed by a significant decrease. A sink is just the opposite, a decrease followed by an increase. Spikes and sinks are used by stock market analyst to describe the behavior of stock prices. Similarly, a doctor may say when blood pressure spikes there is a rapid rise then fall in pressure. Although the general behavior of spikes and sinks are understood more information is need to identify and compare particular instances of the shapes (Fig. 17.2).

The attributes associated with spike and sink shapes are the significance of the increase or decrease and their duration. The significance can be manifested in one or more attributes. The significance of the change can be measured by the absolute, relative, or angular height of the peak point. The absolute height is the absolute value of the peak point. The angular height is defined by the angle created at the peak point. The relative height is defined as the height of the peak point relative to all the other points in the time series. This definition will identify spikes and sinks whose behavior is significantly different then the rest of the points in the time series.

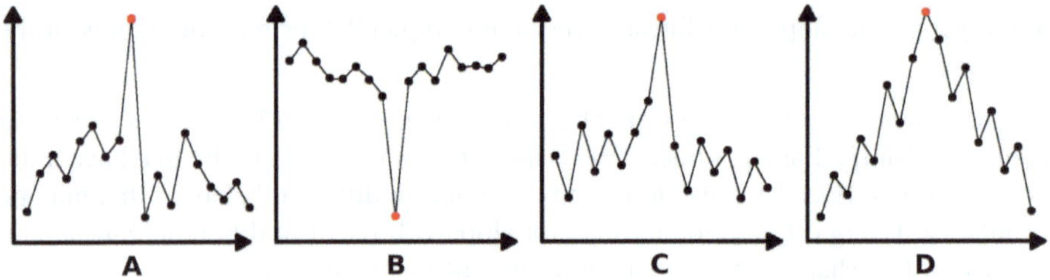

Fig. 17.2 These graphs are examples of spike and sink shapes. The *red dots* are the peak points. Graphs *A*, *B*, and *C* are graphs that may be ranked high based on its relative or angular height. The relative height is a measure of the difference between the peak point and average value of the remainder of the points. The angular height is the measure of the angle created by the two edges that meet at the peak point. An edge may consist of one or more points. Graph *D* is a spike that could be identified using a linear regression calculated over the points in the edges to the right and left of the peak point

For example, the equation, $|(max - mean)|/\sigma$ could be used to define the relative height of a spike or sink.

The relative height attribute of a spike or sink shape is affected by the behavior of all the time points in the time series. The absolute and angular height definitions have the ability to identify spikes and sinks in a volatile time series. Volatile time series are characterized by large changes in opposite directions between a set of consecutive time points. The duration attribute is given by the sum of time points contained in both edges plus the peak point. Constraining these attributes can identify a specific spike or sink shape within a time series.

The absolute, angular, and relative height attributes, as well as the duration and edge slope attributes can be constrained to define different spike and sink shape behaviors and they can be used as a ranking metric to compare and rank the shapes. The duration attribute can be constrained to identify sink and spike shapes that occur over a specific period of time. For instance, a three point and multiple point definition could be defined. The three point shape contains exactly three time points, a peak point and a single point on each side. Three points is the smallest number of points that a spike or sink shape can contain. The multiple point shape contains more than three time points.

The peak height can be constrained to create a definition that will identify shapes which are greater or less than a particular height. The slope of the leading or trailing period of change can also be used to define behaviors of interest for spike and sink shapes. By using these attributes to create shape definitions and rank shapes, particular behaviors of interest can be identified in temporal data sets.

17.3.3 Rise and Drop Shapes

Rise and drop shapes are used to describe a sustained change in the average value. These shapes can be divided into three distinct periods: a period of change that is

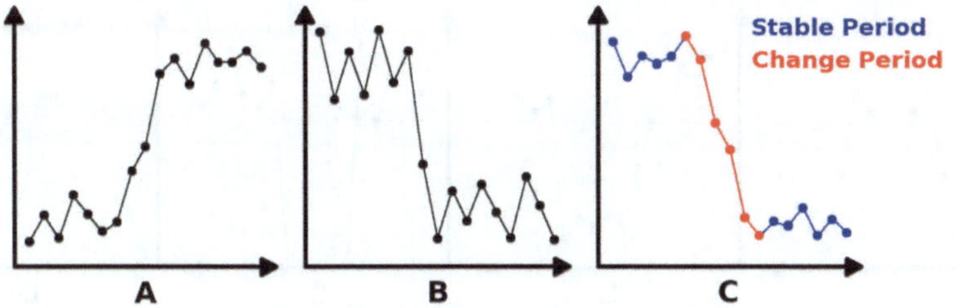

Fig. 17.3 The graphs above are examples of rise and drop shape. Graph *A* is a rise. *B* and *C* are drops. Graph *C* shows the three periods of drop and rise shapes: the leading stable period, the change period, and the trailing stable period

preceded and followed by a periods of stability, Fig. 17.3C. The stable periods are drawn in blue and the period of change in red. A rise shape has a change period that increases in value, while a drop shape decreases in value, as seen in Figs. 17.3A and 17.3B, respectively. Each period must consist of one or more time points; there is a single transition point between each period; and the time points in the shape must be contiguous. Drop and rise shapes contain a minimum of five points. The periods of stability separate these shapes from spikes, sinks and lines.

Stable time points have very low volatility, which could be measured by the standard deviation of the points or some other definition. In drops and rises, if a set of time points is not stable, it is changing. A rise and drop shape describes a person's heart rate at the start and conclusion of a aerobic workout, respectively. At the start of a workout a healthy person's heart rate will transition from a resting rate of approximately 65 beats per minute (bpm) to 140 bpm. During the period prior to and after the transition the active and resting heart rate will be stable until the conclusion of the workout. This is the type of behavior a rise or drop shape could identify.

The length of the periods, the change significance, and the average value of the stable periods are some of the attributes associated with rise and drop shapes. The length of a period is defined by the number of time points contained within that period. The change significance, like the previous shapes, can be defined by the slope of that period, and the slope can be defined in several different ways based on the behavior of interest. The average value of the stable period is the mean of the points in the period.

Period length is the most intuitive attribute to constrain when creating shape definitions for rise and drop shapes. A definition that limits the length of the change period to just two points is useful in identifying rapid change.

17.3.4 Plateaus, Valleys and Gaps

Plateaus, valleys, and gaps are used to describe temporary changes in variable. They differ from spikes and sinks because the temporary value is sustained for a measurable period of time. These shapes consist of leading, intermediate, and trailing stable

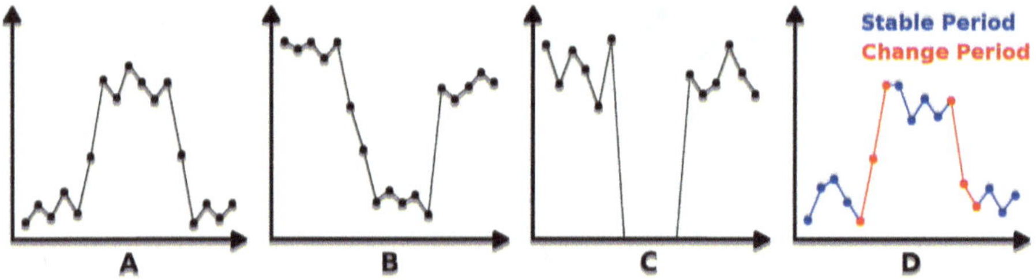

Fig. 17.4 Graphs *A*, *B* and *C* show a plateau, valley and gap shape, respectively. Graph *D* shows the periods associated with plateau, valley and gap shapes

periods, as well as departing and returning change periods, as shown in Fig. 17.4D. A plateau has an intermediate stable period, whose average value is greater than the leading and trailing stable periods (Fig. 17.4A), while a valley has an intermediate period, whose average value is less than the average value of other two stable periods (Fig. 17.4B). A gap is a specific type of valley where the intermediate period's values are zero (Fig. 17.4C). Using the workout example, a plateau describes a person's heart rate during his or her entire workout. Prior to the beginning and after the end of the workout, the heart rate is stable at a resting rate of 65 bpm. At the start of the workout, the heart rate leaves the resting rate and rises to approximately 140 bpm. This heart rate is maintained throughout the workout. At the conclusion of the workout, the heart rate returns to the resting heart rate and remains there. Plateaus, valleys, and gaps are very similar to drops and rises, with one important difference. Drops and rises do not define the behavior that occurs after the trailing stable period. Therefore, several ranking metrics, such as the length of the intermediate stable period (the trailing stable period in the drop and rise shape), have a different meaning in plateaus, valleys and gaps than in drop and rise shapes.

The ranking metrics are similar to the ranking metrics for drops and rises, but they are calculated over the additional portions of the plateaus, valleys, and gaps. Although the calculations are same, the meanings are different. For example, using the workout example, the difference between the mean of leading and trailing stable periods in plateau shapes may signify a strengthening of the heart. On the other hand, the difference between the leading and trailing periods in a rise shape signifies a more strenuous workout.

Definitions that constrain the length of the stable periods are useful when examining plateau, valley and gap shapes. By limiting the length of a particular period, shapes with a specific duration can be identified. Definitions that measure the difference between the leading and trailing stable periods can also be useful.

17.4 TimeSearcher: Shape Search Edition

TimeSearcher: Shape Search Edition (SSE) is an information visualization tool that allows users to identify shapes and rank them according to one or more attributes.

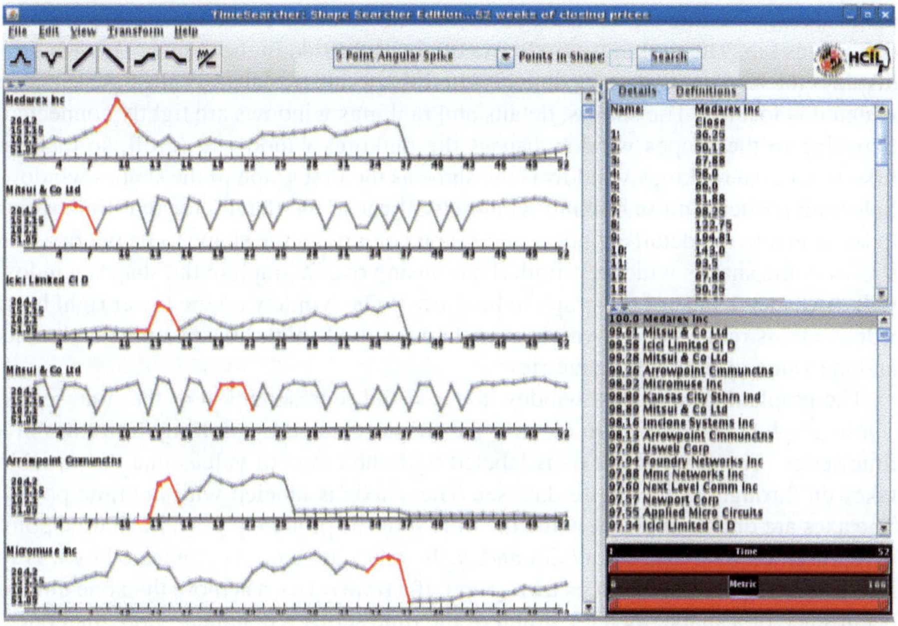

Fig. 17.5 This is a screenshot of TimeSearcher Shape Searcher Edition (SSE). The *upper panel* shows the seven buttons labeled with the shapes that TimeSearcher SSE can identify and rank. Each shape has several definitions that can be selected from the drop down box to the right of the shape buttons. Some of the shape definitions require user defined input, such as the number of time points in the shape. The *left side* contains the shapes window, which displays the currently identified shapes for the loaded data set. The window in the *upper right* contains the details and definitions tab. The details tab displays the time points and values of a particular time series. The definition tab displays an explanation of the selected shape definition. The window in the *left center* is the rankings window. Once a shape and definition have been chosen from the *upper panel* the ranking metric value and label for each shape will be shown in this window. The *lower right corner* contains the dynamic query bars. These bars allow the shapes to be filtered based on the ranking metric and the endpoints associated with a shape

TimeSearcher SSE is an extension of TimeSearcher 1. TimeSearcher SSE can identify several definitions for each of the following shapes, lines, spikes, sinks, rises and drops and they can each ranked according different attributes. The definitions and ranking attributes are primarily static, but some of the definitions require user input (Fig. 17.5).

17.4.1 Interface

TimeSearcher SSE consists of four primary windows. The shapes window on the left side contains time series graphs displaying each of the identified shapes. The tabbed window on the upper right side shows a details view, the time points and associated data values, of a time series in the details tab and the current shape definition in the definitions tab. The rankings window is on the right side in the center. This window displays the ranking metric for an individual shape and the label for the time series in which it is located. The shapes, details and rankings windows are tightly connected. Scrolling in the shapes window causes the rankings window to scroll, so that the first item in the rankings window is the same as the first graph in the shapes window. Selecting an item in the ranking window will cause the details for that time series to be shown in the details window and graph containing the shape to be the first one shown in the shapes window. Similarly, mousing over a graph in the shapes window will cause the details of the graph to be shown. The window on the lower right hand side contains range sliders which filter the identified shapes based on its endpoints and the value of the ranking metric.

The graphs in the shapes window are a visual representation of the time series. These graphs make it easy to identify the shapes created by plotting the values in a time series. The graph's y-axis is labeled with the range of values that the variable takes on throughout the entire data set. The x-axis is labeled with the time points. The axes are drawn in black, while the time series is plotted in gray. Each time point is represented by a small gray dot and each consecutive dot is connected by a gray line. Each shape is shown in its own graph; if a time series has more than one unique occurrence of a shape, then the graph of the time series will appear more than once. Each shape is labeled in the graph with red lines instead of gray; points of interest in the shape are marked by large red dots. A significant point may be the peak point in a spike or sink shape or the change period in a rise or drop shape.

17.4.2 Spike and Sink Shape Identification

TimeSearcher SSE has three definitions for both spike and sink shapes. The definitions define a three, five, and seven point spikes and sinks and each of these shape definitions can be ranked according to its relative and angular height. Each of the shape definitions and ranking metrics are described below:

- **3-Point Spike/ Sink**—a spike or sink shape containing exactly three time points with a single time point on both sides of the peak point.
- **5-Point Spike/ Sink**—a spike or sink shape containing exactly five time points with two time points on both sides of the peak point.
- **7-Point Spike/ Sink**—a spike or sink shape containing exactly seven time points with three time points on both sides of the peak point.
  - *Angular Height*—the measure of the angle created at the point where the edges meet. Figure 17.6A shows the component's angular height calculation. Using the trigonometric function, $\cos(\alpha+\beta) = \cos(\alpha) * \cos(\beta) - \sin(\alpha) * \sin(\beta)$, the angle created by the edges of the spike is equal to $\cos(\alpha+\beta) = (dy1 * dy2 - 1)/\sqrt{(1+dy1^2) * (1+dy2^2)}$ where $dy1 = |y1 - y2|$ and $dy2 = |y2 - y3|$. A linear regression calculated over the points to the right and left of the peak point, defines the increasing and decreasing edges for the 5 and 7-point spikes.

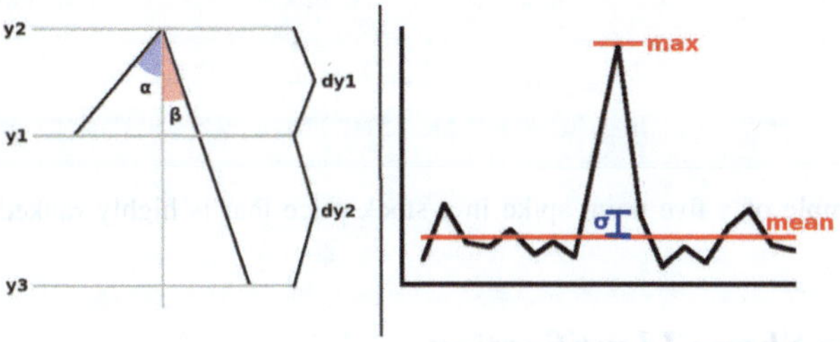

Fig. 17.6 The diagrams above show how the angular and relative height attributes are calculated. The *first image* shows the components of the angular height equation, $\cos(\alpha + \beta) = (dy1 * dy2 - 1)/\sqrt{(1 + dy1^2) * (1 + dy2^2)}$. The angular height a measure of the angle created where the two edge of spikes and sinks meet. The *second image* shows the components of the relative height equation, $|max - mean|/\sigma$. The relative height is the height of a spike or sink relative to the rest of the shape

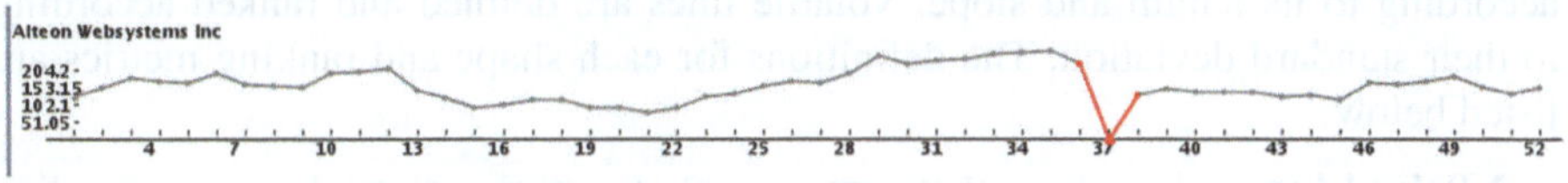

Fig. 17.7 Example of a three point sink ranked according to its angular height. This sink identifies a missing value in this stock market data

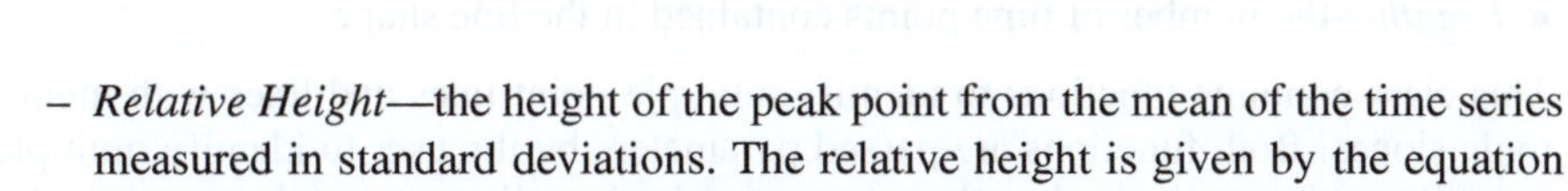

Fig. 17.8 Example of a 31 point spike identified in X-ray diffraction data ranked according to its angular height

– *Relative Height*—the height of the peak point from the mean of the time series measured in standard deviations. The relative height is given by the equation $|max - mean|/\sigma$. Figure 17.6B shows the values of the relative height calculation.

All of the definitions and ranking metrics are static, and require no input from users. Each shape is computed when the data is loaded. Values such as the mean and standard deviation are only calculated once and stored within the internal representation of a time series, an Entity object. The function that identifies the spikes and sinks takes a parameter that defines how many points will be in a spike or sink. These shapes are identified simultaneously. The class attempts to identify shapes as efficiently as possible, by only passing through the data once. Figures 17.7, 17.8, 17.9 show examples of spikes and sinks identified by TimeSearcher SSE.

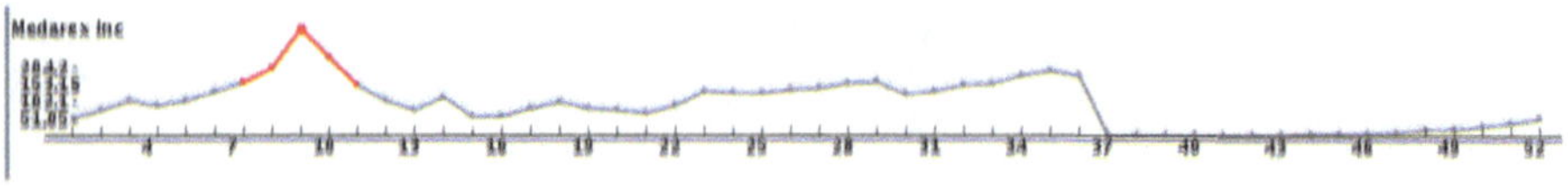

Fig. 17.9 Example of a five point spike in a stock price that is highly ranked according to its angular height

17.4.3 Line Shape Identification

TimeSearcher SSE contains four definitions for both increasing and decreasing line shapes and a single definition for volatile lines. The first three shape definitions for increasing and decreasing lines are two point, multiple point, and monotonic slope line shapes. The fourth definition is a monotonic slope line shape with a constraint placed on the minimum length. The two point and multiple point definitions are ranked according to their slope, while the monotonic slope definition is ranked according to its length and slope. Volatile lines are defined and ranked according to their standard deviation. The definitions for each shape and ranking metrics are listed below:

- **2-Point Line**—a line shape that contains only two time points. An increasing line has a positive slope, while a decreasing line's slope is negative.
- **Multiple Point Line**—a line shape that contains multiple time points. An increasing line has a positive geometric slope, while a decreasing line's slope is negative. There are several ways to measure the slope which are discussed below.
- **Monotonic Slope Line**—a line shape where each line segment's geometric slope has the same sign, positive or negative.
- *Slope*—the geometric slope is given by the equation, $(y2 - y1)/(x2 - x1)$. The slope of a two point line shape or a line segment can be calculated using the geometric slope equation. A multiple point line's slope is a measure of the geometric slope of the linear regression calculated over the points in the line shape. The slope of a monotonic slope line is calculated in the same fashion.
- *Length*—the number of time points contained in the line shape.

This class contains functions to identify multiple point lines and lines with monotonic slopes. Both functions are passed parameters by the user to identify multiple point lines of a particular length and monotonic slope line greater than a particular length. This allows the user to specify a minimum length for the monotonic slope lines, eliminating the two point lines, which are always monotonic. Figures 17.10, 17.11, 17.12 show examples of two increasing and one volatile line identified by TimeSearcher SSE.

17.4.4 Rise and Drop Shape Identification

TimeSearcher SSE contains three definitions for both rise and drop shapes. These definitions are ranked according to their slope and the length of their stable periods.

Fig. 17.10 Example of a fifteen point increasing line ranked according to slope. This line shows the web the term "web" increasing over a fifteen year period

Fig. 17.11 Example of a monotonically increasing line in stock market data ranked highly due to its slope

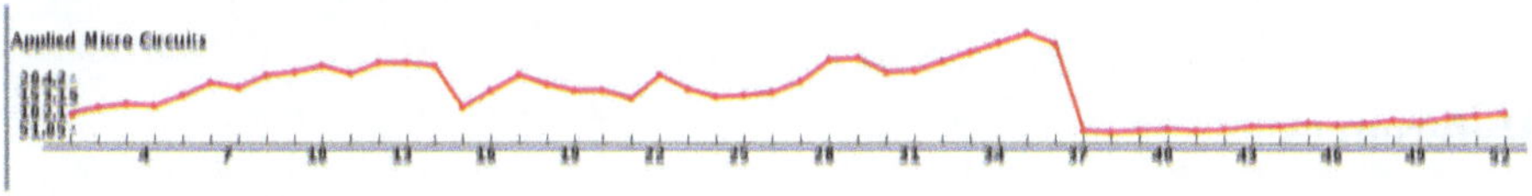

Fig. 17.12 Example of a volatile line shape ranked highly according to its standard deviation

Fig. 17.13 Example of a rise shape in stock market data. The shape is highly ranked according to the length of its stable periods

The definitions defined by TimeSearcher SSE are general definitions described in Sect. 17.3.3 and the same definition except the length attribute of the stable periods is constrained to be a minimum length. Listed below are the definitions:

- **Rise or Drop**—a sustained change in values. These shapes consist of three distinct time periods: a stable period, followed by a period of change, concluding with another stable period.
- **Drop or Rise with Multiple Point Stable Period**—a rise or drop shape that contains multiple points in each of its stable periods.
- *Slope*—the geometric slope of the period of change. The slope of the period of change and a line shape are calculated the same way.
- *Length of the Stable Periods*—the lowest number of time points between the two stable periods.

A point is stable if it lies within one standard deviation of the mean of the other points within the stable period. If a point is not stable then it is changing. Figures 17.13, 17.14 are examples of rise and drop shapes.

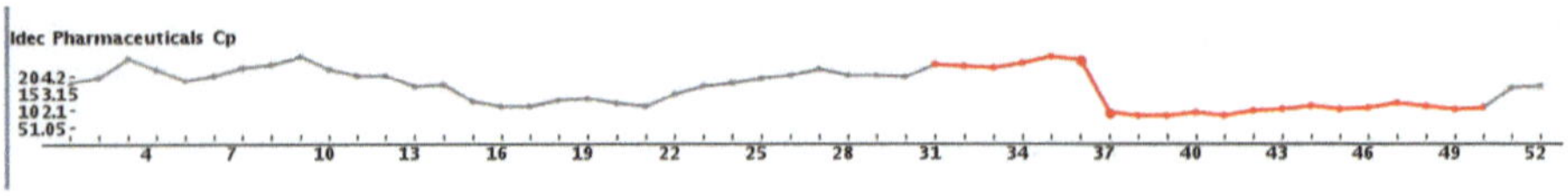

Fig. 17.14 Example of a drop shape in stock market data. This drop was identified using the "stable period greater than *x*" definition which is ranked according to the slope of the change period

17.5 Conclusion

Shapes are used to describe variable behaviors. Most people are familiar with the behaviors that are described by shapes. By providing users attributes to describe and rank shapes particular behaviors can be more easily identified and knowledge discovery becomes a more intuitive process.

References

Agrawal, R., Psaila, G., Wimmers, E. L., & Zaot, M. (1995). Querying shapes of histories. In *Proc. 21st international conference on very large databases* (pp. 502–514). San Mateo: Morgan Kaufmann Publishers.

Balog, K., Mishne, G., & Rijke, M. (2006). Why are they excited? Identifying and explaining spikes in blog mood levels. In *Proc. 11th meeting of the European chapter of the association for computational linguistics*.

Das, G., Lin, K., Mannila, H., Renganathan, G., & Smyth, P. (1998). Rule discovery from time series. In *Proc. of the 4th international conference on knowledge discovery and data mining* (pp. 16–22).

Dettki, H., & Ericsson, G. (2008). Screening radiolocation datasets for movement strategies with time series segmentation. *Journal of Wildlife Management*, *72*, 535–542.

Dubinko, M., Kumar, R., Magnani, J., Novak, J., Raghavan, P., & Tomkins, A. (2006). Visualizing tags over time. In *Proc. of the 15th international WWW conference*.

Fu, T. C., Chung, F. L., Ng, V., & Luk, R. (2001). Pattern discovery for stock time series using self-organizing maps. In *Workshop on temporal data mining, 7th international conference on knowledge discovery and data mining* (pp. 27–37). New York: ACM Press.

Garofalakis, M. N., Rastogi, R., & Shim (1999). Spirit: Sequential pattern mining with regular expression constraints. In *Proc. of the 25th international conference on very large databases* (pp. 223–234).

Guralnik, V., & Srivastava, J. (1999). Event detection from time series data. In *Proc. of the fifth international conference on knowledge discovery and data mining* (pp. 33–42).

Han, J., Dong, G., & Yin, Y. (1998). Efficient mining of partial periodic patterns in time series database. In *Proc. of the fourth international conference on knowledge discovery and data mining* (pp. 214–218). Menlo Park: AAAI Press.

Hochheiser, H. (2002). *Visual queries for finding patterns in time series data*. PhD diss. University of Maryland Computer Science Dept.

Keogh, E., Hochheiser, H., & Shneiderman, B. (2002). An augmented visual query mechanism for finding patterns in time series data. In *LNAI. Proc. of the 5th international conference on flexible query answering systems* (pp. 240–250). Berlin: Springer.

Padmanabhan, B., & Tuzhilin, A. (1996). Pattern discovery in temporal databases: A temporal logic approach. In *Proc. of the 2nd international conference on knowledge discovery and data mining*.

Ryall, K., Lesh, N., Miyashita, H., Makino, S., Lanning, T., Lanning, T., Leigh, D., & Leigh, D. (2005). Querylines: Approximate query for visual browsing. In *Extended abstracts of the conference on human factors in computing systems* (pp. 1765–1768). New York: ACM Press.

Seo, J., & Shneiderman, B. (2004). A rank-by-feature framework for unsupervised multidimensional data exploration using low dimensional projections. In *Proc. of the IEEE symposium on information visualization* (pp. 65–72). New York: IEEE Press.

Shamma, D., Kennedy, L., & Churchill, E. F. (2011). Peaks and persistence: Modeling the shape of microblog conversations. In *Proc. of computer supported cooperative work 2011* (pp. 355–358). New York: ACM Press.

Wattenberg, M. (2001). Sketching a graph to query a time series database. In *Proc. of the 2001 conference human factors in computing systems, extended abstracts* (pp. 381–382). New York: ACM Press.

Yang, J., Wang, W., & Yu, P. S. (2003). Stamp: Discovery of statistically important pattern repeats in a long sequence. In *Proc. of the 3rd SIAM international conference on data mining* (pp. 224–238). Philadelphia: SIAM.

Chapter 18
SSD-C: Smooth Signed Distance Colored Surface Reconstruction

Fatih Calakli and Gabriel Taubin

Abstract In this chapter we address the problem of reconstructing the surface geometry, topology, and color map of a 3D scene from a finite set of colored oriented points. These data sets are nowadays obtained using a variety of techniques, including multi-view stereo reconstruction methods from multiple 2D images. We describe a novel variational method which reduces the problem to the solutions of sparse systems of linear equations. We first use the point positions and orientation vectors to reconstruct the geometry and topology of a watertight surface represented as an adaptively tessellated polygon mesh. The method then smoothly extrapolates the color information from the points to the surface. Experimental evidence is presented to show that the resulting method produces high quality polygon meshes with smooth color maps which accurately approximate the source colored oriented points.

18.1 Introduction

This chapter addresses the problem of reconstructing the geometry and topology of a watertight surface, and a smooth surface color map, from a finite set of colored oriented points. This problem has a wide range of applications in industry, entertainment, virtual reality, archeology, forensics, art, medical imaging, and many other areas. Colored oriented point clouds are nowadays obtained using various optical measuring devices, such as laser scanners and inexpensive structured lighting systems, by other computational means such as multi-view stereo reconstruction algorithms, and also result from large scale simulations. We are particularly interested here in the reconstruction of colored surfaces from multi-view image and video data captured using consumer level digital and video cameras. The problem is particularly challenging due to the non-uniform sampling nature of the data collection

F. Calakli (✉) · G. Taubin
Brown University, Providence, RI 02912, USA
e-mail: fatih_calakli@brown.edu

G. Taubin
e-mail: taubin@brown.edu

J. Dill et al. (eds.), *Expanding the Frontiers of Visual Analytics and Visualization*,
DOI 10.1007/978-1-4471-2804-5_18, © Springer-Verlag London Limited 2012

processes. Common problems to cope with include: non-uniform sampled data due to concave surfaces, missing data due to inaccessible regions, noisy data due to sensor incapabilities, and distorted data due to misalignment of partial scans. As well as other researchers who have contributed to the field, we are particularly concerned with developing algorithms robust with respect to these issues, and to develop efficient algorithms which can scale up to very large data sets.

The prior art in surface reconstruction methods is extensive. We only discuss here some of the existing methods which reconstruct the geometry and topology of the surface from the point locations and orientation vectors. For a more extensive description of the prior art we refer the reader to a recent survey (Schall and Samozino 2005). Despite the long history, the area is still active. One family of algorithms produces interpolating polygon meshes where some of the input points become vertices of the polygons (Bernardini et al. 1999). Most of these algorithms are based on constructing Voronoi diagrams and Delaunay triangulations of the data points, and many come with guaranteed reconstruction quality (Dey 2007). Another family of algorithms are based on implicit function fitting, and produce approximating surfaces which are more desirable in the presence of noise. These methods include Kazhdan (2005), Kazhdan et al. (2006), Alliez et al. (2007), Manson et al. (2008) which reconstruct a binary indicator function; Hoppe et al. (1992), Curless and Levoy (1996), Boissonnat and Cazals (2002), Calakli and Taubin (2011) which estimate a signed distance function; and Carr et al. (2001), Ohtake et al. (2003b), Alexa et al. (2003), Ohtake et al. (2003a), Shen et al. (2004), Fleishman et al. (2005) based on local function fitting and blending. Most of these methods reduce the surface reconstruction problem to the solution of a large scale numerical optimization problem, and use schemes based on space partition data structures such as octrees to reduce the computational and storage complexity.

In Calakli and Taubin (2011) we introduced the Smooth Signed Distance Surface Reconstruction (SSD) method for reconstructing the geometry and topology of a watertight surface. In this chapter we show how to extend this method to the reconstruction of colored surfaces by estimating an additional continuous color map defined on the reconstructed surface geometry. This color map approximates the colors associated with the data points at the point locations, and extrapolate with continuity those colors to areas where the sampling rate is low. The color map estimation step extends the variational formulation in Calakli and Taubin (2011) to accommodate appearance estimation over surfaces defined by implicit functions. As a result, each problem reduces to the solution of a sparse linear system which can be solved independently of the geometry and topology estimation by using an appropriate solver.

We devote Sect. 18.2, Sect. 18.4, and Sect. 18.5 to describe the variational formulation, the discretization, and octree-based implementation, respectively. We present our results in Sect. 18.7. Figure 18.1 shows one example of surface and color map reconstructed with the proposed method. Note the good behavior near boundaries, holes, and regions with uneven sampling.

Fig. 18.1 Reconstruction of the side of a castle model: The input point cloud (*top-left*), surface reconstructed by the proposed algorithm (*top-right*), two views from the surface and color map reconstructed by the proposed algorithm (*bottom*)

18.2 Continuous Formulation

Given a colored oriented point cloud $\mathcal{D} = \{(p_1, n_1, c_1), \ldots, (p_N, n_N, c_N)\}$, where p_i is a surface location sample, n_i is the corresponding surface normal sample oriented towards the outside of the object, and c_i is the corresponding color sample, we are concerned with the problem of reconstructing a surface S defined by an implicit equation $S = \{x : f(x) = 0\}$, where $f : V \to \mathbb{R}$ is the implicit function defined on a bounded volumetric domain V contained in Euclidean three dimensional space, and a smooth color map $g : V \to \mathbb{R}$ defined on the same domain with intensity values, so that $f(p_i) \approx 0$, $\nabla f(p_i) \approx n_i$, and $g(p_i) \approx c_i$, for $i = 1, \ldots, N$.

18.2.1 Surface Reconstruction

If the implicit function $f(x)$ is continuous, then the surface S is watertight. Without loss of generality we will assume that $f(x) < 0$ inside and $f(x) > 0$ outside of the object. As a reference, in both FFT Surface Reconstruction (Kazhdan 2005) and Poisson Reconstruction (Kazhdan et al. 2006) the implicit function is forced to be the indicator function of the volume bounded by the surface S. This function is identically equal to zero outside, to one inside, and discontinuous exactly on S, as shown in a 2D example in Fig. 18.2.

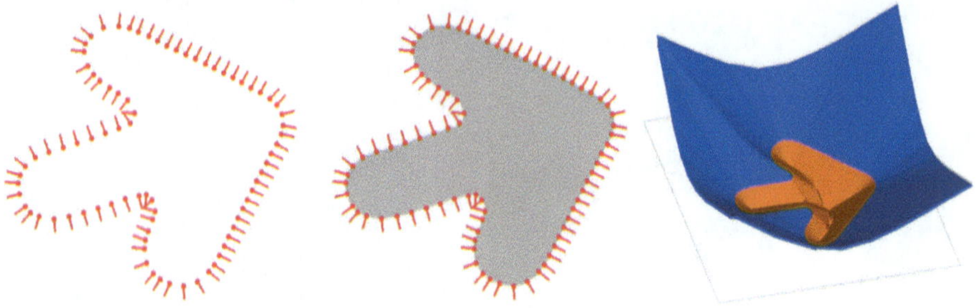

Fig. 18.2 A 2D oriented point cloud (*left*) as samples of a 2D curve which is represented as a level set of an indicator function (*middle*) (gray = 1, white = 0). The graph of the smooth signed distance function (*right*) estimated by our algorithm from the same point cloud

Usually we are only interested in reconstructing the surface S within a bounded volume V, such as a cube containing all the data points, which may result in an open surface at the boundaries of the volume V, particularly when the points only sample one side of the object, there are holes in the data, or more generally if the points are not uniformly distributed along the surface of the solid object.

The gradient $\nabla f(x)$ of a function $f(x)$ with first order continuous derivatives is a vector field normal to the level sets of the function, and in particular to the surface S. We will further assume that the gradient field on the surface S is unit length, which allows us to directly compare the gradient of the function with the point cloud normal vectors. Since the points p_i are regarded as samples of the surface S, and the normal vectors as samples of the surface normal at the corresponding points, the implicit function should ideally satisfy $f(p_i) = 0$ and $\nabla f(p_i) = n_i$ for all the points $i = 1, \ldots, N$ in the data set. Since these two conditions are hard to satisfy in the presence of measurement noise, we require that these conditions be satisfied in the least-squares sense. As a result, we consider the problem of minimizing the following data energy

$$\mathcal{E}_{\mathcal{D}}(f) = \mathcal{E}_{\mathcal{D}_0}(f) + \lambda_1 \mathcal{E}_{\mathcal{D}_1}(f) \tag{18.1}$$

where

$$\mathcal{E}_{\mathcal{D}_0}(f) = \frac{1}{N} \sum_{i=1}^{N} f(p_i)^2 \qquad \mathcal{E}_{\mathcal{D}_1}(f) = \frac{1}{N} \sum_{i=1}^{N} \left\| \nabla f(p_i) - n_i \right\|^2$$

and λ_1 is a positive constant used to give more or less weight to the second energy term with respect to the first term. The normalization by the number of points is introduced to make these two parameters independent of the total number of points. At this point this normalization has no effect, but plays a role after we add a third regularization term.

Depending on which family $\mathcal{F}$ of functions $f(x)$ is considered as the space of admissible solutions, the problem of minimizing the energy function $\mathcal{E}_{\mathcal{D}}(f)$ of Eq. (18.1) may or may not be well conditioned. In particular, this energy function does not specify how the function should behave away from the data points. Many parameterized families of functions have parameters highly localized in space, and the energy function of Eq. (18.1) may not constrain all the parameters. If the unconstrained parameters are arbitrarily set to zero, the estimated surface S may end up containing spurious components located far away from the data points. To address this problem we add the following regularization term to the energy function

$$\mathcal{E}_{\mathcal{R}}(f) = \frac{1}{|V|}\int_V \|Hf(x)\|^2 dx \tag{18.2}$$

where $Hf(x)$ is the Hessian matrix of f, the 3×3 matrix of second order partial derivatives of $f(x)$, and the norm of the matrix is the Frobenius matrix norm, i.e., the sum of the squares of the nine elements of the matrix. The integral is over the volume V where we are interested in reconstructing the surface, $|V| = \int_V dx$ is the measure of this volume.

The total energy function in the proposed formulation is a weighted average of the data and regularization terms

$$\mathcal{E}(f) = \mathcal{E}_{\mathcal{D}_0}(f) + \lambda_1 \mathcal{E}_{\mathcal{D}_1}(f) + \lambda_2 \mathcal{E}_{\mathcal{R}}(f), \tag{18.3}$$

and λ_2 is another positive parameter. Increasing λ_2 with respect to λ_1 produces a smoother result.

Note that the three columns of the Hessian matrix $Hf(x)$ are the partial derivatives of the gradient $\nabla f(x)$ with respect to the three Cartesian variables:

$$Hf(x) = \left[\frac{\partial \nabla f(x)}{\partial x_1} \quad \frac{\partial \nabla f(x)}{\partial x_2} \quad \frac{\partial \nabla f(x)}{\partial x_3} \right].$$

As a result, by forcing the square norm of the Hessian matrix to be close to zero, the regularization term makes the gradient of the function almost constant away from the data points. In the vicinity of the data points the data energy terms dominate the total energy, and make the function to approximate the signed distance function. Away from the data points the regularization energy term dominates the total energy and tends to make the gradient vector field $\nabla f(x)$ constant.

18.2.2 Color Map Reconstruction

We are also interested in estimating the color map g defined on the same bounded volume V. Since the points p_i are regarded as samples of the surface S, and the colors c_i as samples of the surface color at the corresponding points, the color function should ideally satisfy $g(p_i) = c_i$ for all the points $i = 1, \ldots, N$ in the data set. However, we again require that this condition be satisfied in the least-squares sense. As a result, we consider the problem of minimizing the following data energy

$$\mathcal{Q}_{\mathcal{D}}(g) = \frac{1}{N}\sum_{i=1}^{N}\big(g(p_i) - c_i\big)^2. \tag{18.4}$$

Depending on which family $\mathcal{G}$ of functions $g(x)$ is considered as the space of admissible solutions, the problem of minimizing the energy function $\mathcal{Q}_{\mathcal{D}}(g)$ of Eq. (18.4) may or may not be well conditioned. In particular, this energy function does not specify how the function should behave away from the data points. To constraint all the parameters we add the following regularization term to the energy function

$$\mathcal{Q}_{\mathcal{R}}(g) = \frac{1}{|V|} \int_V \|\nabla g(x)\|^2 dx \tag{18.5}$$

where $\nabla g(x)$ is the gradient vector of g, the 3×1 vector of first order partial derivatives of $g(x)$, and the norm of the vector is the L^2-norm. The integral is over the same volume V where we reconstruct the surface, and again $|V| = \int_V dx$ is the measure of this volume. The total energy function in the proposed formulation is a weighted average of the data and regularization terms

$$\mathcal{Q}(g) = \mathcal{Q}_{\mathcal{D}}(g) + \mu \mathcal{Q}_{\mathcal{R}}(g), \tag{18.6}$$

and μ is a positive constant. Increasing μ produces a smoother result. In the vicinity of the data points the data energy term dominate the total energy, and makes the function to approximate the true appearance. Away from the data points the regularization energy term dominates the total energy and tends to make the color function $g(x)$ constant.

18.3 Linearly Parameterized Families

In this section we are concerned with the existence and uniqueness of solution for the variational problems defined by the energy functions $\mathcal{E}(f)$ and $\mathcal{Q}(g)$ of Eqs. (18.3) and (18.6) respectively. We restrict the analysis here to families of functions linearly parameterized by a finite number of parameters. Explicitly, a member of this family can be written as a linear combination of certain basis functions

$$f(x) = \sum_{\alpha \in \Lambda} f_\alpha \phi_\alpha(x) \tag{18.7}$$

where α denotes an index which belongs to a finite set Λ, say with K elements, $\phi_\alpha(x)$ is a basis function, and f_α is the corresponding coefficient. The K basis functions are chosen in advance, and are not regarded as variables in the problem. The function can also be written as an inner product

$$f(x) = \Phi(x)^t F \tag{18.8}$$

where $F = (f_\alpha : \alpha \in \Lambda)$ and $\Phi(x) = (\phi_\alpha(x) : \alpha \in \Lambda)$ are K-dimensional column vectors. Restricting the energy $\mathcal{E}(f)$ of Eq. (18.3) to this function results in a non-homogeneous and quadratic function $F^t A F - 2b^t F + c$ in the K-dimensional parameter vector F. The matrix A is symmetric and positive definite, and the resulting minimization problem has a unique minimum. The global minimum is determined by solving the system of linear equations $AF = b$.

Similarly, when we restrict the color function $g(x)$ to another linearly parametrized function

$$g(x) = \Psi(x)^t G, \tag{18.9}$$

the energy function $\mathcal{Q}(g)$ of Eq. (18.6) results in a non-homogeneous and quadratic energy $G^t BG - 2d^t G + e$ in the K-dimensional parameter vector G. The matrix B is symmetric and positive definite, and the resulting minimization problem has a unique minimum. The global minimum is determined by solving the system of linear equations $BG = d$.

18.4 Discretization with Discontinuous Function

A hybrid of finite-element and finite differences scheme is presented in Calakli and Taubin (2011) to discretize the energy function $\mathcal{E}(f)$ of Eq. (18.3): a finite element discretization for the function $f(x)$, and finite differences discretizations for the gradient $\nabla f(x)$ and the Hessian $Hf(x)$. Since all these terms are written as homogeneous linear functions of the same parameter vector F, the problem still reduces to the solution of linear equations $AF = b$. As this particular discretization is applicable to adaptive grids, we adopt a similar approach to discretize the energy function $\mathcal{Q}(g)$ of Eq. (18.6). We use a finite element discretization for the color function $g(x)$, and finite differences discretization for the gradient $\nabla g(x)$.

To simplify the notation, we first consider a regular hexahedral grid partition of space. We assume that the volume V is a unit cube $V = [0, 1] \times [0, 1] \times [0, 1]$, and that each of the three axes is split into M equally long segments, resulting in M^3 hexahedral cells and $(M+1)^3$ vertices. In this discretization, the indices $\alpha \in \Lambda$ are the grid cell multi-indices $\alpha = (i, j, k)$, for $0 \leq i, j, k < M$. The coefficients g_α are then the values of the color function $g(x)$ at the grid centroids $p_\alpha = ((i + 0.5)/M, (j+0.5)/M, (k+0.5)/M)$. Determining which cell C_α each point p_i falls into reduces to quantization. If $p_i \in C_\alpha$ then

$$g(p_i) \approx g_\alpha. \tag{18.10}$$

Since the piecewise constant function leads to zero first derivatives within each cell, the square norm of the gradient $\nabla g(x)$ is a generalized function supported on the square faces shared by neighboring voxels (as Dirac's δ "function"), and the integral over the volume V reduces to a finite sum over the faces. Hence, we only need an approximation to $\|\nabla g(x)\|^2$ at the faces shared by cells. If C_α and C_β are two such cell that share a face, then we use finite differences

$$\nabla_{\alpha\beta} g = \frac{1}{\Delta_{\alpha\beta}} (g_\alpha - g_\beta) \tag{18.11}$$

where $\Delta_{\alpha\beta}$ is the Euclidean distance between the centers of the cells. As a result, the integral in the regularization term of Eq. (18.5) becomes a sum over all the neighboring cell pairs

$$\mathcal{Q}_\mathcal{R}(g) \approx \frac{1}{|V|} \sum_{(\alpha,\beta)} \frac{|V|_{\alpha\beta}}{\Delta_{\alpha\beta}} (g_\alpha - g_\beta)^2 \tag{18.12}$$

where $|V|_{\alpha\beta}$ is the area of the face shared by cells C_α and C_β, and $|V| = \sum_{(\alpha,\beta)} |V|_{\alpha\beta}$.

18.5 Octree-Based Implementation

A regular grid formulation results in high storage requirements and slow algorithms which limit its appeal. Instead, we adaptively construct an octree based on the location of the data points. In the recursive subdivision algorithm, a cell is split if the number of points contained is larger than a prespecified value, and the cell depth does not exceed another prespecified value. The data set is recursively partitioned into subsets of points $\mathcal{D}_\alpha$ associated with cells C_α. For octrees the multi-indices $\alpha = (L, i, j, k)$ must be augmented with a level (or depth) value L where $0 \le L \le L_{\mathrm{MAX}}$. The correspondence between indices α and cells is 1–1.

The finite-differences discretization presented in the previous section for regular hexahedral grids extends in a natural way to octree grids, without any changes. There is one function value g_α associated with each leaf cell of the octree. As a result, within each cell we use g_α to discretize the function $g(x)$, and use the discretization of the gradient $\nabla g(x)$ of Eq. (18.11), where the weight $|V|_{\alpha\beta}$ of Eq. (18.12) is now the area of the common face.

We first estimate the implicit function $f(x)$ using an iterative cascading multigrid approach described in Calakli and Taubin (2011). We start by solving the problem on a much coarser level than desired using a simple conjugate gradient solver. Then use it to initialize the solution at the next level, which is then refined by the conjugate gradient solver.

We then turn our focus into estimating the color function $g(x)$ on the same level that is used to estimate the implicit function $f(x)$. We need to minimize the total energy of Eq. (18.6)

$$\mathcal{Q}(g) \approx \frac{1}{N} \sum_{\alpha} \sum_{i:p_i \in \mathcal{D}_\alpha} (g_\alpha - c_i)^2 + \frac{\mu}{|V|} \sum_{(\alpha,\beta)} w_{\alpha\beta}(g_\alpha - g_\beta)^2, \tag{18.13}$$

where $w_{\alpha\beta} = |V|_{\alpha\beta} / \Delta_{\alpha\beta}$. Note that this formulation still reduces to the solution of a linear system $BG = d$. After accumulating the elements of matrix B and vector d, for reasonably sized problems one can use a direct solver. Instead, we use an iterative linear solver, namely Gauss-Seidel method. We update one g_α value at a time by using the following update equation

$$g_\alpha = \frac{|V| \sum_{i:p_i \in \mathcal{D}_\alpha} c_i + \mu N \sum_{\beta \in \alpha^*} g_\beta w_{\alpha\beta}}{|V||\mathcal{D}_\alpha| + \mu N \sum_{\beta \in \alpha^*} w_{\alpha\beta}}, \tag{18.14}$$

where α^* are the set of multi-indices of octree leaf cells that share a common face with cell C_α, and $|\mathcal{D}_\alpha|$ is the total number of points in $\mathcal{D}_\alpha$. To compute an RGB color map, we repeat this minimization procedure for each color channel independently.

We use the Dual Marching Cubes algorithm (Schaefer and Warren 2005) to construct a polygonal approximation of the isolevel zero of the implicit function $f(x)$.

Table 18.1 The running time, the peak memory usage, and the number of triangles in the reconstructed surface of the David's head generated with different methods

Method	Time (sec)	Memory (MB)	Polygons
MPU	27	148	378,925
Poisson	43	283	319,989
D4	17	63	365,974
SSD	72	264	346,652

Dual Marching Cubes requires values of the implicit function defined at the centroids of the octree leaf cells. The computed implicit function is defined at the vertices of the primal graph. An implicit function value is computed for the centroid of each leaf cell by averaging the values associated with the eight cell corners. On the other hand, the results of the color function are already defined at centroids of the octree leaf cells, so we can directly transfer coefficients g_α to the mesh with no further function evaluation, i.e., color per vertex attribute on the final mesh.

18.6 Evaluation of Surface Reconstruction Methods

Our algorithm consists of surface reconstruction and color map estimation applied successively. The surface reconstruction step mainly follows the variational formulation presented in Smooth Signed Distance Surface Reconstruction (SSD) (Calakli and Taubin 2011). We include this section to motivate the use of SSD against Multi-Level Partition of Unity Implicits (MPU) (Ohtake et al. 2003a), Poisson Surface Reconstruction (Poisson) (Kazhdan et al. 2006), and Streaming Surface Reconstruction Using Wavelets (D4 Wavelets) (Manson et al. 2008). We evaluate these methods in terms of speed, memory, efficiency, and accuracy. We show that, in terms of the quality of reconstruction, SSD outperforms these other methods even on data sets associated with extreme complications: non-uniform sampling, sensor noise, and missing data. In addition, its performance is still comparable to these methods.

Our initial test case is the head of Michalengelo's David raw dataset of 1 million samples. This dataset is assembled from many range images acquired by a laser scanner. All methods operate on the same data set at a maximal octree depth of 8, and produce surfaces of comparable quality. Table 18.1 summarizes the performance characteristics of each algorithm. Our second test case is the Chiquita model raw dataset comprising 705,375 samples. This dataset was acquired by scanning the real world object with an inexpensive 3D structured lighting system (Crispell et al. 2006). It is an example of *non-uniformly* distributed points with many *inaccurate* normals. Figure 18.3 compares different reconstructions at a maximal octree depth of 9. MPU produces spurious surface sheets. Although D4 Wavelets performs much better, it cannot fill in gaps reasonably. Poisson, and SSD Reconstruction both result in pleasing surfaces with subtle differences. To evaluate the numerical accuracy of the reconstruction results we follow the same strategy as in Manson et al. (2008).

Fig. 18.3 Input point cloud the Chiquita model (*top-left*), and reconstructions using SSD (*top-middle* and *top-right*), MPU (*bottom-left*), Poisson (*bottom-middle*), D4 Wavelets (*bottom-right*) surface reconstruction methods

Table 18.2 Hausdorff distance between real surfaces and reconstructed surfaces. Each row is normalized by the maximum error to provide relative comparison (lower is better)

Model	MPU	Poisson	D4	SSD
Armadillo	1.0000	0.4617	0.2383	0.3514
Dragon	0.8779	1.0000	0.5301	0.6810
Horse	0.0752	0.0827	1.0000	0.0551
Igea	1.0000	0.7761	0.5701	0.4018

We first sample points from a known model, then reconstruct surfaces using each method with this point set. We then compute the Hausdorff distance between each reconstructed model and the known model using Metro tool (Cignoni et al. 1996). Table 18.2 summarizes the result. Note that, in all cases, SSD reconstruction recovers the surfaces with higher degree of accuracy than the Poisson reconstruction. And in two cases (Horse, and Igea) it also outperforms D4 Wavelets.

Fig. 18.4 Reconstruction of a building facade. *Top row*: The input point cloud, and surface geometry reconstructed by the proposed algorithm. *Middle row*: Two views from the surface and color map reconstructed by the proposed algorithm. *Bottom row*: 6 examples from the set of 14 images that are used for shape acquisition

18.7 Results

We apply our algorithm to colored oriented point clouds retrieved using the well-known multi-view stereo (MVS) pipeline consisting of two publicly available algorithms Bundler (Snavely et al. 2006), and the Patch-based MVS (PMVS) (Furukawa and Ponce 2009). The goal of multi-view stereo is to reconstruct a 3D model from images taken from known camera viewpoints. To learn the viewpoints, we use *Bundler* which takes a set of images as input and accurately estimates the camera viewpoint per each image. We then use the Patch-based MVS (PMVS) algorithm which takes the same set of images and the estimated camera parameters as input and produces 3D models represented as colored point clouds with accuracy nearly

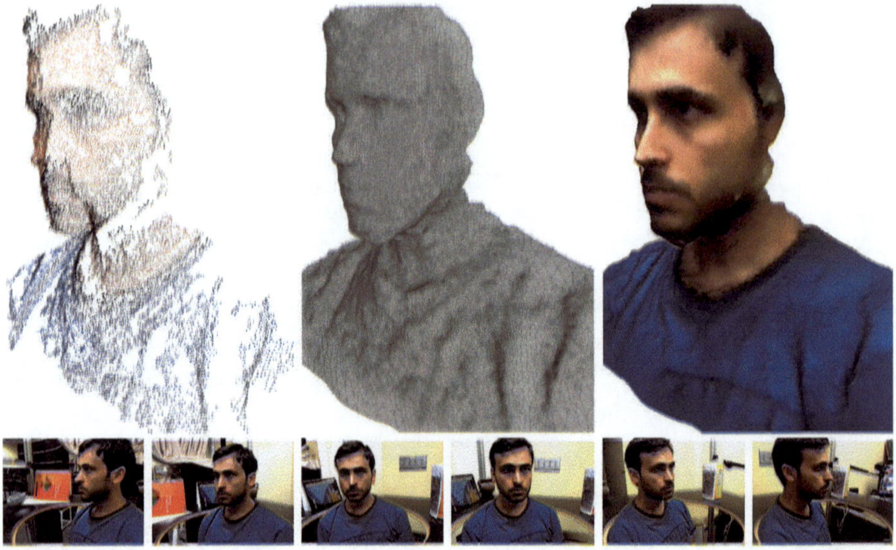

Fig. 18.5 Reconstruction of a human frontal view. *Top row*: the input point cloud (*top-left*), surface geometry (*top-middle*), and color map (*top-right*) reconstructed by the proposed algorithm. *Bottom row*: 6 images that are used for shape acquisition

comparable with laser scanners (Seitz et al. 2006). PMVS is based on the idea of correlating measurements from several images at once to derive globally consistent 3D surface samples. We use a standard digital camera for all the data sets except for the face dataset. In this case, we have to use a set of synchronized cameras as the person could move during data collection procedure. In addition, each camera is calibrated with respect to a common coordinate system.

Our initial test case is the facade of the Applied Mathematics building of Brown University raw dataset of 66,935 points retrieved from 14 photographs. Each image is captured at resolution 1282 × 854 with a standard digital camera. The proposed method results in a model consists of 77,603 polygons when a maximal octree of depth 10 is used. Figure 18.4 shows the reconstruction of the model, and the input point cloud. Our second test case is the frontal view of a human raw dataset of 12,346 points retrieved from 6 photographs. Each image is captured at resolution 1024 × 768 with a time-synchronized camera system consists of 6 cameras. The proposed method results in a model consists of 64,909 polygons when a maximal octree of depth 9 is used. Figure 18.5 shows the reconstruction of the model, and the input point cloud. Our third test case is the cuneiform tablet raw dataset of 333,401 points retrieved from 21 photographs. Each image is captured at resolution 3072 × 2304 with a standard digital camera. The proposed method results in a model consists of 1,034,663 polygons when a maximal octree of depth 11 is used. Figure 18.6 shows the reconstruction of the model, and the input point cloud. Our last test case is the footprint of a human wearing a boot raw dataset of 180,885 points. This dataset is retrieved from 11 pho-

Fig. 18.6 Reconstruction of a cuneiform tablet. *Top row*: the input point cloud (*left*), and surface geometry (*right*) reconstructed by the proposed algorithm. *Middle row*: Two views from surface and color map reconstructed by the proposed algorithm. *Bottom row*: 6 examples from the set of 21 images that are used for shape acquisition

tographs. Each image is captured at resolution 4272 × 2848. The proposed method results in a model consists of 897,273 polygons when a maximal octree of depth 11 is used. Figure 18.7 shows the reconstruction of the model, and the input point cloud.

All the experiments are conducted on a PC with a Intel Core 2 Duo 2.26 GHz processor and a 4 GB ram. A non-threaded in-core CPU implementation takes 3–15 minutes depending on the maximum depth of the tree that will be used for reconstruction. It consumes 90 % of the time for surface reconstruction, and the rest 10 %

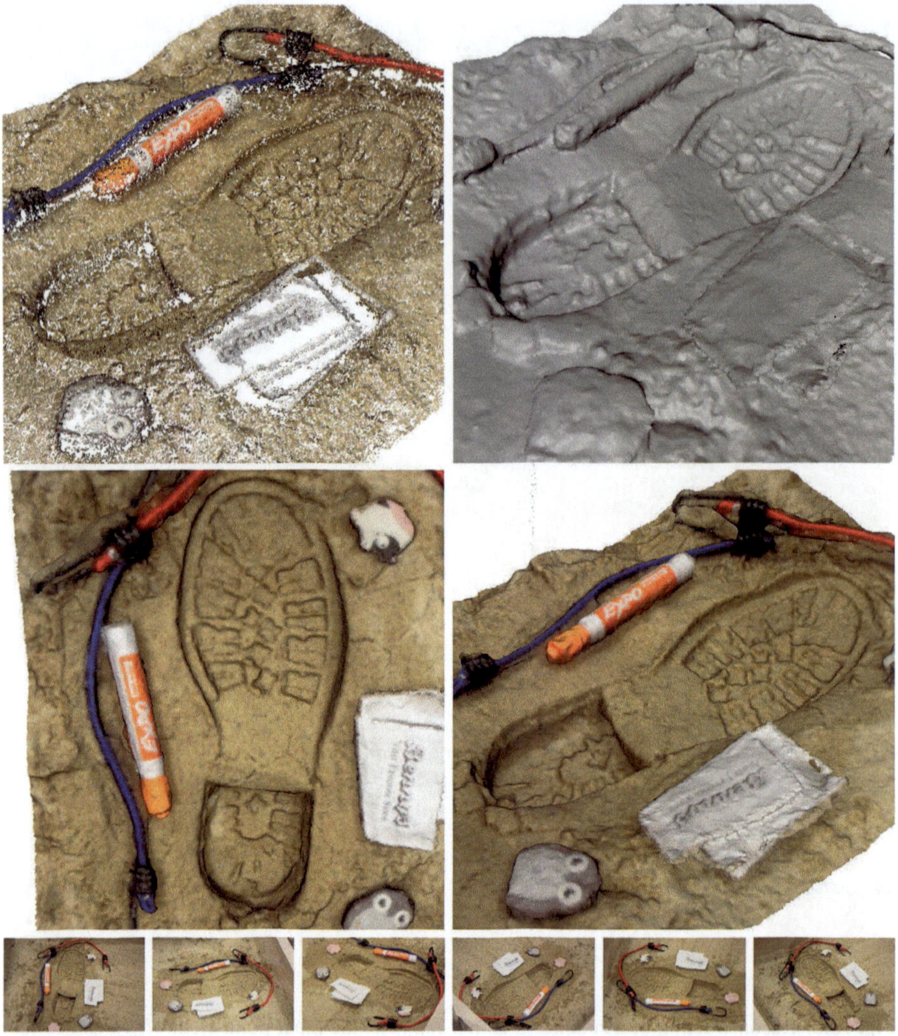

Fig. 18.7 Reconstruction of a shoe print. *Top row*: the input point cloud (*left*), and surface geometry (*right*) reconstructed by the proposed algorithm. *Middle row*: Two views from surface and color map reconstructed by the proposed algorithm. *Bottom row*: 6 examples from the set of 11 images that are used for shape acquisition

for color map reconstruction. We demonstrate that this method produces watertight surfaces with pleasing smooth color maps even on data sets with various complications: non-uniform sampling, sensor noise, and missing regions. In addition, we observe that it is quite in terms of time and memory usage.

18.8 Conclusion

This chapter presented a complete solution to the problem of reconstructing a 3D scene's surface and color map from a finite set of colored oriented points. We used an existing variational formulation for the problem of reconstructing a watertight surface defined by an implicit equation. We then extended this by introducing a new variational formulation for the problem of estimating a smooth appearance defined over the surface. We showed that a simple hybrid FE/FD discretization still reduced the problem to the solutions of sparse linear systems. A proof-of-consent implementation has been shown to produce high-quality polygon meshes with smooth color-per-vertex function.

Acknowledgments The work described herein was supported by the National Science Foundation under Grant No. IIS-0808718, CCF-0729126, and CCF-0915661.

References

Alexa, M., Behr, J., Cohen-Or, D., Fleishman, S., Levin, D., & Silva, C. (2003). Computing and rendering point set surfaces. *IEEE Transactions on Visualization and Computer Graphics*, 3–15.

Alliez, P., Cohen-Steiner, D., Tong, Y., & Desbrun, M. (2007). Voronoi-based variational reconstruction of unoriented point sets. In *Proceedings of the fifth Eurographics symposium on geometry processing* (pp. 39–48). Eurographics Association.

Bernardini, F., Mittleman, J., Rushmeier, H., Silva, C., & Taubin, G. (1999). The ball-pivoting algorithm for surface reconstruction. *IEEE Transactions on Visualization and Computer Graphics*, *5*(4), 349–359.

Boissonnat, J., & Cazals, F. (2002). Smooth surface reconstruction via natural neighbour interpolation of distance functions. *Computational Geometry*, *22*(1), 185–203.

Calakli, F., & Taubin, G. (2011). SSD: Smooth signed distance surface reconstruction. *Computer Graphics Forum*, *30*(7). http://mesh.brown.edu/ssd/.

Carr, J., Beatson, R., Cherrie, J., Mitchell, T., Fright, W., McCallum, B., & Evans, T. (2001). Reconstruction and representation of 3D objects with radial basis functions. In *Proceedings of ACM SIGGRAPH* (pp. 67–76). ACM.

Cignoni, P., Rocchini, C., & Scopigno, R. (1996). *Metro: Measuring error on simplified surfaces*. Paris, France.

Crispell, D., Lanman, D., Sibley, P., Zhao, Y., & Taubin, G. (2006). Beyond silhouettes: Surface reconstruction using multi-flash photography. In *Third international symposium on 3D data processing, visualization, and transmission (3DPVT'2006)* (pp. 405–412). IEEE.

Curless, B., & Levoy, M. (1996). A volumetric method for building complex models from range images. In *Proceedings of ACM SIGGRAPH* (pp. 303–312). New York: ACM.

Dey, T. K. (2007). *Curve and surface reconstruction: Algorithms with mathematical analysis*. New York: Cambridge University Press.

Fleishman, S., Cohen-Or, D., & Silva, C. (2005). Robust moving least-squares fitting with sharp features. *ACM Transactions on Graphics (TOG)*, *24*(3), 544–552.

Furukawa, Y., & Ponce, J. (2009). Accurate, dense, and robust multi-view stereopsis. *IEEE Transactions on Pattern Analysis and Machine Intelligence*, *32*(8).

Hoppe, H., DeRose, T., Duchamp, T., McDonald, J., & Stuetzle, W. (1992). Surface reconstruction from unorganized points. In *Proceedings of ACM SIGGRAPH* (Vol. 26, p. 71).

Kazhdan, M. (2005). Reconstruction of solid models from oriented point sets. In *Proceedings of the 3rd. Eurographics symposium on geometry processing* (p. 73). Eurographics Association.

Kazhdan, M., Bolitho, M., & Hoppe, H. (2006). Poisson surface reconstruction. In *Proceedings of the fourth Eurographics symposium on geometry processing* (pp. 61–70). Eurographics Association.

Manson, J., Petrova, G., & Schaefer, S. (2008). Streaming surface reconstruction using wavelets. *Computer Graphics Forum*, *27*(5), 1411–1420.

Ohtake, Y., Belyaev, A., Alexa, M., Turk, G., & Seidel, H. (2003a). Multi-level partition of unity implicits. *ACM Transactions on Graphics (TOG)*, *22*(3), 463–470.

Ohtake, Y., Belyaev, A., & Seidel, H. (2003b). A multi-scale approach to 3D scattered data interpolation with compactly supported basis functions. In *International conference on shape modeling and applications* (pp. 153–161).

Schaefer, S., & Warren, J. (2005). Dual marching cubes: Primal contouring of dual grids. *Computer Graphics Forum*, *24*(2), 195–201.

Schall, O., & Samozino, M. (2005). Surface from scattered points: A brief survey of recent developments. In B. Falcidieno, & N. Magnenat-Thalmann (Eds.), *1st International workshop on semantic virtual environments*, MIRALab, Villars, Switzerland (pp. 138–147).

Seitz, S. M., Curless, B., Diebel, J., Scharstein, D., & Szeliski, R. (2006). A comparison and evaluation of multi-view stereo reconstruction algorithms. In *Proc. of the 2006 IEEE computer society conference on computer vision and pattern recognition* (pp. 519–528).

Shen, C., O'Brien, J. F., & Shewchuk, J. (2004). Interpolating and approximating implicit surfaces from polygon soup. In *Proceedings of ACM SIGGRAPH* (pp. 896–904).

Snavely, N., Seitz, S., & Szeliski, R. (2006). Photo tourism: Exploring photo collections in 3d. In *ACM Transactions on Graphics* (Vol. 25, pp. 835–846).

Chapter 19
Geometric Issues of Object Manipulation in Task Animation and Virtual Reality

Daniel Thalmann

Abstract This paper reviews the geometric issues in object manipulation in virtual environments. The interaction of real and virtual humans with objects is analyzed for operations such as grasping and reaching. Aspects with regard to smart objects, grasping frameworks, large objects, multiple agents, collision detection and reaching strategies are detailed, and unsolved problems in these areas are identified.

19.1 Introduction

The requirement to model interactions between an object and an autonomous virtual human (VH) appears in most applications of computer animation and Virtual Reality (VR). Applications encompass several domains, such as: VHs living and working in virtual environments, VHs in emergency situations, virtual crowds, human factors analysis, training, education, virtual prototyping, and simulation-based design (Badler 1997). An example of an application using agent-object interactions is presented by Johnson and Rickel (1997), whose purpose is training with regard to the use of equipment in a populated virtual environment. The VH could grasp a simple object or manipulate an object, which has a role to play; a functional object or a smart object. For example, we cannot grasp a door, but we can open it. Finally, before grasping an object, the VH should reach it, which can be difficult if there are many other objects or obstacles around it.

Object interaction in virtual environments is also an active topic and many approaches are available in the literature. In this case, the area of interest is the direct interaction between the user and the environment (Bowman and Hodges 1999; Hand 1997; Poupyrev and Ichikawa 1999). A typical VR situation consists in a user trying to grasp a Virtual Object using a cyberglove. The object could also have a role to play here and become a smart object. Moreover, to feel the object would require a tactile sensation or/and a force feedback effect.

In this paper, we survey the methods we have proposed to solve the different problems in this research area.

D. Thalmann (✉)
Institute for Media Innovation, Nanyang Technological University, Singapore, Singapore
e-mail: danielthalmann@ntu.edu.sg

J. Dill et al. (eds.), *Expanding the Frontiers of Visual Analytics and Visualization*,
DOI 10.1007/978-1-4471-2804-5_19, © Springer-Verlag London Limited 2012

19.2 The Smart Object Approach

A useful approach is to model general agent-object interactions based on objects containing interaction information of various kinds: intrinsic object properties, information on how-to-interact with it, object behaviors, and expected agent behaviors. We introduced the smart object approach (Kallmann and Thalmann 1998, 1999) that extends the idea of having a database of interaction information. For each object modeled, we include the functionality of its moving parts and detailed commands describing each desired interaction, by means of a dedicated script language. The smart objects paradigm has been introduced as a feature modeling (Shah and Mäntylä 1995) approach for interactions of virtual humans with virtual objects (Goncalves et al. 2002; Kallmann and Thalmann 2002). In essence, smart objects provide not only the geometric information necessary for drawing them on the screen, but also semantic information useful for manipulation purposes. The smart objects paradigm is based on extending objects (shapes) with additional information on their semantics. Its focus is on autonomous virtual humans within virtual environments. The semantic information that a smart object carries is mainly about the behavior of the object when an interaction occurs between the object and a virtual human. By "behavior", we mean the changes in the appearance and state of an object as a result of the interaction (i.e., a virtual human opening a door). A feature modeling approach is used to include all desired information in objects. A graphical interface program permits the user to interactively specify different features in the object and save them as a script file. Fig. 19.1 shows an example.

Attributes are the primary means of specifying information on how a virtual human manipulates its environment. They convey various kinds of information (e.g., where and how to approach, to manipulate the object, or to position the hands to grasp it), animation sequences (e.g., a door opening), and general non-geometric information associated with the object (e.g., weight or material properties). The semantic information in the smart object is used by the virtual characters to perform actions on/or with the object, such as grasping it, moving it, and operating it (e.g., a machine or an elevator). Figure 19.2 shows how to define a smart object (here a CD-ROM) and how a virtual character can then use it.

Furthermore, the smart objects paradigm is focused on behavioral animation and virtual human actor-object interactions, where predefined interaction plans and finite state machines are strongly bound to the objects. This imposes a limitation on situations where direct or indirect interactions between agents and multiple objects, or simply multiple objects, are required. Peters et al. (2003) applied the smart objects approach to implementing "attentive" agents. Attention points and face descriptors are specified on objects in the modeling phase, which are then used by a gaze manager to automatically generate gaze behaviors for an agent when they need to look at an object. Three low level gaze functions are used: glance, look, and stare.

Making virtual characters, especially virtual humans, capable of manipulating objects usually requires solutions to two closely related issues: the specification of

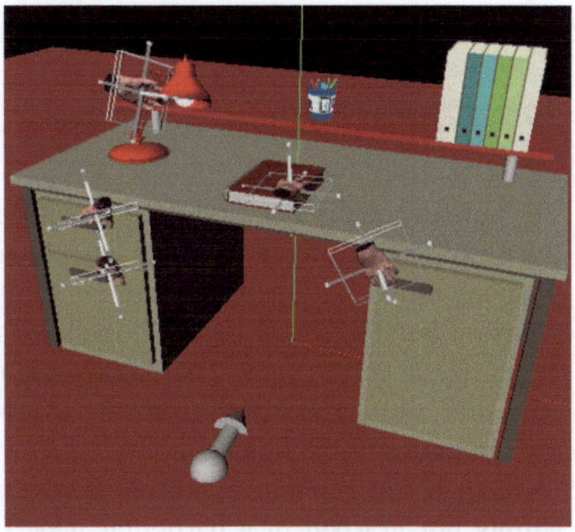

Fig. 19.1 Example of smart objects

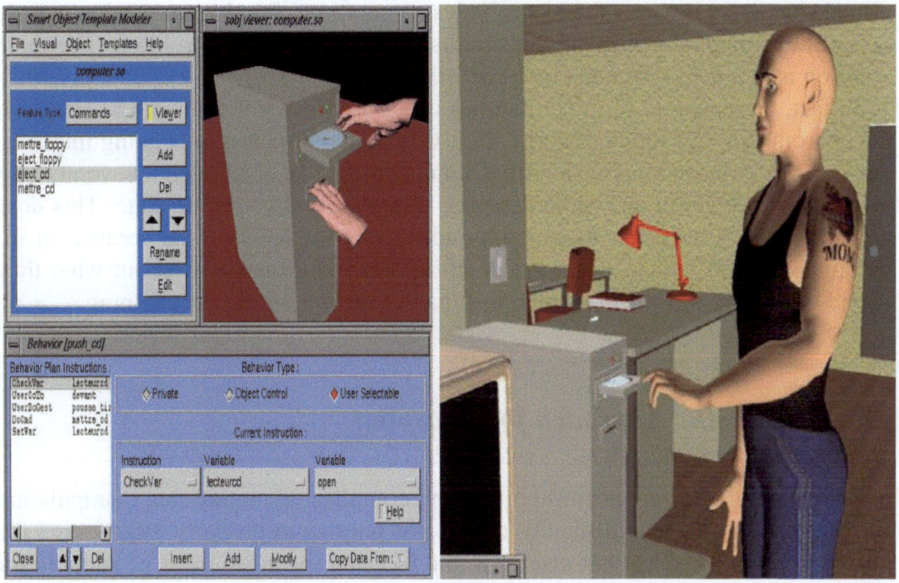

Fig. 19.2 Modeling and simulation phase for a DVD smart object

object behavior and its reflection through animation. The former usually takes place on a more abstract level, whereas the latter is mainly concerned with generation of valid and believable motion for humans and objects. There are works in the literature that have addressed both together, or separately.

19.3 The Grasping Problem

19.3.1 Introduction

The human hand is a complicated articulated structure with 27 bones. Not only must the movements of these joints be calculated, but the reaching motion of the arm and the body must also be considered. For real-time performance with many agents, fast collision-detection and inverse kinematics algorithms (Tolani et al. 2000) will be necessary in most cases. The calculation of the hand and body postures is not the only difficulty in grasping: realistic grasping also requires significant input about the semantics of the object.

Even if the geometric and physical constraints permit, sometimes an object is simply not grasped in a particular way. For example, a door handle must not be grasped by the neck section if the goal is to turn it. A fully automatic grasping algorithm that only takes the geometry of the object into account cannot always come up with solutions that are satisfactory. Fortunately, the grasping problem for virtual characters is easier than its robotics counterpart. Simply put, we do not have to be as accurate and physical constraints are much less of a problem. The main criterion is that the grasp must look realistic.

In fact, the apparent physical realities of a virtual environment can be very different from those of the real world, with very different constraints being imposed. For example, we can imagine a virtual human holding an object that is several times his size and weight in air, while grasping it at a small area on the edge. This does not conflict with the previous examples addressing the reality issue because an autonomous virtual human in a virtual setting has more questions about what they intend to do with the object (semantics) than the actual physics of grasping.

19.3.2 Heuristic Approach for Grasping

Grasping is perhaps the most important and complicated motion that manipulation of objects involves. The difficulty comes not only from properly "wrapping" the fingers around the object but also from the fact that the grasp must be suitable for the intended manipulation. In Cutkosky (1989), a classification of the hand postures commonly used for grasping in manufacturing tasks is given. One of the earlier works on grasping that uses this classification to automatically generate grasping motions is the approach we described in Mas et al. (1997).

This approach is based on three steps:

Heuristic grasping decision. Based on a grasp taxonomy, we proposed a completely automatic grasping system (Mas and Thalmann 1994) for synthetic actors. In particular, the system can decide to use a pinch when the object is too small to be grasped by more than two fingers or to use a two-handed grasp when the object is too large. Figure 19.3a shows the taxonomy.

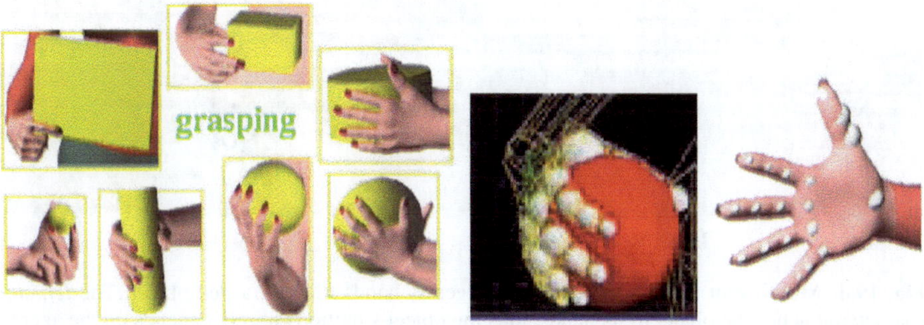

(a) (b) (c)

Fig. 19.3 (**a**) Grasping configurations for heuristic decision (**b**) sensors on a ball (**c**) hand with sensors

Inverse kinematics to find the final arm posture. Inverse kinematics is also commonly used for creation of reaching motions for articulated structures (Baerlocher 2001; Tolani et al. 2000; Wang and Verriest 1998), but it is still difficult to obtain realistic full-body postures without substantial tweaking. On the other hand, database-driven methods (Wiley and Hahn 1997) cope better with full body postures. These methods are based on capturing motions for reaching inside a discrete and fixed volumetric grid around the actor. The reaching motion for a specific position is obtained through interpolation of the motions assigned to the neighboring cells.

Multisensor hand. Our approach (Huang et al. 1995) is adapted from the use of proximity sensors in robotics (Espiau and Boulic 1985), the sensor-actuator networks (van de Panne and Fiume 1993), and our own work on human grasping. In our work the sphere multisensors have both touch and length sensor properties, and have been found very efficient for synthetic actor grasping problem. Multisensors are considered as a group of objects attached to the articulated figure. A sensor is activated for any collision with other objects or sensors. Here we select sphere sensors for their efficiency in collision detection. Figures 19.3b and 19.3c show the multisensors.

19.3.3 Large Objects and Multiple Agents

For large objects, such as furniture, grasping simultaneously involves two or more persons. Therefore, we focused on a multi-agent grasp action (Emering et al. 2000) for encumbering objects (see Fig. 19.4). As the object's weight and geometry is distributed over several hand support points of different agents, the heuristic motion planning schemes have to be different from the ones for an object grasp performed by a single individual.

For large objects which we want to grasp with this action we need power grasps. In contrast to precision grasps, power-grasps seek to maximize hand/object contact

Fig. 19.4 Multi-agent grasping. Sticking the agents' hands to the grasped object. The *left-side* character attaches the object to its hands, thus the object's motion entirely depends on the agent's motion. The *right-side* character uses the holding-action in order to maintain the hands at the object

in order to exert maximal force onto the object. The required grasp-patterns require less finger-mobility but try to have palm contact with the object. As a consequence we can reasonably assume that finger-flexion control will be sufficient. Therefore we opted for a hand/object-wrapping algorithm that entirely relies on finger-sensor information, i.e. without a grasp pattern database. Each sensor controls one finger-flexion degree of freedom. The fingers close or open, depending on the finger-object collisions detected by the sensors. In Huang et al. (1995), the hand first adopts the chosen grasp-pattern defined in the database and then closes the fingers until the sensors detect a collision. In our approach, the fingers might also open, depending on the collision detections. A similar sensor-oriented approach has been described in Rezzonico et al. (1996). Our goal was to correct finger/object penetrations and the detection of force exerted onto the object by analyzing the finger motion. Similarly to Huang et al. (1995), we use a set of twenty sensors, without a palm sensor.

For the reasons explained previously, we require power grasps with palm contact, if possible, and need to introduce a palm sensor. However, we do not use sensors at the fingers' base. Each sensor controls the proximal flexion DOF, but there are no proximal flexion DOF that could be controlled for hypothetical finger-based sensors. Therefore, our approach only requires sixteen sensors per hand. All sensors are spherical and detect collisions with spherical or box-shaped objects. The sensor configuration is illustrated in Fig. 19.5.

When a sensor detects a collision with the object to be grasped, we open the associated DOF. By 'opening' we understand the increase (or decrease) of the joint value results in the opening of the corresponding finger. Similarly, we 'close' the associated DOF if this does not generate new object-collisions. The amount of opening/ closing is regulated by a dichotomous trial-and-error approach. The sensors are grouped according to a defined rank (Fig. 19.5). A rank is a priority number that increases towards the finger tips. Sensors with a same rank perform in parallel and low-ranked sensors perform prior to higher ranked sensors. The idea is to start closing the hand at the finger bases and test if this generates object collisions at the fingers. Then we continue closing the hand at the mid-fingers and test if this generates object collisions at the remaining finger tips. At the final stage we bend the finger tips in order to approach the object's surface as close as possible. This algorithm exploits the hierarchical model of the hand because joint variations at a given

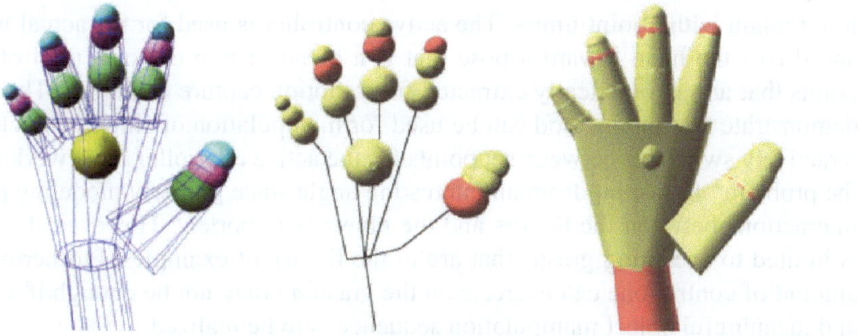

(a) (b) (c)

Fig. 19.5 (**a**) Sensor ranks that are used in the finger/object collision-correction algorithm (**c**) hand palm-view with object-collision detection sensors

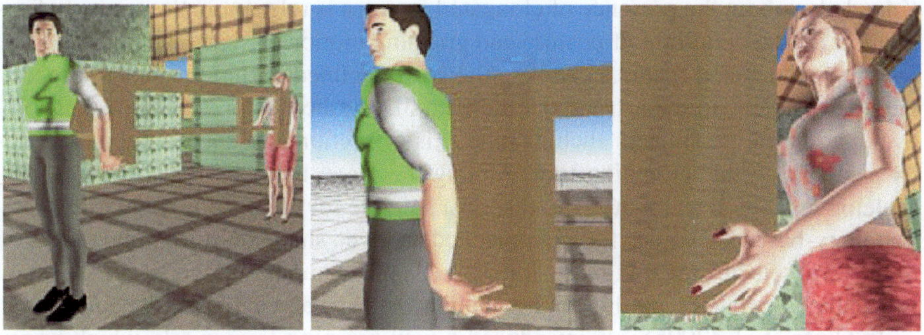

(a) (b) (c)

Fig. 19.6 (**a**) Object hold by two VHs, (**b**) details of the grasping for the first VH, (**c**) details of the grasping for the second VH

node only influence the nodes of the sub-tree. For example, a large object might be grasped frontally by the first VH and from behind by the second VH (see Fig. 19.6).

Another approach used in the Jack system (Badler et al. 1993; Phillips and Badler 1988) that is based on Cutkosy's grasp classification (Cutkosky 1989) is described in Douville et al. (1996). This approach uses specialized controllers for each different type of grasp to close the fingers. It uses parallel transition networks (PaT-Nets) (Trias et al. 1996) to control each finger. Transitions in the PaT-Nets are triggered by collisions between the fingers and the object. Different PaT-Nets are used to simulate different grasp types; the differing responses of the different PaT-Nets actually define how the grasp is to take place.

Another approach in Pollard and Zordan (2005) takes the interactions between the fingers and the object into account by means of dynamics simulation. This work proposes passive and active controllers for the hand. The passive controller is constructed to attract the hand posture toward a naturally comfortable pose and to force it to remain within joint limits. The active controller is used for the actual grasping and drives the hand toward a pose that is a blend of two out of a total of six set points that are automatically extracted from motion capture examples. The authors demonstrate that the method can be used for manipulation of simple objects by interactively switching between set points for the active controller. This work looks at the problem of grasping from an interesting angle since properly modeling physical interactions between the fingers and the object is important. However, the method is limited to executing grasps that are in the library of examples. Furthermore, the amount of control one can exercise on the grasping may not be enough if a specific and meaningful object manipulation sequence is to be realized.

19.3.4 The Tubular Approach

Knowledge about the presence of elongated features is relevant in the context of animation for the definition of posture and grasping motion for virtual humans. While tubular or elongated features can be quite easily defined during the design process, their automatic extraction from unstructured 3D meshes is not a trivial task. Moreover, geometric parameters such as tube axis or section size should be made readily available to the animation tool. Among the many methods for shape analysis, skeleton extraction techniques are the most suitable for identifying tubular features. Topology-based skeletons, for example, code a given shape by storing the evolution of the level sets of a mapping function defined on its boundary. A geometric skeleton is usually associated with this coding, defined by the barycenters of the contours.

In Ciger et al. (2005), we introduced a new grasping framework, which brings together a tubular feature-classification algorithm, a hand grasp posture generation algorithm, and an animation framework for human-object interactions. This unique combination is capable of handling grasping tasks within the proper context of virtual human object manipulation. This is very important because how an object is to be grasped depends strongly on how it is be used. The method has the advantage that it can work with relatively complex objects, where manual approximation with simple geometrical primitives may not be possible or practical. Furthermore, the method supports many intuitive parameters for controlling the grasping posture, such as the finger spread or the thumb configuration. Since the grasp parameters are specified as ranges, it is possible to generate a different posture each time a VH attempts to grasp an object, depending on the current configuration of the VH.

The algorithm to detect tubular features is called Plumber, and it is a specialized shape-classification method for triangle meshes. The Plumber method analyzes the shape of an object by studying how the intersection of spheres centered at the mesh vertices evolve while the sphere radius changes. For example, for a thin limb, the curve of intersection between the mesh and a sphere will be simply connected for a small radius and then will rapidly split into two components when the radius increases and becomes greater than the tube size. A detailed description of the shape analysis technique which uses intersecting sphere and of the Plumber method can

Fig. 19.7 Plumber method: (a) identification of limb vertices, (b) extraction of their connected components and medial loop, (c) iteration, (d) tube and a cap (black) found at this scale

be found in Mortara et al. (2004a,b). We summarize here the main properties of Plumber and describe how the geometric parameters are associated with elongated features. Plumber can identify tubular features whose section and axis can be arbitrarily sized. The size of the tube is kept as a constraint during the identification process. Moreover, since the shape is analyzed using a set of spheres of increasing radius, the recognition follows a multi-resolution schema.

Given a sphere of radius R, Plumber performs the following steps:

1. identify seed-tube regions; these regions will produce one intersection area with the sphere, with two boundary curves of intersection (see Fig. 19.7a);
2. shrink each of the two selected intersection curves along the surface to the medial-loop, whose points are nearly equidistant from the two border loops (see Fig. 19.7b);
3. expand-back the medial-loop by sweeping the extent of the shape in both directions. More precisely, at each iteration we place a sphere of radius R in the barycenter of the new medial loops. If the intersection between the sphere and the surface generates two loops, mesh vertices inside the sphere are marked as visited;
4. the procedure is repeated in both directions until:
    a. no more loops are found, or more than one loop is found on not-visited regions;
    b. the new loop lies on triangles that are already part of another tube, or the length of the new loop exceeds a predefined threshold.
5. the tube skeleton is extracted by joining the loops' barycenters.

As shown in Fig. 19.8, tubular features are recognized at different scales and their geometric description is computed to accommodate interacting features. For the purpose of extracting grasping sites (such as handles) for a virtual human, the radius value can be set with respect to hand anthropometric measures.

After the location of seed tubular regions and the computation of the medial loop, the tubes are recovered by expanding the loop by controlled procedure which, at each step, extends the center-line and at the same time ensures that the surface is tubular around it.

Finally, the barycenters of the medial loops are joined to define the tube skeleton.

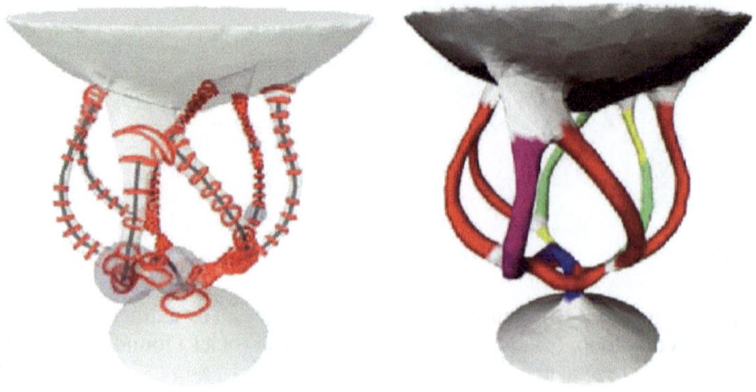

(a) (b)

Fig. 19.8 Tubular features recognized by Plumber on a complex model: (**a**) tube axis and loops, (**b**) tubes colored with respect to their scale

19.3.5 Combining Smart Objects and the Tubular Grasp

Our primary goal is to address grasping issues for VH object manipulation. For this, we propose the flow comprised of the steps given below:

1. Given an object, the tubular or elongated features of an object are recognized and a list of cross-sections is associated to the features.
2. During smart object design, the designer selects the sections of the extracted features that are relevant for grasping. Additional grasping parameters are specified for each of these sections.
3. At run-time, grasping is performed using the data specified in the smart object, as a part of the object manipulation sequence.

The manual specification of the grasp parameters in the second step makes the approach semi-automatic. While we can attempt to derive these parameters automatically, it is very difficult to do so only based on the geometrical properties of the object. To determine which tubular sections of complex object are of relevance to grasping, we need additional input on how the object is to be manipulated. For example, a teapot containing hot tea to be poured into a cup should normally be grasped by the handle, not the neck. The current state of the art in artificial intelligence does not offer a general, working solution for this problem yet, so our practical solution is to make the teapot a smart object and specify the required semantic information during its design. As our approach uses smart objects for simulating manipulation, the grasping parameters will be stored together with other attributes of the object, which are also specified in the design phase.

During the design phase, the designer is presented with the Plumber output and first identifies the tubular regions of the object that are relevant to grasping. These exist as sets of (approximated) cylinders that are connected in a chain configuration. For each such region, the designer then defines the following parameters:

- *Wrist position/orientation* relative to the tubular section. Both can be specified as either fixed or a range of values.
- *Touch tolerance*, essentially specifying how much a finger can "sink" into the object. This value sets the threshold in the capsule intersection algorithm.
- *Thumb configuration* can be specified as closed or on-the-side. If specified as closed, the grasping algorithm will try to make the thumb encircle the section to be grasped, just like the other fingers. If specified as on-the-side, the algorithm will try to make the thumb touch one of the tubes, in a parallel orientation.
- *Finger spread* specifies the angle in between each of the four fingers, effectively defining how much the fingers will be spread.
- *Finger selection* specifies which fingers will be involved in the grasp. These parameters are stored in the object description file, together with all the other attributes. There can be multiple sets of parameters per region.

19.3.6 Collision Detection

Our real-time grasping algorithm is based on approximating the parts of a tubular section and the finger segments with capsules. A capsule (or capped cylinder) is the set of points at a fixed distance from a line segment. Two capsules intersect if and only if the distance between capsule line segments is smaller or equal to the sum of the capsule radii.

Given a finger segment and a tubular region, we first find out which part of the tubular region is most likely to intersect with the finger segment. We accomplish this by intersecting the finger plane with each tube center line segment.

We define the finger plane as the plane perpendicular to the axis of rotation of the distal finger joints. It is dependent on the finger spread parameter.

We then run the capsule intersection test to determine whether the tube and the finger segment intersect.

To determine whether two capsules intersect, we need to compute the minimum distance between points on two capsule line segments. The parametric equations by the line segments are given by $\vec{L}_0(s) = \vec{B}_0 + {}_s\vec{M}_0$ for $s \in [0, 1]$, and $\vec{L}_1(t) = \vec{B}_1 + {}_t\vec{M}_1$ for $t \in [0, 1]$. The squared distance function for any two points on the line segments is $Q(s,t) = |\vec{L}_0(s) - \vec{L}_1(t)|^2$ for $(s,t) \in [0, 1]^2$. The function is quadratic in s and t, and given by

$$Q(s,t) = as^2 + 2bst + ct^2 + 2ds + 2et + f,$$

where $a = \vec{M}_0 \Box \vec{M}_0$, $b = -\vec{M}_0 \Box \vec{M}_1$, $c = M_1 \Box M_1$, $d = M_0 \Box (\vec{B}_0 - \vec{B}_1)$, $e = -\vec{M}_1 \Box (\vec{B}_0 - \vec{B}_1)$, and $f = (\vec{B}_0 - \vec{B}_1) \Box (\vec{B}_0 - \vec{B}_1)$.

The goal is to minimize $Q(s,t)$ over the unit square $[0, 1]^2$. Q is a continuously differentiable function. Therefore the minimum occurs either at an interior point of the square where its gradient is equal to $(0, 0)$ or at a point on the boundary of the square. Eberly and Schneider (2002) includes further details on how this minimization is performed.

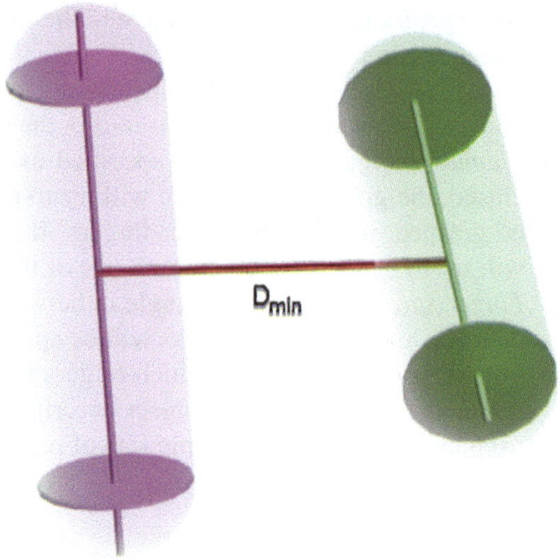

Fig. 19.9 Capsule intersection test

For grasping, we need to determine whether the finger segment "touches" the object, therefore the test method described above is not adequate since it merely reports intersections. Therefore, we introduce the touch tolerance into the capsule collision test inequality as a tolerance value. Let R_{sum} be the sum of the capsule radii, D_{min} the minimum distance between the capsule line segments, and ϵ the touch tolerance (Fig. 19.9).

We can distinguish between three cases:

- $D_{min} > R_{sum}$: The finger segment does not touch the object and it is outside the object.
- $R_{sum} \geq D_{min} > (R_{sum} - \epsilon)$: The finger segment touches the object.
- $(R_{sum} - \epsilon) \geq D_{min}$: The finger segment is inside the object.

In fact, the touch tolerance value implies a relaxed suggestion on how much the capsules can sink into each other. This, in turn, can create the impression of a tighter or looser grasp on the object. This is an advantage of using the capsule intersection test for the collision detection calculations.

The final grasp posture is computed by executing a dichotomy search (similar to the one in Magnenat-Thalmann et al. (1988) in the configuration space of the hand. This space is defined by the range of wrist position and orientation plus the ranges of orientation of the finger joints. Fortunately, its dimensions can be reduced due to the anatomy of the hand (Fig. 19.10):

- The metacarpophalangeal (MCP) joints are biaxial joints, with two degrees of freedom.
- The distal interphalangeal (DIP) and proximal interphalangeal (PIP) joints are uniaxial (hinge type) joints, with only one degree of freedom around the lateral axis.
- We can assume that the DIP joint angle is a function of the PIP joint angle, further reducing the dimensions.

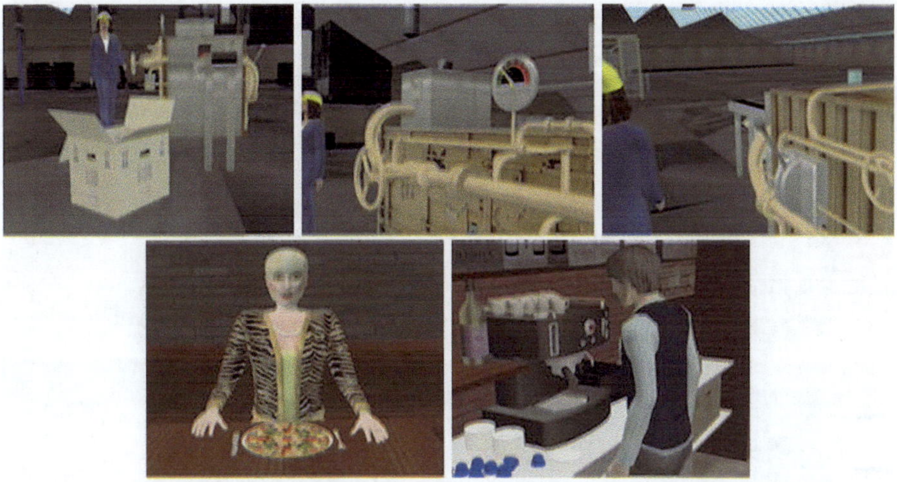

Fig. 19.10 Examples of tubular grasping

19.4 The Reaching Problem

An issue commonly encountered in virtual character animation is the problem of collisions with the environment. This problem is common to locomotion and object manipulation. Most animation algorithms (e.g., inverse kinematics) operate only on the virtual character and do not take the environment into account. When these motions are played, collisions between the virtual human and the scene may occur, detracting from the believability of the virtual environment. If care is taken during the design stage, the probability of collisions happening can be reduced; however, it is not possible to completely eliminate them, especially if we are not able to directly control what is happening in the virtual environment (e.g., if virtual characters are present).

In the field of robotics, researchers have been working on motion-planning methods for robots to avoid collisions (Latombe 1991). These methods can be applied to virtual characters, but a virtual character is an articulated structure with many degrees of freedom; therefore the dimensionality of the search space is very high. Methods based on probabilistic roadmaps (Kavraki et al. 1994; LaValle 1998) are particularly suitable for structures of this complexity. A probabilistic roadmap is a data structure (graph) that is used to capture the connectivity of the search space. Nodes in the roadmap correspond to randomly sampled configurations of the robot (e.g., joint angles). An edge between two nodes in the roadmap means that the robot is able to move between corresponding configurations by means of a local planner. Among these, visibility-based roadmap (Simon et al. 2000) construction techniques aim at reducing the number of nodes while the rapidly exploring random trees (RRT) (Kuffner and LaValle 2000; LaValle 1998) focus on sufficiently exploring the configuration space at the expense of increasing the number of nodes.

The latest trend in motion planning for virtual characters is the use of motion capture data together with roadmap techniques. In Choi et al. (2003), the authors

Fig. 19.11 Reaching examples

attempt to solve the problem of biped locomotion by using randomly sampled feet positions to construct the roadmap, which is augmented afterward with a posture transition graph. Nodes in the roadmap are connected using data from input motion clips. In Kallmann et al. (2003), our motion-planning algorithms are based on probabilistic roadmaps and used to control 22 degrees of freedom (DOFs) of human-like characters in interactive applications. The main purpose is the automatic synthesis of collision-free reaching motions for both arms, with automatic column control and leg flexion. Generated motions are collision free, in equilibrium, and respect articulation range limits. In order to deal with the high (22) dimension of the configuration space, the random distribution of configurations is biased to favor postures most useful for reaching and grasping. Figure 19.11 shows examples.

In addition, there are extensions to interactively generate object manipulation sequences: a probabilistic inverse kinematics solver for proposing goal postures matching predesigned grasps; dynamic update of roadmaps when obstacles change position; online planning of object location transfer; and an automatic stepping control to enlarge the character's reachable space. The work in Yamane et al. (2004) also focuses on the problem of object manipulation. The path of the object to be moved is computed using the RRT algorithm (Fig. 19.12). An inverse kinematics algorithm generates poses that match the object position and orientation. Using soft constraints, it also biases the poses towards those in a posture database. As

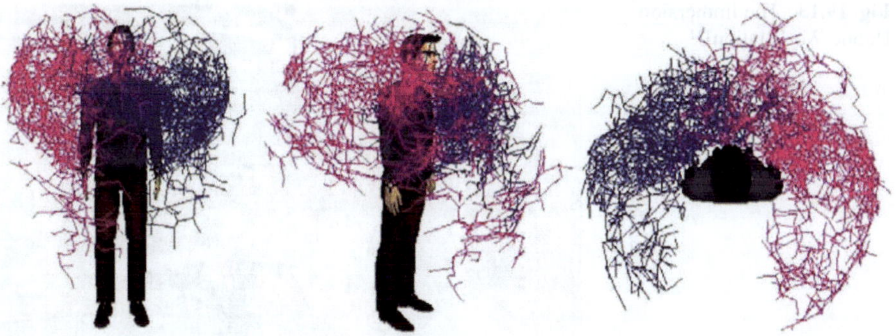

Fig. 19.12 RRT algorithm

commonly seen with many virtual humans motion planning methods, some postprocessing steps are used to increase the realism of the generated motions. The authors aim to reduce the dimensionality of the configuration space by planning only for the position and orientation of the object being manipulated.

Most existing work targeting motion planning for virtual humans assumes that the virtual environment is static. However, if motion planning is to be used for object manipulation, then it is important to consider the dynamics of the environment. Possible changes in the workspace can be included as additional dimensions in the configuration space, but a large number of dimensions is undesirable since it will reduce planning performance. To avoid this, dynamic roadmaps (DRM) can be used. For example, the work of Kallmann and Mataric (2004) proposes a method to construct a dynamic roadmap (Leven and Hutchinson 2000) on top of an RRT planner, for application to a humanoid robot.

19.5 Grasping in VR

19.5.1 Introduction

The role of the hands can be divided into two groups: feeling and interacting. In this section we will focus mainly on interaction, i.e. on the action that occurs when one or two hands have an effect upon one or more objects (and vice-versa). To enable the action of the hands on an object, we need:

- A system for acquiring the posture of the hands. Indeed, the posture is really important for manipulation, because it allows specific grasping of particular objects.
- A system for tracking the position and orientation of the hands in the 3D space. The orientation of the wrist is important and could even be considered as part of hand posture. If we cannot orient the hand, some objects are impossible to grasp.
- A workspace allowing to reach any position of the space close to the chest.

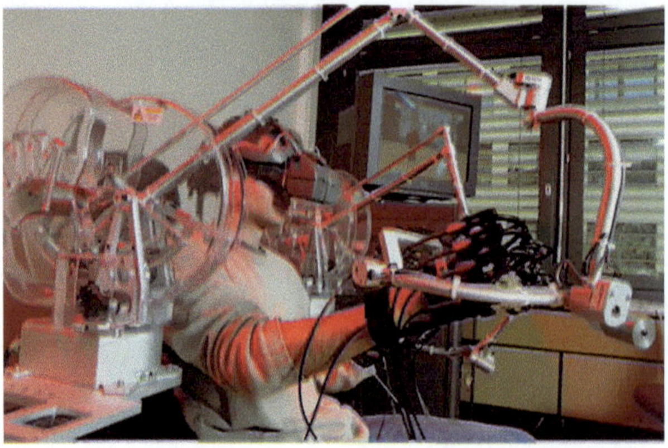

Fig. 19.13 The Immersion Haptic Workstation™

To enable the second part of the assertion, i.e. the action of an object on the hands (which is also related to feeling), we need:

- A system for simulating proprioception on the fingers and on the palm. Indeed, the force feedback prevents user's fingers to penetrate into the objects. Moreover, it provides added information about the nature of a virtual object, and finally it eases the grasping by offering the feeling of contact which is difficult to obtain only with visual/audio feedback.
- For the same reasons, we need a system for applying force feedback on the hands.

19.5.2 Haptic Feedback

Our experience (Ott et al. 2010) is based on the Immersion Haptic Workstation as presented in Fig. 19.13. The organization of the software system is shown in Fig. 19.14.

There are two approaches for two-handed force feedback computation: the direct mapping and the proxy approach.

19.5.2.1 Direct Mapping

Direct mapping consists of positioning a virtual interaction point at the same position as the device itself (hard link). This is the most trivial solution and seems also to be the easiest to implement (but we will show later that it is finally not the case). The calibrated position, rotation and posture of the hands are directly mapped onto the virtual hand. The hand model is thus composed of collision geometries and a skeletal animated visual mesh that uses skinning techniques for increasing realism. The idea behind this technique is to compute collisions between the hands and the virtual objects and to apply a realistic force-feedback for avoiding the collisions.

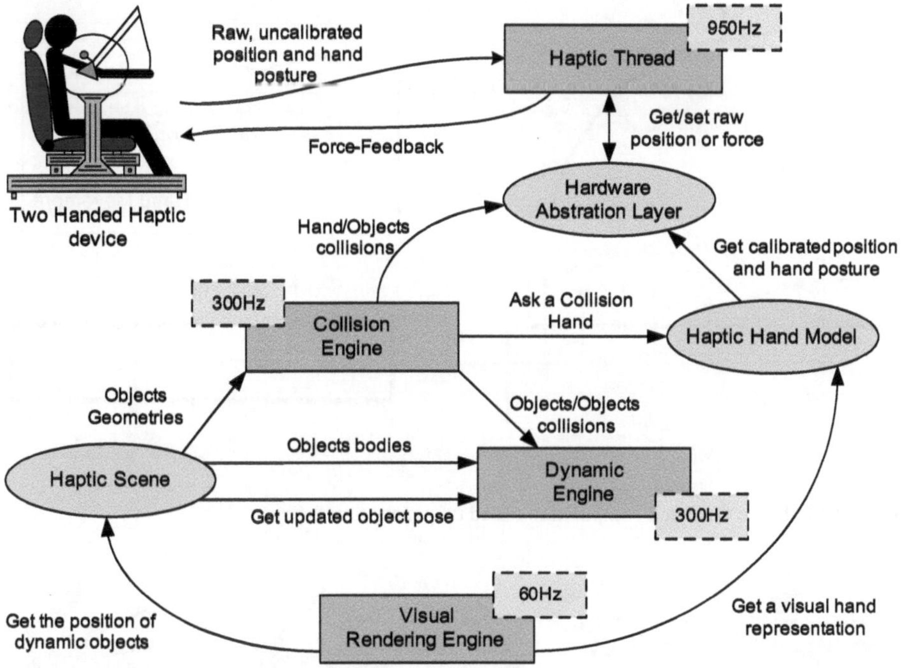

Fig. 19.14 General organization of the haptic software

As already mentioned, the collision detector returns if and where two objects collides. This second information is used to compute the force feedback. For example, if the fingertip enters into a table, two points are returned:

- The deepest point of the phalanx into the table (P_D in Fig. 19.15)
- Another point P_n laying on the table surface that is the closest as possible of P_D

The vector $P_D P_0$ determines the direction of the force feedback, and its norm is used to compute the magnitude of the reaction force. This method gives the impression that an elastic with a zero rest length is link between P_n and the fingertip resulting in a force $F = -k\Delta$. As for every virtual elastics, it is possible to change the spring constant k. In order to avoid the resonance, due to the fact that the user's fingertip is oscillating between a "inside-object"/"outside-object" state, it is also possible to add a damping factor d for smoothing the force magnitude: $F = -(k\Delta + d\Delta')$. In fact, damping is critically important, due to its role in counteracting the energy generation from errors introduced by sensing and discrete time.

The first difficulty with this method is to deal with user's movement. Figure 19.15 presents three particular cases. The first one Fig. 19.15a, shows the resulting force feedback when the user displaces his hand on the surface of a spherical object. We can observe that the force seems to be smooth and the variation of direction gives the impression that the object is a sphere. However, the two other examples show a hand moving on the surface of a table (see Figs. 19.15b and 19.15c) and include

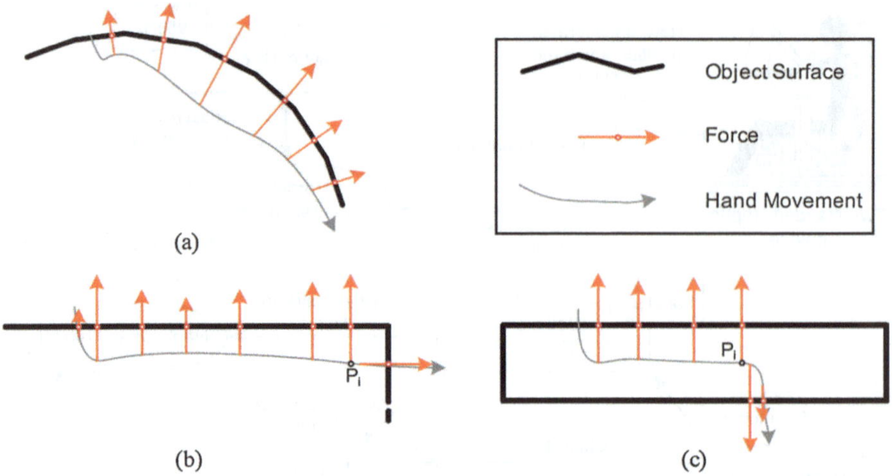

Fig. 19.15 Force feedback computation based on penetration distance

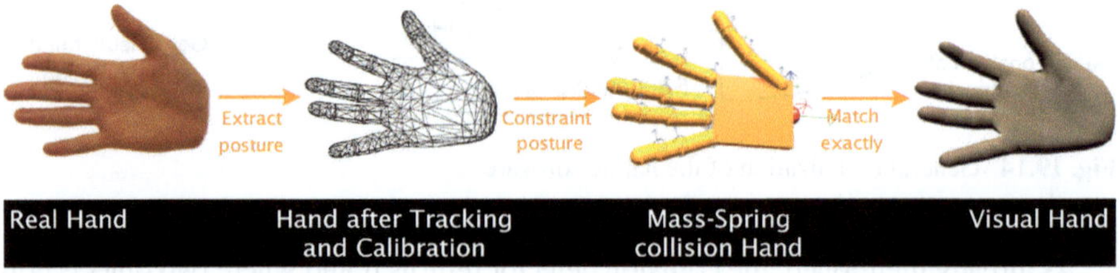

Fig. 19.16 The three hand models

force continuity breaks at particular points P_i. They are due to the fact that the collision detector returns the closest point to P_i laying on the object surface. We can imagine many solutions to avoid this specific problem, but in fact, each solution will present an inconsistency in a particular context.

19.5.2.2 Proxy Approach

This technique consists of using a proxy-based method (Zilles and Salisbury 1995). A proxy is weakly linked to the position of the device, i.e. the Haptic Workstation. Basically, it is based on three hand models (see Fig. 19.16):

- The Tracked Hand (shown in wireframe on the figure). It is in fact the virtual hand skeleton created after calibration. It is supposed to be the exact representation of the real hand position orientation and posture into the Virtual Environment. It is of course not the case, but we assume that the matching is correct.
- The Proxy (Volumes shown on the figure), which is a mass-spring-damper system that has the shape of the hands. Each phalanx and the palm is composed of

a collision geometry, and has also dynamic properties. These elements are linked together with motorized joints parameterized with springs and damping coefficient.
- The Visual Hand. This is the hand that is visually rendered and the only one visible. It is easily created using the visual rendering engine (Peternier et al. 2006).

For each hand, the idea is to couple a proxy hand to the tracked hand using a set of virtual linear and angular springs. As a result of the dynamic simulation, the spring-hand tends to follow the tracked-hand. The visual hand displayed to the user reflects the spring-hand configuration.

This approach follows the "proxy" method proposed for the Phantom (a single-point interaction device), extending it to the whole hand. It has been firstly described by Borst and Indugula (2005): they applied it to the CyberGrasp™ force feedback device which is also a component of the Haptic Workstation™.

It solves the problem of interpenetration between the visual hands and the environment because the spring-hands adapt their pose on the surfaces of the objects. Spring-Hands have basically two constraints:

- A soft constraint to match the best as possible the configuration of the tracked hands. This is achieved by applying specific force and torques on the linear and angular springs.
- A hard constraint to avoid penetration within virtual objects. This is achieved simply by activating the collision detection between the phalanxes/palm rigid bodies and the objects of the Virtual Environment.

19.5.3 Creating Geometric and Dynamic Environments

When creating various applications that have an extensive use of haptic features, the programmers (creators of the application) often face an important problem: the lack of haptic information about the 3D models. The common editing tools for creating Virtual Environments do not always provide the adequate functionalities for adding this kind of information.

In this context, it appears to be necessary to give the opportunity to the haptic programmer to augment the visual Virtual Environment by using an authoring tool, the Haptic Scene Creator. The complexity of a visual mesh requires its decomposition in low level primitives in order to speed up the collision detection. Obviously, this decomposition cannot be done automatically, because it strongly depends on the targeted application and desired level of detail. For this purpose, the Haptic Scene Creator application is a graphical tool that supports the haptic augmentation of any Virtual Environment loadable in our visual rendering engine. It is very intuitive, simple to learn and provides useful automated features to simplify and accelerate the task.

The designer should be able to select visual objects in order to "augment" them. Once selected, the user can manipulate information which is relevant for our dynamic engine and collision detection system.

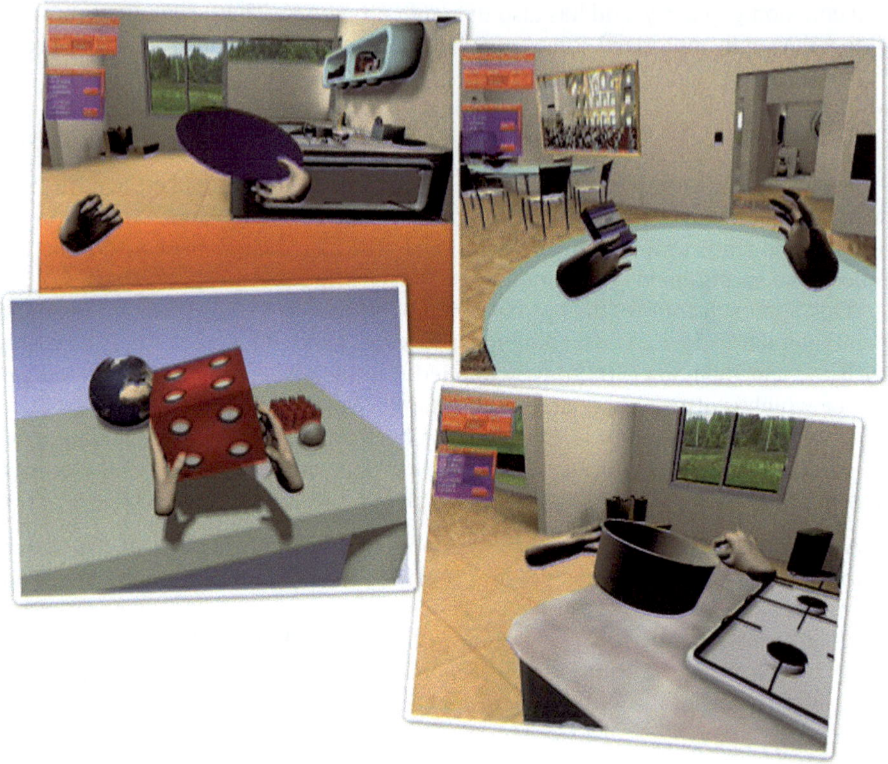

Fig. 19.17 Manipulation and interaction with a haptic house

The dynamic engine needs information related to the "mass" of an object. We remind that the "mass", or body, includes the real mass (or density), the center of gravity and the inertia tensor. Of course the mass/density is easily parameterizable in the editor, but we preferred to hide the inertia tensor to the designer to keep the tool intuitive and accessible. In fact, the center of gravity and the tensor matrix can be computed knowing the size, the position and the density of the geometries linked to the object. Unless some special effects are desired, it provides a reasonable approximation. By automating these computations, the designer will also be able to focus on higher level tasks.

The collision detection system needs to know the shape of an object. Of course, the shape is clearly defined in its visual description. However, using this information only is by far too complex for the computation of the collisions (Ericson 2005). Thus, objects should be approximated with simple geometric primitives (boxes, spheres, capsules). Later on we add more complex geometries such as convex meshes and penetration maps. These geometries are not displayed during the simulation, but it is necessary to visualize them in the editor. Moreover, for each collision geometry linked to an object, its material properties must be parameter-

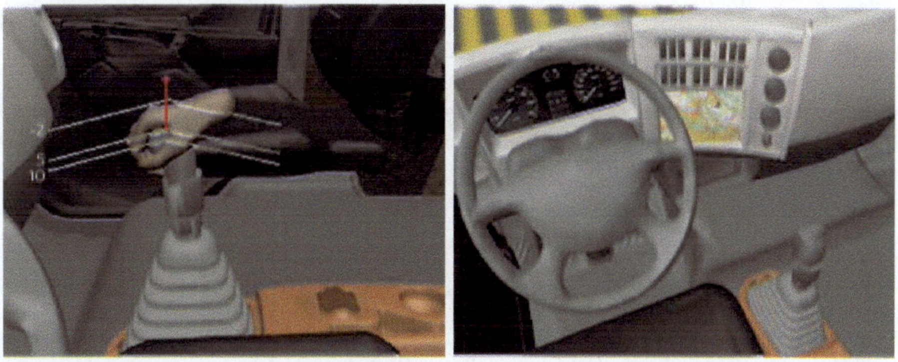

Fig. 19.18 Volvo truck gearbox simulation

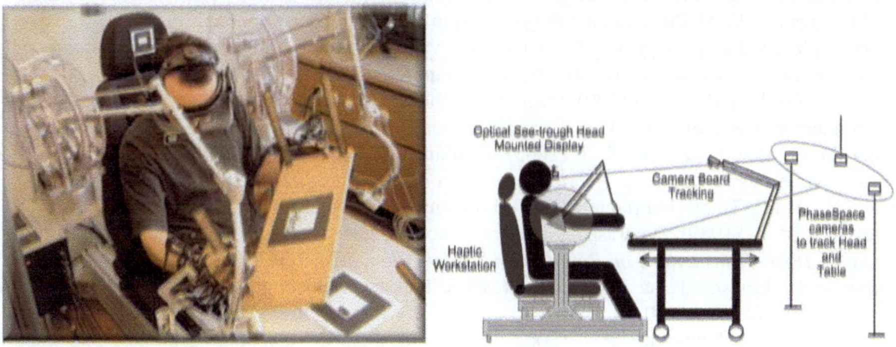

Fig. 19.19 Assembly training under Mixed-Reality condition

izable. These parameters are the static and dynamic friction coefficients and the coefficient of restitution (bounciness).

As shown previously, the Haptic Scene Creator includes many features aiming at simplifying the task of a Haptic application designer. To evaluate it, a designer augmented a visual Virtual Environment. The test scene is a quite complex. It represents a four-room house (kitchen, bathroom, bed, office and living-room), and contains 398 visual nodes. It is presented in Fig. 19.17.

The system was used for several applications: a Volvo truck gearbox simulation (Fig. 19.18) and Assembly training under Mixed-Reality condition (Fig. 19.19).

19.6 Conclusion

This Chapter has provided a review of the various methods and algorithms we have designed in the last 15 years for object manipulation. The problem of manipulating virtual objects by VHs and the user is still not yet completely solved. No general method is available, but there is a hope that with the new Kinect sensor, it will be possible to design new data driven models taking into account information on the depth.

Acknowledgments Most of this research has been performed at the VRlab in EPFL, directed by the author. The author would like to thank students who contributed especially Luc Emering, Tolga Abaci, Marcelo Kallmann, and Renaud Ott.

References

Badler, N. N. (1997). Virtual humans for animation, ergonomics, and simulation. In *IEEE workshop on non-rigid and articulated motion*, Puerto Rico, June 97.

Badler, N. I., Phillips, C. B., & Webber, B. L. (1993). *Simulating humans: Computer graphics animation and control*. New York: Oxford University Press.

Baerlocher, P. (2001). *Inverse kinematics techniques for the interactive posture control of articulated figures*. Ph.D. thesis, École Polytechnique Fédérale de Lausanne (EPFL).

Borst, C. W., & Indugula, A. P. (2005). Realistic virtual grasping. In *Proc. 2005 IEEE conference on virtual reality (VR'05)* (pp. 91–98). Los Alamitos: IEEE Computer Society.

Bowman, D., & Hodges, L. (1999). Formalizing the design, evaluation, and application of interaction techniques. *Journal of Visual Languages and Computing*, *10*, 37–53.

Choi, M. G., Lee, J., & Shin, S. Y. (2003). Planning biped locomotion using motion capture data and probabilistic roadmaps. *ACM Transactions on Graphics*, *22*(2), 182–203.

Ciger, J., Abaci, T., & Thalmann, D. (2005). Planning with smart objects. In *WSCG'2005*.

Cutkosky, M. R. (1989). On grasp choice, grasp models, and the design of hands for manufacturing tasks. *IEEE Transactions on Robotics and Automation*, *5*(3), 269–279.

Douville, B., Levison, L., & Badler, N. I. (1996). Task-level object grasping for simulated agents. *Presence*, *5*(4), 416–430.

Eberly, D. H., & Schneider, P. J. (2002). *Geometric tools for computer graphics*. San Mateo: Morgan Kaufmann.

Emering, L., Boulic, R., Molet, T., & Thalmann, D. (2000). Versatile tuning of humanoid agent activity. *Computer Graphics Forum*, *19*(4), 231–242.

Ericson, C. (2005). *Real-time collision detection*. San Mateo: Morgan Kaufmann.

Espiau, B., & Boulic, R. (1985). Collision avoidance for redondants robots with proximity sensors. In *I third international symposium of robotics research*.

Goncalves, L., Kallmann, M., & Thalmann, D. (2002). Defining behaviors for autonomous agents based on local perception and smart objects. *Computers and Graphics*, *26*(6), 887–897.

Hand, C. (1997). A survey of 3D interaction techniques. *Computer Graphics Forum*, *16*(5), 269–281.

Huang, Z., Boulic, R., Thalmann, N. M., & Thalmann, D. (1995). A multi-sensor approach for grasping and 3D interaction. In *Computer graphics: Developments in virtual environments* (pp. 235–253).

Johnson, W. L., & Rickel, J. (1997). Steve: An animated pedagogical agent for procedural training in virtual environments. *Sigart Bulletin*, *8*(1–4), 16–21.

Kallmann, M., & Mataric, M. (2004). Motion planning using dynamic roadmaps. In *Proceedings of the ICRA 2004 conference* (pp. 4399–4404).

Kallmann, M., & Thalmann, D. (1998). Modeling objects for interaction tasks. In *Proc. Eurographics workshop on animation and simulation*. Berlin: Springer.

Kallmann, M., & Thalmann, D. (1999). A behavioral interface to simulate agent-object interactions in real-time. In *Proc. computer animation 99* (pp. 138–146). Los Alamitos: IEEE Computer Society Press.

Kallmann, M., & Thalmann, D. (2002). Modeling behaviors of interactive objects for real-time virtual environments. *Journal of Visual Languages and Computing*, *13*(2), 177–195.

Kallmann, M., Aubel, A., Abaci, T., & Thalmann, D. (2003). Planning collision-free reaching motions for interactive object manipulation and grasping. In *Proceedings of the Eurographics 2003 conference* (Vol. 22, pp. 313–322).

Kavraki, L., Svestka, P., Latombe, J., & Overmars, M. (1994). *Probabilistic roadmaps for path planning in high-dimensional configuration spaces* (Tech. Rep.). Stanford University Stanford, CA, USA.

Kuffner, J. J., & LaValle, S. M. (2000). RT-connect: An efficient approach to single-query path planning. In *Proceedings of the ICRA 2000 conference* (pp. 995–1001).

Latombe, J. (1991). *Robot motion planning*. Norwell: Kluwer Academic Publishers.

LaValle, S. M. (1998). *Rapidly-exploring random trees: A new tool for path planning* (Tech. Rep. 98-11). Dept. of Computer Science, Iowa State University.

Leven, P., & Hutchinson, S. (2000). Motion planning using dynamic roadmaps. In *Proceedings of the fourth international workshop on the algorithmic foundations of robotics (WAFR)* (pp. 363–376).

Magnenat-Thalmann, N., Laperriere, R., & Thalmann, D. (1988). Joint dependent local deformations for hand animation and object grasping. In *Proceedings of graphics interface '88* (pp. 26–33).

Mas, R., & Thalmann, D. (1994). A hand control and automatic grasping system for synthetic actors. *Computer Graphics Forum*, *13*(3), 167–177.

Mas, R., Boulic, R., & Thalmann, D. (1997). Extended grasping behavior for autonomous human agents. In *AGENTS '97: Proceedings of the first international conference on autonomous agents* (pp. 494–495). New York: ACM Press

Mortara, M., Patanè, G., Spagnuolo, M., Falcidieno, B., & Rossignac, J. (2004a). Blowing bubbles for the multi-scale analysis and decomposition of triangle meshes. *Algorithmica*, *38*(2), 227–248. Special issues on shape algorithms.

Mortara, M., Patanè, G., Spagnuolo, M., Falcidieno, B., & Rossignac, J. (2004b). Plumber: A method for a multi-scale decomposition of 3d shapes into tubular primitives and bodies. In *Ninth ACM symposium on solid modeling and applications SM'04* (pp. 339–344).

Ott, R., Vexo, F., & Thalmann, D. (2010). Two-handed haptic manipulation for CAD and VR applications. *Computer-Aided Design*, *7*(1), 125–138.

Peternier, A., Thalmann, D., & Vexo, F. (2006). Mental vision: A computer graphics teaching platform. In *Proceedings of the 2006 edutainment conference* (pp. 223–232).

Peters, C., Dobbyn, S., McNamee, B., & O'Sullivan, C. (2003). Smart objects for attentive agents, *Journal of WSCG*, *11*.

Phillips, C. B., & Badler, N. I. (1988). JACK: A toolkit for manipulating articulated figures. In *UIST '88: Proceedings of the 1st annual ACM SIGGRAPH symposium on user interface software* (pp. 221–229). New York: ACM Press.

Pollard, N. S., & Zordan, V. B. (2005). Physically based grasping control from example. In *SCA '05: Proceedings of the 2005 ACM SIGGRAPH/Eurographics symposium on computer animation* (pp. 311–318). New York: ACM Press.

Poupyrev, I., & Ichikawa, T. (1999). Manipulating objects in virtual worlds: Categorization and empirical evaluation of interaction techniques. *Journal of Visual Languages and Computing*, *10*, 19–35.

Rezzonico, S., Boulic, R., & Thalmann, D. (1996). Multi-finger manipulation of virtual objects. In *Proc. of the ACM symposium on virtual reality software and technology (VRST'96)*, Hong Kong (pp. 67–74).

Shah, J. J., & Mäntylä, M. (1995). *Parametric and feature-based CAD/CAM*. New York: John Wiley & Sons. ISBN 0-471-00214-3.

Simon, T., Laumond, J., & Nissoux, C. (2000). Visibility based probabilistic roadmaps for motion planning. *Advanced Robotics Journal*, *14*(2).

Tolani, D., Goswami, A., & Badler, N. (2000). Real-time inverse kinematics techniques for anthropomorphic limbs. *Graphical Models and Image Processing*, *62*(5), 353–388.

Trias, T. S., Chopra, S., Reich, B. D., Moore, M. B., Badler, N. I., Webber, B. L., & Geib, C. W. (1996). Decision networks for integrating the behaviors of virtual agents and avatars. In

VRAIS '96: Proceedings of the 1996 virtual reality annual international symposium (VRAIS 96) (p. 156). Washington: IEEE Computer Society.

van de Panne, M., & Fiume, E. (1993). Sensor-actuator networks. In *Proceedings of the of SIGGRAPH-93: Computer graphics*, Anaheim, CA (pp. 335–342).

Wang, X., & Verriest, J. P. (1998). A geometric algorithm to predict the arm reach posture for computer-aided ergonomic evaluation. *The Journal of Visualization and Computer Animation*, *9*(1), 33–47.

Wiley, D. J., & Hahn, J. K. (1997). Interpolation synthesis of articulated figure motion. *IEEE Computer Graphics and Applications*, *17*(6), 39–45.

Yamane, K., Kuffner, J. J., & Hodgins, J. K. (2004). Synthesizing animations of human manipulation tasks. *ACM Transactions on Graphics*, *23*(3), 532–539.

Zilles, C. B., & Salisbury, J. K. (1995). A constraint-based god-object method for haptic display. In *Proc. IEEE/RSJ international conference on intelligent robots and systems* (Vol. 3, pp. 146–151).

Chapter 20
An Analytical Approach to Dynamic Skin Deformation of Character Animation

L.H. You, H. Ugail, X.Y. You, and Jian J. Zhang

Abstract In this paper, we propose a new approach to animate the dynamic skin deformation of virtual characters. This approach is based on a mathematical model which combines a vector-valued second order ordinary differential equation with the equation of motion, and considers the dynamic effects on skin deformation, i.e., how velocity and acceleration affect the deformed skin shapes. We develop an efficient analytical solution of the mathematical model and apply it in some applications of skin deformation. These applications demonstrate the validity of our proposed approach in animating dynamic skin deformation.

20.1 Introduction

The realism of character animation largely depends on the plausibility of skin deformation and a large amount of research effort has therefore been devoted to the animation of skin deformation. In general, dynamic skin shapes can be determined by: 1) formulating the relationship between the displacements of the skin surface points and the joint rotations, 2) interpolating known example skin shapes at different poses, 3) the underlying physics of the skin and anatomy.

The popular and most widely used method in formulating the relationship between the displacements of skin surface points and the joint rotations is the so-called skeleton subspace deformation (SSD) (Lander 1998, 1999; Thalmann et al. 1988; Wang and Phillips 2002; Weber 2000). It was also referred to as linear skin blending (LSB), enveloping and vertex blending. This method determines the new position of a vertex on a skin surface by a weighted linear combination of the vertex rigidly

L.H. You (✉) · J.J. Zhang
National Centre for Computer Animation, Bournemouth University, Bournemouth, UK
e-mail: LYou@bournemouth.ac.uk

H. Ugail
Centre for Visual Computing, University of Bradford, Bradford, UK

X.Y. You
Faculty of Engineering and Computing, Coventry University, Coventry, UK

J. Dill et al. (eds.), *Expanding the Frontiers of Visual Analytics and Visualization*,
DOI 10.1007/978-1-4471-2804-5_20,

transformed by the rotation of each bone. It is simple to use and highly computationally efficient. The original skeleton subspace deformation has the disadvantages of certain anomalies in volume loss especially around joints (the candy-wrapper effect). These disadvantages can be improved by removing the linearity of SSD through introducing extra joints (Mohr and Gleicher 2003) or using curve skeleton skinning (Yang et al. 2006).

The techniques of finding new deformed skin shapes from some known example skin shapes at different poses require scanned or sculpted example skin shapes. New skin shapes at different poses are then produced by interpolation. These techniques involve high computational cost, but can capture some of the complexity of real skin deformation. The pose space deformation (PSD) introduces an interpolation algorithm of example skin shapes to improve SSD (Lewis et al. 2000). It calculates the error of each vertex between SSD and example skin meshes, and uses the error and interpolation algorithm to correct the position of the vertex on the skin mesh produced by SSD. Weighted pose space deformation (WPSD) further improves the quality of skin deformation but requires more calculations (Kurihara and Miyata 2004). The work carried out by Rhee et al. (2006) develops a parallel deformation method using the GPU fragment processors. It calculates the joint weights for each vertex from sample skin shapes automatically, reducing manual intervention and enhancing the quality of WPSD. The method presented by Weber et al. (2007) proposes an example-based skin deformation framework. It enables both interpolation and extrapolation of a very sparse set of example skin shapes, and significantly reduces the computational cost of WPSD by a compact representation of example deformations.

The techniques based on the underlying physics of skin deformation consider the anatomy, elastic mechanics, or biomechanics of skin deformation as a result of the movements of muscles and tendons. The work carried out by Chen and Zeltzer (1992) indicates that the relationship between forces and muscle deformation is complex which does not follow a simple linear variation. Treating muscles as deformable discretized cylinders, Wilhelms and Van Gelder (1997) proposed an improved anatomically based approach. Capell et al. (2002) used volumetric finite element to animate skeleton-driven characters with dynamic elastic deformation. Using linear elastodynamic equation and finite element method, James and Pai (2002) precomputed a volumetric mesh with model analysis and added it to kinematic skinning as deformation texture. Based on length preservation, Larboulette and Cani (2004) proposed a new and easy way to achieve visually realistic dynamic wrinkles. Larboulette et al. (2005) used a new second skinning operation which blends the current flesh volume with its position. In work conducted by Pratscher et al. (2005), the musculature is attached to an existing control skeleton, and change in volume-preserving and pose-based deformations of the musculature is tied to variation in skin shape. Teran et al. (2005) described muscle with a transversely isotropic, quasi-incompressible constitutive model, and presented a finite element technique to simulate skeletal muscles. Von Funck et al. (2006) employed a divergence-free vector field to define deformations of solid shape which is volume and feature preserving and free of self-intersections. Capell et al. (2007) developed a system to give animators the control over the shapes of elastic deformable characters. Using a numerical resolution method, divergence-free vector fields are used to describe the velocity of foldover-free and volume-preserving skin deformation (Angelidis and Singh 2007).

Curves are simpler and easier to describe than surfaces. Using curves to define, manipulate, and animate surface models can simplify the calculations, raise the computational efficiency and reduce the data size of geometric modeling and computer animation. Some researchers have investigated this issue. For example, Shen et al. (1994) used two-dimensional (2D) cross-sectional contours and Hyun et al. (2005) applied 2D elliptic cross-sections to describe human parts. Singh and Fiume (1998) used three-dimensional (3D) parametric curves, and Pyun et al. (2004) extracted wire curves from a facial model, and You et al. (2008) employed 3D characteristic curves to represent character models.

In this paper, we propose an approach to animate skin deformation dynamically using a three-dimensional curve-based representation of skin surfaces. The mathematical model involves deforming 3D curves represented with a vector-valued second order dynamic ordinary differential equation. A key step is to derive an analytical solution of the 3D curves which are used to control the deformation of the skin surfaces.

In what follows, we discuss the mathematical model and analytical solution in Sect. 20.2, the relationships between the curves and skin surfaces in Sect. 20.3, some skin deformation examples in Sect. 20.4, and the conclusions in Sect. 20.5.

20.2 Mathematical Model and Analytical Solution

Using the methodology proposed by Du and Qin (2000) which combines the benefits of partial differential equation (PDE)-based surfaces with physics-based modeling techniques within one single modeling framework, we combine a vector-valued second order ordinary differential equation with the equation of motion to derive the following mathematical model of dynamic skin deformation.

First, we transform skin surfaces into a number of three-dimensional curves defining the skin shapes. Then we deform these curves with the mathematical model presented below. And finally, we use these deformed curves to control the deformations of the skin surfaces.

Assuming the mathematical representation of a three-dimensional curve is $\mathbf{X}(u,t)$ and the force used to deform the three-dimensional curve is $\mathbf{F}(u,t)$ where u is a parametric variable, t is a time variable, $\mathbf{X}(u,t)$ is a vector-valued position function of a three-dimensional curve which has three components $x_1(u,t), x_2(u,t)$ and $x_3(u,t)$, and the vector-valued force function $\mathbf{F}(u,t)$ also has three components $f_1(u,t)$, $f_2(u,t)$ and $f_3(u,t)$, the vector-valued form of the equation of motion used by Du and Qin (2000) can be written as

$$\rho\frac{d^2\mathbf{X}(u,t)}{dt^2}+\eta\frac{d\mathbf{X}(u,t)}{dt}+K\mathbf{X}(u,t)=\mathbf{F}(u,t) \tag{20.1}$$

The first, second and third terms on the left-hand side of Eq. (20.1) represents the effects of acceleration, velocity and position change on the motion of the curve. The position change of the curve is described by the following vector-valued second order ordinary differential equation

$$K\mathbf{X}(u,t) = \alpha \frac{d^2\mathbf{X}(u,t)}{du^2} + \beta \mathbf{X}(u,t) \tag{20.2}$$

where the coefficients α and β are known and called shape control parameters. These coefficients have a significant influence on the shape of the curve.

Inserting Eq. (20.2) into Eq. (20.1), the mathematical model controlling the dynamic deformation of a curve is given by

$$\rho \frac{d^2\mathbf{X}(u,t)}{dt^2} + \eta \frac{d\mathbf{X}(u,t)}{dt} + \alpha \frac{d^2\mathbf{X}(u,t)}{du^2} + \beta \mathbf{X}(u,t) = \mathbf{F}(u,t) \tag{20.3}$$

Character animation requires high computational efficiency. Among various solutions of a mathematical model, the analytical solution is the most efficient. Here we develop such an analytical solution.

If the vector-valued force function at some poses is known, we can find the variation of the force function with the time. For example, if we know the force functions at the poses $t = 0$ and $t = 1$ are $\hat{\mathbf{F}}_0(u)$ and $\hat{\mathbf{F}}_1(u)$, respectively, we can take the variation of the force function with the time to be

$$\mathbf{F}(u,t) = \bar{\mathbf{F}}_0(u) + t\bar{\mathbf{F}}_1(u) \tag{20.4}$$

where $\bar{\mathbf{F}}_0(u)$ and $\bar{\mathbf{F}}_1(u)$ are the vector-valued unknown functions.

Substituting $\mathbf{F}(u,t) = \hat{\mathbf{F}}_0(u)$ at the time $t = 0$ and $\mathbf{F}(u,t) = \hat{\mathbf{F}}_1(u)$ at the time $t = 1$ into Eq. (20.4), solving for the unknown functions $\bar{\mathbf{F}}_0(u)$ and $\bar{\mathbf{F}}_1(u)$, and inserting them back into Eq. (20.4), we obtain the variation of the vector-valued force function with time, i.e.

$$\mathbf{F}(u,t) = \hat{\mathbf{F}}_0(u) + t\big[\hat{\mathbf{F}}_1(u) - \hat{\mathbf{F}}_0(u)\big] \tag{20.5}$$

The force functions $\hat{\mathbf{F}}_0(u)$ and $\hat{\mathbf{F}}_1(u)$ can be represented with a Fourier series as indicated below

$$\begin{aligned}
\hat{\mathbf{F}}_0(u) &= \mathbf{a}_0 + \sum_{n=1}^{N} (\mathbf{a}_{2n-1} \cos 2n\pi u + \mathbf{a}_{2n} \sin 2n\pi u) \\
\hat{\mathbf{F}}_1(u) &= \mathbf{b}_0 + \sum_{n=1}^{N} (\mathbf{b}_{2n-1} \cos 2n\pi u + \mathbf{b}_{2n} \sin 2n\pi u)
\end{aligned} \tag{20.6}$$

where $\mathbf{a}_n$ and $\mathbf{b}_n$ $(n = 0, 1, 2, 3, \dots, 2N)$ are vector-valued unknown constants.

Substituting Eq. (20.6) into (20.5) and carrying out some simple mathematical operations, the force function in Eq. (20.5) becomes

$$\begin{aligned}
\mathbf{F}(u,t) = \mathbf{a}_0 + (\mathbf{b}_0 - \mathbf{a}_0)t + \sum_{n=1}^{N} \big[&\mathbf{a}_{2n-1} \cos 2n\pi u + \mathbf{a}_{2n} \sin 2n\pi u \\
&+ (\mathbf{b}_{2n-1} - \mathbf{a}_{2n-1})t \cos 2n\pi u + (\mathbf{b}_{2n} - \mathbf{a}_{2n})t \sin 2n\pi u\big]
\end{aligned} \tag{20.7}$$

Since the above force function includes the terms of constant 1, t, $\cos 2n\pi u$, $\sin 2n\pi u$, $t\cos 2n\pi u$ and $t\sin 2n\pi u$, the vector-valued function $\mathbf{X}(u,t)$ should also include the corresponding functions so that the differential operations at the left-hand side of Eq. (20.3) can generate these terms. Observing Eqs. (20.3) and (20.7), these functions should have the form of $\mathbf{X}_1(1)$, $\mathbf{X}_2(t)$, $\mathbf{X}_3(\cos 2n\pi u)$, $\mathbf{X}_4(\sin 2n\pi u)$, $\mathbf{X}_5(t\cos 2n\pi u)$ and $\mathbf{X}_6(t\sin 2n\pi u)$.

Substituting $\mathbf{X}_1(1)$ into Eq. (20.3), and making the terms on the left-hand side equal to the corresponding term on the right-hand side, we reach

$$\rho\frac{d^2\mathbf{X}_1(1)}{dt^2}+\eta\frac{d\mathbf{X}_1(1)}{dt}+\beta\mathbf{X}_1(1)=\mathbf{a}_0 \tag{20.8}$$

Assuming that the solution of Eq. (20.8) is $\mathbf{X}_1(1)=\mathbf{d}_0$ and substituting it into Eq. (20.8), the vector-valued unknown constant $\mathbf{d}_0$ is determined and $\mathbf{X}_1(1)$ is found to be

$$\mathbf{X}_1(1)=\mathbf{a}_0/\beta \tag{20.9}$$

For function $\mathbf{X}_2(t)$, Eq. (20.3) is changed into the following form after substituting $\mathbf{X}_2(t)$ into the left-hand side of the equation

$$\rho\frac{d^2\mathbf{X}_2(t)}{dt^2}+\eta\frac{d\mathbf{X}_2(t)}{dt}+\beta\mathbf{X}_2(t)=(\mathbf{b}_0-\mathbf{a}_0)t \tag{20.10}$$

Taking the solution of Eq. (20.10) to be $\mathbf{X}_2(t)=\mathbf{d}_1+\mathbf{d}_2t$, substituting it into Eq. (20.10), the unknown constants $\mathbf{d}_1$ and $\mathbf{d}_2$ are achieved, and the vector-valued function $\mathbf{X}_2(t)$ is obtained below

$$\mathbf{X}_2(t)=(-\rho/\beta+t)(\mathbf{b}_0-\mathbf{a}_0)/\beta \tag{20.11}$$

For the vector-valued function $\mathbf{X}_3(\cos 2n\pi u)$, Eq. (20.3) is transformed into the following differential equation

$$\begin{aligned}\rho\frac{d^2\mathbf{X}_3(\cos 2n\pi u)}{dt^2}+\eta\frac{d\mathbf{X}_3(\cos 2n\pi u)}{dt}-4\alpha n^2\pi^2\cos 2n\pi u\\ \frac{d^2\mathbf{X}_3(\cos 2n\pi u)}{d(\cos 2n\pi u)^2}+\beta\mathbf{X}_3(\cos 2n\pi u)=\mathbf{a}_{2n-1}\cos 2n\pi u\end{aligned} \tag{20.12}$$

Taking the solution of Eq. (20.12) to be $\mathbf{X}_3(\cos 2n\pi u)=\mathbf{d}_3\cos 2n\pi u$, substituting it into Eq. (20.12), we obtain the unknown constants $\mathbf{d}_3$ and the vector-valued function $\mathbf{X}_3(\cos 2n\pi u)$ is found to be

$$\mathbf{X}_3(\cos 2n\pi u)=\mathbf{a}_{2n-1}\cos 2n\pi u/\left(\beta-4\alpha\pi^2n^2\right) \tag{20.13}$$

With the same treatment, we can find the vector-valued function $\mathbf{X}_4(\sin 2n\pi u)$ which can be written as

$$\mathbf{X}_4(\sin 2n\pi u)=\mathbf{a}_{2n}\sin 2n\pi u/\left(\beta-4\alpha\pi^2n^2\right) \tag{20.14}$$

For the vector-valued function $\mathbf{X}_5(t\cos 2n\pi u)$ which is the function of $t\cos 2n\pi u$, Eq. (20.3) becomes the following differential equation

$$\rho\frac{d^2\mathbf{X}_5(t\cos 2n\pi u)}{dt^2}+\eta\frac{d\mathbf{X}_5(t\cos 2n\pi u)}{dt}-4\alpha n^2\pi^2 t\cos 2n\pi u$$
$$\frac{d^2\mathbf{X}_5(t\cos 2n\pi u)}{d(t\cos 2n\pi u)^2}+\beta\mathbf{X}_5(t\cos 2n\pi u)=(\mathbf{b}_{2n-1}-\mathbf{a}_{2n-1})t\cos 2n\pi u \tag{20.15}$$

Taking the solution of Eq. (20.15) to be $\mathbf{X}_5(t\cos 2n\pi u)=(\mathbf{d}_4+\mathbf{d}_5 t)\cos 2n\pi u$, and substituting it into the above equation, we find $\mathbf{d}_4$ and $\mathbf{d}_5$, and the vector-valued function can be written as follows

$$\mathbf{X}_5(t\cos 2n\pi u)=\left[\eta/\left(\beta-4\alpha\pi^2n^2\right)-t\right]$$
$$(\mathbf{a}_{2n-1}-\mathbf{b}_{2n-1})\cos 2n\pi u/\left(\beta-4\alpha\pi^2n^2\right) \tag{20.16}$$

Similarly, the vector-valued function $\mathbf{X}_6(t\sin 2n\pi u)$ can be determined which has the form of

$$\mathbf{X}_6(t\sin 2n\pi u)=\left[\eta/\left(\beta-4\alpha\pi^2n^2\right)-t\right]$$
$$(\mathbf{a}_{2n}-\mathbf{b}_{2n})\sin 2n\pi u/\left(\beta-4\alpha\pi^2n^2\right) \tag{20.17}$$

The resulting vector-valued position function is the sum of those given in Eqs. (20.9), (20.11), (20.13), (20.14), (20.16) and (20.17) which can be written as

$$\mathbf{X}(u,t)=\mathbf{a}_0/\beta+(-\rho/\beta+t)(\mathbf{b}_0-\mathbf{a}_0)/\beta+\sum_{n=1}^{N}\{\mathbf{a}_{2n-1}\cos 2n\pi u$$
$$+\mathbf{a}_{2n}\sin 2n\pi u+\left[\eta/\left(\beta-4\alpha\pi^2n^2\right)-t\right]\left[(\mathbf{a}_{2n-1}-\mathbf{b}_{2n-1})\cos 2n\pi u\right.$$
$$\left.+(\mathbf{a}_{2n}-\mathbf{b}_{2n})\sin 2n\pi u\right]\}/\left(\beta-4\alpha\pi^2n^2\right) \tag{20.18}$$

If the skin shape at the initial pose $t=0$ and the final pose $t=1$ is known, we can generate two linear algebra equations.

First, setting the time variable $t=0$ in the above equation and making it equal to the known skin shape $\hat{\mathbf{X}}_0(u)$ at $t=0$, the following linear algebra equation is reached

$$\mathbf{a}_0/\beta+(-\rho/\beta)(\mathbf{b}_0-\mathbf{a}_0)/\beta+\sum_{n=1}^{N}\{\mathbf{a}_{2n-1}\cos 2n\pi u+\mathbf{a}_{2n}$$
$$\sin 2n\pi u+\eta/\left(\beta-4\alpha\pi^2n^2\right)\left[(\mathbf{a}_{2n-1}-\mathbf{b}_{2n-1})\cos 2n\pi u\right.$$
$$\left.+(\mathbf{a}_{2n}-\mathbf{b}_{2n})\sin 2n\pi u\right]\}/\left(\beta-4\alpha\pi^2n^2\right)=\hat{\mathbf{X}}_0(u) \tag{20.19}$$

Next, we take the time variable $t=1$ in Eq. (20.18) and making it equal to the known skin shape $\hat{\mathbf{X}}_1(u)$ at $t=1$, the following linear algebra equation is obtained

$$\mathbf{a}_0/\beta+(-\rho/\beta+1)(\mathbf{b}_0-\mathbf{a}_0)/\beta+\sum_{n=1}^{N}\{\mathbf{a}_{2n-1}\cos 2n\pi u+\mathbf{a}_{2n}$$

$$\sin 2n\pi u + \left[\eta/(\beta - 4\alpha\pi^2 n^2) - 1\right]\left[(\mathbf{a}_{2n-1} - \mathbf{b}_{2n-1})\cos 2n\pi u + (\mathbf{a}_{2n} - \mathbf{b}_{2n})\sin 2n\pi u\right]\}/(\beta - 4\alpha\pi^2 n^2) = \hat{\mathbf{X}}_1(u) \tag{20.20}$$

Expanding the vector-valued position functions $\hat{\mathbf{X}}_0(u)$ and $\hat{\mathbf{X}}_1(u)$ into the following Fourier series

$$\begin{aligned} \hat{\mathbf{X}}_0(u) &= \mathbf{q}_0 + \sum_{n=1}^{N} (\mathbf{q}_{2n-1} \cos 2n\pi u + \mathbf{q}_{2n} \sin 2n\pi u) \\ \hat{\mathbf{X}}_1(u) &= \mathbf{r}_0 + \sum_{n=1}^{N} (\mathbf{r}_{2n-1} \cos 2n\pi u + \mathbf{r}_{2n} \sin 2n\pi u) \end{aligned} \tag{20.21}$$

where

$$\begin{aligned} \mathbf{q}_0 &= \int_0^1 \hat{\mathbf{X}}_0(u) du \\ \mathbf{q}_{2n-1} &= \int_0^1 \hat{\mathbf{X}}_0(u) \cos 2n\pi u du \\ \mathbf{q}_{2n} &= \int_0^1 \hat{\mathbf{X}}_0(u) \sin 2n\pi u du \end{aligned} \tag{20.22}$$

and

$$\begin{aligned} \mathbf{r}_0 &= \int_0^1 \hat{\mathbf{X}}_1(u) du \\ \mathbf{r}_{2n-1} &= \int_0^1 \hat{\mathbf{X}}_1(u) \cos 2n\pi u du \\ \mathbf{r}_{2n} &= \int_0^1 \hat{\mathbf{X}}_1(u) \sin 2n\pi u du \end{aligned} \tag{20.23}$$

Substituting the first of Eq. (20.21) into (20.19) and the second into (20.20), the following linear algebra equations are reached

$$\begin{aligned} &\mathbf{a}_0/\beta + (-\rho/\beta)(\mathbf{b}_0 - \mathbf{a}_0)/\beta = \mathbf{q}_0 \\ &\mathbf{a}_{2n-1} + \eta/(\beta - 4\alpha\pi^2 n^2)(\mathbf{a}_{2n-1} - \mathbf{b}_{2n-1}) = (\beta - 4\alpha\pi^2 n^2)\mathbf{q}_{2n-1} \\ &\mathbf{a}_{2n} + \eta/(\beta - 4\alpha\pi^2 n^2)(\mathbf{a}_{2n} - \mathbf{b}_{2n}) = (\beta - 4\alpha\pi^2 n^2)\mathbf{q}_{2n} \\ &\mathbf{a}_0/\beta + (-\rho/\beta + 1)(\mathbf{b}_0 - \mathbf{a}_0)/\beta = \mathbf{r}_0 \\ &\mathbf{a}_{2n-1} + \left[\eta/(\beta - 4\alpha\pi^2 n^2) - 1\right](\mathbf{a}_{2n-1} - \mathbf{b}_{2n-1}) = (\beta - 4\alpha\pi^2 n^2)\mathbf{r}_{2n-1} \\ &\mathbf{a}_{2n} + \left[\eta/(\beta - 4\alpha\pi^2 n^2) - 1\right](\mathbf{a}_{2n} - \mathbf{b}_{2n}) = (\beta - 4\alpha\pi^2 n^2)\mathbf{r}_{2n} \end{aligned} \tag{20.24}$$

Solving the above linear algebra equations, we can determine the vector-valued unknown constants $\mathbf{a}_0$, $\mathbf{a}_{2n-1}$, $\mathbf{a}_{2n}$, $\mathbf{b}_0$, $\mathbf{b}_{2n-1}$ and $\mathbf{b}_{2n}$ $(n = 1, 2, 3, \ldots, N)$. Substituting these constants back into Eq. (20.18), the skin deformation at any poses can be obtained with the equation.

20.3 Relationships Between Curves and Skin Surfaces

The relationships between curves and skin surfaces include curve-based representation of skin surfaces and curve-based deformation control of skin surfaces.

20.3.1 Curve-Based Representation of Skin Surfaces

Curve-based representation of skin surfaces describes skin surfaces with a set of curves on skin surfaces. To this aim, we first determine these curves using the method given in our previous work (You et al. 2010).

With this method, we first draw a rough central curve within each part of a character model. From the central curve, we generate some planes perpendicular to the central curve. Then we find the intersecting points between the central curve and the corresponding part. These intersecting points form a curve on the skin surface of the part, and the curve is called an intersecting curve. With this method, we obtain the intersecting curves of a human arm and depicted them in Fig. 20.1. These intersecting curves define the shape of the human arm and provide a curve-based representation of the skin surface of the human arm.

After obtaining the curve-based representation of skin surfaces, these intersecting curves are deformed with the method described in Sect. 20.2. The obtained deformed shapes of the intersecting curves are used to control the skin deformation of the character model with the algorithm presented in the following subsection.

20.3.2 Curve-Based Deformation Control of Skin Surfaces

Curve-based deformation control of skin surfaces is to manipulate skin deformation of virtual characters through deforming the intersecting curves describing the skin surfaces. We still use the method proposed in our paper (You et al. 2010) for this aim.

With this method, we first classify the surface vertices on original character models into two groups: one group of surface vertices are on the intersecting curve and the other group of surface vertices are between two adjacent intersecting curves. Then, we find the geometric relationship between these surface vertices and the adjacent intersecting curves. Finally, we animate skin deformation using this relationship to transfer the deformations of the intersecting curves to the surface vertices of the character models.

If a surface vertex is on an intersecting curve, the new position of the surface vertex after deformation is determined from the deformed shape of the intersecting curve through a simple linear interpolation.

If a surface vertex $\mathbf{p}_o$ is between the ith intersecting curve $\mathbf{c}_i$ and the $(i+1)$th intersecting curve $\mathbf{c}_{i+1}$ as indicated in Fig. 20.2, we use the following algorithm to determine the new position of the surface vertex after deformation.

Fig. 20.1 Curve-based representation

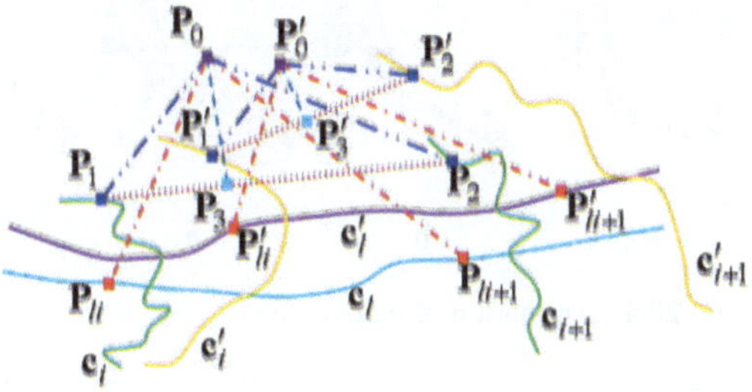

Fig. 20.2 Deformation control by deformed intersecting curves

From the intersecting curves describing a part of a character model, we can determine a central curve $\mathbf{c}_l$ which passes through all the centers of the intersecting curves. After the deformations of the intersecting curves, the central curve $\mathbf{c}_l$ changes its shape and becomes another curve $\mathbf{c}'_l$. Accordingly, the ith intersecting curve $\mathbf{c}_i$ and the $(i+1)$th intersecting curve $\mathbf{c}_{i+1}$ are deformed into $\mathbf{c}'_i$ and $\mathbf{c}'_{i+1}$.

If the center of the two intersecting curves at the central curve $\mathbf{c}_l$ are $\mathbf{p}_{li}$ and $\mathbf{p}_{li+1}$, a plane is created from the three points $\mathbf{p}_o$, $\mathbf{p}_{li}$ and $\mathbf{p}_{li+1}$. Then, we find the intersecting points $\mathbf{p}_1$ and $\mathbf{p}_2$ between the plane and the two intersecting curves $\mathbf{c}_i$ and $\mathbf{c}_{i+1}$ which are the closest to the surface point $\mathbf{p}_o$. Next, we draw a straight line $\mathbf{p}_1\mathbf{p}_2$ and find the point $\mathbf{p}_3$ by making the straight line $\mathbf{p}_o\mathbf{p}_3$ perpendicular to the line $\mathbf{p}_1\mathbf{p}_2$.

After the deformations of the intersecting curves, the intersecting points $\mathbf{p}_1$ and $\mathbf{p}_2$ move to $\mathbf{p}'_1$ and $\mathbf{p}'_2$, and the centers $\mathbf{p}_{li}$ and $\mathbf{p}_{li+1}$ move to $\mathbf{p}'_{li}$ and $\mathbf{p}'_{li+1}$. Through the relationship $\overline{\mathbf{p}'_1\mathbf{p}'_3}/\overline{\mathbf{p}_1\mathbf{p}_3} = \overline{\mathbf{p}'_1\mathbf{p}'_2}/\overline{\mathbf{p}_1\mathbf{p}_2}$, the new position $\mathbf{p}'_3$ of the point $\mathbf{p}_3$ is determined. Upon drawing a straight line passing through the point $\mathbf{p}'_3$ and perpendicular to the line $\mathbf{p}'_1\mathbf{p}'_2$, we find the new position $\mathbf{p}'_o$ of the point $\mathbf{p}_o$ in the plane $\mathbf{p}'_o\mathbf{p}'_{li}\mathbf{p}'_{li+1}$ according to the similarity between the triangles $\mathbf{p}_o\mathbf{p}_1\mathbf{p}_2$ and $\mathbf{p}'_o\mathbf{p}'_1\mathbf{p}'_2$.

Using the above method, the new positions of all surface vertices on the original mesh of the character models are determined and the deformations of skin surfaces of the character model are controlled by the deformed shapes of the intersecting curves.

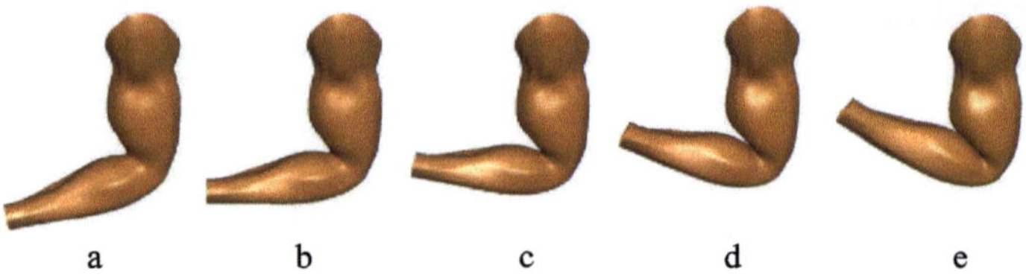

Fig. 20.3 Animation of a human arm

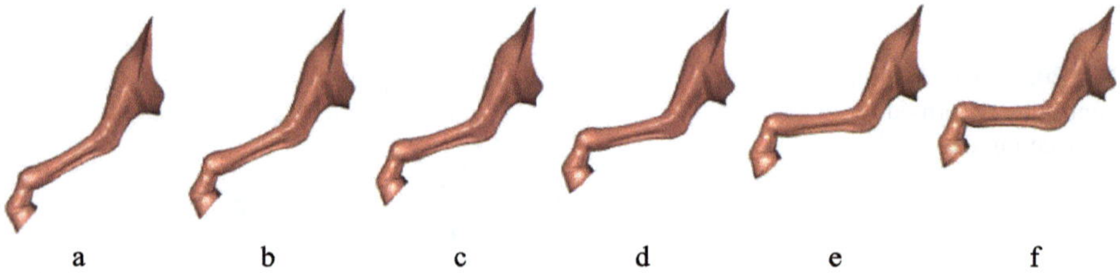

Fig. 20.4 Animation of a horse leg

20.4 Skin Deformation Examples

In this section, we discuss the applications of our proposed approach in animating skin deformation of virtual characters through two examples.

The first example is to animate skin deformation of a human arm caused by the rotation movement of the arm. The skin shapes at the initial pose $t = 0$ and final pose $t = 1$ are known and given in Figs. 20.3a and 20.3e.

From these two example skin shapes, we determine the position functions $\hat{\mathbf{X}}_0(u)$ and $\hat{\mathbf{X}}_1(u)$. After expanding these two position functions into Fourier series through Eq. (20.21), we obtain the Fourier coefficients. Substituting them into Eq. (20.24) and solving the linear algebra equations, we determine the unknown constants $\mathbf{a}_0$, $\mathbf{a}_{2n-1}$, $\mathbf{a}_{2n}$, $\mathbf{b}_0$, $\mathbf{b}_{2n-1}$ and $\mathbf{b}_{2n}$. Introducing these constants into Eq. (20.18), the skin shape at any poses is calculated with the equation. In Fig. 20.3, we depicted the skin shapes at the poses $t = 0.25$, $t = 0.5$ and $t = 0.75$ which correspond to Figs. 20.3b, 20.3c and 20.3d, respectively. These images demonstrate that our proposed approach is able to generate plausible skin deformations.

The second example is to animate the skin deformation of a horse leg in motion. Same as above, the skin shape of the horse leg at the initial pose $t = 0$ and final pose $t = 1$ are known as shown in Figs. 20.4a and 20.4f. With the same treatment, we can determine the skin shape at any poses. The obtained skin shapes at the poses $t = 0.2$, $t = 0.4$, $t = 0.6$ and $t = 0.8$ are shown in Figs. 20.4b, 20.4c, 20.4d and 20.4e, respectively. These images also indicate that the proposed approach can create reasonable skin deformations.

20.5 Conclusions

An analytical approach has been proposed in this paper to tackle the animation of dynamic skin deformation of virtual characters. The mathematical model of the dynamic skin deformation is based on the combination of the equation of motion and a vector-valued second order ordinary differential equation. This treatment takes into account the velocity and acceleration of the virtual character and the skin shape (deformation) is generated accordingly.

In order to generate efficient animation of skin deformations, we have derived an analytical solution of the mathematical model. With two known example skin shapes, this analytical solution can create the skin shapes of the virtual character at any poses.

Two examples have been presented to demonstrate the applications of the proposed approach in animating skin deformation of virtual characters. They indicate that the proposed approach is able to create plausible skin shapes quickly.

Acknowledgments This research is supported by the grant of UK Royal Society International Joint Projects/NSFC 2010.

References

Angelidis, A., & Singh, K. (2007). Kinodynamic skinning using volume-preserving deformations. In *Proceedings of the 2007 ACM SIGGRAPH/Eurographics symposium on computer animation* (pp. 129–140). Aire-la-Ville: Eurographics Association.

Capell, S., Green, S., Curless, B., Duchamp, T., & Popović, Z. (2002). Interactive skeleton-driven dynamic deformations. *ACM Transactions on Graphics (SIGGRAPH 02)*, *21*(3), 586–593.

Capell, S., Burkhart, M., Curless, B., Duchamp, T., & Popović, Z. (2007). Physically based rigging for deformable characters. *Graphical Models*, *69*(1), 71–87.

Chen, D. T., & Zeltzer, D. (1992). Pump it up: Computer animation of a biomechanically based model of muscle using the finite element method. In *SIGGRAPH 92* (pp. 89–98).

Du, H., & Qin, H. (2000). Direct manipulation and interactive sculpting of PDE surfaces. *Computer Graphics Forum*, *19*(3), 261–270.

Hyun, D.-E., Yoon, S.-H., Chang, J.-W., Seong, J.-K., Kim, M.-S., & Jüttler, B. (2005). Sweep-based human deformation. *The Visual Computer*, *21*, 542–550.

James, D. L., & Pai, D. K. (2002). DyRT: Dynamic response textures for real time deformation simulation with graphics hardware. *ACM Transactions on Graphics (SIGGRAPH 02)*, *21*(3), 582–585.

Kurihara, T., & Miyata, N. (2004). Modeling deformable human hands from medical images. In *Proceedings of the 2004 ACM SIGGRAPH symposium on computer animation (SCA-04)* (pp. 357–366).

Lander, J. (1998). Skin them bones: Game programming for the web generation. *Game Developer Magazine*, pp. 11–16.

Lander, J. (1999). Over my dead, polygonal body. *Game Developer Magazine*, 11–16.

Larboulette, C., & Cani, M.-P. (2004). Real-time dynamic wrinkles. In *Proceedings of the computer graphics international (CGI'04)* (pp. 522–525). Washington: IEEE Computer Society Press.

Larboulette, C., Cani, M.-P., & Arnaldi, B. (2005). Dynamic skinning: Adding real-time dynamic effects to an existing character animation. In *Proceedings of the 21st spring conference on computer graphics* (pp. 87–93). New York: ACM.

Lewis, J. P., Cordner, M., & Fong, N. (2000). Pose space deformation: A unified approach to shape interpolation and skeleton-driven deformation. In *Proceedings of the 27th annual conference on computer graphics and interactive techniques* (pp. 165–172). New York: ACM Press/Addison-Wesley.

Mohr, A., & Gleicher, M. (2003). Building efficient, accurate character skins from examples. *ACM Transactions on Graphics*, *22*(3), 562–568.

Pratscher, M., Coleman, P., Laszlo, J., & Singh, K. (2005). Outside-in anatomy based character rigging. In *Proceedings of the 2005 ACM SIGGRAPH/Eurographics symposium on computer animation* (pp. 329–338). New York: ACM.

Pyun, H., Shin, H. J., & Shin, S. Y. (2004). On extracting the wire curves from multiple face models for facial animation. *Computers & Graphics*, *28*(5), 757–765.

Rhee, T., Lewis, J. P., & Neumann, U. (2006). Real-time weighted pose-space deformation on the GPU. *Computer Graphics Forum*, *25*(3), 439–448.

Shen, J., Thalmann, N. M., & Thalmann, D. (1994). Human skin deformation from cross sections. In *Proceedings of computer graphics international*, Melbourne, Australia.

Singh, K., & Fiume, E. (1998). Wires: A geometric deformation technique. In *SIGGRAPH 98* (pp. 405–414).

Teran, J., Sifakis, E., Blemker, S. S., Ng-Thow-Hing, V., Lau, C., & Fedkiw, R. (2005). Creating and simulating skeletal muscle from the visible human data set. *IEEE Transactions on Visualization and Computer Graphics*, *11*(3), 317–328.

Thalmann, N. M., Laperrière, R., & Thalmann, D. (1988). Joint-dependent local deformations for hand animation and object grasping. In *Proceedings of graphics interface* (pp. 26–33).

Von Funck, W., Theisel, H., & Seidel, H.-P. (2006). Vector field based shape deformations. *ACM Transactions on Graphics (SIGGRAPH 06)*, *25*(3), 1118–1125.

Wang, X. C., & Phillips, C. (2002). Multi-weight enveloping: Least-squares approximation techniques for skin animation. In *Proceedings of the 2002 ACM SIGGRAPH/Eurographics symposium on computer animation* (pp. 129–138). New York: ACM Press.

Weber, J. (2000). Run-time skin deformation. In *Proceedings of game developers conference*.

Weber, O., Sorkine, O., Lipman, Y., & Gotsman, C. (2007). Context-aware skeletal shape deformation. *Computer Graphics Forum*, *26*(3), 265–274.

Wilhelms, J., & Van Gelder, A. (1997). Anatomically based modeling. In *Proceedings of the 1997 conference on computer graphics* (pp. 173–180). New York: ACM Press.

Yang, X. S., Somasekharan, A., & Zhang, J. J. (2006). Curve skeleton skinning for human and creature characters. *Computer Animation and Virtual Worlds*, *17*, 281–292.

You, L. H., Yang, X., & Zhang, J. J. (2008). Dynamic skin deformation with characteristic curves. *Computer Animation and Virtual Worlds*, *19*(3–4), 433–444.

You, L. H., Yang, X., You, X. Y., Jin, X. G., & Zhang, J. J. (2010). Shape manipulation using physically based wire deformations. *Computer Animation and Virtual Worlds*, *21*, 297–309.

Part V
Architecture and Displays

Chapter 21
The New Visualization Engine—The Heterogeneous Processor Unit

Jon Peddie

Abstract This chapter presents a brief and partial historical overview of the combination of technological events leading to a new paradigm in visualization—the development and embracing of Heterogeneous Processor Units (HPUs) along with supporting operating systems and development tools across multiple platforms from handheld mobile devices to supercomputers.

HPUs are the result of the evolution of integration of more functions and functionality in semiconductors due to the regular cadence of manufacturing processes shrinking—often referred to as Moore's Law.

The HPU is the integration of powerful serial processors like the ×86 architecture or RISC processors like ARM and MIPS, and highly parallel processors known as GPUs—graphics processor units. These HPUs bring new opportunities to the creation of powerful yet low cost visualization systems.

Abbreviations

HPU	Heterogeneous processor unit;
GPU	Graphics processor unit;
OpenCL	a HPU programming language and tool set;
SIMD	Single instruction, multiple data;
AIB	Add-in board;
FLOPS	Floating operations per second;
SoC	System on a Chip

21.1 Introduction

Late in the first decade of the 21st century three major developments took place independently but with profound implications when combined.

- Two broad-based new operating systems were introduced: Google's Android, and Microsoft's Windows 7.

J. Peddie (✉)
Jon Peddie Research, Tiburon, CA 94920, USA
e-mail: jon@jonpeddie.com

J. Dill et al. (eds.), *Expanding the Frontiers of Visual Analytics and Visualization*, DOI 10.1007/978-1-4471-2804-5_21, © Springer-Verlag London Limited 2012

- Three parallel processing tool sets and environments were introduced: CUDA from Nvidia, Direct Compute from Microsoft, and OpenCL from the open standards body Khronos.
- Multiple examples of advanced processors with CPU and GPU were introduced for the PC and mobile devices from semiconductor suppliers like AMD, Apple, Intel, Nvidia, Qualcomm, Texas Instruments, and others.

Taken singularly, any one of them is a major development and worthy of praise on its own part. But when combined a genuine synergistic major inflection point has been created—a new compute paradigm that will impact all aspects of computing and in particular visualization for decades to come.

21.2 Historical Overview

The story starts in 2000 when fabless[1] semiconductor graphics companies ATI (Toronto, Canada) and Nvidia (Santa Clara, California, USA) independently developed a new class of graphics controllers for the PC with programmable SIMD[2] architectures. Graphics processors are basically a pipeline structure with a logical front-end and a back-end. The front-end processes the elemental constructs of an image using three-dimensional meshes made of triangles. The back-end fills in the triangles and colors them to produce objects and image, and then presents it to the screen (Fig. 21.1).

The front-end is referred to as the vertex processor (for the vertices of the triangles) and the back-end is referred to as the pixel processor or renderer. Because processing of vertexes is a repetition of the same sequence of operations on multiple independent data sets it can be sped up by doing it in parallel using multiple processors operating on the stream of data; thus they are also called stream processors.

In their competitive efforts for market share ATI (founded in 1985) and Nvidia (founded in 1993) had a history of pushing the limits of semiconductor fabrication and architectural development to provide ever greater computing capability while taking advantage of the economics of Moore's Law (Computer History Museum 1965).

Nvidia's GeForce 256 add-in graphics board (AIB) with the NV10 chip released on August 31, 1999 took advantage of Moore's law to a add a hardware transform and lighting (T&L) engine offloading host geometry calculations from the CPU, and

[1] A fabless semiconductor company specializes in the design and sale of hardware devices and semiconductor chips while outsourcing the fabrication or "fab" of the devices to a specialized manufacturer called a semiconductor foundry.

[2] Single instruction, multiple data (SIMD), is a class of parallel computers with elements that perform the same operation on multiple data simultaneously. Thus, such machines exploit data level parallelism.

Fig. 21.1 Graphics pipeline

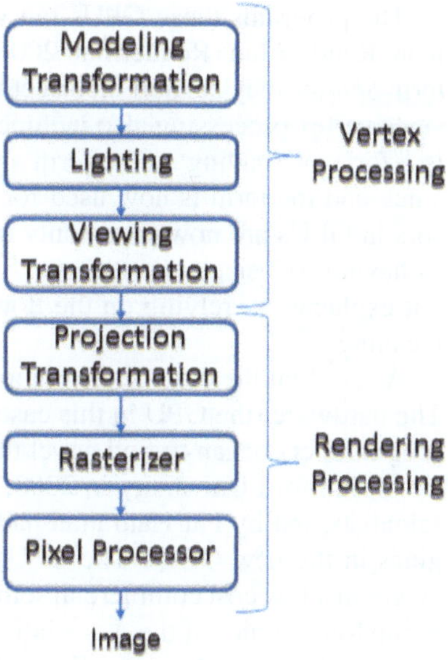

adding hardware motion-compensation for MPEG-2 video. It was also the introduction of a new nomenclature—the GPU—the graphics processor unit.[3]

These efforts in pursuit of parallel processing were realized first by Nvidia in Q2 2001 with their NV20 chip which was used on the GeForce 3 AIB. The NV20 had 1 vertex and 4 pixel processors. In Q3 of 2001 ATI brought out their R200 chip which was used on the Radeon 8500 AIB; it had 2 vertex and 4 pixel processors. However, for both these products, only the front end of the pipe (the "vertex processing") was fully programmable. 2002 saw the introduction of the first fully programmable pipeline processor, ATI's R300 application specific integrated circuit (ASIC[4]) used in the Radeon 9700 AIB. This product had both fully programmable vertex and pixel processing, and offered floating point processing in both parts. Nvidia followed this with their next GPU in early 2003, the NV30. This was the ignition of low cost parallel processors. R300 and NV30 were the first GPU's to really have programmable fragment shading, with NV40.[5]

In 2004 Nvidia introduced their NV40 graphics chip with what was considered astonishing at the time, 6 vertex processors and 16 pixel processor, and was the basis for their GeForce 68000 AIB. Two weeks later ATI brought out their R420 graphics chip, also with 6 vertex processors and 16 pixel processors, which was the basis for their Radeon X800XT AIB. With these new programmable SIMD devices and AIBs, the programmable GPU became a parallel processor.

[3]ATI initially called their unit a VPU—Video Processor Unit, but ultimately gave up the name and adopted the more popular GPU designation.

[4]GPUs are a special class of ASICs, and both terms are used interchangeably.

[5]The Nvidia NV40 also was the first to support Microsoft's Direct X 9 when it had an enhanced shader model (version 3) added which offered long programs and flow control.

The programs these GPUs ran were called "Shader programs." The term came from RenderMan (Renderman 2006), which Pixar introduced publicly in 1989. The term *Shader* may be a bit incorrect when used in the context of vertex programming since vertex processing also includes geometry processing, however, vertex lighting is a form of shading so the term shader has been generalized and used. The name stuck and the term is now used for other graphics pipeline stages too. The processors in GPUs are now commonly referred to as "shaders," i.e., a GPU is described as having 512 shaders or "cores".[6] The terminology is used interchangeably without explanation, relying on the flow of the conversation to establish the context of meaning.

As is often the case in the computing industry, the hardware leads the software. The hardware (the GPU in this case) was introduced to the market and then various programmers began to find novel things for them to do beside just graphics.

At Stanford University in 2003, a group of well known and respected computer scientists, led by Pat Hanrahan had been looking at the potential of the SIMD engines in the new GPUs. The GPUs represented a tremendous amount of compute power in a low cost commercial semiconductor. In 2004 at the annual special interest group for graphics of the Association for Computing Machines (SIGGRAPH-ACM) meeting, Ian Buck from the Stanford team gave a seminal paper on a programming paradigm for the new SIMD processors (Buck et al. 2004), which they called the Brook Project (a play on the streams of a brook).

Brook for GPUs is an extension of the C programming language that allows the inclusion of simple data-parallel constructs, enabling the use of the GPU as a streaming coprocessor. Brook's authors developed a compiler and runtime system that abstracted and virtualized many aspects of the graphics hardware. But what was most attention getting was they showed the acceleration of computation that was possible (with five applications: the SAXPY and SGEMV BLAS[7] operators, image segmentation, FFT, and ray tracing). For those applications they demonstrated that a GPU with their Brook implementation could perform up to seven times faster than a conventional ×86 CPU—it was a major turning point in the computing industry.

However, the programming, was done at the primitive application program interface (API) level using OpenGL,[8] and that was considered awkward and limiting general adoption. Also, the OS of the time Windows XP and variants of Linux did not support multiple incompatible processors. And, as significant as Moore's law was (and is) the process size, expressed in nanometers, limited the number of processors that could be integrated, the frequency they could run at, and the power dissipation. Time was needed for these elements to evolve and merge.

---

[6] A "core" typically now refers to an ALU (arithmetic Logic Unit) capable of at least a fp32 MAD (32-bit floating point Multiply-Add-Divide operation), as distinct from "processors" used in the context above, which is a collection of cores.

[7] SAXPY (Single-precision real Alpha X Plus Y[1]) is one of the functions in the Basic Linear Algebra Subprograms (BLAS) package, and is a common operation in computations with vector processors. SAXPY is a combination of scalar multiplication and vector addition.

[8] OpenGL is a cross-platform API for writing applications that produce 2D and 3D computer graphics.

The use of the GPU for computation is known as "GPU-compute," and somewhat incorrectly sometimes as "GPGPU."[9] GPGPU, also written GP-GPU and GP/GPU, was incorrect at the time because there is little to nothing general purpose (i.e., "GP") about a GPU. Over time, GPUs have become general purpose in their core capabilities, growing into their role as so-called parallel processor devices today. But the initial use of GPUs for general purpose computing was an over statement of the processor's capabilities. A GPU will not run ×86 code, doesn't have an operating system, and won't run applications through an operating system like Linux, Windows, or Apple OS.

Nonetheless, the opportunity was recognized by many in academia and industry. One of the first set of entrepreneurs to exploit this new compute power was PeakStream, founded in 2005. The company included former executives and technical people from Sun, VMWare, Nvidia, and NetApp, and whose Chief Scientist was Prof. Pat Hanrahan of Stanford. Then, almost before the company could get organized, and immediately after they introduced their product in 2006, Google bought the company in 2007—and, apparently, made it disappear—one of the mysteries of the industry.

21.3 Moore's Law and Transistor Feature Size

Predicting the future development of technology probably gained its most widespread attention with the science fiction novels of H.G. Wells, although there interesting and surprisingly accurate forecasts prior to that time. No less a genius than Alan Turing predicted in a 1950 paper that computers would have a billion words of memory by the turn of the millennium (GByte memory in a PC occurred in the mid 1990s). And equally impressive, Douglas Engelbart, a co-inventor of today's mechanical computer mouse, among things, discussed the downscaling of integrated circuit size in a 1960 (or 1959) lecture.

In April 1965, in Electronics Magazine, Gordon Moore published a story titled, "*Cramming more components onto integrated circuits*." In that paper he stated that transistor counts had doubled every year. But it wasn't until 1970 when the visionary VLSI[10] pioneer and Caltech professor, Carver Mead (Fairbairn 2009) used the expression "Moore's law," to illustrate his predictions about VLSI.[11] The term and notion stuck and we have used it ever since. Although originally calculated as a doubling of transistors every year, in the same square area of silicon, Moore later refined the period to two years; it is often incorrectly quoted as a doubling of transistors every 18 months.

[9] Mark Harris, PhD., introduced the term "GPGPU" in 2002 (while an employee of Nvidia), and founded the website www.gpgpu.org that same year.

[10] VLSI—Very Large Scale Integration—semiconductors with hundreds of thousands of transistors.

[11] It was while chatting with a journalist that Mead coined the term Moore's Law.

21.4 Evolution of GPU Development

The graphical processor unit has become more powerful and complex every year since its introduction in 1999. Computer graphics and visualization is a natural home for parallel processing and as resolutions have increased, so has the demand for more complex images and cinematic quality features. This is particularly evident in simulation and visualization systems, high-end PC video games, and the cinema. All three of these application segments, plus several others, have an unrelenting requirement for greater image quality, performance, and lower (or at least the same) costs. As this writer is fond of saying, "*In computer graphics, too much is not enough.*" (Peddie 2005).

GPU development has kept abreast of the development of semiconductor fabrication processes. And with each move to a new and smaller feature size or fabrication node, GPUs have exploited those developments. In fact, they are one of the computing devices most able to take advantage of process density improvements, as GPUs derive their performance naturally from more transistors. Being a parallel device means that more parallel processing can be done and that translates to more performance.

21.5 PC-Based GPUs

By 2011 Nvidia was producing its Fermi class GPU built in a 40 nm semiconductor process that had over 3 billion transistors and 512 unified shaders—the GF110. A "unified" shader is a universal shader or processor that can be employed either as a vertex processor or a pixel processor as the work load demands, or for parallel processing.

In the same time period, AMD, which acquired ATI in 2005, was offering its Cayman processor, also built in a 40 nm processor with 2.64 billion transistors, and it had 1536 unified processors. The AMD device claimed a theoretical performance of 2.7 TFLOPS,[12] while Nvidia claimed a theoretical 1.581 TFLOPS. By comparison, Intel's best ×86 processor of the time, the six-core 1.17 billion transistor core i7 980 PC processor, built in a 32 nm process, had a theoretical peak performance of 107.55 GFLOPS, while AMD's 12-core Magny-Cours built with 1.8 billion transistors was delivering 120 GFLOPS. FLOPS of course is not the only measure of a processor's capability and it's not a really fair way to evaluate GPUs and CPUs since it is so case and usage dependent. However, it is interesting to use as a general comparison, and to illustrate the point about the compute density of GPUs compared to ×86 CPUs.

Because of the SIMD parallel processing nature of a GPU, sometimes referred to as scaling out rather than scaling up (in frequency), some users portray the GPU

[12]In computing, FLOPS (or flops or flop/s) is an acronym meaning FLoating point OPerations per Second. The FLOPS is a measure of a computer's performance, especially in fields of scientific calculations that make heavy use of floating point calculations.

as beating Moore's law. Nowhere is such development needed more than in visualization systems. GPUs in PCs also drive high refresh displays (120/240 Hz) and provide stereovision images (S3D) for visualization applications. A modern AIB can drive at least two screens with resolutions of 2560 × 1600 each, and some AIBs can drive up to six HD+ screens for visualization systems.

21.6 Mobile Devices GPUs

Mobile devices such as mobile phones and tablets have greater constraints in size and power consumption than a PC. Also, it was not until 2010 that smartphones and tablets began to be considered as an alternative to a PC. Nonetheless, the GPUs designed for such mobile devices scaled up to offer four, eight, 16 and more graphics processors. Mobile phones are not considered visualization devices although they are used in augmented reality applications. However, mobile phones can drive a HDTV and could be used in visualization applications. Tablets are used in visualization and presentation applications, and as such need powerful 3D acceleration and GPU-compute capability. GPUs in mobile devices will drive high-refresh (120 Hz) displays and support stereo graphics.

21.7 Introduction of the HPU

Integrating a general purpose CPU (×86 or RISC) with a SIMD-based GPU to create a heterogeneous processor unit (HPU) came in 2010 as the evolution of semiconductor fabrication techniques enabled increased integration. First discussed by the ×86 CPU manufacturer AMD in 2005 after their acquisition of the GPU manufacturer ATI, it took five years for the process technology to catch up with the idea. Heterogeneous computing has been defined as the use of processors with different instruction set architectures (ISA) under direct application programmer control—that is a system that uses a variety of different types of computational units. A generalized block diagram of a HPU is shown in Fig. 21.2.

Heterogeneous processing has been common for years, even before it was practical or possible to integrate individual processing elements. An early example is Intel's 80286 CPU that had an external floating point co-processor: the 80287.[13] Application programs required access to floating point coprocessors with instructions not found on the main CPU, and when the floating point processor was integrated with the CPU in one chip, as Intel did in 1995 with the popular 80386, the Intel ×86 instruction set was extended so that application programs could access the two processors. This was an early example of an HPU being made possible by shrinking semiconductor fabrication process or feature sizes.

[13]The Intel 80286 (also called iAPX 286), introduced on February 1, 1982, was a 16-bit ×86 microprocessor with 134,000 transistors.

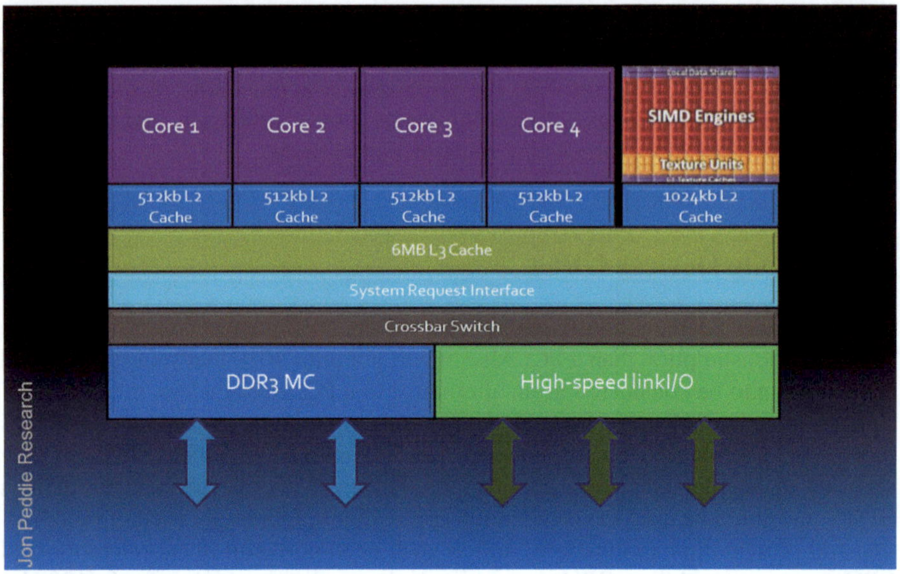

Fig. 21.2 Heterogeneous processor block diagram

Other examples of ×86 or RISC CPUs coupled with FPGAs (field-programmable gate-arrays semiconductors) co-processors, where the FPGA is set up for a specific set of functions similar to an ASIC, have been developed and sold commercially. So the notion and even the implementation of an integrated heterogeneous processor is not new. One can find HPUs of one form or another in many devices, but they may not be programmable. What the GPU suppliers accomplished was the ability to satisfy a large and varied market. Their GPUs are able to run a lot of mass-market software, whether games, scientific visualization or user interfaces, and they are able to bring down the price of their semiconductors by economies of scale in manufacturing. The GPU suppliers added extra programmability with very little silicon area, and distributed their GPUs to a lot of people making it economical to develop software for them.

What is significant about the HPUs introduced in 2010 and subsequently is the use of very popular computing elements such as ARM RISC, MIPS RISC, ×86, and SIMD GPUs which carry a large number of popular software applications, legacy code, and API support. However, without the support of the operating system, using a HPU not be easy.

21.8 Evolution of Operating System Development

Prior to Microsoft's Windows 7 operating system there was no direct support for HPUs in Windows machines. Linux, which is open source, allows for multiple kernels and thereby allows a program developer to give system access to other processors—to give them first class citizenship as it is referred to. Apple's OS, which is based on Linux, provided HPU support in the version named Snow Leopard in mid 2009. Windows 7 came out in the fall of 2009, so by then the PC world was ready for HPUs. A year later AMD introduced their Fusion HPUs.

Grand Central Dispatch (GCD) in the Mac OS X Snow Leopard made it much easier for developers to exploit the power of multicore systems. With GCD, threads are handled by the operating system, not by individual applications. GCD-enabled programs can automatically distribute their work across all available cores, resulting in the best possible performance.

Although Microsoft's Window's 7 offered support for multiple processors, it restricted it by the price. The maximum total quantity of logical processors in a PC that Windows 7 supports is: 32 for 32-bit, and 256 for 64-bit. The maximum number of physical processors of a PC that Windows 7 supports is: 2 for Professional, Enterprise, and Ultimate; 1 for Starter, Home Basic, and Home Premium. With Windows 7, the GPU and CPU exist in a co-processing environment where each can handle the computing task they are best suited to. The CPU is good at performing sequential calculations, I/O, and program flow, and the GPU is well suited for performing massive parallel calculations.

In early 2011 Linus Torvalds, the developer of Linux, announced a new version of the Linux kernel that enhanced support for speeding up operations in SMP (symmetric multiprocessing) systems. Although not specially designed for HPU architectures Linux has been the foundation OS for the DARPA High Productivity Computing Systems Program since 2006, which seeks to exploit the benefits of HPUs.

Mobile devices did not offer direct HPU support through the popular (at the time) Nokia Symbian operating system. However, the Linux based Android operating system from Google did, as did later versions of Apple's iOS used in the popular iPhone and iPad. Intel introduced an OS for their mobile devices called MeeGo also based on Linux, with multiprocessor support. In 2011 Microsoft announced Windows 8 would run on ARM based RISC processors with multiprocessor HPU support—so the market was ready to move forward with HPUs.

"Support" for HPU or multi processors (and "first-class citizenship") means that the other processors in the system have equal access to system memory and peripherals, can be called by applications, and can be scheduled for workload balancing. The processors may implement message passing or shared memory inter-core communication methods.

21.9 HPUs in Various Platforms

HPUs are not unique to the PC or any single platform. HPUs can be found in PCs, Supercomputers, mobile phones, tablets, game consoles, and even automobiles. However, not all HPUs are built the same, nor can they all do the same work.

Physical limitations, power supply and consumption restrictions, and logical applications of the given platform, all play a role in the construction and capability of an HPU.

In the following sections the differences in HPUs for a given platform will be discussed.

21.10 PCs

When Intel first incorporated a small GPU in the same package with a CPU in their popular Clarksfield processor in 2010 many analysts forecasted the end of discrete GPUs, citing the inevitable march of progress and semiconductor integration. The demise of the discrete (i.e., stand-alone) GPU had been forecasted in the past when chipsets had graphics integrated in them in 1997. What they didn't realize then, or in 2010, was the size and power consumption of GPUs, rivaling that of a CPU. One of the reasons AMD and Intel went to multi-core CPU designs was because it was the only way they could offer more computing power (FLOPS) without consuming exponential amounts of electrical power (Watts). The CPU can only be so big, and consume so much electrical power. The GPU has the same issues and a modern PC with a high-end graphics board in it will have four to ten fans running, trying to keep the processors temperature down. So there are problems associated with putting a 250w CPU in the same package as a 250w GPU. The HPUs used in PCs have to compromise on either the SIMD processor or the serial (×86) processor.

AMD's first generation HPUs,[14] introduced in 2011, and code named Llano, have hundreds of GPUs cores and up to four ×86 cores. The ×86 cores are not the most powerful ×86s AMD could build. Intel in their embedded graphics processor (EGP) code named Sandy Bridge has very powerful ×86 cores and only a dozen GPU cores. AMD believes HPUs with powerful SIMDs will be more important to both the consumer products of the future as well as the scientific processors. Intel, with obvious bias toward ×86, is of the view that a powerful multi-core CPU is more important. Intel has been reluctant to designate their processors as HPUs.

21.11 Game Consoles

In 2000 IBM, Sony, and Toshiba began a joint project to develop a new multi-core processor to be known as the Cell (The Cell architecture 2012). In 2005 the company disclosed the device at the ISSCC conference,[15] and in late 2006 Sony began shipping the PlayStation 3 with the Cell in it. The Cell has a front end processor

[14] AMD markets their HPU as an "APU"—accelerate processor unit.

[15] International Solid-State Circuits Conference, held annually in San Francisco and sponsored by the Institute of Electrical and Electronic Engineers (IEEE).

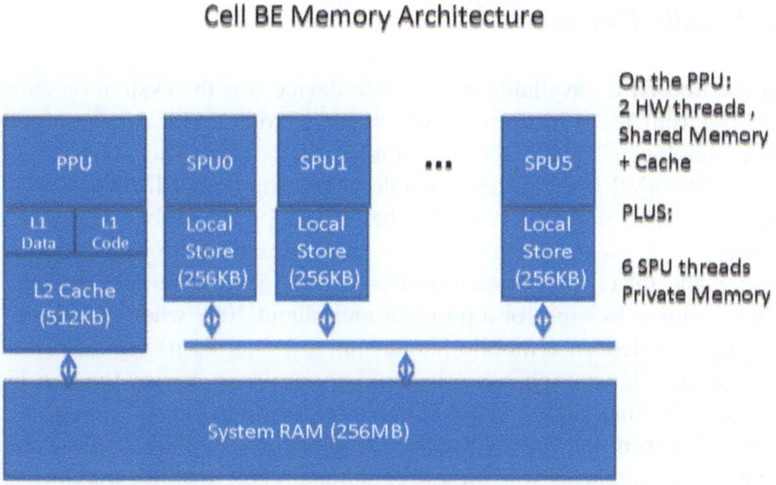

Fig. 21.3 The cell memory architecture. Figure courtesy of Codeplay

based on the 64-bit dual-threaded IBM Power architecture known as the Power Processing Element (PPE) and eight streaming processors elements known as SPEs. The SPEs form a SIMD architecture, and the PPE is very similar to an ×86, and thus the Cell is essentially an HPU. A block diagram of the Cell HPU is shown in Fig. 21.3.

In 2009 IBM ceased development of the Cell architecture, although the chip found its way into one of the world's most powerful supercomputers, and many specialized systems. Some say the Cell was a failed processor, but it was a pioneer in consumer HPUs.

Microsoft introduced the first Xbox in 2001 basically not much more than a repackaged PC. In 2005 the company introduced the Xbox 360 with a dedicated graphics unit (GPU), and an IBM Power multi-core processor—slightly modified versions of the PPE in the Cell processor used on the PlayStation 3. In 2010 Microsoft merged the two designs into one chip (code named Vejle) called the XCGPU to create their HPU for a console platform. The Xbox 360 has a custom operating system (based on Windows NT architecture and Windows XP) developed as a separate project within Microsoft. While the operating system supports many of the same APIs found in Win32, not everything that is in Windows is in the Xbox 360 OS. In addition, Microsoft developed a special version of its Direct3D API for the Xbox platform. Microsoft had an OS that supported a HPU for its Xbox at about the same time Windows 7 was coming out.

Researchers in universities and elsewhere have built small supercomputers by bringing together dozens of game consoles to exploit the low cost computing power. No doubt we will see similar experiments using HPUs in game consoles.

21.12 Mobile Devices

One of the first HPUs available in a mobile device was the system on chip (SoC) OMAP2420 from Texas Instruments which was introduced in 2006 and used Imagination Technologies' "VGP" (Vector Graphics Processor). The VGP is an optional part of the PowerVR MBX cores. Capable of floating point SIMD processing, it is effectively a shader unit. Renesas introduced a chip (SH Mobile G3) in a similar timeframe.

The demand for GPU computation wasn't very great in mobile devices, it was more of a solution looking for a problem until about 2009 when the idea of doing transcoding of video on a mobile phone started to be discussed.[16] Prior to 2009 the GPUs in mobile smartphones were used primarily for driving the user interface (UI), and accelerating games. The API that gave access to the GPUs in smartphones is OpenGL ES from the open standards organization Khronos. In the version 2.0 of OpenGL ES, emphasis was on a programmable 3D graphics pipeline with the ability to create shader and program objects and the ability to write vertex and fragment shaders in the OpenGL ES Shading Language. This was also the rudimentary method of employing the GPU for GPU-compute applications.

The market for smartphones began its significant growth in 2008 and by 2011 had passed PC shipments in unit volume. A powerful computer that fitted into one's pocket, it was only logical that it would exploit the HPU. Right behind it was the introduction of ARM-based tablets, the iconic Apple iPad being the most well known. Seeking to exploit these new market developments, companies brought HPU SoCs to market such as Intel's Moorestown, Marvell's Armada, Nvidia's Tegra, Qualcomm's SnapDragon, Samsung's S5PC100, STMicroelectronics' SPEAr, Texas Instruments' OMAP, and others like VIA's WonderMedia hoping to catch the wave and be part of the growth path. Apple used their own SoC (built at Samsung's fab) for phones and tablets.

Although more HPUs were being built for smartphones than PCs at the turn of the decade, smartphone application developers were slow to exploit the extra power a SIMD and RISC engine with DSP features. OpenCL was ported to ARM-based and other low power processors in 2011 and mobile phones with it, or able to use it, began to be shipped in 2012. This completed the infrastructure needed and HPU applications on mobile devices like smartphones and tablets increased in 2013. The SoC suppliers fell into two camps—those who bought GPU designs (IP—intellectual property), and those who had their own in-house GPU designs. They mostly used ARM, and to a lesser extent MIPS processor designs (IP).

Nvidia, and Qualcomm have their own in-house GPUs. The other SoC builders used either ARM's Mali GPU design, or Imagination Technologies's, or Viviante's. All the GPUs were (and are) OpenGL ES and OpenCL compatible, and therefore capable of providing (exposing) the SIMD capabilities for a HPU.

---

[16]Transcoding is the conversion of a video file from one compression scheme (e.g., MPEG-2) to another such as H.264 or MPEG-4.

Qualcomm is an ARM CPU architecture licensee and has developed its own "Scorpion" CPU core that delivers performance similar to that of ARM's Cortex-A9 but with lower power consumption and greater SIMD performance. To enhance its 3D-graphics expertise, Qualcomm in 2009 acquired the former ATI mobile-graphics unit from AMD (for $65 million), and has since invested in improving the performance of its GPUs for integration into several Snapdragon chipsets for Smartphones and Tablets. Qualcomm's integrated Adreno GPUs use a tile based, unified shader architecture that is similar to XBox 360's "Xenos" GPU, and Adreno supports the latest 3D graphics APIs for Android and Windows Mobile operating systems. Qualcomm will also be supporting OpenCL in the near future.

Nvidia has embraced the ARM architecture for a family of products and a long product roadmap. Addressing the question of how could Nvidia survive in the face of HPUs from AMD and Intel, Nvidia answered by adopting ARM and leveraging from the Microsoft porting of Windows to the ARM architecture. Nvidia came to the HPU market from a visualization context and employed its GPU designs to a low power yet still very powerful design.

Nvidia has also announced the development of a powerful HPU code-named Denver. Similar in general organization to Tegra but with many more ARM and GPU cores, Denver is targeted at the server market as a high-performance computing (HPC) HPU element. Nvidia has adapted its CUDA programming environment to its Tegra, Denver, and other HPU products as well as OpenCL.

21.13 Power Consumption

In mobile devices the challenge is to provide a powerful GPU capability for display and for compute. This means achieving a sub 1 W power envelope for CPU + GPU + Memory. Mobile CPU/GPUs consume about one-percent that of the power of desktop, yet the performance is catching up. At the same time the larger PC-based processors are becoming more power efficient.

Power management in mobile devices is where the technological revolution is happening. The primary OpenCL case will be for imaging and video post processing. Portability of code for these algorithms between different platforms will be a major challenge for some time. Even though OpenCL has a lot of promise, Renderscript from Google, which runs at a lower level, could be disruptive. These technologies are discussed in the next section.

An important factor influencing power consumption is data movement to and from the memory and the HPU. This requires programmers to avoid sending data and instructions off-chip and to use separate smaller units—to keep the data close to the execution units. This is an aspect of HPUs that will gain a lot of attention in the future as programmers seek to exploit the inter-processor communications in a HPU.

21.14 Evolution of GPU-Compute Development Environments

Using the SIMD features of a many-core GPU for computation is usually thought of as parallel processing or parallel computing. However, parallel processing is not an operation that is exclusive to the GPU. The multi- and many-core ×86 and RISC processors can also do parallel processing. Any time multiple compute units run simultaneously to achieve a common result, they performing parallel processing.

21.15 Examples of Multicore Processors

Examples of multicore processors have been, and are with us, in almost every system.

Multicore processors in desktop platforms

×86 based
- AMD Bulldozer—8 physical cores
- AMD Komodo and Terramar—16 and 20 ×86 cores
- AMD Llano and Trinity HPUs—2–4 ×86 cores + SIMD GPU
- Intel Nehelem—6 physical cores
- Intel Ivy Bridge and Haswell—8 14-stage ×86 cores + SIMD

RISC based
- Freescale—4 ARM RISC cores
- Marvell Armada—2/4 ARM RISC cores + SIMD GPU
- Nvidia Tegra and Denver—2/4 and 16 ARM RISC cores + SIMD GPU
- Texas Instruments OMAP—3 to 8 ARM RISC cores + SIMD GPU
- Qualcomm Snapdragon—4 ARM RISC cores + SIMD GPU

GPU based
- AMD Stream SIMD GPU—1600 cores
- Nvidia Fermi SIMD GPU—512 cores

Special purpose and massively parallel devices
- Intel Larrabee/Knights Ferry/Knights Corner—32—80 ×86 cores
- Stream Processors and raster image processors (RIP)
- Ambric—300+ (RIP)
- Tilera—100 cores
- IBM Cell Processor (8 SPUs +1 host processor) RIP except PS3

Multicore DSPs
- Analog Devices Blackfin—16 and 32 cores
- PicoChip PC205—250–300 cores
- Texas Instruments MVP—5 core

Multicore, many-core, magny-core architectures have been available for decades. The promise of doing things faster by doing them simultaneously is too compelling to ignore, and the sooner the work is done the sooner it stops consuming power. The challenge is in the programming of all these cores.

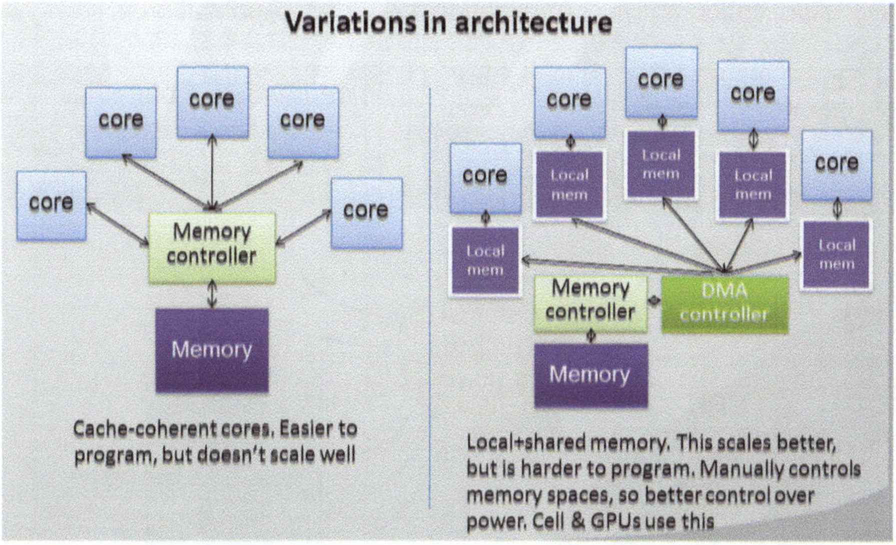

Fig. 21.4 Variations in hardware (courtesy of Codeplay)

21.16 Programming GPU—SIMDs Represents a Challenge

Most current hardware is parallel, most software is not. The challenge for programmers is to keep all the processors busy, and to keep multiple parallel threads of execution synchronized. One of the ways to add that synchronization is to put local memory close to the processor cores, as illustrated in Fig. 21.4. This also helps keep the data on the chip which reduces throughput and speeds up computations.

In addition there are differences in programming models and general industry experience. CPUs are widely understood and standardized. It is relatively easy to develop new a CPU and test it by running existing software. When CPUs evolve instruction sets, and only add new instructions, all the old (legacy) code runs fine, and typically the hardware is separated by the OS.

GPUs evolve much faster than CPUs, with new technologies and standards every year. Programmers need to write new test software for new features. New GPUs often completely change their instruction-set architecture (ISA). That creates a challenge to keep compilers, drivers and OS tightly integrated and developing rapidly. These problems will be with us for many years. Many organizations are working on developing compilers for parallel architectures, with various levels of tool sets and technical support.

21.17 HPU Programming Environments

There are three major parallel processing programming environments for a programmer/developer to choose from:

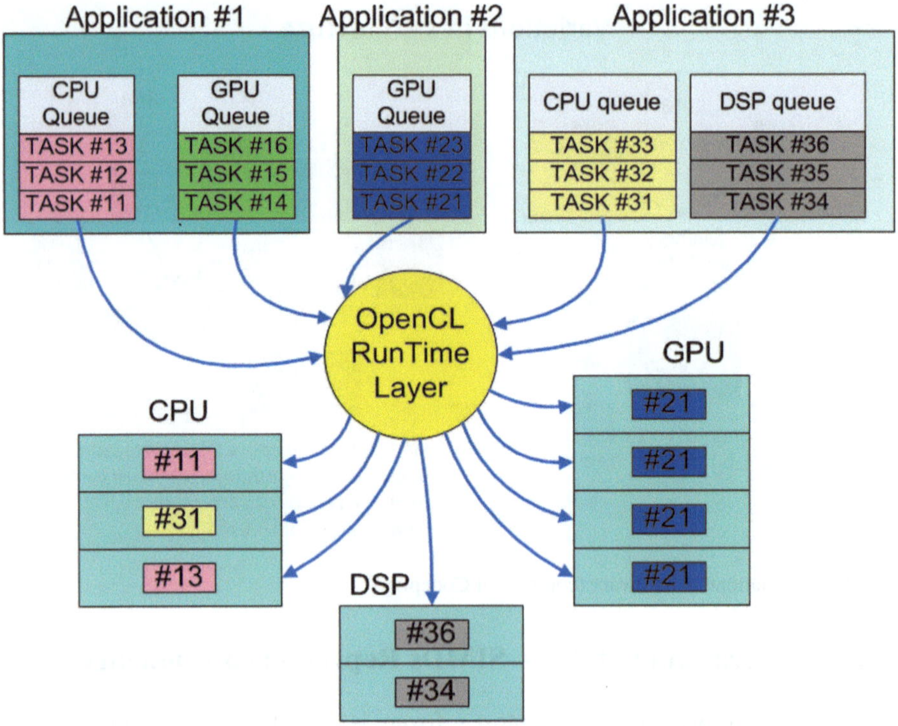

Fig. 21.5 OpenCL can manage multiple tasks with multiple heterogeneous processors (Courtesy of Khronos)

Khronos' OpenCL
Microsoft's DirectCompute "C like"
Nvidia's CUDA—multi-language (C, Fortran)

And several other tools and development systems

CilK (C/C++)
Codeplay VectorC/C++
Google Renderscript
Intel's ArBB (C++ like)
OPenMP
ParaSail
Multi-threaded JAVA

OpenCL stands for Open Computing Language. It is a C-based programming language with a structure that is familiar to programmers. OpenCL was developed by Apple and uses Xcode developer tools. Xcode is a toolset for building Mac OS X and iOS applications and developers can adapt their programs to work with OpenCL. A generalized diagram of OpenCL and its run-time layer is shown in Fig. 21.5.

In most cases it is not necessary to completely rewrite applications to use OpenCL. Developers and programmers only need to rewrite the most performance-intensive parts of their applications in OpenCL. The vast majority of application code can be left unchanged. OpenCL is an open standard that is supported by the industry.

DirectCompute from Microsoft is an application programming interface (API) that supports general-purpose computing on graphics processing units on Microsoft Windows Vista and Windows 7. DirectCompute is part of the Microsoft DirectX collection of APIs and was initially released with the DirectX 11 API but runs on both DirectX 10 and DirectX 11 graphics processing units The DirectCompute architecture shares a range of computational interfaces with OpenCL CUDA.

CUDA (Compute Unified Device Architecture) is a parallel computing architecture developed by Nvidia. Within the CUDA environment are several compliers, C, Fortran, and CUDA for ×86, and third party wrappers are also available for Python, Perl, Fortran, Java, Ruby, Lua, MATLAB and IDL, native support exists in Mathematica. Programmers use C for CUDA (C with Nvidia extensions and certain restrictions), compiled through a PathScale Open64 C compiler. CUDA gives developers access to the virtual instruction set and memory of the parallel computational elements in CUDA GPUs.

Renderscript from Google has a Honeycomb operating system feature. It is an API targeted at high-performance 3D rendering and compute operations. The goal of Renderscript is to bring a lower level, higher performance API to Android developers. It provides three primary tools: A simple 3D rendering API on top of hardware acceleration, a developer friendly compute API similar to CUDA, and a familiar language in C99. Performance gains come from executing native code on the device. The development language for Renderscript is C99 with extensions, which is compiled to a device-agnostic intermediate format during the development process and placed into the application package.

21.18 The Programming Environment

The basic development environment for HPUs is shown in Fig. 21.6.

Such a development environment typically consists of a host library, a limited set of operations by CPU on GPU, a high level kernel language (C) and a compiler for SIMD processors Software running on the GPU has local scope separate from CPU. This is a model of computation that describes launching kernels, defines workgroups, and scheduler behavior.

21.19 When Is Parallel Processing Useful?

Parallel processing is useful any time the data set is large, well organized and susceptible to SIMD operations.

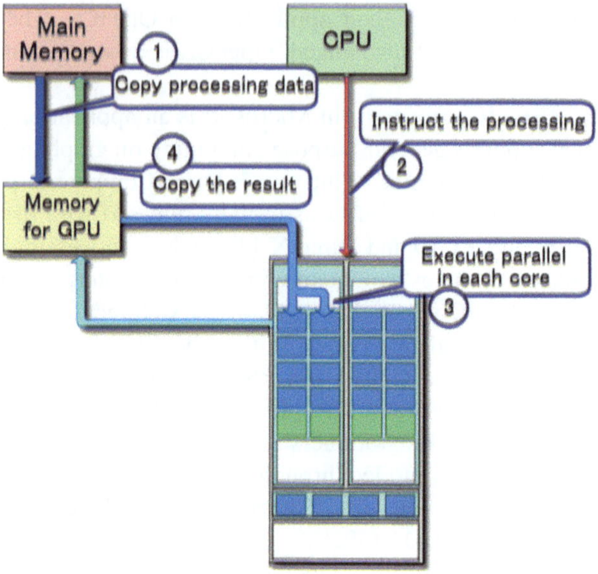

Fig. 21.6 Organization of a HPU programming model such as CUDA or OpenCL (Wikipedia)

Some of the better known examples are:

- Visualization systems
- Post processing with GPU compute
- Image processing and video compression
- Oil and gas most often mentioned applications
- Super Computers with millions of GPUs
- Financial institutions (second only to manufacturing, includes pharmaceuticals)
- Augmented Reality or language translations on a mobile phone

21.20 Visualization Systems and HPUs

Visualization systems consist of personalized two to five monitor systems, 6–48 or more monitors in a visualization wall (as shown in Fig. 21.7), to four to six-sided rooms known as a CAVE and driven by rear projectors.

One PC-based HPU can drive two to five monitors and be mounted on the back of one of the monitors. An HPU in a desk-side system can drive three to four monitors for a local personal visualization system. The cost savings of such a system are enormous. In addition to driving the displays the same HPU can process the data for the display. Multiple HPUs can be used for more complex computation and display options.

Fig. 21.7 The Petit Science Center Visualization Wall is one of the largest (total pixels) tiled display walls in the world (Courtesy of Georgia State University)

21.21 Summary

Critical research in bio-science, design, and manufacturing is compromised due to obstacles to accessible and affordable FLOPS. Very affordable, massively parallel HPUs will reduce that obstacle and essentially put a supercomputer in the hands of all researchers, engineers, and scientists. HPUs will be deployed in visualization systems ranging from multi-monitor installations in individual's offices and laboratories to giant cave installations and ...

As Jim Thomas used to say, *The best is yet to come.*

References

Buck, I., Foley, T., Horn, D., Sugerman, J., Fatahalian, K., Houston, M., & Hanrahan, P. (2004). Brook for GPUs: stream computing on graphics hardware. *ACM Transactions on Graphics (TOG)—Proceedings of ACM SIGGRAPH 2004*, *23*(3), 777–786.

Computer History Museum (1965). "Moore's Law" predicts the future of integrated circuits. http://www.computerhistory.org/semiconductor/timeline/1965-Moore.html.

Fairbairn, D. (interviewer) (2009). Carver mead oral history. Computer History Museum, CHM Reference number: X4309.2008, May 27, 2009, Mountain View, CA.

Peddie, J. (2005). All about getting parallel. Hexus: http://www.hexus.net/content/item.php?item=1094&redirect=yes.

Renderman (2006). CG society of digital artists. http://wiki.cgsociety.org/index.php/Renderman.

The Cell architecture (2012). http://domino.research.ibm.com/comm/research.nsf/pages/r.arch.innovation.html.

Chapter 22
Smart Cloud Computing

Tosiyasu L. Kunii

Abstract Open smart devices such as Android devices as clients of cloud computing as open servers are requiring a transparent and highly universal modeling of the worlds in cloud computing to overcome combinatorial explosion of cloud computing in designing and testing. Hence, appropriate scalable modeling of cloud computing is sought. Extreme diversities, versatility and dynamism of cloud computing applications are shown to be supported by the cloud computing modeling in an incrementally modular abstraction hierarchy (IMAH) with homotopy extension property (HEP) and homotopy lifting property (HLP).

22.1 Introduction

Cloud computing has true potential to free all applications of information technology to social activities such as business, finance, commerce, manufacturing and industry in general, from the constraint of the capacities of individual sites. Also it has been removing the limit of availability of applications through smart devices including smart phones and smart terminals, Android devices in particular, surfing cloud computing spaces.

These potentials of cloud computing become real by the support of scalable computational modeling, overcoming the current combinatorial computational modeling that is causing exponential explosion of computation as serious social problems and hazards.

Dynamically evolving cloud computing worlds in cloud spaces are modularly and hierarchically generated and/or reorganized automatically, eliminating testing by an incrementally modular abstraction hierarchy (IMAH) via attaching functions (also called pasting functions, adjunction functions) that glue equivalent spaces together homotopically, and meeting customers' and suppliers' requirements. The basic principle is information invariants preservation, analogous to material invariants preservation such as mass and energy preservation as invariants in physical worlds

T.L. Kunii (✉)
Iidabashi First Tower 31F, Morpho, Inc., 2-6-1 Koraku, Bunkyo-ku, Tokyo 112-0004, Japan
e-mail: kunii@ieee.org
url: http://member.acm.org/~kunii/

J. Dill et al. (eds.), *Expanding the Frontiers of Visual Analytics and Visualization*,
DOI 10.1007/978-1-4471-2804-5_22,

as seen in physical sciences as the foundation of mechanics, electromagnetism and biology. Such fundamental principle on information invariants is shown to be crucial to effectively utilize cloud computing.

22.2 Cyberworlds

Cyberworlds are being formed in cyberspaces as computational spaces, in cloud computing spaces in particular. Now cyberworlds are rapidly expanding on the Web either intentionally or spontaneously, with or without design (T. L. Kunii 1969, 1998; T. L. Kunii and H. S. Kunii 1999). Widespread and intensive local activities are melting each other on the web globally to create cyberworlds. The diversity of cyberworlds makes it hard to see consistency in terms of *invariants*. The consistency requires for us to abstract the most essentials out of the diversity, and hence the most abstract mathematics. It has been true in science in general, and in the theory of physics to theorize the material worlds in particular.

What are the most essential *invariants* in theorizing cyberworlds? A branch of the most abstract mathematics is topology. For topology to be computable, it has to be algebraic. So, the researches have been conducted for over two decades on *cyberworld invariants* in algebraic topology. *Equivalence relations* define invariants at various abstraction levels.

The first half of the paper serves as an initial summary of algebraic topological resources for studying cyberworlds starting from the very elementary set theoretical level (T. L. Kunii 2003). High social impact application cases of cloud computing such as e-financing, e-commerce and e-manufacturing are presented.

22.2.1 Set Theoretical Design

First of all, we start our design work of cyberworlds from defining a collection of objects we are looking at to construct them in cyberspaces. To be able to conduct automation on such collections by using computers as intelligent machines, each collection has to be a *set* because computers are built as set theoretical machines. The set of all the subsets of X, $\{U \mid U \subseteq X\}$, is called a *power set* of X and denoted as 2^x. It is also called the *discrete topology* of X. The discrete topology is quite useful to design the cyberspace as consisting of subcyberspaces, hence we use discrete topology for cloud computing.

22.2.2 Topological Design

Now, we go into the business of designing the cyberspace as the union of the subcyberspaces of X and their overlaps. The cyberspace thus designed is generally called a *topological space* (X, T) where $T \subseteq 2^x$. Designing a topological space is automated by the following specification:

(1) $X \in T$ and $\varnothing \in T$;
(2) For an arbitrary index set J,

$$\forall j \in J\ (U_j \in T) \rightarrow \bigcup_{j \in J} U_j \in T;$$

(3) $U, V \in T \rightarrow U \cap V \in T$.

T is said to be the *topology* of the topological space (X, T). Given two topologies T_1 and T_2 on X such that $T_1 \subset T_2$, we say T_1 is *weaker* or *smaller* than T_2 (alternatively, we say that T_2 is *stronger* or *larger* than T_1. We also say T_2 is *finer* than T_1, or T_1 is *coarser* than T_2). Obviously the *strongest topology* is the discrete topology (the power set) and the *weakest topology* is $\varnothing$. For simplicity, we often use X instead of (X, T) to represent a topological space whenever no ambiguity arises. When we see two topological spaces (X, T) and (Y, T'), how can we tell (X, T) and (Y, T') are equivalent? Here is a criterion for us to use computers to automatically validate that they are topologically equivalent. Two topological spaces (X, T) and (Y, T') are *topologically equivalent* (or *homeomorphic*) if there is a function $f : (X, T) \rightarrow (Y, T')$ that is continuous, and its inverse exists and is continuous. We write $(X, T) \approx (Y, T')$ for (X, T) to be homeomorphic to (Y, T'). Then, how to validate the *continuity* of a function f? It amounts to check, first, $\forall B \in T'$, $f^{\leftarrow} B \in T$, where $f^{\leftarrow} B$ means the inverse image of B by f, then, next, check the following:

$$B \text{ is open } \Leftrightarrow\ f^{-1}(B) \text{ is also open in } X.$$

22.2.3 Functions

Given a function $f : X \rightarrow Y$, there are a total function and a partial function. For $f : X \rightarrow Y$ iff $\forall x \in X$, $\exists f(x)$, f is called a *total function*. A function $f : X' \rightarrow Y \mid X' \supseteq X$ is called a *partial function*, and not necessarily $f(x)$ exists for every $x \in X$. For total functions, there are three basic types of relationships or mappings: *Injective* or *into*, *surjective* or *onto*, *bijective*, meaning injective and surjective.

22.2.4 Equivalence Relations

For a binary relation $R \subseteq X \times X$ on a set X, R is:
reflexive if $(\forall x \in X)\ [xRx]$: reflexivity,
symmetric if $(\forall x, y \in X)\ [xRy \Rightarrow yRx]$: symmetry, and
transitive if $(\forall x, y, z \in X)\ [[xRy \Rightarrow yRz] \Rightarrow xRz]$: transitivity.

R is called an *equivalence relation* (in a notation $\sim$) if R is reflexive, symmetric and transitive.

Given $x \in X$, a subset of X defined by $x/\!\sim\, = \{y \in X : x \sim y\}$ is called the *equivalence class* of x. Here a class actually means a set; it is a tradition, and hard to be changed at this stage. The set of all the equivalence classes $X/\!\sim$ is called the *quotient space* or the *identification space* of X.

$$X/\!\sim\, = \{x/\!\sim\, \in 2^X \mid x \in X\} \subseteq 2^X.$$

From the transitivity, for each $x \in X$, $x/\!\sim\, \neq \phi$, the followings hold:

$$x \sim y \Leftrightarrow x/\!\sim\, = y/\!\sim, \quad \text{and}$$
$$x \not\sim y \Leftrightarrow x/\!\sim\, \cap\, y/\!\sim\, = \phi.$$

This means a set X is *partitioned* (also called *decomposed*) into non-empty and *disjoint* equivalence classes.

Let us look at simple examples. In e-commerce, to be e-merchandise is an equivalence relation while e-trading is a poset (partially ordered) relation. In e-trading, a seller-buyer relation is asymmetric and hence not an equivalence relation, while an e-merchandise relation is symmetric and hence an equivalence relation because e-merchandise for sellers is also e-merchandise for buyers.

22.2.5 A Quotient Space (an Identification Space)

Let X be a topological space. Let f be a *surjective* (onto) and *continuous* mapping called a *quotient map* (often also called an *identification map*) that maps each point $x \in X$ to a subset (an equivalence class $x/\!\sim\, \in X/\!\sim$) containing x

$$f : X \to X/\!\sim.$$

Here, as explained before, "a map $f : X \to Y$ is surjective (onto)" means

$$(\forall y \in Y)\ (\exists x \in X)\ \big[f(x) = y\big].$$

Suppose we take a surjective map f such that for subset X^0 of X, $X^0 \subseteq X$, X^0 is open $\Leftrightarrow f^{-1}(X^0) \mid y \in A$ is open in X (this means f is continuous), $X/\!\sim$ is called a *quotient space* (or an *identification space*) by a *quotient map* (or an *identification map*) f. There is a reason why a *quotient space* is also called an *identification space*. It is because, as stated before, a quotient space is obtained by identifying each element (an equivalence class)

$$x/\!\sim\, \in X/\!\sim$$

with a point $x \in X$ that is contained in $x/\!\sim$.

22.2.6 An Attaching Space (an Adjunction Space, or an Adjoining Space)

Let us start with a topological space X and attach another topological space Y to it. Then,

$$Y_f = Y \sqcup_f X = Y \sqcup X/\sim$$

is an *attaching space* (an *adjunction space*, or an *adjoining space*) obtained by attaching (gluing, adjuncting, or adjoining) Y to X by an *attaching map* (an *adjunction map*, or an *adjoining map*) f (or by identifying each point $y \in Y_0 \mid Y_0 \subset Y$ with its image $f(y) \in X$ by a *continuous* map f). $\sqcup$ denotes a disjoint union (another name is an "exclusive or") and often a $+$ symbol is used instead.

Attaching map f is a *continuous* map such that

$$f : Y_0 \to X,$$

where $Y_0 \subset Y$. Thus, the attaching space $Y_f = Y \sqcup X/\sim$ is a case of *quotient spaces*

$$Y \sqcup X/\sim = Y \sqcup_f X = Y \sqcup X/\big(x \sim f(y) \mid \forall y \in Y_0\big).$$

The *identification map* g in this case is

$$g : Y \sqcup X \to Y \sqcup_f X = Y_f = Y \sqcup X/\sim = (Y \sqcup X - Y_0) \sqcup Y_0.$$

22.2.7 Restriction and Inclusion

For any function

$$g : Y \to Z$$

the *restriction* of g to X $(X \subseteq Y)$ is:

$$g|X = g \circ i : X \to Z$$

where

$$i : X \to Y$$

is an *inclusion*, i.e.

$$\forall x \in X, \quad i(x) = x.$$

22.2.8 Extensions and Retractions of Continuous Maps

For topological spaces X and Y, and a subspace $A \subset X$, a continuous map $f : X \to Y$ such that $f|A : A \to Y$ is called a *continuous extension* (or simply an *extension*) of a map $f|A$ from A onto X. An extension is, thus, a partial function.

We say that $A \subset X$ is a *retract* of X if there exists a continuous map $r : X \to A$ such that $r(a) = a$ for each $a \in A$. The map r is called a *retraction* of X onto A. We say that A is a *deformation retract* of X if A is a retract of X and $\mathrm{id}_x \simeq i_A \circ r$, i.e., the identity on X is homotopic with a certain retraction $r : X \to A$ composed with the inclusion i_A of A into X. The homotopy between id_x and $i_A \circ r$ is called a *deformation retraction* of X onto A. If there exists a deformation retraction h such that $h(a,t) = a$ for each $a \in A$ and $t \in [0,1]$ then the set A is called a *strong deformation retract* of X and h is called a *strong deformation retraction.*

22.2.9 Homotopy

Homotopy is a case of extensions. Let X and Y be topological spaces, $f, g : X \to Y$ be continuous maps, and $I = [1,0]$. *Homotopy* is defined

$$H : X \times I \to Y$$

where for $t \in I$

$$\begin{aligned} H &= f \quad \text{when } t = 0, \quad \text{and} \\ H &= g \quad \text{when } t = 1. \end{aligned}$$

Homotopy is an extension of continuous maps

$$\begin{aligned} H|X \times \{0\} &= f i_0, \quad \text{and} \\ H|X \times \{1\} &= g i_1 \end{aligned}$$

where

$$\begin{aligned} i_0 &= X \times \{0\} \to X, \quad \text{and} \\ i_1 &= X \times \{1\} \to X. \end{aligned}$$

Topological spaces X and Y are *homotopically equivalent* $X \cong Y$, namely *of the same homotopy type*, if the following condition meets:

For two functions f and h

$$\begin{aligned} f : X \to Y \quad &\text{and} \quad h : Y \to X, \\ h \circ f \cong 1_X \quad &\text{and} \quad f \circ h \cong 1_Y, \end{aligned}$$

where 1_X and 1_Y are identity maps

$$1_X : X \to X \quad \text{and} \quad 1_Y : Y \to Y.$$

Homotopy equivalence is more general than topology equivalence. Homotopy equivalence can identify a shape change that is topologically not any more equivalent after the change. While a shape element goes through deformation processes, the deformation processes are specified by a homotopy and validated by homotopy equivalence. As a matter of fact, from the viewpoint of the abstractness of invariance, homotopy equivalence is more abstract than set theoretical equivalence because, when we change a given set by adding or deleting elements, we can make the set homotopy equivalent by preserving the operation of add or delete and also the added or deleted elements.

22.2.10 Cellular Structured Spaces (Cellular Spaces)

A *cell* is a topological space X that is topologically equivalent (homeomorphic) to an arbitrary dimensional (say n-dimensional where n is a natural number) closed ball $\mathcal{B}^n$ called a closed *n-cell*. An open n-cell is denoted as $\operatorname{Int}\mathcal{B}^n$ (also as $\mathring{\mathcal{B}}^n$ and more often as e^n). $\mathcal{B}^n$ is

$$\mathcal{B}^n = \{x \in \mathbb{R}^n, \|x\| \leq 1\},$$

namely a closed n-dimensional ball, and $\mathbb{R}^n$ is an n-dimensional real number.

$$\operatorname{Int}\mathcal{B}^n = \mathring{\mathcal{B}}^n = \{x \in \mathbb{R}^n, \|x\| < 1\}$$

is an open n-dimensional ball and is an *interior* of $\mathcal{B}^n$.

$$\partial\mathcal{B}^n = \mathcal{B}^n - \mathring{\mathcal{B}}^n = S^{n-1}$$

is the *boundary* of $\mathcal{B}^n$, and it is an $(n-1)$-dimensional *sphere* S^{n-1}.

For a topological space X, a *characteristic map* $\mathcal{F}$ is a continuous function.

$$\mathcal{F} : \mathcal{B}^n \to X,$$

such that it is a homeomorphism:

$$\mathcal{F} : \mathring{\mathcal{B}}^n \to \mathcal{F}(\mathring{\mathcal{B}}^n), \quad \text{and}$$
$$\mathcal{F}(\partial\mathcal{B}^n) = \mathcal{F}(\mathcal{B}^n)\mathcal{F}(\mathring{\mathcal{B}}^n).$$

$e^n = \mathcal{F}(\mathring{\mathcal{B}}^n)$ is an *open n-cell*, and $e^n = \mathcal{F}(\mathcal{B}^n)$ is a *closed n-cell*.

From a topological space X, we can compose a finite or infinite sequence of cells X^p that are subspaces of X, indexed by integer $\mathbb{Z}$, namely $\{X^p \mid X^p \subseteq X, p \in \mathbb{Z}\}$ called a filtration, such that X^p covers X (or X^p is a covering of X), namely,

$$X = \bigcup_{p \in \mathbb{Z}} X^p,$$

and X^p is a subspace of X, namely,

$$X^0 \subseteq X^1 \subseteq X^2 \subseteq \cdots \subseteq X^{p-1} \subseteq X^p \subseteq \cdots \subseteq X$$

(this is called a *skeleton*). The skeleton with a dimension at most p is called a *p-skeleton*.

We also say that $C = \{X^p \mid X^p \subseteq X, p \in \mathbb{Z}\}$ is a *cell decomposition* of a topological space X, or a *partition* of a topological space X into subspaces X^p which are closed cells. (X, C) is called a *CW-complex*.

When we perform cell decomposition, by preserving cell attachment maps, we can turn cellular spaces into reusable resources. We name such preserved and shared information a *cellular database* and a system to manage it a *cellular database management system* (*cellular DBMS*) (T. L. Kunii and H. S. Kunii 1999).

To be more precise, given a topological space X, we *inductively* compose a *filtration* X^p with a *skeleton*

$$X^0 \subseteq X^1 \subseteq X^2 \subseteq \cdots \subseteq X^{p-1} \subseteq X^p \subseteq \cdots \subseteq X$$

as a topological space as follows:

(1) $X^0 \subset X$ is a subspace whose elements are 0-cells of X.
(2) X^p is composed from X^{p-1} by *attaching* (*adjuncting*, *adjoining*, or *gluing*) to it a disjoint union $\bigsqcup_i \mathcal{B}_i^p$ of closed p-dimensional balls via a surjective and continuous mapping called an attaching map (an adjunction map, an adjoining map, or a gluing map)

$$F : \bigsqcup_i \partial \mathcal{B}_i^p \to X^{p-1}.$$

In other words, we compose X^p from X^{p-1} by taking a disjoint union $X^{p-1} \sqcup (\bigsqcup_i \mathcal{B})_i^p)$ and by identifying each point x in $\partial \mathcal{B}_i^p$, $x \in \partial \mathcal{B}_i^p$, with its image $\mathcal{F}(x)$ by a continuous mapping

$$F_i = F | \partial \mathcal{B}_i^p : \partial \mathcal{B}_i^p \to X^{p-1}$$

such that $x \sim f_i(x)$ for each index i. Thus, X^p is a quotient space (the identification space)

$$\begin{aligned} X^p &= X^{p-1} \sqcup \left(\bigsqcup_i \mathcal{B}_i^p \right) \big| \left(x \sim F_i(x) \mid \forall x \in \partial \mathcal{B}_i^p \right) \\ &= X^{p-1} \sqcup_F \left(\bigsqcup_i \mathcal{B}_i^p \right) \end{aligned}$$

and is a case of *attaching spaces* (*adjunction spaces* or *adjoining spaces*). The map F_i is a case of *attaching maps* (*adjunction maps*, *adjoining maps* or *gluing maps*) of a cell $\mathcal{B}_i^p$. A *filtration space* is a space homotopically equivalent to a filtration. The topological space X with the skeleton $X^0 \subseteq X^1 \subseteq X^2 \subseteq \cdots \subseteq X^{p-1} \subseteq X^p \subseteq \cdots \subseteq X$ is called a *CW-space*. As a cell complex, it is called a *CW-complex* as explained before.

We thus obtain a map $\mathcal{F}$ as a case of *identification maps*

$$\mathcal{F} : X^{p-1} \sqcup \left(\bigsqcup_i \mathcal{B}_i^p \right) \to X^{p-1} \sqcup_F \left(\bigsqcup_i \mathcal{B}_i^p \right) = X^p.$$

A characteristic map $\mathcal{F}$ for each n-cell $\mathcal{B}_i^p = \mathcal{F}(\mathcal{B}_i^p) \in X^p$ is

$$\mathcal{F}_i = \mathcal{F} | \partial \mathcal{B}_i^p : \partial \mathcal{B}_i^p \to X^{p-1}.$$

The embedding of X^{p-1} as a closed subspace of X^p is

$$\mathcal{F}|X^{p-1} = X^{p-1} \to X^p.$$

If a CW-space is diffeomorphic, it is equivalent to a *manifold* space.

22.2.11 An Incrementally Modular Abstraction Hierarchy

The following list is the incrementally modular abstraction hierarchy (Ohmori and T. L. Kunii 2012) to be used for defining the architecture of cyberworlds and their modeling for cloud computing:

1. The homotopy (including fiber bundles) level;
2. The set theoretical level;
3. The topological space level;
4. The adjunction space level;
5. The cellular space level;
6. The presentation (including geometry, code et al) level;
7. The view (also called projection) level.

In modeling cyberworlds in cyberspaces, we define general properties of cyberworlds at the higher level and add more specific properties step by step while climbing down the incrementally modular abstraction hierarchy. "Cyberworlds" are the worlds built by cloud computing in "cyberspaces". *Fiber bundles* at the homotopy level define a cyberspace for a cyberworld. A cyberspace is specified by the product of a base space and a bundle of fibers called a fiber bundle. The product space constitutes cyberspaces. The properties defined at the homotopy level are invariants of continuous changes of functions. *Homotopy* is a Greek origin terminology to signify continuous deformation in a general sense. The properties that do not change by continuous modifications in time and space, such as deformation of an object and development of concepts, are expressed at this level as spatiotemporal equivalent properties of cloud computing.

A cyberworld is composed of objects in cyberspaces. At the set theoretical level, the elements of a cyberspace are defined, and a collection of elements constitutes a set with logical operations.

When we define a function on a cyberspace, we need domains that guarantee continuity such that the neighbors are mapped to a near place. Therefore, a topology is introduced into a cyberspace through the concept of *neighborhood*. Another and equivalent way to define topology is by a *power set* as the *strongest topology*, and a *null set* as the *weakest topology*. We mainly use *discrete topology* in modeling information systems, and cyberworlds and cyberspaces as information worlds and information spaces.

Cyberworlds are dynamic. Sometimes some cyberspaces are attached together and/or separated each other. These dynamic changes are described at the adjunction level. When two disjoint cyberspaces are attached together, it constitutes an exclusive union of two cyberspaces where attached areas of two cyberspaces are equivalent. It may happen that an attached space obtained in one way is equivalent to a space attached in another way. These attached spaces can be regarded as a set of equivalent spaces called a *quotient space* that is another invariant.

At the cellular structured space level, an inductive dimension is introduced to each cyberspace.

At the presentation level, each space is represented in a form which may be imagined before designing a cyberworld. For example, if it is a shape, then, geometry is used.

At the view level, also called a projection level, the cyberworlds are projected onto view screens. This level has been well studied and developed as computer graphics, a solid academic discipline, and hence we can safely leave this out in this paper (T. L. Kunii 1999).

Later, we describe cyberworlds of online shopping as an example of e-commerce, assembling chairs as a case of e-manufacturing, and an accounting system to lay global economy as cyberworld economy on a firm ground. We will also show how these examples belong to the identical architecture of cyberworlds. Cyberworlds continue to integrate every system, including conventional systems, into one architecture of cyberworlds, *automatically generating validated systems* as needed. These include e-business, e-commerce, e-production, e-assembling, e-accounting, and e-learning. Hence, as described later, modeling of conventional systems is also important in implementing them as a part of cyberworlds.

22.2.12 Fiber Bundles, Homotopy Lifting Property, and Homotopy Extension Property

Relationships of invariants including the changes of the relationships are clearly specified by fiber bundles. Covering spaces which map cyberworlds to invariant spaces play an essential role in configuring fiber bundles to specify the relationships of invariants. A homotopy lifting property (HLP) and homotopy extension property (HEP), both of which are developed from fiber bundles, represent invariants in changing entities of cyberworlds.

A *covering projection* is a continuous map that is a uniform local homeomorphism. The foundation is on *homeomorphism* that is *topological equivalence*, namely bijection, continuity, and continuity of inverse mapping.

Let $p : C \to B$ be a continuous map. An open subset $U \subset B$ is said to be *evenly covered* by p if $p^{-1}(U)$ is the disjoint union $\bigsqcup_i S_i$ of open subsets of C each S_i of which is mapped homeomorphically onto U by p, namely

1. $\forall b \in B$, $\exists$ an open neighborhood $U \subset B$;
2. $p^{-1}(U) = \bigsqcup_i S_i \mid S_i \subset C$;
3. $\forall i \mid i \in I$, $p|S_i : S_i \to U$ where $S_i \subset C$ is an open subset such that S_i is homeomorphic to U, $S_i \cong U$.

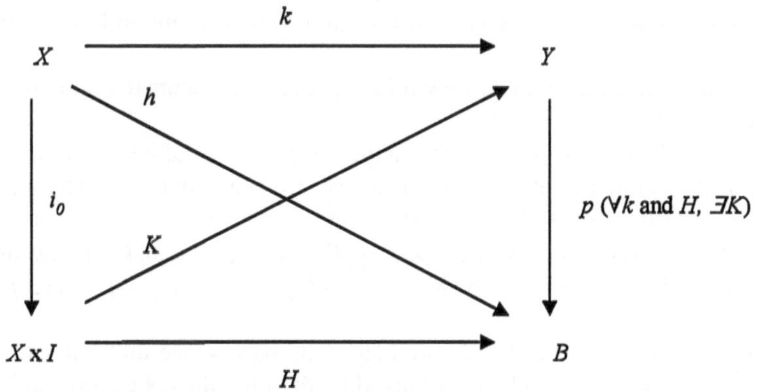

Fig. 22.1 A commutative diagram representing the homotopy lifting property (HLP)

If U is evenly covered by p, any open subset of U is also evenly covered by p. A continuous map $p : C \to B$ is called a *covering projection* if each point $b \in B$ has an open neighborhood evenly covered by p. C is called the *covering space* and B the *base space* of the covering projection. We define a map to be continuous if a preimage of an open set is open, and to be homeomorphic if it is bijective, continuous and its inverse is continuous.

The followings are examples of covering projections.

1. Any homeomorphism is a covering projection.
2. If C is the product of B with a discrete space, the projection $C \to B$ is a covering projection.

A continuous map $p : C \to B$ is called a *local homeomorphism* if each point $c \in C$ has an open neighborhood mapped homeomorphically by p onto an open subset of B. If this is so, each point of C has arbitrarily small neighborhoods with this property.

Special important functions known as *fibrations* and *cofibrations* are derived from the following *dual properties*:

1. Lifting homotopies through a continuous surjection (the *homotopy lifting property, HLP*).
2. Extending homotopies defined on a subspace (the *homotopy extension property, HEP*).

Now, let us introduce these functions. Let $p : Y \to B$ be a continuous surjection. A continuous function $k : X \to Y$ is called a lifting of a continuous function $h : X \to B$ if $p \circ k = h$. A homotopy $K : X \times I \to Y$ is a lifting of a homotopy $H : X \times I \to B$ if $p \circ K = H$ where $I = [0, 1]$.

The existence of a *lifting* of h is an invariant of the homotopy class of h when p satisfies the following *homotopy lifting property* (HLP). The function $p : Y \to B$ has the *homotopy lifting property* (*HLP*) for a space X if, for each continuous function $k : X \to Y$, each homotopy $H : X \times I \to B$ of $p \circ k$ ($H \circ i_0 = p \circ k$) has a *lifting* to a homotopy $K : X \times I \to Y$ of k ($K \circ i_0 = k$) and K is constant on $\{x\} \times I$ whenever H is constant on $\{x\} \times I$.

The *commutative diagram* as shown in Fig. 22.1 represents the homotopy lifting property.

A continuous function $p : Y \to B$ is a type of *fibration* called a *regular Hurewicz fibration* if it has the homotopy lifting property for every space X. Any topological projection $p_B : B \times F \to B$ is a fibration. Further, given any continuous function $k : X \to B \times F$ and homotopy $H : X \times I \to B$ of $H \circ i_0 = p_B \circ k$, there is the *lifting* $K : X \times I \to B \times F$, defined by $K(x, t) = (H(x, t), p_F(k(x)))$ where $p_F : B \times F \to F$.

A covering space is locally the product of its base space and a discrete space. Hence, a covering space can be generalized by defining the concept of fiber bundle, because the total space of a fiber bundle is *locally* the product of its base space and its fiber. The main result of this generalization is that the bundle projection of a fiber bundle is a fibration.

To be more precise, a *fiber bundle* is a quadruple $\xi = (E, B, F, p)$ consisting of a *total space* E, a *base space* B, a *fiber* F, and a *bundle projection* that is a continuous surjection called *F-bundle* $p : E \to B$ such that there exists an open covering $\mathcal{U} = \{U\}$ of B and, for each $U \in \mathcal{U}$, a homeomorphism called a *coordinate chart*

$$\varphi_U : U \times F \to p^{-1}(U)$$

exists such that the composite

$$U \times F_U \overset{\varphi_U}{\to} p^{-1}(U) \overset{p}{\to} U$$

is the projection to the first factor U. Thus the bundle projection $p : E \to B$ and the projection $p_B : B \times F \to B$ are locally equivalent. The *fiber* over $b \in B$ is defined to be equal to $p^{-1}(b)$, and we note that F is homeomorphic to $p^{-1}(b)$ for every $b \in B$, namely $\forall b \in B$, $F \cong p^{-1}(b)$.

Let $i : A \subseteq X$ be the inclusion of a closed subspace. A continuous function $k : X \to Y$ is called an *extension* of a continuous function $h : A \to Y$ provided that $k \circ i = h$. A homotopy $K : X \times I \to Y$ where $I = [0, 1]$ is called an extension of a homotopy $H : A \times I \to Y$ provided that $K \circ (i \times 1_I) = H$.

The existence of an extension of h is an invariant of the homotopy class of h when i has a *homotopy extension property*. To express this property, we view $(A \times I) \cup (X \times \{0\})$ as the union of two closed subspaces of $X \times I$.

A continuous function $H : (A \times I) \cup (X \times \{0\}) \to Y$ is called a *partial homotopy* of $h : X \to Y$ if $H \circ i_0$ and h agree on A where $i_0 : (A \times \{0\}) \cup (X \times \{0\}) \subseteq (A \times I) \cup (X \times \{0\})$. By the gluing theorem, a homotopy $H : A \times I$ such that $H|A \times \{0\} = h|A \times \{0\}$ determines a partial homotopy $H : (A \times I) \cup (X \times \{0\}) \to Y$ of $h : X \times \{0\} \to Y$.

Let us note that the inclusion $i : A \subseteq X$ has the *homotopy extension property* (*HEP*) for the space Y if every partial homotopy $H : (A \times I) \cup (X \times \{0\}) \to Y$ of every continuous function $h : X \times \{0\} \to Y$ extends to a homotopy $K : X \times I \to Y$.

A subspace inclusion $i : A \subseteq X$ is called a *cofibration* provided that it has the homotopy extension property for all spaces Y.

The *fiber* over $b \in B$ is defined to be equal to $p^{-1}(b)$, and we note that F is homeomorphic to $p^{-1}(b)$ for every $b \in B$, namely $\forall b \in B$, $F \cong p^{-1}(b)$.

Let $i : A \subseteq X$ be the inclusion of a closed subspace. A continuous function $k : X \to Y$ is called an *extension* of a continuous function $h : A \to Y$ provided that $k \circ i = h$. A homotopy $K : X \times I \to Y$ where $I = [0, 1]$ is called an extension of a homotopy $H : A \times I \to Y$ provided that $K \circ (i \times 1_I) = H$.

The existence of an extension of h is an invariant of the homotopy class of h when i has a *homotopy extension property*. To express this property, we view $(A \times I) \cup (X \times \{0\})$ as the union of two closed subspaces of $X \times I$.

A continuous function $H : (A \times I) \cup (X \times \{0\}) \to Y$ is called a *partial homotopy* of $h : X \to Y$ if $H \circ i_0$ and h agree on A where $i_0 : (A \times \{0\}) \cup (X \times \{0\}) \subseteq (A \times I) \cup (X \times \{0\})$. By the Gluing Theorem, a homotopy $H : A \times I$ such that $H|A \times \{0\} = h|A \times \{0\}$ determines a partial homotopy $H : (A \times I) \cup (X \times \{0\}) \to Y$ of $h : X \times \{0\} \to Y$.

Let us note that the inclusion $i : A \subseteq X$ has the *homotopy extension property* (*HEP*) for the space Y if every partial homotopy $H : (A \times I) \cup (X \times \{0\}) \to Y$ of every continuous function $h : X \times \{0\} \to Y$ extends to a homotopy $K : X \times I \to Y$.

A subspace inclusion $i : A \subseteq X$ is called a *cofibration* provided that it has the homotopy extension property for all spaces Y.

22.3 Modeling of E-Business and E-Manufacturing

Modeling and visualizing e-business and e-manufacturing are also good application areas for fiber bundles by cloud computing. Let us first look at a case where a customer shops online through the Internet, online book shopping in particular. In trading, being merchandise serves as an equivalence relation to specify invariants through trading processes. Online bookstores post books as merchandise on their homepages with information such as titles, prices, publishers, and reader's reviews. A customer searches for interested books as merchandise through a search engine. Online bookstores are described by a fiber bundle $\xi' = (E', B', F', p')$ composed by a total space E', a base space B' representing books, a fiber F' representing stores and a bundle projection p' from E' to B'. Customers are described by a fiber bundle $\xi'' = (E'', B'', F'', p'')$ composed of a total space E'', a base space B'' representing interest, a fiber F'' representing customers and a bundle projection p'' from E'' to B''. To define online shopping where customers buy interested books through homepages of online bookstores, these bundles are combined into a combined bundle $\xi = (E, B, F, p)$ composed of a total space E representing online market, a base space $B = B' \times B''$, a fiber $F = F' \times F''$ and a bundle projection p from E to B. The relations of these spaces are described later.

22.3.1 The Adjunction Space Level

In cloud computing applications, an adjunction space (also called an attaching space, a gluing space and an adjoining space) is used as a tool to connect and/or integrate any entities with validity through equivalence relations. Considering the social situation such that testing is costing orders of magnitude more than designing, we can safely assert that this automated validation capability of our approach is among those with the largest social impacts. It is particularly so in cyberworlds for cloud computing applications with exploding complexity and growth. We can establish invariance in varied cases of integration at the adjunction space level of the incrementally modular abstraction hierarchy. For example, in a simple case in the real world such as assembling in manufacturing, assembling is performed by assembling parts into a system. The parts are modularly attached together at their adjunction spaces to make assembly efficient and to ease maintenance. In programming, the system is constructed as a set of routines. Very often routines are not designed carefully ignoring equivalences of related parts of modules to cause malfunctions. These designs have a common property that two entities are connected together at the parts as adjunction spaces where equivalence relations hold. This property is handled abstractly by an adjunction mapping.

22.3.1.1 A Case of Online Book Shopping in E-Commerce

A case of online book shopping is analyzed using adjunction spaces. From the fiber bundles of online shopping, a customer $C = F''$ has interest $I = B''$ and an online bookstore $S = F'$ are selling books $B = B'$. We define the customer space $X = (C \times I)$ and the online bookstore space $Y = (S \times B)$ where X and Y are topological spaces. Initially, the customer space X and the online bookstore space Y are assumed independent of each other, and hence the initial state is denoted as $X \sqcup Y$ where $\sqcup$ stands for a disjoint union.

Let us suppose that the customer C having interests I is shopping the books B_0 posted by online bookstores

S_0 on the Web from the set of homepages B of online bookstore S during Web surfing. Since $Y_0 = (B_0 \times S_0)$ are a part of the properties of the online bookstore space Y, $Y_0 \subseteq Y$ holds. The processes of online book shopping on the web as e-business are analyzed and represented as shown in Fig. 22.2. It illustrates how the customer space X becomes related to the online bookstore space Y after the shopping books Y_0 are identified for trading.

This is a case of dynamic situations as explained previously. The adjunction space level we present here precisely represents the *dynamic situations* by an attaching map f, and also represents the situation where "the books are identified for shopping" as the adjunction space of two disjoint topological spaces X (the customer space) and Y (the online bookstore space), obtained by starting from X (the customer space) and by attaching Y (the online bookstore space) to X(the customer space) via a continuous map f by identifying each point $y \in Y_0 \mid Y_0 \subseteq Y$ with its

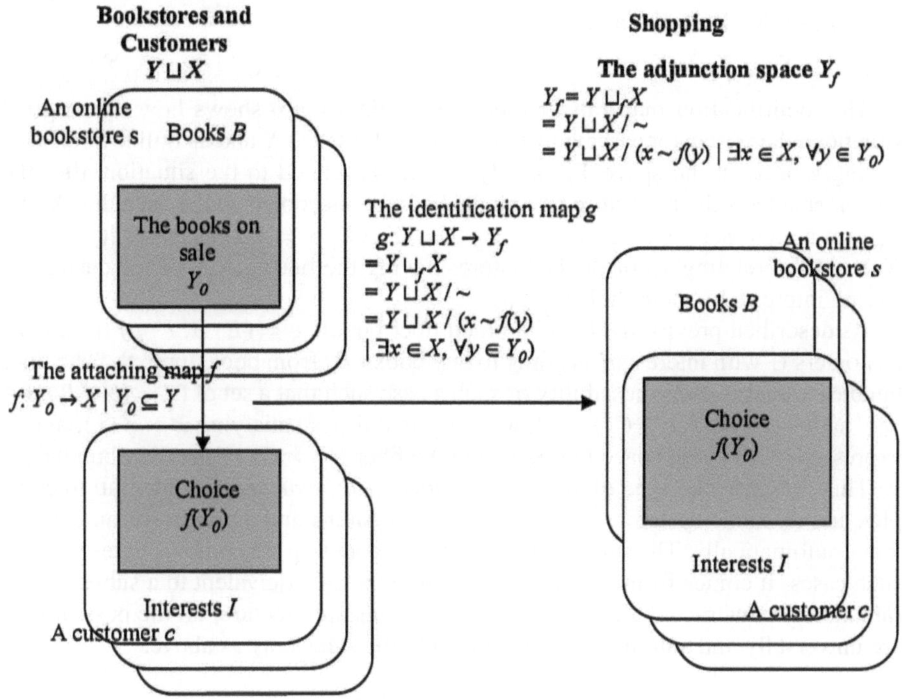

Fig. 22.2 An attaching space of online book shopping

image $f(y) \in X$ so that $x \sim f(y) \mid \exists x \in X, \forall y \in Y_0$. Thus, the equivalence denoted by a symbol $\sim$ plays the central role to compose adjunction spaces at the adjunction space level of the incrementally modular abstraction hierarchy.

Thus, the adjunction space of online book shopping at Y (the online bookstore space) by X (the customer space) on the books of the online store Y_0 is formulated along the line explained so far as follows.

The adjunction space Y_f

$$Y_f = Y \sqcup_f X = Y \sqcup X/\!\sim\, = Y \sqcup X/\big(x \sim f(y) \mid \exists x \in X, \forall y \in Y_0\big)$$

is obtained by identifying each point $y \in Y_0 \mid Y_0 \subseteq Y$ with its image $f(y) \in X$ so that $x \sim f(y) \mid \forall y \in Y_0$. This represents the book shopping process as a *dynamic situation*. To be more precise in explaining the *dynamic situation*, from a set of books B_0 at the online bookstores S_0, the customers C having interests I select $y = (b, s) \in Y_0$ which is a pair of a book and a company. Thus, we can define a function $f : Y_0 \to X$ which specifies $y \in Y_0$ is chosen by $x \in X$. In case that there are many same books b_i in the bookstore s, there are no differences in which book a customer takes. If a customer has no preferences about bookstores, then a book is selected from any bookstore selling this book. These cases are represented as equivalence relations. Hence, $x \sim f(y)$. The customer C continues shopping in this manner to identify numbers of books B of interests I from the online bookstores S. The attaching map f and the identification map g are:

$f : Y_0 \to X \mid Y_0 \subseteq Y$ and
$g : Y \sqcup X \to Y_f = Y \sqcup_f X = Y \sqcup X/{\sim} = Y \sqcup X/\big(x \sim f(y) \mid \exists x \in X, \forall y \in Y_0\big)$.

The identification map (also called the quotient map) shows how the original situation where a customer having an interest in the space X and an online bookstore having a book in the space Y, namely $Y \sqcup X$, is related to the situation after the customer selects the bookstore having the book by its choice $f(Y_0)$ such that X and Y form an adjunction space $Y_f = Y \sqcup_f X = Y \sqcup X/{\sim} = Y \sqcup X/(x \sim f(y) \mid \exists x \in X, \forall y \in Y_0)$ relating Y_0 of the bookstores having the books to X of the customers having interests by their choice $f(Y_0)$.

As described previously, the combined fiber bundle $\xi = (E, B, F, p)$ represents customers C with interests I is going to buy books B_0 from bookstores S_0. The fiber bundle expresses every possibility of such a case such that a set of $(x = (b \in B_0, s \in S_0)$, and $y = (i \in I, c \in C))$. It shows all possibilities satisfying $x \sim f(y)$, and is expressed by the base space $(B_0 \times I)$ and the fiber $(S_0 \times C)$ of the fiber bundle ξ.

This presents one type of versatile *architectural invariance* in integrating complex and dynamic systems, including banking systems and digital government systems, automatically. The same architecture and modeling stated now apples to all of such cases. It comes from the fact that integrations are equivalent to a subset of automatically constructed all the possibilities. In this architecture, all the possibilities are universally and automatically generated in the same way as above.

22.3.1.2 A Case of Assembling for E-Manufacturing

The adjunction space model illustrated above is quite essential and equally applied to manufacturing and also financing in general, making an adjunction space an *architectural invariant*. Modern manufacturing is based on modular architecture for automated assembly and module-based maintainability. Now, all are shifting into cloud computing. As a simple case of manufacturing, let us look at seat assembling. For seat assembling, we can use the previous case of the customers having interests and the stores selling books on the Web, simply by replacing them by the seat and the leg of a chair. Therefore, we can implement them in the identical way as architectural invariance at the adjunction space level to automate the validated implementation. The adjunction space for seat assembling is shown in Fig. 22.3.

22.3.2 Cellular Space Level

The cellular space level is obtained by endowing dimensions to the topological spaces at the adjunction space level. This process to generate the cellular structured space level is almost trivial. Let us show a case of seat assembling. It proceeds as follows.

The seat part is a closed 3 dimensional cell $Y = \mathcal{B}^3_{\text{seat}}$. The leg part $X = \mathcal{B}^3_{\text{leg}}$ is also a closed 3 dimensional cell. The bottom surface of the seat part

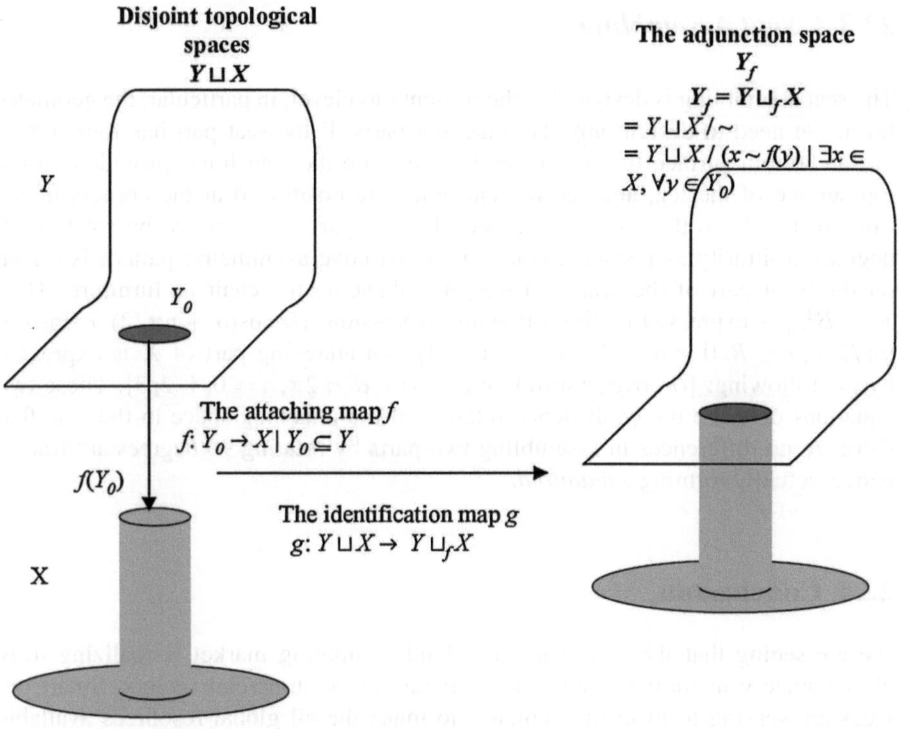

Fig. 22.3 The attaching space of seat assembling

$Y_0 = \mathcal{B}^2_{\text{seat}} \subset Y = \mathcal{B}^3_{\text{seat}}$. The bottom surface is attached to the top surface of the leg part $f(Y_0) = f(\mathcal{B}^2_{\text{seat}}) \subset X = \mathcal{B}^3_{\text{leg}}$.

The adjoining space at the cellular space level is, then:

$$\begin{aligned} Y_0 \sqcup_f X &= \mathcal{B}^3_{\text{seat}} \sqcup_f \mathcal{B}^3_{\text{leg}} = \mathcal{B}^3_{\text{seat}} \sqcup \mathcal{B}^3_{\text{leg}}/\sim \\ &= \mathcal{B}^3_{\text{seat}} \sqcup \mathcal{B}^3_{\text{leg}}/\left(x \sim f(y) \mid \exists x \in \mathcal{B}^3_{\text{leg}}, \forall y \in \mathcal{B}^2_{\text{seat}}\right). \end{aligned}$$

Here, the attaching map f and the identification map g are at the cellular space level of the incrementally modular abstraction hierarchy of seat assembling:

$$\begin{aligned} f &: \mathcal{B}^2_{\text{seat}} \to \mathcal{B}^3_{\text{leg}} \mid \mathcal{B}^2_{\text{seat}} \subset \mathcal{B}^3_{\text{seat}}, \\ g &: \mathcal{B}^3_{\text{seat}} \sqcup \mathcal{B}^3_{\text{leg}} \to \mathcal{B}^3_{\text{seat}} \sqcup_f \mathcal{B}^3_{\text{leg}}. \end{aligned}$$

The surface of the seat part attached to the leg part is: $\partial \mathcal{B}^3_{\text{seat}} = \mathcal{B}^2_{\text{seat}}$, and the top surface of the leg part where the seat part is attached is: $\partial \mathcal{B}^3_{\text{leg}} = \mathcal{B}^2_{\text{leg}}$. The above procedures are identical to that of online book shopping proving that the incrementally modular abstraction hierarchy presented serves as a truly universal architectural foundation of cloud computing for cyberworlds and real worlds. It is also true in visualizing conceptual worlds for cloud computing users' understanding (T. L. Kunii et al. 2003).

22.3.3 Seat Assembling

The seat assembling is designed at the presentation level, in particular, the geometry level. We need to design only the attaching parts. If the seat part has four screws on the bottom surface that would be inserted into the four holes provided on the top surface of the leg, and screws and holes are positioned at the corners of the same rectangle so that once positioned, the seat part is assembled by rotating 90 degrees arbitrarily as needed when some illustrative asymmetric pattern is drawn on the front part of the seat as a way of enhancing the chair as furniture. Then $Y_0 = \mathcal{B}^2_{\text{seet}}$ is expressed by the following expression: $\{(r\cos(\alpha + n\pi/2), r\sin(\alpha + n\pi/2)) \mid r \in R, 0 < \alpha < 2\pi, n = 0, 1, 2, 3\}$. An attaching part of X is expressed by the following: $\{(r\cos\alpha, r\sin\alpha) \mid r \in R, 0 < \alpha < 2\pi, n = 0, 1, 2, 3\}$. These two equations describe the equivalence relation of the attaching space in the way that there are no differences in assembling two parts by rotating 90 degrees arbitrarily, hence, actually forming a *manifold*.

22.4 Conclusions

We are seeing that the emergence of cloud computing market is realizing truly global society including industrial, financial, and commercial sectors. Smart devices are serving to meet the demands to make the all global resources available to individuals. Cloud computing services are now widely available, some open and some closed: Google, Amazon, and Microsoft to name a few. Yet, the real hazard is waiting to burr the whole benefit, suffering from the combinatorial explosion of computation, inevitable in the current cloud computing models.

The proposed approach fundamentally resolves the hazard, since cloud computing become scalable via automatically validated information combinations via homotopic equivalences in adjunction spaces in both top-down and bottom-up manners via HEP (homotopy extension property) and HLP (homotopy lifting property), respectively in an incrementally modular abstraction hierarchy. Implementation of cellular data systems for cloud computing information management is now made available as a commercial product named Cellular Data System, CDS (T. L. Kunii and H. S. Kunii 1999). The incrementally modular abstraction hierarchy, IMAH, is also further developed to include parallel procedures (Ohmori and T. L. Kunii 2012). It makes cloud computing more effective in practice.

References

Kunii, T. L. (1969). Invitation to system sciences—poetry, philosophy and science in computer age. *Journal of Mathematical Sciences*, 54–56. In Japanese.

Kunii, T. L. (1998). The philosophy of synthetic worlds digital genesis for communicating synthetic worlds and the real world. In T. L. Kunii, & A. Luciani (Eds.), *Cyberworlds* (pp. 5–15). Berlin: Springer.

Kunii, T. L. (1999). Homotopy modeling as world modeling. In *Proceedings of computer graphics international '99 (CGI99)*, Canmore, Alberta, Canada, June 7–11 (pp. 130–141). Los Alamitos: IEEE Computer Society Press.

Kunii, T. L. (2003). Algebraic topological modeling for cyberworld design. In *Proceedings of international conference on cyberworlds*, 3–5 December 2003, Marina Mandarin Hotel, Singapore (pp. xx–xxvi). Los Alamitos: IEEE Computer Society Press.

Kunii, T. L., & Kunii, H. S. (1999). A cellular model for information systems on the web—integrating local and global information. In *International symposium on database applications in non-traditional environments (DANTE'99)*, Heian Shrine, Kyoto, Japan, November 28–30, 1999 (pp. 19–24). Los Alamitos: IEEE Computer Society Press. Organized by Research Project on Advanced Databases, in cooperation with Information Processing Society of Japan, ACM Japan, ACM SIGMOD Japan

Kunii, T. L., Ibusuki, M. Pasko, G. A., Pasko, A., Terasaki, D., & Hanaizumi, H. (2003). Modeling of conceptual multiresolution analysis by an incrementally modular abstraction hierarchy. *IEICE Transactions on Information and Systems*, *E86-D*(7), 1181–1190.

Ohmori, K., & Kunii, T. L. (2012). A formal methodology for developing enterprise systems procedurally: Homotopy, pi-calculus and event-driven programs. In *Proceedings of international conference on cyberworlds*, 20–22 October 2010, Singapore (pp. 223–230). Los Alamitos: IEEE Computer Society Press. http://dx.doi.org/10.1109/CW.2010.47.

Chapter 23
Visualization Surfaces

Turner Whitted and Steven Drucker

Abstract Large displays suitable for visualization applications are typically constructed from arrays of smaller ones. The physical and optical challenges of designing these assemblies are the first topic addressed here. The bandwidth and computation required to feed these collections exceed that of almost any single computer or graphics processor which leads to the second topic of processor arrays and interconnections for large displays. Finally we conclude with an overview of the atypical human factors to be considered when designing and evaluating interactions with large displays as they are applied to visualization tasks.

23.1 The Value of Scale and Detail

In the days of slide rule calculations visualization via pencil and paper was a natural exercise. With data and computation on a scale of petabytes and petaflops, simply finding a piece of paper large enough to serve as a meaningful conveyance presents an overwhelming challenge.

Within this data-rich environment we are searching for large display technologies, new means of computing display content, new approaches to moving data to displays, and new mechanisms for interacting with what we see. The challenges of this work have produced a number of novel systems and architectures, most based on conventional graphics techniques. However the scale of data and presentation requires a rethinking of how these conventional components are connected and used.

In our experience building large display surfaces we have yet to encounter a viewer claiming that our display was too large or too detailed. Formal user studies for both large desktops (Czerwinski et al. 2003) and display walls reinforce this sentiment. While experiences for large desktops and walls are distinct, there is value in scale and detail for both environments (Fig. 23.1).

For large desktops, either conventional multi-monitor arrangements or large semi-immersive single displays, the modes of interaction retain the devices and

T. Whitted (✉) · S. Drucker
Microsoft Research, Redmond, USA
e-mail: jtw@microsoft.com

J. Dill et al. (eds.), *Expanding the Frontiers of Visual Analytics and Visualization*,
DOI 10.1007/978-1-4471-2804-5_23, © Springer-Verlag London Limited 2012

Fig. 23.1 Dsharp rear projection large desktop prototype (Gary Starkweather, Microsoft Research)

affordances of WIMP (window, icon, menu, pointing device). The measurable benefit is user efficiency.

Display wall uses differ from that of both desktops and the well worn passive viewing experience of television. Viewing distances can vary from 5 meters to less than 40 cm. Multiple users with multiple modes of interaction may use the display at the same time. No pointer, touch surface, pen or mouse will suffice as a single input device. No matter what the means of interaction, the ability of display walls to combine scope, detail, collaboration in one surface has shown its value in numerous applications (Fig. 23.2).

In some cases projectors have been employed to create surfaces that extend well beyond planar rectangles. The well-known CAVE™ (Cruz-Neira et al. 1993) surrounds viewers with a complete virtual environment. UNC's Office of the Future (Raskar et al. 1998) takes a different approach by projecting virtual environments into real spaces. In addition we have seen projectors employed to extend desktops onto office walls as a hybrid of desktops and display walls. While the detail available in the projected image is degraded, the opportunity to share with other viewers as well as the "freedom" from desktop monitor clutter has advantages. These examples are a reminder that visualization surfaces come in many sizes and shapes and do not simply fall into the two categories of large desktop displays and display walls.

While this spectrum of surfaces is diverse, there are common technologies as well as common issues of scalability, maintainability, and usability shared across

Fig. 23.2 Tiled flat panel display wall (Microsoft Research vX Project)

the spectrum (Ni et al. 2006). In the following sections we examine details of the physical mechanisms of large displays, the architecture of graphics clusters for driving large displays, and lessons learned from interacting with such displays.

23.2 Large Display Mechanisms: Projection

Projection is the most obvious of large display technologies. While front projection onto large screens at desktop resolutions in darkened rooms is the norm for passive presentations, it is less than optimal for most interactive applications. Aside from the issues of contrast and shadowing, desktop resolution is simply inadequate for visualization when spread across a large screen.

Rear projection from multiple projectors is far superior. The compactness of the active component (the projector) combined with the low cost of the passive component (the screen) made this the starting point of many experiments. Each projector is aimed at its own section of the screen with minimal overlap of areas lit by adjacent projectors. Pixel count on the projection screen is simply number of projectors times the resolution of each projector minus the areas of overlap. If the pixel density is too low for effective interaction, the solution is to simply add more projectors.

Projectors themselves come in various flavors. Each has one or more light sources, a light modulator, and optics for focusing modulated light on the screen. The modulator may be reflective or transmissive. If the light source covers the entire visible spectrum, then the modulator may contain filters for red, green, and blue. Alternatively separate light sources for red, green, and blue may be modulated by monochromatic reflectors or transmitters. Note that this arrangement dictates time division multiplexing of the light sources if a single modulator is employed or totally separate modulators for each color. The two dominant modulation mechanisms are liquid crystal displays (LCDs) as a transmissive modulator, and micro-electro-mechanical (MEMs) mirrors as a reflective modulator. These internal details of projectors would not typically be accessible to builders of display walls, but the characteristics of specific projector classes may affect design choices (Clodfelter et al. 2003).

Regardless of the type of projector employed there are common calibration steps required to make projection displays usable. As mentioned above, multiple projectors must be aligned so the regions covered form the desired array and overlap slightly along boundaries of adjacent projectors. This presents two challenges. In the first place, manual alignment is neither sufficiently accurate nor stable over long periods of time. In addition precise mechanical alignment is a time consuming process. If coarse mechanical alignment is done initially, then some automatic self-alignment is essential for maintaining the visual quality of the combined projections.

The second alignment challenge is compensation for irregularities of illumination across the surface of a large display. If the areas lit by two adjacent projectors do not overlap then dark seams will appear on the screen. If the areas do overlap, then overly bright seams will appear on the screen. Additionally, projection lamps degrade over time at different rates producing non-uniformity of both luminance and chrominance over the surface which also requires compensation. The solution is to include a compensation step as part of the alignment procedure that computes corrections which are later applied during rendering to images cast by individual projectors and insures a smooth transition in the region of overlap (Raskar et al. 1998). This process is typically done in software using cameras aimed at the projection surface as the alignment sensing mechanism. Once the alignment procedure produces a model of geometric, intensity, and color distortions a mapping is defined and applied by adding a distortion compensation and color correction texture mapping stage to the display's rendering pipeline.

An underappreciated feature of projection walls is the bi-directionality of the optical path. Lights directed at or shadows cast on the projection surface can be detected by cameras co-located with the projectors. Since cameras are generally included for purposes of alignment and calibration it is a bonus to apply them to sensing for interaction, although additional infrared cameras may be needed for touch interfaces (Wilson 2005).

The foremost problem of rear projection is the volume of space between the array of projectors and the screen. For this reason such installations will not usually fit into existing work spaces and require expensive construction. In many cases the need for custom spaces is expected and readily accommodated. There are commercial short-throw projection tiles as thin as 30 cm[1] but they are usually intended for signage in public places and not for interactive visualization. There are optical mechanisms for "thin" projection (Travis et al. 2000), but to date these have not

[1] http://www.christiedigital.com/en-us/digital-signage/pages/default.aspx.

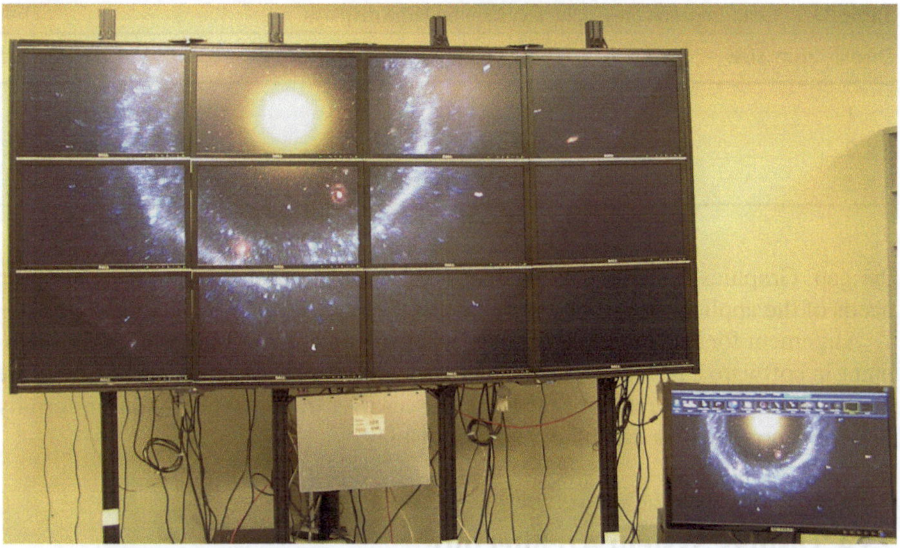

Fig. 23.3 Large display assembled from unmodified LCD panels (WorldWide Telescope, Microsoft Research)

been tiled or built at a size suitable for large scale visualization. In short, there are numerous challenges to installing large displays based on projection but the utility of such displays and the continuing development of projection technologies hold much promise for interactive applications.

23.3 Large Display Mechanisms: Modular Flat Panels

Flat panel displays (FPDs) include a light source and modulators in a single planar package. The light source is either a linear fluorescent lamp or a linear array of LEDs diffused through a plastic light guide covering the entire back of the panel. The modulator is an LCD panel with red, green, and blue subpixels. Building a display wall from FPDs has been an almost casual exercise in some cases. Most installations consist of an array of off-the-shelf monitors with cables running to one or more workstations as illustrated in Fig. 23.3.

While thin compared to projection spaces, tiled FPDs have their own unique problem of seams between tiles. Typically the seam is 30 to 40 mm for panels enclosed within their original desktop frames. We have reduced the seam to as little as 13 mm if the LCD panels are removed from their frames and tightly tiled along with their backlights while some commercial installations report seams as thin as 7 mm.

Compensation for the inter-tile gap may or may not be enabled. When graphical objects move across the surface any abrupt shift in position is disconcerting. Accounting for the gap in the graphics hardware or software yields continuous motion with no abrupt shifts. However this compensation results in data being hidden by

Table 23.1 Load imposed on graphics system by large displays

Display array size	Number of pixels	Video bandwidth
1 × 1	2,073,600	466 MB/s
3 × 2	12,441,600	2.8 GB/s
7 × 5	72,576,000	16.3 GB/s

the gap. Graphics systems may enable or disable the compensation depending on needs of the application (Robertson et al. 2005).

Alignment for FPD arrays is entirely mechanical, eliminating the need for alignment in software calibration procedures. However both projectors and FPDs share the problem of deterioration of the light sources over time as well as non-uniformity of light sources across the full extent of a display.

23.4 Display System Architecture

To gain some perspective on the load imposed on the graphics system by large displays consider the numbers in Table 23.1, assuming HD resolution for each display tile.

No single graphics processor can supply the pixel throughput required to fill a wall. The first systems challenge for display walls is building a display processor which scales with the display.

The basic configuration of any large display surface combines multiple display tiles with multiple display processors. The term display processor in this context generally refers to a complete PC incorporating a CPU, one or more GPUs, memory, and a network interface. Given the low cost and high performance of commercial desktop graphics systems, combining clusters of these components is the preferred path for building scalable graphics processors. With this approach come a number of challenges: connecting multiple graphics processors to multiple displays, providing a usable software platform, and insuring scalability in the aggregate system.

A conceptually simple arrangement of display tiles and processors is to dedicate one graphics server processor to each tile. With this arrangement interprocessor connections are required only at the front of each graphics pipeline. An additional client processor acting as master can host user applications and distribute graphics commands to the dedicated display processors over a network (WorldWide Telescope 2008) as shown in Fig. 23.4.

While simple, a one-to-one assignment of graphics processor to display tile may not be the most efficient arrangement of resources. A many-to-many arrangement provides an opportunity to balance rendering loads across the full array of display processors. The Princeton display wall (Samanta et al. 1999; Wallace et al. 2005) accomplished this by partitioning the rendering task among display processors according to load and then moving rendered pixels across the network to the display processor attached to the target display for each partition. Alternatively one may

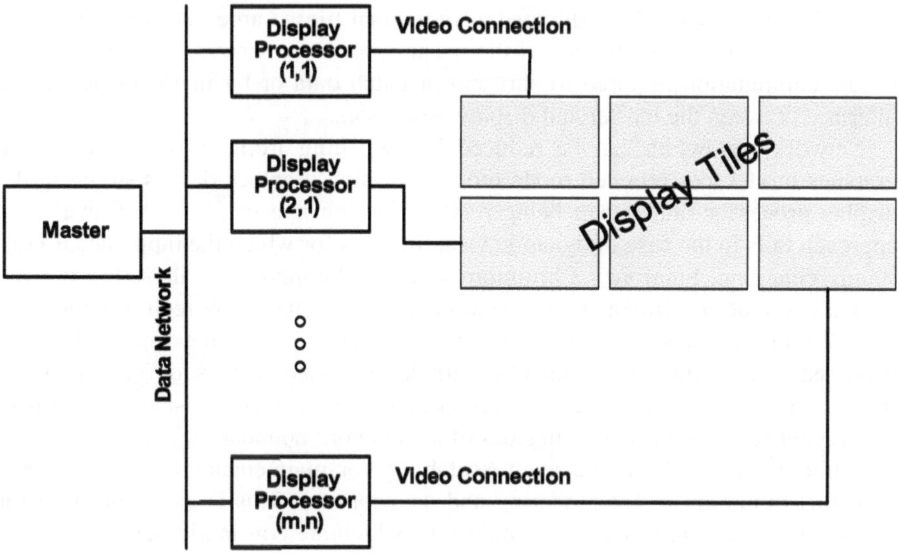

Fig. 23.4 Typical parallel display processor configuration

insert a switch for routing pixels from any display processor to any display tile as with Stanford's Lightning-2 (Stoll et al. 2001). In this case graphics commands are distributed to multiple processors at the front end of the pipeline and then pixels are routed to the appropriate displays from the back end of the pipeline without any additional load imposed on the front end data network.

The economy of using off-the-shelf components for large display assemblies can be a curse as well as a blessing. Conventional components adhere to standards which may not lend themselves to scaling. For example, decoding JPEG images has an inherently sequential front end stage followed by an inherently parallel back end stage. Regions of the compressed image cannot be distributed to the multiple display processors without executing the sequential part of decoding on a single processor. The single processor, the master unit in the configuration of Fig. 23.4, then becomes a bottleneck. In short, the standard JPEG format does not scale to large displays. As an attempt to overcome this limitation researchers at Princeton have proposed an attachment to JPEG files which directs the distribution of undecoded images to the appropriate display processors (Chen et al. 2002). In a similar fashion Lightning-2 routes pixels through its crossbar using addresses embedded in "header" pixels of a DVI video stream. This header is not part of the DVI standard but is essential for building a scalable system from commodity interfaces. Both of these examples serve as reminders that imaging, video, and interconnection standards aren't intended to fit large scale systems.

While the cluster of display processors shown in Fig. 23.4 handles the increased resolution of large displays it does nothing to relieve congestion of graphics data and commands in the master processor. Simple software systems for visualization pass graphics commands and data to the display processors either by broadcast or by sorting into bins of data directed at individual tiles. Large data sets will show no improvement in performance if the master processor becomes saturated, either by the computation required to sort and dispatch data or by inefficiencies in the interface between the master and display processors.

Network bandwidth can be reduced by switching from an immediate mode graphics model to a retained mode model in which graphics data is stored in the display processor rather than being reissued by the master for each frame. This approach fails in the case of dynamic visualizations for which the input data is constantly changing. Stanford's Chromium system (Humphreys et al. 2002), derived from a string of experimental visualization systems including WireGL (Humphreys et al. 2001), provides an infrastructure for distributed processing which addresses these issues at several levels. One of its simplest enhancements is to format network traffic to make most efficient use of available bandwidth and to consciously optimize data layout for the CPUs on both sides of the network boundary.

While not generally appreciated, scalability for maintenance of large displays is just as important as for rendering and data transfer. This is especially true for today's experimental visualization platforms which are constantly being altered or upgraded. To address this need the Princeton display wall has a collection of automated maintenance tools for tasks ranging from software upgrades to projector alignment (Chen et al. 2002).

23.5 Interaction

Passive (non-interactive) large displays have been in wide use for decades. They have been used to monitor or show complex systems from nuclear power plants, flight control, oil & space exploration or even advertising. They typically are controlled primarily by a single source, but viewed by many participants who need access or are shown the same information.

Interactive large displays are a more recent development, though the roots of interaction with large displays have been explored for over 30 years in both the academic and popular community. In the academic world, Richard Bolt's early 'Put-that-there' system (Bolt 1980) was a seminal paper in exploring combined speech plus pointing systems. More recently, the movie *Minority Report* explored a natural, gestural interface which allowed a user to symbolically manipulate a data rich environment. While that system was completely faked for the purposes of the movie, the actual system was realized by the special effects consultant for the move (Underkoffler 2010) using a VICON optical tracking system. More recently, the advent of the Microsoft Kinect system has made crude optical tracking cheap and widely available, producing a swath of gestural controlled systems both for games and for other activities.

It certainly makes sense that interactive large displays are a popular area of research. Work has shown that there are significant cognitive benefits to using a large display surface even for doing basic windows, mouse, and keyboard interaction (Tan et al. 2006). A large display can provide a great opportunity for collaborative work since multiple people can see and interact with the same surface. Large or projected displays have often been used as presentation devices, but allowing interaction by touching on the screen (Han 2005) helps give viewers immediate context for changes to the display.

Yet, to date, none of these systems have gained widespread acceptance. Some problems inherent in pushing interactive large display research have been the following: cost (as outlined in previous sections), interaction modality, tracking technology, fatigue, and learnability.

For example, voice as an interaction modality has been used in several systems, but poor recognition performance and restricted vocabularies present challenges for widespread adoption. In addition, appropriate voice interaction tends not to be obvious to end users (Oviatt 1999).

Touch and more recently multi-touch are popular techniques for directly manipulating the representation of objects and have been used for large displays as well. However in large displays, the sheer size of the display limits convenient access to many parts of the surface (Baudisch et al. 2003). In addition, being close to the display prevents a convenient overview of the entirety of the surface.

Gestural interaction has challenges in both finding an appropriate tracking technology and in accuracy and end-user discovery and education. Tracking technologies that have been explored have ranged from expensive optical tracking systems[2] to infrared lasers (Cheng and Pulo 2003) to electromagnetic techniques.[3,4] Accuracy and tracking volumes are constant tradeoffs that need to be balanced. And multi person tracking can impose even further challenges.

A significant problem in interacting with any large display is fatigue. Holding ones arms in the air for gestural control or pointing cannot be sustained for long periods (Cabral et al. 2005). One solution to this problem has been the addition of peripheral devices which can be controlled locally but which affect the output of the larger display. Peripheral devices have the added advantage of being able to use familiar metaphors for interaction and there have been significant investigations on the adaptation of conventional interaction metaphors to use on large displays (Malik et al. 2005).

23.6 Future

Discussions of future displays often turn to holography or other 3D technologies. While continuing to dream about such 3D experiences we would do well to address the cost and availability of more simple large displays. Today's display walls are expensive and rare. As with computers of the 1960s they are a resource to which

[2]http://www.vicon.com/applications.

[3]http://www.ascension-tech.com/realtime/RTflockofBIRDS.php.

[4]http://www.polhemus.com.

users must travel instead of a ubiquitous commodity available to any user anywhere. Once ubiquity is achieved, there will be a sea-change in the interaction techniques and styles used. Visions of future interactive surfaces have the feel of science fiction where any man-made object can suddenly take on the appearance of a map, a virtual whiteboard, or a theater screen (Funkhouser and Li 2000). These visions append the qualities of ubiquity and compactness, or rather thinness, to current practice. The term "digital wallpaper" implies both of these qualities along with low cost. A stimulus for this view is the emergence of thin, flexible displays printed onto rolls of plastic as if they were literally wallpaper. The display mechanisms range from organic light-emitting diodes (OLEDs) to electrophoretic materials.

What is missing from this vision is the circuitry to deliver digital content to these surfaces or to even transfer the energy needed to light them up. Furthermore, displays on every potentially visible surface aren't particularly appealing if an air conditioned closet full of processors is required to drive every wall. There are proposals for embedding processing into the same wallpaper as the display, but they are embryonic. Missing also are the fully evolved means and modes of interaction specific to large surfaces and not just adopted from desktop practice. In spite of these hurdles the vision is too compelling to ignore. When the vision becomes reality we will find ourselves regarding "visualization" as just another element of everyday life alongside indoor plumbing and broadband access.

References

Baudisch, P., Cutrell, E., Robbins, D., Czerwinski, M., Tandler, P., Bederson, B., & Zierlinger, A. (2003). Drag-and-pop and drag-and-pick: Techniques for accessing remote screen content on touch- and pen-operated systems. In *Proceedings of interact 2003*, Zurich, Switzerland, August 2003 (pp. 57–64).

Bolt, R. (1980). Put-that-there: Voice and gesture at the graphics interface. In *Proceedings of SIGGRAPH 80* (pp. 262–270). http://dl.acm.org/citation.cfm?id=807503.

Cabral, M., Morimoto, C., & Zuffo, M. (2005). On the usability of gesture interfaces in virtual reality environments. In *Proceedings of the 2005 Latin American conference on human-computer interaction (CLIHC '05)* (pp. 100–108).

Chen, H., Wallace, G., Gupta, A., Li, K., Funkhouser, T., & Cook, P. (2002). Experiences with scalability of display walls. In *Proceedings of the immersive projection technology (IPT) workshop*. http://www.cs.princeton.edu/~funk/ipt02.pdf.

Cheng, K., & Pulo, K. (2003). Direct interaction with large-scale display systems using infrared laser tracking devices. In *Proceedings of the Australasian symposium on information visualisation* (pp. 67–74).

Clodfelter, R., Sadler, D., & Blondelle, J. (2003). Large high resolution display systems via tiling of projectors. Barco simulation products. http://www.barco.com/projection_systems/downloads/Large_high_res_display_systems.pdf.

Cruz-Neira, C., Sandin, D., & Defanti, T. (1993). Surround-screen projection-based virtual reality: The design and implementation of the CAVE. In *Proceedings of SIGGRAPH '93* (pp. 135–142).

Czerwinski, M., Smith, G., Regan, T., Meyers, B., Robertson, G., & Starkweather, G. (2003). Toward characterizing the productivity benefits of very large displays. In *Proceedings of IFIP INTERACT03: human-computer interaction* (pp. 9–16).

Funkhouser, T., & Li, K. (2000). Guest editors' introduction: Special issue on large displays. *IEEE Computer Graphics and Applications*, *20*(4), 20–21.

Han, J. Y. (2005). Low-cost multi-touch sensing through frustrated total internal reflection. In *Proceedings of the 18th annual ACM symposium on user interface software and technology* (pp. 115–118).

Humphreys, G., Eldridge, M., Buck, I., Stoll, G., Everett, M., & Hanrahan, P. (2001). WireGL: A scalable graphics system for clusters. In *Proceedings of SIGGRAPH 2001* (pp. 129–140).

Humphreys, G., Houston, M., Ng, R., Frank, R., Ahern, S., Kirchner, P. D., & Klosowski, J. T. (2002). Chromium: A stream processing framework for interactive rendering on clusters. In *Proceedings of SIGGRAPH 2002* (pp. 693–702).

IEEE Computer Graphics and Applications (2000). Special issue on large format displays, July-August 2000.

IEEE Computer Graphics and Applications (2005). Special issue on applications of large displays, July-August 2005.

Malik, S., Ranjan, A., & Balakrishnan, R. (2005). Interacting with large displays from a distance with vision-tracked multi-finger gestural input. In *Proceedings of UIST 2005* (pp. 43–52).

Ni, T., Schmidt, G., Staadt, O., Livingston, M., Ball, R., & May, R. (2006). A survey of large high-resolution display technologies, techniques, and applications. In *Proceedings of the IEEE conference on virtual reality* (pp. 223–236).

Oviatt, S. (1999). Ten myths of multimodal interaction. *Communications of the ACM*, *42*(11), 74–81.

Raskar, R., Welch, G., Cutts, M., Lake, A., Stesin, L., & Fuchs, H. (1998). The office of the future: A unified approach to image-based modeling and spatially immersive displays. In *Proceedings of SIGGRAPH 1998* (pp. 179–188).

Robertson, G., Czerwinski, M., Baudisch, P., Meyers, B., Robbins, D., Smith, G., & Tan, D. (2005). The large-display user experience. *IEEE Computer Graphics and Applications*, *25*(4), 44–51.

Samanta, R., Zheng, J., Funkhouser, T., Li, K., & Pal Singh, J. (1999). Load balancing for multi-projector rendering systems. In *Proceedings of SIGGRAPH/Eurographics workshop on graphics hardware* (pp. 107–116).

Stoll, G., Eldridge, M., Patterson, D., Webb, A., Berman, S., Levy, R., Caywood, C., Taveira, M., Hunt, S., & Hanrahan, P. (2001). Lightning-2: A high-performance display subsystem for PC clusters. In *Proceedings of SIGGRAPH 2001* (pp. 141–148).

Tan, D., Gergle, D., Scupelli, P., & Pausch, R. (2006). Physically large displays improve performance on spatial tasks. *ACM Transactions on Computer-Human Interaction*, *13*(1), 71–99.

Travis, A., Payne, F., Zhong, F., & Moore, J. (2000). Flat panel display using projection within a wedge-shaped waveguide. In *Conference record of the 20th international display research conference* (pp. 292–295).

Underkoffler, J. (2010). http://www.ted.com/talks/john_underkoffler_drive_3d_data_with_a_gesture.html.

Wallace, G., Anshus, O., Bi, P., Chen, H., Chen, Y., Clark, D., Cook, P., Finkelstein, A., Funkhouser, T., Gupta, A., Hibbs, M., Li, K., Liu, Z., Samanta, R., Sukthankar, R., & Troyanskaya, O. (2005). Tools and applications for large-scale display walls. *IEEE Computer Graphics and Applications*, *25*(4), 24–33.

Wilson, A. (2005). PlayAnywhere: A compact interactive tabletop projection-vision system. In *Proceedings of UIST 2005* (pp. 83–92).

WorldWide Telescope, Microsoft Research (2008). http://www.worldwidetelescope.org/help/SupportHelp.aspx#MultiMonitorCluster.

Part VI
Virtual Reality and Augmented Reality

Chapter 24
The Development of Mobile Augmented Reality

Lawrence J. Rosenblum, Steven K. Feiner, Simon J. Julier, J. Edward Swan II, and Mark A. Livingston

Abstract The goal of this chapter is to provide a high-level overview of fifteen years of augmented reality research that was sponsored by the U.S. Office of Naval Research (ONR). The research was conducted at Columbia University and the U.S. Naval Research Laboratory (NRL) between 1991 and 2005 and supported in the later years by a number of university and industrial research laboratories. It laid the groundwork for the development of many commercial mobile augmented reality (AR) applications that are currently available for smartphones. Furthermore, it has helped shape a number of ongoing research activities in mobile AR.

24.1 Introduction

In 1991, Feiner, working at Columbia University, received an ONR Young Investigator Award for research on "Automated Generation of Three-Dimensional Virtual Worlds for Task Explanation." In previous work, his Computer Graphics and User Interfaces Lab had developed IBIS, a rule-based system that generated 3D pictures that explained how to perform maintenance tasks (Seligmann and Feiner 1989, 1991), and an AR window manager that embedded a stationary flat panel display

L.J. Rosenblum (✉)
National Science Foundation°, Washington DC, USA
e-mail: lrosenbl@NSF.GOV

S.K. Feiner
Columbia University, New York, USA

S.J. Julier
University College London°, London, UK

J.E. Swan II
Mississippi State University°, Starkville, USA

M.A. Livingston
Naval Research Laboratory, Washington DC, USA

°Current affiliation; research performed at the Naval Research Laboratory.

J. Dill et al. (eds.), *Expanding the Frontiers of Visual Analytics and Visualization*,
DOI 10.1007/978-1-4471-2804-5_24,

Fig. 24.1 The Columbia Touring Machine in 1997. *Left*: A user wearing the backpack and operating the hand-held display. *Right*: A view through the head-worn display (recorded by a video camera looking through the head-worn display)

within a surrounding set of 2D windows presented on a home-made, head-tracked, optical see-through display (Feiner and Shamash 1991). The goal of the new ONR-funded research was to expand this work to generate 3D virtual worlds that would be viewed through head-tracked displays. Beginning in the summer of 1991, Feiner and his PhD students Blair MacIntyre and Dorée Seligmann modified IBIS and combined it with software they developed to render 3D graphics for their head-tracked, optical—see-through, head-worn display. The new system, which they later named KARMA (Knowledge-based Augmented Reality for Maintenance Assistance), interactively designed animated overlaid graphics that explained how to perform simple end-user maintenance for a laser printer (Feiner et al. 1992, 1993). This was the first of a set of ONR-funded projects their lab created to address indoor AR.

In the course of their work, Feiner had realized that despite the many difficult research issues that still needed to be solved to make indoor AR practical, taking AR outside would be a crucial next step. He had heard about work by Loomis and colleagues (Loomis et al. 1993) using differential GPS and a magnetometer to track a user's head and provide spatial audio cues in an outdoor guidance system for the visually impaired. Inspired by that work, Feiner decided to combine these position and orientation tracking technologies with a see-through head-worn display to create the first example of what his lab called a Mobile AR System (MARS). Starting in 1996, Feiner and his students developed the (barely) wearable system shown in Fig. 24.1. This system was mounted on an external frame backpack, and was powered by a battery belt (Feiner et al. 1997). A stylus-based hand-held computer complemented the head-worn display. The system was connected to the Internet using an experimental wireless network (Ioannidis et al. 1991).

The initial MARS software was developed with colleagues in the Columbia Graduate School of Architecture and conceived of as a campus tour guide, named the "Touring Machine." As the user looked around, they could see Columbia's buildings and other major landmarks overlaid by their names, as shown in Fig. 24.1, obtained from a database of geocoded landmarks. Using head-orientation to approximate gaze tracking, the object whose name stayed closest to the center of a small circular area at the middle of the head-worn display for a set period of time was automatically selected, causing a customized menu to be presented at the top of the display. The menu could be operated through a touch pad mounted on the rear of the hand-held display, allowing the user to manipulate the touchpad easily while holding the hand-held display. This controlled a cursor presented on the head-worn display. One menu item overlaid the selected building with the names of its departments; selecting a department name would cause its webpage to be displayed on the hand-held display. The overlaid menus viewed on the head-worn display were also presented on the hand-held display as custom web pages. A conical cursor at the bottom of the display pointed to the currently selected building.

The software was split into two applications, written using an infrastructure that supported distributed applications (MacIntyre and Feiner 1996). The tour application on the backpack was responsible for generating graphics and presenting it on the head-worn display. The application running on the hand-held computer was a custom HTTP server in charge of generating custom web pages on the fly and accessing and caching external web pages by means of a proxy component. This custom HTTP server communicated with an unmodified web browser on the hand-held computer and with the tour application.

24.2 Program Development

24.2.1 Research Issues

Many important research issues would need to be addressed to make the Touring Machine into more than a research prototype. After Rosenblum's completion of a two-year tour at the ONR European Office (ONREUR) in 1994, he founded and directed the NRL Virtual Reality Laboratory (VRL). Rosenblum had seen the potential of Feiner's research and had included it in talks he gave about the ONR computer science research program in Europe while at ONREUR. In early 1998, Rosenblum suggested that Julier, then a VRL team member, and Feiner put together a proposal to ONR that would explore how mobile AR could be developed to make practical systems for use by the military. This funding was awarded and, for NRL, was supplemented by an NRL Base Program award. The program, called the Battlefield Augmented Reality System (BARS™) (Julier et al. 2000a,b; Livingston et al. 2002), would investigate how multiple mobile AR users on foot could cooperate effectively with one another and with personnel in combat operations centers, who had access to more powerful computing and display facilities. The proposed work would build on the Touring Machine at Columbia and on previous NRL research using the VRL's rear-projected workbench (Rosenblum et al. 1997) and CAVE-like multi-display environment (Rosenberg et al. 2000). Several challenges became apparent: building and maintaining environmental models of a complex and dynamic scene,

Fig. 24.2 Situated documentary. A 3D model of an historic building, long since demolished, is shown at its former location

managing the information relevant to military operations, and interacting with this information. To achieve such a system, the architectures for the software to encapsulate these features had to be developed. Although this also required high-fidelity tracking of multiple mobile users, our primary focus was on the information management and interaction components.

24.2.2 Information Management

Situated documentaries. In contrast to the spatially-located text that the Touring Machine supported, it was clear that many applications would benefit from the full range of media that could be presented by computer. To explore this idea, Columbia developed *situated documentaries*—narrated hypermedia briefings about local events that used AR to embed media objects at locations with which they were associated. One situated documentary, created by Feiner and his students in collaboration with Columbia colleagues in Journalism, presented the story of the 1968 Columbia Student Strike (Höllerer et al. 1999). Virtual 3D flagpoles located around the Columbia campus were visible through the head-worn display; each flagpole represented part of the story and was attached to a menu that allowed the user to select portions of the story to experience. While still images were presented on the head-worn display, playing video smoothly on the same display as the user looked around was beyond the capabilities of the hardware, so video was shown on the

Fig. 24.3 The need for information filtering. *Left*: "raw" data, a confusing clutter of many different labels and objects. *Right*: filtered output draws the foreground building for context, the path the user is following, and a potential threat

hand-held display. In developing our situated documentaries, we were especially interested in how multimedia AR could improve a user's understanding of their environment. One example presented 3D models of historic buildings on the head-worn display, overlaid where they once stood, as shown in Fig. 24.2. The user could interact with a timeline presented on the hand-held display to move forward and backward in time, fading buildings up and down in synchrony with a narrated presentation.

Some of the key scientific contributions of the Columbia/NRL research were embodied in our development of a model for mobile AR user interfaces (Höllerer et al. 2001), comprising three essential components: information filtering, UI component design, and view management.

Information filtering. The display space for a mobile AR system is limited, and, in order to utilize the technology in a 3D urban environment, it was clear that effective methods were needed to determine what to display. Based in part on the user's spatial relationship to items of interest, algorithms were developed (Julier et al. 2000a,b) to determine the information that is most relevant to the user. *UI component design* determines how the selected information should be conveyed, based on the kind of display available, and how accurately the user and objects of interest can be tracked relative to each other. For example, if sufficiently accurate tracking is possible, a representation of an item can be overlaid where it might appear in the user's field of view; however, if the relative location and orientation of the user and object are not known with sufficient accuracy, the item might instead be shown on a map or list. *View management* (Bell et al. 2001) refers to the concept of laying out information on the projection plane so that the relationships among objects are as unambiguous as possible, and physical or virtual objects do not obstruct the user's view of more important physical or virtual objects in the scene. Our work on view management introduced an efficient way of allocating and querying space on the viewplane, dynamically accounting for obscuration relationships among objects relative to the user. Software implementations of these three components were included in our prototypes (Fig. 24.3).

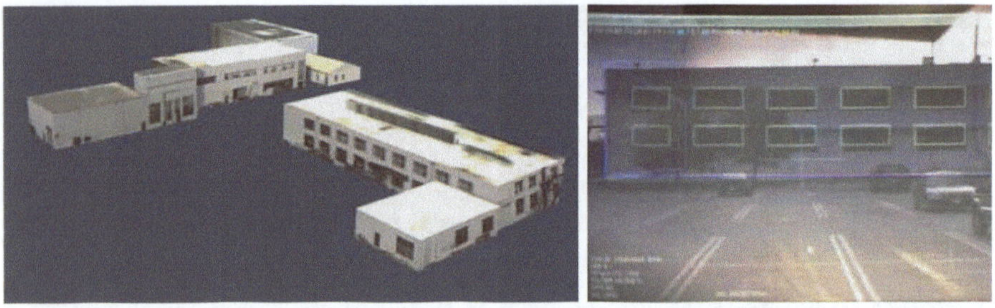

Fig. 24.4 *Left*: Campus model geared towards visualization (without semantic elements). *Right*: The model shown in AR with a wireframe overlay. Note the misalignment in the top-left corner caused by optical distortion in the head-worn see-through display. This is one of the challenges of mobile AR systems

Authoring tools. Authoring mobile AR experiences using our early systems was tedious, and relied on coding large portions of the experience in textual programming languages, along with creating databases using conventional tools. This required that programmers be part of any authoring team. Inspired by multimedia authoring systems (for example, Macromedia Director), AR authoring tools were developed to allow content developers to create richer AR experiences (Julier et al. 1999, 2001). A key concept was to combine a 2D media timeline editor, similar to that used in existing multimedia authoring systems, with a 3D spatial editor that allowed authors to graphically position media objects in a representation of the 3D environment (Güven and Feiner 2004) (Fig. 24.4).

24.2.3 Development Iterations

The earlier development of BARS was carried out in two distinct phases. The Phase I mobile system was a high performance (for its time) mobile hardware platform with the correct software and graphical infrastructure to be able to deliver information about a dynamically changing environment to a user with limited interaction capabilities. The initial BARS prototype consisted of a differential kinematic GPS receiver, an orientation tracker, a head-worn display, a wearable computer and a wireless network. The BARS software architecture was implemented in Java and C/C++. The initial user interface had simple graphical representations (wireframe icons) and was enhanced using information filtering. Techniques for precise registration were developed, including algorithms for calibrating the properties of the head-worn display and the tracking system. To mitigate the problem of information overload, a filtering mechanism was developed to identify the subset of information that must be shown to the user. Accurate models of some of the buildings and

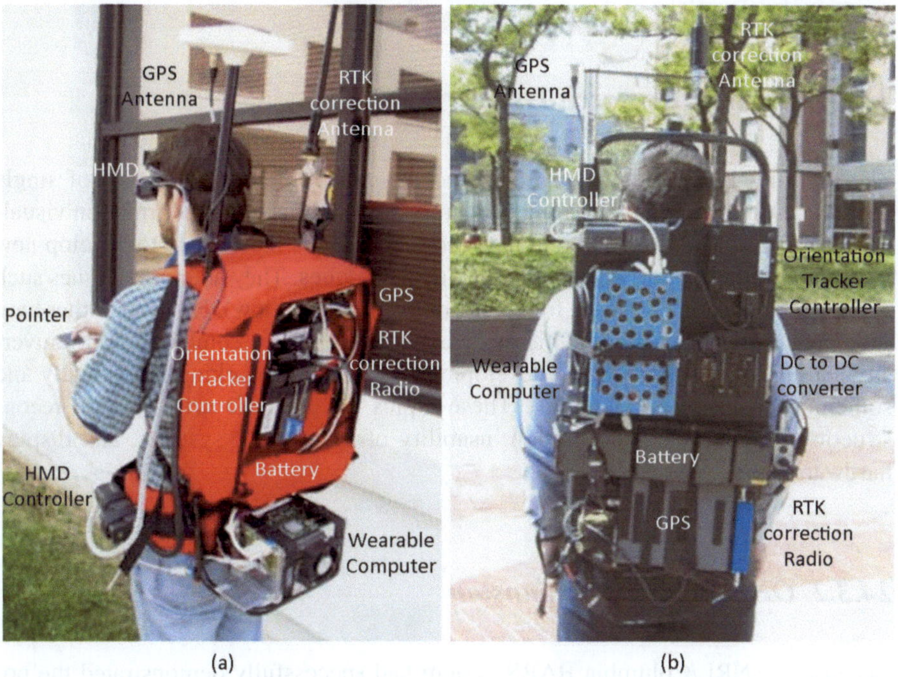

Fig. 24.5 The experimental mobile augmented reality systems

building features were developed for both NRL and Columbia. The Phase II system integrated the mobile AR system into a multi-system collaborative environment. The BARS system architecture was extended to allow multiple, distributed systems to share and change a common environment. Preliminary implementations of components were completed.

Two systems were developed—one based on consumer grade hardware, the other using embedded computers. There was a direct tradeoff of capability and weight versus usability. Both systems used Sony Glasstron optical see through head-worn displays, and a loosely integrated tracking solution consisting of a real-time kinematic GPS receiver and an orientation sensor. The first demonstration of BARS was in November 1999. NRL and Columbia demonstrated early versions of some of this joint work at ISWC 2000, showing the new backpack systems (Fig. 24.5). At SIGGRAPH's Emerging Technologies Pavilion (Feiner et al. 2001), we first demonstrated integration with wide-area tracking in a joint effort with InterSense; Eric Foxlin contributed an early version of the IS-1200 tracker technology and large ceiling-mounted fiducials.

24.3 Program Expansion

24.3.1 Further Research Issues

The preliminary prototypes demonstrated the capabilities and potential of single user AR. One area of shortcoming was in the user interface and information visualization. NRL and Columbia continued their research in these areas to develop new information filtering algorithms and display techniques. They addressed issues such as the "X-ray vision" problem for occlusion (described below). However, other hard problems remained. Additional issues were addressed by a combination of university and industrial research and development (sometimes working individually and sometimes with NRL/Columbia). These topics included 3D urban terrain reconstruction, tracking and registration, usability of mobile AR systems, and display hardware.

24.3.2 ONR Program Expansion

Because the NRL/Columbia BARS system had successfully demonstrated the potential of mobile AR, Andre van Tilborg, then the Director of the Mathematical, Computer, and Information Sciences and Technology Division at ONR, asked Rosenblum, who was working part time for ONR while serving as Director of the Virtual Reality Laboratory at NRL, to assemble a primarily university-based research program to complement the Columbia/NRL research program and assure that the field advanced. We believe this program, combined with the NRL/Columbia effort, was the largest single effort through that time to perform the research necessary to turn mobile AR into a recognized field and that it provided the basis for advances on an international scale.

The program was based upon several options available within ONR and U.S. DoD for funding research and totaled several million dollars annually for approximately five years, although most PIs were funded for differing periods during that time. The majority of the awards were the typical three-year ONR research grants for university projects (similar to those of the National Science Foundation), but also included two industrial awards as well as related research conducted under a DoD Multidisciplinary University Research Initiative (MURI), which was a $1M/year award for five years to researchers at the University of California Berkeley, the Massachusetts Institute of Technology, and the University of California San Francisco. Only a portion of the MURI research, relating to the reconstruction of 3D urban terrain from photographs, applied directly to the ONR mobile AR program. Institutions and lead PIs involved in this program were:

- Tracking and Registration (Ulrich Neumann, University of Southern California; Reinhold Behringer; Rockwell)

- Usability of Mobile AR systems (Debbie Hix, Virginia Polytechnic Institute and State University; Blair MacIntyre, Georgia Institute of Technology; Brian Goldiez, University of Central Florida)
- 3D Urban Terrain Reconstruction (Seth Teller, Massachusetts Institute of Technology; Jitendra Malik, University of California at Berkeley; William Ribarsky, Georgia Institute of Technology)
- Retinal Scanning Displays (Tom Furness, University of Washington; Microvision, Inc.)

Also, two separately funded NRL projects funneled results into BARS:

- 3D Multimodal Interaction (NRL and Phil Cohen, Oregon Graduate Institute)
- Interoperable Virtual Reality Systems (NRL)

The remainder of this subsection briefly summarizes a few of these projects.

The Façade project at Berkeley acquired photographs (of a limited area) and developed algorithms to reconstruct the geometry and add texture maps, using human-in-the-loop methods. This research inspired several commercial image-based modeling packages. The Berkeley research went on to solve the difficult inverse global illumination problem: given geometry, light sources, and radiance images, devise fast and accurate algorithms to determine the (diffuse and specular) reflectance properties (although this portion of the research was not directly related to mobile AR).

The 3D urban terrain reconstruction research at MIT made seminal algorithmic advances. Previous methods, including the Berkeley work, relied on human-in-the-loop methods to make point or edge correspondences. Teller developed a sequence of algorithms that could take camera images collected from a mobile robot and reconstruct the urban environment. Algorithms were developed for image registration, model extraction, facade identification, and texture estimation. The two main advances of this research were to provide a method that did not require human intervention and to develop algorithms that allowed for far faster reconstruction than was previously possible. The model extraction algorithm was shown to be $O(N + V)$, where N is the number of images and V is the number of voxels, while previous methods were $O(N * V)$.

One missing component in the development of mobile AR prior to the ONR program was integrating usability engineering into the development of a wearable AR system and into producing AR design guidelines. VPI, working jointly with NRL, performed a domain analysis (Gabbard et al. 2002) to create a context for usability engineering effort, performed formative user-based evaluations to refine user interface designs, and conducted formal user studies both to understand user performance and to produce design guidelines. An iterative process was developed, which was essential due to the extremely large state space generated by the hundreds of parameters that arise from the use of visualization and interaction techniques. The team developed a use case for a platoon in an urban setting and tested BARS interaction and visualization prototypes using semi-formal evaluation techniques with domain experts (Hix et al. 2004). Out of these evaluations emerged two *driving problems* for BARS, both of which led to a series of informal and formal evaluations: (1) AR depth perception and the "X-ray vision" problem (i.e., correct

Fig. 24.6 *Left*: an accurately aligned marker on a window can be hard to achieve with tracking errors. *Center*: a larger boundary can guarantee to enclose the desired object if tracking error is bounded. *Right*: Text indicators can direct users to the correct point when tracking errors prevent correct registration

geospatial recognition of occluded objects by the user), and (2) text legibility in outdoor settings with rapid and extreme illumination changes. For the text legibility problem, VPI and NRL designed an active color scheme for text that accounted for the color capabilities of optical see-through AR displays. Appropriate coloring of the text foreground enabled faster reading, but using a filled rectangle to provide a background enabled the fastest user performance (Gabbard et al. 2007).

Tracking the user's head position against the real-world scene remains one of the difficult problems in mobile AR. Research at the University of Southern California developed an approach based on 2D line detection and tracking. Features included the use of knowledge that man-made structures were in the scene. The nature of these structures permitted use of larger scale primitives (e.g. windows) that provided more geometrical information for stable matching. This approach proved more robust than the use of point like features. A line-based auto-calibration algorithm was also developed.

Because tracking head-motion and aligning the view correctly to the real world is so difficult, methods are needed to convey registration uncertainty. Note that this tends to be task dependent since placing a label on a building requires quite a different accuracy than identifying a specific window. Joint research by Georgia Tech and NRL resulted in a methodology for portraying uncertainty (MacIntyre et al. 2002). The statistics of 3D tracker errors were projected into 2D registration errors on the display. The errors for each object were then collected together to define an error region. An aggregate view of the errors was then generated using geometric considerations based on computing an inner and outer convex hull and placed over the scene (Fig. 24.6).

The one disappointing area of the research program was in the attempt to produce the hardware for the AR display. The Sony Glasstron did not have sufficient brightness for the augmented image to be seen in bright sunlight; it was nearly unusable under that condition. Program management felt that the Microvision retinal scanning display, using a laser to scan an image directly onto the eye, had the potential to overcome the scientific issues involved in producing a display with sufficient resolution and field of view and would produce sufficient luminance to work under conditions ranging from bright sunlight to darkness. While Microvision made advances in their display technology, they did not produce a display that completely met the needs of mobile AR. The University of Washington performed basic research to scan bright images on the retina while also tracking the retinal and head position using the same scanning aperture. The research was theoretically successful, but (at least in the time period of the program) it was not transitioned into a commercial product.

24.3.3 The "X-Ray Vision" Problem and the Perception of Depth

Our domain analysis revealed that one challenge of urban operations is maintaining understanding of the location of forces that are hidden by urban infrastructure. This is called the "X-ray vision" problem: Given the ability to see "through" objects with an AR system, how does one determine how to effectively represent the locations of the occluded objects? This led us to develop visualization techniques that could communicate the location of graphical entities with respect to the real environment. Drawing on earlier work at Columbia to represent occluded infrastructure (Feiner and Seligmann 1992), NRL implemented a range of graphical parameters for hidden objects. NRL and VPI then conducted a user study to examine which of the numerous possible graphical parameters were most effective. We were the first to study objects at far-field distances of 60–500 meters, identifying visualization parameters (Fig. 24.7) such as drawing style, opacity settings, and intensity settings that could compensate for the lack of being able to rely on a consistent ground plane and identifying which parameters were most effective (Livingston et al. 2003). NRL began to apply depth perception measurement techniques from perceptual psychology. This led us to adopt a perceptual matching technique (Swan et al. 2006), which we used to study AR depth perception at distances of 5–45 meters in an indoor hallway. Our first experiment with this technique showed that user behavior with real and virtual targets was not significantly different when performing this perceptual matching against real reference objects (Livingston et al. 2005). We later used the technique to study how AR depth perception differs in indoor and outdoor settings (noting an underestimation indoors and overestimation outdoors) and how linear perspective cues could be simulated outdoors to assist users (Livingston et al. 2009). The studies have produced some conflicting data regarding underestimation and overestimation. This remains an active research area, with many parameters being investigated to explain the effects observed in the series of experiments.

24.3.4 Integration of a Component-Based System

The software architecture had to support two goals: coordination of all the different types of information required and providing flexibility for the different systems under test. NRL implemented a substantial amount of the system using the Bamboo toolkit (Watsen and Zyda 1998). Bamboo decomposed an application into a set of

Fig. 24.7 *Left*: one of the concept sketches for how occluded buildings and units might be represented in BARS. *Right*: a photograph taken through our optical see-through display with a similar protocol implemented

modules that could be loaded in a hierarchical manner with dependencies between them. Into this framework, NRL researchers could plug in UI components, such as the event manager for display layout, designed and tested at Columbia (Höllerer et al. 2001).

One example of the success of this architecture was the demonstration at the International Symposium on Mixed and Augmented Reality in November 2004. Into the NRL BARS framework (with video to provide a multi-person AR view of Washington, DC) were integrated Columbia's view management for placing labels and VPI's rules for providing color or intensity contrast to ensure label legibility. Another success was a variation on the BARS system to integrate semi-automated forces, providing a realistic training scene for military call-for-fire. This system was demonstrated at Quantico Marine Corps Base in October 2004.

24.4 Ongoing Research

The ONR Mathematical, Computer, and Information Sciences and Technology Division program helped to launch major efforts within the U.S. Department of Defense to build usable mobile AR systems for military applications. These programs focused on applications, but recognized the need for fundamental research and enabled continued efforts in the basic research as well as applied research domains. These programs enabled some members of the ONR AR program to continue their work. This section focuses on recent NRL and Columbia research and development.

Two particularly broad efforts, both inspired by the NRL-led work, are the operationally-focused DARPA Urban Leader Tactical Response Awareness and Visualization (ULTRA-Vis) program, and the DoD Future Immersive Training Environments (FITE) Joint Capability Technology Demonstration; a follow-up ONR program called Next-generation Naval Immersive Training (N2IT) carries on the training research.

NRL participated in both of these programs, based on its experiences with both the training applications for urban combat skills and the human factors evaluations, which apply to both training and operational contexts. User interface techniques continue to be a critical element of the research (Livingston et al. 2011). NRL in recent years has also continued to study the human factors issues described above. Livingston and Feiner collaborated on exploring AR stereo vergence (Livingston et al. 2006). Livingston and Swan have maintained collaboration on the depth perception and X-ray vision research (Livingston et al. 2009; Swan et al. 2007), as well as other human factors issues. We became interested in using perceptual-motor tasks, which have been widely applied in perceptual psychology, to study AR depth perception (Jones et al. 2008; Singh et al. 2010). Recent work has studied reaching distances, which are important for other AR applications, such as maintenance. At NRL, the original operational context of "X-ray vision" continues to be a topic of interest (Livingston et al. 2011). NRL continues to offer technical support to ONR programs sponsoring research on improving see-through displays and tracking systems appropriate for training facilities.

Columbia was funded through the Air Force Research Laboratory, and later through ONR, to examine the feasibility and appropriate configuration of AR for maintenance of military vehicles (Henderson and Feiner 2010, 2011). Feiner and his students have also continued to explore a broad range of research issues in AR. The concept of situated documentaries has led to the study of *situated visualization*, in which information visualizations are integrated with the user's view of the environment to which they relate, with applications to site visits for urban design and urban planning (White and Feiner 2009). Interacting with a scale model of an environment in AR is a challenge; in some cases, performance can be improved when 3D selection is decomposed into complementary lower dimensional tasks (Benko and Feiner 2007). Leveraging the ubiquity of handheld devices with built-in cameras and vision-based tracking, Columbia has investigated the advantages of having users take snapshots of an environment and quickly switch between augmenting the live view or one of the snapshots (Sukan and Feiner 2010).

24.5 Predictions for the Future

24.5.1 Consumer Use

When mobile AR research began, few people saw the potential applications as having a deep impact in the consumer market. However, if one compares our early image to images of tourist guides available for mobile phones (Fig. 24.8), it is apparent that our vision of mobile AR has reached the consumer market, even if the application requirements in the military domain have proven more challenging to fulfill.

Even though AR is no longer merely a laboratory curiosity, we believe that many challenges remain.

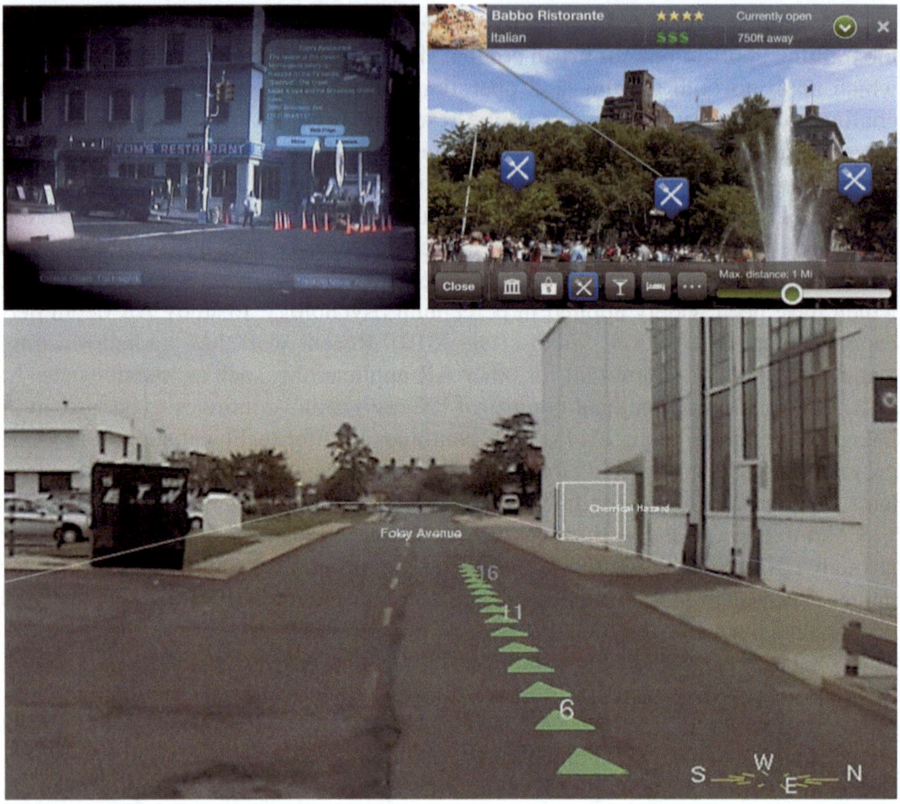

Fig. 24.8 *Top left*: The Touring Machine showed the potential of AR to guide a user through an unknown urban environment (Bell et al. 2002). *Top right*: An image from Mtrip Travel Guides shows a modern implementation of commercial AR guidance. Image ©2011 Mtrip Travel Guides, http://www.mtrip.com; used by permission. *Bottom*: BARS was envisioned to be able to provide urban cues integrated in 3D. This BARS image shows a compass for orientation and a route for the user to follow in addition to a street label and the location of a hidden hazard

24.5.2 Tracking

There have been many advances in hardware design. Tracking sensors are now readily available. Almost all recent mobile phones contain built in GPS and IMU (magnetometers, accelerometers and gyroscopes) sensors. However, despite this wide availability of sensing devices and decades of intensive research, tracking remains one of the most significant challenges facing AR. Non-line-of-sight and multi-path means that GPS position solutions can contain errors of between tens and hundreds of meters. Metallic structures can introduce angular errors of 180 degrees with compasses. As mobile devices improve in power, we are already seeing vision-based algorithms for tracking new environments being applied to consumer AR games. However, many of these systems rely on the assumption that the entire world is static.

We believe that, in the short term, very accurate tracking will only be available in two cases. The first set of cases will be niche applications (such as surgical assistants, maintenance and repair of delicate equipment, or fabrication in highly specialized fields). These can justify the use of expensive, intrusive, and dedicated equipment. Second, we believe that vision-based algorithms can be used effectively to track planar targets (e.g., the discrete markers of ARToolKit or the clusters of natural features used in the Qualcomm AR SDK). As a result, we believe these markers will proliferate.

In the long-term, we believe that tracking systems cannot be based on metric information alone. Apart from the hybrid use of sensors, a great deal of high-level semantic information is not being exploited by tracking systems. Scene understanding can be used to process an image and recognize potentially stable objects, such as buildings, to be used as landmarks for tracking.

A related question is whether absolute 3D spatial models are required in many mixed-reality applications. If an augmentation can be defined relative to recognizable landmarks in the real world, it may be necessary only to have accuracy relative to that landmark. For example, a proposed extension to a building must connect to that building accurately, whether or not the 3D model of the building is accurate relative to some external coordinate system. We also believe that the use of robust interfaces, cognizant of the structure of the environment, the ambiguity of information, and the impact of errors can be used to adapt the display to mitigate the effects of tracking errors.

24.5.3 Form Factor

Many current AR applications are based on hand-held devices such as mobile phones. For many reasons (e.g., ease of being carried or fit into a pocket), the devices cannot become substantially larger. However, this leads to a mismatch—the camera has a wide field-of-view (in some cases, more than 60°), but the angle subtended by a hand-held display is very small (typically 12–16°). As a result, this introduces many user interface challenges. Apart from issues such as fatigue, such displays can monopolize a user's attention, potentially to the exclusion of other things around them. This is clearly unacceptable for dangerous tasks such as disaster relief. Even in tourism applications, a tourist needs to be aware of the environment to navigate effectively. Furthermore, hand-held devices, by definition, also need to be held, which can make many common tasks that could benefit from AR hard to perform.

We believe that if AR is to realize its full potential, hand-held form factors, despite much of the hype they are receiving now, simply are not adequate. Rather, AR systems will need to be based on head-worn displays—eyewear—which must become as ubiquitous as earphones. For that to happen, AR eyewear must be comfortable, good-looking, of sufficient optical quality that they feel like looking through properly fitted eyeglasses, and relatively inexpensive. Many of the other hardware barriers to mobile AR have fallen, thanks to small but powerful sensor-laden smartphones, coupled with affordable high-bandwidth data access, and rapidly improving tracking ability. Consequently, we are now seeing far-sighted consumer electronics companies, both large and small, exploring how to develop appropriate AR eyewear.

24.6 Summary

We have been very fortunate to work on mobile AR at a pivotal time in its development. Through the research programs described, we were able to explore many important issues, and it is good to see that some of the once impractical ideas we investigated are now incorporated in applications running on consumer devices. However, despite its promise, mobile AR has a substantial way to go to realize its full potential. If AR is to become an effective, ubiquitous technology, many fundamental research and development challenges remain to be overcome.

Acknowledgments The authors wish to thank Yohan Baillot, Reinhold Behringer, Blaine Bell, Dennis Brown, Aaron Bryden, Enylton Coelho, Elliot Cooper-Balis, Deborah Hix, Joseph Gabbard, Brian Goldiez, Tobias Höllerer, Bryan Hurley, Marco Lanzagorta, Dennis Lin, Blair MacIntyre, Douglas Maxwell, Ulrich Neumann, Gregory Schmidt, Erik Tomlin, Ross Whitaker, Suya You, and Catherine Zanbaka. We appreciate the support we had over this extended time period from ONR. In particular, we thank Andre van Tilborg, Wen Masters, Paul Quinn, and Ralph Wachter. We also thank Randy Shumaker and John McLean for their support for the NRL portion of the research. Opinions expressed in this article are those of the authors and do not represent official positions of the Naval Research Laboratory, the National Science Foundation, or any other institution.

References

Bell, B., Feiner, S., & Höllerer, T. (2001). View management for virtual and augmented reality. In *ACM symposium on user interface software and technology* (pp. 101–110).

Bell, B., Feiner, S., & Höllerer, T. (2002). Information at a glance. *IEEE Computer Graphics & Applications*, *22*(4), 6–9.

Benko, H., & Feiner, S. (2007). Balloon selection: A multi-finger technique for accurate low-fatigue 3D selections. In *IEEE symposium on 3D user interfaces* (pp. 79–86).

Feiner, S., & Shamash, A. (1991). Hybrid user interfaces: Breding virtually bigger interfaces for physically smaller computers. In *ACM symposium on user interface software and technology* (pp. 9–17).

Feiner, S., & Seligmann, D. (1992). Cutaways and ghosting: Satisfying visibility constraints in dynamic 3D illustrations. *The Visual Computer*, *8*(5–6), 292–302.

Feiner, S., MacIntyre, B., & Seligmann, D. (1992). Annotating the real work with knowledge-based graphics on a see-through head-mounted display. In *Graphics interface '92* (pp. 78–85).

Feiner, S., MacIntyre, B., & Seligmann, D. (1993). Knowledge-based augmented reality. *Communications of the ACM*, *36*(7), 52–62.

Feiner, S., MacIntyre, B., Höllerer, T., & Webster, T. (1997). A touring machine: Prototyping 3D mobile augmented reality systems for exploring the urban environment. In *International symposium on wearable computers* (pp. 74–81).

Feiner, S., Bell, B., Gagas, E., Güven, S., Hallaway, D., Höllerer, T., Lok, S., Tinna, N., Yamamoto, R., Julier, S., Baillot, Y., Brown, D., Lanzagorta, M., Butz, A., Foxlin, E., Harrington, M., Naimark, L., & Wormell, D. (2001). Mobile augmented reality systems. In *28th international conference on computer graphics and interactive techniques (SIGGRAPH 2001). Conference abstracts and applications* (p. 129).

Gabbard, J. L., Swan II, J. E., Hix, D., Lanzagorta, M., MA, Livingston, Brown, D., & Julier, S. J. (2002). Usability engineering: domain analysis activities for augmented reality systems. In *SPIE: Vol. 4660. Stereoscopic displays and virtual reality systems IX* (pp. 445–457).

Gabbard, J. L., Swan II, J. E., Hix, D., Si-Jung, K., & Fitch, G. (2007). Active text drawing styles for outdoor augmented reality: A user-based study and design implications. In *IEEE virtual reality* (pp. 35–42).

Güven, S., & Feiner, S. (2004). A hypermedia authoring tool for augmented and virtual reality. *The New Review of Hypermedia and Multimedia 9*, 89–116.

Henderson, S., & Feiner, S. (2010). Opportunistic tangible user interfaces for augmented reality. *IEEE Transactions on Visualization and Computer Graphics, 16*(1), 4–16.

Henderson, S., & Feiner, S. (2011). Exploring the benefits of augmented reality documentation for maintenance and repair. *IEEE Transactions on Visualization and Computer Graphics, 17*(10), 1355–1368.

Hix, D., Gabbard, J. L., Swan II, J. E., Livingston, M. A., Höllerer, T., Julier, S. J., Baillot, Y., & Brown, D. (2004). A cost-effective usability evaluation progression for novel interactive systems. In *Hawaii international conference on system sciences (HICSS-37)*.

Höllerer, T., Feiner, S., & Pavlik, J. (1999). Situated documentaries: embedding multimedia presentations in the real world. In *International symposium on wearable computers* (pp. 79–86).

Höllerer, T., Feiner, S., Hallaway, D., Bell, B., Lanzagorta, M., Brown, D., Julier, S., Baillot, Y., & Rosenblum, L. (2001). User interface management techniques for collaborative mobile augmented reality. *Computers and Graphics, 25*(5), 799–810.

Ioannidis, J., Duchamp, D., & Maguire, G. Q. Jr (1991). IP-based protocols for mobile internetworking. In *ACM SIGCOMM* (pp. 235–245).

Jones, J. A., Swan II, J. E., Singh, G., Kolstad, E., & Ellis, S. R. (2008). The effects of virtual reality, augmented reality, and motion parallax on egocentric depth perception. In *Symposium on applied perception in graphics and visualization* (pp. 9–14).

Julier, S., Feiner, S., & Rosenblum, L. (1999). Augmented reality as an example of a demanding human-centered system. In *First EC/NSF advanced research workshop*.

Julier, S., Lanzagorta, M., Baillot, Y., Rosenblum, L., Feiner, S., Höllerer, T., & Sestito, S. (2000a). Information filtering for mobile augmented reality. In *IEEE international symposium on augmented reality* (pp. 3–11).

Julier, S., Baillot, Y., Lanzagorta, M., Brown, D., & Rosenblum, L. (2000b). BARS: Battlefield augmented reality system. In *NATO symposium on information processing techniques for military systems* (pp. 9–11).

Julier, S., Baillot, Y., Lanzagorta, M., Rosenblum, L. J., & Brown, D. (2001). Urban terrain modelling for augmented reality applications. In *3D synthetic environment reconstruction* (Chap. 6, pp. 119–136). Dordrecht: Kluwer Academic Press.

Livingston, M. A., Rosenblum, L. J., Julier, S. J., Brown, D. G., Baillot, Y., Swan II, J. E., Gabbard, J. L., & Hix, D. (2002). An augmented reality system for military operations in urban terrain. In *Interservice/industry training, simulation, and education conference* (p. 89).

Livingston, M. A., Swan II, J. E., Gabbard, J. L., Höllerer, T. H., Hix, D., Julier, S. J., Baillot, Y., & Brown, D. G. (2003). Resolving multiple occluded layers in augmented reality. In *2nd international symposium on mixed and augmented reality* (pp. 56–65).

Livingston, M. A., Zanbaka, C., Swan II, J. E., & Smallman, S. (2005). Objective measures for the effectiveness of augmented reality. In *Proceedings of IEEE virtual reality (poster session)*, Bonn, Germany (pp. 287–288).

Livingston, M. A., Lederer, A., Ellis, S. R., White, S. M., & Feiner, S. K. (2006). Vertical vergence calibration for augmented reality displays. In *IEEE virtual reality* (Poster Session).

Livingston, M. A., Ai, Z., Swan II, J. E., & Smallman, H. S. (2009). Indoor vs. outdoor depth perception for mobile augmented reality. In *IEEE virtual reality* (pp. 55–61).

Livingston, M. A., Karsch, K., Ai, Z., & Gibson, G. O. (2011). User interface design for military AR applications. *Virtual Reality*, *15*, 175–184.

Loomis, J. M., Klatzky, R. L., Golledge, R. G., Cicinelli, J. G., Pellegrino, J. W., & Fry, P. A. (1993). Nonvisual navigation by blind and sighted: Assessment of path integration ability. *Journal of Experimental Psychology, General*, *122*(1), 73–91.

MacIntyre, B. M., & Feiner, S. (1996). Future multimedia user interfaces. *Multimedia Systems*, *4*(5), 250–268.

MacIntyre, B., Coelho, E. M., & Julier, S. J. (2002). Estimating and adapting to registration errors in augmented reality systems. In *IEEE virtual reality* (pp. 73–80).

Rosenblum, L., Durbin, J., Doyle, R., & Tate, D. (1997). Situational awareness using the VR responsive workbench. *IEEE Computer Graphics and Applications*, *17*(4), 12–13.

Rosenberg, R., Lanzagorta, M., Kuo, E., King, R., & Rosenblum, L. (2000). Immersive scientific visualization. In *NRL review* (pp. 137–139).

Seligmann, D., & Feiner, S. (1989). Specifying composite illustrations with communicative goals. In *ACM symposium on user interface software and technology* (pp. 1–9).

Seligmann, D., & Feiner, S. (1991). Automated generation of intent-based 3D illustrations. *Computer Graphics*, *25*(4), 123–132.

Singh, G., Swan II, J. E., Jones, J. A., & Ellis, S. R. (2010). Depth judgment measures and occluding surfaces in near-field augmented reality. In *Symposium on applied perception in graphics and visualization* (pp. 149–156).

Sukan, M., & Feiner, S. (2010). SnapAR: Storing snapshots for quick viewpoint switching in handheld augmented reality. In *IEEE international symposium on mixed and augmented reality* (pp. 273–274).

Swan II, J. E., Livingston, M. A., Smallman, H. S., Brown, D. G., Baillot, Y., Gabbard, J. L., & Hix, D. (2006). A perceptual matching technique for depth judgments in optical, see-through augmented reality. In *IEEE virtual reality* (pp. 19–26).

Swan II, J. E., Jones, J. A., Kolstad, E., Livingston, M. A., & Smallman, H. S. (2007). Egocentric depth judgments in optical, see-through augmented reality. *IEEE Transactions on Visualization and Computer Graphics*, *13*(3), 429–442.

Watsen, K., & Zyda, M. (1998). Bamboo—a portable system for dynamically extensible, networked, real-time, virtual environments. In *Virtual reality annual international symposium* (pp. 252–259).

White, S., & Feiner, S. (2009). SiteLens: Situated visualization techniques for urban site visits. In *ACM SIGCHI conference on-human factors in computing systems* (pp. 1117–1120).

Chapter 25
Multimodal Interfaces for Augmented Reality

Mark Billinghurst and Minkyung Lee

Abstract Recent research in multimodal speech and gesture input for Augmented Reality (AR) applications is described. Although multimodal input has been researched for desktop applications, 3D graphics and virtual reality interfaces, there have been very few multimodal AR applications. We review previous work in the area and then present our own multimodal interfaces and user studies conducted with those interfaces. Based on these studies we provide design guidelines for developing effective multimodal AR experiences.

25.1 Introduction

Augmented reality (AR) is a technology that overlays computer-generated information onto the real world (Azuma 1997). In 1965 Ivan Sutherland described his vision of the "Ultimate Display" in which computers can simulate reality, and he built a head mounted display for viewing graphics in the real world (Sutherland 1965), creating the first AR interface. In the forty years since there have been a wide range of different AR prototypes developed and the first commercial applications have begun appearing. However, in many ways AR interfaces for these applications are still in their infancy.

As Ishii says, the AR field has been primarily concerned with "... considering purely visual augmentations" (Ishii and Ullmer 1997) and while great advances have been made in display and tracking technologies, *interaction* has usually been limited to either passive viewing or simple browsing of virtual information. Few systems provide tools that let the user effectively interact, request or modify this information. Furthermore, even basic AR interaction tasks have been poorly addressed, such as manipulation, copying, annotating, and dynamically adding and deleting virtual objects.

M. Billinghurst (✉) · M. Lee
HIT Lab NZ, University of Canterbury, Christchurch, New Zealand
e-mail: mark.billinghurst@hitlabnz.org

M. Lee
e-mail: minkyung.lee@hitlabnz.org

J. Dill et al. (eds.), *Expanding the Frontiers of Visual Analytics and Visualization*,
DOI 10.1007/978-1-4471-2804-5_25, © Springer-Verlag London Limited 2012

Azuma points out that AR technology has three core attributes (Azuma 1997); it combines real and virtual images, the images are registered in three-dimensional space, and it is interactive in real time. Thus there is a strong connection between the real and virtual worlds. In our research we have been developing AR interaction techniques based on the user's natural real world behavior, and in particular their speech and gestures. Many current AR applications adopt general Virtual Reality (VR) (Nakashima et al. 2005) or GUI interaction techniques (Broll et al. 2003). However, these methods are designed for fully immersive virtual environments or desktop interfaces, and largely ignore the connection between AR content and the real world. Thus, there is a need to research new interface metaphors ideally suited for AR.

Computer interfaces that combine speech and gesture input are an example of a multimodal interface (MMI). MMI have previously been found to be an intuitive way to interact with 2D and 3D graphics applications (Bolt 1980; Cohen and Sullivan 1989; Oviatt et al. 2004). However, there has been little research on the use of multimodal input in AR interfaces, and especially usability evaluations of AR multimodal interfaces. In this chapter we provide an overview of multimodal input in AR, beginning with a summary of related work in the field and then describing our own research in the area. We summarize our work in a set of guidelines for developing effective multimodal interfaces for AR systems, and then describe directions for future work.

25.2 Related Work

The first research on multimodal interfaces dates back to the Bolt's "Put-that-there" work (Bolt 1980). In this case a user was able to use pointing gestures and speech to manipulate 2D icons on a screen. Many multimodal interfaces after Bolt's work were map or screen-based 2D applications (Tse et al. 2006). For these, pen-based or touch screen input and speech was enough to support a gesture based interface on a 2D surface. For example, QuickSet (Cohen et al. 1997) supported multimodal input in a military planning application.

Interfaces that combine speech and hand gesture input are an intuitive way to interact with 2D and 3D graphics desktop applications (Hauptmann 1989). This is because the combination of natural language and direct manipulation can overcame the limitations of unimodal input (Cohen and Sullivan 1989; Oviatt et al. 2004). Unlike gesture or mouse input, voice is not tied to a spatial metaphor (Cohen et al. 1989), and so can be used to interact with objects regardless of whether they can be seen or not. However, care must be taken to map the appropriate modality to the application input parameters. For example, Kay (1993) constructed a speech driven interface for a drawing program in which even simple cursor movements required a time consuming combination of movements in response to vocal commands.

Earlier researchers have used speech input with hand tracking devices or DataGloves (Koons and Sparrell 1994; Latoschik 2001; LaViola 1999; Weimer and

Ganapathy 1989) to explore multimodal input in 3D graphics environments. For example, Koons and Sparrell (1994) combined two-handed DataGlove gestures with speech to allow users to arrange 3D objects in a virtual scene. LaViola (1999) developed multimodal interfaces for virtual reality applications that allowed users to create, place, modify, and manipulate furniture using 3D hand gestures and speech. MMI was also used for interacting with 3D virtual content (Chu et al. 1997) or to navigate through virtual worlds (Krum et al. 2002). Ciger et al. (2003) presented a multimodal user interface that combined a magic wand with spell casting. The user could navigate in the virtual environment, grab and manipulate objects using a combination of speech and the magic wand. Although this research provides a natural way for people to use their hands to interact with 3D virtual objects, they had to wear encumbering data gloves and a number of tracking devices. This could reduce the naturalness of the hand gesture interfaces made.

More recently, computer vision-based hand tracking techniques have been used in systems such as "VisSpace" (Lucente et al. 1998) to estimate where users were pointing (Rauschert et al. 2002). This overcomes the disadvantages of using DataGloves for capturing hand gesture input; however, these systems did not support natural manipulation of 3D objects as they were only concerned with where users were pointing.

There has also been research conducted on how to combine speech and gesture input. Latoschik (2001) presented a framework for modeling multimodal interactions, which enriched the virtual scene with linguistic and functional knowledge about the objects to allow the interpretation of complex multimodal utterances. Holzapfel et al. (2004) presented multimodal fusion for natural interaction with a humanoid robot. Their multimodal fusion is based on an information-based approach by comparing object types defined in the ontology.

Although multimodal input has been studied in 3D graphics and VR, there has been relatively little research in AR multimodal interfaces. One of the first systems developed was Heidemann et al. (2004) who used an MMI to acquire visual knowledge and retrieve memorized objects. Speech input was used to select interface menu options and 3D pointing gestures were used to select the object. However, the main interaction was navigating in 2D, and their AR MMI did not involve any 3D object manipulation.

Kölsch et al. (2006) developed a multimodal information visualization system with 2D natural hand gesture, speech, and trackball input in a wearable AR environment. They used HandVu (Kölsch et al. 2004) to recognize the users' hand gestures in 2D. However, their MMI could not be used to manipulate virtual objects in 3D space and they did not evaluate the system usability.

Olwal's SenseShape (Olwal et al. 2003) and its later extended version (Kaiser et al. 2003) were the first truly 3D AR multimodal interfaces. In this case users had to wear a data glove and trackers to give gesture commands to the system. However the focus of their interface evaluation was on the system's mutual disambiguation capabilities and not usability.

Thus, there have only been only few examples of AR MMIs, and none of them have used computer vision techniques for unencumbered 3D hand interaction. There has also been very little evaluation of AR MMIs, especially exploring the usability of AR MMIs. In the rest of the chapter we will present two multimodal AR systems that we have developed, results from user studies evaluating those systems, and general lessons learned that could be applied to the design of multimodal AR interfaces.

25.3 Speech and Paddle Gesture

The first system that we developed involved speech input and paddle gestures (Irawati et al. 2006a,b). This was based on extending the earlier VOMAR AR application for virtual furniture arranging (Kato et al. 2000). VOMAR allows users to arrange virtual furniture in empty rooms using marker-attached paddle gestures. This was extended by adding speech input and a semantic multimodal fusion framework. The goal was to allow people to easily arrange AR content using a natural mixture of speech and gesture inputs.

25.3.1 Multimodal System

The multimodal system developed was a modified version of the VOMAR application (Kato et al. 2000) based on the ARToolKit AR tracking library (ARToolKit website 2012). We used the Microsoft Speech API (Microsoft Speech API 2012) for speech input and Ariadne (Denecke 2002) as the spoken dialog system. Figure 25.1 shows the system architecture. The AR Application allows a user to interact with the system using paddle gestures and speech. It is responsible for receiving the speech commands from Ariadne, recognizing paddle gestures, and fusing the speech and paddle gesture input into a single interpretation. Ariadne and the AR Application communicate with each other using the middleware ICE (ICE website 2012). A Microsoft Access database was used to store the object descriptions, to specify the speech grammar, and to enable the multimodal fusion.

The AR application involved the manipulation of virtual furniture in a virtual room, although the multimodal interaction techniques could be applied to various other domains. When the user looked at a set of menu pages through a head mounted display with a camera attached to it, they saw different types of virtual furniture on the pages (Fig. 25.2). Looking at the workspace, a large piece of paper with specific tracking markers, they saw the virtual room. The user could then pick furniture from the menu pages and place them into the room using paddle and speech commands.

Gesture input was through using a paddle held in the user's hand, with an attached marker that was tracked by the AR system and allowed the user to make gestures to interact with the virtual objects. A range of static and dynamic gestures were recognized by tracking the paddle (Table 25.1).

Speech input was recognized by the Microsoft Speech API and sent to the Ariadne spoken dialog system for spoken dialog understanding. To create a speech

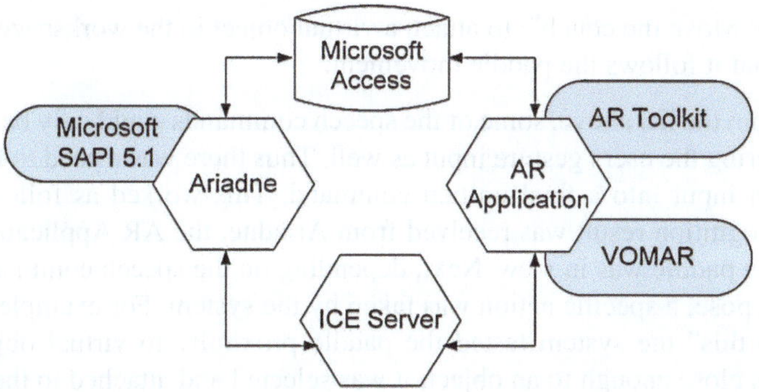

Fig. 25.1 Multimodal architecture

Fig. 25.2 Using the multimodal application

Table 25.1 Paddle gestures recognized

Static Gestures	Paddle proximity to object Paddle tilt/inclination
Dynamic Gestures	*Shaking:* side to side motion of the paddle *Hitting:* up and down motion of the paddle *Pushing:* pushing paddle while touching an object

grammar structure, objects were imported from an SQL database which contained an OBJECT_NAME attribute for all the names of virtual objects that could be manipulated by the user.

The following types of speech commands were recognized by the system:

- **Create**—"Make a blue chair": to create a virtual object.
- **Duplicate**—"Copy this": to duplicate a virtual object.
- **Grab**—"Grab table": to select a virtual object.
- **Place**—"Place here": to place a selected object in the workspace.

- **Move**—"Move the couch": to attach a virtual object in the workspace to the paddle so that it follows the paddle movement.

As seen from the list above, some of the speech commands could only be understood by considering the users gesture input as well. Thus there was a need to fuse gesture and speech input into a final unified command. This worked as follows: when a speech recognition result was received from Ariadne, the AR Application checked whether the paddle was in view. Next, depending on the speech command type and the paddle pose, a specific action was taken by the system. For example, if the user said "grab this" the system tested the paddle proximity to virtual objects. If the paddle was close enough to an object, it was selected and attached to the paddle.

When fusing the multimodal input, our system considered object properties, such as whether the object could have things placed on it or if there was space under it. These properties are used to resolve deictic references in the speech commands from the user. For example, if the user said "put here" while touching a virtual couch with the paddle, the possible locations referred to by 'here' are 'on the couch' or 'under the couch'. By checking the object properties of the couch, the system understands that 'here' refers to the position 'on top of the couch'. In case the object properties cannot disambiguate user input, the position of the paddle is used by the system. For example, the system checks the paddle in the z (up-down) direction. If the z position of the paddle was less than a threshold value (for example the height of a desk), the system understands 'here' as 'under the desk'.

The system also provided visual and audio feedback to the user by showing the speech recognition result, and an object bounding box when an object is touched. In addition, audio feedback is given after the speech and paddle gesture command, so the user can immediately recognize if there is an incorrect result from the speech or gesture recognition system.

25.3.2 Evaluation

To evaluate our multimodal AR interface, we conducted a user study (Irawati et al. 2006b). The goal was to compare user interaction with the multimodal interface to that with a single input mode. There were 14 participants (3 female and 11 male). The user study took about forty-five minutes for each user during which users had to build three different furniture configurations using three different interface conditions: (A) Paddle gestures only, (B) Speech with static paddle position, and (C) Speech with paddle gestures.

Before each trial, a brief demonstration was given so that the users were comfortable with the interface. For each interface condition the subjects were trained by performing object manipulation tasks until they were proficient enough to be able to assemble a sample scene in less than five minutes. A list of speech commands was provided on a piece of paper, so the user could refer to them throughout the experiment.

Table 25.2 Average trial completion times

	A: Paddle only	B: Speech and static	C: Speech and gesture
Time (sec.)	165 s	106 s	147 s

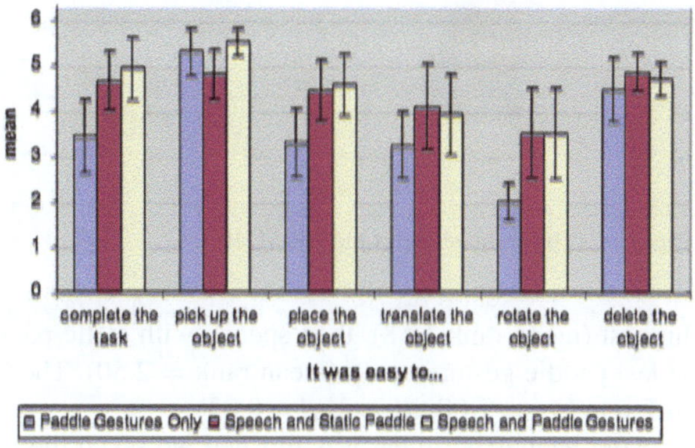

Fig. 25.3 Subjective survey results (95 % CI with Bonferroni adjustment)

A virtual model of the final goal was shown, then the furniture removed from the scene, and the user asked to reproduce it, using a picture of the final scene as a reference. After each trial, users were asked questions about the interface usability, efficiency and intuitiveness. After all trials users rated the three interaction modes and commented on their experience. Trial completion times and object placement accuracy were recorded.

Results for average completion times across the three interface conditions are shown in Table 25.2. When using speech and static paddle interaction, participants completed the task significantly faster than when using paddle gestures only, an ANOVA test finding ($F(2, 22) = 7.25$, $p = 0.004$). The completion time for the speech with paddle gestures condition did not differ significantly from the other two conditions. The results show that the use of input channels with different modalities leads to an improvement in task completion time. Similarly, we found that users had difficulty translating and rotating objects using paddle gestures alone, and were significantly more accurate in rotating objects in the multimodal conditions (B and C).

After each trial, users were given a subjective survey where they were asked on a 6-point Likert scale if they agreed or disagreed with a number of statements (1 = disagree, 6 = agree) (see Fig. 25.3). Users felt that completing the task in condition C was easier than condition A ($F(2, 26) = 5.55$, $p = 0.01$). They also thought that placing objects was easier in condition C than in condition A ($F(2, 26) = 4.59$, $p = 0.02$). Users reported that object rotation was easier in conditions B and C than with condition A ($F(1.15, 14.97) = 7.80$, $p = 0.01$). Thus, users found it hard to place objects in the target positions and rotate them using only paddle gestures.

We also asked the users to rank the conditions from 1 to 3 (with 1 as best rating) in terms of which they liked most. Speech with paddle gestures was ranked

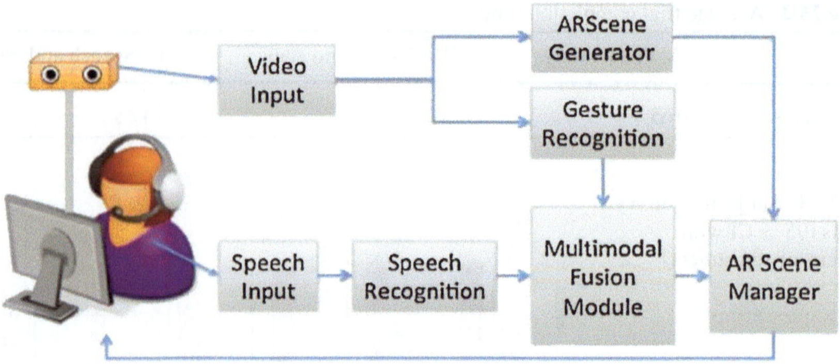

Fig. 25.4 The architecture of the AR MMI

highest (mean rank 1.58), then speech with static paddle (mean rank = 1.91), and at last paddle gestures only (mean rank = 2.50). These rankings were significantly different ($\chi^2 = 7.00$, $df = 2$, $p = 0.03$).

After each experiment was finished we asked the users to provide general comments about the system. Most agreed that it was difficult to place and rotate the virtual objects using only paddle gestures. Many users were impressed with the robustness of the speech recognition (the system was not trained for individual users). The users mentioned that accomplishing the task using combined speech and paddle commands was a lot easier once they had learned and practiced the speech commands.

In summary, the results of our user study demonstrated how combining speech and paddle gestures improved performance in arranging virtual objects over using paddle input alone. Using multimodal input, users could orient the objects more precisely in the target position, and finished an assigned task a third faster than using paddle gestures alone. The users also felt that they could complete the task more efficiently. Paddle gestures allowed the users to interact intuitively with the system since they could in- teract directly with the virtual objects.

25.4 Speech and Free-Hand Input

More recently we have developed an AR MMI that combines 3D stereo vision-based natural hand gesture input and speech input. This system is made up of a number of components that are connected together (see Fig. 25.4). They include modules for capturing video, recognizing gesture and speech input, a fusion module for combining input modalities, an AR scene generation, and manager modules for generating the AR output and providing feedback to the user.

This system is based on an earlier study where we observed how people use natural gesture and speech input in an AR environment (Lee and Billinghurst 2008). From this we found that the same gestures had different meanings based on the

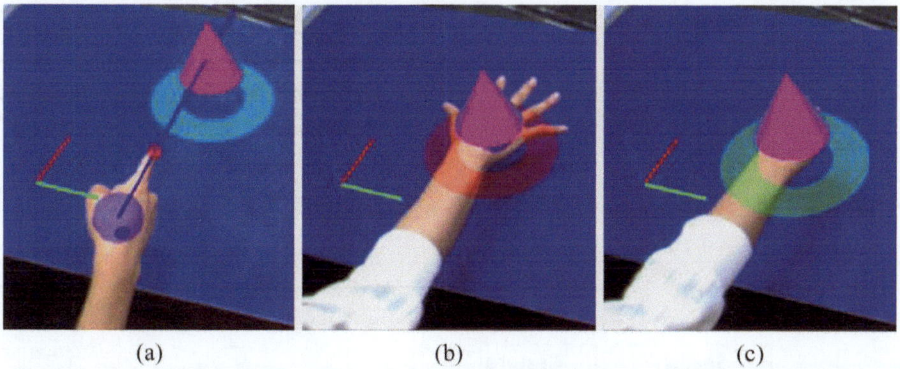

Fig. 25.5 Hand gestures interacting with a virtual object; (**a**) pointing gesture, (**b**) open hand gesture, and (**c**) close hand gesture

context; the meaning of a gesture is varied according to its corresponding speech command. Users mostly triggered gestures before the corresponding speech input, meaning that a gesture-triggered time window is needed to capture related commands. We also found that people used three different types of gestures: (1) open hand, (2) closed hand, and (3) pointing.

In order to capture these gestures we developed a stereo computer vision system involving five steps: (1) Camera calibration (off-line), (2) Skin color segmentation, (3) Fingertip detection, (4) Fingertip estimation in 3D, and (5) Gesture recognition. For camera input we used a BumbleBee camera (Point Grey Research Inc 2009) that provided two 320×240 pixel images at 25 frames per second.

Camera calibration (Borgefors 1986) and skin segmentation (Chai and Bouzerdoum 2000) was done using standard computer vision techniques. Fingertip positions were estimated by (1) drawing the convex hull around the hand, (2) finding the center point of the hand, (3) removing the palm area to leave only segmented fingers, (4) finding the contour of each finger blob, (5) calculating the distance from points on each contours to the hand center, and (6) marking the furthest point on each finger blob as a fingertip. When the fingertip locations and camera calibration matrices are known, we can estimate the 3D position of the fingertips in real-time, accurate from 4.5 mm to 26.2 mm depending on the distance between the user's hand and the cameras.

Finally, gesture recognition was performed by considering the number of fingertips visible; an open hand has five fingertips; closed hand has no fingertips; and a pointing gesture has only one fingertip. A moving gesture is recognized from a continuous movement of the closed hand. The gesture recognition results in a semantic form that includes arrival time, type of gesture, position in 3D, and function. Figure 25.5 shows the three hand gestures we implemented.

For the speech input, we used the Microsoft Speech API 5.3 with the Microsoft Speech Recognizer 8.0, trained with a male voice to achieve accuracy of over 90 %. We use a set of speech commands that are integrated later with the gesture input (see Table 25.3).

Table 25.3 Supported speech commands

Color	Shape	Direction
Green	Sphere	Backward
Blue	Cylinder	Forward
Red	Cube	Right
Yellow	Cone	Left
		Up
		Down

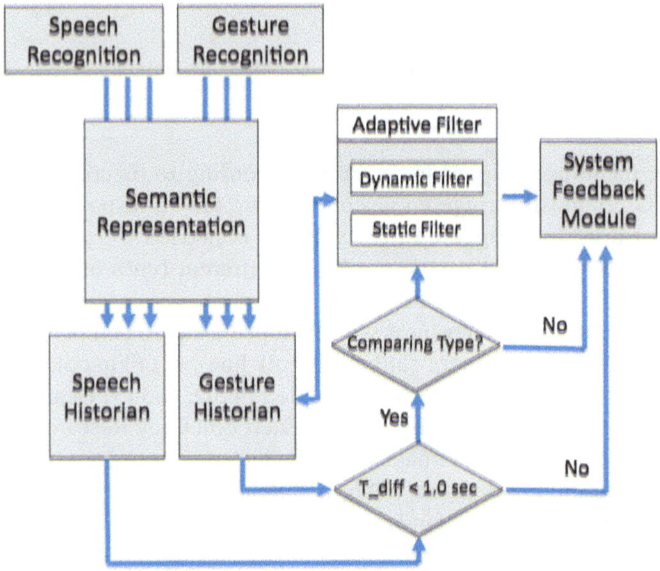

Fig. 25.6 The multimodal fusion architecture

To combine the gesture and speech input we implemented a multimodal fusion architecture more complex than in the earlier paddle interface (see Fig. 25.6). Recognized speech and gesture input are passed to the semantic representation module with their arrival time, where they are given semantic tags. The output from the semantic representation module is passed to historians that store input for 10 seconds in case future commands need them. In around 95 % of AR multimodal commands, a gesture is issued up to one second earlier than the related speech input (Lee and Billinghurst 2008). If speech and gesture input occur within one second of each other they are compared and passed to a filter module if they are complimentary. If the time difference is bigger than one second or the command types not the same, the input is considered as a unimodal one and passed to the system feedback module.

The adaptive filter module combines commands of the same type into a single multimodal command by filling out the information needed as a result of the type comparison. There is a Dynamic Filter for moving commands and a Static Filter

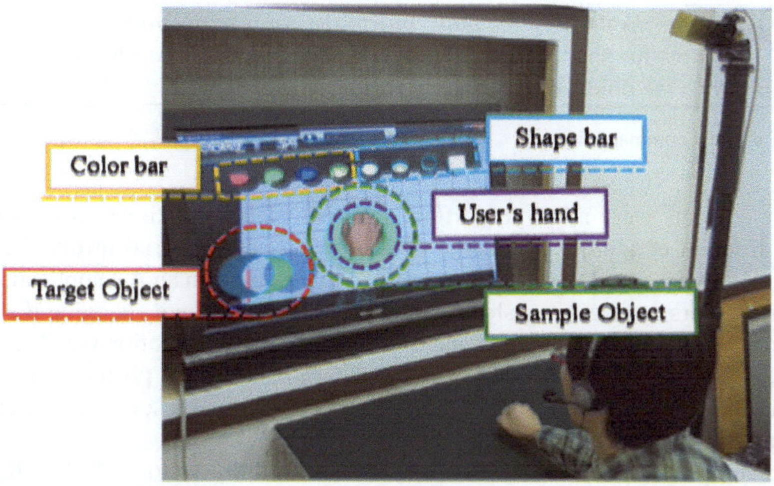

Fig. 25.7 Multimodal AR application

for other commands such as pointing and touching. The Dynamic Filter handles commands related to moving virtual objects and so needs to have the starting point and the destination point as input. The Static Filter only needs to have a single input point. Once all necessary information is successfully filled out, the output of the Adaptive Filter module is passed to the system feedback module that changes the AR scene according to the outputs.

The target AR multimodal application was for 3D object manipulation and scene assembly. In the next section we describe the application developed with this system and an evaluation conducted with it.

25.4.1 Evaluation

To test the AR multimodal architecture we developed a simple test application. The user sat in front of a large plasma screen, on which was shown the AR view from the BumbleBee camera located above them. The AR view showed their hand and a color bar with several colors and a shape bar with several shapes. On the left side of the table was a colored object and the goal of the application was to select the same shaped object from the shape bar, color it and move it to the target (see Fig. 25.7).

To test the system we used three different interface conditions: (1) a speech-only interface, (2) a gesture-only interface, and (3) a MMI. For the speech- and gesture-only conditions, the subjects were asked to use only a single modality, however in the MMI condition, they could use both of them in any way they wanted to. There were twenty participants in the experiment, eighteen male and two female, with ages from 25 to 40 years old. They were familiar with AR applications but had little experience with speech interfaces, gesture interfaces, and MMI. A within-subjects design was used so all participants experienced all conditions.

1. *Change the* color *of the pink cone to the color of the target object.*
2. *Change* the shape *of the cone to the shape of the target object.*
3. *Move the* object *to the target position.*

Fig. 25.8 Trial command list

The subjects were asked to perform ten task trials three times each using the three different conditions for a total of 90 trials. Each task trial involved using a particular interface to interact with a sample virtual object in an AR application. For each trial users were given a short task list that involved them changing the visual characteristics of a virtual object and moving it to a target location (see Fig. 25.8). When the target object is moved to within 5 mm of the target position, the system will recognize it as a successful completion of the trial and reset the AR scene and start another task automatically.

We compared the three interfaces using the usability factors of (1) efficiency, (2) effectiveness, and (3) satisfaction. The measured factors were (1) the task completion time, (2) the number of user and system errors, and (3) user satisfaction (questionnaire), respectively. We used a one-way repeated measure ANOVA to test the results for a significant difference and performed a post-hoc pairwise comparison with the Bonferroni correction.

We measured the time between when users started and finished a trial with the given interface conditions. There was a significant difference in the task completion time across conditions ($F(2, 18) = 8.78$, $p < 0.01$). After post-hoc pairwise comparisons we found that the task completion time with the gesture only interface was significantly different from the time with the speech interface ($p < 0.01$) and the MMI ($p < 0.01$). It took longer to complete the given tasks with the gesture interface (mean = 15.4 s) than the speech interface (mean = 12.4 s) and the MMI (mean = 11.9 s). However, we did not find any significant difference in task completion time between the speech-only interface and the MMI condition.

User errors were used to measure the effectiveness of the system. To measure this, we observed the video of users interacting with the system and counted the number of errors made. The average number of user errors with speech input was 0.41 times per task, with gesture input was 0.50 times per task, and the average number of user errors with MMI was 0.42 times per task. There was no significant difference in the average number of user errors across the different interfaces ($F(2, 18) = 0.73$, $p = 0.5$).

System errors are dependent on the speech and gesture recognition accuracy and the multimodal fusion accuracy, which is percentage of correctly recognized commands. This is also found from analyzing video of people using the application. The average accuracy of the speech interface was 94 %, and of the gesture interface was 86 %. We found experimentally that the accuracy of the MMI was 90 %, showing that the fusion module helped to increase the system accuracy slightly from the raw gesture accuracy by capturing the related speech input and compensating for error.

We also collected user feedback using surveys of each modality, and the MMI. The subject answered questions on a Likert scale from 1 (very low) to 7 (very high).

Table 25.4 Subjective survey results for object interaction

Survey question	Gesture	Speech	MMI	P value
1. How natural was object manipulation	4.60	5.60	5.80	$p < 0.01$
2. How easy was changing object color	4.05	5.60	5.60	$p < 0.01$
3. How easy was changing object shape	4.00	5.90	6.00	$p < 0.01$
4. How easy was it to move the objects	4.75	4.70	5.70	$p < 0.01$

Table 25.5 Subjective survey results for overall interface evaluation

Survey question	Gesture	Speech	MMI	P value
5. How efficient was the interface	4.45	5.15	6.05	$p < 0.01$
6. How fast was the interface	4.40	5.05	6.15	$p < 0.01$
7. How accurate was the interface	4.40	5.05	5.60	$p < 0.01$

Table 25.4 shows average feedback on questions related to object manipulation and changing properties. In all of these questions there was a significant difference between the average results, with the speech and MMI conditions significantly higher than the gesture only interface, except for question four, where the MMI was rated significantly easier than both the gesture alone and speech alone conditions.

Table 25.5 shows average feedback on questions related to interface performance (the efficiency, speed, and accuracy of the interfaces). Overall, users felt that the MMI was the most efficient, fastest, and accurate interface. In Q5 and Q6 the MMI was rated significantly higher than both the speech and gesture only interfaces, while in Q7 the MMI was rated better than the gesture only condition, and there was no difference from the speech only condition.

After the experiment trials, we asked users to rank the preferred interface condition. In total 70 % of users preferred the MMI over the unimodal interfaces, 25 % preferred the speech only and only 5 % preferred the gesture only interfaces. Users said the MMI was the preferred interface because they could use the two different modalities simultaneously or sequentially and so they could complete the task more quickly and efficiently. They also felt that the two different modalities compensated for each other and let them do the task more accurately. For example, speech was used to change the color of the sample object, and gesture was useful in changing the position of the object. They said they least preferred the gesture input as they found it physically demanding and they had to search the control menu to find the target colors and shapes. It took longer and was less accurate than using the other interface conditions.

We counted the number of commands which were used to complete each trial and found a significant difference between the number of commands used in each condition ($F(2, 18) = 11.58$, $p < 0.01$). From the post-hoc tests, we found that subjects issued more commands with gesture only interface (mean = 6.14) than with the speech only interface (mean = 5.23) or MMI (mean = 4.93). However, there was no significant difference in the number of commands between the speech only interface and MMI.

We classified the commands into two types: (1) *Characteristic*—involving object characteristics such as the shape and color and (2) *Movement*—involving physical motions such as grabbing, moving, and dropping. There was no significant difference between the numbers of characteristic commands with the different types of interfaces. However, we found a significant difference in the number of movement commands with each interface condition ($F(2, 18) = 3.82$, $p < 0.04$). The speech only modality (mean = 28.5) required fewer commands than the gesture only modality (mean = 35.3) for moving the objects ($p < 0.03$). We found no significant difference between number of speech and MMI commands or between number of gesture and MMI commands for moving the objects.

We also measured the proportions of simultaneous and sequential multimodal commands during the study. On average, only 21 % of MMI commands were issued simultaneously while 79 % were triggered sequentially. Speech commands preceded gesture commands in only 1.1 % of a simultaneously integrated MMI.

By comparing the task completion times for the three different interface conditions, we found that the MMI significantly reduced interaction time compared to the gesture only interface. This is partly because using the speech input in the MMI took less time than the gesture only condition. Previous research (Kaiser et al. 2003) has found that speech input is helpful for descriptive commands, such as changing the color, while gesture input is useful for spatial commands, such as pointing or moving an object. The MMI takes advantage of the complementary nature of the two input modalities, combining descriptive and spatial commands. As a result, we observed that the MMI was more efficient than the gesture interface for this AR application. However, we did not find any significant difference in the efficiency between the speech only interface and the MMI.

These findings also agreed with the user feedback that we received. The subjects preferred the MMI condition over the gesture only interface. Although speech recognition produced slightly fewer errors, they felt that the MMI was overall more accurate than the speech only input condition. This is because performing the tasks well typically required a combination of speech and gesture input.

25.5 Lessons Learned

From these two multimodal AR interfaces and user studies with the system, we learned a number of important design lessons that could help people develop better multimodal AR interfaces in the future.

Match Affordances: Firstly, it's very important to match the speech and gesture input modalities to the appropriate interaction methods. We were using speech to specify commands and gestures to specify parameters (locations and objects) for the commands. It is much easier to say "Put that there" rather than "Put the table at coordinates $x = 50$, $y = 60$".

Provide Feedback: With imprecise input recognition it is important to provide feedback to the user about what commands are being sent to the system. In the paddle application we showed the results of the speech recognition on-screen and gave audio feedback after the gesture commands. This enabled the user to immediately recognize when the speech or gesture recognition was producing an error.

Simple Command Set: It is also important to use a speech and gesture command set that is easy for users to remember. In our first case, we only had a limited speech grammar and five paddle gestures. Using combined multimodal input reduces the amount of commands that users need to remember; for example it was possible to say "Put that there", rather than "Put the vase on the table".

Use Context: The interaction context can be used to disambiguate speech and gesture input. In our case the fusion engine interprets combined speech and gesture input based on the timing of the input events and domain semantics providing two types of contextual cues.

Use Gesture-Triggered Fusion: In the second application, in only 1 % of the multimodal commands did the speech input precede the gesture input. We also found a similar pattern in an earlier study where 94 % of gesture commands preceded speech input (Lee and Billinghurst 2008). Thus, multimodal AR applications may need to have a gesture-triggered MMI fusion architecture.

25.6 Conclusions and Future Work

In this chapter we have reported on developments in multimodal input for Augmented Reality applications. In general, although speech and gesture input has proven useful for desktop and immersive graphics applications, there has been little research on how multimodal techniques can be applied in an AR setting. Those few interfaces that have been developed have typically relied on special input hardware and/or have not conducted user studies to evaluate the interface.

Over the past several years we have developed a range of different multimodal AR interfaces and we report on two of them; one that used paddle and speech input for furniture arranging, and one that supported free hand gesture input for changing object properties. Both used a different system architecture, but both demonstrated how combining speech and gestures improved performance over using gesture or speech input alone.

In the future, we need to study task performance in a variety of AR environments such as an AR navigation task or AR game application with different display types (HMD and handheld displays) and balanced user genders. Performance may be improved by adding a feedback channel to give the user information about the fusion result and showing if there are system failures occurring. We could also use this to build a learning module into the multimodal fusion architecture that would improve the accuracy of the MMI based on the users' behavior. In this way we could develop AR MMI that are even more effective.

References

ARToolKit website (2012). http://www.hitl.washington.edu/artoolkit.

Azuma, R. T. (1997). A survey of augmented reality. *Presence: Teleoperators and Virtual Environments*, *6*(4), 355–385.

Bolt, R. A. (1980). "Put-that-there": Voice and gesture at the graphics interface. In *Proc. annual conference on computer graphics and interactive techniques* (pp. 262–270).

Borgefors, G. (1986). Distance transformations in digital images. In *Computer vision, graphics and image processing* (pp. 344–371).

Broll, W., Stoerring, M., & Mottram, C. (2003). The augmented round table—a new interface to urban planning and architectural design. In *Proc. INTERACT'03* (pp. 1103–1104).

Chai, D., & Bouzerdoum, A. (2000). A Bayesian approach to skin color classification in YCbCr color space. In *Proceedings of IEEE TENCONO'00* (Vol. 2, pp. 421–424).

Chu, C. P., Dani, T. H., & Gadh, R. (1997). Multimodal interface for a virtual reality based computer aided design system. In *Proceedings of 1997 IEEE international conference on robotics and automation* (Vol. 2, pp. 1329–1334).

Ciger, J., Gutierrez, M., Vexo, F., & Thalmann, D. (2003). The magic wand. In *Proceedings of the 19th spring conference on computer graphics* (pp. 119–124).

Cohen, P. R., & Sullivan, J. W. (1989). Synergistic user of direct manipulation and natural language. In *Proc. CHI '89* (pp. 227–233).

Cohen, P. R., Dalrymple, M., Pereira, F. C. N., Sullivan, J. W., Gargan Jr., R. A., Schlossberg, J. L., & Tyler, S. W. (1989). Synergistic use of direct manipulation and natural language. In *Proceedings of ACM conference on human factors in computing systems (CHI '89)* (pp. 227–233).

Cohen, P. R., Johnston, M., McGee, D., & Oviatt, S. (1997). QuickSet: Multimodal interaction for distributed applications. In *Proc. international conference on multimedia* (pp. 31–40).

Denecke, M. (2002). Rapid prototyping for spoken dialogue systems. In *Proceedings of the 19th international conference on computational linguistics* (Vol. 1, pp. 1–7).

Hauptmann, A. G. (1989). Speech and gestures for graphic image manipulation. In *Proc. CHI '89* (pp. 241–245).

Heidemann, G., Bax, I., & Bekel, H. (2004). Multimodal interaction in an augmented reality scenario. In *Proceedings of international conference on multimodal interfaces (ICMI'04)* (pp. 53–60).

Holzapfel, H., Nickel, K., & Stiefelhagen, R. (2004). Implementation and evaluation of a constraint-based multimodal fusion system for speech and 3D pointing gestures. In *Proceedings of the 6th international conference on multimodal interfaces* (pp. 175–182). New York: ACM Press.

ICE website (2012). http://www.zeroc.com/ice.html.

Irawati, S., Green, S., Billinghurst, M., Duenser, A., & Ko, H. (2006a). Move the couch where?: Developing an augmented reality multimodal interface. In *Proc. ICAT '06* (pp. 1–4).

Irawati, S., Green, S., Billinghurst, M., Duenser, A., & Ko, H. (2006b). An evaluation of an augmented reality multimodal interface using speech and paddle gestures. In *Proc. of ICAT '06* (pp. 272–283).

Ishii, H., & Ullmer, B. (1997). Tangible bits: Towards seamless interfaces between people, bits and atoms. In *Proceedings of CHI '97*, Atlanta, Georgia, USA (pp. 234–241). New York: ACM Press.

Kaiser, E., Olwal, A., McGee, D., Benko, H., Corradini, A., Li, X., Cohen, P., & Feiner, S. (2003). Mutual disambiguation of 3D multimodal interaction in augmented and virtual reality. In *Proceedings of international conference on multimodal interfaces (ICMI '03)* (pp. 12–19).

Kato, H., Billinghurst, M., Poupyrev, I., Imamoto, K., & Tachibana, K. (2000). Virtual object manipulation on a table-top AR environment. In *Proceedings of the international symposium on augmented reality (ISAR 2000)* (pp. 111–119).

Kay, P. (1993). Speech driven graphics: A user interface. *Journal of Microcomputer Applications*, *16*, 223–231.

Kölsch, M., Turk, M., & Tobias, H. (2004). Vision-based interfaces for mobility. In *Proceedings of MobiQuitous'04* (pp. 86–94).

Kölsch, M., Turk, M., & Tobias, H. (2006). Multimodal interaction with a wearable augmented reality system. *IEEE Computer Graphics and Applications*, *26*(3), 62–71.

Koons, D. B., & Sparrell, C. J. (1994). ICONIC: Speech and depictive gestures at the human-machine interface. In *Proc. CHI '94* (pp. 453–454).

Krum, D. M., Omotesto, O., Ribarsky, W., Starner, T., & Hodges, L. F. (2002). Speech and gesture control of a whole earth 3D visualization environment. In *Proceedings of joint Eurographics-IEEE TCVG symposium on visualization* (pp. 195–200).

Latoschik, M. E. (2001). A gesture processing framework for multimodal interaction in virtual reality. In *Proc. AFRIGRAPH 2001* (pp. 95–100).

LaViola, J. J. Jr. (1999). A multimodal interface framework for using hand gestures and speech in virtual environment applications. In *Gesture-based communication in human-computer interaction* (pp. 303–341).

Lee, M., & Billinghurst, M. (2008). A wizard of oz study for an AR multimodal interface. In *Proceedings of international conference on multimodal interfaces (ICMI '08)* (pp. 249–256).

Lucente, M., Zwart, G. J., & George, A. D. (1998). Visualization space: A testbed for deviceless multimodal user interface. In *Proceedings of AAAI spring symposium on intelligent environments*. AAAI TR SS-98-02.

Microsoft Speech API (2012). http://en.wikipedia.org/wiki/Microsoft_Speech_API.

Nakashima, K., Machida, T., Kiyokawa, K., & Takemura, H. (2005). A 2D-3D integrated environment for cooperative work. In *Proc. VRST '05* (pp. 16–22).

Olwal, A., Benko, H., & Feiner, S. (2003). SenseShapes: Using statistical geometry for object selection in a multimodal augmented reality system. In *Proceedings of international symposium on mixed and augmented reality (ISMAR '03)* (pp. 300–301).

Oviatt, S., Coulson, R., & Lunsford, R. (2004). When do we interact multimodally? Cognitive load and multimodal communication patterns. In *Proc. ICMI '04* (pp. 129–136).

Point Grey Research Inc (2009). http://www.ptgrey.com/products/stereo.asp.

Rauschert, I., Agrawal, P., Sharmar, R., Fuhrmann, S., Brewer, I., MacEachren, A., Wang, H., & Cai, G. (2002) Designing a human-centered, multimodal GIS interface to support emergency management. In *Proceedings of geographic information system* (pp. 119–124).

Sutherland, I. (1965). The ultimate display. In *International federation of information processing* (Vol. 2, pp. 506–508).

Tse, E., Greenberg, S., & Shen, C. (2006). GSI DEMO: Multiuser gesture/speech interaction over digital tables by wrapping single user applications. In *Proc. ICMI '06* (pp. 76–83).

Weimer, D., & Ganapathy, S. K. (1989). A synthetic visual environment with hand gesturing and voice input. In *Proc. CHI '89* (pp. 235–240).

Part VII
Technology Transfer

Chapter 26
Knowledge Exchange, Technology Transfer and the Academy

Rae Earnshaw

Abstract The relationship between the academy and the business community is currently perceived to be important to the future of both parties. Universities provide graduates to meet the needs and requirements of society and industry, and the latter supplies products and services to meet the needs of the market place. Whether public or private, industry increasingly seeks to use tools and techniques that increase efficiency and effectiveness, whilst at the same time maximizing quality and minimizing cost. The current trend towards companies outsourcing their R & D requirements to reduce corporate overheads and optimize staffing levels means that Universities can utilize the opportunity and bid to supply this expertise. Universities also generate their own spin-outs from intellectual property they create, as well as licensing technology to industry, rather than transferring it. However, the relationship between university and industry is not without its challenges, chief of which is the historical commitment of the academy to advance knowledge whether it is directly applicable or not. In addition, there are many fundamental and important long term research issues that many would argue are the primary duty of the academy to address, which may have no direct application in the short to medium term. This is resulting in increasing tensions in the academy, and in the priorities for national and international funding agencies. There can also be significant cultural differences and reward models between the academy and industry which give rise to difficult issues for staff at the interface. This chapter reviews the current developments and the issues at the interface between business and the academy.

26.1 Introduction

As economies advance it is argued that they migrate from resource-based to knowledge-based production. Thus knowledge and innovation are two of the factors behind job creation and economic growth. This in turn affects the social context and also public and economic policy. Many national governments have therefore

R. Earnshaw (✉)
University of Bradford, Bradford, UK
e-mail: R.A.Earnshaw@bradford.ac.uk

J. Dill et al. (eds.), *Expanding the Frontiers of Visual Analytics and Visualization*,
DOI 10.1007/978-1-4471-2804-5_26, © Springer-Verlag London Limited 2012

sought to address the challenges implicit in this observation and, in particular, provide motivation and incentives to increase the collaboration between industry and the academy in the expectation that there will be direct benefits to a nation's economy and overall global competitiveness. In turn, the academy has sought to address the challenges and opportunities where they align with their institutional mission. Clark (1998) used the phrase "*entrepreneurial universities*" to characterize the aspects of promoting technology transfer within national systems of learning and innovation.

http://en.wikipedia.org/wiki/Knowledge_transfer

26.2 The Bayh-Dole Act

Before the passing of the Bayh-Dole Act in 1980, the ownership of any intellectual property generated by research funded by the US government was undefined. The Act, which passed into US legislation, resulted in all US Universities, small businesses and non-profit organizations being able to utilize the intellectual property arising from such funding. It was a recognition of two factors. Firstly, before the Bayh-Dole Act the US government had accumulated 30,000 patents of which only 5 % had been licensed commercially. Clearly this was a significant waste of assets and there was much greater scope for direct commercialization if those involved with generating the patents could also exploit them. Secondly, after World War II it was clear that there was significant potential in US Universities to contribute directly to the rapidly developing fields of science, engineering, medicine, and health.

http://en.wikipedia.org/wiki/Bayh%E2%80%93Dole_Act

The effects of the Bayh-Dole Act in its early years on US research and technology transfer is summarized by Mowery et al. (1999), Mowery and Nelson (2004).

26.3 Technology Transfer Systems in the USA

Technology transfer systems in the USA and Germany are set out in detail in Abramson et al. (1997). The following types of technology transfer are being used dependent on the particular context—

- Consultancy—where the member of the academy provides advice to industry for a fee.
- Personnel Exchange—where a member of the academy relocates to industry (usually for a fixed and predefined period) or a member of an industrial company relocates to an academy research laboratory (similarly for a fixed period).
- Co-operative research—where the academy and industry enter into a joint relationship. Such an arrangement could be via a University-Industry Research Center. With significant critical mass this could increase its attractive power to both government and industry funding agencies compared to applications from single research groups. Such a center can provide the framework for collaborative

research and development where technology transfer is an integral part of the mission.
- Spin-off companies—where the academy translates the IP directly into a spin-off using members of the academy to develop the company (whether full or part-time) and using industry expertise for marketing and to secure venture capital to pump prime development and expansion.
- Licensing of Patents—where the academy licenses its patents to industry to develop and manufacture products, and the academy receives a license fee from industry. Many US Universities have Patent Offices within their research divisions that advise and support the development of patents and also market them to industry.
- Courses and Workshops designed to meet the needs of industry and led by the academy.

26.4 Technology Transfer in Germany—The Fraunhofer Model

In Germany, industrial research is conducted principally by the 60 institutes of the Fraunhofer Society. They receive 20–30 % of their total income from the government based on the degree to which they generate contract work for public and commercial clients. Thus the agenda is primarily demand-driven and much of the work is of an applied nature. However, the classic research ethos is maintained by appointing directors of Fraunhofer Institutes who are also professors with research programs within their Universities. Thus the Fraunhofer establishes a direct bridge between the academy and industry. It is also particularly relevant for European multi-partner research grants where a combination of academic and industrial expertise is often required in the consortium. The Fraunhofer gives priority to work directed to the areas of health, security, communication, energy and the environment. As a result, the work undertaken by researchers and developers can have a significant impact on people's lives. The advantage of the institutes being organized into one overall framework provides opportunity for the development of an overall national strategy which is coherent and ensures added-value across the network. In addition, it can provide access by all the institutes to specialist centers of expertise or high cost equipment (e.g. for nanotechnology).

http://www.fraunhofer.de/en/about-fraunhofer/

http://www.fraunhofer.de/en/institutes-research-establishments/

The accumulation of fundamental research can lead to the establishment of an institute as summarized by Earnshaw (1998) in the areas of computer graphics, visualization, and virtual reality at the University of Darmstadt.

http://ieeexplore.ieee.org/xpl/freeabs_all.jsp?arnumber=656784

http://www.igd.fraunhofer.de/

26.5 Lambert Review

In the UK in 2003, the Lambert Review was initiated to address the following three objectives—

- To recognize the changing nature of industrial R&D such as outsourcing, and the increasingly global nature of R&D due to the Internet and international competition.
- To benefit from successful role models of collaboration between the academy and industry that had already benefited the UK economy.
- To make recommendations for the future.
  http://www.hm-treasury.gov.uk/d/lambertemergingissues_173.pdf

The review recognized that research in the academy operated on international networks, particularly that in the internationally-leading institutions. There was potential therefore for industry to benefit by linking in with these. The review noted that a key performance indicator was the total spend of the UK on R&D as a percentage of the Gross Domestic Product (GDP). When compared with leading nations such as the USA and Germany it was noted to be lower and needed to be increased. The review supported the UK government's third-stream funding (i.e. in addition to teaching and research) established in 2001 and proposed that this be expanded. This Higher Education Innovation Fund (HEIF) provides funding direct to institutions to support business/academy collaborations.

"*The Government Treasury advised that*:

- *the best form of knowledge transfer comes when a talented researcher moves out of the university and into business, or vice versa. [p12]*
- *the most exciting collaborations arise as a result of like-minded people getting together—sometimes by chance—to address a problem. [p12]*
- *encouraging academics and business people to spend more time together should be a high priority for knowledge transfer professionals. [p12]*
- *the innovation process is non-linear, so knowledge transfer is not simply a question of channeling clever ideas from researchers down a production line into commercialization. "Great ideas emerge out of all kinds of feedback loops, development activities and sheer chance. This is another reason why it is so critical to build dynamic networks between academic researchers and their business counterparts." [p12]*
- *diversity is good, both in mission and in funding. "The type of business collaboration that would make sense for one kind of university might be either impossible or irrelevant for another." [p13]*
- *proximity matters when it comes to business collaboration. [p13]*
- *"business-university collaborations need careful and consistent management by both sides, and a number of joint programs have failed for lack of such attention". [p13]*
- *an emphasis on knowledge transfer requires institutions to put in place new mechanisms for establishing institutional priorities. [p13]*

- *universities are more complex to manage than businesses, with a variety of different stakeholders—academics, students, and funders. [p13]*
- *that the large number of pots of ring-fenced financing is 'the source of endless unnecessary frustration'. [p13]*"

  http://en.wikipedia.org/wiki/Lambert_Review

The UK operates a dual funding system for research. Firstly, an amount is distributed to each institution determined by a periodic (usually every 5 years) national and international audit of research quality in each discipline in each institution (the Research Assessment). This amount is known as the Quality Related (QR) funding stream and remains constant for the next 5 years to provide a secure and stable baseline for funding research, and is supplied to institutions on an annual basis. In 2011–2012 the Higher Education Funding Council for England will distribute a total of £1.5 billion via this mechanism. The second aspect is the funding of grant proposals submitted to the national research councils. Thus the HEIF stream added to this and provided direct funding to support the development of academy/industry collaborations. This can also be used to support and strengthen central Technology Transfer Offices in institutions. £150 million per annum has been allocated by the Higher Education Founding Council for England for the period 2011 to 2015. This can be compared to the total of £3 billion annually available from the research councils (to cover all the areas of science, engineering, biosciences, medical, economics and social science, arts and humanities) by peer review of grant bids.

http://www.hefce.ac.uk/econsoc/buscom/heif/
http://www.bis.gov.uk/policies/science/knowledge-transfer/heif

26.6 Case Studies

26.6.1 MIT, Cambridge and Tokyo

Hatakenaka (2003) investigated the industry academy collaborations at MIT, Cambridge and Tokyo. The purpose of the study was to identify the nature of change taking place in these partnerships, and to understand the underlying factors that influence that change, and to explore the underlying process of change. In general, each of these institutions developed an agenda to contribute to, and benefit from, collaboration with industry, whilst at the same time maintaining an internationally leading reputation in all areas of research.

26.6.2 Johns Hopkins University

A counter example is Johns Hopkins University which has consistently advanced knowledge through scientific discovery and scholarship and which has traditionally not supported interaction with industry in order to ensure that such enquiry was free from commercial interests (Brody 1999; Feldman and Desrochers 2001). Although technology transfer is provided for at Johns Hopkins, the academy has been slow to accept it because of the long tradition of the University.

26.6.3 University of Utah

At the University of Utah, one of the first things President Young did after arriving in 2005 was to move the technology commercialization office under the direction of the business school. He then combined three separate technology transfer areas under one organization called "Technology Ventures". However, "*the 3-part mission of the organization remains*:

1. *Create enterprises in Utah that are technology leaders in their markets and provide quality jobs for the citizens of Utah.*
2. *Support technology development for existing Utah businesses and enterprises founded on University technologies so they prosper and expand in Utah.*
3. *Generate returns on the University's technologies for investment in new research, to support and retain current faculty, and to hire world-class scientists.*"

http://www.geekwire.com/2011/incoming-uw-president-michael-young-strong-track-record-supporting

It is also reported that the University of Utah spin-outs had attracted some $250 million in venture capital. More than 100 start-ups have been spun out of the university in the past five years, leading to more than 15,000 direct and indirect jobs in the state.

26.6.4 National Visualization and Analytics Centers

The National Visualization and Analytics Center (NVAC) is a national and international resource providing strategic leadership and coordination for visual analytics technology and tools. The unique partnerships created under NVAC between national laboratories, university research centers, scholars, and other government agencies represents an on-going commitment to collaboration in the discipline of visual analytics. NVAC provides stewardship for the Research and Development Agenda, ensuring that a continual stream of advanced analytical tools for information discovery are developed and implemented for stakeholders. This owes much to the pioneering spirit and leadership qualities of Jim Thomas.

http://nvac.pnl.gov/
http://www.vacommunity.org/Contributing+Members
http://nvac.pnl.gov/about.stm

26.7 Challenges, Cultural and Social Issues

The following issues characterize the interface between the academy and industry.

26.7.1 Time scale

The academy operates on a much longer time frame for R&D than industry which is generally concerned with this year's balance sheet, this year's products and this year's share price. In particular, some institutions concentrate primarily on pure, "blue-skies" research and do not wish to be concerned with interaction with industry (except perhaps to obtain sponsorship grants). Thus there can be a very real issue between short-term technological progress and longer term research on what are regarded as the more important fundamental questions (called "Grand Challenges" in some disciplines).

26.7.2 Reward Models

Reward models in the academy for faculty who work at the industrial interface are generally not well defined, or even if they are defined, are deemed by some tenure and review committees to be of less academic value than research grants and publications of high scholarly value in journals of a high impact factor. Even if the modification of the traditional reward models is agreed by the institution, the culture on the ground can be slow to change. Where the peer review of the progress of a faculty member also includes external peer review, those who provide it may have a different view to those of the institution where the work has been supported. Whilst there is general agreement on academic excellence as defined by traditional metrics in the academy, there is no general agreement on how excellence is defined in knowledge transfer, or whether it should even be included in the evaluation of academic excellence.

26.7.3 Value of Applied Research

Applied research is regarded by some institutions as of lesser academic value compared to pure research. Peer review of research grant proposals or publications in applied research can often result in these being ranked lower than those in pure research. It is noted that early in their life cycle during the development of disciplines they have to concentrate on the pure academic aspects in order to establish themselves amongst their fellow disciplines in the academy. An example is computer science. It clearly began with hardware and programming but had to establish itself on a wider front to gain academic respect and standing. However, when disciplines are well established they can do applied research without question (e.g. medicine, surgery, pharmacology) and those within these disciplines no longer talk in disparaging terms about applied research within their discipline. It is now perceived to enhance them. However, in emerging disciplines, such as computer science, there can be a tendency to still regard the more practical aspects as merely "applications" and of lower academic merit compared to other areas of the discipline.

26.7.4 Technology Transfer Culture

Institutions with a strong technology transfer culture in the faculty often result in undergraduates and graduate students being entrepreneurial and setting up their own companies (sometimes before even completing their courses and graduating). This could be regarded as an advantage to those on the course of study, but some faculty can regard this as a diversion from concentrating on the course material. It can be argued that the syllabus is designed to prepare a graduate for 2–4 career changes during their working life and to concentrate on the immediate career can be too short-sighted.

26.7.5 Communication and Values

Communication protocols in academia can be different in the academy to those in industry. Most academic institutions are collegiate in nature and decisions are often based on an informal consensus within the faculty. Industry on the other hand can be more formal and may require board meetings for any decisions to be approved by senior management. There can also be differences in the stated values in the missions of the respective organizations which can give rise to tension and misunderstandings.

26.7.6 Differences Across Discipline Areas

Some disciplines, such as those in the applied sciences, lend themselves more naturally to collaboration with, and technology transfer to, industry. Discovering a new technique or process in science or engineering can lead to improvements in the design and manufacture of products and services. However, there is less natural affinity in the arts and social sciences, where there is less potential intellectual property to patent and exploit. The academic discipline of economics has an uneasy relationship with the market place and its financial complexities and no single theory appears to win favor in all, or even any, circumstances. For example, experts differ widely on what to do in times of economic recession in order to stimulate growth. This asymmetry between disciplines can create tension in the academy when its mission includes technology transfer or improvement of society in general. The academy can give different internal priories to its various academic disciplines with corresponding financial implications. Some institutions allow financial cross-subsidy between revenue generation areas and those areas in deficit in order to allow the institution as a whole to remain in balance. This can enable the academy with a given academic footprint to deal with fluctuations in student demand in the market place for its courses, and in the varying research priorities that may be set by governments over time. Others ring fence the revenue generation so that it can benefit the areas producing it, and provide motivation for growth and expansion of these areas. By contrast, deficit areas need to be restructured to become viable, or closed down, with consequent implications for the careers of faculty members and support staff. In addition, the academy may use different financial models at different times, which can create uncertainty in the planning processes for academic areas and can affect the tenure and job security of academic staff.

Patent generation is much less common in the academic areas of the arts, humanities and social sciences, so this raises the issue of how to promote, value, and reward knowledge transfer in these areas. However, some areas of the academy have been particularly successful in exploiting interdisciplinary research, though there can still be challenges within the academy due to the budget ring-fencing of faculties and deans wishing to protect their respective disciplines. Structures within the academy may need to be modified to take full advantage of new research opportunities which cross traditional academic boundaries.

26.7.7 Performance Metrics

Metrics for evaluating knowledge transfer can be diverse and give different results for different disciplines and different contexts. Examples of possible metrics are number of patents, patent value, spin-off companies, commercialization, public value, private value, impact value, etc. Currently there is no general agreement on what might constitute a core set of performance metrics. Some feel that quantitative metrics favor engineering and the sciences, whilst qualitative metrics favor the arts and social sciences. The UK is currently moving towards a research evaluation based on impact factors derived from a relatively small number of case studies for each discipline in each institution. However, it is clear that there will be significant subjective elements involved in this evaluation. The Russell Group's opinion on the Warry report's proposal can be noted, "that an individual competent in the economic impact of research should be accommodated on each Research Audit Panel": "*There is no evidence to date of any rigorous way of measuring economic impact other than in the very broadest of terms and outputs. It is therefore extremely difficult to see how such Panel members could be identified or the basis upon which they would be expected to make their observations. Without such a rigorous and accepted methodology, this proposal could do more harm than good.*"

http://www.csc.liv.ac.uk/~leslie/impact/impact.html

The incorporation of impact factors into research grant proposals and the periodic audit of research quality has been strongly opposed by key academics in the UK. More than 18,000 academics, including six Nobel Prize Winners, have written to the UK government to condemn the current plans to include economic impact in the evaluation of research.

"The scholars are concerned that making university research more accountable to the wider economy will stifle the sort of curiosity-driven research that has led to groundbreaking discoveries and Nobel prizes".

"History shows us that in many cases it is basic research, undertaken purely out of curiosity to understand more about our world, that has delivered revolutionary breakthroughs," Dr Kirby-Harris said. "X-rays, lasers and semiconductors—technologies widely used in every aspect of our lives—all stem from discoveries made through fundamental research, undertaken without any immediate application in mind."

Sir Tim Hunt, one of six Nobel Prize winners to sign the petition, said: *"The impact guidelines will discourage academics from making discoveries and will encourage people to come up with unoriginal research proposals. The whole idea of research is to find out things you didn't know before. The fruits of basic research are unpredictable and to seek to control them in this way is not in the interests of the country."*

http://www.independent.co.uk/news/science/nobel-laureates-dont-put-money-before-science-1860138.html

http://www.nybooks.com/articles/archives/2011/jan/13/grim-threat-british-universities/

26.7.8 Diversification of Academic Mission

Governments have sought to diversify the missions of their academic institutions by getting them to concentrate on their strengths and select from the principal areas of teaching, research, widening access, and knowledge transfer. However, it is generally the case that institutions that do the best research also by definition have the best IP and are more highly regarded by industry. Lesser institutions can end up by being squeezed out of both research and knowledge transfer, which clearly was not the government's original intention.

26.8 Conclusions

This chapter has provided an outline of the development of collaborations between the academy and industry and reviewed how governments have sought to influence the mission and agenda of the academy in order to address what are perceived to be more near-term economic and social requirements. Many eminent scientists, particularly a number of those involved in significant research leading to the award of a Nobel Prize, have criticized key aspects of these developments. In particular, they are concerned that this could result in the suppression and devaluing of long term research on the more fundamental research questions which in the history of the academy have led to significant advances.

The chapter has also reviewed issues at the interface between the academy and industry and noted that some of these are significant and have not been resolved, or in some cases, not even been fully recognized or addressed.

However, there are clearly significant mutually beneficial aspects to developing such collaborations for the R & D income they provide, the critical mass of researchers that they generate, the ability to attract future R & D grants, and the contributions to society and the economy that can follow.

There is a current trend in funding agencies to allocate larger grants to larger research groups in order to address major research challenges and also to increase international competitiveness. In addition, the aggregation of research groups across institutions in the academy creates research hubs in particular discipline areas. These can also be attractive to industry because of their larger critical mass and potential international reach, and can bring in additional sponsorship and support. However, this does have the effect of marginalizing those institutions not represented in the research hubs and the academy could become increasingly stratified and divided.

References

Abramson, H. N., Encarnacao, J. L., Reid, P. P., & Schmoch, U. (Eds.) (1997). *Technology transfer systems in the United States and Germany*. Washington: National Academy Press. ISBN 0-309-05530-X.

Brody, W. (1999). *From minds to minefields: Negotiating the demilitarized zone between industry and academia*. Remarks delivered for the Biomedical Engineering Lectures Series by William R. Brody, President, The Johns Hopkins University, Tuesday, April 6. http://www.jhu.edu/~president/speech/biolec.html.

Clark, B. (1998). *Creating entrepreneurial universities*. Oxford: International Association of Universities and Elsevier Science.

Earnshaw, R. A. (1998). Fraunhofer Institute—Building on a decade of computer graphics research. *IEEE Computer Graphics and Applications*, *18*(2), 10–16. doi:10.1109/38.656784.

Feldman, M., & Desrochers, P. (2001). Truth for its own sake: Academic culture and technology transfer at the Johns Hopkins University. *Minerva*, *42*(2), 105–126. http://www.cs.jhu.edu/~mfeldman/Minerva102.pdf.

Hatakenaka, S. (2003). *University-industry partnerships in MIT, Cambridge and Tokyo: Storytelling across boundaries. Studies in higher education*. Dissertation, Routledge, 11 Dec 2003.

Mowery, D. C., & Nelson, R. R. (2004). *Ivory tower and industrial innovation: University-industry technology before and after the Bayh-Dole act. Stanford Business Books*. Stanford: Stanford University Press. 30 Apr 2004.

Mowery, D., Nelson, R., Sampat, B., & Ziedonis, A. (1999). The effects of the Bayh-Dole act on U.S. University research and technology transfer. In L. Branscomb, F. Kodama, & R. Florida (Eds.), *Industrializing knowledge* (pp. 269–306). Cambridge: MIT Press.

Chapter 27
Discovering and Transitioning Technology

John Dill and David J. Kasik

Abstract This paper examines how complex computing technology is discovered and migrated into more general use. Computing technology that has proved useful to, and enabled by, the Boeing Company and General Motors is described. The accompanying analysis shows the time to transition the technology into general use. Observations are made on the sources of technology discovery, and factors that are further slowing discovery and transitioning of new technology.

27.1 Introduction

The gift of time has allowed a retrospective look across long careers. Computer graphics bit us early, and our passion for the field continues unabated.

It has been a privilege to work at all levels of computer graphics and user interface development, from computer animation to bit-level device drivers to user interface management systems to developing an integrated, full-scale CAD/CAM system to visualization applications for thousands of users. Professional experience has provided an understanding of the implications of scale and complexity at a scientific laboratory, an automotive company, academia, and an aerospace company.

During this time, transitioning technology from research and development to widespread production has presented a continuing challenge. This paper will not present a thesis that technology transition has suddenly become easy. There is no evidence that the task has become any less of a challenge or any less work.

Instead, technology is examined and the way transition itself has changed over the last forty years. The approach is to look at graphics and interactive techniques that Boeing and General Motors have published and contributed to the international community. What is of particular interest is how surprisingly long it has taken for

J. Dill (✉)
Simon Fraser University, Surrey, Canada
e-mail: dill@cs.sfu.ca

D.J. Kasik
The Boeing Company, Seattle, USA
e-mail: david.j.kasik@boeing.com

J. Dill et al. (eds.), *Expanding the Frontiers of Visual Analytics and Visualization*,
DOI 10.1007/978-1-4471-2804-5_27,

technology to become widely adopted. After describing these contributions, the current state of technology development is explored because of its increasing effect on technology transition. Finally, a joint industry-academia model is described that has accelerated both technology development and transition.

27.2 Projects

27.2.1 General Motors

GM's history in computer graphics goes back almost as far as computer graphics itself, starting with work in the late 50s that culminated in the seminal 1964 papers by Jacks (1964) and Hargreaves et al. (1964). A detailed early history of the development that led to the DAC-1, Design Augmented by Computer, is well described in Krull's (1994) historical overview. DAC was one of the earliest graphical computer aided design systems. Developed by General Motors, IBM was brought in as a partner in 1960 and the two developed the system and released it to production in 1963. It was publicly unveiled at the fall Joint Computer Conference in Detroit 1964. Although intended primarily to establish feasibility, GM used the DAC system for some production design into the late 60s. Since at this point the promise was high, further development was assigned to the Manufacturing Development division which evolved and developed the software into the successor CADANCE system (Dill 1981; Krull 1994). A portion of the original research and development group remained at GM Research and began investigating new approaches to the components needed for a system to support CAD, including the basic time-shared operating system (MCTS, an offshoot of Multics), programming language (Malus, a PL/1-like derivative), hierarchical file system, and support for remote graphics (all early systems were based on graphics stations connected via hard-wired "channels" to the mainframe).

GM has had a substantial impact on a variety of different computing disciplines, including programming language development, file system design, free-form surface design, operating system aspects including approaches to virtual memory management, computational geometry, solid modeling, HCI and parametric design. Finally, like Boeing and others, GM realized its business was automobiles, not software, and switched to commercial CAD systems (many if not most of which trace their roots to the DAC and CADANCE systems).

27.2.2 The Boeing Company

The Boeing Company has a long history in the development of advanced computing technology. As an aerospace industry leader, Boeing was an early adopter of digital computers for design, development, and support of commercial and military products. As an early adopter, there were numerous computing capabilities that required internal development. In addition to the logical contributions needed to advance aerospace technology, numerous current and former staff members have made significant contributions to computer science.

In order to provide focus, the projects described in the next few pages are limited to work in computer graphics and interactive techniques that resulted in significant and influential publications. Boeing has had a substantial impact on a number of different computing disciplines, including computational geometry (both non-uniform rational b-splines (NURBS) and parametric evaluators), database management system techniques, engineering flight simulators, networking, and international standards.

Also omitted are projects in which Boeing was an early adopter of state-of-the-art computing technology. Computing vendors and researchers often approach Boeing to evaluate new technology. Part of the reason is that Boeing is known for its use of advanced technology and its willingness to experiment. More significantly, Boeing represents a large market and an excellent reference account. Some have argued that Boeing has at least one copy of just about every form of new computing technology. Limiting the scope to externally published technology means that the early use of 3D graphics devices is omitted, as well as model-based definition to provide product manufacturing information for 3D models, 3D instructions for manufacturing and support, raster-to-vector conversion, and motion tracking for manufacturing.

27.2.3 Computer Graphics

As in many fields in computer science, computer graphics grew out of a community of like-minded individuals. The basic capability to draw on a screen was carried over from analog devices that traced vectors on screens (e.g. oscilloscopes) or used stepping motors to move pens across paper (e.g. plotters). Wikipedia (2011a) indicates that the field was unnamed until Bill Fetter, a Boeing technical illustrator, coined the term computer graphics in 1960. While much of the foundational work in hardware was being done in universities and government laboratories, the nascent field of computer graphics was unnamed until someone at an industrial company provided an acceptable name.

One of the issues that arose as graphics developed was that it required a significant amount of computing just to display the geometry that the rest of the system had generated, in fact more computing to display than to generate. Since, at the time, graphics stations were a major expense, much effort was devoted to determining which parts of the computational chain should be performed on which hardware component (host, satellite, intelligent terminal) (Dill and Thomas 1975).

27.2.3.1 Evolution

Computer graphics moved slowly through universities, laboratories, and industry through the 1980's. There were clearly significant events along the way, including the use of graphics for computer-aided drafting and design at General Motors, McDonnell-Douglas, Lockheed, Ford, and others; animation and hidden surface algorithm development at the University of Utah and Ohio State; the raster revolution; and early computer games. The Battelle Computer Graphics Conference in 1974 addressed the issue that computer graphics always seemed to be just a year away. Wikipedia (2011a) indicates that computer graphics "*has made computers easier to interact with, and better for understanding and interpreting many types of data. Developments in computer graphics have had a profound impact on many types of media.*" The advent of widespread graphics occurred in the early 1990's. At that point, relatively inexpensive personal computers defined a simpler user experience through the graphical user interface, and both graphical input and output became pervasive and cost effective

27.2.4 Human Model

Early uses of computer graphics focused on providing a computer interface to repetitive tasks like drafting, plotting graphs, and developing animation sequences. Bill Fetter found a fascinating use of computer graphics to evaluate designs in terms of ergonomic quality. Exploring reach and visual field issues caused him to develop the first digital man-model in 1964 as described in Wikipedia (2011b). The studies were conducted for the bridge of a ship. Not only did Fetter develop individual case studies, but he also examined reach paths (shown in Fig. 27.1) that were plotted on a continuous roll of paper. Boeing legend indicates that a film camera recorded the individual images on the continuous plots to produce animations.

An early analogous study at GM made use of interactive graphics and geometric analysis to study the placement of rear-view mirrors, as the driver's eye position varied over a standard elliptical area.

27.2.4.1 Evolution

Human modeling has moved from the realm of computer programmers and artists to become a special class of software for staff members trained in ergonomics. Today's systems (e.g., Siemens Jack, Dassault Digital Model, ICIDO Ergonomics) are significantly more sophisticated in visual presentation and include extensive libraries to evaluate classes of people and evaluation of muscle stress resulting from multiple joint positions. Even with more scientific knowledge about ergonomics, automating manufacturing assembly or support disassembly/assembly sequences continues to be a research problem. While digital human models are of significant use, specialized knowledge and costly systems have limited deployment, especially when compared to 3D digital design.

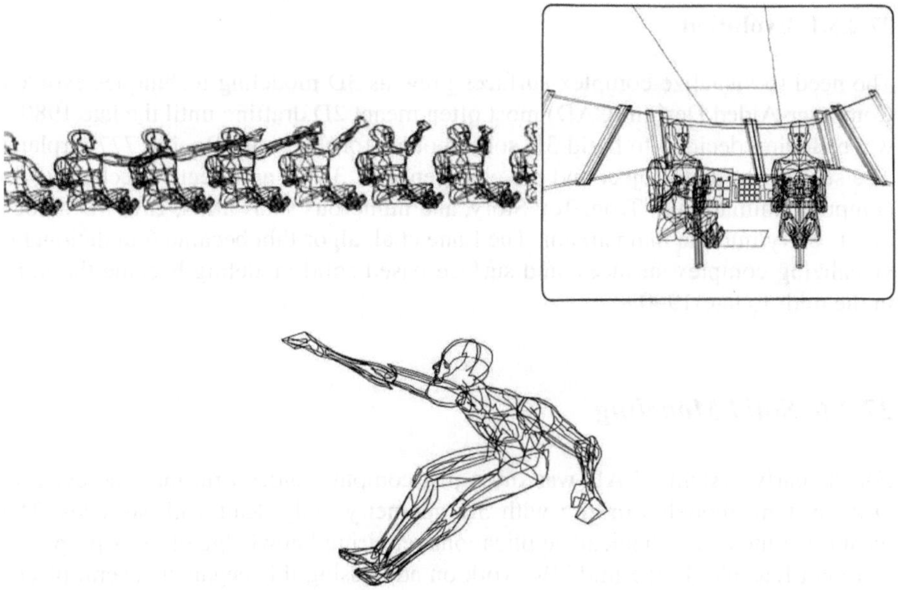

Fig. 27.1 Human model plots (reproduced by permission of Boeing)

27.2.5 B-Spline Surface Rendering

Computational geometry is a natural companion to computer graphics. Computer-aided drafting requires the definition of geometric forms to automate drafting tasks (e.g., tangents, intersection, measurement). Moving to 3D geometric definitions provides the basis for complete digital product design. Individual companies, led by the automotive industry, developed multiple surface definitions (Coons patches, Overhauser surfaces, Bezier patches, Gordon surfaces, b-spline surfaces, etc.). As shaded graphics images emerged in the mid-1970's, there was a need to advance basic algorithms beyond planar polygons and constructive solid geometry. Jeff Lane, who came to Boeing from the University of Utah, and Loren Carpenter, who developed his own shading technology as a Masters student at the University of Washington while working full-time at Boeing, were co-authors of the first paper for rendering general B-spline surfaces (Lane et al. 1980).

Warn (1983) at GM Research developed advanced lighting models for various advanced rendering systems.

One free-form surfaces area still awaiting further development is aesthetic evaluation. GM Research's Mathematics Department did some very early work on this with design staff, showing the value of higher level derivatives (the human eye is a good differentiator!) such as first and second derivatives of curvature. Relatively little effort has been made to better understand surface curvature and its contributions to aesthetics, though GM Research did develop a preliminary method (Dill 1981) that began to appear in commercial systems a decade later.

27.2.5.1 Evolution

The need to visualize complex surfaces grew as 3D modeling techniques evolved. Computer-Aided Design (CAD) most often meant 2D drafting until the late 1980's, when Boeing decided to build 3D solid models for the entire Boeing 777 airplane. The success of that project and the emergence of 3D as an effective technique for computer animation in Tron, Toy Story, and numerous short films, gave 3D modeling its entry into the mainstream. The Lane et al. algorithm became foundational in visualizing complex surfaces, and surface-based solid modeling became the norm in the mid- to late-1990's.

27.2.6 Solid Modeling

For the early systems, CAD was often just computer-aided drafting, and even the DAC system, though working with 3D geometry, only dealt with surfaces. This meant that most "mechanical" applications requiring knowledge of mass properties were not feasible. In the mid 70s, work on addressing this began at several places, including Herb Voelcker's group at the University of Rochester which developed a Constructive Solid Model (CSG) approach. Based on this theory, Boyse at GM Research developed a full 3D solid modeling capability called GMSolid, some of which was added to CADANCE in the late 70s (Boyse 1978, 1982). The 1980s saw very active development in this field both in academia and industry, with CSG and the Boundary Representation (BRep) being the primary approaches. Today, almost all commercial CAD systems are based on one of these, with BRep being by far the most common. Again it took an appreciable fraction of a human generation for this technology to transition from laboratory to first industrial use to commodity.

27.2.7 Fractals

Loren Carpenter made *Vol Libre*, the first fractal film, in 1979–1980 while working on the internal TIGER CAD/CAM research system. The film, available online (Carpenter 1980), accompanied a SIGGRAPH80 paper on how to synthesize fractal geometry with a computer. There are 8–10 different fractal generating algorithms in the film. Each frame was computed on a VAX-11/780 in about 20–40 minutes. The final result was produced on a microfilm recorder. The paper and film were based on fractal algorithms by Mandelbrot (1982) and received a standing ovation at the SIGGRAPH conference (Fig. 27.2).

27.2.7.1 Evolution

Carpenter used an anti-aliased version of the software to create the fractal planet in the Genesis Sequence of Star Trek 2, the Wrath of Khan. Combined with Reeves

Fig. 27.2 Still from VolLibre (reproduced by permission of Loren Carpenter)

(1983) particle fire, the sequence made a lasting impression that carried over to additional Star Trek films. Fractals have become a standard method for generating not only synthetic landscapes but also numerous artistic images using specialized algorithms.

27.2.8 User Interface Management Systems

In 1979, Boeing decided to fund TIGER, an ambitious project to build a new generation CAD/CAM system. A key design goal was to make the system highly portable while retaining an easy-to-use graphical user interface and high performance interactive 3D graphics. Kasik (1982) developed the concept of a User Interface Management System (UIMS) to not only make the user interface easier to navigate but also improve programmer productivity and make the resulting system easier to maintain. The UIMS changed the way programmers described interactive dialog. Instead of inserting command sequences in line with algorithms, the UIMS prescribed an architecture in which the user interface invoked the application based on a dialog description file. Loren Carpenter programmed the first version of the UIMS while working on *Vol Libre*.

Fig. 27.3 Wire bundle Instructions via Augmented Reality (reproduced by permission of Boeing)

27.2.8.1 Evolution

The entire UIMS concept was popular until the early 1990's. There were numerous publications, academic research, and some commercial products. The popularity of the external dialog specification language faded as programmers wanted more control of the application's look-and-feel and migrated to customizable user interface toolkits. The UIMS-introduced concept of the user interface invoking the application, most often implemented with a callback mechanism, is still the basis of modern user interface toolkits.

27.2.9 Augmented Reality

The notion of overlaying instructions on top of video started in the late 1980's. Boeing got into the business early through Tom Caudell and David Mizell because of the intricacies involved in aircraft manufacture. Figure 27.3 shows a form board for laying out wire harnesses manually and with instructions overlaid on lenses in a head-mounted display. As the field grew, Caudell coined the term augmented reality as documented in Wikipedia (2011c).

27.2.9.1 Evolution

The basic concept of augmented reality as a way of presenting instructions remained a strong industrial and academic research topic through the 1990's. Eventually, performance and the weight of the video capture/display head gear caused the overall concept to wane. There has been a resurgence since the late 2000's as low cost mobile devices became equipped with embedded cameras. Together with fast image processing algorithms, augmented reality is beginning to emerge in the consumer marketplace for applications that superimpose locations on images acquired

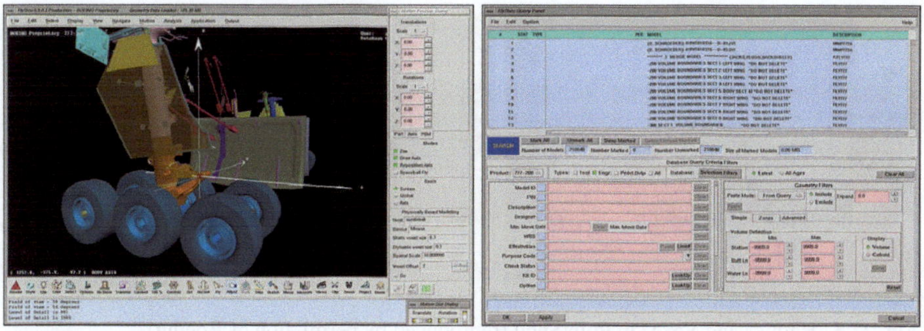

Fig. 27.4 Typical FlyThru Geometry and Query Panel (reproduced by permission of Boeing)

with the built-in cameras. In addition, industrial companies are pushing to provide not only location documentation but also maintenance and assembly instructions. Rosenblum et al. detail the progress of augmented reality in a chapter in this book.

A somewhat related effort at GM Research, VisualEyes, Randall Smith investigated the use of large VR displays to try to reduce the need for a large number of full-size clay models and other mockups. Though useful, it ultimately was dropped because of difficulties with stereo vision.

http://www.evl.uic.edu/core.php?mod=4&type=4&indi=60

http://www.evl.uic.edu/core.php?mod=4&type=1&indi=134

27.2.10 FlyThru/IVT

Boeing took a big step in the late 1980's when the company designed the 777 using solid modeling techniques. The project was the first to move from drawings to solid models to represent detailed interior part design as well as exterior surfaces. The scale of the number of models involved was unprecedented. Dozens of mainframe computers handled the computing workload. One of the significant side benefits was that the fit of the design could be investigated in three dimensions, a job previously relegated to building a series of expensive mock-ups to detect incorrect part positioning. Abarbanel and McNeely (1996) led the development of FlyThru, an application that proved critical to Boeing's success. The software extracted 3D geometry from the geometry configuration management system and made it available through a search query (right image in Fig. 27.4) that was similar to the configuration management system.

The software reduced complex geometry to bounding boxes when Silicon Graphics workstations encountered performance problems. Basically, users wanted to see more and more geometry, and the boxes were an effective workaround when interactive performance degraded. The amount of geometry to be displayed was limited to the amount of memory in an SGI system.

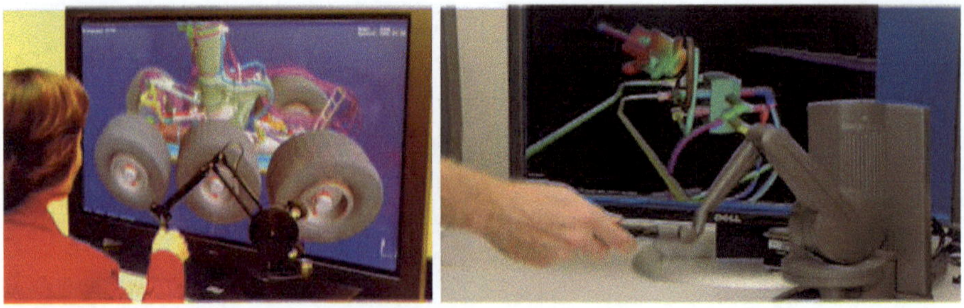

Fig. 27.5 Haptics and VoxMap PointShell (reproduced by permission of Boeing)

27.2.10.1 Evolution

FlyThru became a commercial product that had little market success. The Integration Visualization Tool (IVT), has been in production use in Boeing since the early 2000's and runs on PC hardware. All large CAD/CAM companies and numerous small companies sell viewers that are similar to the basic capabilities originally included in FlyThru. FlyThru and its IVT successor excel in reliably providing a large user group with current, configuration-managed geometry.

27.2.11 Voxmap PointShell

The task of aerospace product maintenance has many of the same issues as maintenance of any complex product. Aerospace products bring additional challenges because of the complexity of the systems needed for electrical, hydraulic, fuel, heating ventilation, air conditioning, and other functions. The mid-1990s saw experimentation with haptic systems to enhance manufacturing and maintenance technicians' ability to 'test drive' assembly/disassembly sequences as shown in Fig. 27.5. The key factor was to compute collisions fast enough (1000 Hz) to give the user immediate tactile feedback even when the geometry was complex. VoxMap PointShell was McNeely et al.'s (1999) entry into the real-time collision business. The fundamental algorithm fits solid models with voxels and then computes voxel-voxel collisions rather than polygon-polygon intersections.

27.2.11.1 Evolution

While the notion of haptic devices for maintenance planning never became popular in Boeing, VoxMap PointShell did. The algorithms are used in FlyThru and IVT to compute a list of unwanted part collisions interactively for small amounts of geometry and on a nightly basis for an entire airplane. Boeing has licensed VoxMap PointShell to other companies. While there are a large number of collision-collision detection algorithms, VoxMap PointShell remains one of the fastest and most scalable.

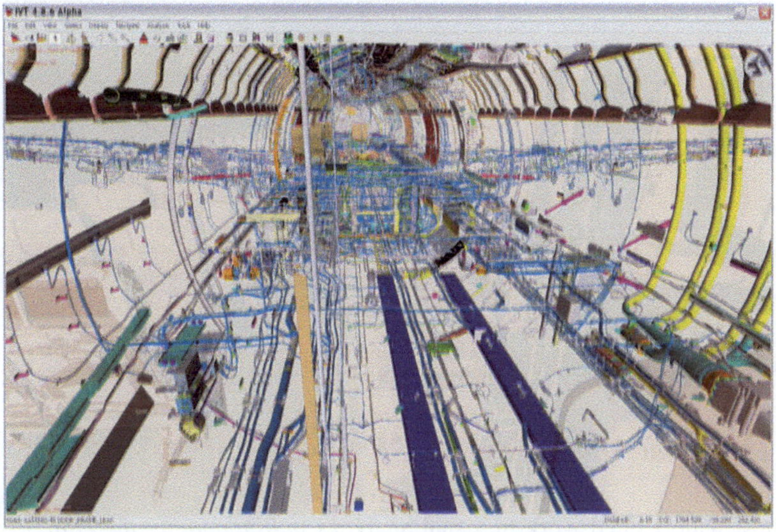

Fig. 27.6 Airplane systems in context (reproduced by permission of Boeing)

27.2.12 Massive Model Visualization

As PCs and add-on graphics cards became faster and less expensive to accommodate digital video games, another set of researchers became interested in rendering geometric models that exceeded physical memory in the PC and/or the graphics card. Boeing pushed the research community to experiment on even more complex models, such as those corresponding to a commercial airplane. Commercial airplanes are notoriously difficult to render, because of the sheer data volume. In addition, hydraulic tubes, wire harnesses, fuel lines, and ducts run the length of the model. Furthermore, there are few planar surfaces along the airplane skins or in interior parts. The approach used was to make a complex test case, the first 777, easily available outside Boeing. Yoon et al. (2008) used the term 'massive model' to describe the large scale of geometric models and the overall system implications in providing interactive response on conventional hardware (Fig. 27.6).

27.2.12.1 Evolution

Boeing has implemented a production massive model version of IVT. Users are presented with the same interface; they can just visualize more. The current state-of-the-art with massive model visualization requires preprocessing, so power users dominate those in the company who utilize this version of IVT. Research in the field is on-going, and a few companies (ICIDO, Right Hemisphere) are building massive model visualization systems.

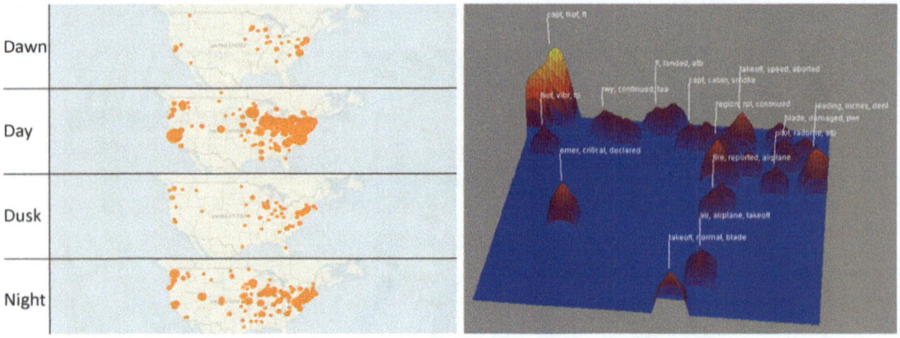

Fig. 27.7 2D and 3D visual analytics examples (reproduced by permission of Boeing)

27.2.13 Visual Analytics

The most widely cited work in visual analytics is *Illuminating the Path*, (Thomas and Cook 2005), which set the research agenda for the field. Both authors attended the inaugural workshop and were lead chapter authors (Fig. 27.7).

27.2.13.1 Evolution

Boeing has taken steps to transition visual analytics technology to production use through a series of research projects in the U.S. and Canada. The effort not only engages key universities in basic research that pertains to visual analytics (e.g., how visual analytics tool experts and Boeing subject matter experts work with one another, impact of different display styles), but it also defines educational programs that expose students to visual analytics tools and techniques.

27.3 Observations

Buxton (2010) observed that new computing concepts move from radical to commodity in increments of two or three decades. Table 27.1 contains an analysis of the migration of technology in which Boeing played a significant role from the outset. The start times span 5 decades.

Table 27.2 summarizes the amount of time it took to expand adoption of the technology, most often without direct Boeing intervention. Computer graphics has moved from specialized use in product development to games and entertainment. The economies of scale, particularly in games, have made computer graphics available on all interactive devices. Man-model technology requires specialized use that has gradually increased and is not yet widely used across product design. B-spline rendering techniques are included in any system that does surface modeling. Such

Table 27.1 Evolution (reproduced by permission of Boeing)

Technology	Boeing start	Evolution
Computer graphics	1960	CAD (1980's) -> entertainment (late 1990's). Now everywhere.
Man-model	1964	2 internal systems until late 1990's. Mostly COTS today
B-spline surface rendering	1980	NURBS started dominating CAD geometry in mid-to-late 1990's
Fractals	1980	Fractals became commonplace in mid-1990s
User interface management systems	1981	Precursor published in 1976. Became COTS in 1980's and fizzled in mid-1990's
Augmented reality	1990	Lots of academic research through late 2000's. Finally becoming 'real' with mobile maps.
FlyThru/IVT	1992	CAD vendors built/acquired similar systems in the early 2000's
VoxMap PointShell	1997	Collision detection embedded in many electronic games, surgical trainers, etc. Boeing has sold a few VPS licenses.
Massive model visualization	2004	Full production in Superviewer. One COTS package (Right Hemisphere), no CAD vendors.
Visual analytics	2004	Primary use in intelligence community. Early experimental use in Boeing.

Technology	GM start	Evolution	Timing
Solid modeling	1977	Academia early 70s, use in GM 1980, early industrial use, mid 80s, standard after 90s	20 years to commonplace in cad
Free form surfaces	1963	Early developers 60s/70s; commercial CAD 80s	5 years to 1st use; 10–15 to reasonable use
Human-computer Graphical interaction	1963	Light-pencil and light-pens replaced by mouse and WIMP interfaces in 70s	10–15 years to "standard" mouse/keyboard config
Quantitative measures of aesthetics	1980	In commercial CAD 90s; Still not often used.	
Graphics display	1963	First industrial (CAD) use; IBM 2250 mid/late 60s; First inexpensive display (Tektronix storage display) 70s. Now common.	10 years to significant industrial use; another 10 to common use
VR/CAVE	1995	Much early promise; dropped due to several issues including stereo problems.	
Cycle of moving the actual computation closer to the display	1970	Continual change from early 70s	Ongoing move to continually smaller form factors.

Table 27.2 Duration analysis (reproduced by permission of Boeing)

Technology		Boeing start	Evolution
Computer gra	20 yrs to CAD. 10 to games. 20 to commonplace		entertainment (late 1990's). Now
Man-model	45 yrs to reasonable use	1964	2 internal systems until late 1990's. Mostly COTS today
B-spline surfa	20 yrs to commonplace	1980	NURBS started dominating CAD geometry in mid-to-late 1990's
Fractals	15 yrs to commonplace	1980	Fractals became commonplace in mid-1990s
User interface	15 yrs to reasonable use. little use in 2011		rsor published in 1976. Became COTS in s and fizzled in mid-1990's
Augmented R	20 yrs to some use	1990	Lots of academic research through late 2000's. Finally becoming 'real' with mobile maps.
FlyThru/IVT	20 yrs to reasonable use	1992	CAD vendors built/acquired similar systems in the early 2000's
VoxMap Point	20 yrs to reasonable use	1997	Collision detection embedded in many electronic games, surgical trainers, etc. Boeing has sold a few VPS licenses.
Massive model visualizat	Still emerging	2004	Full production in Superviewer. One COTS package (Right Hemisphere), no CAD vendors.
Visual analytics	Still emerging	2004	Primary use in intelligence community. Early experimental use in Boeing.

systems are used in product manufacturing, arts and entertainment, and other industries. Fractals have expanded from modeling methods for natural objects to arts to methods of controlling motion. User interface management systems have come and gone. Augmented reality is re-emerging because of advances in the mobile computing market. FlyThru/IVT set the stage for the development of 3D viewers that are increasingly prevalent. Collision detection with VoxMap PointShell and others is essential in games, surgical simulators, and other applications. Recent technologies like massive model visualization and visual analytics are still in the early stages of adoption.

The bottom line is as follows. The transition of Boeing-discovered technology to widespread adoption is measured in terms of decades, which is similar to Buxton's observation for other forms of computing technology. There seems to be no extra incentive for people to adopt new computing technology just because it comes from Boeing.

27.4 Implications

What does this all mean in terms of moving strong technologies into widespread use? Moving into widespread use must account for the time to both discover and transition technology.

As described in the previous section, technology transition moves slowly, a pattern that has been observed in multiple computing fields. We do not see technology transition suddenly moving quickly.

Of more concern is the rate of development of new technology, which has been slowing since the early days of computing (prior to 1990 for computer graphics and interactive techniques). When combined with the naturally slow technology transition process, moving to widespread use is becoming slower. Factors slowing new technology development include:

- Sources of new technology
- A fragmented technical community
- Business climate
- Immediate return on investment

27.4.1 Sources of New Technology

Product design and manufacturing improvements drove research from the 1960s through the 1980s. There were a number of significant improvements, including basic z-buffer and ray-tracing rendering algorithms, solid and surface modeling, fractals, touch-screen interfaces, plasma panels, gestural interfaces, and multi-window interaction technology. Product manufacturing companies often did the basic work or directly participated in research efforts with academia. Computing companies then improved the basic technology significantly. The problems in product development companies led them to recruit highly skilled computing staff. The fundamental problems, especially the problem of scale, were so challenging that those companies were attractive places to work.

As computer graphics for product manufacturing became more of a commodity, arts and entertainment built on the successes and became the dominant driver in the mid-1980s. Clear improvements were built on the foundation started in product manufacturing from the previous three decades. Examples include generalized texture mapping, computational photography, 3D cameras, 3D printers, scanners, and photorealism. The primary source of the new technology moved from industry to academia and computing companies. Product manufacturing companies opted out of research and moved to a buy-not-build model.

The significance of improvements driven by arts and entertainment has decreased over the past ten years. Computer graphics pervades all forms of interactive devices. What was once highly specialized and costly is now a commodity. It is not clear what, or who, will drive the next steps (see Kasik 2011).

27.4.2 Fragmented Technical Community

As the graphics industry has grown, smaller communities of interest have emerged and spun off. The bellwether SIGGRAPH conference spawned numerous smaller conferences and publications. Having all the players in the same place in computer graphics' early days naturally led to alliances that made step-level improvements move from the laboratory to commodity with fewer impediments. Over time, separate technical communities broke away from SIGGRAPH and developed their own publications and conferences. Examples include virtual reality, computational geometry, computer-human interaction, game developers, information visualization, scientific visualization, and visual analytics. All fundamentally rely on computer graphics and interactive techniques yet have difficulty in insuring that new needs are driven back into the base computer graphics community.

Moreover, product manufacturing companies that invested significantly in pushing the state-of-the-art and routinely collaborated with the graphics industry and researchers are doing so sporadically. As graphics became a commodity, these companies decreased their reliance on in-house talent and started relying on the graphics industry and academia for innovation. As noted in the previous section, large product-development companies (General Motors, Lockheed, Boeing, etc.) have generally stopped supplementing and inspiring research. The same trend is occurring in arts and entertainment. As a result, there is less serious collaboration and less communication between industry and the broader research community.

27.4.3 Business Climate

The business climate for inventing and making technology widely available has changed significantly. A substantial contributing is the decrease in the number of key companies supplying technology from twenty or more to less than five. Decreased market competition tends to slow dramatic innovation. Being conservative in a smaller pool increases the likelihood that a company will stay in business. This has happened in the computing industry with hardware (CPUs, GPUs), operating systems, computer-aided design software, animation packages, database management systems, and others.

Furthermore, the current business climate shows an increased desire to protect intellectual property. Academia and industry are both putting significant effort in developing complex intellectual property agreements. This is a significant change from early evolution, where academic and industrial work was published early and often. As a result, significant results were shared quickly and with few restrictions.

27.4.4 Immediate Return on Investment

Funding agencies and research managers often demand that research results have substantial impact within three to five years. University, government, and industrial researchers are asked to estimate the probability of success and provide a business case for their work. A low likelihood of success or a poor business case dooms many good ideas.

The desire to have a big win quickly seems to be driven by a misperception. Many think that transitioning success is an overnight phenomenon. As documented here, success and widespread adoption takes decades, not years. We tend to forget that fundamental discoveries that occur rapidly still take a long time to enter the mainstream.

27.5 One Successful Approach

As described in the previous section, there are a number of different factors that slow widespread adoption of new technology, including both technology transition and technology discovery.

From an industry perspective, none is more serious than how industry has become disconnected from the research community. It has become difficult for industry to describe problems with sufficient clarity for the research community. Intellectual property concerns on both sides constrain direct connection.

Some Boeing projects have found a way to form a direct link with researchers at three Canadian universities. The dominant subject started with visual analytics, and the project has been extended to include textual analytics. Moreover, the success has led to investigation of other Boeing problems in material science in Canada, mesh compression and crowd simulation in Saudi Arabia, and visualization in Brazil.

The key to making these projects work centers on bi-directional cooperation between Boeing and the universities. Intellectual property and proprietary information agreements were hammered out before the research started. The team jointly fashioned a research agenda that allows the researchers to pursue an independent line of thinking. Boeing staff provides problem statements, data, and non-computing subject matter expertise. The Boeing technical program manager provides guidance and counsel to students conducting the research in much the same way the rest of the faculty does. The net result is that researchers get to devise their own technical strategies and suggest promising new approaches while working on Boeing-defined problems that involve large amounts of technical data.

Further smoothing the technology transition involves people. Boeing has hired students directly as full-time employees and interns. Even during specific research projects, many students come to Boeing to review results and get additional ideas about specific problems. Boeing benefits because students get to see the environment and understand problems prior to an internship or full-time employment.

27.6 Conclusion

Computer graphics and interactive techniques have become remarkably successful and mature. Evidence for this comes from observing both research, which is moving incrementally, and successful graphics technology companies, which have coalesced into a few large players.

Even in the early days when discovery of new computer graphics and interactive techniques happened more quickly, transitioning the technology into widespread use was still time-consuming.

What we have to realize about technology is that transition will continue to move slowly and that development moves at different rates depending on the technology maturity. No matter the rate of innovation, technology transition is a contact sport. Jim Thomas succeeded in discovering and transitioning complex technology because he had the vision, the passion, and the patience to succeed.

References

Abarbanel, R., & McNeely, W. (1996). FlyThru the Boeing 777. In *Computer Graphics* (p. 124). http://dl.acm.org/citation.cfm?id=253800.

Boyse, J. W. (1978). *Preliminary design for a geometric modeller* (GM Research Report GMR 2768). GM Research Laboratories.

Buxton, W. (2010). *NUI: What's in a name*. Presentation at Microsoft Development Center, Copenhagen, Oct. 2010. http://channel9.msdn.com/posts/TechTalk-NUI-Whats-in-a-Name.

Carpenter, L. (1980). Vol Libre. http://vimeo.com/5810737.

Dill, J. (1981). An application of color graphics to the display of surface curvature. In *Proceedings SIGGRAPH 1981* (pp. 153–161). http://dl.acm.org/citation.cfm?id=806801, http://mrl.nyu.edu/~elif/thesisprop/Dill81.pdf.

Dill, J. C., & Thomas, J. J. (1975). On the organization of a remote low cost intelligent graphics terminal. In *Proceedings of SIGGRAPH 1975* (pp. 1–8). http://delivery.acm.org/10.1145/570000/563733/p1-dill.pdf?ip=143.53.47.47&acc=ACTIVE%20SERVICE&CFID=69066836&CFTOKEN=13870923&__acm__=1321522150_3aeff8c0cdde06e293c958129246d82b.

Hargreaves, B., Joyce, J. D., Cole, G. L., Foss, E. D., Gray, R. G., Sharp, E. M., Sippel, R. J., Spellman, T. M., & Thorpe, R. A. (1964). Image processing hardware for a man-machine graphical communication system. In *Proceeding AFIPS '64* (Fall, Part I, pp. 27–29). New York: ACM.

Jacks, E. L. (1964). A laboratory for the study of graphical man-machine communication. In *AFIPS conference proceedings: Vol. 26* (Part 1, pp. 343–350). Arlington: AFIPS Press. http://dl.acm.org/citation.cfm?id=1464082.

Kasik, D. (1982). A user interface management system. *Computer Graphics*, *16*(3), 99–106. http://dl.acm.org/citation.cfm?id=801268.

Kasik, D. (2011). The third wave in computer graphics and interactive techniques. *IEEE Computer Graphics and Interactive Techniques*, *31*(4), 89–93. http://www.computer.org/portal/web/computingnow/0811/whatsnew/cga.

Krull, F. (1994). The origin of computer graphics within general motors. *IEEE Annals of the History of Computing*, *16*(3), 40–56. https://design.osu.edu/carlson/history/PDFs/CGatGM.pdf.

Lane, J., Carpenter, L., Whitted, T., & Blinn, J. (1980). Scan line methods for displaying parametrically defined surfaces. *Communications of the ACM*, *21*, 1980. http://dl.acm.org/citation.cfm?id=358815.

Mandelbrot, B. (1982). *Fractals: Form, chance, and dimensions*. New York: WH Freeman and Co.

McNeely, W., Puterbaugh, K., & Troy, J. (1999). Six degree-of-freedom haptic rendering using voxel sampling. In *Proceedings of ACM SIGGRAPH, 1999* (pp. 401–408). http://arnetminer.org/viewpub.do?pid=593684.

Reeves, W. (1983). Particle systems—a technique for modeling a class of fuzzy objects. *Proceedings of SIGGRAPH 1983, Computer Graphics*, *17*(3), 359–376. http://dl.acm.org/citation.cfm?id=801167, http://dl.acm.org/citation.cfm?id=357320.

Thomas, J., & Cook, K. (Eds.) (2005). *Illuminating the path*. New York: IEEE Press. http://nvac.pnl.gov/agenda.stm.

Warn, D. (1983). Lighting controls for synthetic images. *Computer Graphics*, *17*(3), 13–21. http://dl.acm.org/citation.cfm?id=801127.

Wikipedia (2011a). Wikipedia. http://en.wikipedia.org/wiki/William_Fetter.

Wikipedia (2011b). Wikipedia. http://en.wikipedia.org/wiki/Computer_graphics.

Wikipedia (2011c). Wikipedia. http://en.wikipedia.org/wiki/Augmented_reality.

Yoon, S., Stephens, A., Kasik, D., & Manocha, D. (2008). *Real-time massive model rendering*. Morgan-Claypool.

Chapter 28
Technology Transfer at IBBT-EDM: Case Study in the Computer Graphics Domain

Fabian Di Fiore, Eddy Flerackers, and Frank Van Reeth

Abstract In this paper we will report on the founding of Ultra Pictura as a case study of technology transfer from academia to industry. Ultra Pictura specializes in capturing and recreating animated painterly artwork techniques. By means of a proprietary digital paint and render platform Ultra Pictura offers animation production studios a service solution that enables artists to create totally new and original 2D painterly animation styles for animated backgrounds, characters as well as special effects.

Ultra Pictura was founded in October 2010 as a spin-off initiative of the Interdisciplinary Institute for BroadBand Technology (IBBT). IBBT is a research institute founded by the Flemish government to stimulate R&D in innovative ICT services and applications in close collaboration with government and industry. By offering both research support and go to-market assistance, IBBT creates the right eco-system for the translation of research results into marketable products creating real social and economic benefits. Through the use of tools and hands-on training and coaching, researchers (academics as well as individuals) learn to take their innovations to market and thus maximize the valorisation potential of the research results. The final step in the IBBT's innovation pipeline is the venture stage which ultimately leads to the creation of new innovative start-ups.

F. Di Fiore (✉) · E. Flerackers · F. Van Reeth
Expertise Centre for Digital Media, Hasselt University – tUL – IBBT, Wetenschapspark, 2, BE-3590 Diepenbeek, Belgium
e-mail: fabian.difiore@uhasselt.be

E. Flerackers
e-mail: eddy.flerackers@uhasselt.be

F. Van Reeth
e-mail: frank.vanreeth@uhasselt.be

J. Dill et al. (eds.), *Expanding the Frontiers of Visual Analytics and Visualization*,
DOI 10.1007/978-1-4471-2804-5_28,

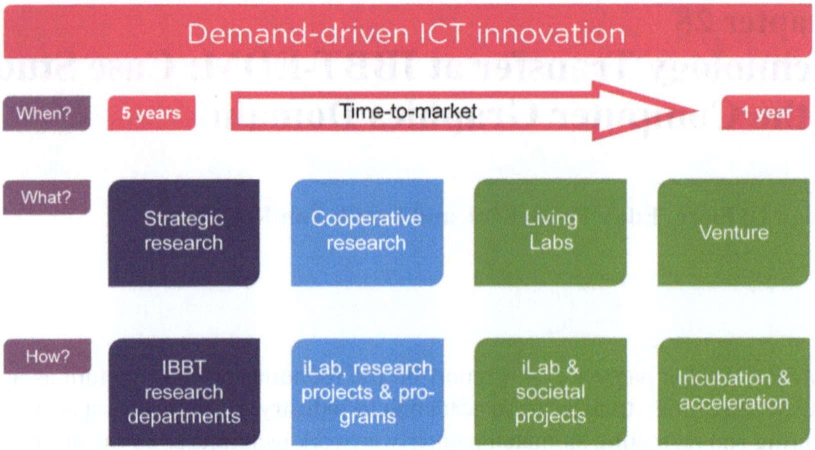

Fig. 28.1 IBBT demand-driven ICT innovation: from idea to business

28.1 Interdisciplinary Institute for BroadBand Technology (IBBT)

IBBT is a research institute founded by the Flemish government to stimulate R&D in innovative ICT services and applications in close collaboration with government and industry. IBBT develops interdisciplinary demand-driven solutions so as to maximize the economical and societal impact of the research results. To this end, about twenty ICT research groups from Flemish universities have been put together to take on this challenge. These academic researcher groups collaborate with teams from large companies, SME's, non-profit organizations and government representatives both in local and European research projects.

By building upon the joint expertise of these groups, the IBBT has become a strategic research partner to the industry and the society in Flanders and abroad. Furthermore, by providing both research support and go to-market assistance, IBBT is creating the right eco-system for the translation of its research results into marketable products creating real social and economic benefits. Figure 28.1 depicts IBBT's pipeline for turning a successful new business idea into a reality. The following subsections will elaborate on the different steps involved.

28.1.1 Strategic Research

IBBT's research organization is structured in five research departments (see Fig. 28.2) with a special focus on the most important technological challenges for the upcoming decade: *Digital Society*, *Future Health*, *Future Internet*, *Future Media & Imaging*, and *Security*. The main goal of the organization's departments is to obtain more critical mass through focus and efficient leadership in order to have in

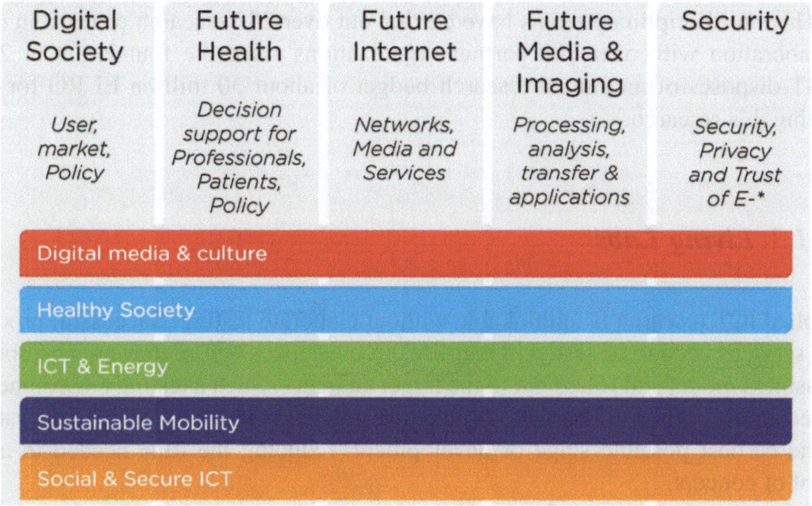

Fig. 28.2 IBBT strategic research organization. (*Top row*) Five research departments. (*Bottom rows*) Research subjects

place the conditions necessary to reach the required level of world-class research in the different domains. To this end, each department elaborates the expertise of a multidisciplinary team of researchers coming from several research teams.

28.1.2 Cooperative Research

IBBT plays many roles in the creation and execution of interdisciplinary collaborative projects between IBBT research groups and external partners such as companies, governments, and non-profit organizations. It can provide infrastructure, equipment, services such as testing, bring partners together and provide some of the financing. Always keeping in mind the need to create economically-effective solutions that are marketable and user-oriented.

Project proposals are formed bottom-up by the external partners, need to be demand-driven and within the framework of the IBBT innovation themes (see Fig. 28.2), and are always submitted by a consortium in which several partners can participate. There are no restrictions regarding organizational form, so governments as well as non-profit organizations, SME's, large companies and local branches of multinationals can participate next to the IBBT research groups. IBBT finances up to 50 % of the total research cost. The external partners have the possibility to apply for financial support from the Flemish Government Agency for Innovation by Science and Technology.

The goal of the research projects is to deliver real results by means of prototypes which can then be turned into applications to daily life by our partners or spin-off companies.

The interdisciplinary teams have carried out over 250 research projects in close collaboration with over 700 partner organizations since the foundation in 2004. IBBT disposes of an annual research budget of about 30 million EURO for supporting this research.

28.1.3 Living Labs

Applied ICT research is unthinkable without elaborate testing. Successful products and services need to be tested in real-life circumstances before they are absorbed in a business model and rolled out to the target audience. Such a testing environment is called a living lab. A living lab evaluates the practical feasibility of ICT innovations at the earliest possible stage of development, reducing the time needed to attain proof of concept.

Two complementary infrastructures are provided by IBBT. The first, *iLab.o*, helps to set up a large-scale trial outside the lab environment. Representative users will get the chance to test ICT innovations over a longer period of time in their daily environment. iLab.o also provides the selection, recruitment and coaching of the test users. The second infrastructure, *iLab.t*, provides lab infrastructure to evaluate technical feasibility, performance, and service quality of ICT innovations at the earliest possible stage. The collaborators at iLab.t measure the performance and service quality of your ICT innovation and compare it with existing standards.

Notice that in a living lab a large number of users gets to interact with new products and services in their daily—both professional and private—life. This heavy user involvement distinguishes a living lab from traditional market and user research. It is also worthy of note that these kinds of living lab activities are based on a scientific research methodology while leaving room to innovate and develop further.

28.1.4 Venture

The final step in the IBBT's innovation pipeline is the venture stage. Through the use of tools and hands-on training and coaching, our researchers (academics as well as individuals from the research partners) learn to take their innovations to market and thus maximize the valorisation potential of the project results, leading to the creation of new innovative start-ups.

The complete venture co-operation model consists of six components, each of which focuses specifically on major themes or issues that newly formed companies must face.

IPR focuses on the protection of intellectual property. After all, companies do not always realize that acquired knowledge, original ideas or inventions can be used by others if they are not guarded and protected.

iStep training programs address specific topics which are of importance when starting up a company: choosing a business model, creating a business plan, explaining IPR, team building, defining a marketing strategy, drawing up a financial plan etc.
iBoot aims for teams to look at their projects from a number of different angles, such as technology, marketing, finance etc., and to study any potential opportunities and risks in detail with the help of a number of professional coaches. At the end of the iBoot the different teams have to present their project to a jury of experts, including venture capitalists, who then give feedback and advice.
iStart focuses specifically on the further development and commercialization of technology and the results of research projects. Participants have the opportunity, as a real potential entrepreneur under the wings of IBBT, to create a business model, to develop prototypes, to carry out market research and field trials and, on the basis of these, to present a strategy for commercialization and a financial plan. Using the results of this incubation phase it is assessed whether the company in question is ready to take the next step. Also, on the basis of a number of criteria it is decided whether the product has to be internally or externally taken further, or whether licensing possibilities are present or if a project may possibly lead to the setting up of a spin-off, etc.
iCubes deals with finding a home for your business. Spin-offs and innovative companies which establish themselves here can count on every possible facility including furnished offices and meeting rooms, reception desk and secretarial office, and a ready-to-use IT and telecommunications infrastructure.
iVenture is an investment fund of IBBT that also invests in IBBT spin-offs in the preseed phase of the research. iVenture is only aimed at projects within the IBBT eco-system and in this way provides preseed, start-up and early-stage funding (via a system of convertible loans) for setting up start-ups.

28.2 Expertise Centre for Digital Media (EDM)

The Expertise Centre for Digital Media (EDM) is a research institute of Hasselt University (UHasselt) and has been active in Information & Communication Technology (ICT) R&D since 1987 (EDM 1987). EDM employs a team of about 70 ICT specialists in fundamental, basic & applied research as well as contract R&D. EDM currently has two main activity domains: Visual Computing and Human Computer Interaction. Its key objective is to be a leading research institute in multimedia, human-computer interaction, computer graphics and virtual environments.

The research at EDM is partially funded by Hasselt University, generally meant for faculty, teaching assistants and fundamental research projects. The majority of the research budget, however, has an external origin (governments, non-profit-organizations and industry), IBBT being a main source of this funding.

EDM is involved in the Interdisciplinary institute for BroadBand Technology (IBBT) from the beginning (2004) and takes part in the core department 'Future Internet'. The core of this department is to provide a platform that will support the natural interaction between humans and their environment, enabling services in a wide range of application domains and interconnecting the world in order to obtain a sustainable smart society.

Through the years EDM gave birth to ten spin-off companies of which ANDROME is the leading one. ANDROME also takes the role of parent company for almost all other spin-offs.

28.3 ANDROME

ANDROME is a spin-off company of the Expertise Centre for Digital Media (EDM) and has been active in animation related R&D projects since more than twenty years (Androme 1990). Complementary to its other important strand of its R&D activities in the networked media domain, the animation related R&D has always been considered as an important pillar on which future business opportunities can be developed.

The research projects at ANDROME are mainly funded by organizations like the EU, Flemish Government Agency for Innovation by Science and Technology, and the IBBT.

28.4 Case Study: Ultra Pictura

Currently IBBT has three spin-off companies that were founded by EDM and ANDROME: TinkerTouch (TinkerTouch 2010), Camargus (Camargus 2010) and Ultra Pictura (Ultra Pictura 2010). The following sections will elaborate on the case of Ultra Pictura.

28.4.1 Company Summary

Ultra Pictura offers animation production studios that are constantly looking for new artistic ways of expression, a service solution that enables artists to create totally new and original 2D painterly animation styles for animated backgrounds, characters as well as special effects. Figure 28.3(a) shows what presently happens in 2D animation production: due to creative and technical constraints, animated characters are flatly colored over a painterly colored background. Figure 28.3(b) indicates what Ultra Pictura can offer: using its creative insights and innovative software tools, animated characters can be colored in the same painterly style as the underlying backgrounds.

Working with Ultra Pictura's services will have a profound impact on the overall look of animated storytelling and alleviates creating new styles of animated imagery, with the potential to open a completely new animation category beyond traditional two-dimensional animation and three-dimensional computer animation. Figure 28.4 illustrates the myriad of potential styles that we can address.

(a) (b)

Fig. 28.3 (**a**) Traditional 2D animation production. (**b**) The Ultra Pictura production

28.4.2 From Idea to Business

Ultra Pictura was founded in October 2010 as a spin-off initiative of ANDROME, EDM and IBBT. In addition, it has a strategic alliance with production company Walking The Dog (Walking The Dog 2000) giving the company the opportunity to work for and with important players in the animation business. The Ultra Pictura team, hence, has respective firm roots in the market at issue regarding business/development (software company link), production/marketing (producer/animation studio link) and research & development.

Table 28.1 lists all past activities involved in setting up the company. EDM has been working in computer graphics and animation since 1987, which has given rise to a substantial amount of know-how in these fields (Di Fiore 2004; Van Laerhoven 2006). Over the years, the EDM (and hence IBBT) activity domains have been extended to include non-photorealistic animation and rendering (NPAR).

ANDROME has been active in R&D on 2D animation since its involvement in 1997 in ERASTA, a European ESPRIT FP4 R&D project. Various R&D projects—funded internally, through the EC and through IWT[1]—as well as commercial projects followed, resulting in a total investment of about 3.8 MEUR.

The research efforts of EDM and ANDROME on stylized animation were started in the EU research project CUSTODIEV (IST EU R&D project FP V, October 2002–March 2005). The main R&D topic involved around animating image sequences in the 'carte à gratter noir' (scraper board) style as well as image sequences in airbrush styles (Di Fiore and Van Reeth 2003; Di Fiore et al. 2006; Henzen et al. 2005).

IBBT became involved through the organization of its first iBoot, in which a team was selected and supported to work on a business study around painterly stylized animation during Q2 of 2008. The iBoot was followed by an IBBT incubation project on painterly stylized animation (Q4 2008–Q1 2010) of which the main goal was to

[1] Flemish government agency for Innovation by Science and Technology.

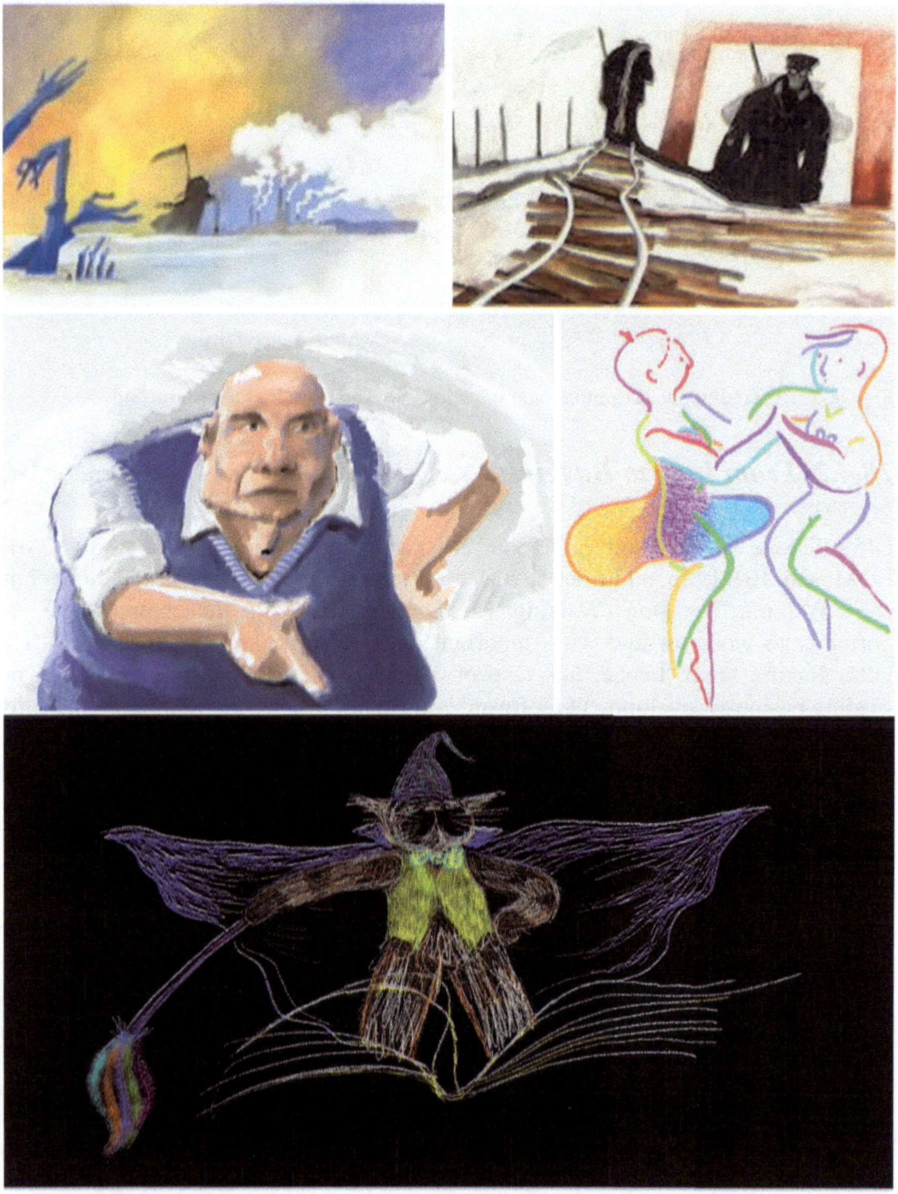

Fig. 28.4 Artworks illustrating the content styles which can be animated through Ultra Pictura. (*1st row*) © Marie-Anne Bonneterre. (*2nd row*) *Left*: © Bart 'Pokke' Van Bael. *Right*: © Lesley Keen. (*3rd row*) © Lesley Keen

step in with a new approach to highly stylized animation offering a new perspective on computer-assisted animation production in which the problem of 'animation

Table 28.1 Ultra Pictura: from idea to business

Period	Activity	Funding	Partners
1987–...	R&D on computer graphics and animation		EDM
1997–2002	R&D on 2D animation	European (ESPRIT FP4) and National (IWT)	ANDROME EDM
2002–2005	R&D on 2D stylized animation	European (IST EU R&D FP5)	ANDROME EDM CNBDI (France) Siriol (UK) Glasgow University (UK) Philips (NL)
2008	iBoot on stylized animation	IBBT	ANDROME Walking the Dog IBBT-EDM
2008–2010	iStart	IBBT	ANDROME
2009–2011	R&D on stylized animation	National (IWT)	ANDROME
2009–2011	R&D on business modeling	IBBT	ANDROME Walking the Dog IBBT-EDM IBBT (other)
2010, October	Founding of Ultra Pictura		ANDROME IBBT Walking the Dog
2011	iVenture	IBBT	Ultra Pictura

sameness' in 3D animation and of 'coloring sameness' in traditional animation are tackled.

Aside the technological R&D, together with ANDROME new business modeling opportunities were investigated in a cooperate research project during the period Q2 2009–Q1 2011. Finally, the IBBT iVenture investment fund provided early-stage funding (via a convertible loan) for setting up the company.

28.4.3 Company Management

At present Ultra Pictura organizationally is arranged around a core team of three people as fixed personnel and a floating number of people which are hired on a free-lance basis depending on the need in the commercial subcontracting/production activities. A management committee has been set up, with the core team and representatives of the board, in which the medium- to longer-term activities of Ultra Pictura are discussed.

The core team consists of (i) a creative director with an extensive background in animation as well as business development, and (ii) two technical directors, former employees of IBBT-EDM, each having a Ph.D. in computer science. The CEO of ANDROME will act in the initial years as CEO of Ultra Pictura. The vice director of IBBT-EDM is a member of the management committee as representative of ANDROME and to maintain the innovation link towards IBBT; the CEO of Walking the Dog is member of the management committee as representative of Walking the Dog and to maintain the link towards the market.

28.5 Conclusions

We have described the key aspects in the setting up of Ultra Picture to transfer technology from academia to industry in the area of animation production techniques. The Institute for Broadband Technology provided the right kind of environment to develop and facilitate this initiative from the viewpoint of the academic researchers and also from industry.

Acknowledgments We gratefully express our gratitude to the European Fund for Regional Development, the Flemish Government, and to IBBT which have kindly funded part of our research activities.

References

ANDROME (1990). http://www.androme.com.

Camargus (2010). http://www.camargus.com.

Di Fiore, F. (2004). *A 2.5d modelling and animation framework supporting computer assisted traditional animation*. Dissertation submitted in partial fulfillment of the requirements for the degree of doctor of philosophy: Computer science, transnational University Limburg: School of Information Technology, Expertise Center for Digital Media, Limburgs Universitair Centrum, Universitaire Campus, B-3590 Diepenbeek, Belgium.

Di Fiore, F., & Van Reeth, F. (2003). Modelling in 2D enabling fluid stylised animation. In *Proceedings of GraphiCon, international conference on computer graphics & vision* (pp. 124–130).

Di Fiore, F., Van Reeth, F., Patterson, J., & Willis, P. (2006). Highly stylised drawn animation. In *Lecture notes in computer science: Vol. 4035. Computer Graphics International (CGI2006)* (pp. 36–53).

EDM (1987). http://www.edm.uhasselt.be.

Henzen, A., Ailenei, N., Di Fiore, F., Van Reeth, F., & Patterson, J. (2005). Sketching with a low-latency electronic ink drawing tablet. In *Proceedings of the 3rd international conference on computer graphics and interactive techniques in Australasia and South East Asia (GRAPHITE 2005)* (pp. 51–60).

TinkerTouch (2010). http://www.tinkertouch.com.

Ultra Pictura (2010). http://www.ultrapictura.com.

Van Laerhoven, T. (2006). *An extensible simulation framework supporting physically-based interactive painting*. Dissertation submitted in partial fulfillment of the requirements for the degree of doctor of philosophy: Computer science, transnational University Limburg: School of Information Technology, Expertise Center for Digital Media, Limburgs Universitair Centrum, Universitaire Campus, B-3590 Diepenbeek, Belgium.

Walking The Dog (2000). http://www.walkingthedog.be.

Chapter 29
Building Adoption of Visual Analytics Software

Nancy Chinchor, Kristin Cook, and Jean Scholtz

Abstract The impact of visual analytic software can only be fully realized if attention is focused on the development of approaches to facilitate broad adoption. While all technology adoption efforts face obstacles, the highly visual and interactive nature of visual analytics software as a cognitive aid poses particular technological and cultural challenges that must be addressed. Successful adoption requires different techniques at every phase of the technology adoption life cycle, from the innovators and the visionary early adopters to the more pragmatic early majority and finally to the less technologically-oriented late majority. This chapter provides an overview of the technology adoption life cycle and describes the particular challenges of technology adoption for visual analytics software. A case study of visual analytics technology adoption is considered, and the role of organizational culture is examined. Finally, an extensive set of guidelines is presented for facilitating visual analytics software adoption throughout the entire technology adoption life cycle.

29.1 Introduction

Although visual analytics is a relatively new research area, it has reached sufficient maturity that several visual analytics software tools are widely available, with still more innovative research in the pipeline. Both private industry and government organizations are exploring the capabilities offered by visual analytics to enable more effective ways of gaining insight from complex information. The impact of these innovative software programs can only be fully realized if attention is focused on techniques for supporting visual analytics software adoption. This chapter focuses on ways to effectively address the challenges of visual analytics software adoption.

Researchers in visual analytics define this field as the science of analytical reasoning facilitated by interactive visual interfaces (Thomas and Cook 2005). Visual

N. Chinchor (✉) · K. Cook · J. Scholtz
Pacific Northwest National Laboratory, Richland, WA, USA
e-mail: chinchoreclectic@gmail.com

You cannot acquire experience by making experiments. You cannot create experience. You must undergo it. Albert Camus (1913–1960)

J. Dill et al. (eds.), *Expanding the Frontiers of Visual Analytics and Visualization*,
DOI 10.1007/978-1-4471-2804-5_29, © Springer-Verlag London Limited 2012

analytics emerged from the need to more deeply analyze complex information in ways that support both formal and informal analytical techniques. Visual analytics draws from information visualization, scientific visualization, cognitive psychology, human-computer interaction, and data mining, which are well-established research areas. Progress in these fields enabled the visual analytics research agenda to emerge quickly. In 2004, approximately 40 researchers interested in visual analytics met to discuss the challenges needed to advance the field. This collaboration resulted in *Illuminating the Path* (Thomas and Cook 2005). In 2006 a group of information visualization researchers held an initial Visual Analytics Science and Technology (VAST) Symposium as part of the IEEE VisWeek Conferences, as a forum for discussing research progress in the field. Participation in VAST has increased each year, and in 2010, it was made a full-fledged conference along with the Information Visualization and Visualization conferences. In 2010, over twenty visual analytics researchers again met to update the agenda and to describe what had been accomplished in the intervening five years and what challenges had yet to be overcome. The results were published in a special journal edition (Kielman and Thomas 2009). Although both *Illuminating the Path* and the special journal edition were concerned with the transition of visual analytics software, they did not address the more user-centered challenge of technology adoption.

In the final chapter of *Illuminating the Path*, "Moving Research into Practice," the authors discuss ways to accelerate the process of moving research results in visual analytics into the real world. There are actually two processes involved here: transition and adoption. The process of transitioning software is a step-by-step procedure that involves evaluating components of the visual analytics software, ensuring that security and privacy requirements have been addressed, providing support for interoperability so that the tools can be deployed in existing architectures, and ensuring that the technology is integrated into the user's work processes. Each organization has a transition process that must be followed with different requirements that must be met and different groups or managers who need to sign off. However, transition is not the final objective. It is necessary to go further to ensure that the technology is adopted by the end users in the organization and also able to be used effectively. Measures of success for adoption are more qualitative than quantitative and focus on changes in standard business processes and cultural changes in an organization.

Adoption of new and potentially disruptive visual analytics technology into an existing operational enterprise can be difficult. Common issues include having the infrastructure necessary to support the new technology, customizing training for users, integrating the technology into current processes, and securing the time, managerial support, and necessary funds to support the adoption process. In addition, work is needed to take advantage of the new ways of problem solving enabled by visual analytics. New software tools that are incremental improvements on currently used tools are much easier for the majority of users to adopt. A new version of a spreadsheet or word processing tool provides new capabilities and may take some time to get used to, but the user's process is not affected. Adopting a totally new tool changes not only how the user does her work but also how she collaborates with colleagues and how she presents work products to management and to outside customers. In other words, both the user and those she works with and for must embrace the technology.

Visual analytics tools require a new way of thinking and some reliance on software algorithms. Not only must the end user trust the visualizations of their data, they also have to interact with these visualizations and interpret their meaning. In a sense, visual analytics tools are unproven. Users do not know whether these tools will help them with their problems. Organizations have users from many different demographics; some older, some less interested in technology than others, some with more analytic expertise, some with higher and more demanding workloads, and some with problems in different domains. All of these factors and more affect the attitude that the end users have towards new unproven software.

As users embrace new business processes, such as the use of visual analytics tools, the culture of the organization evolves. Users who have adopted the new tools and processes move ahead with the organization. Managers and customers begin to expect work products developed using newer processes and tools. What strategies can be used in helping the full range of users, from highly technical to less technically savvy, adopt these new tools? In the following sections, some issues in technology adoption are discussed and a case study of an organization's efforts in adopting a visual analytics tool is presented. In the final section of this chapter, some guidelines for adoption strategies are provided. These guidelines are based on the experiences of the authors in their efforts in the organizational adoption of visual analytics technology. Because each organization is unique, specific step-by-step procedures are not appropriate. Rather, the guidelines are organized according to situations that may be encountered during technology adoption. To understand issues that may arise, it is necessary to understand in general how technology is integrated into organizations.

29.2 The Technology Adoption Life Cycle

The process of technology adoption is complex and dynamic. Geoffrey Moore, in his book *Crossing the Chasm* (1999), articulates what has become a widely accepted description of the technology adoption life cycle.

Moore identifies five distinct categories of technology adopters ranging from the earliest to latest groups to embrace a new technology: innovators, early adopters, early majority, late majority, and laggards. These groups are distributed across a bell curve. Each of these five groups has unique motivations and priorities. Technology adoption does not proceed smoothly from innovators to early adopters to the early majority, late majority, and laggards, because each of these groups has different motivations, needs, and constraints. These discontinuities among user groups must be overcome in order to achieve broad adoption in an organization.

Innovators are technically savvy people who actively seek and embrace new technology, even if just out of curiosity. They are willing to take greater technological risks than the other groups and are intrigued by technology even without clear line of sight to an important application. Innovators are more open to research-grade software or alpha or beta releases. Innovators are typically few in number but their opinions are influential. With the prevalence of social media, it could be argued that the influence of innovators has further expanded because of their ability to share their opinions broadly through blogs and other public forums. However, innovators are generally much more technically oriented than the broad user base being targeted for most new technologies, so gaining favor among the innovators is valuable but not sufficient for broad technology adoption.

Early adopters, by contrast, are not technologists but innovative users. They are a relatively small group of potential users who are able to envision how a new technology could enable them to accomplish their goals. Early adopters may have important needs that are not currently addressed in existing solutions, for example. They rely on their own expertise to guide them, rather than looking for references or endorsements from others. They are willing to go to some extra effort to use a new tool if it helps them solve an important problem or brings important new capabilities to them. In visual analytics deployments, early adopters may be senior members of the user organization and are often responsible for developing new problem-solving and analytic techniques to be used by the group. Their organizations give them some level of flexibility to explore new or alternative approaches (or they determinedly find ways around organizational limitations) rather than being constrained to the existing infrastructure and tool suites. Because visual analytics software presents opportunities for addressing problems that could not previously be addressed, early adopters often embrace the capabilities that it presents.

Early adopters are motivated by addressing their own unmet goals, not by exploring technology for technology's sake. To be able to move beyond the innovators into use by early adopters, visual analytics technologies must demonstrate that they enable early adopters to do something significant that their current techniques and technologies cannot provide.

The early majority, roughly one-third of the population according to Moore, are pragmatists. They are comfortable with new technologies, but are seeking productivity improvement rather than revolutionary innovation. In visual analytics deployments, the early majority are likely to be working in a well-established infrastructure that includes established data repositories or data sources, as well as a fixed set of tools to support their work processes. They work under tight deadlines and do not have the degree of flexibility early adopters may have.

The remarkable gap between the early adopters and the early majority is the "chasm" referred to in the title of Moore's book. An overwhelming number of promising technologies fail to make the transition between these two groups. To move adoption beyond the relatively tiny group of early adopters to the large early majority, a visual analytics technology must move beyond the purview of the individual early adopter's workstation and become part of the established enterprise infrastructure. In other words, the software needs to be integrated into the organizational workflow. The software must be capable of interfacing with other software tools in the user's workflow and complementing their use. It must be able to routinely tolerate data imperfections in enterprise data systems without failing. The software must truly be mature at this stage—capable of being easily installable, maintainable, and scalable to meet the organization's needs. In addition, a robust training and support infrastructure must be in place. If the new visual analytics software is augmenting existing capabilities, then new workflows must be developed to take advantage of the new capabilities. If the new visual analytics software is replacing another tool, then the visual analytics software may also have to provide the key capabilities of the old software in addition to its new capabilities, as a type of bridge for users to adopt the new software.

Reaching the early majority, while critical, is not sufficient to achieve full technology adoption; the late majority must also be engaged. The late majority, roughly another one- third of the population, are traditionalists who are conservative about technology adoption and avoid potentially disruptive innovations, even when those disruptions are positive ones. In visual analytics deployments, they too work under tight deadlines and may have developed very finely honed manual or semi-automated processes for performing their analytic tasks.

To move beyond adoption by the early majority into use by the late majority, technologies must become very easy to use while remaining useful. While technically savvy users may be comfortable with visual analytics tools that provide a wide range of options, late majority users may be much more comfortable with well-designed software that can easily be customized to the user's task, with extraneous options hidden away. Simpler, lighter-weight versions of visual analytics tools may be needed in order to reach this group. Another option is to provide configuration options in the interface that permit users or administrators to minimize the number of options available, resulting in a much simpler user interface.

The final group in the life cycle, the laggards, is characterized as individuals who avoid technology wherever possible. In visual analytics deployments, laggards are those people who, even with training and full organizational support for the technology, still revert back to their old techniques if permitted to do so. Laggards may still use some of the innovative data analytics algorithms if they can be made automatic and invisible, and they may benefit from well-designed information presentation tools, but laggards are not good candidates to use the interactive visual interfaces that are at the core of visual analytics.

The characteristics of various user groups certainly affect the adoption of any technology. However, as mentioned earlier, there are other challenges specific to visual analytics technologies. Six of these are discussed in the next section.

29.3 Adoption Challenges for Visual Analytics

A number of challenges must be overcome to achieve broad-scale adoption of visual analytics tools in a given organization. Of the six challenges listed below, the first four are identified in Chapt. 6 of *Illuminating the Path* and the latter two have been identified through the experience of the authors in technology adoption.

Challenge One: New visual analytics tools, algorithms, and approaches must be evaluated to ensure that they operate correctly and offer a significant advance over existing processes. Recommendations to deal with this challenge involve developing evaluation methodologies for the various levels of visual analytics technologies: component level, system level, and work environment level. While additional work is needed, several publications at recent VAST conferences have taken on this challenge. The VAST Challenge that accompanies this conference (Costello et al. 2009; Grinstein et al. 2006, 2007, 2008, 2009, 2010; Plaisant et al. 2008) has helped researchers to understand the work tasks and data for which visual analytics tools are needed. In the five-year history of the challenge, the sophistication of the VAST Challenge tasks has grown, which reflects the community's growing visual analytics capabilities.

Challenge Two: Security and privacy must be addressed. Different organizations have different security requirements. It is vital that researchers are aware of security requirements and address these early on in their work. Additionally, privacy is a concern when data contains personal information about individuals. Privacy is more of an issue with the current ability to collect information about individuals such as location data based on mobile device use and social networking. Researchers in visual analytics need to be aware of privacy protections and how those concerns vary in the global environment.

Challenge Three: Visual analytics software must support interoperability to facilitate collaboration, rapid evaluation, and smooth deployment. Software tools in an organization are not used in isolation. Analysts use many different tools, depending on their needs. Furthermore, when groups of analysts work together, they must be able to coordinate—and this means that the software tools they use must be able to coordinate as well. Visual analytics tools will be more readily adopted if it is easy to get data in and get results out. Interoperability issues are not research issues, but are practical issues that need to be considered at the system level and at the work environment level. Evaluation efforts should measure interoperability issues at both of these levels. As pointed out in *Illuminating the Path*, specific challenges for interoperability include the interface between visual analytics tools and other software; supporting analysis of dynamic data, very large data sets, and data from multiple data sets; supporting work and data from diverse application domains; ensuring that visual analytics tools work with a variety of hardware and operating systems; and ensuring the performance requirements are still met.

Challenge Four: Visual analytics tools must be integrated into existing work processes. Technology insertion requires many new partners outside of the research team and the actual end users. These partners come from the IT infrastructure team in the organization, from the management team, and from the training department. Managers must be convinced of the usefulness of the technologies to provide monetary support for the transition efforts. The IT infrastructure may want to see results of evaluations, know that security and privacy have been addressed, and feel confident that the visual analytics tools work on the organization's infrastructure and satisfy the appropriate interoperability issues. At this point, the IT team will do its own testing to ensure that the software tool satisfies organizational criteria for transition.

Challenge Five: Users of the domains targeted by visual analytics software are extremely busy and have time constraints. How can they be persuaded to try out the software? While a few users are probably those who discovered the software and had contacts with the researchers, these are the innovators or the early adopters. Even these users are busy and need to quickly see the value that a new technology can provide. This is particularly true for software that is a fundamental change or paradigm shift. Visual analytics moves away from reasoning with numerical information—a well-known, comfortable methodology for information analysts—to reasoning visually. For the software to be beneficial to the organization, it needs to be more widely adopted among users within the organization, from innovators to at least the late majority. One way to convince users to try out new software is to produce utility metrics. Most employees are evaluated on their work for raises and promotions. The evaluation measures might be number of publications produced, number of patents received, or number of new customers brought in, for example. Showing a user how a software tool can contribute to a measure that is meaningful to that user helps to demonstrate the utility of that software tool. Builders use power tools because they increase the rate at which carpentry tasks can be completed. Power software tools increase the rate at which software tasks can be completed. If visual analytics tools enable analysts to solve problems that previously eluded them, analysts will quickly adopt those tools.

Challenge Six: Training analysts to use the software is also an issue. Most training focuses on how to use different features in the user interface. While this is certainly needed, the difficult part of adopting a new tool is determining how it fits into the analysts' current processes. Analysts in all domains have methodologies that they use. Do the new tools support these methodologies? If so, how? Training in visual analytics tools needs to be focused on how to use the features to attack the different problems the user has. The problem is to identify the persons who both understand the problems and can provide the training. What is needed is a combination of expertise with the visual analytics tool and expertise in the analytic problems in that particular application domain. In reality, this expertise will likely come from a team of people: a technology-savvy analyst working with a software developer skilled in using the visual analytics software. Training differs depending on the stage of adoption. Early adopters and early majority users are most interested in finding out how to use the new software and what problems can now be solved. While these users need support for exploration, late majority users are focused on a more prescriptive approach. They are interested in basic functionality and a guide to routine uses with perhaps a hint of the tool's additional capabilities.

Of the six challenges described above, the first four can be classified as technological challenges. That is, they are centered mainly on aspects of the software and are needed in order to cross the chasm. The last two challenges, however, are cultural challenges and span the technology adoption life cycle. These are more difficult to deal with because every organization is unique and it is difficult to produce a step-by-step list of things to do. Rather, it is necessary to understand how users of new technology perceive the value of that technology. Isomursu et al. (2011) analyzed the perceived value of a software tool from the perspective of three different end-user groups: teachers, students, and parents. The three groups participated in an experiment with software that automatically recorded class attendance in a grade school. Students were given identification cards to swipe against a card reader when they entered class. Originally, the expectation was that both teachers and parents would benefit. Teachers would no longer have to call roll and parents would be able to log in to the system to determine that children were safely in class, eliminating the need to call the teacher. Isomursu was able to show that the software tool brought value to all three groups, not just the teachers and parents. The students felt that being trusted with this responsibility gave them status among their peers and they were proud that they could help both their teachers and parents. It is important to note that these values were perceived and that subjective perception of value is not necessarily the same as objective measures.

Cockton (2004) argues that a focus on "quality in use," or usability, is not enough for end users when considering the use of technology. Software usability is evaluated in context. That is, users are asked to perform tasks, and measures are taken of the time needed, the errors made, and the user's general satisfaction in performing the tasks. While usability is important, Cockton argues that the fit between the users' tasks and the software matters more than usability. However, value matters more than fit. In the case of software used in an organization, there are more end user groups involved than just analysts; management and customers must also see benefit and value in the new software tools in order for adoption to be widespread.

Adoption is simplified in some cases. The software may be applicable to a smaller set of problems, be useful for only a few types of data, or the users may be more homogeneous. Essentially, the software tool is more focused. Widespread adoption in this case is actually achieved even though a much smaller set of end users are involved. This does not mean that any of the challenges above can be ignored. It just means that overcoming the challenges can be accomplished more easily because the scope is limited.

The adoption process for visual analytics software has some important differences from adoption processes for other software. Visual analytics software requires evaluating computation, presentation, and interpretation on the user's part. In any application domain where analysis is done, the analysts are the ones responsible for the analysis and recommendations. There are multiple implications when software processes data and presents it to the analyst. First, the analyst must be convinced that this processing is accurate, or at least that it is as good as the analyst could do. Because analysts often are unable to find and review all the relevant data, they must make their recommendations based on a subset of data. There is no correct answer—only the analyst's best estimate of the situation and her recommendations based on the current situation and her knowledge of past history. Analysts do not have access to the behind the scenes computations that are used to produce the visualizations, but they must somehow build trust in the software. As with collaborations with others, trust is built up over time. Only after collaborators work together on problems do they develop trust in one another. Likewise, analysts develop trust in the software as they work with it successfully. Using the tools on data sets that the analysts are familiar with will also help build trust. For example, if software tools find the same or more relationships in a data set as the analyst found, she will be more inclined to trust the software tool with new data.

In addition, visual analytics software sometimes relies on user interpretation of complex visualizations. Colors, line widths, spacing, icons, and such are interpreted differently by different users. Users will ask many questions. Some examples include the following: Does the visualization accurately portray what is in the data? Can I select and view the raw data? Do I understand the display? If not, do I understand it after an explanation is provided? Can I manipulate the data in the display to support my tasks? Can I restrict the display to just the data I want? Again, as users work with the visual analytics software, they will make these decisions for themselves. However, researchers and developers need to perform evaluations during the research and development cycle to ensure that the data processing is correct (a technology evaluation) and that users are able to correctly interpret the results (a user-centered evaluation). To complicate this issue, evaluation work needs to take into account different types of data and different types of users with different problems to solve.

The evaluation needs to include seeing how analysts might need to change their processes when using visual analytics software. When innovators and early adopters use these tools, they should be encouraged to write methodology papers and share them with others who could benefit from using the tool. Understanding how to approach a problem with a new tool is a big step that will help others get on board more quickly. This understanding includes recognizing any data manipulations that have to be made to use the software, including data clean-up or techniques for dealing with missing or uncertain data.

Visual analytics is still a young research area, and new evaluation methodologies must be developed for assessing visual analytics software, including measuring the accuracy of the visual representations and the ease with which users can interpret the visualization. New ways must be developed to measure values that are important to user groups. It is important that researchers and developers include end user groups early in the process of developing visual analytics software. Visual analytics tools will only be adopted if the users find value in them.

29.4 Case Study: Moore's Life Cycle Applied to an Organization

The case study described in this section applied Moore's life cycle to an organization that is meeting the challenges of a media revolution. The organization has collected and reported on global traditional media for more than 50 years. As the influence of new media increased, a small team was dropped into the organization with the mission of modernizing collection and reporting. This embedded team became the early adopters and the agents of culture change in the organization.

The characteristics of the organization both assisted and retarded the adoption of new software techniques. The organization was committed to its mission, maintained global coverage using a complex computer network, and was held to high standards of production. Although the mission of the organization required change, the organization resisted change because even small changes could have significant ripple effects. The resistance was in part due to lack of resources, the complexity of day-to-day operations of the organization, and a lack of methods for analyzing the veracity of new media and what could be rigorously inferred from citizen journalism. Overall, the organization could be considered the late majority or laggard as far as technology was concerned. Newer staff members and some senior analysts embraced technological change. However, upper and many middle managers were much more risk-averse.

The embedded team had strategies for parallel cultural change and modernization of the desktop given the characteristics of the organization. The main strategy was outreach to the other offices in the organization for two main reasons. The team had been embedded from outside and needed to understand the mission of the organization from the workers who kept it running. The embedded team had to demonstrate service to the organization because it was using organizational resources.

Not only did the embedded team have to promote its offerings in briefings worldwide, but it also had to forge one-to-one working relationships with the mainstream analysts. The outreach meant a consistent effort to fully engage and answer all questions that were posed. When people had a problem they were working intensely, the embedded team members offered to join in and raise productivity by adding the view from new media or by providing rigorously collected data from new media.

The organization often had conducted pilot evaluations of software in their environment. When the embedded team proposed a pilot evaluation, many people believed that they would be giving their opinion during the pilot and then would most likely never see the software again. This chasm was identified early by the embedded team. To get pilot participants, the embedded team carried out more well-designed pilot studies with full support of all stakeholders and then identified and chose early adopters for the pilot. Following the pilot, the team made it possible for the users to continue working with the piloted visual analytics product without interruption. The team made certain that analytic products came out of the pilot and were disseminated to the community or, at the very least, briefed to management. The embedded team formed a good relationship with the supporting information technology organization so that system support that was integral to piloting and production was provided in a timely and controlled manner. The continued availability of the piloted software and transition of the software into production operation helped transform the small group of early adopters into an early majority group by group, because the embedded team continuously worked with engineering and the analysts to demonstrate tool utility. Successful adoption was planned for by the information technology team and the embedded team before the pilots started, thus causing the chasm to narrow and lowering the amount of work needed to bridge the chasm after the pilot.

To understand what the other groups in the organization were concerned with and what issues there were where new media would play a critical role, the embedded team conducted outreach at every turn. On some issues, the team experimented and developed methods of analyzing different types of data from online journalism and social media, and disseminated these methods to the rest of the organization through formal products.

The cultural change through interaction with key people and management throughout the organization overshadowed the adoption of new software. Cultural change was necessary for new media to be understood for what it represented and for new methods of collection, analysis, and reporting to be applied. The support of the key senior members of the organization helped lessen some of the fear of change and break down unnecessary barriers.

The embedded team realized and illustrated that social media must be looked at as a communal expression rather than single sources. The embedded team considered visual analytics software to be the only approach that could accurately aggregate social media for repeatable analytic conclusions. Influential bloggers must be paid attention to because they are on-the-ground commentators who are trusted for a reason. Determining who is influential in the blogosphere and on the internet in general requires the use of visual analytics technology.

The understanding of new media and the use of visual analytics software increased through the team leveraging education and the application of analytic methodologies to new media. External events such as the ubiquitous use of social media made the team's contribution invaluable and pushed visual analytics software along the bell curve of adoption. The embedded team knew to ride the wave by providing mass training to the early and late majorities as soon as systems were available on the desktops in the larger training rooms. Training working groups together as a single team and identifying designated trainers within those groups was the most efficient way to get widespread good practices group-by-group.

A milestone of the embedded team's success was when products that used visual analytics software won awards from the organization's management for handling large amounts of data. As a result, the embedded team was called upon more and more and became the "go-to" part of the organization.

29.5 Cultural Implications of Adoption

Culture change can create the climate for adoption of new technologies, and the introduction of new ways of doing business using new technologies will change the culture.

Culture can be defined as "the set of shared attitudes, values, goals, and practices that characterizes an institution or organization."[1] Cultural change is behavioral change in the organization. Normally, change would not be attempted unless it was a natural next step in the organization's set of shared attitudes, values, goals, and practices. Dialog, logical solutions to problems, behaving in a new way as an example, and training can all lead to behavioral change in an organization. Resistance to change can be nullified by showing that goals can be achieved better as a result of change and that values are conserved during every step of the change. Methodologies serve as pathways to change of behavior for those who want to change or need to see the full path before taking the first step.

[1] Merriam-Webster Online Dictionary, http://www.merriam-webster.com/.

Building a culture of "opportunity-seeking" can be a precursor to building adoption of visual analytics software. Certain triggering conditions that alter the status quo can create a climate for embracing greater innovation by an organization. For example, the revolution in using social media for political action can affect analysts' approaches for keeping up with that external change.

Visual analytics tools revolutionize the ability to collaborate across time and space in the organization. Previously, collaboration in analytic enterprises was driven through means such as email and instant messaging, and collaboration was not timely or easily coordinated. Through the use of visual analytics capabilities, collaboration is enabled as a part of the analytic business processes. It is a learning process for people to develop and accept this new approach for collaboration. It requires that users adopt different processes for collaboration and involves transition as portions of the team transition to the new technology and others do not. It enables collaboration as a part of the task completion process.

Technology adoption is also a budget problem as well as an organizational issue. It requires hardware, software licenses, and staff to support it in the computing infrastructure. Information technology infrastructure groups are incentivized to minimize risk and manage tight budgets. However, they need to be brought along with the changes needed to meet mission goals. The organization as a whole has to act rationally and understand the steps that must be taken.

While management can insist on change, everyone has to be moved along the way one step at a time. The agents of change must act reverently to move people and take opportunities to work with people rather than expecting them to move alone. Moving people to change is a communal activity, but, just like viral marketing, it takes place by one person talking to another person. When the momentum has built, the agent of change can enhance it by working with its natural resonance. Training can maintain the momentum and multiply it.

29.6 Recommendations for Building Visual Analytics Technology Adoption

Adoption of a visual analytics solution is a highly collaborative, multidisciplinary activity that ideally involves not only the adopting organization but also the visual analytics research and development team. It is often difficult for the research and development team to learn how to smooth the deployment path, because there are limited sources of guidance available to the team. Conferences and journals predominantly focus on sharing of research results, and many research teams are satisfied with performing and publishing innovative research. For teams for whom success is measured in deployments rather than in publications, there are no analogous conferences or journals in the visual analytics community.

The recommendations described in this section come as a result of lessons learned through technology transition and adoption experiences of the authors as well as extensive discussions and interviews with others who have been engaged in technology transition and adoption of other types of analytical software. Lessons have been learned through both success and failure, and those are reflected here.

29.6.1 Initiating the Adoption Process

Not all research and development in visual analytics is intended to result in a deployable software product. It is important that research be conducted to answer fundamental questions about the use of visualization, interaction, and data representations and transformations to support analytical reasoning.

However, when the visual analytics research is ultimately intended to produce a deployable software tool, this research should be directly informed by a clear understanding of unmet user needs. Making the link to the potential user organization is a critical step in the evaluation and maturation of visual analytics software. The technology may well be extremely innovative, but to be adopted by end users, the technology must solve critical problems or address unmet needs for an organization.

Ideally, researchers and engineers can team with a few visionary early adopters from an early stage in the research and development process. Von Hippel (1986) describes the concept of "lead users"—people who currently have important needs that are representative of the needs that will be felt more generally by others in the months or years to come. Lead users can articulate problems and needs that can help focus applied research efforts and drive innovation with long-term impact.

Commonly, visual analytics research is performed with a hypothesized need in mind without any direct involvement by a user organization. Access to target users or user surrogates for visual analytics can be very difficult to gain. Not only do analysts typically have great demands on their time, but they often work with very sensitive data, whether in the medical, security, business and finance, or legal domains. These security and privacy considerations often limit what can be shared with a researcher without extensive special arrangements.

Regardless, the research and development team must articulate the problem being solved by their software. While it is appropriate to begin with a hypothesis about a problem that should be solved, this is a question that must be explored throughout the research and development process.

To develop a deeper understanding of the analytic problem in the absence of direct user engagement, the research team should endeavor to perform their own analyses on analogue problems of interest to them. For example, a text analysis tool could be used to determine which new car to buy. In the absence of direct user feedback, personal experience with using the software to perform an analysis can be extremely informative to the research and development team. The team can gain an understanding of the software's strengths and weaknesses to determine whether the software is of value in performing an analysis.

It is also helpful to identify groups that can act as user surrogates to participate in evaluations of designs and prototypes. Because visual analytics depends greatly on users' interpretation of visualization and understanding of the associated analytic interactions' functionality, user feedback plays an important role in the evolution of visual analytics software. Two examples of user surrogates are retirees who worked in the target user domain or students training for careers in the user domain.

A valuable resource at this stage is the collection of VAST Challenge data sets and tasks (Reddy et al. 2011). Not only does the VAST Challenge provide data for analysis, but it also provides a task definition and answers. VAST Challenge data sets have been created for a wide range of problems. The VAST Challenge was started in 2006 and continues today as a feature of the IEEE VisWeek program. The number of participants has increased from single digits (6 and 7) in 2006 and 2007 to more than 50 in the following years. In the first two years, the VAST Challenge consisted of a single but heterogeneous data set along with a situation that participants were asked to assess. Since 2008, the VAST Challenge has consisted of a set of mini-challenges, each with its own homogeneous data set and questions. Participants can choose to use their visual analytics software to analyze one or more mini-challenges. If participants are able to analyze all the mini-challenges, they can participate in the Grand Challenge, which requires them to pull together the results of all the mini-challenges to describe the overall situation. For example, the 2009 VAST Challenge consisted of three mini-challenges. The scenario was a cyber security incident within an embassy. An employee was suspected of leaking information to a criminal organization and participants were asked to identify the employee and provide evidence and to identify the structure of the criminal organization. The first mini-challenge one contained records of badge and network traffic in the embassy. The second mini-challenge contained social network information about the criminal organization, and the third mini-challenge three contained video data from cameras located in the business district near the embassy. Ground truth is embedded in all three data sets so that teams are able to get accuracy feedback as well as more qualitative feedback on the utility of their tool in the analytic process. This effort has helped researchers and developers design and evaluate their tools, regardless of whether they participate in the actual challenge, as the problems and data sets are available to the community.

To find the appropriate user organizations for a new visual analytics technology, several steps are helpful:

1. Understand the target user base. Read about the target users and analytic processes to understand their needs and constraints.
2. Develop compelling demonstrations of the software using data and tasks that closely relate to potential users' applications and show them broadly. For the potential impact to be understood, visual analytics software must be seen in action. However, the choice of data and task used in a demonstration is critical. Potential user groups seeing a visual analytics software tool for the first time can have difficulty translating a data set of Shakespeare plays or baseball statistics to their own analogous text or financial data applications. If the data used in a demonstration is interesting and familiar to the users, it helps engage them in the demonstration and makes it easier for them to map the software into their own needs and processes.

3. Make the new software as visible as possible, so that innovators and early adopters have a chance to see it in action. While it is common for visual analytics research to be published in technical forums, it is less common for it to be published in the popular press or the publications of the potential user domain. These outlets can help draw attention to the capability. For visual analytics software, it is particularly important that the software be demonstrable on the internet, even if only in video form, because of the highly visual nature of the software.
4. Network extensively and creatively to find opportunity-seeking people who can validate the value of your software in solving important problems.

It can be difficult to know who can assume responsibility for helping a new technology move into broad deployment. While it is important that some organizations inside an agency or company has explicit responsibility for technology transition and technology adoption, this is not often the case. Where research has been funded by a specific research organization, the research organization is often willing to fund use by innovators and early adopters, in the form of pilots. These pilots may not be sufficient demonstration of value to get user organizations to be willing to assume the full cost of deployment and support. As a result, the research organization may need to fund initial portions of the deployment as well, so as to demonstrate the broad value to the organization and make the return on investment obvious to the user organization.

Once the key step of identifying a linkage between the user organization's needs and the technology's capabilities has been accomplished, the technology developers must do everything possible to be responsive to the organization's needs. Throughout the remainder of the process, the development team needs to see their job as one of removing barriers to deployment. These barriers are often not of the development team's making, but that scarcely matters. The important thing at this stage is to work smoothly with the user organizations involved to remove those barriers as effectively as possible.

29.6.2 Building Interest Among Innovators

To succeed in building interest among innovators, it is important first and foremost to demonstrate that you have created something that is new and interesting. In visual analytics applications, innovators may be technologists who are assigned to search for new technologies more generally, but they are more likely to have some specialized knowledge of the analytical process to go along with their technical prowess. Innovators generally will also have thorough knowledge of other software that addresses the problems your software addresses.

Innovators may sometimes be associated with specialized capabilities such as analytic testbeds, which can be used to demonstrate the value of new analytic software in a realistic environment. Innovators can offer unique insights in the early stages of software development. Innovators with testbeds can run formalized experiments on the software and provide explicit feedback in terms of strengths and weaknesses. These experiments can be informative, but they also must be conducted with care. The evaluation of visual analytics software is a complex topic and subject of ongoing research. The complexity arises from a large number of variables that affect utility of the software in addressing an analytic problem: the suitability of the analytic task, the success of the automated data analytics, the effectiveness of the visualization for this task, the suitability of the interactions to support the required task, the usability of the software, and the level of subject matter expertise and computer expertise required of the user. While simple evaluations can consider user satisfaction and accuracy on simple tests, a true evaluation may not be possible until the analyst has achieved a level of proficiency with the software. The time required to conduct informative utility evaluations is often prohibitive at this stage.

Because they are so well informed about the problems and available solutions, innovators are a key source of early feedback for the visual analytics team in refining concepts and identifying strengths and weaknesses. The keys to success with innovators are to be well-informed about how your approach compares to others, communicate with the innovators on a technical level, and be responsive to their feedback. This feedback will be important to helping position the software for use by early adopters.

29.6.3 Technology Adoption by Early Adopters

While innovators think in terms of "technology first, analytics second," the early adopters are solidly focused on analytics first and foremost. Feedback from innovators helps shape the software so that it is better suited for use by early adopters. However, it can be expected that engagement with early adopters will bring even greater change to the software as it gets its first true test in the rigors of operational use.

This may be accomplished in the form of a 10–20 user pilot. In these pilots, users are given training on the software and asked to perform specific tasks using the visual analytics software for a period of time. Pilots can be designed to be brief, intense exercises in which the users work with the piloted software exclusively over a few weeks, or they may be longer, more sporadic activities during which the users work with the software to perform the regular tasks for which it is targeted over a course of several weeks or months. These longer pilots are often more representative of the actual working conditions in which visual analytics software is used, and so they provide additional insights into the challenges of intermittently using more complex software and new analytical processes. They help identify issues associated with training and support that will be important to more wide-scale usage.

For successful trial by early adopters, the software must be installed in a low-risk environment where the users can experiment with the software without jeopardizing the operational computing environment. This may be an established test environment or an isolated computer on which the software can be installed. To achieve maximum value during use by early adopters, it is important to ensure that the users can access the software from their offices; otherwise, time pressures prevent the users from making use of the software despite their best intentions. Ideally, software should be accessible from the users' normal workstations. This may be a limitation for some visual analytics software tools, as users' workstations will not generally have specialized graphics cards or excess computing capacity. Where visual analytics software can be developed using basic commodity hardware, it becomes much simpler to deploy.

Recruiting participants in a pilot can be a challenge, especially in longitudinal studies during which participants may be pulled away due to other job requirements. Also during longer pilots, new users may express interest in participating in the pilot, even well after it has begun. When an infrastructure can be established to permit users to conduct quick experiments to determine whether or not their problem is appropriate to the software tool's capabilities, it becomes much simpler to identify the right participants for a pilot, both at its inception and throughout the pilot process.

Within a pilot, one of the challenges is to enable the users to develop trust in the software, especially in visual analytics software, where the algorithms are invisible to the user. One approach to building this trust is to have users conduct analysis on data they have previously analyzed to see if they can use the software to support their previous conclusions. Performing a previous analysis using the software can help users gain a feeling for the software's strengths and weaknesses as well as identifying how the processes differ.

Pilots represent an important opportunity for refining the software tool in preparation for broader deployment. This time of extended use by early adopters provides an opportunity to learn about how people can make productive use of the technology. It also offers examples of the frustrations and challenges that users may encounter. In this stage, developers can identify workflow issues that arise and implement improvements to better accommodate the customary workflows. Analysts will often use visual analytics software differently than the research and development team expected. These uses may or may not actually work as the user expects. If these creative uses do not actually work, they provide important clues to new functionality that may be needed. Likewise, users may directly request new features or capabilities. Users embrace visual analytics software more fully when they understand that they can influence the tool to better fit their needs.

A pilot is important preparation for the major task of "crossing the chasm" into use by the early majority and beyond. The pilot lets both the user organization and the development team identify challenges posed by the computing architecture and data sources present in the analytic environment. One of the greatest technical barriers to deployment of visual analytics software is the fact that data are much more messy and complex than test data sets typically emulate. For example, data may not be formatted consistently across an entire data repository, data quality may vary, data from different tables or sources may directly conflict, or there may be much more (or much less) data than necessary. In addition, visual analytics tools may need to be applied against a wide variety of data sources, so the process to set up interfaces to the data must be simple, flexible, and reliable. Changes may be needed in the software in order to support the wide variety of data challenges encountered during the pilot.

Challenges can also arise from limitations in network bandwidth, security policies, or hardware capabilities. Every operational setting has its own particular characteristics, so even after a successful deployment in one environment, previously unencountered challenges can arise in future pilots in other environments.

Given that the pilot represents the operating environment in microcosm, the lessons learned here may provide important opportunities to tune the operation of the software to better support the operating constraints of the broader organization. The pilot also provides insights into new analytic methodologies that the software supports. As the software is adopted by the early and late majority, these new methodologies become the core of training exercises and usage in a new analytic workflow.

Finally, it is important to capture success stories during the pilot. These stories help people understand how the visual analytics software enables new analytical approaches and solves new problems. These stories not only provide partial justification for moving the software into broad deployment but also help illustrate the potential impact of the software and help organizations justify the investment in broader implementation.

29.6.4 Adoption by the Early Majority

If use by the early adopters has proved successful, then the software must continue to evolve to build a better fit between the organization's needs and the software's capabilities. Through the pilot, the user organization will have developed a much greater understanding of the strengths and weaknesses of the software and have a greater understanding of the software's fit within their organizational workflow.

With the benefit of a successful pilot, the chasm to the early majority is greatly diminished. However, there is still much to be done to successfully attain adoption of a visual analytics software tool by the early majority. The software must be rigorously tested and be highly reliable, even in an operational environment. The software must tolerate messy data and network infrastructure issues. User documentation must be assembled, not only covering the functionality of the software itself but also documenting the software as it should be used in accomplishing the user's analytic tasks.

To enable successful adoption by the early majority, training plays a central role. Visual analytics software enables new analytical processes, but it also requires new analytical thinking. Analysts who have their own established work processes must find a way to translate these processes into a fundamentally different type of software platform that makes extensive use of visualization. While some visual thinkers take to this approach naturally, that is not a universal experience.

Training is an important step in helping visual analytics software become approachable by the early majority. Classes should not focus on "buttonology"; instead, they should be task-centric. Ideally, training should make use of the user's own data. The use of the tool itself should be explained in the context of the task that the user needs to perform. Accompanying documentation should be task-focused as well. Showing users how to perform analytic tasks on their own data and providing supporting documentation that they can refer to following the training greatly increases the chances of the users actually trying to work with the software.

Training provides an opportunity for lessons learned that the development team can use to further improve the software. Not only do misunderstandings surface about the meaning of the visualizations, the analytic interactions, or other software functionality, but unaddressed needs may be uncovered that are necessary to support the user's workflow. Training should be performed only after the software has been made available on the user's desktop and interfaces to the user's data and other critical tools in the workflow have been established. If users cannot work with the software on their data immediately after the training, then the training should be delayed.

Following training, it is important to provide a support system to answer usage questions and address technical issues. New users need proactive support to reinforce how to apply their training to their analytic tasks. It can be very helpful to periodically reach out to see if they are using the software and address any issues they are encountering. Users experiencing challenges with the software do not necessarily seek help even when it is readily available. However, these same users often respond well to direct outreach.

As new users become experienced users, it is important to continue capturing success stories and give users an opportunity to share their own success stories with one another through user groups. Visual analytics software enables people to address previously unaddressable problems, but creativity is required on the part of the users to move their processes and mindsets beyond limitations imposed by previous tools (or the lack thereof). User groups make it possible for users to learn new techniques and use cases from one another. These groups are also a great resource for identifying further unmet needs that should be considered for future versions of the software.

29.6.5 Adoption by the Late Majority and Laggards

Adoption by the late majority builds upon the substantial infrastructure assembled for adoption by the early majority. However, additional work is needed to support adoption by this less technically savvy group. First and foremost, the software and associated analytic techniques must be simplified wherever possible to provide direct support to the analytic workflow with a minimum of unnecessary options or extra steps. Lightweight, limited functionality versions of visual analytics tools can be useful for late adopters. In some cases, more technically savvy users may do more of the complex steps of preparation and setup of analyses, and then push the resulting visualizations out to the late majority users for their analysis.

Where possible, templates should be provided to support the late majority in performing complex tasks. By enabling users to follow a step-by-step process, they can accomplish more complex analyses with less worry and less chance of getting lost in the process.

Training for the late majority must also evolve. In addition to class-based training, one-on-one task-based training may be required. Step-by-step how-to videos and written documentation may provide a more sustainable approach to providing ongoing support following initial training.

While the late majority can learn to use visual analytics software, laggards are not likely to ever do so. However, laggards can still benefit from some of the analytic calculations that underlie visual analytics software tools, provided that these analytic results can be expressed in a way that is straightforwardly mapped to a step in the user's analytic process and the user can develop trust in the tool. Well-defined analytic processes that have been defined by more experienced analysts can also be used even by laggards, if the visual analytics software's user interface has been carefully designed to support this use.

29.6.6 Adaptive Approaches for Technology Adoption

Experience has shown that changing conditions may make an organization more or less able to change. For example, organizations that are rewarded for accuracy and penalized for errors are less likely to take the risks associated with incorporating innovation into their workflow. Organizations that typically work under extreme time pressures may be reticent to take on new technologies, even if it is clear that the technology could offer some level of improvement, due to the time required to make the change.

However, when new organizations are stood up and processes have not become entrenched, it is possible to introduce innovation with a minimum of complexity. Likewise, when an organization is faced with an urgent new priority that cannot be addressed by current capabilities, even a conservative organization must find a way to adapt to new demands, even if this means using new technologies. In cases like these, adoption of new technologies becomes much more important organizationally and it becomes much easier to overcome common barriers.

29.7 Conclusion

For visual analytics technologies to succeed throughout the technology adoption life cycle, they need first to be truly novel to gain the attention of the innovators. But that is not sufficient. They must solve an unmet operational need, with a revolutionary benefit that merits early adoption by visionary users. If successful with these early adopters, the visual analytics tool must mature from a great one-off software tool to a true software product that can fit into the organization's computing infrastructure and work processes. If this hurdle is overcome, then the focus must turn to continued refinement and simplification to help gain usage by the less technically savvy in the organization.

Visual analytics research and development is essentially a human-centered development activity. Because visualizations must be interpreted by the user, research hypotheses about what constitutes a meaningful and informative visualization must be confirmed in concert with the target users. Interactions enabled by the software must directly support analytic processes that are required to address the analyst's tasks. Data analysis processes underlying the software must be well suited to the users' data. For visual analytics tools to make an impact, the data, the visualization, and the interactions must fit the users' needs. In order for this to happen, it is essential that users be consulted throughout the technology adoption cycle.

Although numerous challenges are associated with adoption of visual analytics technologies, there are enormous payoffs for those who are successful. The user organization can successfully tackle fundamentally different and harder challenges than they could previously have dealt with. If they stay engaged throughout the process, the research and development team gain a much greater insight into the analytic process and the needs of their users. And furthermore, as trust is built between the software researchers and developers and the user community, a wealth of new research challenges will be identified that can provide a foundation for years of meaningful research and development.

References

Cockton, G. (2004). From quality in use to value in the world. In *Proceedings of CHI 2004*, Vienna, Austria, April 24–29, 2004 (pp. 1287–1290). New York: ACM.

Costello, L., Grinstein, G., Plaisant, C., & Scholtz, J. (2009). Advancing user-centered evaluation of visual analytic environments through contests. *Information Visualization*, *8*(2009), 230–238.

Grinstein, G., O'Connell, T., Laskowski, S., Plaisant, C., Scholtz, J., & Whiting, M. (2006). VAST 2006 contest—a tale of alderwood. In *Proceedings of IEEE VAST 2006*, Baltimore, MD (pp. 215–216).

Grinstein, G., Plaisant, C., Laskowski, S., O'Connell, T., Scholtz, J., & Whiting, M. (2007). VAST 2007 contest—blue iguanodon. In *Proceedings of the IEEE symposium on visual analytics science and technology*, Sacramento, CA (pp. 231–232).

Grinstein, G., Plaisant, C., Laskowski, S., O'Connell, T., Scholtz, J., & Whiting, M. (2008). VAST 2008 challenge: introducing mini-challenges. In *Proceedings of IEEE symposium on visual analytics science and technology*, Columbus, OH (pp. 195–196).

Grinstein, G., Plaisant, C., Scholtz, J., & Whiting, M. (2009). VAST 2009 challenge: an insider threat. In *Proceedings of IEEE VAST 2009*, Atlantic City, NJ (pp. 243–244).

Grinstein, G., Konecni, S., Plaisant, C., Scholtz, J., & Whiting, M. (2010). VAST 2010 challenge: arms dealings and pandemics. In *Proceedings of VAST 2010 conference*, Salt Lake City, UT (pp. 267–268). New York: IEEE.

Isomursu, M., Ervasti, M., Kinnula, M., & Isomursu, P. (2011). Understanding human values in adopting new technology—a case study and methodological discussion. *International Journal of Human-Computer Studies*, *69*, 183–200.

Kielman, J., & Thomas, J. (2009). *Information Visualization—Special Issue: Foundations and Frontiers of Visual Analytics*, *8*(4).

Moore, G. (1999). *Crossing the chasm: marketing and selling high-tech products to mainstream customers* (revised edn.). New York: HarperBusiness.

Plaisant, C., Grinstein, G., Scholtz, J., Whiting, M., O'Connell, T., Laskowski, S., Chien, L., Tat, A., Wright, W., Gorg, C., Liu, Z., Parekh, N., Singhal, K., & Stasko, J. (2008). Evaluating visual analytics: the 2007 visual analytics science and technology symposium contest. *IEEE Computer Graphics and Applications*, *28*(2), 12–21. Accessed August 22, 2011.
Reddy, S., Plaisant, C., Scholtz, J., & Grinstein, G. (2011). Visual analytics benchmark repository. http://hcil.cs.umd.edu/localphp/hcil/vast/archive/. Accessed August 22, 2011.
Thomas, J., & Cook, K. (Eds.) (2005). *Illuminating the path: the research and development agenda for visual analytics*. Los Alamitos: IEEE Computer Society.
Von Hippel, E. (1986). Lead users: a source of novel product concepts. *Management Science*, *32*(7), 791–805.

Author Index

J. Dill et al. (eds.), *Expanding the Frontiers of Visual Analytics and Visualization*,
DOI 10.1007/978-1-4471-2804-5,

MIX
Papier aus verantwortungsvollen Quellen
Paper from responsible sources
FSC® C105338

If you have any concerns about our products,
you can contact us on
ProductSafety@springernature.com

In case Publisher is established outside the EU,
the EU authorized representative is:
Springer Nature Customer Service Center GmbH
Europaplatz 3, 69115 Heidelberg, Germany

Printed by Libri Plureos GmbH
in Hamburg, Germany